NEW YORK
PANORAMA

NEW YORK PANORAMA

A COMPANION TO THE WPA
GUIDE TO NEW YORK CITY

WITH A NEW INTRODUCTION
BY ALFRED KAZIN

*A Comprehensive View of the Metropolis,
Presented in a Series of Articles
Prepared by the Federal Writers' Project
of the Works Progress Administration
in New York City*

PANTHEON BOOKS
NEW YORK

Library of Congress Cataloging in Publication Data
Main entry under title:

New York panorama.

Reprint. Originally published: New York: Random
House, c1938. (American guide series)
Includes index.
1. New York (N.Y.)—Description—Guide-books.
I. Federal Writers' Project.   II. Series: American guide
series.
F128.18.N435   1984   917.47'10443   84-42701
ISBN 0-394-54147-2
ISBN 0-394-72731-2 (pbk.)

Display design by Naomi Osnos

Manufactured in the United States of America
First Pantheon Edition

WORKS PROGRESS ADMINISTRATION

HARRY L. HOPKINS, *Administrator*

ELLEN S. WOODWARD, *Assistant Administrator*

HENRY G. ALSBERG, *Director of Federal Writers' Project*

HARRY L. SHAW, JR., *Director, Federal Writers' Project of
New York City*

Preface

THE "panorama" of New York presented in this series of articles has certain qualities in common with an actual panorama of the city, as seen from the crest of one of its giant skyscrapers. In neither does the broad view embrace a compositional pattern that is wholly tidy, and harmonious. What manifests itself in either case is the more or less fortuitous and empirical result of group activity. And on that account, perhaps, within the broader implications of our analogy, the work may be a more faithful and fitting reflection of its subject than could be achieved by any rigidly formal treatment.

As prepared by the Federal Writers' Project of New York City, this volume represents the collective labor of many persons—writers, research workers, editors, supervisors, photographers and others. While naturally seeking no individual credit for their own part in a cooperative task, they would be remiss in both courtesy and gratitude if they failed to acknowledge the invaluable assistance given them by many persons outside the Project. They are particularly grateful to Hiram Motherwell, Publicity Director of the Welfare Council of New York City, who assembled the data utilized in the article on Social Welfare; and to the following expert consultants in other fields: Frederick L. Ackerman, architect; Franklin P. Adams, author and columnist; Brooks Atkinson, drama critic of the New York Times; Alfred H. Barr, Jr., Director of the Museum of Modern Art; Paul F. Brissenden, Assistant Professor of Economics, Columbia University; Stephen Duggan, Director of the Institute of International Education, Inc.; Lewis Gannett, literary editor of the New York Herald Tribune; James Shelley Hamilton, National Board of Review of Motion Pictures; Charles H. Houston, Special Counsel for the National Association for the Advancement of Colored People; James A. Hubert, Executive Director of the New York Urban League, Inc.; Vladimir D. Kazakevich, New York Chapter of the American Institute of Banking; Lawrence J. Keefe, Secretary to the Port of New York Authority; Max Lerner, editor of the Nation; Audrey McMahon, Assistant to the Director of the Federal Art Project; Frank Monaghan, Director of Library and Research, New York World's Fair, 1939; Lewis Mumford, author and architectural critic; Dan Parker, sports editor of the New York Mirror; James Powers, sports edi-

v

tor of the New York *News;* Terry Ramsaye, editor of the *Motion Picture Herald;* Carl Randau, President of the Newspaper Guild of New York; Rebecca B. Rankin, Librarian of the Municipal Reference Library, New York; Chester A. Reeds, American Museum of Natural History; Lester Rosner, Research Director of the American Labor Party of New York State; Margaret Schlauch, Associate Professor of English, New York University; Robert A. Simon, music critic of the *New Yorker;* Thomas P. Smith, Jr., Executive Division, Office of the Comptroller, New York; Mark Villchur, Chief of the Division of Foreign Language Press, Foreign Language Information Service, New York; M. R. Werner, author; Frederic A. Willis, Assistant to the President, Columbia Broadcasting System, Inc.; and Carl Zigrosser, art critic. Thanks are due to Joseph Gaer, Chief Field Supervisor of the Federal Writers' Project and Waldo R. Browne, Associate Editor of the Washington staff, under whose editorial supervision this volume was prepared. A word of thanks must also be accorded to the publishers for their helpful cooperation and their patient forbearance in the face of many difficulties.

It should be obvious that, in the discussion of twenty-six widely diverse subjects by many different writers, various individual opinions are bound to find expression. These latter are not necessarily the opinions of the Works Progress Administration or the sponsors of this book or the consultants whose names appear above.

The present volume, although complete in itself and sold separately, constitutes in effect the general introduction for a detailed guide book to New York City, prepared by the Federal Writers' Project, which will appear at an early date in the same general format and under the same sponsorship and publishing auspices.

Contents

Illustrations

Traffic at Columbus Circle
Train Shed at Pennsylvania Station
Motor Traffic on Fifth Avenue
Staten Island Ferry
    Courtesy of New York Department of Docks
Traffic in Times Square
"Subway" Platforms in Brooklyn

ART IN NEW YORK   between 468 and 469
Metropolitan Museum of Art, Roman Court
    Courtesy of the Museum
The Cloisters, Fort Tryon Park
Metropolitan Museum
    Courtesy of the Museum
Machine Art and Modern Murals at the Museum of Modern Art
    Courtesy of the Museum
Whitney Museum of American Art, Gallery and Sculpture Court
    Courtesy of the Museum
Wax Dioramas in the Museum of the City of New York
    Courtesy of the Museum
Museum of the City of New York, Entrance Hall
    Courtesy of the Museum
Hispanic Society of America, and Court of Its Museum
    Courtesy of the Society
Brooklyn Museum
    Courtesy of the Museum
National Academy of Design
Federal Art Project Class, Leonardo da Vinci School
Outdoor Sculpture Exhibit on Park Avenue

Unless otherwise indicated, all the photographs reproduced in this book
are by staff photographers of the Federal Writers' Project.

Introduction

New York Panorama, twenty-six essays by members of the Federal Writers' Project, represents a still unequaled history and guide to New York's many activities in its last age of innocence before World War II. It was published in 1938, a year before *The WPA Guide to New York City*.

The Federal Writers' Project, like many other innovative, generous, and inspiring acts of the New Deal, was axed (under prodding by a Congress always hostile to writers, artists, and intellectuals drawing $50 to $103.50 a month from the federal treasury) well before Franklin Delano Roosevelt announced that "Dr. Win-the-War has replaced Dr. New Deal." It lasted just four years, 1935 to 1939, and in the nation at large included in its ranks such future celebrities as Ralph Ellison, Saul Bellow, Richard Wright, John Cheever, Conrad Aiken, Harold Rosenberg, Samuel Putnam, Studs Terkel, Katherine Dunham, Frank Yerby, Loren Eiseley, and Margaret Walker. Jerre Mangione, in his history of the Writers' Project, *The Dream and the Deal,* says that other now well-known names asked him not to disclose that they had been on the project.

I was twenty-three years old in 1938 and like other writers of my generation was convinced that my country, too, was starting out in the thirties —starting all over again in a turbulent decade that was full of hope for a better America despite the Depression and the threat of war. The hope and promise of the time were symbolized in government-sponsored books like *New York Panorama* and by the Federal Writers' Project itself, which in its embattled four years employed 6600 unemployed writers, journalists, editors, and research workers. Its main production was the American Guide Series, a series of books meant to give the United States a detailed portrait of itself. The scope ranged from geographical and travel information to folklore, architecture, and other phases of cultural and ethnological history. One of America's greatest cultural historians, Constance Rourke, was a consultant to the valuable *Index of American Design.* And there are few interpretations of the "American Renaissance" in nineteenth-century New England as lasting as Conrad Aiken's essay in the Massachusetts State Guide.

As late as 1941, just before Pearl Harbor, America's median income was

$1,070; in other words, as many people had annual earnings below that figure as had incomes above it. One-half of one percent of Americans at the top received as much income as the whole third of the people at the bottom. A migratory farm family earned $1.50 for chopping cotton over a fourteen-hour day. In the depths of the Depression, prices were often lower than they had been in the nineteenth century; it was not unusual to eat a whole dinner for fifty cents in a decent if not fashionable restaurant. (The liberal columnist and founder of the Newspaper Guild, Heywood Broun, genially explained the suddenly conservative grumblings of a rival columnist, Westbrook Pegler: "Peg recently paid as much as $2 for dinner.") But as *New York Panorama* notes in its soundly factual chapter on social welfare, "New York As Good Samaritan," relief in New York in one year alone, 1936, public and private, amounted to $310 million.

In the worst of the Depression a quarter of America's work force was unemployed. When Roosevelt came into office in March 1933, the national income was less than $50 billion. (By midsummer 1945, thanks to the expansion of the war period, the liquid assets of the American people were three times that.) One of the best records of the Depression period, Matthew Josephson's *Infidel in the Temple,* quotes a famous surgeon recalling that his millionaire patients lived "in a state of sheer terror." Henry Ford at the outset of the economic crisis dismissed eighty percent of his two hundred and fifty thousand workers, but maintained a private army of a thousand thugs "to guard his grandchildren" against the unemployed. On the East River docks a vast emergency shelter housed thousands of men every night. In mid-Manhattan the public squares and parks were filled with crowds of homeless men carrying their belongings in paper bags. At the low point of the "crisis" (ended only by the war) one out of three families was in distress. On May Day 1931, when sixty thousand people gathered in Union Square to protest unemployment, the police trained machine guns on them.

By 1938, when *New York Panorama* appeared, the New Deal had not yet lost out to the international crisis. The fiery Fiorello LaGuardia was Mayor of New York, and things had improved just enough for a note of determined cheerfulness to salt-and-pepper the *Panorama*'s description of contemporary New York. ("Old New York," from Peter Stuyvesant to the Jazz Age, was pleasanter to write about.) In 1938 the Spanish Republic was still resisting Franco (whose allies were Hitler, Mussolini, and a good many right-wing sympathizers in the British Foreign Office and the Catholic Church). Stalin, though busily shooting most of the "Old

Bolsheviks," was promoting a Popular Front against Fascism. Hitler, Mussolini, and the Japanese militarists were clearly itching for war, but Russia somehow or other and despite everything would surely be a barrier to the Axis powers.

Or so it seemed to many intellectuals and writers, especially in New York. New York in 1938 was not quite the "world capital" it would become during World War II, when some of the greatest European painters thronged Fifty-Seventh Street. (As Yehudi Menuhin said, "One of the great war aims is to get to New York.") By the 1940s, and especially in the unexpected postwar expansion of the economy, New York became the greatest possible world center. But even in the depressed thirties it was the most cosmopolitan of American cities, the center of publishing and printing, a major subject of American writing. It was linked to European politics, art, music, literature, by its masses of foreign-born and their many intellectual and creative children. Ever since the early twentieth century (when the *New York Times* became a modern newspaper and a unique resource to educated people), the city typified a restless intelligence in relation to the international scene that was still unknown in Washington, engulfed by the 1930s in the search for national "recovery."

Given the times and given New York, there is an obvious sympathy in *New York Panorama* with labor, with the poor, and even a discreet tinge of old-fashioned left-wing populism. It is like going down memory lane to read the caption under one photograph in the book—"Rockefeller Center's Sunken Plaza—For Those Who Can Afford It." Or this one: "Campus of City College, Where Students Take Life and Politics Seriously." This caption is so discreet as to be unintelligible to the Harvard and Yale children of City College alumni. What the caption writer did not say was that City College students of my generation battled each other ideologically night and day, attacked visiting Italian Fascist students, and were denounced by the college's president as "guttersnipes."

Given the spirit of the age and the temper of some members of the Writers' Project, it is now laughable, if not pathetic, to read in this book's chapter on the press, "Newspaperman's Mecca"—"The *Daily Worker*, official organ of the Communist Party of the United States, occupies an important place among New York's labor newspapers. Many well-informed persons outside the labor movement now find it necessary or desirable to supplement their reading of the regulation newspapers with a perusal of the *Daily Worker* in order to obtain a balanced and comprehensive view of current affairs." It would be dishonest to omit from the New York described in the *Panorama* the radicalism of the time, though it was confined to a limited group. I am bemused by the fact that some of those 1930s radicals are now among Ronald Reagan's most fervent supporters. Thinking in ideologies is a habit hard to shake off.

The transformation of the city since 1938 makes *New York Panorama* an often-amusing period piece as well as a brisk record of what the writers in 1938 thought of as "Old New York." The changes brought about by World War II and its aftermath have turned the 1930s into "Old New York"!

New York in 1938 still had the "el"—the elevated railroads darkening Third, Sixth, and Ninth Avenues. The *Panorama* judiciously notes that trolleys were still running, but would soon be missed. A plane flying seven thousand feet above the Alleghenies manifested the "neotechnic" age which so riveted the anonymous writers; flaunting their expertise along with their literary talent, they wrote of pilots with "senses extended in the antennules of a hundred instruments." Floyd Bennett Field was still New York's "international" airport. No LaGuardia, no Idlewild or Kennedy. Little helmeted Greek "Mercury" figures sat atop the Fifth Avenue traffic lights. The famous avenue still had double-decker buses (fare one slim dime)—and some of the upper decks, by gosh, were open. A *New Yorker* cartoon of the period portraying couples entwined on the upper deck emphasized one couple not so occupied. The conductor in the cartoon (conductors used to go around with a little machine into which you inserted your dime, and which then *rang* with a merry clang) is saying to the one gent on the upper deck not embracing a girl, "Will you please put your arm around her! You're being conspicuous!"

In 1938 all men "going out to business" (and many just going out into the street) wore fedoras, and many of the women wore hats. Clothes in winter were somber. In Berenice Abbott's wonderful photographs of Depression crowds crossing Fifth Avenue and Forty-Second Street—the "crossroads of the world"—you can still see how much more formal, mannered, upright, and "correct" people were—or had to look. (Society still exacted greater obedience than it does today—on the surface.) Broadway was "The Great White Way"; there was still vaudeville at the Palace and "stage shows" along with the "feature film" at Radio City Music Hall. As the *Panorama* accurately notes, Radio City boasted the "largest and emptiest mural" around. There were "movie palaces"—the Paramount, the Astor, the Capitol—on the same side of Broadway as the Astor Hotel, where, when in New York, Toscanini dwelt (and chased divas). There were "movie palaces" even in downtown Brooklyn, where the RKO Albee (or was the name the other way around?) seemed to be constructed of nothing but marble. As the *Panorama* comments about the New York Paramount, "Its owners spent a million dollars and made every nickel show."

Despite the Depression, young people—then as now—always had money and time enough for entertainment. As a young freelance trudging weekly to the *Times* on Forty-Third Street in the hope of getting a book to review, I would have to push my way through the tremendous crowds outside the Paramount waiting impatiently to hear Frank Sinatra or Benny Goodman. "The Great White Way" was raffish, of course, but somehow had *style* and was even funny. There was a large electric Camels cigarette sign that showed a figure blowing out real smoke. Broadway was not as lowdown as it has become since porn invaded the movies, and drug dealers, transvestites, and pimps made it dangerous to walk Forty-Second Street.

New York has always been strong on boosting itself, and the *Panorama* is not shy about setting out the facts and figures that prove New York the "biggest," the "richest," the "smartest." An obvious amount of civic pride—sweet and genuine, not manufactured to decorate campaign buttons and T-shirts as it is now—fills its pages and innocently inflates its style. In 1938 the Empire State Building *was* the tallest building in America—in the world! The Chrysler Building *was* a perfect demonstration of Art Deco at its most monumental, just before Art Deco died. "There stand the inconceivable spires of Manhattan," runs one sentence presenting New York as the "wonder city" "to the men and women of the small towns, the sierras, the cornlands and grasslands, the seaboard coves and Gulf bayous—farmers, automobile mechanics, packrats, schoolteachers. . . ."

The writers of this book had to get a lot of things in, and fast. The style had to be all-inclusive, vivid in the documentary style of the period and up-to-the-minute for people still impressed with themselves for living in the "neotechnic age":

Perhaps only the industrial engineer begins to comprehend the technical changes in transportation between Chaucer's time—or even Whitman's—and the 1930's. Unless the traveler drives his own car, he must resign himself to the helmsmen of the neotechnic age—locomotive engineers, ships' quartermasters, bus drivers, transport pilots—whose responsibilities have been reapportioned into a vast complex of schedules, maintenance men, radio directional and telephone signals, cartographers, traffic lights, instrument panels and routine instructions, all centered on New York.

Long before New York was threatened with bankruptcy and it became necessary for discouraged citizens to insist that the city was the "Big Apple" and that they "loved" New York, there was a real, tough, endlessly resistant New York civic pride typified by the enduring legend of Al Smith from Oliver Street, the street-wise adroit dancing rhythms (in everything he said, did, walked) of Jimmy Cagney from Yorkville, the proud sentimentality of Irving Berlin from the lower East Side, the ironic lyricism of George Gershwin from Brooklyn. In the days when the vast electric sign on Broadway promoting Lucky Strikes featured endorsements by the reigning "stars of stage and screen," Fanny Brice was amazed to hear that a friend had turned down "a fortune" to recommend the weed. "My God," Fanny screamed, "I would endorse a chewing tobacco for half a buck!"

It is diverting to read in New York Panorama that since 1907 New York "taxicabs have been a perpetual source of discussion, first as to their desirability in the horse-and-buggy era, later as to the number necessary for the city's needs. The outcome . . . will very likely continue to have very little effect on the men who drive the cabs. Drawn from many nationalities and including all types, they know New York from end to end."

Less diverting, in a period when law officials battling the billion-dollar drug traffic are quoted in the New York Times as conceding that "the volume is burying us," is the news from 1937 that the drugs regularly seized in New York ports (mostly opium) amounted in one fiscal year to $2 million. More entertaining is the chapter on sports, which dutifully notes that the great city of New York boasts three major baseball teams. Not a word about the Brooklyn Dodgers! Nary a mention of Ebbets Field! But History has taken its revenge. The extended discussion of the Polo Grounds will mean nothing to a generation that probably thinks the Giants started in San Francisco. It will miss entirely the sarcasm behind this passage: "The Giants are gentlemen off and on. One of the greatest defensive combinations ever, they defend themselves at one and the same time from hot grounders, internecine strife and public vilification." On the other hand, how nice it is in 1984 to read of such discarded follies as this: ". . . the National Negro Baseball League in . . . New York is represented by the Black Yankees, who play at Dyckman Oval. Though Negroes have been playing professionally since the 1880s, and have developed more than one authentic star of the diamond, none has yet appeared in major league baseball."

The competitively refined tone of the different writers here is sometimes archly at variance with the subject. "Stickball," played in ancient
Brooklyn without a stick as "punchball," is described as "easily the city's
greatest summer game. For this variant, the required equipment is a rubber
ball, a broomstick, and a street with or without traffic. Primarily a kid's
game, it often enough pulls papa off the front stoop of an evening to do
or die against the kids from the next street." I am glad the writers got
papa off the stoop. What they don't say is that in the thirties every
decent street had a team of its own and that competition was organized
by neighborhood.

Considering what has happened to Eighth Avenue, now bedeviled by
porn commercializing every imaginable (and unimaginable) sexual
fantasy and combination, it is touching to read that in 1938 it was an
avenue not only of pawnshops but also of rooming houses and small hotels
typifying backstage poverty. Thanks to this book, I am happy to remember
the Civic Repertory Theater on Fourteenth Street under the inspired
leadership of Eva Le Gallienne, where at sixteen I first saw Ibsen. The
book makes me fond even of the old left-wing Theater Union, though its
raucous productions are overpraised. A last hurrah for the wonderful
Group Theater (I had forgotten that it was originally a subsidiary of the
Theater Guild), which made possible the career of Clifford Odets and
Awake and Sing, Paradise Lost, Golden Boy, Rocket to the Moon. The
emphasis in the book on "social issues" in the theater now seems so old-
fashioned (Broadway is sillier than ever) that I can smile benevolently
at the homage to long-forgotten *New Theater Magazine,* "which under
the audacious editorship of Herbert Kline soon became the most important
publication of its kind in America. It fought for truth in the theater and
introduced in its pages such sensational hits as *Waiting for Lefty, Bury
the Dead* and *Hymn to the Rising Sun.*"

Ah, time in its flight! Where now are Betty Boop, gravel-voiced Lionel
Stander, mock-pugnacious Jimmy Durante ("Schnozzola"), the Trans-Lux
Newsreel Theaters on Broadway? Where the New York *Sun,* the *Herald
Tribune,* Walter Winchell, the Yacht Club Boys "at one of the more
exclusive upper East Side night clubs poking fun at alphabetic government
agencies in such a way as to please their special audience"? Where are
Charlie McCarthy, the *Brooklyn Daily Eagle,* the *Bronx Home News,* the
old "Swamp" district just off Brooklyn Bridge, David Stern's New York
Post, the McAlpin Hotel, the "gloomy isolation" of the Villard Houses
on Madison Avenue? Whatever happened to "Thirteenth Avenue," to

the private railroad siding once provided for the *really* top guests at the Waldorf Astoria, a hotel built over the tracks of the New York Central? Any news of the three sweet wonderful Rhinelander Houses, once the boast of lower Fifth Avenue, of the "noble simplicity" that once dominated the eastern corner there? Where are the crowds that used to hang around taxi dancers at dance "palaces" like the Savoy and Roseland? Why did the great book-printing companies of New York disappear—companies that made it possible to get a book out in a few months? To the little Japanese colonies in New York once engaged in importing gift junk? Where is Tammany Hall now, where the Orozco and Rivera murals at the New School? Where the "traction interests" that once held New Yorkers fief to private companies like the Interborough Rapid Transit Company, the Brooklyn and Manhattan Company? Where, indeed, is "rapid transit," and does anybody else remember when Spanish was the mother tongue of just 200,000 residents of New York? When milk was delivered every morning by a "milkman" driving a horse-drawn wagon, when Welfare Island contained the City Penitentiary? Anybody still around who remembers Jimmy Walker, the crooked Brooklyn sheriff with his "little tin box," reformer Samuel Seabury? Thomas E. Dewey, who on page 77 enters *New York Panorama* with such a flourish?

On August 7, 1935, he opened his investigation and caused the arrest of the first racketeer. By September 11, when the indicted man had pleaded guilty to an extortion charge, the public began to see in this 33-year-old special prosecutor the newest hope of law and order. . . . On April 18, 1936 . . . the powerful "Lucky" Luciano . . . found himself jailed in New York City in the unheard-of bail of $350,000, which he could not raise; and on June 18, he was sentenced to a prison term of from 30 to 50 years. . . .

Of course *we* know that "Lucky" got out of jail soon enough. He is supposed to have earned his freedom by ordering the Mafia to assist U.S. troops in the invasion of Sicily. Or so rumor has it. Anyway, history in New York is fabulous, and the answer to "Where are they now?" is that they are all in this book. Of course there are omissions and even a few slight errors. The great landscape artist and creator of Central Park was Frederick Law Olmsted, not Olmstead. John Brown was executed not at Harper's Ferry but Charlestown, Virginia. "Caribbean" is twice misspelled. But more important, the book makes one sigh for the days when "In addition to being America's greatest commercial center, New York is also this country's major industrial city. More workers are paid more wages for producing more goods in more manufacturing establishments here than in any other American city—or indeed, than in any one of 43 states."

New York has not been the same since it became altogether too much of a white-collar town. There is good reason to believe that despite the corporate wealth frothing at the top, New York has never recovered the sound financial base it had as a producer of industrial goods.

New York Panorama ends on an anticipation of the World's Fair that opened in 1939, just on the eve of World War II. The fair, with its Trylon and Perisphere, its "Futurama" and other visions of the super-technical age that indeed.came to pass, is now another barely recoverable memory of what, despite the terribleness of the thirties, *was* an age of innocence. By contrast with that age, New York now seems almost too hectically "important" to be described in a book like *New York Panorama*. The world is pouring in more than ever. But who would have believed in the 1930s that New York would be full, on such a scale, of masses of refugees from Latin and Central America, China and Korea, Russia and Eastern Europe (when they can get here)? Who would have believed, in the age of "anti-Jewish education quotas," that Columbia University would in the 1980s pick a Jew as president? That New York would steal the idea of modern art from Paris and become the world capital of modern art? Wonders on wonders. But also madness on a scale never dreamed of in the depths of the Depression, also destitution and neglect to which the employed seem totally indifferent, fear of the city on the part of many who have left and of the many more who cannot leave.

Grover Whalen, once New York's official greeter of Channel swimmers and other celebrities, was president of the New York World's Fair Corporation. One of the many valuable time-capsule Great Sayings of New Yorkers commemorated in *New York Panorama* was pronounced by Whalen when he returned from the Paris Exposition of 1937. He was

optimistic on the subject of peace. Should his prediction of world peace turn out to be correct—or even, perhaps, if it doesn't—it is reasonably certain that on April 3, 1939, commemorating Washington's inauguration in New York City exactly 150 years earlier, the biggest and costliest of all expositions will open at Flushing Meadow Park, Queens. For the first time in its history, Greater New York will be host to the world; and as a press release of the corporation suggests, this announcement in itself is "enough to set the world agog—for the world well knows New York's reputation for carrying through to spectacular success."

How right that was! Only the other day I read in the *New York Times* that the World Trade Center "is a city unto itself." It feeds 30,000 people a day, is a 110-story complex of six buildings with 6 sixteen-acre underground levels beneath them. The World Trade Center has a resident business population of 50,000, a daily transient population of 80,000. One of its engineers boasts that "with all pumps running, we could pump water from West Street to New Jersey."

New York not only "sets the world agog." It sets itself agog. Of course there are discontented white-collar types who complain, as a character does in Christopher Knowlton's *The Real World,* "Doesn't it scare you that you may live here and do pretty much what we do today until the day you retire, and the only difference will be you eat in better restaurants?" But here is the mayor of New York, the Honorable Edward I. Koch: "Somehow or other, truly or falsely . . . when you see yourself as a New Yorker you talk faster, you walk faster and you think faster." That is the everlasting New York—"panoramic" as all get-out.

June 1, 1984   ALFRED KAZIN

Metropolis and Her Children

THE RUMOR of a great city goes out beyond its borders, to all the latitudes of the known earth. The city becomes an emblem in remote minds; apart from the tangible export of goods and men, it exerts its cultural instrumentality in a thousand phases: as an image of glittering light, as the forcing ground which creates a new prose style or a new agro-biological theory, or as the germinal point for a fresh technique in metal sculpture, biometrics or the fixation of nitrogen. Its less ponderable influence may be a complex of inextricable ideas, economic exchanges, associations, artifacts: the flask of perfume which brings Fifth Avenue to a hacienda in the Argentine, the stencil marks on a packing case dumped on the wharf at Beira or Reykjavik, a flurry of dark-goggled globe-trotters from a cruise ship, a book of verse

> Under the stone I saw them flow
> express Times Square at five o'clock
> eyes set in darkness

read in a sheepherder's hut in New South Wales, or a Harlem band playing *Young Woman's Blues* from a phonograph as the safari breaks camp in Tanganyika under a tile-blue morning sky as intensely lighted as the panorama closed by mountains in the ceiling dome of the African section at the American Museum of Natural History.

The orbit of such a world city as New York also intersects the orbits of other world cities. New York, London, Tokyo, Rome exchange preferred stocks and bullion, ships' manifests and radio programs—in rivalry or well-calculated friendship. During the 1920's, for example, a jump spark crackled between New York and Paris. The art of Matisse, Derain, Picasso commanded the Fifty-Seventh Street market. The French developed a taste for *le jazz* and *le sport;* in an atmosphere of war debts and the Young Plan, the Americanization of Europe was mentioned. Paris, capital of the

Valutaschweine, became the bourne of good and gay New Yorkers, the implicit heroine of a comedy by Philip Barry or a novel by Ernest Hemingway. The French replied, though not always in kind. Georges Duhamel pronounced a jeremiad against the machine apocalypse in America and Paul Morand, an amateur of violence, explored the sensational diversity of New York. These were symptomatic. The comments of Jules Romains went deeper and established fixed points for contrast with a later period.

All the rays of force alive in the modern world move inward upon the city, and the burning glass of its attraction concentrates them in the flame that is New York. Historically, it has been to an exceptional degree a city of accumulation: its methods promotion and commerce, its principle aggrandizement. About a nucleus of Dutch and English—even French Huguenot—settlers it subsequently collected swarm after swarm of Irish, German, Italian, Jewish and Russian immigrants, a proportion of other nationalities, and Americans of many stocks from the seaboard and the interior. For the most part, those immigrants who remained in the city were compacted into districts especially suited to their exploitation, districts as verminous and sunless as the Cloaca Maxima. Here, in dwellings that reproduced the foetor of the slave ship in all but the promise of eventual liberty held out to the more intelligent or ruthless, they formed a crawling agglomeration. This was the frontier of New York and the grim apotheosis of the frontier in the United States, preserved almost untouched into the third decade of the 20th century.

The shawled refugees from European want and oppression, most of whom crossed the ocean in immigrant ships under conditions of the utmost squalor, were also transported by a succession of great New York trade vessels: the Black Ball and other Western Ocean packet lines, the world-ranging Donald McKay clippers, the first wood and iron steamships. These were conned through the Narrows by men off the superb Sandy Hook pilot schooners which had been worked out from the designs of Isaac Webb in the 1830's, the hollow-entrance experiments of Griffiths in the 1840's, and the later masterly work of George Steers in such craft as the *Moses H. Grinnell* and the *America,* for which the *America's* Cup was named. Great numbers of immigrants and New Yorkers moved inland by way of the Hudson River sloops and steamboats, the Conestoga wagons, the Erie Canal barges and the railroads. Very early, therefore, the history of New York began to be a history of the successive phases in American transportation. As its lines of influence spread out into the interior, thickened and were fixed, it became more and more the commanding American city, the maker or merchant of dress silks and pannikins and spices, wines and beds and grub hoes. Long before the paramount age of sail ended, New York had taken on its alternate character as a great two-way transfer point and classification yard for men and goods and ideas moving between the other countries of the world and the great central plain of America. It has consolidated and enlarged this character with a multiplicity of functions which help to determine its position as the first city of the Western Hemisphere.

Approach to the City

For the American traveler coming home from Cape Town or St. Moritz or the Caribbean, and for those others who converge upon the city from Chicago and El Paso and Kildeer and Tonopah, New York has a nearer meaning. It is, in whatever sense, a substitute home town—a great apartment hotel, as Glenway Wescott wrote, in which everyone lives and no one is at home. In other eyes it may be a state fair grown to magnificence, a Main Street translated into the imperial splendor of Fifth Avenue. To such travelers the city is a coat of many colors—becoming to each, but not quite his own. It is both novelty and recognition that pleases him: the novelty of its actual and amazing encompassment, the recognition of great shafts and crowds and thoroughfares remembered from a hundred motion pictures, rotogravures and advertisements.

The man from another city will perhaps be least discommoded, his sense of the familiar both intensified and expanded. But to the men and women of the small towns, the sierras, the cornlands and grasslands, the seaboard coves and Gulf bayous—farmers, automobile mechanics, pack-rats, schoolteachers—New York cannot help but stand as a special order: the place which is not wilderness, the place of light and warmth and the envelopment of the human swarm, the place in which everyone is awake and laughing at three in the morning. These things are not altogether true, of course—but magic does not need to be true.

The traveler will know many things about New York and there will be guides to tell him many more, in the particular and the large; but he will see by looking, and find out by asking, and match the figure to the phenomenon. He may know that New York City is made up of five boroughs, four of which—Brooklyn, Queens, Richmond, the Bronx—compose like crinkled lily pads about the basking trout of Manhattan. He will not know, perhaps, that he and the other men and women who travel with him helped to make up a total of 68,999,376 visitors to the city in 1936, an off year. If he is an agronomist, he may find a certain perverse irony in the fact that the 198,330 acres of the five boroughs, without any tillage worth mentioning, supported an estimated population of 7,434,346 in 1937.

But it is less likely that the visitor who moves down one of those enormous radials that converge on New York from Seattle and Galveston and Los Angeles and Chicago will understand how Thomas Campanella's vision of a City of the Sun, published in 1623, has influenced the growth of such a modern metropolis as New York. Nor will he be aware, perhaps, that the verses of Walt Whitman and the paintings of "The Eight" and the landscape architecture of Olmsted the elder, quite as much as the Roeblings' Brooklyn Bridge and the Hoe press and the steel converters of Kelly and Bessemer, helped to create the social climate of the emerging city.

In the larger aspects of New York he may glimpse not only the results of the Randall Plan of 1811, but evidences of the influence of Geddes, Norton, Wright, McClellan, Bassett, Delano, Burnham, Keppel, James, the Olmsteds, Lewis, Whitten, Howard, Unwin, Wilgus, Mumford, Adams, McAneny, Stein, Perkins, Walsh, the indefatigable Moses, and a hundred others of the noble guild of city planners, up to and including the work of the Regional Plan of New York and Its Environs, the Port of New York Authority, the New York Department of Parks and the New York City Planning Commission. He will wish to know how the city changes, the extent and character of its physical property, and something about the nature and complexity of its functions. But he will understand that plant and function are never more than indicators of a series of cultural choices and directions. Finally, he will be made aware of these choices and directions at their source, in the character, convictions and behavior of New Yorkers themselves: the faces, vivid or distracted, washed in neon light the color of mercurochrome, faces of men and women who work and eat and make love in catacombs under the enormous pylons of their city.

The traveler approaches in bare winter or rainy autumn, in keen seaboard spring or the dog days. He drives a faded sedan with a child slung in a hammock cradle in the rear; or he takes the hot bouillon and crackers of the great airlines. He walks the glassed-in promenade deck of the *Normandie* or the open boat deck of the *Nieuw Amsterdam;* or he lounges in the doorway of the *Manhattan's* radio room. In the streamlined club cars of the Yankee Clipper, the Twentieth Century, the Royal Blue, the Broadway Limited, or in the day coaches of slower trains, he turns the pages of a national or trade journal published in New York—*Women's Wear, Collier's, Life, Variety, Printers' Ink*—and watches the conglomerate backyards of Albany-Bridgeport-Trenton slide past the window. Painted with slipstream whorls, his blunt-nosed bus trundles out of the lunch stop and bores Manhattan-ward again, the whipcord back of the driver twisted as he pulls out and around a great dark pantechnicon truck with small lamps at its clearance points.

The traveler is a fuel company executive returning from a trip through the West, a copy of *Saward's Coal Annual* wedged into the briefcase beside him; an elementary school principal from Lewiston, bound for special courses at Barnard College; a Cleveland printer out of a job, a men's wear buyer from Jacksonville, a Brooklyn clergyman on his return trip from Rome, a Pittsburgh engineer coming back from a South American cruise, a San Francisco divorcee loosed in Reno and remarried to a Hollywood fashion designer commuting to New York. These make up a composite American as alive and definite as Chaucer's pilgrims or Whitman's cameradoes of democracy.

But perhaps only the industrial engineer begins to comprehend the technical changes in transportation between Chaucer's time—or even Whitman's—and the 1930's. Unless the traveler drives his own car, he must resign himself to the helmsmen of the neotechnic age—locomotive engineers, ships' quartermasters, bus drivers, transport pilots—whose responsibilities have been reapportioned into a vast complex of schedules, maintenance men, radio directional and telephone signals, cartographers, traffic lights, instrument panels and routine instructions, all centered on New York.

The helmsmen themselves are aware of their place in this network. The locomotive engineer knows it, intent on the block signals aimed at and swallowed by the rush of his train, a full minute to be made up between Poughkeepsie and Grand Central Terminal. The bus driver gunning his coach in heavy traffic over US1 from New England, or the Albany Post Road, or the Sunrise Highway, or the loop over the Pulaski Skyway into the Jersey City mouth of the Holland Tunnel feels responsibility like a small knot between his shoulder blades: the need for quick and certain decisions, the judgment of space and time and the intent of drivers and a small boy heedless on a bicycle.

The pilot of Flight 16 eastbound, crossing the Alleghenies in cloud at

7,000 feet, knows it well. When his tally of instruments—altimeter, clock, air speed, bank and turn, artificial horizon—indicates that he has passed the outer marker, he reports by radio to the company dispatcher at Newark Metropolitan Airport, chief terminus for the New York district. Passengers rub at the bleared windows. But as he nears the inner marker at Martin's Creek, the mist begins to fade apart into soft translucent islands drenched with sun and the voice from the Newark radio control tower comes in with the tone of a man speaking clearly in the same room: "WREE to Western Trip 16, Pilot Johnson. Stuff breaking up fast. You are cleared at 3,000 feet to the range station. You're Number Two airplane."

In the chart-room of a transatlantic liner inbound from Cherbourg to New York, 200 miles off Fire Island in a pea-soup fog, the blasts of the automatic ship's siren at intervals of one minute vibrate amongst the polished metal or enameled instruments: the chronometers, telephone, radio compass, loudspeaker, mercury and aneroid barometers, gyro course-indicator and other devices of the new scientific navigation. The senior watch officer checks his chronometers against time signals from Nauen, Arlington and the Eiffel Tower. A seaman at the radio directional compass slowly swivels the frame of his antenna ring until the note of the Fire Island radio beacon—plangent as a tuning fork, but crisper— is loudest in his headphones. Making a cross-check, the junior watch officer sets down fathometer depth readings on a length of tracing paper in such a way that it can be laid over the chart for comparison with course and position marks.

Immobile in the dark wheelhouse, the helmsman concentrates on the lighted compass before him. No longer must he watch for the telltale flutter of the leech, or nurse his ship in weather seas. In the 330 years between Henry Hudson's *Half Moon*, steered into the future New York Harbor with a wheel-and-whipstaff rig that resembled a four-armed capstan with elongated bars, and the great express ships of the 1930's, already obsolescent in view of operating costs, irreducible vibration and other factors, the helmsman's responsibilities have been shorn away by engineers and technicians. The automatic steering device, or "Iron Mike," has even in part replaced him.

These new helmsmen of land and sea and air are the creatures of demanding time, their senses extended in the antennules of a hundred instruments. So they must necessarily regard the city a little as the gunnery officer does his target; but they too feel its magnetism. It comes to the traveler a great way off, like the intimation of any other dense human engagement. The expectant nerves contract, the mind is sensitized in advance. A familiar visitor, a New Yorker, waits for the sense of the city's resumed envelopment; but the bus passenger coming down over the Boston Post Road from New England watches traffic slow and thicken as the environs towns become larger, draw together, give off the effect of a brisker life. There is a moment in which he asks himself: "Are we in the city yet? Is this New York?" The visitor by rail, if he approaches from the south, may get hardly a glimpse of the towers before he tunnels under the river and coasts to a stop along the platform at Pennsylvania Station. Coming in from the north, he cannot help but be struck by the infinite pueblo of the Bronx.

But to the traveler by air, especially from the north or east, the city appears with the instancy of revelation: the slowly crinkling samite of its rivers and New York Harbor vaporous beyond, the Bronx splayed out and interwoven with the tight dark Hudson Valley foliage, Brooklyn and Queens and Staten Island dispersed in their enormous encampments about the narrow seaward-thrusting rock of Manhattan. Seen thus from above, the pattern of the island suggests a weirdly shaped printer's form. It is as if the lead rules had been picked out for avenues between the solid lines of type which are buildings. The skyscrapers—those characters too pointed to be equalized by the wooden mallet of the makeup man—prickle up along the lower rim of Central Park, through the midtown section, and most densely at the foot of the island.

These last are what the homebound traveler by water sees as his vessel comes through the Narrows into the Lower Bay, a journey and journey's end which has always somehow the quality of a public triumph. There stand the inconceivable spires of Manhattan—composed, repeating the upthrust torch of Liberty, at first almost without the sense of great weight, the distraction of archaic and heterogeneous detail. The forms of "gypsum crystals," a giant's cromlech, a mass of stalagmites, "the Cathedrals and Great White Thrones of the National Parks," an Arizona mesa, a "ship of living stone," a petrified forest, "an irregular tableland intersected by shadowy cañons," a mastodon herd, "a pin-cushion," the Henry Mountains in Utah, "a vertical aggregation," dividends in the sky: such metaphors reflect its diversity of association. As Melville's *Redburn* indicates, the term *skyscraper* itself—a noun full in the homely tradition of the American vernacular—was once synonymous with *moon-sail* and *cloudraker* as the name for a ship's topmost kites.

Le Corbusier, celebrated French architect in the International style, refers to this massed upthrust as "the winning of a game: proclamation by skyscraper." And in the third book of Jules Romains' *Psyché,* Pierre Febvre thinks of it as "a rivalry of tumefactions constructed in haste on the rock of Manhattan, a typical fragment of American unreality." Taken together, both images—a sense of the grandiose subjective exemplified in architectural terms, and the perhaps consequent suggestion of imperfectly realized forms—help to clarify a profound intimation of the familiar experienced by many travelers, even those who have no acquaintance with the city. In one of the Regional Plan volumes, this intimation is dramatized, simply enough, by photographs on facing pages: one of lower Manhattan, the other of Mont-Saint-Michel, the ancient fortress rock of France, a cluster of towers about which the tides swirl like level avalanches.

The visual analogy is striking, but it does not end there. The image of the medieval castle-town has gone deep into the consciousness of western man. Preserved in masonry at Mont-Saint-Michel and Carcassonne, stylized in the perspectives of a hundred medieval and Renaissance painters, translated into fantasy in the fairy tales of Andersen and Perrault and the towers of Cloud Cuckoo Land, popularized in the colors of Dulac and Rackham and Parrish and the mass-production lampshade, it reappears in the apparition of lower Manhattan evoked by the new technology: the medieval image of power, the infantile or schizoid fantasy of withdrawal, the supreme image of escape to the inaccessible.

The Concept of the City

Historically, as Robert L. Duffus points out in *Mastering a Metropolis,* cities "have tended to grow up *around* something—a fortification, a temple, a market-place, a landing-place." In other words, the selection of site and arrangement have usually been determined by a choice of social function, a definite cultural emphasis. Sometimes it was relatively accidental. On the principle that travelers may be customers, a market town grew up at a crossroads. The walled towns of the Middle Ages, usually grouped about a castle for efficient defense, retained to some extent the lines of a military camp; but the exigencies of space within the walls made for a certain homogeneous and charming irregularity. The radial plans of the Renaissance, of which Karlsruhe is the most striking example, probably developed from the Greek and Roman cities clustered around a central temple or forum, although they retained some of the medieval irregularities.

Parallel with the unplanned growth of cities, there has always been a tradition of planned cities, conceived either as Utopias—by Plato in his *Republic*, More in his *Utopia*, Campanella in his *City of the Sun*, Bellamy in his *Looking Backward*, Samuel Butler in his *Erewhon*, to name only a few—or by architects and city planners for actual realization in stone and mortar. The geometrical design for Alexandria, and Wren's project for the rebuilding of London after the great fire were examples of this kind. Notable among them was the plan for Washington. Challenged by the unexpectedly possible, Jefferson studied the city patterns of Europe and with Washington and L'Enfant evolved the American capital city.

But it is significant that in general the tradition of abstract design, surviving through the Renaissance, through Karlsruhe and Palladio and Wren into the era of L'Enfant's Washington and Haussmann's renovation of Paris, is basically eclectic, corresponding almost exactly to the anachronistic revivals of the classic orders or the Gothic in architecture. But the criticism is not merely negative; it implies a basic disregard of the primacy of cultural function, of the possible and fruitful coordination between plant and function and environment in a new order of the city.

In any case, for good or ill, planned cities did not by any means represent the dominant mode in urban evolution. If there was one, it can only be called agglomeration; the gathering of flies around a stain of honey. More often than not, that honey was commerce, additionally sweetened by the perquisites of a capital city. Philip II, for example, deliberately built up the municipal strength of Paris as an offset to the challenge of the nobles, thus contributing to the new nationalism and the upswing of the merchant classes. Tudor London, clamorous with trades and spiky with the masts of ships, added central cells of industry to the commercial swarming of the city. After the great fires of the next century, Wren suggested that wherever possible industries should be relocated on the outer margins of the city—a recommendation seconded by Walter Curt Behrendt and the New York Regional Plan in the 1930's.

The advent of what Sir Patrick Geddes called the paleotechnic period, early in the 19th century, with its criteria of absolute utilitarianism, gradually created the inhuman ratholes of London and Glasgow and Birmingham and New York and Berlin—that "home city of the rent barracks." Dickens described a composite of industrial cities as Coketown. "It had a black canal in it, and a river that ran purple with ill-smelling dye"; and "the piston of the steam engine worked monotonously up and down, like the head of an elephant in a state of melancholy madness. It contained several large streets all very like one another, inhabited by people exactly like one another, who all went in and out at the same hours, with the same sound upon the same pavements to do the same work, and to whom every day was the same as yesterday and tomorrow, and every year the counterpart of the last and the next."

New York City, of all the great communities in the modern world, has been most acted upon by the agencies incident to the 19th century revolution in industry and techniques, most subject to the devastating consequences of 19th century *laissez faire* and the tensions of excessively rapid growth, most influenced by the multiplication and hypertrophy of functions, most compromised by a street plan which united some of the inconvenient features of the rigidly classical and the narrowly utilitarian, most unstable in the number and distribution of its population, most opportunistic in land uses, most anarchic in the character of its building, and most dynamic in the pulse and variety of its living ways.

In a history of some 330 years, of which hardly more than a century has been taken up with major growth, New York has somehow condensed and accommodated the stresses of 20 centuries in the evolution of Rome or Paris. Such drastic foreshortening exacted a price and developed an opportunity. The price was paid and is being paid in the primary conception of the city as merely an accumulation: the largest size, the greatest number (even of units of quality), and the highest speed. It was paid in the ruthlessness—and the complementary meliorism that all this would somehow right itself—of what may be called the utilitarian imperative, which cut off waterside areas from public use, gobbled up available park sites, covered blocks with sunless tenements and no less sunless apartment houses, made night and day indistinguishable under the overhanging scarps of lower Manhattan, fostered duplication and peculation and high taxes in municipal government, and centered a terrific volume of traffic in a few sectors already overburdened by subway and elevated concentration, the lack of through highways and the density of building.

These became commonplaces, even rules of thumb. At a certain point, the practical effect was that a man could not go to the theater or visit a friend without a wholly disproportionate expenditure of time, energy, ingenuity and money. But in the deepest sense—the sense, that is, in which these processes were at once an expression and reflection of the New Yorker's cultural attitude toward his city—such factors tended to become psychological vested interests. The healthy dynamism of a developing metropolis was perpetuated as neurotic action for its own sake. The original necessity of enduring noise, dirt, conflict, confusion as symptoms of a transitional phase developed into a taste for the mindless intoxicant of sensation. Tall buildings convenient for intracommunication in such activities as finance became tall buildings for the sake of mere height and vainglory. In fine, the psychology of swift growth—its quick sense of the expedient, its prompt resource, its urgent energy, its prodigality in human waste, its impatience with deeper interrelationships and effects, by-products or details—was carried over and intensified in a period which demanded consolidation, an assay of cultural attitudes and values, planning, a new concept of the city.

By 1938 the signs of this new attitude were already sharply manifest. Long before that, in 1931, Thomas Adams could write: "There is no city in the world that has a greater influence than New York. . . All over this continent it is imitated, even where it is said to be feared. Men say New York is a warning rather than an example, and then proceed to make it an example. Outside America, New York is America, and its skyscraper a symbol of the spirit of America. It is not only the largest city in the world, it is the greatest and most powerful city that is not a capital of a nation." There were jeremiads and panegyrics; this was a temperate statement of the fact.

All through the 1920's, New York had been not only the symbol of America but the daemonic symbol of the modern—the fortunate giant in his youth, the world city whose past weighed least heavily upon its future. Had not Paul Morand testified that the latest skyscraper was always the best? It was a city infallible in finance, torrential in pace, unlimited in resource, hard as infrangible diamonds, forever leaping upon the moment beyond. "You can get away with anything," said Ellen Thatcher in John Dos Passos' *Manhattan Transfer*, "if you do it quick enough." Speed—with its dividend, sensation—became the master formula in every human activity and technique: Wall Street, dancing, crime, the theater, construction, even death. "Don't get much time to sleep," said a Broadway soda clerk. "I have to sleep so fast I'm all tired out when I get up in the morning." This was rueful Eddington, the telescoping of time and space—a cliché of the period—in terms of the wear and tear on human metabolism. Photographers, draughtsmen, commentators all attempted to catch this loud moment or to translate it in terms of indefinite extension. An aseptic skyscraper city, an immense machine for living, was projected by such draughtsmen and writers as Hugh Ferriss, Sheldon Cheney, Raymond Hood and Norman Bel Geddes (of whom an anonymous satirist remarked in 1937 that he suffered from "an edifice complex").

In this period too New York had broken out full sail as the American capital of the arts and a world capital of major importance. This was in itself an extraordinary phenomenon. Other large, recently colonial cities —Melbourne, Rio de Janeiro, Toronto, even Mexico City—had shown no such versatile and autochthonous upsurge. It could be explained only in part by a reference to great concentration of wealth and commerce— as usual, a concentration in which artists had little share and against which, for the most part, they swung the shoulder of revolt. This cultural definition came out of the native genius of the city itself and was inseparably collateral with it. To a remarkable degree, the formulation and interpretation of that genius became the first task of the artist in New York.

Historians of another age may find the cultural rivalries of the Eastern seaboard cities in the middle of the 19th century as fruitful a source of social interpretation as their contests in trade. Philadelphia had receded, Charleston and Baltimore settled into their graceful mold. But Boston, as Van Wyck Brooks has superbly recreated it in *The Flowering of New England*, produced a culture articulated in all its parts. It is necessary to indicate more closely here the relative scale of that culture. Its perfect symbol, perhaps, was the figure of Hawthorne confronting the Marble Faun. Its faithfulness to a special Anglo-American tradition at once defined its limits and committed it to contest with the assimilative turbulence of its more democratic neighbor to the southward. Even in Emerson, perhaps, there was something of the merely benign clergyman; even in Thoreau, a little of the truant schoolboy decorating his metaphorical hut at Walden with the knickknacks of Athens and Rome. And even in Emily Dickinson's triumph of the microcosmic, it was possible to feel the sedate child who withdraws from the world to thread in quietude the quicksilver necklaces of the imagination. The neat coherence of parts, the good scholars competing for the prizes of the intelligence, the inflexibility of ethical referrents, the absence of that excess which is also the evidence of supreme vitality, the frugality and unanimity of pattern—all these were the sedate lamplight of a provincial culture, a culture comparable to that of Ghent in the late 14th century or 18th century Dublin and Stockholm.

But there were giants to the southward—men who had consorted with the buffalo and leviathan, who were privy to enormous griefs and ecstasies, who had faced the tremendous gales of the world in their most disintegrative onslaught. These men—Whitman and Melville—were of another breed, another stature; and they proclaimed themselves men of Manhattan. They came of the same Dutch-English stock, bred by that Empire State through which the commerce of the nation had begun to pour. *Moby Dick* appeared in 1851, *Leaves of Grass* in 1855. Both books were shunned or excoriated. Then and later, the culture of New York resembled the tumultuous cross-rips of Hell Gate. Museums, opera, the theater, libraries, lecture halls, schools, the superb education of street and waterfront: these were lavishly available, and Whitman in particular made good use of them. But the dominant tenor of the city was savage in its commercial excesses, ravenous in land use (though the salvaging of Central Park began a few years before the Civil War) and brutal in its disregard for health, amenities, the elementary kindness of life. The deeper significance of such personalities as Whitman and Melville is that they were archetypes of the city's character-to-be. Their decisive feeling for the supreme importance, the frequent nobility of the common man, their immersion by choice in his hopes and occupations—these were as foreign to the men of Boston, with their uneasy self-awareness in the role of scholar-gentlemen, as they would have been to that earlier New Yorker, the James Fenimore Cooper who wrote *The American Democrat.*

"He who touches the soil of Manhattan and the pavement of New York," said Lewis Mumford, "touches, whether he knows it or not, Walt Whitman." Certainly it was Whitman who conceived the city as an image of the democratic process—an historic reversal, it may be noted, of Thomas Jefferson's primary design. The city spoke out of Whitman's fiber: out of the broadest and most intimate lines of *A Broadway Pageant* and *Crossing Brooklyn Bridge,* out of

> Walt Whitman, a kosmos, of Manhattan the son,
> Turbulent, fleshy, sensual, eating, drinking
>   and breeding,

or out of

> . . . submit to no models
> but your own O city!

But in *Democratic Vistas* he faced all the implications of his image: splendor in the amplitude and onrush, "the sparkling sea-tides" and "masses of gay color" which were New York, but confession that to the cold eye appeared "pervading flippancy and vulgarity, low cunning, infidelity" and the rest, even to a degree beyond the average of mankind. But there were poets to be called up, poets to make "a literature underlying life"; to fertilize it, to create again and again the corrective vision of the city in an order more nobly human than itself. Whitman said it and said it plain:

A great city is that which has the greatest men and women.

Did he not help to make good his own words?

But in its essence, Whitman's concept of New York as a symbol of the democratic maelstrom was a neo-romantic one. It rejoiced in the splendor of the fact, hewed close to it, made it Homeric. But was it not, even in that society of transitional latitude, precisely a begging of the question as to *what* means were to be applied to the creation of *what* forms for *what* ends—ends, that is, which might be translated concretely from the abstract *liberty, equality, fraternity, plenty?* Affirmation of greatness to nurture greatness, exultation in diversity for the use and promise of diversity, acceptance of barbarous poverty and wrong in the name of a more humane future, faith in the destiny of the free man intermingling freely with his fellows: these demanded a confident and practical vision of the city as a whole—a vision broader than Campanella's, as instrumental as the machine lathe—formulated and canalized in terms of New York's own native function and genius.

On the contrary, Whitman's noble disorder, with its hospitality to everything human, tended to emphasize precisely those impulses toward unoriented mass, energy, diversity which came to their anarchic ultimate at the end of the 1920's. It was Whitman's dynamic, with its dramatization of the common impulse, that prevailed in the evolving folkways of New York. Even in 1937, the city was most often presented in terms of speed, energy, quantity rather than as a correlative for human use and aspiration. Nor is it enough to point out, as Marie Swabey does in *Theory of the Democratic State*, that the natural criteria of democracy are predominantly quantitative. The confusion inheres in the fact that big numbers have so often been used as if they were equivalent to definitions of quality— as if a tremendous number of housing units, even slum dwellings, somehow indicated a corresponding total of human happiness.

Side by side with the most devouring greed, it has almost always been possible to find a superb generosity of life in New York—even, in the late 1930's, signs of a nascent change of heart. If the vainglory of power began to give way a little to the order of a genuine and mature society, there were men to be thanked for it—too many names for this place. These were the men who created and recreated values; who translated those values, under one form or another, into instruments of civic welfare; and who implemented the common aspiration. Together with that aspiration, the sum of their vision and accomplishments determined the living concept of New York: that basic unity, that prerequisite and final virtue of persons, which must be vital to the coherence of any human organization.

There were engineers—the Roeblings of Brooklyn Bridge, Clifford M. Holland of the Holland Tunnel, Nelson P. Lewis of the Board of Estimate and Apportionment, Singstad and Amman of the Port Authority—whose probity blossomed in highways and tunnels, or in the piers and cables of a bridge: such a bridge as Hart Crane had envisaged, a figure of the flight of time and the passage of mankind across the gulf. Stubborn bands and lone fighters—John Peter Zenger of the New York *Weekly Journal*, whose trial in 1735 vindicated free expression in the press; Nast and Parkhurst and the Lexow Committee; Seabury and the City Affairs Committee of the 1920's—these and a hundred others struck for the integrity of a free commonwealth. Scientists and research technicians, who worked with sludge digestion tanks and chlorination and polyphase alternators, created a fresh environment available to the social imagination of an ampler culture. A John Dewey reground the tools of the mind; a Thorstein Veblen challenged the directions of American civilization, especially those directions which New York had long controlled.

"A very little boy stood upon a heap of gravel for the honor of Rum Alley" in Stephen Crane's exact nightmare of the slums; John Dos Passos' Ellen Thatcher murmured: "I think that this city is full of people wanting inconceivable things"; and Thomas Wolfe's Eugene Gant cried: "Proud, cruel, everchanging and ephemeral city, to whom we came once when our hearts were high . . ." These were novelists answerable to the truth of the living. There were men who created vivid museums, set up liberal schools, fought to establish capable hospitals. Even politicians who hoped for nothing but their own advantage sometimes inadvertently contributed to the civic total, as Tweed did in setting out the pleasant boulevard along Broadway north of Sixty-Fifth Street, later routed by the subway.

Painters and photographers—Albert Ryder and Thomas Eakins, the ancestors; Steiglitz and Paul Strand and Berenice Abbott; the genre work of Sloan, Glenn Coleman, Reginald Marsh, Lawson, Glackens, Kenneth Hayes Miller; John Marin's vision of the skyscrapers in a vibrating rondure of forms; Demuth's *My Egypt* and Billings' and Sheeler's stylization of industrial masses—these and others literally created the human face of the city for the endowment of its citizens. The work of Hardenbergh and R. H. Hunt, among the older men, and of McKim and Stanford White in the 1890's; Goodhue's churches and Snyder's neo-Gothic schools; the loft buildings of Ely Jacques Kahn; the skyscraper designs of Harvey Wiley Corbett and Raymond Hood; the model apartment groups laid out by Clarence Stein and Henry Wright, which helped to anticipate the Federal Government's plans for housing developments in the 1930's: these were among the factors that made New York architecture the most exciting and various, if not always the soundest, in the world. Too, Whitman had his poets—not often prophets, but men and women who struck a dark accusatory music from the city's agonism: Edna St. Vincent Millay, Hart Crane, Louise Bogan, Archibald MacLeish, Horace Gregory.

Forecast by such lively wine salesmen of the arts as James Huneker, a more thorough school of cultural commentators whose origins were mainly literary set out in the early 1920's to reexamine the pattern of New York as a prefiguration of the new America. Randolph Bourne's voice, and such books as Harold Stearns' *Civilization in the United States,* Waldo Frank's *Our America,* Paul Rosenfeld's *Port of New York,* Van Wyck Brooks' *America's Coming of Age* and William Carlos Williams' *In the American Grain* managed to make themselves heard above the noise of traffic. Lewis Mumford's broad and precise imagination, the warmth and vitality of his interpenetrating sense of the whole distinguished half a dozen volumes that culminated in the definitive *Technics and Civilization* and *The Culture of Cities.* There were, finally, the innumerable common heroes in the patient and immense body of the city: the workers in laboratories and hospitals who died of X-ray burns or a finger pricked at an autopsy; the riveter tumbled from his hawk's perch, falling voiceless and alone; orange-helmeted sandhogs coughing with silicosis or twisted with the bends; and the men who could work no more, the unremembered ones Stephen Crane found in the city's scratch houses in *An Experiment in Misery,* whose successors were still there when Joseph Mitchell published his sketch, *A Cold Night Downtown,* in 1938.

Together these engineers and artists and milk-wagon drivers forged a concept of the city, a unity for the city, out of the collective character and history of its inhabitants, just as the individuality of Paris was defined by Villon's reckless verses, the gardens of Marie Antoinette, Julian the Apostate's addresses to "my dear Lutetia," Victor Hugo, the engineer Eiffel,

Marie Curie's dedication and Jules Romains' great antiphonal hymn. This unity, in fact, is at the root of the caricature visualized by outsiders as "a real New Yorker"—a certain large and shrewd liberality of thought and behavior, easy wit, compulsive energy, a liking for risk and the new, curiosity, restlessness.

There are those who consider that it is impossible to find any unity in the chaotic pattern of New York; or that, romantically enough, the emergence of unity would cancel its major charm. But the uneconomic and antisocial nature of many of the city's living ways demand a clear reorientation. The potential unity necessary to such reorientation already exists in the New Yorker's own concept of his city. In this shared consciousness —generated by a look, a grin, an anecdote as cabalistic to outsiders as the shop talk of mathematicians—the complex of the metropolis finds its organizing principle, deeper than civic pride and more basic than the domination of mass or power. To the degree that this principle, this wise geolatry, can be instrumented by the forms and processes appropriate to it, New York will emerge in greatness from the paradox of its confusions.

Habitat Map

Not so long ago, as time is reckoned in geology—something like 100,000 years ago, perhaps—the Hudson entered the Atlantic south-east of Long Beach and about 125 miles out from what is now Sandy Hook. From an airplane, if the weather is bright, the old channel may be seen as a wide dark streak on the sea. In those days the whole northeastern coast was a mile higher than it is now; the Palisades were twice as high (glaciers hadn't yet choked the Hudson bed); and Manhattan, not then an island, was a long chain of great hills. For 85 miles beyond what is now Sandy Hook the river flowed with smooth swiftness across the coastal plain. "Then," writes William Beebe, who has cast his nets into the gorge, "without warning, its waters plunged into the maw of a canyon mightier than man has ever seen."

Attaining a width of seven miles farther out, the gorge here is about a mile wide and soon reaches a depth of 1,600 feet. Four miles farther along the canyon, where the continental shelf is submerged 1,000 feet, the gorge bottom takes almost a mile of Mr. Beebe's sounding wire. Here the full burden of the old Hudson—which drained the area of the Great Lakes and had the Housatonic, Passaic and Hackensack as tributaries—cascaded 36 miles down a great valley to the Atlantic basin, whose floor is 2,000 to 4,600 fathoms deep. The United States Coast and Geodetic Survey has undertaken to chart Hudson Canyon with an automatic sounding instrument, the fathometer; and soon, even in the foggiest weather, ships will be able to steam straight into New York Bay by following the canyon's course.

The Hudson carved its mighty gorge more than 10,000,000 years ago, when eastern North America was being elevated anew. More than 40,000,-000 years before that, during a previous elevation, the Hudson ate its way across the highlands of upstate New York.

After the gorge was cut, subsidence of the land embayed the Hudson, made an estuary of it as far as Albany, the tides ebbing and flowing up through this whole distance of 150 miles. The ragged coastal contour around New York City has not changed much since the last glacier left its terminal debris on Long Island and Staten Island some 35,000 years ago and began melting its way back to Labrador. It used to be claimed that the coast was sinking a quarter of an inch a year, or about two feet a century, but geologists now dispute this—which is encouraging. For the land wouldn't have to subside very much to change Manhattan into a group of islets and reefs; and 100 feet of uplift would cause the ocean to retreat far out beyond Sandy Hook, making the present waterways unnavigable. Such changes have happened and are likely to happen again, but not in any layman-reckoned time.

And by the bye, no earthquake is likely to topple the American Babylon into the sea either. The glacier here at its end couldn't have been more than a half mile thick, hence the post-glacial uplifts—and the rock faulting that causes quakes—have been slight. Around Quebec the ice was two miles thick, with 8,500,000,000 tons to the square mile, and there the uplift has been greatest. Tremors arising there and in New England may be felt to the southward; but no quakes have occurred in New York or are likely to occur.

Harbor Outline

The present mouth of the Hudson at the Battery is 18 miles from the entrance to New York Harbor. Divided into Lower Bay and Upper Bay, the Harbor is like a giant hour-glass. Through its neck, the Narrows, the sand- and refuse-laden tides ebb and flow. The entrance to Lower Bay is the five-mile stretch of ocean northeastward from Sandy Hook, New Jersey, to Rockaway Point, Queens. Ambrose Channel, seven miles long, 2,000 feet wide and dredged to 40 feet, is the chief of the three channels crossing Sandy Hook Bar and allowing ships into and through the Lower Bay. The harbor occupies a northwestern angle toward which southwesterly winds sweep from a great distance, and in the gateway the wind-driven shore currents meet and deposit some of their materials. The Hudson too carries down its sediment. Thus the bar grows, hooking away from the wind. The bar can obstruct but never close the harbor, for the rush of ebb tide sweeps pretty clean. Sandy Hook and its bar, and Coney Island and Rockaway Beach facing the sea on the South Shore of Long Island, are marked coastal irregularities. The shoreline here is straightening itself out. First the reefs and barriers become dry land, then the lagoons behind them.

The south part of the Lower Bay, adjacent to Sandy Hook, is Sandy Hook Bay; near Staten Island it is Raritan Bay, five miles by seven. Both bays are shallow, shoaling to three fathoms or less over extensive areas. The Narrows, connecting the Lower Bay with the Upper Bay, is a strait about a mile wide between Staten Island and Long Island. As one enters the Lower Bay, Coney Island stands to the right. Farther off is the Rockaway peninsula, shielding Jamaica Bay from the ocean. Jamaica Bay, shallow and thick with islets, is eight miles by four, about the same size as the Upper Bay.

As one continues northward through the Main or Anchorage Channel of the Upper Bay, Brooklyn lies to the east and Jersey City to the west, while straight ahead the towers of Manhattan thrust at the sky. Main Channel is a half mile wide and 40 to 90 feet deep. There are two other channels in the Upper Bay: one to the east, Buttermilk Channel, leading to the East River and separated from Main Channel by a broad shoal and Governors Island; the second to the west, Kill van Kull, now dredged to 30 feet and giving access to Newark Bay.

Newark Bay is an estuary extending south from the confluence of the Passaic and Hackensack Rivers to Staten Island, a distance of about five miles. It is about 1½ miles wide. The channel up the bay, leading to the rivers and branching off to Port Newark Terminal as well, is dredged to 30 feet.

The most extensive shallows in the Upper Bay are in the western part. Almost in mid-channel lies Liberty or Bedloe Island. Near by, Ellis Island is really three islands joined by causeways and has been built up from three to 27 acres. Governors Island, now pear-shaped, has also been added to. In the early days cattle could cross to the island at low tide from what is now the Red Hook section of Brooklyn.

The Upper Bay is continued in the Hudson and East Rivers. The latter, really a tidal strait to Long Island Sound, is 16 miles long, 600 to 4,000 feet wide, and has a through channel of 35 feet at low water. There are three main islands in it, under the authority of Manhattan: Welfare (formerly Blackwell's), Randall's and Ward's Islands. The latter two help to support Triborough Bridge.

The Hudson's width decreases gradually from 3,670 feet at the Battery to 2,770 feet opposite Fourteenth Street, increasing again to the greater part of a mile at the northern boundary of Manhattan. Its channel is 40 feet deep. The Dutch called the Hudson the North River and the Delaware the South River because these rivers, respectively, flowed through the extreme northern and southern territories held by the Dutch. From the Battery to about Fourteenth Street, where Manhattan loses its triangular shape, the Hudson River today is officially the North River, known as such by many native New Yorkers.

The rise and fall of the tide in the harbor averages only about four feet, thus permitting the pier system. Ships of every size may enter or leave at any time; but if vessels larger than the *Queen Mary* or the *Normandie* are built, they may have to wait for flood tide. The total water frontage of New York City is 578.4 miles.

Topography by Boroughs

Occupying about 323 square miles in the southeastern corner of the State, New York City is 36 miles long at its longest and 16½ miles at its widest. It comprises the five boroughs: (1) Manhattan (about 22 square miles, the smallest borough); (2) the Bronx (almost twice as large); (3) Brooklyn-Kings (about 3½ times as large); (4) Queens (the largest borough, more than five times as large); and (5) Richmond-Staten Island (more than twice as large). The Bronx is the only borough on the mainland. With the exception of Brooklyn and Queens (on western Long Island, east and south of Manhattan), each borough is separated from the others by water; even a part of the boundary of these two boroughs is formed by historic Newtown Creek, a four-mile tidal arm of the East River. Long Island is 120 miles long, 23 miles wide.

On the map, the central borough of Manhattan, about 12½ miles long and 2½ miles at its extreme width, looks like a small stone cleaver about to hack at the huge loaf of Long Island. The northern handle of this cleaver, beginning where the East River branches off into the Sound at Bronx Kills, is in the main bounded by the Harlem River, which becomes the United States Ship Canal (this traces in part the course of the old Spuyten Duyvil Creek) near the point where it flows into the Hudson at Spuyten Duyvil. The whole waterway is eight miles long. On the west or Hudson side, Spuyten Duyvil is 13 miles by water from the Battery; on the east, Bronx Kills is 8½ miles above the Battery.

Adjacent to the north is the fist-and-cuff-shaped area of the Bronx, with its bony knuckles in Long Island Sound and its cuff formed by the Westchester County boundary line. Opposite Manhattan to the west are the high columns of the Palisades and the port cities of Weehawken, Hoboken and Jersey City. In the harbor lies Staten Island, southwest of Manhattan.

Shaped like Africa, it hugs the mainland of New Jersey to the west, from which it is separated only by the waterways, Kill van Kull and Arthur Kill.

The staired and serried skyscrapers of Manhattan, rising from the bay to rival the Cathedrals and Great White Thrones of the National Parks in beauty and grandeur, are made possible by a tough bed of rock, Manhattan schist: a thick, unyielding, coarsely crystalline rock glinting with mica. This metamorphic formation, found on a major portion of the island, is near or at the surface uptown (there are exposures in Central Park); and the first step in the construction of many a tower of commerce or lofty domicile was the stubborn blasting of a cellar. South of about Twenty-Third Street, however, the island is covered with glacial drift of varying depths, washed down from the higher part of the island. At Trinity Church it is 26 feet to bedrock; 90 feet at City Hall; while at Tombs Prison (on part of what was once the site of the large Collect Pond used by Fitch in 1796 for his experiments with the first screw-propeller craft), the builders found 40 feet of made ground, 30 feet of black mud, 5-10 feet of blue clay and 80 feet of gravel—total to bedrock, about 155 feet.

Manhattan schist crops up again on Governors Island, and there's a prong of it on Staten Island, which gives that body of land its third chief geological feature. The others are its hills of serpentine rock and its terminal moraine. Schist is also the basal rock of Brooklyn and Queens; but except for a few exposures (in Astoria and Long Island City) it is buried beneath hundreds of feet of glacial till. From Bay Ridge to Bath Beach, east of the Narrows, this drift material goes down from 200 to 500 feet respectively to bedrock; 500 feet at Woodside; and 650 feet at Greenport.

Over a period of two centuries and more, Manhattan's face has been lifted and relifted unceasingly. Abrupt ledges of rock have been levelled, deep narrow valleys filled, forests cleared. Where pools and meandering streams made great areas of marshland, canals have been dredged and the drained land filled. As the city expanded, miles of similar swampland in Brooklyn, Queens and Harlem have been reclaimed to provide space for buildings and homes. Battery Park, together with Water, Front and South Streets, are all on made land. In fact, the shoreline of Manhattan was once Pearl Street on the east; and on the west—below Fourteenth Street—it ran along Greenwich Street. Washington Square, Gramercy Park, Madison Square, Tompkins Square are all located on one-time swamps.

The swift converging currents of the Hudson and East Rivers no longer wear away the precious shoreline of the island, as they did at a good rate in the city's earliest days, when the tip of Manhadoes (Island of the Hills) was a great deal narrower. A rocky promontory projected from the shore, forming a natural breakwater, and in this sheltered cove Indians landed their canoes. Its boulders helped to construct the ramparts of Fort Amsterdam. At that time the Battery was a receding bluff which fronted the Hudson between the present Bowling Green and Trinity Church.

Broadway was laid out over an Indian trail that ran along a chain of hills from the Battery to the vicinity of Canal Street, where another trail cut east to Maiginnac, or Corlear's Hook, and west to the Village of Lapinikan, where the Indians crossed the forest-fringed Hudson to Hobokan, Hacking and on south to the Delaware. Covered with oak, hickory and chestnut, the chain of ragged hills extended to Canal Street, where valleys and marshland on both sides of the hills spread across the island—so low that at high tide water flowed from river to river. In the valleys and the grassy dales between hills were the log houses and fields of the first settlers. Cowpaths across the marshes gave access to the upper part of the island, precipitous and wild, in whose somber forests and impenetrable thickets of grapevines, creepers, blackberry and raspberry bushes lurked the wolves, foxes, bears and panthers that preyed on the farmers' stock. The plentiful deer and turkeys, too, sometimes destroyed his crops.

On the North River there was but one inlet or slip, that at the foot of Oswego, now Liberty Street; but there were many on the East River, Coenties Old Slip being the first of them. Extending a mile along the shore at the foot of Rivington were Marinus Willet's and Stuyvesant's Meadows. Here, by common repute, the pirates Kidd and Blackbeard buried their treasure. At Grand, Houston, Fifth, Seventh, Tenth and Thirtieth Streets the island's edge was frayed by marshes. At the western end of Canal Street the Lispenard Meadows—70 acres of salt marsh used as a skating pond in winter—was connected by the Lispenard Creek to the Collect or Fresh Water Pond. Tombs Prison on Centre Street stands at what was about the middle of this famous Collect Pond. Called bottomless, it actually measured from 40 to 70 feet deep. Contemporaries spoke of it as a lovely sheet of water, and it was celebrated both for its fish and as a fine place for skating.

Many of the hills on the lower part of the island were 100 to 130 feet above tidewater. One such was Bunker's Hill, at the junction of Grand and Elm Streets, commanding the bay and Staten Island, the Hudson, Jersey and the high ridge of Long Island. Corlear's Hook was broken by hills, some 80 feet high, strewn with big boulders; and on a large knoll rising just north of Collect Pond criminals were hanged. In an adjoining hollow Negroes suspected of inciting riots were burned alive. A fort, still standing a decade or so after the Revolution, topped the hill at Provost (now Franklin) and Varick Streets. Murray Hill remains as a rather inconsiderable elevation between Third Avenue and Broadway from Thirty-Second to Forty-Second Streets.

Between the hills were waterholes, and sometimes a stream issued, winding to east or west. The area along the East River north of Central Park was marked by creeks and muddy estuaries. Harlem Lane began at about 130th Street on the west and flowed into Hell Gate at Ninety-Second Street. Harlem Creek meandered to the Hudson from Goldfish Pond, a basin between Lenox and Seventh Avenues, 117th and 119th Streets. At 110th it crossed to Fifth Avenue and entered the Harlem Marsh. A streamlet ran from a little pond in Manhattan Square to the large lake in Central Park, then on down to the East River. Minetta Brook, troublesomely rediscovered by subway sandhogs in the 1920's, started at about University Place; flowed through a section of the old Potter's Field in Washington Square; on past Sandy Hill; collected into a pond north of Richmond Hill; and then, beyond Varick Street, fell off into a salt marsh before finding its way to the North River. This brook separated Greenwich Village from the contemporary city. Another brook ran through Tompkins Square to the soggy meadows of the East River; and a stream flowing along Broad Street had a branch, the Beaver Canal, running down Beaver Street.

In 1670 there were several public wells in the middle of the city's streets, their indifferent water being drawn with buckets, not pumped. The source of the most potable water was one of the springs feeding Collect Pond, at a point on the present Park Row between Baxter and Mulberry Streets. This became known as the Tea-Water Pump. The "tea-water man" bought this water at four pence the hogshead and peddled it about the village for a penny bill a gallon. Tea-Water Garden became a center of social activity where village boys played and matrons gossiped.

The overflow from the pump created a pool of stagnant water; and the Collect Pond degenerated at the end of the 18th century into a foul, disease-breeding cesspool. In 1774 Christopher Colles built a reservoir near the "New Gaol," which was more commonly known as Debtors' Prison. "Good pitch pipes, well-hooped with iron," were used to distribute the water to subscribing households. The Revolution caused suspension of this development, and service was not resumed until the beginning of the 19th century, when Aaron Burr organized the Manhattan Company. This company dug a well near Broadway, north of the present Spring Street, the only use of which, as it turned out, was to serve as the "hiding place for the body of beautiful Gulielma Snow in one of New York's most famous murder mysteries." Another well was sunk in Reade Street. This tapped the subterranean springs of the old pump and gave the growing city a small supply of water.

The springs which provided the city's early water supply have been a continual source of trouble. All attempts effectually to block their flow have failed. Adjoining basements ooze with their seepage, and engineers say that if the walls of the IRT subway station at Canal and Lafayette Streets were pierced, water would gush forth as from a fountain.

The first successful attempt to relieve Manhattan from dependence on the uncertain flow of private and public wells was made in 1842, when the municipal authorities tapped the Croton River with an aqueduct having a capacity of 35 million gallons a day. Brooklyn was served by private wells until 1859. At that time a city water system was installed, using the surface and subterranean streams of Long Island—sources which remain an essential part of the system today. In 1917 the first supply of water from the Catskill system was available—250 million gallons daily.

In 1936 the municipally owned and operated system supplied 913,-000,000 gallons of water daily to New York City and sold about 20,-000,000 gallons daily to other communities. Costs of construction to January 1, 1936, amounted to well over $513,000,000. Experts agree that this system is the greatest in the world, and that the water is unexcelled in purity and palatability. Principal sources are four watersheds in the Catskill Mountains and the Putnam and Westchester hills, which have an aggregate drainage area of 968 square miles. Aqueducts as large as railroad tunnels carry this water from the reservoirs to the city. Much of the terrain about the reservoirs is under public ownership, beautifully landscaped, and maintained as restricted parks. About the Croton watershed alone there are some 10,000 acres of such land. Work going forward in 1937 was intended eventually to swell the present huge water supply by 60 percent, developing new watersheds in the upper tributaries of the Delaware River. There are still five private companies operating driven wells which supply some 59,000,000 gallons daily to localities in Brooklyn and Queens.

The island of Manhattan rises in the north, with its highest places on the upper West Side; perhaps for this reason the section was not built up until later than the upper East Side. A ridge on the West Side, rising gently northward from Fifty-Ninth Street, forms the imposing Cathedral Plateau which drops down again from 116th to 125th Streets—this latter section called the Hollow Way in Washington's time—and rises once more to St. Nicholas Heights.

Descending in terraces toward the Hudson, to the east it falls suddenly through Morningside Park—a declivity which extends northward from 110th Street to Coogan's Bluffs—into Harlem Flats, an alluvial plain. In many parts of this craggy area there were rather deep bowls, as at Seventy-Sixth Street, since filled in with debris from neighboring bosses of rock. These pits, as late as 1880, held the shacks of the period's Hoovervilles. Mount Morris, in the section of that name at Fifth Avenue between 120th and 124th Streets, is itself the terminal peak of an interrupted ridge.

The ridge on the West Side rises again to Washington Heights proper, from 155th to 176th Streets, and toward the Hudson reaches the highest natural altitude in Manhattan—267.75 feet—near the site of old Fort Washington, just north of 181st Street and Fort Washington Avenue. This elevation extends into Fort Tryon Park. Just to the eastward, there is another sharp depression at Dyckman Street; then the ridge climbs into Inwood Park. Inwood Hill, northern tip of the island, is 232.75 feet in height. The street level at High Bridge water-tower, on the high bluff overlooking the Harlem River, is 203.25 feet.

Several transverse ravines, caused by faulting, lie in this handle section of Manhattan. These were probably courses worn by the four or more glaciers that scraped across the northern part of the island during the last ice age. In Manhattan and the Bronx the glaciers have grooved and potted the rock. Striated slabs, and granite boulders known as "travelers," are especially prevalent in Bronx Zoological Park. Most famous is the Rocking Stone, large as a small house, which hails from New England. Similar boulders tinted with greenish mica and milky quartz are found near the ball field in Central Park. Mount Tom, at Eighty-Third Street and the Hudson, is smoothed and planed by the ice, its base furrowed with glacial grooves.

Inwood dolomite, a limestone, is found in large quantities in the Inwood and Harlem sections. It is an organic rock, formed by the metamorphosis of animal and vegetable deposits. An intrusion of granite near the Hudson between Forty-Eighth and Fifty-Fifth Streets used to be quarried, and can still be seen in a vacant lot opposite the *Normandie's* dock.

Granite veins occur all through the schist, and it is in these veins that precious and semi-precious stones are found: garnets, amethysts, opals, tourmalines, beryls, chrysoberyls and what not. Ninety-nine species and 170 varieties have been found in Manhattan, a record probably not excelled in the United States by any other locality of the same size. A deposit of garnets which netted a small fortune for the finder was uncovered at Broadway and Sixty-Fifth Street in 1888. Later, the largest perfect garnet crystal ever found in this country was thrown out of a ditch in West Thirty-Fifth Street, used as a doorstop in a shop, and eventually turned over to the New York Mineralogical Club, which exhibits its collections in the American Museum of Natural History. Apatite, columbite and menaccanite of rare or unusual size are among the minerals found on Manhattan Island. Although some amber has been taken from Staten Island, the other four boroughs of the city, whose foundational rock has been less disturbed by blasting in connection with construction work, have yielded relatively few mineral specimens.

Fordham gneiss is the chief basal rock of the Bronx; it is also found in the ledges of Spuyten Duyvil. The hills of the Bronx are a part of the foothills and worn extensions of the Green Mountains and the Berkshires. The highest point in the Bronx is Riverdale Hill—284.5 feet—at Iselin Avenue and West 250th Street. Other high elevations, varying from 210 feet to 141, are at Jerome Avenue, near East 233d Street; Van Cortlandt Park at Jerome and Moshulu Avenues; Spuyten Duyvil; the Grand Boulevard and Concourse at East 199th Street; and the Hall of Fame Terrace.

The Bronx River, which courses through the center of the borough with a depth varying from a few inches to ten feet and a width of from ten to 300 feet, is fed by its tributaries: Sprain Brook, Hutchinson Brook and the Sheldrake River. It is 15 miles long and empties into the East River 11 miles northeast of the Battery. In the main the borough of the Bronx reproduces the geological features of Manhattan. Its group of north and south ridges declines eastward to the Sound from the high bluff of the Fordham section and Van Cortlandt Park.

The bold escarpment of the Palisades, the most striking surface feature in the New York area, gives the Hudson a world-wide reputation for scenic majesty. The cliffs are formed of a volcanic rock, 350-1,000 feet thick, and rise to 700 feet. The vertical columns, developed during the cooling stage of the rock, suggested the ridge's name. The skeleton of a dinosaur that looked rather like a crocodile was uncovered at the foot of these Palisades. Jerseyite or not, he was christened *Rutiodon manhattanensis*.

With the exception of the Palisades, the New Jersey terrain near New York City is low-lying and marshy, as motorists crossing the Pulaski Skyway can testify. A large lake—Lake Hackensack—occupied the region below the Passaic River and west of the Hudson during the retreat of the last glacier. The Newark Lowland is a plain developed on inclined weak strata consisting of red sandstones and shales of Triassic rocks. Intrusive sheets of resultant volcanic rock form prominent residual ridges, such as the Palisades and the Watchung Mountains.

Queens is sharply divided into North Shore (on the Sound) and South Shore (on the ocean) by northerly hills running the length of Long Island. Flushing Meadow Park, chosen for the site of the 1939 World's Fair, is a filled-in marsh used for years as a city dump. On the south shore there is much made land. In the northeastern sector, the glacial margins and outwash channels are particularly plain. The outermost margins, now fronting on the East River and the Sound, were once the shores of the Atlantic Ocean. Little Neck Hill—266.48 feet in elevation—between Alley Pond Park and the Nassau County line, is the highest point in Queens. West of this point, Alley Pond Park includes, besides the Alley Pond, a flourishing bird sanctuary hospitable to quail, pheasants, Canadian geese, pelicans and heron.

In Brooklyn, large areas of Flatlands, Greenpoint, Williamsburg and Red Hook have been raised above sea level. With the exception of the Brooklyn Heights bluff, and the morainic belt under parts of Greenwood Cemetery, Prospect Park and the site of the Brooklyn Museum, Brooklyn is extremely flat. Unlike the terminal moraine on Staten Island, the morainic knobs and kettle holes in Brooklyn and Queens constitute the most conspicuous topographical feature. This has largely determined, in the choice of sites for parks, cemeteries and railway beds, the development of the two boroughs. To the south is a glacial outwash visible a little above sea level. This terminal moraine, marking the southern boundary of the glacier, extends in a semicircle from Cape Cod to Seattle.

The rounded hills on Staten Island, rising from the harbor and Kill van Kull, extend in a northeast-southwest chain 300-380 feet high and are of serpentine rock. At Richmond, in the center of the island, they disappear under the Fresh Kill Meadows. Morainic hills drop into the sea at Prince's (or Princess) Bay, near Tottenville, at the southwestern corner of the island. Innumerable boulders are scattered along the desolate shore of the Kill van Kull; and in the southwestern part of Staten Island there are sand dunes, marshland and much loneliness. Between the moraine and the flatlands the sea wind sweeps over pools of fresh water, patches of cedars, deserted houses and ragged acres of weed and brush between the farmlands. Todt Hill, 409.239 feet above sea level, is one of the highest elevations on the Atlantic Coast between Maine and Florida; but there is a point on Long Island—High Hill, near Huntington—approximately as high.

Climate

New York's annual mean temperature is about 50 degrees Fahrenheit, which coincides pretty closely with that of Paris, London and Berlin. But extremes, sudden variations and strong winds make the climate a bit trying to strangers. A drop of 20 degrees in a few hours is not uncommon. The weather's inconstancy is aggravated by the high average rainfall of Atlantic cities in the United States—nearly double that of Europe's metropolises. Furthermore, one year's weather may be extremely unlike the next.

Autumn is perhaps the preferred season. Late September rains are likely to be soon over, and one may reasonably count on a prolonged spell of fairly settled weather, clear skies and a mellow Indian summer. Late spring, with its patches of green poignantly concentrated in the city's squares, is lovely and poetic. For that matter, even during the bridge-expanding stress of July and the muggy dog days of August, when shirt-sleeved millions sit panting on the stoops, there are New Yorkers (not all out of town either) who will rise to assert that their city is the best summer resort in the world. Heat waves are often caused by what is termed the "Bermuda High"—an area of high air pressure over Bermuda which sends warm humid air to the Atlantic seaboard. The official record is 102.3 degrees, recorded on July 9, 1936. It was during this heat wave that the drawbridge across the Harlem River expanded and couldn't be closed, halting traffic for several hours. Changes in temperature cause the roadway of the George Washington Bridge to flex like a bow, producing up-and-down variations of as much as six feet at its midmost point.

The lowest temperature ever recorded was 14 degrees below zero on February 9, 1934. The great blizzard of 1888 is still a favorite topic among older New Yorkers. The blizzard's fury caught the city unprepared, for neither Government nor individual weather prophets (not even the man who made predictions exclusively for the *Herald*) foretold the approach of the storm. It began on Sunday night, March 11, in the form of a heavy rain lashed by wind. Shortly before midnight the rain changed to hail and the temperature fell, while the bruit of the gale increased until the wind was zooming at 60 miles an hour. Dry snow followed the hail, driven in blinding clouds. All day Monday the storm continued. Traffic practically ceased. Many persons who braved the outdoors were later found frozen to death. Monday night was the wildest and darkest the city has ever experienced. Chimneys, windows, awnings, fences were blown down. Not until 6 A.M. on Tuesday did the snow stop, the wind abate. In some places drifts completely covered street lamps and street cars. A week elapsed before the first train got through from Philadelphia. Another blizzard in 1920, not quite so severe, brought great hardship and financial loss.

New York Harbor is remarkably free of fog; but during cold spells, ice floes in the Hudson lodge against the piers, and in 1934 and 1935 they interfered seriously with shipping. The average velocity of the wind in the city is 15 miles an hour, stronger than in other important American cities. The heaviest gale ever recorded in New York whipped the city on February 22, 1912: velocity 96 miles an hour. A storm which swept the Atlantic coast late in 1932 brought a swarm of Arctic birds, called dovekies, and dashed many of them against the skyscrapers. Thousands were found all over the city, their limp bodies draped on telephone wires, in the streets, on the lakes and lawns of the parks. In 1878 a cyclone brought sooty terns—tropic birds from the West Indies and the Caribbean. Some of them were found alive at Lake Ronkonkoma, Long Island.

Animals, Trees and Flowers

Close-packed blocks of buildings and teeming mankind haven't exterminated all native plant and animal life in the metropolitan area. Many species of wild birds nest in the five boroughs. In Central Park, although the number is now declining, 168 varieties have recently been noted; in Prospect Park, 200 species. There are 15,148 acres of park land within the city, for plant and animal conservation, including six bird sanctuaries, two of them in Central Park. Geese, pelicans and herons are among the species protected. The Staten Island reservation comprises 51 heavily wooded acres, a salt marsh for waterfowl, and a strip of dense underbrush for quail, pheasants and similar species. Nut trees in the parks attract chipmunks and red and gray squirrels. A few snakes are around too, harmless hog-nose and garter snakes, though occasionally a rattler or a copperhead turns up along the Palisades. In the outlying districts you may startle a rabbit, or vice versa. Lizards are fairly common, and the ponds and streams breed salamanders, frogs and turtles.

The pollution of the Upper Bay and the North and East Rivers doesn't stop countless would-be fishermen from fishing; but in the waters of Staten

Island, Pelham Bay and the Sound more than 60 kinds of fresh and salt water fish, some edible, are actually caught. Occasionally, perhaps, even a Manhattan pier fisherman may catch something—more than likely a hook-wary shad, once abundant in the Hudson. Ellis Island was earlier called Oyster Island because of the fine oysters plentiful thereabouts; and oysters, clams, crabs, lobsters and eels, as well as such curiosities as starfish, sea-horses and jellyfish, can still be taken inside the city limits.

Within 50 miles, more than 247 species of fish exclusive of those below the 25-fathom level have been caught. Sand and brown sharks are common in this latitude. Females of the latter variety enter the bays in midsummer to give birth to their young. The true tropical man eater or white shark has been taken in this vicinity only once. In the early years of the 18th century sharks so infested the East River around the Catherine Slip Market that men were hired to catch them from the dock. Sam Way, one of the best with a handline, often got as many as seven a day, 14 feet or more in length (the story, no doubt, was a good deal longer than the fish).

Few people would believe that there are still more trees in New York than buildings, but there are—more than a million of them, nearly all belonging to the city. There'd be more if it were not for leaky gas mains and reckless motorists, chief causes—in Manhattan at least—of tree mortality. Horses used to kill city trees by eating the bark. In the 17th century, plum, pear and cherry trees grew wild in the woods. In the middle of the next century the streets were shaded by beech, elm, locust and lime trees, criticized by visitors as offering homes for tree-toads, whose "clamorous voices" stirred their ire. Remnants of the primitive woods survive in the squares and parks, along the streets and in outlying sections such as Forest Hills in Queens, the Edenwald section of the Bronx, and on Staten Island. The virgin Hemlock Forest in Bronx Park, containing about 3,000 trees, is particularly notable.

The majority of New York's trees, however, are foreign varieties—mostly planes, and stock from earlier imports of Norwegian and Japanese maples. Poplars, once so common, are forbidden now. They require plenty of water, and to get it a poplar sometimes drives its roots into sewers and water mains. For some reason, Chinese trees seem best able to endure New York's soot. The ailanthus, or Chinese tree of heaven, is locally called "the backyard tree."

May spice and button bush—swamp shrubs—frequently are used by landscape gardeners for their beautiful, fragrant blooms. Holly, not generally found so far north, grows wild on a few spots of vacant land, particularly on Staten Island. Dogwood, its white blossoms made inviolate by city ordinance, is common in the outskirts of town; and bayberry, once gathered by housewives who perfumed linen with its leaves and moulded candles from its berry wax, grows on many sandy spots. The laurel, whose bud-clusters break into pink bloom toward the end of June, is fairly common. Flowers still manage to grow in vacant lots and on rooftops, notably in the Gardens of the Nations at Rockefeller Center. Wooded or bushy spots sometimes conceal lady slippers. Where leaf mould is thick and rich the Indian pipe lifts its pallid stalk and bowl. Cardinal flowers appear along a few shaded streams. Numerous other blooms may be found throughout the warm months by watchful botanists.

There are about 19,000 horses in New York—as many as there ever were. The milk companies and others find it more economical to stick to the hoofbeats-at-dawn tradition. (Stories about milk horses, who get about a good deal at night, crop up time and again in the city's folk humor.) New York has something like 300,000 dogs and 500,000 cats. The number of rats and mice and cockroaches must be empirically reckoned.

Some kinds of birds—pigeon, sparrow, gull and chimney swift—have learned new habits and are much at home even downtown. (Loosed in Central Park in 1863 were 14 sparrows, the first imported from Europe. They increased rapidly and were so well liked that swanky dwellings were built for them in the parks. Many people also kept them in their homes as pets.) Bats also persist and thrive downtown. An occasional butterfly pirouettes through Wall Street's canyon, nor do the towers of finance deter the ant from building his sandhill. In fact, insects—beetles and lady-bugs and caterpillars—do pretty well downtown, all things considered.

Fantastic Metropolis

VIEW OF MID-MANHATTAN FROM THE 67TH FLOOR OF ROCKEFELLER
CENTER

OLD ABRAHAM DE PEYSTER IN THE MIDST OF SKYSCRAPERS

Above: WEATHERBEATEN FISHING BOATS MOORED TO THE PIERS OF SOUTH STREET, THE OLD "STREET O' SHIPS"

Below: THE ARCHITECTURAL GIANTS OF 42ND STREET RISING BEYOND ST. GABRIEL'S PARK

THE CANYONS AND TURRETS OF LOWER MANHATTAN AS SEEN FROM
THE AIR, BY DAY; AND AS THEY LOOM FROM THE BAY, BY NIGHT

BALCONIES OF THE ELEGANT 1880'S LOOK OUT ON THE HARD ANGLES
OF MODERN FUNCTIONAL DESIGN

PATTERN OF A CITY ON THE FABRIC OF NIGHT

BUSY EXECUTIVES IN ROCKEFELLER
CENTER CAN ENJOY THE QUIET
BEAUTY OF ROOF GARDENS, HIGH
ABOVE FIFTH AVENUE TRAFFIC

OLD TRINITY CHURCH AT THE HEAD OF WALL STREET

Trading-Post to Cosmopolis

THE HISTORY of New York has been primarily influenced by its physical situation on a great harbor at the mouth of a great river. Linked to the trading bent and activities of the early settlers, this led almost inevitably to the creation of a commercial metropolis made up of people from every country in the world.

New York has contributed substantially to the nation of which it is the greatest city. It has long dominated American commerce and finance; and it has been the gateway through which millions of immigrants have passed to other parts of the country after first receiving their baptism in American ideals and opportunities.

A great number of immigrants remained, and they were joined by people from all sections of the United States. These two groups constituted and still constitute New York. They are the brains and the brawn that have created a commercial empire in which the cultural phases of life have not been neglected during the long struggle upward from trading post to cosmopolis.

Before the White Man

The builders of that cosmopolis were preceded by three groups of Algonquian Indians. On Manhattan Island—which constituted New York City until 1874—the Indians were neither a great nor a rich people. They existed in some 94 communities housing several thousand people, where they lived in fear of powerful enemies who had driven them to the sea and were levying tribute from them. Huddled together for safety, their existence was precarious and primitive. They achieved no particularly outstanding qualities.

Such living conditions had apparently existed for several generations before the appearance of even the earliest explorers, and it is not improbable that the Indians may have welcomed the Dutch as they did because they were thinking of a possible alliance against brutal foes among their own people. Whatever the motive, it is a matter of record that they never turned on the white man until he turned on them. For years they carried on a fairly extensive trade with the Dutch and English, this constructive phase of their relationship being marred, unfortunately, by the illicit traffic in rum that developed later, particularly in the Dutch period, and taxed the ability and patience of more than one provincial administration.

Discovery and Exploration: 1524–1609

More than a century before that situation arose, the Indians had come in contact with an early explorer of New York's magnificent harbor. In 1524, 85 years before Hudson's failure to find the northeast passage to the Orient's riches had turned him westward along our shores, Giovanni da Verrazano, an Italian explorer serving the King of France, visited the lower and upper bays. In May of the following year, Estéban Gómez, a Portuguese navigator representing the Emperor Charles V of Spain, was probably in the vicinity of New York, but his explorations, like those of Verrazano, failed to result in Spanish activity here. The rest of the 16th century, according to Stokes, "was a period of myth and mystery so far as the neighborhood of Manhattan Island was concerned."

With the advent of the 17th century, the first of the great Dutch trading companies, which created in 50 years a world empire comparable to the British Empire, was organized. Formation of this and similar companies, in the midst of war with Spain, was the result of the need for new sources and new markets to serve Dutch trade.

On April 25, 1607, the Dutch became masters of the sea by defeating the Spanish fleet at Gibraltar; and on January 8, 1609, the Dutch East India Company contracted with Henry Hudson, an English explorer-for-hire, to find a new route to the Indies by way of the northeast, around the northern coast of Russia and Siberia. Hudson failed to find that passage. Instead, for reasons much too confused to be considered historically reliable, he turned west and rounded what is now Sandy Hook on September 2, 1609. Nine days later, he had moved into the Upper Bay of New York's present harbor, from which base his explorations up the river convinced him that a passage to the Orient was impossible in that direction. On October 4, 1609, he passed out of sight of Sandy Hook on his way home, his chief contribution being explorations of the harbor's lower and upper bays and of the river named after him.

He was followed by a ship sent to the Hudson in 1610 by several Amsterdam merchants. Little is known about this ship, which some authorities believe was commanded by Hendrick Christiaensen, who, according to the Dutch historian Wassenaer, was the first after Hudson to sail the river and is known as the most active skipper in numerous voyages to the Hudson during 1610–16, his career being cut short in 1616 when he was killed by an Indian at Fort Nassau on Castle Island, near what is now Albany. In 1612, Christiaensen entered into a partnership with Adriaen Block, and the two visited the Hudson in a ship captained by one Ryser. By 1613, this partnership was apparently well established, Christiaensen having command of the *Fortune* and Block being in charge of the *Tiger*.

The *Tiger* burned in New Netherland early in 1614 and was replaced by the *Onrust* or, as the word is usually translated, the *Restless*. One authority is of the opinion that the *Tiger* burned in the neighborhood of Manhattan Island, and that the *Restless* was built on or in the vicinity of the island; another maintains that both events occurred not far from Albany. In any event, it is known that the *Restless* passed through Hellegat (Hell Gate), and that Block made important discoveries along the New England coast.

Block's major contribution to exploration was his map of 1614. The original was lost, but an anonymous Dutch copy, the so-called "Figurative Map" of 1614, is still preserved in the archives of the States-General at The Hague. On this map, the name of New Netherland appears for the first time, and Manhattan Island is also represented for the first time as an island, thus indicating the thoroughness of Block's explorations. One chart and two maps had preceded Block's in the early 17th century; but his was by far the most accurate of its time, and it contributed greatly to his own and other subsequent explorations in 1614–16.

Evidence has been offered, but no definite proof established, to support the theory that the "pretended Dutch governor" seen on Manhattan Island in 1613 by Samuel Argall, an English explorer, was Block. Though doubt may exist as to this claim, there can be no question that Block laid the foundations for exploration by Dutch adventurers in 1612–14 which led to the granting of the United New Netherland Company's charter in 1614.

During the next 12 years, several more or less unproductive voyages to the New World, and the formation of other trading companies, preceded the first real settlement on Manhattan Island. On June 3, 1621, the Dutch West India Company, formed to weaken Spain's military and commercial powers, was granted a monopoly that superseded all others in America. Three years later, it sent out its first colony, which arrived at the mouth of the Hudson River in May 1624 and proceeded upstream to Albany. No settlement was made on Manhattan Island. A second contingent, including cattle, arrived in April 1625. The cattle were first landed on what is now Governors Island and then moved to Manhattan, where some of the colonists remained only a very short time before proceeding with the cattle to Albany to join the first company. The stay of this group on Manhattan Island was merely a stop-over; there still was no real settlement on the island.

The Era of Dutch Control: 1626–1664

Hudson's explorations in 1609 had given the Dutch an exploratory title to the territory, so that the Dutch period dates technically from 1609. But what was later to become New York was not established as a permanent settlement until Peter Minuit, third governor-general of the Dutch West India Company, landed in New Netherland on May 4, 1626, attempted to settle on Governors Island, and then moved to Manhattan. From that time until September 8, 1664, when the town and its fort were formally surrendered to the English, the city of New Amsterdam was under Dutch control.

New Amsterdam was originally one of several trading posts in New Netherland. This latter was a province organized and controlled by a Dutch trading company deriving its charter from the States-General of the Netherlands. Unlike various English provinces, New Netherland's boundaries were not specifically defined with respect to its field of operations. Instead, the province was composed of a rather loose association of trading posts. There were three on the Hudson River, three on the Delaware River, and one on the Connecticut at Fort Hope. Several of these preceded the permanent settlement of New Amsterdam on the lowest point of Manhattan Island. New Amsterdam eventually became the governmental and commercial center of New Netherland.

The date of the settlement of New Amsterdam and the details regarding it are highly controversial. It is certain, however, that the first known settlement on a permanent basis was not undertaken until after the arrival of Peter Minuit's group. They found, according to one authority, a site prepared at the lower end of Manhattan Island, where a blockhouse was being built. That unfinished blockhouse was the beginning of what later became Fort Amsterdam.

The history of Fort Amsterdam is a story of continual struggle on the part of Dutch governors-general and citizens to create adequate defenses despite the glaring neglect of the settlement by the Dutch West India Company and the States-General of Holland. At no time did it constitute a real defense. Begun in 1626, and almost completely rebuilt ten years later, it was crumbling away in 1646. In 1647, Peter Stuyvesant, seventh governor-general, noted that it resembled "more a mole hill than a fortress, without gates, the walls and bastions trodden under foot by men and cattle." In 1650, it did not have "one gun carriage or one piece of cannon in a suitable frame or on a good platform." Fourteen years later, it was so useless from a defensive standpoint that it could not resist the English men-of-war in the harbor and thus prevent surrender to the English. Within its poorly constructed walls were the governor-general's house, a double-roofed church with a square tower, barracks, prison, whipping post and gallows. There was no well or cistern.

In 1626, Peter Minuit bought Manhattan Island from the Indians for 60 guilders, or about $24. This transaction was carried out according to instructions by the Dutch West India Company in Holland to Willem Verhulst, second governor-general and Minuit's predecessor. Knives, beads and trinkets constituted the "money" used.

This period of Dutch control falls quite naturally into two major divisions: pre-Stuyvesant and Stuyvesant. Before that colorful character's appointment as governor-general on July 28, 1646, and his arrival at New Amsterdam on May 11, 1647, six governors-general in succession had struggled with the new colony's problems, the administration of William Kieft (1637-46) being the longest in those first 22 years of New Netherland's history.

Prior to Kieft, the material progress of the company's colonial venture had not justified the more than $165,000 that had been poured into it. Kieft did not improve matters. His administration was marked by the bloody and expensive Indian War of 1643-45, which occurred as a result of his bellicose attitude toward the natives and his unwarranted slaughter of a number of them in February 1643. Other events of his regime included the granting of a large tract of land to spur tobacco growing; a mutiny among the garrison at Fort Amsterdam and its suppression; the issuance on May 10, 1640, of the first militia regulations, whereby all men were ordered to get good guns and report to their respective corporals in the event of trouble; and the appointment on December 11, 1642, of George Baxter as English secretary of the province, this move being made because "of the number of English" who had "numerous law suits."

The most important act of Kieft's administration was his consultation with a "Board of Twelve Men," elected August 26, 1641, on the subject of adequate punishment for an Indian murderer. Although this board had no judicial authority and few important functions, and was abruptly dissolved by Kieft on February 8, 1642, it may very properly be termed the beginning of representative government in the province.

Kieft's term came to an end when the directors at Amsterdam recalled him, primarily because of a lack of profits for the company's venture, but also because of the number of protests and complaints from the people. He was lost at sea on September 27, 1647, while on his way to the Netherlands to defend his administration before the company's directors at Amsterdam.

His successor, Peter Stuyvesant, who arrived at New Amsterdam on May 11, 1647, was the seventh and by far the best known of the Dutch West India Company's colonial administrators. His 17-year regime had the effect of eclipsing the other 21 years of Dutch occupation. Opinions may differ as to his true historical stature, but none can deny that oblivion would long ago have overtaken anyone less gifted in political manipulation and sheer showmanship. He was by all odds the most colorful figure of these years.

Under him, the first distinctly municipal form of government came into being in New Amsterdam on February 2, 1653, when Stuyvesant and his council proclaimed the creation of a body resembling our present-day aldermen, as well as of a bench of justices. Limited though both of these bodies were in real authority, they constituted the first major concession to people who had come to the New World as little more than man-power for the Dutch West India Company. They fed the desire for a greater share in governmental affairs, and were followed by several assemblies, all convened by Stuyvesant. The first had 19 members, representing New Amsterdam and seven outlying towns in Long Island and Westchester. This group, which met December 10, 1653, was the most truly representative assembly yet called in New Netherland and the forerunner of others, all subject to call and dismissal by the governor-general, but all advancing the idea of giving the commonalty a voice in public affairs.

Soon the municipal government began to function with increasing regularity, until the demands of the various assemblies and the city fathers resulted in a "common council," at which the first definite citizenship rights were proposed. These demands were granted when the great and small burgher-rights were created by law on February 2, 1657. The great burgher-right conferred citizenship upon all former as well as present provincial officials, burgomasters, *schepens* (corresponding to present-day aldermen), Dutch clergymen, and certain commissioned officers of the city regiment. The common or small burgher-right was given to all male inhabitants "who had kept fire and light within the City one year and six weeks," to all native-born, and to those who had already married or should thereafter marry native-born daughters of burghers. Between April 10 and May 3, 1657, the burghers were registered, citizenship thus becoming an accomplished legal fact for the first time in the city's history.

Commercially, the Dutch West India Company was a total failure; and in 1661, New Amsterdam was bankrupt. Symptomatic of this situation, no doubt, was the commonalty's disregard of laws and ordinances designed to promote colonial interests. Again and again the people appear to have paid not the slightest attention to acts of the provincial and city governments, despite the severity of punishments inflicted on some who were prosecuted, such punishments including branding, public lashings, use of the rack and similar measures.

The attempt to replace the thatched roofs and badly plastered wooden chimneys, both of which constituted a serious fire hazard, well illustrates the almost contemptuous disregard of many laws. Repeated ordinances and "final" warnings had no effect; indeed, the officer of the City Court who issued the "last and final" notice of 1657 reported that the people merely laughed at him as he read the order. Another example of this attitude is evidenced in connection with the ordinances which, beginning in 1638 and continuing steadily almost to 1664, were issued to control excessive drinking. The use of liquor in the province had grown from mere lack of moderation to proportions so menacing as to threaten prosperity and progress. Yet neither the provincial nor the city government could make the slightest headway in effective restraint or control. Still further proof of the lack of respect for governmental edicts is revealed in the public attitude toward ordinances calling upon the citizens to concentrate on Manhattan Island, to fence their lands and to form villages or hamlets for protective purposes. Not one of these commands was carried out as issued, and none was obeyed even to a decent degree until sheer necessity compelled it.

In addition to this lack of law observance, which in many cases amounted to nullification, the province was faced with a mounting burden of taxes that produced precious little in the way of justifiable or tangible results. The "evil genius" more responsible for this, probably, than any other individual was Cornelius van Tienhoven, who as provincial secretary helped himself to no small part of the hard-won taxes from 1638 to 1656, thus all too often making new and heavier taxes necessary. Dismissed finally from office, he committed suicide rather than face the charges brought against him. The combination of Van Tienhoven and a governor-general who was so lax about submitting any financial accounting that his superiors were forced repeatedly to call upon him to do so, together with a populace either unwilling or unable to face the stern realities of colonial life, finally bankrupted New Amsterdam.

Although religious freedom existed in New Amsterdam, yet from the time when Jonas Michaelius became the first regularly ordained clergyman and organized what is now the Collegiate Church, to the very end of the Dutch regime, not a single religious organization other than the Dutch Reformed Church was permitted to erect a house of worship on Manhattan Island. Nevertheless, other denominations, the Lutherans in particular, did organize small congregations with comparatively little persecution.

Obviously, these years provided many "firsts" in the history of New York. The first recorded murder occurred in May 1638; the first assessment list was made up in 1653; the first official price-fixing occurred on September 11, 1653, when a duly convened assembly "froze" the prices of many articles; the first crop control program in the United States was set up March 20, 1653, when tobacco planters were ordered to devote certain parts of their holdings to "hard grain for Bread" in order to prevent famine; the first "overtime" pay for workmen was inaugurated on August 27, 1656, when "extra weighing out of hours" at the weigh-house was put on an added-charge basis; the first recorded lottery was run off in March 1655, "Bibles, Testaments and other books" being used to provide a profit for the promoter and funds for the poor; the first attempt at silkworm culture in the nation was made in 1657; the first recorded "third degree" was carried out on June 25, 1661, when a woman charged with stealing stockings was "placed on the rack, and threatened with torture" to make her talk; the first unemployment "home relief" on a local-community basis was inaugurated on October 26, 1661; and the first law against "loan sharks," very numerous in New Amsterdam at the time, was passed in 1661.

The end of the Dutch West India Company's venture began on March

22, 1664, when King Charles II of England gave to his brother, the Duke of York, a grant in America covering territory that included the highly desirable New Netherland holdings. The ink on this grandiloquently worded grant was hardly dry before the English began to convert its words into actualities; and a fleet of four warships under command of Colonel Richard Nicolls, first deputy-governor of the Duke's territories, forced formal surrender of New Amsterdam on September 8, 1664. Nicolls promptly renamed the place New York.

Even in these last days of Dutch rule, the lack of preparedness for emergencies was evident, there being no adequate fort or guns or military stores with which successfully to resist invasion.

Yet it was these Dutch who had established the first permanent settlement on Manhattan; who had settled a number of outlying towns such as Breuckelen, Vlissingen (Flushing), Midwout (Flatbush), Heemstede (Hempstead), Ameersfoort (Flatlands), Middleburgh (Newton), and Gravesend; who had started a common school as early as 1638 and a Latin school in 1652; who had laid out a "city," no matter how crudely; who had developed friendly relations with the Indians, despite Kieft's blunders; and who had, above all else, laid the foundations for a commerce which was to become the backbone not only of the English regime but of all future development in this part of the New World.

English Control at Its Height: 1664–1763

After the oath of allegiance to the British monarch and the Duke of York had been proclaimed by Governor Nicolls on October 28, 1664, control of New York shifted from the Dutch merchants to the Duke as an individual proprietor, with the right to establish whatever form of government might please him.

Unquestionably the most important single event under English control was the establishment of the right to a free press. This occurred as a result of Governor William Cosby's dismissal of Lewis Morris, long chief justice of the province, because of Morris' dissenting opinion in a case involving the governor. The strong popular opposition to this move did not worry Cosby, who controlled the courts and the meeting of the legislature, through his legally granted powers; and who, furthermore, had the unqualified support of the city's only newspaper, William Bradford's *New-York Gazette*. To provide a medium for presenting their case, the Morris supporters started another paper, the *New-York Weekly Journal*, under the editorship of John Peter Zenger. The *Journal* stated its opinions bluntly until, as the result of charges made against him in the issue of October 7, 1734, Governor Cosby ordered Zenger's arrest. Zenger's New York counsel was promptly "disbarred," but Andrew Hamilton of Philadelphia came to the rescue with so able a defense that the jury acquitted Zenger. This victory had its immediate effect, newspapers thereafter becoming the medium through which the people openly secured a knowledge of their rights, thus aiding the growth of a spirit of independence and hastening separation of the colonies from England.

The second major achievement under English rule was in the realm of religious freedom. The Quakers held their first meeting under a roof in 1671; the Lutherans established their own church, also in 1671; the French Church, on the north side of Pine Street, east of Nassau, was built in 1704; the Presbyterians erected a church on Wall Street, the first of that denomination in the city, and were permitted by the common council to worship in what was then City Hall while their edifice was being constructed. In 1707, when Governor Cornbury jailed the "nonconformist" ministers of these same Presbyterians, the courts tried and freed them despite the governor's attitude, thus definitely establishing a remarkably liberal degree of religious toleration in the province of New York.

The charter which resulted from the general assembly called in 1683 by Governor Dongan, and subsequent additions thereto, was one of the three major groups of laws in force within the colony of New York from 1665 to 1691. The first was the Duke's Laws of 1665, a code drawn up by Colonel Richard Nicolls, first governor of the Duke of York's province, and approved at a meeting of 34 deputies from 17 towns at Hempstead on March 1, 1665. The Duke's Laws were the basis of government until 1683, when an assembly elected according to the Duke's instructions to Thomas Dongan, fourth governor, met at New York on October 17th. This first general provincial assembly passed 50 statutes which constituted the law during 1683–1685. The assembly sat three times, twice in 1683 and once in 1685. With its permanent dissolution by Dongan in 1685, the law-making function of the province fell to the governor and his council. This executive council passed laws in the king's name which superseded those enacted by the assembly of 1683.

Of these three major groups of laws from 1665 to 1691, the charter of 1683, which was in force 1683–85, is the best known. It included a charter of liberties, provided for new customs duties, and claimed the taxing power for the assembly. Its "Charter of Libertyes and Privileges" is credited to Matthias Nicolls, a leading Englishman of the province. This charter was approved by King James II, but was never sent back to New York because of involved reasons upon which historians do not agree. A charter was granted to the city by Governor Dongan in 1686. Included in the provisions of this instrument, which continued in force 45 years, was the English form of municipal government, under a mayor, sheriff, aldermen, etc., the right of electing aldermen, assistant aldermen, and sub-constables being granted to the voters in the several wards. This, in addition to the provision for making freemen of natural-born subjects of the king, or those who had been naturalized by the mayor, recorder and aldermen, constituted the major liberal gains. For signing this charter, Governor Dongan was paid 300 pounds sterling on authority of the common council.

A Gilbert and Sullivan touch was provided in this period when, as the result of war between England and the Netherlands, New York was "captured" from the English by the Dutch on August 9, 1673, was renamed New Orange, changed its form of government back to that of the Dutch, and went through another oath-taking ceremony. Then, because of a treaty of peace signed in Europe, the entire show was staged over again, this time with Sir Edmund Andros, third governor of New York, acting as master of ceremonies in the "surrender" of the town back to the English on November 10, 1674.

Fourteen years later, King James II annexed New York and East and West Jersey to the recently created Dominion of New England. Sir Edmund Andros, former governor of the province of New York, was appointed captain-general and governor-in-chief of the Dominion of New England. Andros reached New York on August 11, 1688, had the seal of the province broken in the presence of the council according to royal command, and ordered that the seal of New England should thereafter be used.

But behind the formalities of Andros' reception lay factors that were rapidly pushing many of the people toward revolt. The heavy cost of maintaining defenses was resulting in high taxes; the English on Long Island viewed with alarm the dissolution of the general assembly of 1683 and the creation of an executive form of government in which the governor and his council made the laws without recourse to popular opinion; merchants denied the legality of taxes and customs imposed by an all-powerful executive council; and many feared the growing power of Roman Catholics in England, where the king was of that faith, and of Roman Catholic officials in the colonies. This last reason was perhaps the greatest contributing cause of the revolt that manifested itself in America when James II fled from England and the revolution there was capped by the ascension to the throne of William and Mary.

Governor Andros of the Dominion of New England was seized and imprisoned in Boston, and the Dominion collapsed as a political entity, each part resuming its former independent state. In New York, Lieutenant-Governor Nicholson tried to control the growing unrest there. On May 31, 1689, Jacob Leisler, a captain of the militia, seized the fort and set himself up as head of the government. From December 11, 1689, when he had gained supreme command of the situation, until March 19, 1691, Leisler controlled the province of New York. Among his more constructive acts was the calling of a municipal election, whereby Peter Delanoy became the first mayor chosen by popular vote, and the decided efforts he made toward colonial unity as a weapon against the French and English.

On November 14, 1689, King William III approved the appointment of Colonel Henry Sloughter as governor of New York, but delay in fitting out Sloughter's ships resulted in the arrival before him, at New York, of one of his subordinates, Major Richard Ingoldsby. Leisler refused to recognize Ingoldsby because the latter was not accredited by the king to take command of the province. When Governor Sloughter himself arrived, he clapped Leisler and others into jail, and executed Leisler and his son-in-law for treason on May 16, 1691. This created bitter political dissension which endured for many years. An act of Parliament in 1694 reversed Sloughter's and the trial court's verdict and vindicated Leisler's seizure of the government.

Piracy, which began to manifest itself in New York waters about this time, was subsequently suppressed by the same administrator who made an agreement in 1695 with Captain William Kidd to fit out a privateer and share in the prizes captured, and who later sent Kidd back to England to be hanged for piracy. This was the Earl of Bellomont. He arrived in New York as governor of the province in 1698, and almost immediately began a long series of reports to the lords of trade in England, in which he constantly stressed the prevalence of piracy around New York. Accusing his predecessor, Governor Fletcher, of aiding the freebooters, Bellomont issued a proclamation on May 9, 1698, calling for the arrest of all known pirates and the suppression of piracy. From that day until April 16, 1700, when the notorious Captain Kidd and 40 other pirates landed in England to be tried, Bellomont's reports to the lords of trade pleaded steadily for good judges from England, an honest and able attorney-general, a man-of-war commanded by a trustworthy captain, and pay and recruits for the four foot-companies of soldiers in the city—these, he averred, were the only means to put down piracy.

Despite corrupt customs officials and a populace "impudent in abetting and sheltering Pirates and their Goods," Bellomont personally ordered the seizure, examination and imprisonment of his former partner, Captain Kidd; and to the commissioners whom he had appointed to examine Kidd's ship he forwarded jewels valued at £10,000 which Kidd had presented to Lady Bellomont during his term as the Earl's partner.

Bellomont's unrelenting war against the pirates resulted in the dispatching of a man-of-war from England in 1699, and the king's order of February 10, 1700, which required that certain pirates be sent from New York to England with all witnesses and evidence against them. Among the prisoners was Captain Kidd, who, together with several of the others, was hanged soon after reaching England. With Kidd's execution, piracy in New York waters dwindled.

Among the more constructive local administrations of this period were those of Abraham de Peyster and William Peartree. As mayor of New York from 1691 to 1694, Colonel de Peyster was very much interested in balancing the budget, his proposal of 1694 to sell certain vacant lots in the city to pay off the municipal debt being one of similar suggestions that were supported by the common council. Yet he was not niggardly with respect to civic improvements, as was demonstrated in 1696 when he was appointed by the common council to consider the building of a new City Hall—a project to which he gave much time and thought. In 1698 and in 1709, De Peyster was appointed to the governor's council, and in 1701 he was appointed deputy auditor-general of the colony. Both in and out of these and other offices, De Peyster's efforts were often directed toward projects not customarily associated with the interests of his class at the time.

Colonel William Peartree, who served as mayor from 1703 to 1706, is credited with having effected several public improvements. On May 11, 1706, he caused the citizens to begin work on fortifications of the city, these being described in the *Manual of the Corporation of the City of New York* (1853) as "the first erected at the Narrows," the "principal incentive" therefor being cited as "the entrance of a French privateer within the harbor, which put the whole city in consternation." In 1705, the *Manual* continues, Colonel Peartree was entrusted "with the command of an expedition, consisting of a brigantine and two sloops, fitted out by several of the principal shipping merchants of the city, to cruise after a certain French privateer which had been depredating upon merchant vessels bound for this port." Peartree established the first free grammar school, as well as a school for Negro slaves. He also improved conditions in the jail and provided a debtors' prison in the City Hall.

One particularly disgraceful episode that stands out against the more constructive achievements of the period was the so-called "Negro plot" of 1741. It began when several fires broke out in swift succession, was whipped up by lightning-like gossip implicating the colored inhabitants, and resulted finally in the imprisonment of more than 100 Negroes, the burning of 29 at the stake and the transporting of 88. Three whites were also executed before the hysteria died down.

Among the many events of these years were the founding of the first mercantile exchange in 1670; the death of Peter Stuyvesant two years later; the establishment of part of the Boston Post Road in 1671, and a regular post between New York and Boston the following year; the appearance in 1680 of the first "trust" in American history, when coopers organized for the express purpose of raising the prices of casks; the setting up of the first printing press and the establishment on November 8, 1725, of the city's first newspaper, the *New-York Gazette;* the opening in 1731 of the first public library when 1,642 books received from the Society for the Propagation of the Gospel in Foreign Parts were made available at City Hall; the organization of New York's first labor union, in 1747, when 100 mechanics protested against the low wage scales in neighboring provinces and combined to increase their own; and the granting of a charter on October 31, 1754, to King's College, now Columbia University, financial support of which was made possible by a lottery.

The Revolutionary Period: 1763–1783

The Treaty of Paris in 1763 freed the colonies from dependence on the British government for protection against the French and Indians by eliminating the former from what was to be the United States and by making peace with the latter. This led to swift development of the movement toward union of the colonies—a result long foreseen by competent observers, who knew that only fear of the French and Indians had kept the colonies in line.

The second force that now drove the colonies together and brought on the Revolution was a series of stupid blunders made by the British government under a young king too ignorant and unyielding to compromise on vital issues. Soon His Majesty's Government and the colonies were opposed on two fundamental issues: enforcement of the navigation laws, which would ruin a rich smuggling trade that was technically illegal but had been openly carried on for more than 100 years without official interference; and insistence by the home government on raising a permanent revenue from the colonies through direct taxation, the Stamp Act of 1765 and the Townshend Acts of 1767 being prominent examples of these unwise measures.

On October 7, 1765, the so-called Stamp Act Congress met at City Hall in New York, with 28 delegates seated from Massachusetts Bay, Rhode Island, Connecticut, New York, New Jersey, Pennsylvania, Maryland, South Carolina, and "the counties of New Castle, Kent and Sussex on Delaware." A "declaration of the rights and grievances of the colonists in America" was agreed to on October 19 and set forth in 14 articles, chief among which were the protest against "taxation without representation," the demand for the right to trial by jury, and the statement that the Stamp Act manifestly tended "to subvert the rights and liberties of the colonies." Three days later, the Congress approved an address to the king, a memorial to the lords, and a petition to the House of Commons. On October 25, the Congress adjourned after the clerk had been directed to make a copy of the proceedings for each of the colonies, and two sets to be dispatched to England.

Among the "radical" organizations that did much at this time to consolidate opposition to England's sudden enforcement of the Navigation Laws in 1763, and to taxes levied in 1765 and 1767, were groups constituting the Sons of Liberty. They first made their direct influence felt when the Stamp Act laid a tax on all legal documents executed within the colonies. When the stamps for this tax arrived on October 22, 1765, the people were in an ugly mood, as threatening manuscript placards throughout the city evidenced. "The first Man," read one of these placards, "that either distributes or makes use of Stampt Paper let him take care of His House, Person & Effects." By November 1, the government's refusal to surrender the stamps resulted in riots. Mobs, led by Sons of Liberty groups, roamed the town, broke open the governor's coachhouse, and burned it and the palisades they had ripped away in Bowling Green. Then they broke into and sacked the house of Major James, who had been appointed to enforce the regulations, and proceeded to train cannon on the city. Finally Lieutenant-Governor Colden turned the stamps over to the common council and they were put in the City Hall under care of the city watch. A few days later, the new governor, Sir Henry Moore, arrived and tried to placate the people by dismantling the fort and removing artillery stores placed there by Major James.

Four years later, the New York assembly met and was asked by Colden to make provision for the king's troops. The assembly did so in return for issue to it of £120,000 in paper currency. The people, whose opposition to supporting the troops had previously been manifested, saw in this measure a betrayal by their own assembly; and clashes occurred between the people, led by Sons of Liberty groups, and the soldiers.

When the Stamp Act of 1765 was repealed by Parliament in 1766, a declaratory act was passed asserting Parliament's right to tax America. On the basis of this declaratory act, duties were laid in 1767 on all paint, paper, glass and tea imported into the colonies. In March 1770, these taxes were repealed, with the exception of that on tea, which was maintained as evidence of Parliament's authority to tax the colonies. It was openly opposed by merchants throughout the Dominion of New England, but only Boston was selected for punishment because of such opposition. The admiration of many New York merchants for Boston's continued defiance of the tax resulted finally in the election on May 16, 1774, of the Committee of Fifty-One at Fraunces Tavern and the adoption of a resolution to help Boston.

On July 4, 1774, the committee nominated Philip Livingston, John Alsop, Isaac Low, James Duane and John Jay as representatives to the general congress of the colonies that the committee had proposed. Two days later, the radical faction of the committee, dissatisfied with conservative action, called a public meeting in what is now City Hall Park and passed stinging resolutions that resulted in withdrawal of 11 members from the committee. The general congress of the colonies, held at Philadelphia early in September 1774, adopted the "Association," an agreement pledging the colonies to non-importation of British goods. That agreement was kept to the letter only by New York.

News of the battles of Lexington and Concord reached New York on Sunday morning, April 23, 1775. Bands of citizens marched to the City Hall, seized the government and confiscated all arms. A Committee of One Hundred, chosen to bring order out of the existing chaos, was forced to proceed cautiously because of the many loyalists, a large party of whom planned to turn the city over to the English. Repeated clashes between these loyalists and the patriots marked the very severe winter of 1775–76.

Washington arrived in the city on April 13, 1776, fought the Battle of Long Island, and fell back to a fortified camp on Brooklyn Heights, from which he moved his forces to Manhattan on August 29. The English concentration of a superior force threatened the Americans, who now evacuated the city proper and entrenched themselves on territory along the Hudson at Washington Heights. The opposing forces clashed finally at the Battle of Harlem Heights, fought over an area lying roughly between the present Riverside and Morningside Drives, from 120th Street southward to 103d Street. The English were defeated, but Washington did not have a force sufficient to dislodge them from the city, which they had occupied on September 15, 1776, and which they held, under a military government, for the next seven years.

On April 20, 1777, a representative convention at Kingston, N. Y., adopted a constitution giving the choice of governor to the people for the first time, George Clinton being elected in June and inaugurated July 30.

Four years later, Lord Cornwallis surrendered at Yorktown; and after two years of battling with an obstinate king, the definitive treaty of peace was signed September 3, 1783, by the American commissioners and His Majesty's Government.

During the English occupation of New York, a devastating fire destroyed about one-fourth of the city, September 21–3, 1776. But this disaster was as nothing compared to the horror of the prison ships in Wallabout Bay and the makeshift prisons on land, in which some 12,000 American prisoners of war, including 2,637 men left to garrison Fort Washington and later captured, died as a result of being deprived of food by grafting commissaries. Property belonging to royalists was marked and protected; all other was confiscated by the Crown. The city became a refuge for tories from all parts of the country. One of the most dramatic episodes of the period was Nathan Hale's execution as a spy on September 22, 1776.

Against the pleasant fact that no taxes were levied on the citizens (expenses were met by revenues from wharf-dues, tavern licenses, etc.) was the unpleasant and unprecedented rise in the cost of living. Landlords increased their rents as demand rose sharply, and some of the necessities of life soared 800 percent above normal prices. These factors, together with the disastrous fire of 1776 and the extremely severe winter of 1777, produced a steady increase in poverty, which became one of the major problems faced by the British commandants during the occupation. Considerable damage was done to the churches of Dissenters, the military seizing and using them for prisons, stables, hospitals and storehouses.

Despite such conditions, the town was gay. Beach bathing, a little theater on John Street, band concerts, and even bull-baiting served to keep the tories and British officers amused. The outstanding social event was the visit of Prince William Henry, third son of the king, in 1781. He was the first person of royal lineage to visit America.

The city's physical progress was remarkable considering the handicaps of the period. The population increased from about 12,000 in 1763 to 21,863 for city and county in 1771. New streets were opened and developed as the city grew to the northward at a rapid pace. More churches were built, including St. Paul's, the Brick Presbyterian, and the city's first Methodist Church. The Chamber of Commerce, designed to encourage industry and trade, and the Marine Society, founded to promote maritime knowledge and to care for widows and orphans of sea captains, were formed in 1768. Two years later, New York Hospital was chartered, although the fire of 1776 and the war prevented its actual operation as a hospital until 1791.

On December 5, 1783, not a British flag remained in the harbor. A new nation had been born, and New York stood ready to enter upon an era of growth and prosperity such as it had not yet enjoyed.

Reconstruction and Consolidation: 1783–1811

City, State and nation went through a period of adjustment and reconstruction that began immediately after the treaty of peace was formally signed with England in 1783 and continued until the War of 1812. During the intervening years, decided progress was made in several directions.

State matters concerned the legislature, which met in the city from January 1784 to November 1796 (except for five sessions, held elsewhere). Governors Clinton and Jay occupied the Government House, begun in 1790 to house State and Federal officers. Legislative acts directly concerning the city included the incorporation in 1784 of the "Regents of the University of the State of New York," this act changing the name of King's College to Columbia College; the altering of ward designations from names such as Dock, East, etc., to First, Second, etc.; the act of 1799 providing for gradual abolition of slavery throughout the State; and the petition of 1802 to construct a bridge across the East River, the first proposal of its kind and one that was heartily ridiculed.

Federal matters ccncerned the Congress, which met in New York City from its first session of January 11, 1785, to August 30, 1790, when it moved to Philadelphia. After the adoption of the Constitution, Congress met for the first time under the terms of that instrument on March 4, 1789, in Federal Hall, which stood on the site of the present Subtreasury building. There, electors chose George Washington as first President on April 6, 1789, the inauguration taking place 24 days later on the balcony of Federal Hall. Washington's stay in New York was marked by gracious entertainment, walks "round the Battery," long drives in the family coach with Mrs. Washington and her two children, theater parties, and even a fishing trip to Sandy Hook in 1790. The President also sat for the portraits by Trumbull and Savage that hang today in City Hall.

Important religious developments took place in the city after passage by the legislature in 1784 of an act allowing all religious bodies to be incorporated—an act as important to religious equality as the Declaration of Independence to political freedom. The Catholics, who had been prohibited from exercising their form of worship in Great Britain and the colonies, laid the cornerstone of St. Peter's, the first Roman Catholic church in New York, on October 5, 1785, at the southeast corner of Church and Barclay Streets. Twenty-three years later, a Roman Catholic See was created in New York. The first convention of the Protestant Episcopal Church in the State of New York was held here on June 22, 1785, and this body was later organized as an independent branch of the mother church, just 90 years after Trinity Church had been chartered by Governor Fletcher.

Building activity began to increase greatly. In 1800, about 100 buildings, half of them three-story structures, were under way. Seven years later, more new houses were built than in any previous year, while between 600 and 700 dwellings and shops were begun in the spring of 1810.

Between 1783 and 1812, commerce and industry suffered a serious slump, then enjoyed a recovery, and subsequently went into another decline that resulted in panic. In February 1784, the *Empress of China* sailed for Asiatic waters flying the American flag that had been adopted in 1777— the first American ship to set out for the Orient with those colors. The Bank of New York was organized in 1784 as the city's first financial institution; and the first fire insurance company was founded ten years later under the name of Mutual Assurance Company. In 1792, an agreement was effected among stock brokers that later resulted in formation of the New York Stock Exchange. Prior to 1792, outdoor trading had been conducted near a buttonwood tree that stood between Nos. 68 and 70 Wall Street.

The energies of the people were not, however, devoted entirely to commercial adjustment and physical reconstruction. Amusements and sports occupied no little of their time, with theaters, pleasure gardens, circuses and various other diversions vying for patronage.

Pleasure gardens were numerous. Best known were those owned by Joseph de Lacroix, a French restaurateur, at No. 112 Broadway, where ice cream and open-air concerts were featured; and at the Bayard Mansion, between Broadway and the Bowery just below the present Astor Place, where private boxes under shade trees were the "ringside tables." Circuses were great favorites. From 1786 to 1808, eight of them held forth. They featured exhibitions of horsemanship, grandiose stage spectacles, bull-baiting and wild animal combats.

The sporting gentry had their fill too. On August 13, 1789, they staged a yacht race off Sandy Hook that was the forerunner of the present America's Cup races. Horse-racing in Greenwich Lane, fox-hunting and (in November and December of 1784) buffalo hunts with hounds, in which buffalo brought from Kentucky were used, rounded out the sports of the day.

Various societies that continue to this day were organized. The "Society of Tammany or Columbian Order in the City of New York," established in 1786 as a social and philanthropic organization, was developed into the present political machine by a long line of astute leaders from Aaron Burr down to Charlie Murphy. It was not the first Tammany Society in the United States, others having preceded it in Pennsylvania, Virginia and New Jersey. Two other organizations formed at this time were the New York Academy of Fine Arts (1802) and the New York Historical Society (1804).

The closing year of this period, 1811, was extremely important in the city's history. On March 22, commissioners appointed in 1807 to lay out streets, roads and public squares submitted their report. With it they transmitted a map drawn in triplicate by John Randel, Jr., from surveys made by him for the commissioners. One of the originals of that map, the most important of its kind in the entire history of New York, hangs today in the great Public Library at Forty-Second Street and Fifth Avenue, its faded ink marking the end of little old New York and the beginning of a great metropolis.

The plan of 1811 divided the greater part of Manhattan Island into rectangular blocks separated by north and south avenues 100 feet wide, and east and west cross streets laid out to 155th Street. Avenues that could be extended to Harlem were designated by ordinal numbers, from First at the east to Twelfth at the west; with four short avenues, A, B, C and D, east of First Avenue.

Squares and other open spaces included Bloomingdale Square, from Fifty-Third to Fifty-Seventh Streets, between Eighth and Ninth Avenues; Hamilton Square, from Sixty-Sixth to Sixty-Eighth Streets, between Third and Fifth Avenues; Manhattan Square, from Seventy-Seventh to Eighty-First Streets, between Eighth and Ninth Avenues; Harlem Marsh, from 106th to 109th Streets, between the East River and Fifth Avenue; and Harlem Square, from 117th to 121st Streets, between Sixth and Seventh Avenues.

Like nearly all attempts to effect improvement, the plan of 1811 aroused the customary chorus of opposition from self-appointed defenders of the "people's rights." Fortunately, the courts sustained the commissioners, and the haphazard community now began to develop along the lines of a planned system of thoroughfares that persists, basically, to this day.

It was in this period of adjustment and reconstruction that De Witt Clinton began a distinguished public career in city and state that covered about a quarter of a century. Graduated in 1786 from Columbia College, he was appointed mayor of New York in 1803 and served ten terms in that office during the ensuing years to 1815. Then, in the period from 1817 to 1828, he served two terms as governor of the State. Although his name is most prominently associated with the development of early inland waterways, notably the Erie Canal, Clinton was a pioneer participant in numerous other important activities. He was the first president of the Society for Establishing a Free School in the City of New York (later the Public School Society), the Literary and Philosophical Society of New York, the American Academy of Fine Arts and the Institution for the Relief of the Deaf and Dumb. He died at Albany on February 10, 1828.

The War of 1812

Work on the commissioners' plan of 1811 was interrupted in 1812 by the declaration of war against England on June 18, various diplomatic measures employed by President Jefferson having failed to stop both the French and English policy of search and seizure of American ships and the impressment of their crews. New York City's part in the war consisted chiefly in supplying men and money for the erection of fortifications to defend the harbor. In addition, New York was prominent in fitting out privateers that preyed on British commerce and naval forces, the city's activities in this respect being second only to those of Baltimore.

Of especial interest during these years was the development of steamboat navigation. As McMaster points out, there were no steamboats outside New York at this time, "but such was the commercial importance of that city that eight found employment in administering to the wants and conveniences of its citizens." One of those who helped to make possible that development was Cadwallader D. Colden, grandson of an English colonial governor and himself mayor of New York for three terms, in 1818–21. It was Colden who in 1812 acted as attorney for Robert Fulton and his associates before the common council, and secured an extension of Fulton's contract with the city, thus assuring the success of the Steam Boat Ferry Company and the subsequent expansion of steamboat navigation. Later, after Colden had become mayor, he evidenced his interest in another important public problem by presenting to the common council Robert Macomb's idea of bringing water to the city from Rye Pond. Although the Macomb plan was not carried out, it served to stimulate discussion of this and other schemes that led to definite action some two decades later. Colden's *Memoir of the Canal Celebration* is one of the best contemporary accounts of the ceremonies in New York in 1825 when the Erie Canal was completed.

Also important in this period was the establishment in 1812 of the State's public school system and the refusal of the Free School Society, which controlled practically all of New York City's non-sectarian elementary education, to submit to administration by the State authorities, though it accepted its share of school funds from the State. Not until many years thereafter did the city's public schools become a part of the State system.

Material Prosperity and Civic Lethargy: 1815–1841

The end of the War of 1812 marked the opening of a burst of commercial activity. Imports, which had been seriously curtailed for several years, now flooded the port of New York. So huge was the total that, after merchants' demands were met, many cargoes of goods were sold directly to the consumer. This resulted in cutting off the market for the merchants, running citizens into debt for purchases far beyond their means, and the collapse of home industries developed during the past decade to replace imports from Europe. Hard times set in, and the winter of 1815–16 was one of great suffering. Soup kitchens spread rapidly, until by March 1, 1816, they were feeding between 6,000 and 7,000 persons.

But the depression soon passed. The famous Black Ball and other packet lines began their sailings to Europe, South America and the Indies. The seven-million-dollar canal system connecting New York with the interior was completed in 1825. Steam railroad transporation within and out of the city was initiated and expanded. Such improvements, coupled with an eager market for imports on the one hand and home products now protected by the tariff of 1816 on the other, resulted in unprecedented business activity, particularly as the flood of immigration was swiftly creating a shortage in housing and other related fields.

Duties collected on imports ran as high as ten million dollars in one year; merchants from all parts of the country came to New York to transact business; about 1,500 mercantile houses are said to have been established in the first half of 1825; and hotel and transportation revenues soared. Twelve banks with a combined capital of 13 millions and ten marine insurance companies capitalized at ten millions were inadequate to handle the enormous business in their fields; and applications were made to the legislature for 27 more bank charters and 31 other corporation charters, the new companies having a total capitalization of 37½ million dollars. Even the nationwide financial panic of 1837 failed to have an extended effect on the upswing. By 1841, the 185 commercial failures in New York, the attendant riots, and the suspension by banks of specie payments were fairly well in the background, and the boom was on again.

Meanwhile, civic pride was crying aloud in the wilderness of commercial frenzy. Pauperism was plentiful at the lower end of the economic scale. The liquor traffic was running riot, the newly opened almshouse being taxed to the limit by many who spent their relief allowances in the 1,900 licensed grog shops and 600 other sources of supply in the city. A housing shortage was created by the population increase from 96,373 in 1810 to 312,710 in 1840, facilities being so inadequate that the universal moving day of May 1 found people gathered with their goods in the park or lodged in the jail until their unfinished houses could be made ready. Building was speedily and poorly done; sanitary measures were secondary to swift completion.

Deep-seated antagonisms of native or naturalized Americans toward immigrants began to be manifested in riots and mob violence. Revision of the charter in 1834 and consequent direct election of the mayor produced in Tammany an overnight affection for these immigrants, who soon discovered that he who giveth on election day taketh away on all others. The inevitable reaction on the part of these thousands of newcomers was either cynicism or apathy toward municipal affairs. Thus, with those at the top of the social structure interested primarily in economic rather than civic gains, and with the others antagonistic or indifferent, civic pride went with the wind.

Streets were filthy and in poor repair. The great fire that broke out on December 15, 1835, consuming more than 600 buildings at a loss of about 17 million dollars, demonstrated the utter inadequacy of the fire-fighting personnel and equipment. This fire destroyed the heart of the business section and nearly all of the old Dutch town that had survived the fires of 1776 and 1778. More than 17 city blocks were laid waste in the streets east of Broadway and south of Wall Street, and not until buildings in the path of the fire were blown up was it checked. Nearly all of the fire insurance companies were bankrupted by this disaster. Policing, performed by the unemployed, was too inefficient to cope with the riots of 1833–35. The inadequate wells and pumps that provided the only available drinking water were responsible for four epidemics between 1818 and 1834. An initial scourge of yellow fever had scarcely died down when the dread disease reappeared on an even wider scale in 1822. Then a third occurred in 1823, thousands fleeing the city and remaining away until November. Nine years later, cholera swept the city, killing 3,500 persons in 105 days.

Early in the 19th century, an English visitor to New York had particularly noted "the colored people, the custom of smoking segars in the streets (even followed by some of the children), and the number and nuisance of the pigs permitted to be at large." By 1837, the scene had changed considerably.

One hundred years ago, about one-sixth of Manhattan was compactly covered with houses, stores and paved streets, the rest being given over to farms and gardens. Broadway, extending for three miles from the Battery to the junction of Fifth Avenue and Twenty-Third Street, was still the finest thoroughfare. Houses were mostly of brick, two to six stories high. Of the 60-odd hotels, only three were operated on the European plan, with rates ranging from $2 to $3.50 weekly, while the rest offered board and lodging on the American plan for from $1 to $2.50 a day. Of the five theaters, the Park, in Park Row, was the oldest, largest and most fashionable; box seats cost $1, admission to the "pit" was 50 cents and to the gallery 25 cents. Other places of fashionable resort included the Battery; Castle Garden, which had been ceded by the United States to the city in 1823 and had served since as a place of public entertainment; and Niblo's Garden, at the corner of Broadway and Pine Street, one of the most frequented spots during the summer months.

Churches numbered about 150 in 1837, the Presbyterians leading with 39 and the Episcopalians ranking second with 29. Educational facilities were surprisingly good for the time. Columbia College, on the site bounded by Murray, Barclay, Church and Chapel Streets, and the University of the City of New York, on the east side of Washington Square, constituted the principal non-sectarian institutions of higher learning. The General Theological Seminary of the Protestant Episcopal Church, at the corner of Ninth Avenue and Twenty-First Street, and the New York Theological Seminary of the Presbyterian Church, on Wooster Street above Waverly Place, were two of the leading sectarian schools. Labor had its own Mechanics' School, established in 1820 by the General Society of Mechanics and Tradesmen to educate children of deceased or unfortunate members. Public schools maintained by the Public School Society totaled 49, of which eight were for Negroes; the enrollment exceeded 12,000 white and 1,000 colored pupils. In addition, there were several private schools and seminaries. The press had expanded rapidly beyond the seven daily, five semi-weekly and five weekly newspapers of 1817. In 1837, the city had more than 50 newspapers.

In 1837, Philip Hone, who had been mayor in 1826–27 and was one of the city's leading social and political figures, built a new house at the southeast corner of Broadway and Great Jones Street, and there continued his diary, begun in 1828 and regularly maintained until almost the day of his death in 1851. This diary constitutes a record unrivalled in its field, its more than two million words being the most complete contemporary picture of a period in which its author played a prominent role. Politically, Hone's real importance, as Allan Nevins has pointed out, "was as a counsellor and agent of the great Whig leaders—of Webster, Clay, Seward, Tallmadge, and Taylor. No man had a greater influence with the New York merchants." Apart from his political activity, he served as an officer, director, or trustee of many business, social welfare and civic organizations. In these other posts, he contributed steadily to the development of the city he loved, and through his diary he recorded and often interpreted the growth of that city from about 200,000 population to more than 500,000.

The Pre-Civil War Period: 1842–1860

By 1842, New York had entered upon an era of remarkable expansion in population, wealth and commerce. Population leaped from 312,710 in 1840 to 813,669 in 1860. The clipper ship carried the American merchant marine to its glorious peak in 1860, creating great fortunes as the American flag became supreme in the trade with China, in the California gold rush and on the Atlantic; until in 1860 American merchant tonnage represented not far from one-third of the world-total. The lower part of the city was crowded with buildings, the upper section began to develop by 1853, and in 1860 the total assessed valuation of all real estate had increased 206 millions of dollars over the figures for 1842. The passenger elevator, without which modern New York architecture would be impossible, made its first screw-propelled appearance in 1859 at the Fifth Avenue Hotel. Express services for packages had been developed by 1843; postage stamps for prepaid letters were inaugurated in 1846 by the New York postmaster and extended nationally in 1847; and the telegraph climaxed the speeding of communications when the first New York line was opened in 1845.

It was in this period that land for Central Park was purchased and construction of that beautiful development was begun. In 1850, the need for more parks was stressed by civic organizations; and in 1851, authority to buy land was approved by the legislature, and commissioners of estimate and assessment were appointed to secure land for a park. In 1856, the Central Park Commission, consisting of the mayor, street commissioner and several prominent citizens, was created. Designs for the park were submitted in 1856–57, those of Frederick Law Olmstead and Calvert Vaux being selected. Land was acquired in 1856, work was begun in 1857 and the park was considered completed on the basis of the Olmstead-Vaux plans in 1876. To Andrew H. Green, executive officer and president of the Central Park Commission from 1857 to 1870, was given chief credit for the work.

Hard times swept over the city in the same year that Central Park was begun, about 40,000 laborers being thrown out of work. Hunger meetings were held in public centers, particularly Tompkins Square. People marched through the streets demanding bread and work. Threats were made against public buildings, and troops were called out to guard the Custom House and the Subtreasury. Damage was done to private property, but no deaths were recorded as a result of these disturbances. Improved business conditions solved the problem, which had threatened to get completely out of hand when such gangs as the "Dead Rabbits" and the "Bowery Boys" took advantage of the situation in violence and looting.

Politically, this period was marked by two distinct developments. Slavery became a national issue, splitting the Democratic Party. In New York, attention was centered on the charter, which was amended five times without really correcting the lack of centralization of power that contributed no little to the efficiency of Mayor Fernando Wood's corrupt political machine and the development of a technique whereby "Boss" Tweed later plundered the city.

Progress was made, however, in dealing with the three most important municipal problems: an adequate supply of water, public education and improvement of the police department. Of these, water supply was by far the most pressing, and construction of the Croton system became the greatest single advance of the period.

The second great advance of this period was in the field of public education, which the Free School Society had dominated since 1805 and in which it had effected several improvements, including those of 1828, when it opened the first of its more than 60 primary schools. Although the Society had been sharing in the State's school funds, it had not and still was not operating under the regulations of the State-wide public education act of 1812.

In 1831, the old question of permitting religious societies to share in public educational funds was re-opened when the Roman Catholic Benevolent Society requested the common council to help its orphan asylum with a grant from the school fund. The council acceded to this request, thus reversing its position of 1824, despite objections by trustees of the Public School Society. Nine years later, the Catholics went considerably beyond their former request when the trustees of the Catholic Free Schools applied to the common council for aid. On this occasion, the Public School Society's objections were sustained by the council's denial of the application.

The Catholics struck back at the common council's refusal to grant them aid by pointing out that the use of the King James Version of the Bible, as well as of other books that they deemed unacceptable to their church, virtually excluded them from sharing in the facilities of the common school system if they were to maintain their religious integrity. The subsequent deletion of objectionable matter from text-books failed to satisfy the Catholics, who carried the issue to the legislature, where it was taken up in 1841. Then the Catholic groups organized and entered municipal politics. They were badly beaten in the subsequent mayoralty election.

As a result of this agitation, and of recommendations by Governor William H. Seward, the legislature enacted a law in April 1842 that provided for management of schools sharing in public funds by officials elected by the people; extended the State's public school system to include New York City; and, most important of all, prohibited allotment of public funds to any school that taught or practiced a sectarian doctrine. This was followed by creation of school districts within the city, one to each ward, where the voters elected two commissioners, two inspectors and five trustees of common schools. These ward commissioners became the board of education for the city of New York.

The first ward school was opened in 1843. Five years later, 24 such schools had been organized. By 1853, after clashes with the new board of education, the Public School Society had transferred its 17 schools and other property to the city. In that year the Society, which had done so much for public education in New York, voluntarily dissolved. After 1856, the board of education completely controlled the schools.

The third contribution of this period to municipal betterment was the development of the police department on a more efficient administrative and personnel basis. The department had long been woefully inadequate. In 1833 and again in 1844, public officials had sharply criticized it. As the Watch Department, it consisted of 1,525 regular and 300 special officers. Its 100 marshals were paid on a fee system that very obviously depended on the existence (and even the instigation) of crime. Night watchmen worked at other jobs during the day, and found it practically impossible to stay awake on their posts. There were no uniforms and there was little discipline.

In 1844, the legislature passed an act empowering the city to organize a regularly paid day-and-night police force. Both mayor and common council refused the necessary approval; instead, they created a municipal force by city ordinance. One of the amusing results of this move was Mayor Harper's attempt to get the policemen into uniform, a proposal rejected by the men on the ground that, as free-born American citizens, they did not propose to wear "livery" and look like servants.

By 1845, the failure of the locally-created police force was so obvious as to lead to approval of the legislative act previously rejected by the mayor and the common council. Under this act, the city was divided into regular police districts, each with its local police court; the chief of police was appointed by the mayor with the approval of the common council; captains, assistants and "roundsmen" were appointed for each ward by the mayor after being nominated by the ward's aldermen, assistant aldermen and assessors. The duties of the force were many. In addition to the usual police work, they lighted street lamps, sounded alarms and acted as street inspectors, health wardens, fire wardens, dockmasters and in other capacities.

On June 19, 1845, George W. Matsell was appointed the first chief of this new organization, which managed to acquit itself in such a manner as to win official commendation from Mayor Havemeyer in 1848. Incidentally, Matsell later published the *National Police Gazette;* and he was the author of *Vocabulum, or The Rogue's Lexicon,* the first considerable glossary of New York underworld slang.

The department was further improved in 1853, when revision of the city's charter created a Board of Commissioners to appoint officers, such appointments to stand during good behavior and to be revocable only "for cause." The free-born American citizens having resigned themselves to the idea of wearing "livery," a uniform was adopted, consisting of a blue coat with brass buttons, gray trousers and blue cap. This was the first completely uniformed, tax-supported, full-time police force in the city's history.

Four years later, at the time of Mayor Fernando Wood's second administration, this force had become so inefficient and corrupt that the State legislature voted to abolish the Municipal Police, setting up in its stead a Metropolitan Police under five commissioners appointed by the governor. Outraged, Mayor Wood struck the appropriate pose; and the Municipals and Metropolitans had it out in a spirited hurly-burly on the steps of City Hall. The Metropolitans, outnumbered, got much the worst of the fracas until the Seventh Regiment, fortuitously marching down to the Boston boat, was called in. The mayor submitted to arrest; and the authority of the Metropolitan Police was subsequently established.

An affair of international interest in this period was the "Exhibition of the Industry of All Nations," held in 1853–54. Inspired by the Crystal Palace Exposition of 1851 in London, civic-minded New Yorkers incorporated a company to promote and stage a similar exposition on a municipally-granted site now occupied by Bryant Park, west of the present Public Library. The building, of iron and glass, resembled the famous Crystal Palace of the English exposition; and in it a total of 4,000 exhibitors from Germany, Belgium, France, Switzerland, Holland, Austria, Italy, Sweden,

Norway, Mexico, Turkey and other countries displayed their wares to approximately 1,250,000 visitors.

The Civil War: 1861–1865

Human nature being what it is New York's part in the Civil War is almost invariably associated with the dramatic Draft Riots of 1863 rather than with the more prosaic record of men, money and supplies that the city contributed generously toward the winning of the war.

The riots were precipitated by many factors, among these being the previous hard times and the anti-militarist and anti-Union sentiment entertained by large groups of New York Democrats. The main factor, of course, was resistance to the draft, in particular the popular indignation aroused by the actual setting up of drafting lotteries in Provost Marshals' offices throughout the city.

As J. T. Headley, a contemporary chronicler, points out in his *Pen and Pencil Sketches of the Great Riots,* most of the conscripts "were laboring men or poor mechanics, who were unable to hire a substitute . . . If a well-known name, that of a man of wealth, was among the number, it only increased the exasperation, for the law exempted everyone drawn who would pay three hundred dollars towards a substitute. This was taking practically the whole number of soldiers called for out of the laboring classes. A great proportion of these being Irish, it naturally became an Irish question and eventually an Irish riot."

Street battles began on Monday, July 13, and continued into Thursday evening. Mobs sometimes numbering 10,000 persons—the total of those involved was estimated at from 50,000 to 70,000—smashed the lotteries and, joined by the gangs that flourished under Mayor Wood, looted stores and burned buildings. Fury ruled the island from Union Square on the south to Shantytown on the north. Along with opposition to the draft went resentment toward Negroes as the precipitating cause of the war. The Colored Half Orphan Asylum, a substantial building on Fifth Avenue between Forty-Third and Forty-Fourth Streets, was burned, and many Negroes were killed.

By July 16, when troops recalled from the front took over the city, casualties were as numerous as in some of the important battles of the Revolution and the Civil War. Estimates run all the way from 400 to 2,000 killed, with about 8,000 wounded. Property valued at between $1,200,000 and $5,000,000 was destroyed. "Investigation," says Bassett, "showed that the allotments of the Democratic enrollment districts were excessive, and when the error was corrected the draft proceeded quietly." In the end, exactly 2,557 men were actually enrolled out of the 77,862 examined for service under the draft in New York State.

New York City, however, contributed thousands of volunteers. By April 23, 1861, the fifth, sixth, seventh, eighth, twelfth, twenty-first and sixty-ninth State regiments of volunteers were on their way to, or already at, the front. In 1862, the city's troops were guarding the upper Potomac line; in 1863, 12 regiments of the National Guard were used to check the Confederate advance on Pennsylvania and to defend Baltimore, their work being cut short when they were recalled to prevent further rioting in the city.

In addition, troops were equipped and moved, in the early days of the war, by the Committee of Union Defense of the City of New York, this remarkable organization sending 36 regiments to the front and expending about $800,000. Of even greater importance was the Sanitary Commission, outgrowth of the Women's Central Association of Relief. It received and spent about five million dollars, and distributed supplies worth about 15 millions. Its work in caring for the sick and wounded, and in the prevention of disease, cannot be too highly praised.

The city's total war contribution to the national treasury, including that of banks and other financial institutions, was estimated by Mayor Updyke at 400 million dollars. Despite such expenditures, however, New York was not seriously crippled by the war. True, the physical growth of the city, as well as its population growth, had been checked, the population actually decreasing nearly 100,000 from 1860 to 1865. But the huge business of equipping and forwarding troops had so supplanted the former trade with the South that the commercial and financial structures more than held their own.

The Tweed Ring: 1865–1874

Perhaps the most important development of the decade immediately following the Civil War was the beginning of a profound change in the source of New York's wealth. Heretofore, the city had been dependent almost entirely on foreign and inland trade; now it began to develop those manufactures which today constitute an enormous share of its economic resources and power. This development was accompanied by excessive speculation, by many dubious or dishonest promotional activities, and by the welding of corrupt relations between business and politics. To these factors was due, in no small measure, the rise of the Tweed Ring, probably the greatest plunderers of a great city the world has ever known. The leading members of the ring consisted of William M. Tweed, Peter B. Sweeny, Richard Connolly and A. Oakey Hall, all of whom held important posts in the city government. The extent of their looting has never been accurately ascertained, because of the disappearance of records and the manner in which their transactions were carried out. Estimates vary from a minimum of 30 million dollars to a maximum of 200 millions, the latter figure including all the issues of fraudulent stock with which the ring was associated. Seventy-five million dollars is a fairly conservative figure.

It is impossible to give definite dates for the entire period in which the ring operated, Tweed's own testimony on the subject being none too definite. But it was chiefly active from about 1867 to 1871. During those years, the construction and equipment costs for public buildings were somewhat startling. Items for one building, for example, included $7,500 for thermometers, $41,190.95 for brooms, $531,594.22 for plastering, and $1,-294,684.13 for repairs to that plastering before the building was completed.

One of the favorite devices whereby the ring looted the city treasury was that of raising accounts. If, for example, a bill was presented for $5,000, the creditor was told that the city could not possibly pay that amount, but that it would willingly discount a bill for $10,000. Thereupon, the creditor would present a new bill at the higher figure and receive the amount of his original bill, while the ring would pocket the difference. On most transactions the difference was comparatively small in 1869. By 1870, re-submitted bills were normally 67 percent higher than the original bills. Later, they were 85 percent greater.

Credit for bringing about the exposure and downfall of Tweed and his associates belongs to George Jones, proprietor, and Louis J. Jennings, editor, of the New York *Times*, and to Thomas Nast, brilliant cartoonist of *Harper's Weekly*. When Jennings had finally secured a sufficient amount of incriminating evidence from within the organization itself, Jones was offered five million dollars to suppress publication of the facts, while Nast was approached with a bribe of $500,000. But the ring had at last come up against men who could not be bought; and on July 8, 1871, the *Times* began publication of its exposé, as Nast kept hammering away with his cartoons.

The result, from the standpoint of justice, was disappointing. Tweed was the only important member of the ring to go to prison. He died in Ludlow Street Jail on April 12, 1878, nearly six years after his first arrest, subsequent escape, flight to Spain and extradition to stand trial here.

Territorial Expansion: 1874–1898

Two years before the nation celebrated the 100th anniversary of the Declaration of Independence, the limits of New York City were expanded, for the first time in its history, beyond the shores of Manhattan Island.

On January 1, 1874, the townships of Kingsbridge, West Farms and Morrisania (which were then part of the Borough of the Bronx in Westchester County) became a part of New York City by authority of the State legislature. Today the area constitutes that part of the Borough of the Bronx (in Greater New York) lying west of the Bronx River.

On November 6, 1894, a proposal to consolidate certain localities adjacent to New York was submitted to popular vote. Included among these localities was an area within Westchester County that had not been annexed in 1874. This part of the county now voted against the proposal. But the adverse majority was so small that it was ignored by the annexationists; and on July 1, 1895, the whole section east of the Bronx River became a part of New York City, as a result of Senator Robinson's Annexation Bill. This action occurred three years prior to the effective date of the enabling legislation that created Greater New York. The territory thus taken included Throg's Neck, Unionport, Westchester, Williamsbridge, Bronxdale, Olinville, Baychester, Eastchester, Wakefield and Bartow.

The history of the area embraced in these two annexations north of the Harlem River is very confused, representing the coalition of several villages that had been assembled little by little in an uneven manner. The first recorded settlement was that of Jonas Bronck, "a Dane or Swede" who arrived in New Amsterdam with his Dutch wife in 1639, and settled in 1641 near the mouth of the river named after him. In addition to Bronck, the most prominent names in the earliest history of the Bronx are those of Mrs. Anne Hutchinson, who settled in 1643 at Pelham's Neck; John Throckmorton and a few others, who came in October 1642 to what is now Throg's Neck; and Jonkheer Adrien Van Der Donck, who was made a patroon and settled on a tract of land extending about eight miles north of Spuyten Duyvil.

In 1874 and 1895, the annexations already noted made the old Borough of the Bronx, in Westchester County, part of New York City under the then existing charters. In 1896–97, the charter of the proposed Greater New York was prepared, submitted to the people and approved. On January 1, 1898, the area comprising the 1874 and 1895 annexations north of the Harlem River, which was already part of New York City, became the Borough of the Bronx in Greater New York.

Since that time, the Bronx has developed at a rapid rate. In 1900, its population was 200,507; 25 years later, it exceeded one million; and in 1936 it was only 288,001 less than Manhattan's, as compared to 1,477,720 less in 1916. Today, the Bronx ranks third in population among the five boroughs, fourth in area and fourth in assessed valuation.

When Greater New York became a legal fact in 1898 by virtue of enabling legislation, the Bronx was already an established part of New York City. Not so, however, the areas that were to become the Boroughs of Brooklyn, Queens and Richmond.

The flourishing city of Brooklyn had a background almost as old as that of New York itself. In 1636, the first grant of land was made there to A. Bennett and Jacques Bentyn at Gowanus, where they erected a house. The following year, Joris Jansen de Rapalje and his wife, Catelyna Trico, came to live on adjacent land known as the Waal-boght. It was this same Catelyna Trico who, outliving her husband by many years, became known as "the mother of Brooklyn" by virtue of her eleven children and subsequent descendants, numbering 145 in 1679.

In 1645, settlers between the Waal-boght and Gowanus Kill (a section roughly approximating the present Fulton, Hoyt, Smith Streets district) founded a town called Breuckelen, the name being the same as that of an ancient village in the Netherlands. It was granted local officials in 1646 as other towns—Roode Hoek (Red Hook), so named because of its rich red soil, Gowanus, Nieu Utrecht and Ameersfoort (Flatlands)—developed on Long Island. Later, English settlers came to Gravesend, Jamaica and Flushing.

After the English seizure of New Amsterdam in 1664, Breuckelen became, successively, Brockland, Brocklin, Brookline, and finally Brooklyn. In 1816, it was made an incorporated village; in 1834, a city; and in 1898, the Borough of Brooklyn in Greater New York. Its population at the time of consolidation was considerably less than Manhattan's. In 1923, it passed Manhattan's figure. Today, it leads all of New York's boroughs in population, stands second only to Manhattan in assessed valuation, and is second in area with 47,660 acres.

Adjacent to Brooklyn and southeast of Manhattan lies another of the areas consolidated in 1898, the Borough of Queens. The first settlement in this territory was made at Flushing Bay, the formal charter of Vlissingen (Flushing) being dated 1645. The first provincial laws to recognize Vlissingen officially were the so-called Duke's Laws, proclaimed in 1665 by Governor Nicolls and his council, sitting as a court of assizes at Hempstead before deputies assembled for the purpose from Vlissingen and other Long Island and Westchester towns. This code was designed principally for what was then known as Yorkshire, a political entity, composed of Long Island, Staten Island and what was then Westchester County.

In 1683, Governor Dongan of the province of New York issued writs for the election of a general assembly that met October 17 at New York and resulted in the creation of Queens County from a part of Yorkshire. Even then, Queens was famous for its two race courses, New Market and Beaver Pond, the mile-long course around Beaver Pond at Jamaica being especially well known. On May 27, 1823, a race run there for a $20,000 purse was witnessed by a crowd estimated at between 40,000 and 50,000 persons.

In 1929, Queens went over the one million mark in population, and by 1936 its total of 1,280,805 was not far behind that of the Bronx and was fourth among Greater New York's boroughs. In assessed valuation, it was well ahead of the Bronx. In area, it ranks first by a wide margin, its total of 70,370 acres being practically four times greater than Manhattan's, and larger even than the Manhattan and Brooklyn areas combined. It is in Queens, at the historic Flushing Meadows, that the World's Fair of 1939 will be held.

Southwest of Manhattan lies Staten Island, another of the territories incorporated in Greater New York. This island, which became the Borough of Richmond under the 1898 consolidation, resembled and still resembles early New York more than any other division of the modern city. For here remain such hills and other natural beauties as long ago disappeared in Manhattan's leveling process.

The early history of Staten Island is extremely difficult to trace, as far as the first actual settlers are concerned. It is known that three attempts to colonize the territory by the patroon system failed, although David P. de Vries, who went there in 1636, and Cornelius Melyn, who arrived in 1640, loom importantly in the island's history.

The first permanent settlement was made by Peter Billiou and eighteen others in 1661, the settlement being named Oude Dorp, meaning Old Town. Three years later, after the English had captured New Amsterdam and changed its name to New York, British names were given to other parts of the province, including Staten Island, which now became a division of "Yorkshire" known as the "West Riding." Later, the Indians sold the entire island to a man named Ryssel, who soon discovered the Indian aptitude for selling the same thing repeatedly, and at a higher price each time.

There were only some 200 families on the island when it became the English county of Richmond on November 1, 1683, under Governor Dongan. On March 7, 1788, Richmond became a county of New York State. One hundred and ten years later, it was incorporated in Greater New York as the Borough of Richmond.

In 1698, the population of Richmond consisted of 654 whites and 73 Negroes. Four years later, it had decreased to a total of 505; and in the nine years following 1703, there was a gain of less than 800. Eleven years later, the inhabitants numbered 1,506, of whom 255 were Negroes. By 1771, the total of 727 in 1698 had increased to 2,847—an average gain of only 30 persons a year. The first Federal census of 1790 listed 3,835 persons. Fifty years later, the figure was 10,965; and by 1936, it had reached 172,169.

The Greater New York charter that had translated the popular vote of 1895 into the legal fact of consolidation in 1898 had been very strongly criticized at public hearings held in January 1897. The Bar Association, Board of Trade, Clearing House Association, City Club, Union League Club, Reform Club, and Real Estate Exchange had expressed their opinions in no uncertain terms. Even Mayor Strong of New York, ex-officio member of the Charter Commission that had framed the instrument, reversed his position when the charter was submitted for his approval as mayor. But the legislature overrode his veto by large majorities in both houses. The criticism did not cease after January 1, 1898, when Greater New York became a fact despite these protests. On the contrary, it mounted until the 1898 charter was revised in 1901. The revised instrument, which became effective January 1, 1902, was virtually a new charter throughout.

Prosperity and Progress: 1879–1909

By 1879, the nation had begun to recover from the panic of 1873, and New York entered upon a phase of its modern growth which, while not devoid of the corruption that had characterized the Tweed era, was marked at least by increasingly determined efforts to better the governmental structure and thus to control in a greater degree the various factors contributing to an unbelievably rapid expansion.

By 1909, 300 years after Henry Hudson's arrival in New York's magnificent harbor, the city was not only the undisputed colossus of the western hemisphere, but a giant among world-giants as well. The three decades between 1879 and 1909 constitute the first phase of New York's development as a modern city.

Politically, the period contributed evidence of a civic pride lacking for years. In 1882, the first of several organized public attempts to defeat corruption was staged. Although unsuccessful, it contributed to the legislative investigation of 1884, which was particularly interesting because of the appearance on the New York scene of a young man named Theodore Roosevelt, who headed the Assembly committee and submitted a report lashing, among other things, the Police Department. Ten years later, Roosevelt became president of the Board of Police Commissioners. In that post, he succeeded in doing a job sufficiently sound to bring himself to the attention of the nation, which later made him President.

The election of William R. Grace as mayor in 1884 was the first victory for good government in this period. Two years later, the idea of independent tickets had so far progressed as to make possible the first labor-union candidate for mayor—Henry George, the single-taxer. Both he and his Republican opponent, Theodore Roosevelt, were defeated by Abraham S. Hewitt, the Democratic nominee.

From 1888 to 1894, Tammany completely dominated municipal affairs. Then came the famous exposures of Police Department graft by the so-called Lexow Committee of 1894. These shocking revelations resulted in the nomination of a fusion candidate, William L. Strong, who defeated Tammany and turned in a generally good administration. But Strong lost political support because he and his adherents did not give enough thought to political realities, with the result that Tammany won the 1897 election.

Again the community regretted its choice, and once more fusion defeated corrupt politicians by the election in 1901 of Seth Low and the temporary smashing of Tammany's power in Manhattan, Brooklyn and Richmond. This was the victory that carried William Travers Jerome into the district attorney's office in New York County and loosed a one-man crusade against Tammany which that organization is not likely to forget. Low was followed by George B. McClellan, a Tammany candidate whose independence, particularly in his second term, cut the Hall to the quick.

The awakening of civic pride, as the result of political developments demanding greater interest in the community by its citizens, was accompanied by other developments in various fields. Street improvements on an important scale began in 1889. Two years later, there were 365 miles of paved thoroughfares. Electricity for lighting began to replace gas in 1880; and in 1887 the tremendous task of moving electric light wires from the forests of poles to underground conduits was initiated.

This latter move turned out to be of great advantage in the building boom that reached its peak in 1901, probably the year of greatest activity in real estate and building that New York has ever known. Many rambling old structures below City Hall were replaced by modern office buildings. Within a few years, the skyscraper began to dominate lower Manhattan, center of the city's big-business activities. The Flatiron, Singer, Metropolitan Life and Woolworth Buildings exemplified a new and distinctly American type of commercial architecture.

Residential construction was particularly prominent on Fifth Avenue, where the Vanderbilts, Carnegies and other wealthy families were building elaborate mansions; and to the north in Morningside Heights, Washington Heights and the Bronx, where large tracts of land were being utilized as apartment house sites.

New public buildings included the Criminal Courts, the Custom House, and the Hall of Records, all completed by 1907; the Municipal Building, begun toward the end of this period; the Metropolitan Opera House, opened in 1883; and Carnegie Hall, completed in 1891. Two large department stores began construction of new quarters at Greeley Square; the new Pennsylvania Station was started; and Longacre Square became the center of unparalleled real estate and building developments that resulted in the Times Square of today.

New educational structures were projected or opened. On Morningside Heights, Barnard, Teachers and Columbia Colleges, together with Union Theological Seminary, constituted a noteworthy group. New York University opened its uptown center in 1895, and City College dedicated similar quarters in 1908. In 1895, 15 new buildings and annexes were being built for public school use. Public high schools were inaugurated with the opening of the first three in September 1897.

Along the waterfront and in the parks, important improvements were also effected. In 1897, five new piers were under construction, and plans for seven more had been approved. Between 1904 and 1909, about 35 miles of new wharfage were constructed. Park development had progressed so steadily that the New York Improvement Commission recommended, in

1907, a city-wide parkway system connecting the independent borough systems—a recommendation that, in its basic features, is now (1938) being carried out by Park Commissioner Moses.

With the close of the Hudson-Fulton Celebration of 1907, this first phase of the development of modern New York was well advanced. The first transatlantic radio message, the first successful flight of a heavier-than-air craft, the first skyscraper and the first subway were accomplished facts. Engineering and scientific genius had provided the bases upon which the city was now developing physically.

New York had become a colossus. It had the money, the power and the ability to maintain and to strengthen its undisputed supremacy. It had the room to grow even more huge. It had a throbbing, almost a terrifying, vitality. It had unlimited ambition, and the power to translate that ambition into reality. Yet this power, this hugeness, this vitality were essentially those of a frontier town sprawling beyond its limits. New York knew comparatively little and cared less about the world beyond its borders. It was satisfied to have and to hold. Despite its world-wide commerce, it could hardly be called world-conscious in anything save rates of exchange.

The new colossus had grown in bone and sinew and muscle. Now it was about to develop intellectually through a broadening of its interests; it was about to become truly cosmopolitan

From Metropolis to Cosmopolis: 1910–1937

In this period, at least three factors contributed to the second phase of New York's modern development. They were the administrations of Mayors Gaynor and Mitchel, the revelations of the Seabury and Dewey investigations, and the development of a cosmopolitan viewpoint as the result of the World War and a later domestic crisis.

William J. Gaynor, who was elected mayor in 1909 and served until his death on September 10, 1913, has been described as combining "the gift for literary gossip and philosophy of Philip Hone, the clever wit and satire of the elegant A. Oakey Hall, and the simple earnestness of Peter Cooper." Certainly Gaynor was unusual. He challenged the Tammany machine that had nominated him; he refused so steadily to yield to patronage demands that the machine denied him a renomination; he sued his most enthusiastic journalistic supporter, the World, for libel; he fought William Randolph Hearst, the publisher, to a standstill; and he probably lost the Presidency of the United States by declining the proffered aid of Colonel House, the man who is credited with putting Woodrow Wilson in the White House and who had first sought Gaynor as the nominee.

Before becoming mayor, Gaynor had been a reporter, lawyer, vice crusader, writer and a justice of the Appellate Division of the New York Supreme Court. He was considered an authority on libel and slander, and his judicial experience was marked by continual effort to reduce the long and involved terminology of the law to brief and exact statements of fact, as well as by a viewpoint remarkably liberal for those days. "Nothing is more distressing," he stated in an article published more than 30 years ago, "than to see a bench of judges, old men as a rule, set themselves against the manifest and enlightened will of the community in matters of social, economic, or commercial progress." The plain people were his primary interest, and it is said of him that he understood them as did no other man of his time. Intolerance of any kind, particularly racial, was abhorrent to him. He was the champion especially of the Jews, and he had many powerful Jewish friends.

Gaynor's emphasis upon brevity of speech throughout his public career was never better demonstrated than during the simple inaugural ceremonies at City Hall after his victory of 1909. His speech consisted of exactly 31 words: "I enter upon this office with the intention of doing the very best I can for the city of New York. That will have to suffice. I can do no more." About six months later, he was shot by a dissatisfied employee of the Dock Department on the deck of the *Kaiser Wilhelm* as he was about to sail for Europe. The bullet was never removed, and three years later he died as a result of the wound.

Denied a renomination by Tammany in 1913, Gaynor entered a three-cornered contest independently, only to die before the campaign got under way. This left the regular Tammany nominee and a young man named John Purroy Mitchel as the candidates. Mitchel had been nominated by the "Committee of 107," a fusion organization created to beat Tammany and also to prevent the re-election of Gaynor. He won by about 120,000 votes, and became mayor on January 1, 1914.

Although only 34 years old, Mitchel had been in politics for seven years, as assistant corporation counsel, commissioner of accounts, president of the Board of Aldermen, and acting mayor for a time in Gaynor's regime. Like his predecessor, he gave New York good government in the face of a still powerful Tammany machine and an electorate by no means as politically aroused or well-educated as it is today. Theodore Roosevelt regarded him as having "given us as nearly an ideal administration . . . as

I have seen in my lifetime, or as I have heard of since New York became a big city"; and Oswald Garrison Villard wrote of his regime: "Never was the fire department so well handled, never were the city's charities so well administered, nor its finances grappled with upon such a sound and far-sighted basis . . . Under him the schools progressed wonderfully, while prisons were carried on with some semblance of scientific and humanitarian management."

Among Mitchel's various services to the city were a thorough reorganization of the police department under Arthur Woods as commissioner, the cleaning up of gambling and vice at Coney Island, the preparation of a corporate stock budget that showed just where the city stood on public expenditures, the supervision of a complete schedule of city property that stopped purchase by the municipality of its own holdings, the mapping of the city's zoning plan, the launching of investigations that led to the removal of two borough presidents, and initiation of the West Side improvement program that has now been finally achieved. Despite these constructive services, Mitchel was beaten by Tammany in 1917, his defeat being attributed to various reasons, not the least of which was a lack of diplomacy in the handling of delicate political situations. He enlisted at once in the Army, was commissioned a major in the air service, and was killed in a fall from a scout plane during the last stage of his training period, on July 6, 1918.

His successor, John F. Hylan, became mayor on January 1, 1918, and from that day to January 1, 1934, Tammany Hall was in undisputed control of New York's government. Few mayors of New York have been so savagely criticized as Hylan, and fewer still could better hold their own in the rough and tumble school. That he was personally honest even his worst enemies conceded. Three investigations during his administrations failed to turn up anything worth while. Indeed, most of the departments were run surprisingly well, with practically none of the old-fashioned graft. This was credited to "Boss" Murphy's "enlightened" leadership of Tammany Hall rather than to Hylan. The latter, according to many observers, was merely a figurehead.

Yet Hylan had forced himself on the powerful Charlie Murphy as the Tammany candidate in 1917 with no more background than about 11 years of service in rather obscure judicial posts. His strategy was beautifully simple. It consisted of setting up the "Allied Boards of Trade and Taxpayers' Associations of Brooklyn," an organization with headquarters in a battered letterbox at No. 1028 Gates Avenue, where Hylan had his law office, and a membership composed of himself, two fellow lawyers and a vaudeville entertainer. For 12 months prior to the 1917 campaign, this "alliance" poured out caustic criticism of Mayor Mitchel, while Judge Hylan repeated that criticism before many civic organizations throughout the city. Curiously enough, it never occurred to anyone to look into the "Allied Boards of Trade and Taxpayers' Associations of Brooklyn" until just a few days before the election. It was too late then, for Hylan had made himself a front-page figure. Throughout the eight years of his regime as mayor, Hylan was one of the most effectively publicized men New York has ever known.

During these superbly press-agented administrations, the kind of government that Mayor Gaynor had initiated and Mayor Mitchel had carried forward came to an end, especially after Mayor Hylan's record plurality of more than 420,000 in 1921 had convinced Tammany that continuation of a more or less *laissez faire* policy would do quite well. Nevertheless, Mayor Hylan did have to his credit an uncompromising stand against the "traction interests," as he termed them, which some authorities contend saved the city millions of dollars.

In 1925, Tammany turned for its candidate from the elderly, plodding, bewildered, unflinchingly honest Hylan to the young, effervescent, cocksure, night-clubbing James J. Walker; and Walker's election justified the Hall's strategy. From 1925 to 1930, Tammany gave New York what has been well described as "high, wide and handsome government." Then the Hall began to turn an anxious eye toward a certain Mr. Samuel Seabury, who in August 1930 was appointed a referee by the Appellate Division of the New York Supreme Court, First Judicial Department, to conduct an investigation into the magistrates' courts of Manhattan and the Bronx. In March 1931, Governor Roosevelt selected Mr. Seabury to investigate and report on charges against Thomas C. T. Crain, district attorney of New York County; and a month later he was made counsel to the Joint Committee of the New York State Senate and Assembly, created to investigate various departments of government of the city of New York. Under all of these appointments, Mr. Seabury had power merely to investigate, report and make recommendations.

The recommendations submitted by Mr. Seabury on the reorganization of the magistrates' courts more directly affected the average New Yorker than the inquiry into District Attorney Crain's activities or even the investigation by the Joint Committee. But it was in this last that the dramatic clash between Seabury and Mayor James J. Walker focused attention on testimony so damaging to Tammany Hall as to make possible an anti-Tammany victory in 1933 and an even more crushing defeat of the Tiger in 1937.

Most amusing of all the testimony was that of James A. McQuade, then Tammany leader of the Fifteenth Assembly District in Brooklyn and Register of Kings County. It was brought out that McQuade had deposited about $520,000 over a period of six years, on a total salary for that period of less than $50,000. Questioned about this, McQuade replied that "33 other McQuades" were dependent on him. "They were," he said, "placed on my back, I being the only bread-winner, so to speak, and after that it was necessary to keep life in their body, sustenance, to go out and borrow money." Such borrowed money, McQuade explained, accounted for the $470,000 above and beyond his visible earnings. With it, he saved the "33 other McQuades."

One direct result of this investigation was the sudden resignation of Mayor James J. Walker before Governor Franklin D. Roosevelt had a chance to hear all the evidence that Seabury adduced. Indirectly, the Seabury revelations are credited with being a tremendous factor in the election of Fiorello H. La Guardia in 1933 on a fusion ticket. On the occasion of this election, William Travers Jerome remarked: "Tammany goes out, and Tammany comes back in, and you've got to be realistic about it." So far Mr. La Guardia, an excellent politician, has been very realistic about it, indeed much too realistic to suit Tammany, which went down to another smashing defeat in the re-election of Mayor La Guardia on November 2, 1937.

Mayor La Guardia's first administration had to its credit a long list of public improvements. Among these were the tearing down of the notorious City Penitentiary on Welfare Island to make way for a hospital, and the transfer of the convicts to a new city prison on Riker's Island; the Ward's Island sewage disposal plant; the great Triborough Bridge, in use since July 11, 1936; an increase in number of the city's hospital beds; the first real start made on slum clearance; the magnificent parks, boulevards and bridges, and the hundreds of new playgrounds, created in most cases with the help of Federal funds.

Thomas E. Dewey was the second major investigator of this period. On July 1, 1935, he was appointed by District Attorney William C. Dodge of New York County as a special deputy assistant district attorney "to conduct an investigation of vice and racketeering before an extraordinary grand jury." The idea of so appointing Mr. Dewey was not Mr. Dodge's; it had been urged upon Tammany's district attorney by Governor Herbert H. Lehman. Four Republican leaders of the bar had declined to serve, and had joined in seconding Governor Lehman's recommendation.

Mr. Dewey came to his new position with a broad knowledge of racketeering methods and personalities, having already, as special assistant to the U. S. Attorney-General, placed several racketeers in government penitentiaries. From the day of his appointment to July 29, when he and the first eight of his assistants were formally sworn, Mr. Dewey was busy laying preliminary plans. On August 7, he opened his investigation and caused the arrest of the first racketeer. By September 11, when the indicted man had pleaded guilty to an extortion charge, the public began to see in this 33-year-old special prosecutor the newest hope of law and order.

On October 25, it was reported, a new group took over all major rackets in New York, Brooklyn and Newark. This group virtually asked Mr. Dewey what he was going to do about it. On April 18, 1936, they had their answer. On that day, the powerful "Lucky" Luciano (Lucania) found himself jailed in New York City in the unheard-of-bail of $350,000, which he could not raise; and on June 18, he was sentenced to a prison term of from 30 to 50 years, with other members of his gang getting similarly stiff sentences. This was Mr. Dewey's most sensational conviction. It drove the vice gang to cover, and was followed by impressive victories in the case of other rackets, notably those in the restaurant and poultry businesses.

The rackets that had flourished for years in New York, exacting tribute from rich and poor alike, were now definitely on the run—a condition confidently expected to continue as long as Thomas E. Dewey has the power to make indictments and to prosecute them. This power was assured him when he was elected District Attorney of New York County in November 1937.

But neither the Seabury nor the Dewey investigations, important though both of those were to good government and law enforcement, constituted the really significant contribution of the period now under review. That lay in another and not nearly so evident a field; and it changed New York from a sprawling and overgrown colossus into a cosmopolitan city.

This development began with the World War. Millions were put under arms. Nationality met nationality, and found it not at all a bad experience. Thousands went overseas; and even in very bitter circumstances, they managed to survive contact with "foreigners." Intimacy bred an understanding of the other fellow such as these clannish New Yorkers had never before possessed.

The war ended. But millions who had been taken out of their complacent little group-existence did not cease to be interested in things they had seen, heard and read about. The press, more than anything else, had broadened the viewpoint not only of those who had gone to fight but of those who stayed at home. However restricted by censorship, it had still furnished news, and in so doing had expanded its foreign service far beyond the 1910 standard. By 1926, the old system of maintaining only London and Paris offices, and there picking up stuff via the foreign news agencies, was no longer adequate. The war had doubled or tripled the number of correspondents. Papers had been forced to send men to places never before directly covered. During the war, correspondents had naturally written about the war. Now, they were writing about the problems that the struggle had left in its wake.

America found itself linked to nation after nation through loans. New York was the financial center of the country. It was interested in loans, in economic losses, in the effects of those losses on industry and jobs. Presently the papers were printing a tremendous amount of foreign political news. New Yorkers read it; for they began to sense that the politics of Russia, of Europe, of the Far East had a great deal to do with loans and trade and jobs. Nations that had been little more to the average New Yorker than a stereopticon slide now became vital to his well-being. He didn't understand the situation, but he did see a lot about it in the papers. And as he read, the world shrank. "Foreigners" were now neighbors; Europe and the Soviet Union and the Far East were inextricably mixed up, somehow, with prosperity and profits and work in New York.

From 1915 to 1926, when foreign news was steadily increasing in the press, Washington news was decreasing. This condition reflected the curious fact that, although New Yorkers had learned to know the world, they were still strangers to the United States. Beyond the city limits, everything was "the sticks"—useful as a market for New York products, to be sure, but unimportant otherwise. The factors having to do with the purchasing power of that market were as little known to the average New Yorker as the same foreign trade factors once had been. For years New York had been virtually the capital of the United States. The money was there, the power was there, and national policies were created by that money and that power. Washington was merely the loudspeaker through which New York announced itself—and the inconsiderable amount of Washington news proved it.

The election of 1932 changed all that. The nation, facing a very serious emergency, turned its eyes to Washington in 1933 precisely as it had turned them to Europe in 1914–18. The future of the country depended to a large degree on what was done in Washington. People wanted to know. Again the press met their demands, and again New Yorkers expanded their viewpoint.

Today the long march and countermarch from colony to cosmopolis, from Peter Minuit's little settlement on the lower tip of Manhattan Island to the vast machine of the modern city, has gained for the moment a stabilization point. Worship of the grandiose is no longer enough. New York has grown up to the beginnings of a cosmopolitan maturity. What she will do with it, how she will divert the terrific flume of her energy into the orderly dynamos of social realization, the years ahead must determine.

Where New Yorkers Live

SOME NEW YORKERS LIVE BEHIND WROUGHT-IRON BALCONIES OF THE
MID-19TH CENTURY

STABLES TURNED STUDIOS IN MACDOUGAL ALLEY, GREENWICH VILLAGE

DWELLERS ON CENTRAL PARK WEST LOOK OUT UPON BRIDLE PATHS AND
LANDSCAPED GARDENS

PUSHCARTS AT THE FRONT DOOR, CLOTHES-LINES AT THE BACK, FOR
EAST SIDE TENANTS

A PARK AVENUE ADDRESS IS A SOCIAL ASSET

WEALTHY NEW YORKERS MAY LIVE IN RESIDENCE HOTELS OVERLOOKING
CENTRAL PARK

THE LESS FORTUNATE MAY LIVE IN SHACKS IN BARREN ISLAND,
BROOKLYN

A QUIET STREET IN ST. GEORGE, STATEN ISLAND, ACROSS THE BAY

OLD RESIDENCES ON BROOKLYN HEIGHTS, FOR A CENTURY THE CENTER
OF FASHIONABLE LIFE IN BROOKLYN

SPACIOUS WASHINGTON SQUARE, AT THE FOOT OF FIFTH AVENUE

COMPACT, ULTRA-MODERN KNICKERBOCKER VILLAGE, ON THE SITE OF
A FORMER TENEMENT AREA

SUTTON PLACE, AT THE MANHATTAN END OF QUEEENSBORO BRIDGE,
WHERE TERRACED GARDENS OVERLOOK THE EAST RIVER

WORKERS' COOPERATIVE APARTMENTS IN THE BRONX

New World Symphony

"ON THE island of Manhate, and in its environs," reported in 1646 Father Jogues of the Society of Jesus, "there may well be four or five hundred men of different sects and nations: the Director General told me that there were men of eighteen different languages." Roundly the good father damned this confusion of tongues, likening the spirit created thereby to the "arrogance of Babel." Scarcely ten generations later, persons of foreign stock resident in New York City had increased some ten thousand times, until in 1930 the foreign born and their children accounted for almost three-fourths of all the city's residents.

Much of what has come to be considered peculiarly "American" is the direct contribution of persons of foreign stock. Freedom of belief? The Dutch of New Amsterdam, more concerned with trade than with theology, early established a tradition of religious toleration that drew settlers from almost every country of Europe. Democracy? A century before the United States became a nation, and two centuries before New York was incorporated in its present form as a city, a "Gen¹¹ Assembly of All the Freeholders," representing Dutch, English, French, Portuguese, Swedes, and Finns, met in 1683 and, abetted by the governor, Colonel Thomas Dongan, an Irishman, took steps to end a feudal and unrepresentative rule. Political freedom? When a tide of new political ideas surged through Europe in the 18th century, immigrants brought some of these ideas to the American colonies, and Filippo Mazzei, an Italian, wrote in an American newspaper the words "all men are by nature created free and independent" which were paraphrased by Thomas Jefferson in the Declaration of Independence. Business, and that most "American" of American institutions, the Chamber of Commerce? The courtly company that founded the New York Chamber of Commerce in 1786 included among its charter members two gentlemen of Dutch origin who were born in New York, a French Huguenot, four native born of English stock, an Englishman, a Scot, and two of Irish stock, probably Irish born. Material wealth and physical grandeur? During the great migration from Europe after 1880, it was predominantly these "men of different sects and nations" who erected physical New York—its streets, bridges, tunnels, railroads, wharves, and buildings, creating with their own hands much of its material wealth, yet somehow finding leisure to leave to their city a considerable legacy in science and the arts, in social improvement and political leadership.

In the process the immigrant gave far more than he received. His rich agrarian culture he exchanged for the poverty-stricken culture of industrial society. He traded his native string orchestras and folk tunes for commercial tumpety-tump; expressive group dances for cheap dancehalls; traditional historic or romantic rhymed narratives for machine-made fiction and the distortion of contemporary history in the news columns. A few folk traditions, encouraged by religious groups and such organizations as International House, remain. Thus the Swedes of New York still preserve some of their native crafts and gather round the *smörgasbord;* the Neapolitans annually parade the effigy of their martyred patron, San Gennaro, along Mulberry Street between booths filled with sweetmeats, candles and offerings; the Finns celebrate a non-existent harvest, dancing the *Ploughman Waltz* over a soil imprisoned in concrete; in autumn Hungarians escape to the countryside for the *szureti mulatsagok,* the festival of the grape; Dutch children dance the *Boer's romton* and celebrate St. Nicholas' Eve on December fifth; German meistersingers hold annual singing contests; the *koumbaros,* godfather, still maintains his position of authority in many Greek households; Russian singers still chant epics thousands of unwritten lines long; Ukrainians still sing *Oh, Don't Go, Gritzu* and *The Wide Dnieper Weeps and Moans;* on Easter Sunday Czech young men still have the privilege of spilling water on young women they meet and of placing their hats in the kitchen sink to be filled with Easter eggs; Rumanians dance *La Hora* and celebrate on May tenth their day of independence; Yugoslav women occasionally wear headdresses with floating veils and capes richly embroidered and trimmed with gold braid; Poles dance the *mazurka,* the *krakowiak* and the *polka;* New York orthodox Jewry still celebrates on the Passover the miraculous crossing of the Red Sea by Moses and the Children of Israel, and in a mood of nostalgic nationalism still plants trees on *La'g b'omer* in the rite of ever-recurring spring-millenial remembrance of their agricultural past in Zion. Foreign colonies still exist in New York, retaining their food stores, newspapers, mutual benefit societies, steamship agencies, banks, and are still colorful, teeming and "picturesque."

But customs based on agrarian ways, however tenderly fostered, could not long survive the impact of industrial society; nor could a body of traditional modes of thought long withstand its modern equivalent—the language and social practices associated with a job. Foreign-born residents of New York did not drop their traditional social patterns without a struggle, but organized, as had the Yankees in New England two centuries before them, their group against the world, attempting to build up their own cultural and economic institutions, challenging the new world in a group instead of taking the individual plunge into American life. But the world was moving much faster than in 17th century New England, and the tremendous pressure of industrial society succeeded in dissolving most of these national groups. No longer does a foreign colony in New York have the status of a genuine "foreign quarter," where the leaders of the foreign group live, contributing to its life. The foreign sections of the city shift ever more freely, disintegrate ever more quickly; each year better paid workers migrate from the upper level of the colony to other parts of the city; each year poorer members of other foreign stocks filter in below. The colony becomes less and less a center of national culture, a focusing-point of tradition—and more and more plain slum.

As recently as 1924, Konrad Bercovici wrote: "A map of Europe superimposed upon the map of New York could prove that the different foreign sections of the city live in the same proximity to one another as in Europe: the Germans near the Austrians, the Russians and the Rumanians near the Hungarians, and the Greeks behind the Italians. People of western Europe live in the western side of the city. People of eastern Europe live in the eastern side of the city. Northerners live in the northern part of the city and southerners in the southern part. Those who have lived on the other side near the sea or a river have a tendency to live here as near the sea or the river as possible. . . . A reformation of the same grouping takes place every time the city expands. If the Italians move further up Harlem, the Greeks follow them, the Spanish join them, with the French always lagging behind and the Germans expanding eastward."

This ingenious generalization, if it was ever true, is so no longer. The major groups of Italians, Germans, Irish and Jews are widely distributed throughout the city. In Manhattan the Italians live in the vicinity of City Hall Park, near Battery Park, in Greenwich Village south of Washington Square, in the southeast quarter of the lower East Side, in Hell's Kitchen, in the northern part of Chelsea, in Madison Square, in Columbus Circle, near the Queensboro Bridge, in Yorkville and near Harlem Bridge. They predominate in the English Kills, Brooklyn Heights and Fort Greene sections of Brooklyn; make up two-thirds of the inhabitants of the South Brooklyn section; and are found in fourteen other well-defined neighborhoods of Brooklyn from Highland Park to Coney Island. They are well distributed throughout the Bronx and Queens, and make up 28.9 percent of the total foreign white stock in Richmond. The Jews are found on the lower East Side, in Central Park West, south of Columbia University, near Mount Morris Park, near City College, and in Washington Heights, in Manhattan; they make up nine-tenths of the population of Brownsville in Brooklyn, are well distributed through the other neighborhoods of Brooklyn, are scattered through Queens, and are heavily concentrated in the Bronx. The Irish are found in Manhattan from Battery Park to Manhattanville, where they make up one-third of the population, and in Brooklyn, the Bronx and Queens. The Germans are scattered even more widely, many of them living in Queens and Richmond. Many Greeks live in Chelsea, Manhattan; many Poles around Battery Park and on the lower East side near Tompkins Square; English in Queens and Richmond; Hungarians in Yorkville; Scandinavians in Brooklyn, the Bronx and Richmond; Czechoslovaks near Battery Park and in Yorkville. Only 4,000 of the 18,000 Chinese in New York live in Chinatown (Pell and Mott Streets).

The New Yorker of foreign white stock, having made tremendous contributions to the city for 300 years, is now in process of becoming socially invisible. As soon as he can "get on," that is, as soon as he is accepted economically on the basis of individual merit without invidious reference to racial origin or cultural inheritance, he is considered to be "assimilated." In New York the chief obstacle to absorption seems to be not cultural differences but physical traits.

The process of becoming socially invisible is accelerated by the tendency toward intermarriage in the second generation between members of different foreign white stocks. Thus the ratio of intermarriage for men and women of all nationalities, as a group, is about 14 of every 100 marriages. In the second generation, intermarriage is approximately three times as frequent. Within each group, three main forces work to produce amalgamation with other groups. The first is the preponderance of marriageable men over marriageable women, the major cause of intermarriage in the first generation. The second is a diminution of intensity of group consciousness in the second generation. The third and most important factor is the rise in economic status, which encourages intermarriage in both the first and second generations. Strong religious preferences are factors that discourage intermarriage by the Jews, who intermarry the least, the Italians, who intermarry almost as infrequently, and the Irish.

"There are more Italians in New York City than in Rome, Milan, or Naples," runs the familiar assertion, "more Irish than in Dublin, more Jews than in any other city in the world." Such statements mean little, however, unless there is first some agreement as to just who are the "Italians," "Irish," and "Jews." New Yorkers loosely use the term "Italian," for instance, to cover several categories of residents: a person of "Italian descent"; an "Italian-speaking" person; any citizen of Italy, regardless of mother-tongue, who lives in New York; or even a person who "looks like an Italian" or has an "Italian-sounding" name. Even if the term is limited to denote only a person born in Italy, the "Italian" may still be, if he comes from the Riviera, French in stock, Teutonic if he comes from the Val d'Aosta, Albanian if from Calabria or Sicily, Slav if from Cividale, or Spanish (Catalan) if from Sardinia. If the "Italian" came to New York since the World War as a native of one of the "redeemed" provinces of Austria, he may have been born a German, a Slovene, or a Croat.

Popular use of the term "Jew" is still more confusing. A "Jew," as the term is currently employed, may be a member of one of a dozen ethnic groups, whose skin may be white or black; who speaks Yiddish and reads Hebrew, speaks Yiddish and speaks Hebrew, or who speaks and reads neither; who belongs to one of the three major groups of Judaism, or none; whose place of origin may have been Poland, Africa, Oceania, or Oklahoma.

Implicit in popular use of national designations, but clearly coming to light in such general expressions as "racial groups" and "newer races" used to denote persons of foreign stock, is a mythological concept of race, and the mystical idea of a nationality that can somehow transcend geographical and political frontiers. The United States Census Bureau, however, confronted with the realistic task of tabulating the population, indulges in no such fourth-dimensional boundary jumping. It does attempt to make a rough division of the population by color; "white" (somewhat more accurately defined by the schoolmaster in *A Passage to India* as "pinko-gray"), "Negro," and "other." The last group includes Indians, Chinese, Japanese, and, since 1930, Mexicans. The native white population is usually divided into two groups: (1) those of native parentage (both parents native to the United States), (2) those of foreign parentage (both parents foreign born), and of "mixed" parentage (one parent native and the other foreign born). The foreign white stock, as defined by the Census Bureau, is composed of two distinct elements: the foreign born white and the native white of foreign or mixed parentage. Foreign born whites are classified according to country of birth. Native whites of foreign or mixed parentage are classified according to the country of birth of the father, except that where the father is native and the mother foreign born the classification is according to the country of birth of the mother.

In considering the foreign white stock resident in the five boroughs of New York City, then, only the first generation (the foreign born) and the second generation (the native born of foreign or mixed parentage) can be accurately examined. Accordingly, when reference is made to an "Italian" living in present-day New York, the term indicates one of the following: a person born in one of the political subdivisions of Italy existent in 1930; a person both of whose parents were born in Italy, or one of whose parents was born in the United States and the other in Italy, or whose father was born in Italy and whose mother was born in some other foreign country. In the instance of the Jews, a group which has no single country of origin and for which separate treatment is given in a subsequent section of this article, figures from the *American Jewish Year Book,* published under the sponsorship of the American Jewish Committee, have been used. The Negroes, who play so important a part in the life of the city, are treated in a separate article.

The United States Census Bureau figures for 1930 are not only the most complete and the most reliable, but are further significant because in 1930 the United States had the largest foreign born population in its history—14,204,149. In that year, also, 38,727,593 were immigrants or the children of immigrants. In 1931 there were more aliens who left the United States than entered it, the net loss for the year 1930–31 being 10,237 aliens. Each year thereafter showed an ebbing of the tide which from 1820 to 1930 had brought to the United States 37,762,012 immigrant aliens.

The stemming of this tide began with the quota laws of the early 1920's. The first quota law had been passed in 1921. Under the quota law proclaimed in operation as of July 1, 1929 there could be admitted yearly a maximum of only about 153,900 alien immigrants. This quota did not apply to Canada, Mexico, or independent countries of Central and South America, but did apply to such Filipinos as were not then citizens of the United States. Total exclusion, with certain exceptions, continued to be applied, as it had been for years, to the so-called "yellow races" of China and Japan. The Ellis Island Committee, a non-partisan group of men and women appointed in 1933 to inquire impartially into conditions at Ellis Island and the welfare of immigrants generally, urged that the immigration quotas, in view of widespread unemployment, be maintained without substantial amendment. The Committee recommended, however, the amending of the quota law to avoid the separation of husband and wife, parents and children, which has been an evil ever since the quota law was passed; and the opening of asylum to political and religious refugees from other countries.

In 1930 the foreign white stock resident in New York City numbered 5,082,025, or 73.3 percent of the total population of 6,930,446. Of the boroughs of New York, the Bronx led with 82 percent foreign white stock, followed by Brooklyn with 77.9 percent, Manhattan with 67 percent, Richmond with 65.5 percent, and Queens with 64.3 percent.

The Italian group alone numbered 1,070,355 or 21.1 percent of the total foreign white stock in New York. It ranked first in Brooklyn, Richmond and Manhattan, but second to the Russians in the Bronx and to the Germans in Queens. The Italians were followed by the Russians with 945,072 (18.6 percent) and the Germans with 600,084 (11.8 percent). The Irish from the Irish Free State, to which could be added the 1.5 percent from Northern Ireland, followed with 535,034 (10.5); and the Poles with 458,381 (9 percent). Austrians numbered 5.7 percent of the total foreign white stock in New York City, English 3.5 percent, Hungarians 2.3 percent, Rumanians 1.8 percent, Swedes 1.3 percent, Norwegians 1.2 percent; while the French, Lithuanians, Danes, Latvians and Belgians fell below one percent. Jews, variously estimated at from one and three-quarters millions to two millions, illustrate the fact that the boundaries of European nations cut arbitrarily across minority groups. And the majority of immigrants from a foreign country may not necessarily be of the dominant stock of their native land. An overwhelming proportion of Russians in New York City, for instance, are Jews, as are large sections of the Poles, Rumanians, Austrians, and others. Of Russian immigrants from 1881 to 1906, it is estimated that 2 percent were Slav and 98 percent non-Slav, largely Jews. Of the 216,000 Russians who entered the country in 1906, 125,000 were Jews, and the rest included many of Lithuanian, Finn, and German stock.

Central, southern and eastern Europe contributed over half the foreign white stock of New York, as compared to less than one-third originating in northwestern Europe, less than one-tenth from the Americas, and 1.5 percent from all other countries. On the whole, those from northwestern Europe and Germany represented an older immigration.

The large proportion of foreign white stock among New Yorkers (73.3 percent compared with 31.5 percent for the United States as a whole) is nothing new. It goes back, in fact, far earlier than 1820, when statistics of the country of origin of foreign immigrants to the United States began to be kept.

Charles M. Andrews remarks in *The Colonial Period of American History* that in 1664 "the Duke of York became the proprietor, not only of an oddly fashioned territorial area but of an equally strange assortment of peoples—Dutch, English, French, Swedes, and Finns." Of the early inhabitants of New York Andrews writes, "Racially these people were of great variety, Dutch, Walloons, French, English, Portuguese, and, after 1655, Swedes and Finns. There were a few Jews, and many Negroes from Brazil and elsewhere." On Manhattan and in the present Westchester county the Dutch, a trading people, constituted three-fourths of the total population, the English, largely farmers, less than one-fourth, and the French and other nationalities the remainder.

To the Dutch, French, English, Irish and Scots exerting important influences upon early New York should be added the Germans, present from its earliest settlement in New Amsterdam, of which the first director general, Peter Minuit, is claimed as a German. By arrangement with the British government, groups of Germans were brought over from the war-torn provinces of Holstein and the Palatinate in 1708 and 1709. About 1706 the Jews erected their first synagogue on Mill Street, the only such for a hundred years. Not until the revolutionary year 1848, however, did the great tide from northwestern Europe begin, to continue until the early days of the Civil War. In 1820, but 8,385 immigrant aliens entered the ports of New York, Philadelphia and Boston. In the decade 1821–1830 a total of but 143,439 new immigrants arrived, as contrasted with a total for the decade 1841–1850 of 1,713,251.

In Ireland, Scotland and England, in Germany and northwestern Europe, peasant peoples, racked by wars, decimated by famine, repressed by governments still retaining many of the elements of feudalism, listened to incredible tales of America—and believed. Agents of the firm of Rawson and McMurray of New York were typical of many others in making such assertions as that (1837) a migrant from the British Isles could get "£10

British money per month and his diet, as wages; that everyone was on a perfect equality in America; that the common laboring man received high wages and sat at the same table with his master . . . and that with ease an independent fortune could be made." No sooner did they touch the American shore, however, than these hopefuls fell prey to "a new class of grafters—runners, agents, brokers, etc., who lived on the immigrants, finding the new arrivals gullible because of their inexperience in the American situation" (L. G. Brown, *Immigration*). These agents, often of the country of the very people they victimized, herded the new arrivals into boarding houses, and "proprietors of these establishments were always interested in giving insufficient and indifferent food and accommodations. In all cases their profits were measured by this economy, and in some instances, when they made a bad speculation in relation to a ship's entire passengers, cruelty, evasion, and neglect were resorted to as the only means by which they could escape bankruptcy. . . . The buildings employed were usually selected in the suburbs of the city, rather for economy than for adaptation, and almost necessarily deficient in ventilation. . . . So odious did these places become that hundreds of sick and destitute quitted them in terror and disgust." In 1830 the Mayor of New York sent a message to the President of the United States concerning the pauperism and crime being bred among the immigrants in the city, who were crowded into what a generation before had been the homes of the old Knickerbockers and their descendants, but which had become filthy and overcrowded tenements. In 1848 a committee of the New York Assembly investigated and reported on frauds perpetrated on immigrants, and in 1852 a State legislative committee was appointed to investigate the work of the New York commissioners of immigration. Not until 1864, when the first wave of immigration had passed its peak, did Congress establish a general immigration assistance office in New York City.

Many proposals were made, both during this period and later, to impose a head tax on immigrants, to limit their numbers, and to deprive them of the right to vote. Labor unions sought a "protective tariff" against the influx of cheap labor. The "Know-Nothing" or American Party was formed to protest against this tide of aliens, especially against such as "owed allegiance to the Pope of Rome." In an effort to control the arrival of "undesirables," New York passed about 1848 a law requiring a bond of $300 which made the shipowners and passenger agents responsible for those who were sick or destitute for a period of five years—a responsibility that was evaded by agents, who provided private "hospitals" and "poor-houses" of their own. After immigrants had acquired the vote, appeals were made to them to vote for candidates of the same country of origin, as for example this circular, issued about 1856 in New York City: "Irishmen to your post, or you'll lose America. By perseverance you may become its rulers. By negligence you will become its slaves. Your own country was lost by submitting to ambitious rulers. This beautiful country you gain by being firm and united. Vote the tickets Alexander Stewart, Alderman; Edward Flanagan, Assessor; both true Irishmen."

In 1861 only 91,918 immigrants arrived in the United States; in 1881 their number rose to 669,431. In the decade 1881–1890 there entered 5,246,613 immigrant aliens, as contrasted with 1,713,251 in the period from 1841–1850. Each of the years 1905, 1906, 1907, 1910, 1913, and 1914 brought to the United States over a million. In general, periods of prosperity in the United States coincided with periods of heavy immigration. Thus both immigration and prosperity were high in 1873 and low in 1879; rising in 1882, falling in 1885; high in 1892, low in 1897; and the long period of prosperity from 1900 to 1915 coincided with the high peak of immigration.

This second great wave originated not in northwestern Europe like the first, but in countries of eastern and southern Europe. "A line drawn across the continent of Europe from northeast to southwest," says John R. Commons in *Races and Immigrants in America*, "separating the Scandinavian Peninsula, the British Isles, Germany, and France from Russia, Austria-Hungary, Italy, and Turkey, separates countries not only of distinct races but of distinct civilizations. It separates Protestant Europe from Catholic Europe; it separates countries of representative institutions and popular government from absolute monarchy; it separates lands where education is universal from lands where illiteracy predominates; it separates manufacturing centers, progressive agriculture, and skilled labor from primitive hand industries, backward agriculture, and unskilled labor."

Such generalizations should not be interpreted to mean, however, that the immigrants of the second wave, coming from southeast of this imaginary line, were inferior to earlier immigrants or to earlier "American" stock. Dr. Ales Hrdlicka, after a statistical examination of descendants of older American stock and of fourteen national groups of white immigrants who arrived in the United States before the World War, stated that "the results were, in brief, that not in one single item, except stature, has it been possible to discover, in the healthy, non-crippled, non-defective immigrant from any of the different nationalities in Europe, any inferiority.

. . . If through such investigation it is impossible to find a substantial, meaning difference from the sound older stock that has peopled America, there surely cannot exist between the older stock and the newer comers any substantial superiority or inferiority." A census monograph on the occupations of immigrants and their children by Niles Carpenter, based on the 1920 United States Census, extended these investigations into the economic field. While available statistics were too meager for any general conclusions, they indicated that the "older" immigrant no more chose certain occupations than the "newer" arrivals, and that "the distinctions between 'old' and 'new' immigration cannot be taken to imply any significant differences in the economic behavior" of the races and nationalities under consideration. Concerning the mixture of the various stocks Dr. Hrdlicka remarked: "So far as science is able to see, there has not been, to this moment, a trace of any bad effect of these mixtures on the American people; much rather otherwise. Probably a good part, perhaps a very important part already of the power and strength of the American people is the result of these very mixtures."

The immigrants of the second great wave came from the lowest economic stratum. Thus one-quarter of the Italians coming over in the great wave after 1881 are supposed to have had their passage paid by friends and relatives in the United States. The Italians were not fleeing political or religious persecution, or, as in the case of the Jews of Russia, the Armenians and Syrians of Turkey, and the Slavs of Hungary, oppression by other national groups in power. The Italians attempted to avoid, by migration, exploitation by another class of their own race. In the southern Italian provinces and Sicily, where the power of the landlords was greatest, rental of farm land was high and crop prices low. Agricultural laborers in Italy received in 1900 from 8 to 32 cents a day in wages, yet had to consume 85 percent of their wages for food, as against 62 percent in Germany and 41 percent in the United States. Some idea of the low standard of living in southern Italy can be had from the fact that a peasant in Apulia was accustomed to consume 10 pounds of meat a year, although paupers in English workhouses were alloted 57 pounds each per year.

The overwhelming majority of the immigrants, with the exception of the Jews, were of an agrarian tradition and training. An examination of the occupations of 15 ethnic groups listed in the 1920 census supports this contention, showing that of the total number in these groups, 13.5 of the farmers were Irish, but in the United States only 1.3 percent were engaged in this occupation, turning instead to railroad construction and operation, and the steel industry. Irish women furnished 81.3 percent of domestic servants within these groups. The Scandinavians either migrated westward into farming areas, or became domestic servants and textile operatives in the city.

These agrarians, cast suddenly into a highly industrialized city, were forced to make in a few months an about-face in modes of living which had been transmitted to them unchanged since the Middle Ages. In their homes they continued to employ primitive methods of sanitation which, though harmless in an agrarian civilization, in the crowded tenements of New York induced disease. In their native countries they were by no means unskilled at tilling the soil, but in New York they dropped into the ranks of common labor, and as such built New York's railroads, bridges, buildings and streets.

Many immigrants who technically entered the port of New York never had the slightest contact with the life of the city. An eye-witness (Dr. Hrdlicka) tells of "droves of immigrants taken at Castle Garden by *padrones* or agents, led like a flock through gloomy downtown New York and over the ferry to Hoboken, where trains of old cars were waiting to carry them directly to the Pennsylvania coal fields and factories. . . . They never heard, never saw, never felt the real America, they were kept rather away from American influence and contact, lest such a contact might open their eyes and help them to revolt against the conditions of their labor. Their employers did not want prospective Americans, they wanted only the human beasts of labor."

In New York the alien immigrant soon learned a few necessary American words; thus the Italian of a decade's residence began to astound more recently arrived compatriots with such expressions as *giobba* (job), *sanguiccio* (sandwich), and *sonomagogna* (son of a gun). With the acquisition of American words came the acquisition of something of the American's sweeping largeness of idea. To the peasant in his native village, a native of the next village was a "foreigner." In New York, however, he had to mix with natives of his whole province or district, and here began his first lesson in the democratic process. From the native of a village he became, while living in New York, the native of a province, and even the native of a single country.

Even when the immigrant adopted America as his country, he still was set apart from other Americans by language and customs, often by the nature of his job. If a recent arrival, and hence the poorest and worst paid, he sometimes was recruited to break a strike of other workers, thus erecting a further barrier against himself. Often by joining an American labor union the alien immigrant first began to absorb some of the traditions of American democracy. The immigrant's children, however, went to New York schools, read New York papers, took part in New York amusements and sports, and became hardly distinguishable from children of native stock. In 1938, however, 180 foreign language periodicals were still being issued, in 27 languages, in Greater New York; these included 30 daily newspapers.

Generalizations as to occupations and contributions of foreign stocks in New York are frequently made, but rest on slight statistical information. Thus the Ukrainians of New York, many of whom work as window washers and dish washers, have made great contributions to sport; the Irish, whose unskilled hands first labored at building the city, have made many contributions to journalism, the theater, building and construction, and city politics; the Italians, most of whom began as day laborers, and many of whom were later concentrated in the clothing industry, contributed to science, music, art and politics; the Yugoslavs, besides repairing furnaces and houses, have furnished scientists, inventors, musicians and literary men to New York; the Scandinavians, mechanics and craftsmen, have made important contributions to music and to the maritime industry; the Jews, although usually associated in the popular mind with industry, commerce, and trade, have made significant contributions to the arts and sciences, as well as to education and social welfare.

In the pages which follow are sketched, in barest outline, something of the history and contributions of some of the numerically important foreign stocks of the city.

Italians

Italians have shared in the growth and history of New York City ever since its harbor was entered by Giovanni Verazzano, the Florentine navigator, in 1524—eighty-five years before Henry Hudson set eyes on Manhattan Island. In New Amsterdam were a number of Italians—among them one Mathys Capito, in 1655 a clerk of the Municipal Bookkeeping Office. When in 1657 a group of Waldensians—Italian Protestants—came from Piedmont in Italy to settle finally in Delaware, some are believed to have settled at Stony Brook, Staten Island.

Staten Island was an early haven for Italian political refugees. Here a small group of revolutionary leaders and exiles lived after the unsuccessful Italian uprisings of 1820, 1821, 1830 and 1848 against Austrian rule. Among these exiles were Giuseppe Garibaldi, leader of his country's revolutionary forces, and Felice Foresti, later professor of Italian at Columbia College and United States Consul to Genoa. The oldest Italian settlement in Manhattan was the "Mulberry Bend" district in the vicinity of Mulberry Street, later to become an area of notorious overcrowding, poverty and squalor. In 1880 the Italian population of New York, chiefly North Italians, was only 12,000. It was not until after 1880, when the United States inaugurated its open-door immigration policy and a flood of Italian immigrants, encouraged to migrate by their own government, began to sweep in through New York harbor, that "Mulberry Bend" and other Italian settlements in the city reached their greatest density of population.

America needed these immigrants: industrial expansion and the building of new railroad trunk lines in the West had created a demand for great numbers of unskilled laborers. They came chiefly from the south of Italy—from Sicily, Sardinia, Apulia, Calabria—but North Italians from Venetia, Lombardy and Piedmont were among them too.

Large numbers of the newly arrived immigrants were subjected to exploitation at the hands of some of their fellow-countrymen who had preceded them. These were the *padrones,* agents who took charge of the immigrants from the moment they arrived and thenceforth preyed upon them in every possible way. The *padrone* found his client a job, installed him as a slum tenant, and acted as his banker, profiting by each transaction. In addition to acting as employment agent and interpreter, he often induced clients to quit their employers, rehiring them to some other company and making an extra fee in the operation. Many of the *padrones* became men of considerable wealth and influence. Some Italian laborers, dazed and cowed by this treatment, became strike-breakers, and thus earned the hatred of other sections of the population.

But the Italian worker did not long remain blind to the advantages of union organization. In 1900, when excavation was begun on the Lexington Avenue subway, 4,000 Italian immigrants were brought in to displace Irish and Polish laborers. Under the spur of intolerable conditions, these Italians organized a union, struck for higher wages, shorter hours, better working conditions, and won their strike. Their victory marked the first participation in the organized labor movement by Italians in America. It was followed in 1904 by another victorious strike involving 5,000 Italian excavators and bricklayers working on the construction of the Bronx Aqueduct.

Italians, first brought into New York's needle trades by employers to fight off the trade unions, now comprise one of the most important sections of organized labor in the needle industries. At present the roster of organized Italian labor in the city includes 100,000 members in the International Ladies' Garment Workers Union; some 15,000 in the Amalgamated Clothing Workers Union; about 100,000 in various branches of the bulding trades unions; and a large representation in the longshoremen's union, the musicians' union, and barbers', waiters' and shoe workers' unions. Besides protecting his economic interests, many of these unions make important provision for meeting the cultural and educational needs of the Italian worker.

Italian workers have consistently gained in skill and specialization. A statistical investigation of jobs held by Italian bridegrooms reveals that in 1916 the percentage of laborers among them was 32.5. By 1931 the percentage had fallen to 10.6—clear indication of a constant betterment of position among this group. Their specific occupations were in 1931, in order of numerical importance, laborers, chauffeurs, barbers, tailors, shoemakers, clerks, painters, mechanics, salesmen, bakers, plasterers, carpenters, cooks, pressers, butchers, ice dealers, waiters, printers, bricklayers, drivers, operators, icemen, machinists, plumbers, electricians, cabinet makers, upholsterers, grocers, fruit dealers, laundry workers, restaurant workers, auto mechanics, cutters and masons. A fuller list would include doctors, lawyers, merchants, contractors, engineers, executives and a considerable number of workers in the highly skilled crafts.

No account of New York's cultural development would be complete without reference to Italian contributions. Italian musicians were in New York before the Revolution. In 1774 Nicholas Biferi established a music school in the city, and gave harpsichord recitals the following year. Lorenzo da Ponte, famous as the librettist of several of the Mozart operas, came to New York in 1805 and later became first professor of Italian language and literature at Columbia College, doing much to advance Italian opera in the city and to champion the cause of Italian culture generally. The increasing popularity of Italian opera led in 1854 to the establishment of the Academy of Music on Fourteenth Street, and here Adelina Patti made her debut in 1859. In 1883 the Metropolitan Opera House opened, destined to bring to New York Caruso, Toscanini, Galli-Curci,

Cavalieri, and the others in its long roll of musical celebrities. Toscanini's subsequent career as conductor of the New York Philharmonic Symphony Society orchestra did much to raise the level of musical appreciation in the country as a whole. The wealth of Italian art works in the city's museums attests to the grip of Italian tradition on American culture. In literature, the rich cultural heritage of Italy was introduced to Americans rather by writers of native stock—Washington Irving, William Cullen Bryant, William Dean Howells, Edith Wharton—than by Italians.

The Italians of New York have participated widely in the civic and social life of the city, contributing many of its public officials. The city's Italians never voted as a racial bloc, although many of them were active in the Italian Federation of Democratic Clubs. Only a small minority of New York's Italian population takes enough interest in the internal politics of the mother country to align itself in fascist and anti-fascist groups.

Evidence of the community spirit of Italians is provided in the existence of their numerous benevolent, philanthropic, medical, cultural, educational, sports and business clubs and institutions in the city. Among these are the Italy-America Society, a cultural group; the Haarlem House, the *Casa del Popolo,* the Mulberry Community House, and other community houses; the Italian Welfare League, the Italian Community Councils and the *Ordine dei Figli d'Italia* (Sons of Italy) among the social service agencies; and Columbus Hospital and the Italian Medical Center among the medical institutions.

The *Casa Italiana* was presented to Columbia University in 1927 by New York's Italian community. Its bureau of information provides data from Italian archives and libraries; it contains an Italian reference library; it arranges exchange fellowships between Italian and American universities; and its educational bureau devotes itself to the study and publicizing of cultural and social changes that affect Italian immigrants and their descendants in America.

The great majority of Italians in New York are Roman Catholics. Their churches in Manhattan include St. Joachim's at 26 Roosevelt Street, built in 1888; the handsome church of Our Lady of Pompeii at Bleecker and Carmine Streets; and the Church of Our Lady of Mt. Carmel at 115th Street near First Avenue. Some of New York's most colorful spectacles are provided by the celebration of Italian saints' days and religious festivals. There are also some 30 churches, chapels and missions which minister to the needs of Protestant Italians in Greater New York. (For a full treatment of the Italians, see *The Italians of New York,* 1938.)

Germans

German immigrants began to arrive in New Netherland as early as 1630, and it seems altogether likely that a fifth, possibly a fourth, of the inhabitants of New Netherland prior to 1664 were of German origin. Throughout the second half of the 17th century, the immigrants coming from Amsterdam to New Amsterdam included natives from all sections of Germany—Northern Germany, the lower Rhine district, Westphalia, Friesland, the Hanseatic cities, Hessia, Thuringia, the Elbe districts, Suabia and the German-speaking cantons of Switzerland.

The most prominent and colorful personality among these German-born immigrants was Jacob Leisler, for a short time during the English Revolution of 1688 the virtual ruler of the city. Leisler called the first congress of American colonists together. It was supposed that a plan was made to conquer Canada, and that an expedition by water and land, aided by a force of Mohawk warriors, was prepared. Evidently the leaders fell out among themselves and the plot failed of execution. The new British governor of New York, Colonel Henry Sloughter, entered charges against Leisler and his son-in-law, Milborne, both of whom were hanged on the spot where Pearl and Centre Streets now meet. Leisler was later exonerated, an indemnity was paid to his heirs, and his remains were transferred with distinguished honors to the grounds of the Dutch Reformed Church.

The early years of the 18th century brought to New York a large influx of immigrants from the Palatinate, a German province on the Rhine devastated and impoverished by the wars of Louis XIV and by the destruction of its vineyards in the severe winter of 1708-9. British lords of trade objected that "should these people be settled on the Continent of America, they will fall upon Woollen and other Manufactories to the prejudice of the Manufactures of this Kingdom now consumed in these parts." These fears were allayed with the assurance that "such mischievous practice may be discouraged and checqued much easier" in America than elsewhere. Of 3,000 of these Germans who sailed for America in 1709, more than one-third died on the voyage from bad food and contaminated water. The British authorities of New York did little to protect these immigrants and even allowed their exploitation by swindlers and speculators. Many who remained in the city were compelled to work in a condition of virtual serfdom, while those who could do so migrated to upper New York State and Pennsylvania.

Among the Germans from the Palatinate who arrived in 1711 was an orphan, John Peter Zenger. Apprenticed to William Bradford, owner of New York's first newspaper, the *New-York Gazette,* Zenger later started a newspaper of his own, the *New-York Weekly Journal,* and launched a vigorous campaign against corruption among the city's British officials. "We see men's deeds destroyed," he wrote, "judges are literally displaced, new courts erected without the consent of the legislature, by which it seems to me trials by Jury are taken away when a governor pleases; men of known estates are denied their votes. . . . Who is there in the province that can call anything his own, or enjoy any liberty longer than those in the administration will condescend to let them, for which reason I left [the administration], as I believe more will." British officials retaliated by bringing a suit for libel against Zenger, who was finally sentenced to jail. But the more Zenger incurred British wrath, the more popular he became with the people of New York. His acquittal after relentless prosecution was occasion for public demonstrations throughout the city. Another German youth, John Jacob Astor, who arrived in the city in 1783, was at the time of his death in 1848 one of the wealthiest men in America.

By 1834 New York had enough Germans to support a weekly newspaper, the *Staats-Zeitung,* printed on a handpress and edited by Gustav Adolph Neuman. Its circulation that year was 2,000; by 1840 it had 5,000 readers. In 1850, under new ownership, it began to be issued as a daily newspaper.

Carl Schurz, who took part in the German revolution of 1848, escaping in romantic fashion, came to the United States in 1852 and quickly became a leader in American life. He campaigned for Lincoln in 1860, was United States minister to Spain in 1861, and later served as major-general in the Union Army. At one time he was part owner of *Die Westliche Post* in St. Louis, on which Joseph Pulitzer afterwards worked, and was later on the editorial staff of the New York *Evening Post,* the *Nation* and *Harper's Weekly.* He was elected to Congress from Missouri, and for four years was Secretary of the Interior. He lived in New York from 1881 until his death in 1906. His lifelong friend, Abraham Jacobi, born in Germany of Jewish parents, became a specialist in children's diseases in New York and was president of the American Medical Association in 1912 and 1913.

Radical German immigrants who came to New York after the defeat of the German revolution in 1848 founded the Free Workers' School, one of the earliest experiments in workers' education in the United States.

Headquarters were finally established on Second Avenue in Faulhaber's Hall. Here were taught for the first time in America the theory and philosophy of socialism under the guidance of Germans who had received their inspiration from Marx and Engels.

In 1859 the Paulist Fathers, a new Catholic order in America, was founded by Father Isaak Thomas Hecker and its headquarters established at Columbus Avenue and Fifty-Ninth Street. In 1865 Father Hecker founded the *Catholic World*, a monthly magazine, and a year later he created the Catholic Publication Society, now known as the Paulist Press.

Among the first to answer President Lincoln's call for Civil War volunteers were local regiments composed largely of Germans. These included the Steuben Regiment, Blenkons Artillery, the Turner Regiment, First Aster Regiment, the Fifth German Rifles, the Sigel Rifles, and the Steuben Rangers. The *Staats-Zeitung*, then under the editorship of Oswald Ottendorfer, supported the government vigorously throughout the war. Ottendorfer was later active in the fight against the Tammany ring.

In the second half of the 19th century brewing in New York came under the virtual monopoly of German-Americans. In 1859 Peter Doelger founded the brewery firm of his name. In 1854 Anton Hupfel founded the brewing company which also bears his name today. The Lion Brewery, which has been in continuous operation since 1850, was the first to bring the Pilsener style beer to the American table. In 1883 Piel's beer began to foam as the result of the establishment of a gigantic brewery in Brooklyn. Other New York breweries founded in this period by German immigrants or persons of German stock are Pilser Brewing Company, Eberhart Brewing Company, Ebling Brewery, John Eichler Brewing Company, and Jacob Ruppert Brewery.

As the German population of the city increased during the latter part of the 19th century, a settlement known as "Little Germany" began to extend along the East Side, from Houston Street to what is now known as Yorkville. Tompkins Square, its center, was popularly known as *der Weisse Garten*—the white garden. Until the influx of Italians and Slavs at the turn of the century, almost all of the lower East Side was dotted with German beer halls, German clubs and German stores. Today there still stand landmarks of that period: the old Catholic Church of St. Nicholas on Second Street east of First Avenue, St. Mark's Church on St. Mark's Place near Second Avenue, Beethoven Hall on Fourth Street, Luchow's restaurant on Fourteenth Street, Teutonia Hall on Sixteenth Street, and Scheffel Hall on Third Avenue near Seventeenth Street.

By 1896 the Free Workers' School, which had conducted most of its activities on Saturdays and Sundays, underwent reorganization and expansion because of the Raines Law forbidding any institutions other than hotels to remain open on Sundays. A house was rented at 206 East Eighty-Fourth Street and the name of the organization was changed to the Workmen's Educational Association. In 1898, the Workmen's Educational Association established a Home Association, and in 1906 moved to the present Labor Temple, one of the largest centers of social activities in present-day Yorkville. Until the World War the Association enjoyed both popularity and prosperity, but anti-German feeling evidently discouraged membership. Prohibition, which virtually brought an end to the Association's lighter festivities, dealt the organization an even greater blow. It lost many of its German members and had to seek the support of other national groups. Today relatively few of the organizations that meet in Labor Temple conduct their activities in the German language. Anti-German feeling during the World War also resulted in many German firms operating under American names. This was especially true of the banks.

In 1930 the population of German stock in New York was 600,084. Of these, 237,588 were born in Germany, while 362,496 were born in the United States of German or mixed parentage. Germans were more numerous than any other foreign white stock in Queens, where they were 26.6 percent of the total foreign white stock; second only to the Italians in Richmond, where they were 14.5 percent; and in Manhattan they were exceeded by the Italians and Irish, representing 11.3 percent. In the Bronx they made up 10.3 percent of the foreign white stock; in Brooklyn, 7.6 percent.

In Harlem the Germans have been crowded out by Italians and Slavs. Formerly populated almost entirely by Germans, Harlem today still has the landmarks of its German days, such as the Harlem Casino, the Alhambra, and a number of churches. Yorkville, centering around East Eighty-Sixth Street, is at present the only section in Manhattan with a fairly compact German population.

Forty years ago the Bronx was almost exclusively a German district. Now, in spite of the large quota of Germans in that part of the city, the German element is noticeable only in scattered sections of the borough. Among these are the Morrisania section around Third Avenue and 161st Street, the Van Cortlandt section, Pelham Bay, Franz Sigel Park and Crotona Park.

Brooklyn once had a large number of German sections such as the Borough Hall vicinity, the Myrtle Avenue section, DeKalb Avenue, the Bedford section, Bay Ridge, Bensonhurst, Flatbush, Ridgewood and Williamsburg. At present only the Ridgewood section has a more or less compact German population.

In many sections of Queens a large proportion of the population is of German origin. These sections include Astoria, Woodside, Middle Village, Steinway, Maspeth, Newton, Elmhurst, Corona, Flushing. More than half the population of Jamaica is of German stock. The residents of Staten Island are largely of German origin. In Stapleton certain signs of German community life have survived. But as a whole, the German element of the city is being rather rapidly absorbed.

Irish

Those of Irish stock in New York (in 1930 numbering 614,000, of whom 535,000 were from the Irish Free State) due to their kinship with the dominant Anglo-Saxon culture easily adapted themselves to new conditions, without isolating themselves for any great period from the main stream of American life. Thus the Irish have never created anything like an Irish quarter in New York; they have always lived "all around the town."

Most of the Irish who came to this city before the American Revolution were Protestants from the North, although the first record of an Irishman in the colony of New Amsterdam is that of a Catholic, Hugh O'Neal, who was married in 1643 to the widow of Adriean de Donck, a Dutch farmer of the Bronx. In 1683 another Irish Catholic, Sir Thomas Dongan, became governor of the English province of New York, and was responsible for the charter which has come down to us in modified form. Sir Thomas opposed the keeping of slaves, opened the first free common school in America in 1685, and proclaimed the doctrine of religious tolerance.

Sir Thomas' compatriots in the little colony, slightly more than 400, were the town's blacksmiths, tailors, weavers, woolcombers and cobblers. Several managed to attain a higher estate; there was, for instance, Anthony Duane of County Galway, after whom a street was named, whose son, James, was New York's first mayor after the Revolution. Thomas Lynch, a shipping agent and importer, established a thriving business on Dock Street. William Mooney, the "Liberty Boy," was the founder and first Grand Sachem, in 1789, of the Society of Tammany, then called the Columbian Order.

The great wave of Irish immigration that began in the middle 1800's had its impetus in the Irish famine of 1846–47, bringing more than two million Irish to the United States in less than 20 years. Most of these settled in New York. They brought with them a passion for political and religious freedom and hatred for the English. The poverty and political persecution of the Irish in Ireland account for much of the subsequent development of the Irish in America. Most of the Irish were peasants whose ancestors had been farmers for centuries. Because they associated poverty with life on the land, they preferred to remain, for the most part, in the large cities. Totally unequipped to cope with the problems of a highly industrialized community such as New York, they were forced down to the level of the lowest economic groups.

Tammany, although it had been founded by an Irishman, was not controlled by the Irish in the first few years of its existence. In 1817 the Irish group within the organization made its first successful bid for control when it succeeded in electing Thomas Addison Emmett, a distinguished Irish lawyer, to Congress. From that time on Tammany became increasingly Irish, and Irish political leaders built Tammany into the city's most powerful political organization. "Honest John" Kelley, Richard Croker, Charles Murphy, "Big Tim" Sullivan were some of those who perfected the technique which enabled that organization to acquire control of every branch of municipal activity and to hold it for almost a century.

Most of Tammany's continued power and prestige lay in its ability to provide jobs and political preferment for its supporters, and for the Irish immigrants who were constantly pouring into the city during these years. The process of filling vacancies in the police and fire departments with Irish gave to these branches of the municipal service an Irish complexion which has persisted to this day. Other department vacancies were filled with deserving political henchmen.

Much of the hostility which the Irish encountered on their first arrival in this country was due to their Catholic faith. In many cities there were even anti-Catholic riots, but from the beginning the Catholic Church has been allowed to develop in New York with little friction. Its growth in this city owes a great debt to Irish membership and to three great Irish prelates—Cardinals McCloskey, Farley and Hayes. The church preserved much of the Irish cultural heritage ruthlessly suppressed by the English invader, and a great deal of the Celtic genius thus had its only outlet within the church. The church continued to play a great part in the life of the Irish American, and has always reflected him at every stage of his development. In the beginning outside contributions were necessary to build the city's first Catholic church, St. Peter's, erected in 1786—a simple structure to which Charles IV of Spain gave $1,000. By 1879 there stood, as a symbol of the progress which had been made since that time, the magnificent St. Patrick's Cathedral, erected entirely from funds raised among local Catholics.

The Irish of New York have always participated in the dramatic, literary and industrial activities of the city. To Broadway they have given some of its finest actors, dramatists and producers. For a period the American stage was dominated by such Irish figures as John Drew, Ada Rehan, Chauncey Olcott, among the actors; Augustin Daly, among the producers; and, among the playwrights, Dion Boucicault, James A. Herne and William Harrigan.

Among composers have been Victor Herbert and Edward MacDowell; among singers Geraldine Farrar and John McCormack. Horace Greeley and E. L. Godkin were among the outstanding journalists of Irish stock who helped make New York a newspaper capital. Irish men of letters have included Finley Peter Dunne, Lafcadio Hearn, Harvey O'Higgins and Joyce Kilmer.

In medicine the Irish gave to the city Dr. John Byrne, one of the earliest researchers in cancer, and William McNeven, a pioneer of American medicine. To the industrial development of the last century the Irish contributed such inventors and engineers as Christopher Colles, Patrick B. Delaney, Robert Fulton, John Phillip Holland, John Bart McDonald and John Joseph Carty. One of the earliest department stores in the city was founded by Alexander Stewart, and one of the most successful American shipping lines by W. R. Grace, another Irishman.

English, Scotch, Welsh

The first mass migration of Englishmen to New York came in 1664 when Colonel Richard Nicolls forced the surrender of Peter Stuyvesant, rechristened the hitherto Dutch town of New Amsterdam and became the first British governor of New York. In the first years of British rule, English and Welsh arrived in large numbers and settled for the most part on the tip of Manhattan below Wall Street and in the southwestern area of Staten Island.

While Scotch settlers had trickled into the city since its founding, it was not until 1764 that they began to arrive in any considerable numbers, as the result of the border wars between England and Scotland. With them came the "Ulster Scots" or Scotch-Irish who had settled in Northern Ireland before migrating to the colonies. The heavy flow of Scotch and Scotch-Irish continued for ten years.

By the end of the eighteenth century, a colony of several hundred Scotch weavers, mainly from Paisley, had settled in what was then called the Village of Greenwich.

Little remains of these settlements, and today New York's more than six percent of the nation's total British population is scattered through the city. Tottenville, Staten Island, is the only thing resembling a "British quarter"; the site of an old English colony, it still houses some of the descendants of the early settlers. In 1930 New York's English population was 178,703, Welsh 5,000, and Scotch 71,187.

British influence has made itself felt on the governmental structure as well as on the economic and cultural tone of New York. In the formative period of the city's history it was British enterprise that raised the city to commercial and maritime importance. It was in this same period of English rule that the molds were cast of the city's political structure, much of which has remained to this day.

British shipping interests which first made New York an important seaport still figure largely in the city's commercial life. Chief among the lines which handle New York's sea-going traffic is the British-owned Cunard White Star Line.

Relic of the days when England set the pattern for American literature are the many New York publishing houses which have grown out of American branches of long established British concerns. These include Thomas Nelson & Son, The Macmillan Company, and Longmans, Green & Company.

English influence on New York architecture is seen in many of the city's churches and in the manor-like homes of Westchester. Churches of English origin are Trinity Church, St. Mark's in the Bouwerie, First Presbyterian Church, rebuilt on the corner of Rutgers and Henry Streets in 1796, and the Scotch Presbyterian Church on Grand Street which dates from 1756.

The Van Cortlandt Manor House in Van Cortlandt Park, the Philipse Manor House in Yonkers and the Jumel Mansion overlooking the upper reaches of the Harlem River are among the more celebrated copies of the

English country house. Modern counterparts are seen in Westchester imitations of this style.

Chief among the old English landmarks which dot the city is Fraunces Tavern at Pearl and Broad Streets, celebrated rendezvous before and after the Revolution. Ye Olde Chop House at 118 Cedar Street was also a well-known resort of Colonial days, patronized by Franklin, Burr, Madison and Thomas Paine.

The city's water supply system owes its origins to a British model used in London in 1613. English metal construction set the patterns for Brooklyn Bridge and New York's sewers followed the designs of British engineers.

Famous Britishers in New York's history are Gilbert Blackford, instrumental in founding the Aquarium; Samuel Gompers, of Jewish origin, the first president of the American Federation of Labor; Thomas and John Henderson of the Anchor Steamship Line; Duncan Phyfe, a Scot who created beautiful examples of American furniture and in 1795 opened a shop on Fulton Street, on the site of the present Hudson Terminal Building; John Paul Jones; Peter Fleming, the surveyor who laid out the grades for New York State's first railroad; Archibald Gracie, founder of the Lying-in Hospital, the Cedar Street Presbyterian Church and the Chamber of Commerce. James Lenox and Andrew Carnegie were Scots linked with New York's growth. Chief Justice Charles Evans Hughes is the son of a Welsh minister. Commodore Perry and Henry Ward Beecher were of Welsh descent.

Chief among the British organizations are the Societies of Saint George, Saint Andrew and Saint David, the patron saints respectively of England, Scotland and Wales. St. George's Society, with headquarters at 19 Moore Street, gives its annual dinner on St. George's Day, April 23, and throughout the year carries on philanthropic work among British residents in the city. St. Andrew's Society, a Scotch organization with headquarters at 105 East Twenty-Second Street, is similar to St. George's Society in aims and functions, climaxing its activities with dinner on St. Andrew's Day, November 30, the main feature of which is the ceremonial serving of the haggis, borne in by Highland bagpipers as Robert Burns' *Address to the Haggis* is recited. The Welsh St. David's Society at 289 Fourth Avenue carries on philanthropic work and stimulates and preserves interest in the Welsh language, literature and customs.

Other British organizations in New York include the Daughters of the British Empire, which maintains the Victoria Home for the Aged, near Ossining; the British Apprentice's Club, made up of cadet officers of the English merchant marine; the British Great War Veterans of America; the British Luncheon Club; the Over-Seas League, and the British Club of New York. The last three are social organizations with a general membership of English-born New Yorkers.

The British Empire Chamber of Commerce, a semi-official institution operating under a license from the British Board of Trade, has offices in the British Empire Building at 620 Fifth Avenue, where it maintains a permanent exhibition of British products, and publishes a monthly trade paper, the *British World*.

The English Folk Dance Society at 637 Madison Avenue is a branch of the English Folk Dance and Song Society founded by Cecil Sharp in 1911.

The Federation of Scottish Societies includes among its member organizations several lodges, the Caledonia Club, the Celtic Society and the Gaelic Society.

The English-Speaking Union of the United States, an organization to promote mutual understanding between the English and American peoples, has 13,000 members in this country, and is affiliated with the English-speaking Union of the British Empire, which has a membership of more than 10,000.

Russians

The references to Russian immigration, as reported by the United States Census Bureau, do not give even an approximate picture of the number and importance of the Russians in New York as an ethnic or linguistic group. All immigrants from Russia, which is populated by more than 80 nationalities representing many ethnic, linguistic, racial or religious groups, are classified as "Russians" in the census, even though they do not speak Russian.

Of the four important waves of immigration from Russia, the first, which arrived in 1880, was largely composed of Jews from Poland and Ukrainia who fled pogroms and unbearable economic conditions. The second influx began about 1890, with Slavs of the peasant class well in the majority. The Russian revolutionary upheaval of 1905 and its subsequent defeat gave a new impetus to emigration, and this third wave continued until the World War and the revolution of 1917. Although a large proportion of these political refugees was not ethnically Russian, these immigrants, largely of the educated classes, possessed a common tradition and language that gave them the designation of the "old Russian colony." Between 1920 and 1925, at the end of the civil war in Russia, thousands of the members of the nobility and upper classes fled Russia. Together with some of the older Slavic immigrants, they formed what has come to be known as the "new colony" as distinguished from the "old colony" of pre-revolutionary immigrants. The new group, numbering about 5,000, lives near Madison Avenue and 121st Street and along Broadway from 135th Street to 157th Street. They are, of course, violently opposed to the present Russian government.

Four Russian dailies represent as many shades of political opinion, and New York contains many Russian fraternal and cultural associations. Russian contributors to American arts and sciences include such outstanding men in New York as Nicholas Roerich, Vladimir G. Simkhovich, Igor Sikorsky, Serge Rachmaninoff and the Fokines.

In 1930 Russian white stock of all classes and racial origin living in New York numbered 945,072, or 18.6 percent of the total foreign white stock in the city.

Ukrainians

One of the most important groups of people from southern Russia and the eastern part of the former Austrian province of Galicia is made up of Ukrainians, known also as Ruthenians or Little Russians. They are all ethnically Slavs and most of them are of peasant origin. Of all Slavic languages theirs is most akin to Russian. Those who come from Galicia belong to the Greek Catholic or Greek Uniate faith, those from the Russian Ukraine are Eastern Orthodox. About 80,000 Ukrainians, representing the largest Slavic element, live in New York and publish a daily newspaper in their language.

Greeks

Large-scale Greek immigration began in the 1890's. A few of the arrivals before this time were Turkish subjects from Crete and the Aegean Islands. In the 110 years up to 1930 421,489 Greeks entered the United States. New York has the largest Greek colony in the nation, with more than 25,000 of the total 174,526 foreign-born Greeks in the United States in 1930. Chicago is second with about 15,000.

Most of the city's Greeks live in three main areas. The most populous is in the Thirties west of Sixth Avenue; the oldest is on Madison Street, between Catherine and Pearl; the third, largely residential, is on Second Avenue in the Thirties. But one must not expect to find in any of these regions a distinctly Hellenic settlement; a few shops and restaurants alone give evidence of the national origin of many of the inhabitants. None of the more prominent Greek churches is located in these neighborhoods. The new Greek residential section on Washington Heights centers around the church of St. Spyridon at Wadsworth Avenue and 179th Street.

Holy Trinity Orthodox Greek Church, built in 1904 and subsequently burned, was rebuilt at 31 East Seventy-Fourth Street as the cathedral of the archdiocese of all Orthodox churches in North and South America. On January 6, Epiphany Day, Greeks march in procession through the streets, led by priests in their sumptuous robes, with ikons borne by acolytes. The chief priest carries a cross to the water's edge at the Battery, and others cast the cross into the waves, blessing the sea; the cross is then rescued by a believer who plunges into the chill water and brings it to shore. March 25 marks the coincidence of the feast of the Annunciation of the Virgin with the anniversary of Greek Independence Day, when every Greek who can do so takes part in the joint celebration. On this occasion the Consul General usually attends the service at Holy Trinity.

New York has a Greek day school (Forest Avenue, Bronx, attached to the Church of Zoodochos Peghe) and about 50 afternoon and evening schools where some 2000 pupils are instructed in the Greek language. Two principal newspapers in Greek are published in New York, and there are several Greek book shops.

Although they are rarely worn in public, native Greek costumes may be purchased in the shops in the Greek quarters. Greek restaurants of all kinds abound, but to enjoy the real native cuisine one must go to those eating places in the Greek quarters patronized by Hellenes.

There are two Greek theatrical troupes which from time to time give performances in the vernacular of plays by modern authors (consult the Greek newspapers *Atlantis* and *Keryx* for time and place). Greek programs are heard daily over the radio.

Best known of the Greek societies are the American-Hellenic Educational Progressive Association and the Greek-American Progressive Association. Philaptochos (Ladies Charity Organization), closely affiliated with the church, has 600 branches in the United States.

Of all the businesses in which American Greeks are engaged, the selling of cut flowers is easily the first. There are many Greek importers and manufacturers of Turkish and Egyptian cigarettes. Not the least among New York's business enterprises operated by Greeks are motion picture theaters, candy shops, lunch rooms and night clubs.

Rumanians

New York's Little Rumania was one of the city's most interesting foreign colonies during the great migration from the 1890's to the early 1900's. Its restaurants were notable not only for their Rumanian delicacies but also for their clientele: bearded men with derby hats, shabbily dressed wives and children, drinking the sour wines of the homeland while listening to Rumanian ballads played by a tiny native orchestra.

Today New York's five or six hundred Rumanian gypsies in the lower East Side and other sections of Manhattan constitute the city's only closely-knit Rumanian colony. The 88,000 Rumanian Jews in New York live scattered throughout the five boroughs. About 5,000 Rumanians from Transylvania and Bukovina are largely of the Eastern Orthodox faith and, like the Rumanian Jews, are scattered throughout the city. Most of these worship in a special chapel attached to St Nicholas' Russian Orthodox Cathedral at 15 East Ninety-Seventh Street, Manhattan. The Rumanian Jews usually worship in the synagogues nearest their homes, but there are two congregations which were founded during immigration days and which still have a definite Rumanian stamp: the First Rumanian-American Congregation, 89 Rivington Street, Manhattan, and the First Brooklyn Rumanian-American Congregation, 224 Hopkins Street, Brooklyn.

A major national holiday is celebrated by Rumanians in New York on May 10, in commemoration of the liberation of Rumania in 1877 from Turkish rule.

With few exceptions, most of the Rumanian restaurants in New York cater to a Jewish clientele. Experts agree, however, that the food resembles the native Danubian cuisine rather closely. Meals in Rumanian restaurants are often accompanied by Rumanian gypsy music.

A large Rumanian bookstore in New York is the Rumanian Book Depository Company's shop at 37 East Twenty-Eighth Street. It carries a large stock of Rumanian and English books, magazines, and newspapers and serves readers in all parts of the United States. Despite the fact that there are larger or more significant Rumanian groups in Ohio, West

Virginia, Colorado and Pennsylvania, where the farmer and laborer of Transylvania and Bukovina are more at home than in the metropolis, New York is the cultural capital of Rumanians in America. The Institute of Rumanian Culture is in New York; Leon Feraru, an outstanding authority on Rumanian literature, is Professor of Romance Languages at Long Island University; the first Rumanian Symphony of George Enesco was introduced in America by Arturo Toscanini and the Philharmonic Orchestra; and a well-known Rumanian-American writer, Konrad Bercovici, has for years lived and worked in New York.

Hungarians

The countrymen of Louis Kossuth and Joseph Pulitzer constitute one of the city's smaller foreign groups. Particularly striking is their parade on May 15, a holiday for Magyars in New York, when they assemble on East Eighty-Second Street and march in honor of Louis Kossuth, whose statue stands impressively on Riverside Drive.

There were Hungarians in America as long ago as during the Revolutionary days, when one of them, Michael de Kovats, fought as a colonel in Washington's army. Most of them, however, came here after the ill-fated Hungarian revolution of 1848. Today there are in the city some 150,000 residents of Hungarian stock, about 90,000 of whom are Jews.

From 1880 to 1914, 230,000 Hungarians entered the port of New York, and nearly half of these settled in the city to form the largest single Hungarian group in the country. Most of the others went on to Pennsylvania, Ohio, Indiana, and Illinois, where they became miners, steel workers, and agricultural laborers. Those who remained in New York settled at first on the lower East Side in the vicinity of Houston Street and Avenues A and B, but with the coming of newer immigrants the colony began to move. Since 1905 it has been a relatively permanent part of Yorkville between Seventy-First and Seventy-Ninth Streets, east of Lexington Avenue.

Most Hungarians in New York are employed in the food industries and in the needle and building trades. A few are musicians, among them Erno Rapee, conductor of the Radio City Symphony Orchestra, and Emery Deutsch, music director for station WABC.

The people of Hungarian birth or parentage in the city maintain four Protestant (Hungarian Reformed) churches, two Catholic churches and 30 synagogues. These groups also conduct church schools, largely for teaching the Hungarian language, tradition, and culture to American-born children of immigrants.

Most of the Hungarian clubs and societies in the city are chartered as sick and benevolent associations, and two or three date from the 1850's. The best known of those more recently established is the Ady Endre Society, founded after the World War to aid political refugees from Hungary. It sponsors literary forum evenings annually and publishes a Hungarian language weekly, *Az Ember* (The Man). Another group, the Culture Society, was founded in 1931 and is known in the Hungarian colony for its dramatic productions, musicales, and lectures. *Efyleti Elet* (Club Life), a monthly publication with 15,000 circulation, is the official organ of many Hungarian organizations. Eight publications are issued in Hungarian in New York, including the Hungarian daily, *Amerikai Magyar Nepszava*.

The Elore Hungarian Players, 380 East Eighty-First Street, an affiliate of the Hungarian Workers' Federation, is a leading Hungarian dramatic company in America. All plays are presented in Hungarian, usually at the Fifth Avenue Theater and at the Heckscher Foundation.

The Tobis Theatre, First Avenue and Seventy-Eighth Street, is the sole permanent Hungarian motion picture house in the country. Probably it is the only one in the world that shows Hungarian pictures exclusively, for in Hungary, where only about fifteen pictures are produced annually, the theaters often show American and British films.

The Hungarian stores in New York are the chief importing and distributing agencies in this country for Tokay wines, Budapest salami, and goose livers, the latter a favorite Hungarian delicacy. The stores have a nationwide trade, sending their wares to the Hungarian-born miners and steel workers throughout the country.

It is in the unpretentious eating places of Yorkville and the lower East Side that authentic Hungarian delicacies are to be found. The large and gaudy places boasting gypsy music and elaborate cuisine are seldom so truly Hungarian.

Czechoslovaks

Czechoslovakia has contributed more than 40,000 to the population of the New York area, and since the World War, when that country won its independence and formed a democratic government, Czechs and Slovaks here have combined many of their interests. Earlier each gathered in widely separated vicinities in Manhattan, the Czechs in the lower part of Yorkville, between Seventy-First and Seventy-Fifth Streets, east of Second Avenue, and the Slovaks downtown from Fourth to Seventh Street east of Avenue A. Now some Slovaks are moving into the northern district. About 15,000 Czechs live in Queens County, chiefly in Astoria, with smaller groups in Winfield, Woodside, Corona and Jackson Heights.

Most of the Czechoslovaks in New York are Roman Catholics, but there are many American Czechs who are not affiliated with any church. The Roman Catholic Czechs attend the Church of Our Lady of Perpetual Help, 323 East Sixty-First Street, and St. John the Martyr's, 254 East Seventy-Second Street. Protestants attend the Jan Huss Church (Presbyterian), 349 East Seventy-Fourth Street, and the Madison Avenue Presbyterian Church at Seventy-Third Street. There are four Slovak churches, one Roman Catholic, with a large congregation, St. Nepomucky Church at Sixty-Sixth Street and First Avenue. The other churches of this language group are the Slovak Baptist, Seventh Day Adventist and Slovak Lutheran.

Czechs and Slovaks keep alive their traditions and languages by maintaining separate schools where after public school hours children are taught history and the native speech. The Sokol (Falcon) Athletic Union of New York and other organizations are especially concerned with calisthenics and sports. Other groups present native dramas, folk songs and forms of entertainment which have their origin back in the home country. The largest meeting place is Bohemian National Hall, 335 East Seventy-Third Street, Manhattan, where forty-eight organizations meet regularly. Among the most popular choral groups are the Huss Choir, Jan Huss House, Seventy-Fourth Street near First Avenue, and the Sokol Singing and Dramatic Society, 420 East Seventy-First Street. Czechoslovakia has contributed prominent artists to the musical and theatrical world.

The daily newspaper *New Yorkske Listy* (Czech) was established in 1879 and *New Yorksky Dennik* (Slovak) in 1912. *Slovak v Amerike* is a semi-weekly periodical and *Tydenni Zpravy* is a weekly.

At Jan Huss House, on Seventy-Fourth Street near First Avenue, there is a Czech museum.

Balkan Slavs

New York City has 10,600 persons of Yugoslav stock—Serbs, Croats and Slovenes—of whom 6,500 were born abroad. Established about 1890, the earliest Yugoslav colony in New York City was centered around Twenty-Third Street and Tenth Avenue, Manhattan. The colony now extends along Ninth and Tenth Avenues between Twenty-First Street and Fortieth Street. There are many Balkan Slavs in Astoria, Long Island. Of the entire Balkan group in the city the Bulgarians are fewest in number, comprising only about 100 families and 300 transients, most of whom live in upper Manhattan.

Croats, Serbs and Slovenes have sharply defined cultures. The Croats and Slovenes are influenced by Austrian and Hungarian cultures, while the Serbs have acquired many Turkish traditions and customs.

Croats and Slovenes are generally Roman Catholic; the Croatian church, SS Cyril and Methodius, is located at 552 West Fiftieth Street, the Slovene church at 62 St. Mark's Place. The Serbs, few in number and without a church of their own, attend the Russian Orthodox Church on Houston Street near Second Avenue, where services are conducted in the ancient Slavonic church language. The Slovenes also have an auditorium at 253 Irving Avenue, Ridgewood, Brooklyn. Several Yugoslav schools have been established in the city; a Croatian school is affiliated with the church on West Fiftieth Street, and others are supported by New York Yugoslav societies, which number more than 100 and sponsor cultural, political and mutual aid programs.

Art, music, drama, literature and the dance, education, science and industry—all have been enriched by Yugoslav New Yorkers. A few of these are Nichola Tesla and Michael I. Pupin, noted scientists; Henry Suzzallo, sociologist and president of the University of the State of Washington; Prof. R. R. Radosavljevich, educational psychologist; Louis Adamic, author; and Tashamira, the interpretive dancer.

Yugoslavs have their own restaurants where native foods may be enjoyed and special occasions celebrated. Music is supplied by a native tamburitza orchestra and an evening often ends with the kolo—the ancient national dance—performed by both patrons and professionals.

The holiday most widely observed by Yugoslavs is celebrated on December 1, anniversary of the establishment in 1918 of the Kingdom of Serbs, Croats and Slovenes (later called Yugoslavia), when these three peoples were united under one flag. The feast of SS Cyril and Methodius, who converted the Slavs to Christianity in the ninth century and translated the Scriptures into Slavic, is observed on June 7 by Yugoslavs of both Roman Catholic and Greek Orthodox faith.

Four Yugoslav newspapers are published in New York: *Svijet,* Croatian daily; *Glas Naroda,* Slovenian daily; *Srbski Dnevnik,* Serbian daily; *Hrvatski List,* Croatian newspaper issued three times a week.

Estonians

Scattered about the city—in the Bronx, Harlem and the East Side— are about 6,000 Estonians, one of the latest groups to emigrate. Most of them left Estonia, whose people are closely related to the Finns, after the unsuccessful revolution of 1905 in Russia.

Estonians in New York are engaged chiefly in various forms of skilled labor. They publish a weekly newspaper in their native language and they support two social organizations and three churches of their own. Periodically they hold music festivals at which many of the men and women appear in the Estonian peasant costume.

Lithuanians and Letts

After 1868, Lithuanians came to New York in considerable numbers, as a result of oppression in the homeland. According to the Federal census of 1930, there were 31,000 persons of Lithuanian parentage in the city at that time.

Three newspapers published in the Lithuanian language do much to maintain the group's national identity. Ranging in allegiance from Catholic Nationalist to Communist, these organs are intimately bound up with organizations almost equally diverse: sick and death benefit societies, religious, artistic, literary, musical, social, and other groups. Local 54 of the Amalgamated Clothing Workers of America is composed entirely of Lithuanians.

The largest colonies of Lithuanians are in Williamsburg, Brooklyn and Queens. Several Lithuanian Roman Catholic Churches in the city have well-trained choirs. An outstanding musical group is the Aidas Chorus. A school for children and a radio station, WMBQ, with seven Lithuanian announcers, help to keep the language alive. A sports federation includes eight baseball teams.

The Lithuanians and Letts who came from the Baltic provinces of Czarist Russia speak languages related to each other, which form a special branch of the Indo-European family.

Most of the 16,000 Letts in New York left their native country—now independent Latvia—after the Russian revolution in 1905. Concentrated in Brooklyn and the Bronx, the Letts work principally as bricklayers, carpenters and unskilled laborers. Many of the women are engaged in the needle trades and in domestic service.

Letts have founded several clubs and societies for persons of their nationality. The largest of these has its own dramatic group, a chorus and a string orchestra.

There is no permanent Lettish church, but two congregations, Baptist and Lutheran, hold services once a month in Judson Memorial Church on Washington Square and in the John Street Church.

Scandinavians

In spite of the fact that they are more nearly akin to the Anglo-Americans than any other group from the European continent, the Scandinavians of New York have preserved much of their native culture and modes of life. Many live in the Bay Ridge section of Brooklyn, which is full of Danish, Norwegian and Swedish shops, restaurants, bookstores and churches. The majority of Scandinavians who came over in the great immigration of the 19th century settled in the vast farming regions of the Middle West to follow the traditional agricultural life of their fathers. Thus New York has only 20,000 residents of Danish stock out of the more than 500,000 in this country, 63,000 of Norwegian stock out of 1,100,098, and 71,000 of Swedish stock out of more than one million and a half.

The first Scandinavians came to New York with Henry Hudson in 1609; there were a few Danes among the crew of the *Half Moon* when it entered New York Bay that year. Until late in the 19th century there were hardly more than one thousand in the entire city. A Norwegian, Claes Carstensen, may have determined Brooklyn as a residence for most of the Scandinavians who subsequently settled in New York, when he purchased in 1642 some 60 acres of land in the section later known as Williamsburg. In 1704 the Norwegian and Danish residents of the city erected a stone chapel on lower Manhattan near Broadway and Rector Street.

The Scandinavians who remained in New York became, for the most part, mechanics, seamen and skilled workers in the building trades. More than 60 percent are members of trade unions. They are especially numerous in such unions as the Carpenters', Bricklayers', Painters', and

International Seamen's. The leaders in the movement for unionization have been those Swedes who came to New York after the Swedish general strike of 1909.

Most of the Scandinavians in this city are Lutherans, each nationality maintaining its separate church. The first Swedish church in the city, however, was the Swedish Immanuel Methodist Episcopal Church, of which the first services were held in 1845 on an old ship anchored in the Hudson River. *Den Norske Sjomandskirke* (Norwegian Seamen's Church), which has been maintained chiefly for Norwegian sailors since 1878, has always had its pastor selected by church and governmental authorities in Norway.

The Swedes are especially well known for their talented singers, some of whom have been featured on the stage of the Metropolitan Opera House. Many Swedes have won distinction in engineering.

The Danes have also been prominent in musical and professional life. Jacob A. Riis, a Danish immigrant, became a well-known journalist. His articles in the New York *Tribune* and other newspapers on the disease-ridden slums of New York, along with such books as *The Making of an American* and *How the Other Half Lives,* were important contributions to sociological literature.

Scandinavians have established numerous benevolent, charitable and social organizations, as well as several newspapers. Danes and Norwegians have one newspaper each, with a circulation of 4,100 and 9,000 respectively; the Swedes have five newspapers with a total circulation of 14,000. All Scandinavians unite in the celebration of Leif Erickson Day on October 9; the Danes alone observe *Grundslovsdagen,* or Constitution Day, on June 5; the Swedes celebrate on November 6 the anniversary of the death of their great national hero King Gustavus Adolphus, at the battle of Lützen.

Peoples of the Near East

During the later decades of the 19th century, Turkish massacres drove Armenians and Syrians to American shores in steadily increasing numbers. The wave of near-East immigration reached its peak in the last decade of that century. In 1896, a number of Turks joined the exodus when Sultan Abdul Hamid II, in a precedent-breaking decree, permitted his own nationals to leave the empire.

Of the three near-Eastern groups, the Syrians have the largest population in the city, numbering 30,000 throughout greater New York. The Armenians come next with 22,000, while the Turks in New York number only about 300.

Only 1,000 of the city's Syrians live in Manhattan, along Washington Street between Morris and Rector Streets. The largest Syrian colony in the city lies between De Graw and State Streets, running from the East River to Hoyt Street in Brooklyn. A smaller settlement has grown up in the Bay Ridge section of Brooklyn.

New York's Armenians live for the most part between Twenty-First and Thirty-Second Streets, in the district east of Lexington Avenue. Other colonies center about Bathgate and Washington Avenues in the Bronx; along Amsterdam and St. Nicholas Avenues between 181st and 191st Streets in Washington Heights; and near Fifteenth Street and Fourth Avenue, Brooklyn.

The Turks are settled mainly along Rivington and Forsythe Streets in Manhattan.

While the Syrians are mainly importers, dealing in embroideries, laces, linens, brassware, pottery, exotic foods and Asiatic objects of art, the Turks are for the most part unskilled laborers, while the Armenians participate in the whole range of the city's occupations.

Armenians and Syrians in the city are almost without exception Christian, the former adhering to the Gregorian Church while the latter have formed a number of sects related to the Greek Orthodox and the Greek and Roman Catholic Churches. St. Joseph's Roman Catholic Church at 57 Washington Street, best known Syrian church in the city, conducts services in Syrian.

The Turks are exclusively Mohammedans. The only real mosque in the city, at 108 Powers Street in Brooklyn, claims most of the devout. Some belong to the Mohammedan Unity Society at 67 West 125th Street.

The Syrians are the most nationally-conscious group of the city's near-Eastern population, boasting three Arabic dailies, a tri-weekly and a semi-monthly. Leading newspaper is *Al-Hoda* (The Guidance) published at 55 Washington Street. Other publications include *Al-Islash* (The Reform), *The Syrian Eagle,* Democratic Party organ; the tri-weekly *Mirror of the West;* and the semi-monthly news magazine, *As-Sameer.*

Armenian left-wing groups publish the daily *Panvor* (Worker), which is the only near-Eastern publication comparable to the Syrian press in the city. Armenians also publish two New York weeklies, *Gotchnag* (The

Church Bell), a religious and literary magazine, and *The Armenian Spectator*, a political magazine dedicated to Armenian independence from Turkey and in opposition to Soviet Armenia.

The only Turkish publication is a monthly bulletin put out by the Turkish Aid Society, 2344 Eighth Avenue, the only strictly Turkish organization in the city.

Few of the customary holidays of these nationalities are observed in the city, and these are mainly political. Armenians celebrate April 24, All-Armenian Martyrs Day, commemorating the Armenian victims of Turkish pogroms during the World War, and May 20, Armenian National Independence Day, celebrating the autonomy of Soviet Armenia.

The Syrians in New York, 85 percent of whom are Lebanese, hail the founding of the republic of Lebanon on September 1. The principal Turkish political holiday is October 27, anniversary of the founding of the Turkish republic in 1923.

New York has come to rank high in Arabic literary history as the final home of Syria's leading modern poet, Kallil Gibran, who lived in the city for many years and died here in 1931.

Orientals

Simultaneous with the tide of European immigration to the east coast of the United States during the last half of the 19th century, waves of Chinese and Japanese began to pour into the west. The Chinese, mainly from Canton province, began to settle in this country during the middle of the century. In 1852 Commodore Perry broke through Japanese isolation and paved the way for future migrations. Later, Chinese were driven eastward by the west coast anti-Chinese disturbances that led finally to the exclusion acts barring Chinese and Japanese immigration, and many eventually settled in New York.

While 1930 figures give the city's Chinese population as 18,000 and the Japanese as only 2,000, the latter wield an influence in New York's commercial life considerably greater than the former's. Headed by the powerful Tokyo House of Mitsui, whose local offices cover a floor of the Empire State Building, New York's Japanese are mainly engaged in large scale importing. With the exception of a number of domestic and restaurant workers, the Japanese are reasonably prosperous.

In sharp contrast, the Chinese are mainly small shopkeepers, art and curio dealers, domestic workers and laundrymen. They live in some of the city's worst tenements. Their few doctors, artists and teachers have a clientele largely limited to their own countrymen. "Chinatown," so familiar to out-of-town sightseers, is in the Bowery district northwest of Chatham Square.

Many of the city's Japanese and several hundred Chinese in New York are Christian. The only Buddhist temple in the city is in the private apartment of a Japanese priest, many of whose congregation are white Americans, the rest Japanese. Devout Chinese Buddhists worship in their own homes, repudiating the two joss houses in Chinatown as tourist attractions.

Chinese fraternal organization, which once centered about the much publicized tongs, has shifted, and the nature of the tongs themselves has changed. Once marked by racketeering, gambling and bloodshed, tong affairs have been quiet for some years. For the most part the tongs have returned to their original character of benevolent and protective societies. The main tongs in Chinatown are still the Hip Sings at 61 Doyers Street, and the On Leong Tong at 41 Mott Street. The Chinese Consolidated Benevolent Society, enrolling members of both organizations, now adjudicates all tong disputes.

The Chinese publish three dailies in New York, largest of which is the liberal *Chinese Journal,* which boasts a circulation of 9,000. Other papers include the *Chinese Nationalist Daily,* organ of the Kuomintang's New York branch, and the *Chinese Republic News,* featuring mainly Chinese Masonic lodge news. There is also the *Chinese Vanguard,* a weekly published by the left-wing Chinese Workers' Club.

The Japanese in New York publish two periodicals, the *Japanese Times* and the *Japanese American.* Both reflect the official Japanese government views.

New York's Chinese and Japanese have, like most other nationalities, dropped most of their native customs. The holidays celebrated in the city are political rather than religious or traditional. Chinese New Year's day, which may occur anywhere from the first of January to mid-February, is still celebrated with dragon parades and firecrackers, but is almost the only occasion for large-scale observance. The Chinese commemorate the birth and death of Sun Yat Sen and the founding of the Chinese Republic, while the Japanese bow to the Emperor's picture on his birthday.

Both of these groups are fervidly patriotic, but only the Chinese maintain a complete school for their children, at 64 Mott Street. Smaller Japanese schools are attached to various Japanese Christian churches. A

Chinese dramatic society stages plays, and two Bowery movie houses show Chinese films after 10 P.M.

Following in the wake of the far-Eastern migrations that landed first on the Pacific Coast came the Koreans and Filipinos, some of whom crossed the continent to settle in New York. Koreans filtered in with the flood of Chinese and Japanese immigrants, until they reached their present population of about 200 in the city.

The Filipinos came in much larger numbers, their influx reaching its height after 1910. Until the establishment of the Philippine Commonwealth in 1935 they were classed as "nationals," an intermediate category neither citizen nor alien. They are now considered alien and their immigration is limited to 50 per year, thereby stabilizing their population in the city at the present figure of 4,000.

Small colonies of Filipinos have grown up along Second Avenue between Thirteenth and Sixteenth Streets and on Sixty-Fourth and Sixty-Fifth Streets between Broadway and Amsterdam Avenue in Manhattan. In Brooklyn there is a settlement along Sands, Concord and Nassau Streets and another along Columbia and Hamilton Avenues.

The Koreans form no colony but are scattered throughout the five boroughs. Like the Filipinos, they are chiefly employed as domestic and restaurant workers. A few Koreans are importers.

While the Koreans are mainly Protestant in religion, the Filipinos are generally Catholic. Both groups are highly patriotic. The Koreans publish a fervidly nationalist weekly, *New Korea,* while the Filipinos continue to celebrate as their chief holiday the anniversary of the death of José Rizal, national hero executed by Spaniards when they ruled the country. Other national occasions observed by Filipinos include National Heroes Day and the anniversary of the founding of the Philippine Commonwealth.

The 500 Hindus and the 100 Persians in New York are for the most part fairly prosperous merchants and importers.

Hindu immigration followed shortly after the visit of Swami Vivekananda to the World Religious Conference at Chicago in 1893. In the years immediately following the conference more than 2,000 Punjab farmers came to settle near Stockton, California, but those that came farther east were mainly merchants, missionaries or students.

Foremost Hindu religious organization is the Vedanta Society at 34 West Seventy-First Street, founded by Swami Vivekananda and now under the direction of his disciple, Swami Bodhananda. The society publishes a monthly, *Vedanta Darpana* (Mirror of Vedanta). The World Fellowship of Faiths, with headquarters in the Hotel New Yorker, is the only other important Hindu organization in the city; it publishes a quarterly, *Appreciation,* and a semi-annual, *Dharma* (The Law).

The only Persian societies in the city are the Association for Persian Art and Archaeology and the Iran Society, both cultural organizations.

Spanish-Speaking People

Spanish is the mother-tongue of some 200,000 residents of New York. The great majority of these have come from the Carribean region, chiefly Puerto Rico, and the rest from Spanish America and Spain.

Of the city's four Spanish-speaking districts or *barrios,* the largest is in lower Harlem, stretching from 110th Street to 125th Street between First and Manhattan Avenues, and from 101st Street to 125th Street for two or three blocks east of Madison Avenue. This *barrio,* as well as the one in the Red Hook district of Brooklyn, is mainly Puerto Rican. In the past ten years another colony, made up originally of more well-to-do Puerto Ricans, has been growing up on Washington Heights, between 135th and 153d Streets along Broadway and Amsterdam Avenue. Other Spanish-speaking families have been moving into this district, as they emancipated themselves from the slums of Harlem and the lower East Side; but it is doubtful whether this will develop into a closely-knit colony, as its way of life differs little from that of its neighbors, the trend being towards at least an outward absorption. Another *barrio* is to be found in lower Manhattan, close to the Brooklyn Bridge, mainly around Cherry and Roosevelt Streets. The people here are largely from the Spanish provinces of Galicia and Catalonia. In conversation with other Spanish-speaking people they use Spanish proper (Castilian), but among themselves they speak Gallego (similar to Portuguese) and Catalonian (a derivation from Provençal).

The shifting *barrios* followed the usual social trend, from slums to West Side districts, but the racial factor also came into play in the case of the Spanish-speaking people. Before the World War there were few Carribeans in the city, and the old Spanish *barrio* above Canal Street was made up chiefly of Spaniards proper and South Americans. After the war came the first large influx of Puerto Ricans, many of whom later shifted to Harlem. One of the causes of this shift seems to have been the difficulty encountered by many of the darker or colored Puerto Ricans in finding homes in the old district. Others followed, as the color line or racial prejudice is little known among these islanders, and before long most of the Puerto Ricans were concentrated in lower Harlem.

While the great majority of Spanish-speaking people came here to escape hopeless poverty, a large proportion of the others came as a result of political repression. Each violent overturn of a regime in Latin America brought refugees to New York. Ever since Latin America freed itself from Spanish rule, New York has been a center of opposition movements by refugees; and many historical figures, including ex-presidents, dictators and cabinet officials, have spent years of exile here. The movement for the independence of Cuba was greatly aided by the revolutionary junta in New York, under the leadership of the Cuban patriot, José Marti. When the exiled adherents of a cause returned to the homeland, following a revolution, their opponents often took their place here as exiles. In the case of Spain, almost all the refugees who came here were workers forced to flee from the homeland following the periodical violent suppression of labor movements. Only a small proportion of Spaniards have emigrated here, as most Spanish emigrants leave their country for economic reasons, settling in Latin America where the mother-tongue is spoken.

Although the Spanish-speaking people are often lumped together as a single group, they represent a rich variety of social and racial elements. The few who come from Argentina, Chile and Uruguay are usually Latins with little Indian mixture. Mexicans have a large admixture of Indian blood, and can be easily recognized as mestizos. The few Peruvians, Ecuadorians and Dominicans have Indian and mulatto admixtures; while many Puerto Ricans and Cubans have some Negro blood. Intermarriage is common among the Spanish-speaking people, but generally follows class lines, which in turn run parallel to racial shades. In general, social status forms a stronger line of cleavage than complexion.

As is true of most immigrant groups, the standard of living is low among the Spanish-speaking people as a whole. For the majority of these people, coming to New York has meant a shift from a backward agricultural to a highly industrialized economy, and many of them have become unskilled laborers and domestic servants. Among the women, large numbers have gone into the needle and millinery trades, often doing piecework at home for starvation wages. Families are usually large, living quarters are greatly overcrowded, and undernourishment is widespread. The depression brought great suffering, three or four out of five families being thrown on relief.

Another element is made up of those in the skilled trades, particularly as mechanics, motor car drivers, electricians, linotype operators, pressmen, etc. Most have learned these trades in New York, but many of the Spaniards came here as skilled mechanics. In contrast with the rest of the Spanish-speaking people, few workers, skilled or unskilled, are to be found among the South Americans here. These few are usually connected with banks or export and import firms as translators, correspondents, and in other capacities. This element avoids the slum *barrios,* being able to afford homes in the Washington Heights section or in the rooming-house district between Central Park West and Amsterdam Avenue.

The Puerto Ricans have a special significance. They come here as American citizens, and form the great mass of the Spanish-speaking people in New York. The acute over-population of the island and its desperate economic condition with more than three-fourths of the inhabitants chronically unemployed, have caused a continued exodus limited only by the difficulty of securing the necessary steamship fare. Virtually all of the 150,000 Puerto Ricans in New York have come here since 1918. It is noteworthy that nearly all emigrating Puerto Ricans come to this city. Perhaps the chief reason is that the steamship lines land most of them here, but there are other reasons as well. In 1918, the Federal government imported some 15,000 unemployed workers from Puerto Rico for the war industries in Georgia, the Carolinas, Louisiana and Arkansas. The end of the war threw these thousands out of work, and they were given the choice of free transportation back to the island or shifting for themselves. Most of them chose to stay in this country; but chiefly because of racial discrimination in the South, they drifted northward and finally settled in New York.

Migratory workers comprise the bulk of New York's Mexican population, and for this reason no particular locality in the city can be designated as Mexican. In 1930 some 3,000 Mexicans were recorded as living in New York City. Works by three noted Mexican artists, Orozco, Rivera and Siqueiros, are on view in the city. There are four frescoes with social themes in the Orozco Room at the New School for Social Research, and 21 panels by Rivera at the New Worker's School. Siqueiros conducted an experimental workshop on Fourteenth Street in 1936.

Spanish social organizations and clubs in this city are mainly concerned with mutual benefits, charity and entertainment. They are usually based on provincial lines; thus, those coming from Spanish Galicia have the *Centro Gallego,* those from Asturias the *Centro Asturiano,* etc. The Latin

Americans also have their political clubs, including socialist, communist and syndicalist organizations.

Since the beginning of the present century, many Spanish-language publications have appeared and disappeared in New York, in connection with the rise and fall of political activities and revolutionary movements in the home countries. Among the more permanent efforts was the *Puerto Rico Herald,* founded in 1908 by Luis Muñoz Rivera, an early Puerto Rican patriot; this weekly supported the first movement for Puerto Rican home-rule under the American flag. The first Spanish-language daily in New York was *La Prensa,* founded in 1916 as a weekly. It was originally supported largely by Spaniards, but in recent years it has become the organ of the whole Spanish-speaking community. It provides more news from Latin America and Spain than any other New York newspaper. It is politically independent, although it supports the Loyalist cause in the present Spanish conflict. A new daily with a decided liberal trend, *La Voz,* founded in 1937, also makes its appeal to all elements in the Spanish-speaking community. There are several weeklies, representing various social and political trends, but publications of this type are usually short-lived. A monthly magazine, *La Nueva Democracia,* represents the liberal and Protestant point of view, and is mainly directed against political dictatorships in Latin America.

While most Spanish-speaking persons are born Catholic, few of the men are church-goers. There are five Catholic churches in New York. Nuestra Señora de la Esperanza, Nuestra Señora de la Madalla Milagrosa, and Parroquia de la Santa Agonia are uptown, Nuestra Señora de la Guadalupe is downtown, and the Parroquia de San Pedro is in Brooklyn. The Protestants have sermon halls and one church, the Spanish Evangelical Church on West 115th Street. Many followers of the French spiritualist Kardec are to be found among the Spanish-speaking people.

On Saturday nights, the Puerto Rican section of Harlem is alive with music and merry-making. There are only about 8,000 Cubans in New York, but it is Cuban music that accompanies the dancing everywhere among the Spanish-speaking people—and indeed has invaded New York's night life in general. A number of cafés and cabarets with Cuban atmosphere have appeared during the last few years. In addition to the many inexpensive Spanish restaurants and cabarets catering especially to the Basque, Gallego, Catalan or Asturian compatriots of the proprietors, there are several night clubs frequented not only by the Spanish-speaking population but also by many others in search of slightly exotic entertainment. Such cabarets, with

Spanish dancers, Spanish food, and Spanish, Cuban and Argentine music, where New Yorkers try to show the natives how the tango and the rhumba should be danced, can be found in Greenwich Village, on the outskirts of Harlem, and in other parts of the city.

Two regular Spanish radio programs are broadcast from stations WHOM and WBXY, and a weekly musical program is sent out from a Spanish cabaret in Greenwich Village over WEAF. Harlem is the home of two theaters that specialize in the showing of films produced in Spanish-speaking countries.

The city's Spanish-speaking population celebrates annually on Columbus Day their *Dia de la Raza* (Day of the Spanish Race), when a parade is held which ends at the statue of Columbus in Columbus Circle.

Jewish People

According to the best available estimates, about 1,750,000 present-day residents of New York City are designated as Jews. Members of this group have never been able to agree as to the basis of their cohesion. Are they a race, a people, a religious confraternity, a singular cultural constellation, or merely a "remarkable accident of history"? There are, for instance, those Jewish assimilationists who stand solidly upon the assumption that what makes a man a Jew is his adherence to Judaism. The orthodox Jews, on the other hand, think of themselves as both a religious group and a nation, a conception obviously derived from the theocratic nature of the Jewish state in Biblical times. The political Zionists, excepting of course the religionists among them, generally take the view that the Jews are a people, a national entity possessing an ancient historic and cultural past.

Besides these large groups, there is the considerable body of assimilationists who for various reasons deny that the Jews are either a race, a nation, or a religious confraternity. First they cite historical evidence in the attempt to invalidate the contention that the Jews are pure and distinctive racially. They point to the fact that intermarriage was widespread in ancient times between Jews and non-Jews, even non-Semites, particularly with the Canaanites, Philistines, Moabites, Amorites, Assyrians, Babylonians, Persians, Medes, Greeks, Romans and Egyptians. They further bring to bear the considerable body of facts testifying to the mingling of many strains and the fusion of widely diverse stocks in which Jews were involved during the centuries after the Dispersion and throughout the entire Christian era.

The Jews of New York come from nearly every country under the sun, talk fluently in nearly every known tongue and dialect, and mentally reveal the imprint of an infinite variety of cultures. Physically, too, they are as diverse as there are types in the ethnological museum. Professor Franz Boas, the eminent anthropologist, once made a careful study of the somatic traits of several thousand New York Jewish immigrants and their progeny. He discovered among them Jews who were blond, brunette and redheaded; Jews with blue, gray, brown and black eyes; Jews with round skulls and long skulls; Jews with straight, hooked, retroussé, long and short noses; Jews who looked Nordic, Mediterranean, Mongolian, and Negroid; Jews with thin lips and thick lips; in short, Jews who resembled members of all the known types and races of mankind.

But however Jews may differ in their definitions and conceptions of what constitutes a Jew, there can be no doubt that through more than three centuries a more or less cohesive group of individuals classified as Jews, originally professing various foreign national loyalties and still largely representative of diverse cultures, has played a prominent part in the economic, cultural, professional, and philanthropic life of New York City.

The first Jewish settler in New Amsterdam was Jacob Barsimon. He arrived on the *Preboom* from Holland on July 8, 1654. In the following month, 23 Jewish refugees from Brazil disembarked from the *St. Catherine* at the Battery. These men, women and children were descendants of those Jews who had been expelled from Spain and Portugal by Ferdinand and Isabella in 1492, and who had gone to live under scant sufferance in Holland. When the Dutch secured a foothold in Brazil, these 23 had been among those who had emigrated in 1624, hoping their lot would be a happier one. Unfortunately, nemesis in the form of the conquering Portuguese and the ubiquitous Holy Office forced them to flee for their lives from Brazil.

The new arrivals received an openly hostile reception from Governor Peter Stuyvesant; he petitioned the Dutch West India Company in Amsterdam for permission to expel them from New Netherland so that "these blasphemers of the name of Christ . . . be not allowed further to infest and trouble this new colony." But the company, with a prudent eye on its guilders, replied on April 26, 1655, that "it would be unreasonable and unfair" to comply with the Governor's request. Despite this ruling, Stuyvesant denied the Jews the right of citizenship, prohibited them from engaging in retail trade and put obstacles in their way when they asked permission to purchase a burial ground.

Even after the English had wrested the Colony from the Dutch in 1664 the tiny Jewish community continued to struggle under the burden of many discriminations and humiliations. It was not until 1686 that the Jews of New York were permitted to hold public religious services. They then proceeded to organize the Shearith Israel Congregation, and erected a synagogue on Beaver Street a few years later.

Most of these early Jews engaged in commercial pursuits; the rest were small manufacturers or skilled workers. By 1687, New York had its Jewish butchers, chandlers, hairdressers, saddlemakers, goldsmiths and watchmakers. Two decades later, New York Jews were carrying on an extensive trade with the West Indies and Portugal. The Jewish community grew slowly but steadily. By 1738 a number of Jews were members of the New York militia; and in 1740, when the Royal Naturalization Act was promulgated, they acquired the rights and privileges of citizenship.

In 1769 a number of New York Jews signed the first historic document concerning civil rights in America, the Non-Importation Resolution. Although at the outbreak of the War for Independence no more than 2,500 Jews were living in the colonies, of whom 400 resided in New York, a number of Jews fought in the Continental Army or gave it material support. Rabbi Gershom Mendes Seixas preached sermons against British tyranny and in defense of human liberty, fleeing for his life when the British invaded New York. Hayim Solomon, a Polish Jew, gave his entire fortune to the Continental Congress when funds were desperately needed.

At the close of the 18th century the Jewish population of New York consisted principally of descendants of the Spanish and Portuguese Jews, numbering approximately 4,000. There was also a small group of German and Polish Jews. Later, during the first and second decades of the 19th century, Jews began to arrive from Germany and Poland, as a result of the period of reaction in Europe after Napoleon's defeat. By 1840 the Jewish population had increased to almost 10,000. Most of the German and Polish Jewish immigrants settled on the lower East Side. They were soon joined by other German Jews who emigrated after the debacle of the republican revolution of 1848 in the German states. The German element of the Jewish community soon became dominant. Many of them started as peddlers, but before long had become clothing manufacturers, storekeepers, traders and professionals. Among the workers many entered the fur and jewelry trades, and quickly became adjusted to the American scene.

At the outbreak of the Civil War the Jews of New York volunteered by thousands. They were pro-Union and abolitionists, many of them having brought over their equalitarian idealism from the revolutionary Europe of 1848.

Jewish immigrants still continued to arrive in large numbers from the German states. By 1880 fully 80,000 Jews were residing in the city. In May 1881, Czar Alexander III of Russia promulgated the infamous May Laws which further restricted the rights of the already persecuted and impoverished Jews in the Russian Empire. Mobs attacked the Jewish quarters in the cities, towns and villages. The Jewish masses thought only of flight, especially to America. Russian Jews, and later Jews from Galicia, Poland, Rumania and other countries, poured into New York. Since the metropolis contained the largest Jewish community in the country, and in addition offered the greatest economic opportunities, a vast number of Jews decided to settle there.

By 1914 there were more than a million Jews in New York, most of them on the lower East Side, where they lived in squalid and overcrowded tenements, suffering like the other immigrant groups from poverty, malnutrition and unsanitary conditions. The majority of these immigrants worked in the rapidly developing garment trades. Some became manufacturers or contractors, who frequently established workshops in their own tenement homes. Thus arose the sweatshop, with its accompanying evils of exploitation, disease and child labor. These conditions gave rise to a notable proletarian literature in Yiddish, characterized by morbid speculation about the futility of life in the face of overwhelming wretchedness and poverty, and even more markedly by a spirit of outrage and rebellion against exploitation and human degradation.

By 1888 several small Jewish trade unions were organized in the United Hebrew Trades. Although the latter started out as a strictly Jewish labor body, its present membership is composed of at least 60 percent Gentiles. Its influence has subsided recently, due to the fact that the international bodies of its member unions have taken over all work of organization. Perhaps the most influential of these internationals is the Ladies Garment Workers Union, founded in 1900. It has at present a membership in New York of 190,000 workers, organized in about 200 locals; virtually two-thirds of the members are women and about half are Jewish.

Two other powerful Jewish labor internationals operate in the city. One is the Amalgamated Clothing Workers of America. It was organized in 1914, and has now a New York City membership of about 20,000, of whom about half are Jews. The International Fur Workers Union, organized in 1904, and with a membership of 10,000 in the city, is about 80 percent Jewish.

The efforts of these unions did much toward driving the labor-sweater out of the apparel industry and bettering working conditions. Higher wages and shorter hours made it possible for thousands of Jewish workers to move out of wretched tenements into brighter and cleaner homes in the healthier neighborhoods of the Bronx, Brooklyn, Queens and Staten Island.

Jews now occupy an important place in manufacturing, wholesaling and retailing, as both workers and employers. They have also taken a prominent place in the professional life of the city. With the economic depression of recent years, the overcrowding of the professions has become an even acuter problem than hitherto, particularly for Jewish professionals. Anti-Semitism has made its appearance in a number of educational institutions. Jews, no matter how talented, find it difficult to get appointments on the faculties of some institutions, and certain professional schools have established quotas for Jewish students.

The multiplicity of community problems raised by the enormous growth of Jewish population in New York has resulted in the establishment of many Jewish social welfare agencies, charity organizations, hospitals, homes, centers and asylums. More than 90 of these are now organized in the Federation for the Support of Jewish Philanthropic Societies, which acts as a central coordinating agency in raising and allocating funds. A similar Federation in Brooklyn performs the same service for its member institutions within that borough. The city also has a number of independent social welfare organizations and several thousand Jewish benevolent and mutual benefit societies.

At the same time, extensive relief work is carried on by New York Jews for Jewish communities and institutions abroad. The Joint Distribution Committee, organized in 1914 for war relief work, is still actively functioning as a distributor of millions of dollars, collected from Jews all over the country, to needy Jews in Germany, Poland, Rumania and elsewhere, for the settlement of German Jewish refugees in Palestine and South America, and for colonization in the Crimea of Jews from the old Russian ghettos. The Icor, an association to aid the colonization of Jews in the Soviet Union, including Biro-Bidjan in the Far East, was organized in 1924.

Zionist organizations active in New York for the establishment of a homeland in Palestine are the conservative Zionist Organization of America, the labor Poalei Zion and Zirei Zion Federation, the ultra-orthodox Mizrachi Zionist Organization, the Hadassah, which provides hospital and medical service to Jewish settlements in Palestine, the Junior Hadassah, and Avukah, the intercollegiate Zionist Society.

The various schisms that divide all religious sects also exist among the Jews. But, in general, religious Jews may be divided into two major groups. Those from western, eastern, and central Europe are usually described as *Ashkenazim;* and those from the Mediterranean countries, North Africa and Asia are called *Sephardim.* These two appellations actually refer only to the kind of liturgies customary among the Jews of these countries. The Jews of New York are preponderantly Ashkenazim. By and large the Sephardim are ultra-orthodox. But the Ashkenazim are divided into four camps: the orthodox, the chassidic, the conservative and the reformed. Each has its own synagogues, employing different liturgies and ceremonies; they also differ widely in theology.

The Shearith Israel Synagogue, founded by Spanish-Portuguese Jews toward the end of the 17th century and now situated at Central Park West and Seventieth Street, is the leading orthodox synagogue of the Sephardim in New York. It has an imposing interior, and its ceremonials and liturgy are characterized by great dignity and simplicity. The Jewish Center Synagogue, at 131 West Eighty-Sixth Street, is a leading center of orthodoxy; and the Congregation B'nai Jeshurun, at 270 West Eighty-Ninth Street, is one of the outstanding conservative houses of worship. Perhaps the best-known Reform Temples are the Central Synagogue at 652 Lexington Avenue and the Temple Emanu-El at Fifth Avenue and Sixty-Fifth Street.

Clustering around the hundreds of synagogues and temples in New York are various denominational Jewish educational systems. There are 480 Jewish religious schools of all varieties, with an attendance of some 65,000 children. About half of the latter attend the orthodox-conservative *Talmud Torahs,* in which the Bible, Jewish history and the Hebrew language are the principal studies. In addition, about 10,000 children attend after regular school hours the ultra-orthodox type of religious school—the *Cheder,* in which the verbal translation of the Hebrew Pentateuch into Yiddish is the sole educational activity.

There are six *Yeshivas,* or orthodox schools of higher Hebrew studies, in New York. The best known of these is the Yeshiva College, at 187th Street and Amsterdam Avenue. Besides the work of its Hebrew Teachers Institute, its principal function is to train orthodox rabbis. Devoted to the same tasks, although on a larger scale, is the Jewish Theological Seminary, at Broadway and 122d Street. Most of the younger orthodox rabbis and teachers of America are trained in its Seminary and Teachers Institute. The Jewish Institute of Religion, at 40 West Sixty-Eighth Street, is the only reform rabbinical seminary in New York.

There are other types of Jewish education, mostly of a non-religious kind, with emphasis on Jewish culture and the Yiddish language and literature. The Jewish National Workers Alliance, a Labor-Zionist organization, has 18 schools, with an attendance of about 1,000; the Sholem Aleichem schools, supported by progressive nationalistic Jewish workers, are 20 in number and are attended by 1,200 children; the Workmen's Circle Schools, of socialist tendencies, number 50 and have about 3,000 pupils; then finally the International Workers Order has a number of Jewish schools, with an attendance of about 3,000.

The two foremost Jewish newspapers of New York, the *Daily Forward,* a socialist organ, and the *Morning Freiheit,* an exponent of communism, have been prominent forces in the Jewish labor movement. The former has a circulation of approximately 170,000, the latter of about 50,000. Two other influential Yiddish dailies are the Zionist-nationalistic *Day* and the orthodox-conservative *Morning Journal,* each of which has a circulation of about 83,000. In addition to these dailies, New York is the home of a number of Jewish periodicals, issued weekly, monthly or quarterly and published in Yiddish, Hebrew or English, which represent a wide range of social, political, economic and cultural viewpoints.

Portrait of Harlem

THOUGH always restricted by tradition to certain residential areas, trades and professions, the Negro. has lived and labored in New York for more than three hundred years. He is one of the most vivid figures in the city's history; and in terms of progress and chronology, his continuous adjustment to New York's ever-changing environment, the manner in which he has reacted to the handicaps and penalties imposed upon him because of class and color, make a record of dramatic interest and social challenge.

In 1930, 327,706 Negroes were residents of New York, the largest single concentration of Negro population anywhere in the world. Though Negroes are to be found in all five boroughs of the city, by far the largest number—some 250,000 in all—live in Harlem, an area of Upper Manhattan roughly circumscribed by 155th Street on the north, 110th Street on the south, the Harlem and East Rivers on the east, and Amsterdam Avenue on the west. In addition, the Manhattan area also contains small Negro colonies in Greenwich Village, Chelsea, the East Side, San Juan Hill and Yorkville. Brooklyn has the largest Negro population outside of Manhattan, with more than 68,000 residents centered for the most part in the Stuyvesant Heights and Brownsville sections. Negroes are also scattered in many small settlements throughout Queens, Bronx and Richmond. Before the depression, economic security afforded a few the opportunity to migrate from Harlem to the comparatively luxurious Merrick Park development in Jamaica.

The earliest available records show that 11 Negroes were brought to the settlement of New Amsterdam in 1626 in the capacity of slaves. For nearly one hundred years thereafter, the majority of Negroes in the settlement were either indentured servants or slaves. Under the rule of the Dutch colonists, many Negroes were granted freedom, for the Dutch often did not know what to do with them and a rigorous system of slavery had not yet been established. Though regarded as slaves, Negroes had the right to travel, assemble, marry and own property; and they were also afforded some degree of legal protection. It was not until 1664, when the English conquered the Dutch, that slavery became a profitable, flourishing and oppressive institution modeled upon the slave system of Virginia. In 1694 the colony possessed about 2,170 slaves, and in 1709 open slave-markets were operating in New York. Living for the most part in the center of the city, in Greenwich Village near Spring and Broome Streets, and near the establishments that employed them, most of the Negroes in early New York labored as domestics, chimney sweeps and ship calkers. A few, who had obtained freedom from their masters through determination and frugality, owned small businesses.

The first school for Negroes in New York was opened in 1704 by Elias Neau for the Society for the Propagation of the Gospel in Foreign Parts. It was intended for religious instruction only—as was a school opened in 1760 by several clergymen. The first secular educational institution was the African Free School, organized chiefly by the New York Manumission Society and opened in 1787. Forty-seven years later, when Negro children were transferred to the public school system, there were seven African Free Schools in the city.

An early protest indicating spirit on the part of the Negro population was registered in 1710, when a slave brought suit against his master for wages. Another incident of the Negroes' early struggle for human rights occurred in 1712, when a group of slaves, smarting under a sense of intolerable wrong, met in an orchard in Maiden Lane and planned an insurrection against the whites. Severely suppressed by the militia, the insurrection brought savage retaliation. Out of it, however, grew fear and respect for the Negroes which found expression, on the one hand, in legislation to control them, and on the other, in many attempts to abolish the slave trade.

A much more important insurrectionary event in the colonial period was the plot of 1741. It is clear from available records that this insurrection was planned, and Negroes as well as poor whites took part. The population of New York at that time numbered some 10,000, about one-fifth of whom were Negro slaves; there were also several hundred white indentured servants whose lot was no less harsh. With the outbreak of nine fires in different parts of New York, rumor spread that the slaves were trying to burn the city and murder the entire population. During the ensuing terror, every Negro seen on the streets was arrested. Whites became implicated when a search for stolen goods led to the tavern of John Hughson, whose servant girl was arrested and made to confess knowledge of the insurrection under torture. Her story was so fantastic as to involve all of the Negro population and a considerable portion of the white. A special session of the Grand Jury was held, and the ensuing trial lasted throughout the summer. Public hysteria and panic, intense in New York, spread throughout the country. Of 154 Negroes cast into prison, 13 were burned at the stake, 18 hanged, and 71 transported to the West Indies. Twenty whites were arrested, John Hughson, his wife, and John Ury, an unfrocked Catholic priest, being later executed.

Between 1741 and 1766, increasing numbers of Negroes succeeded in purchasing their freedom. During the Revolution they were accepted for military service by both America and England. New York was one of the few States to reward Negro soldiers with freedom; and in 1799 an act was passed conferring gradual emancipation and ending slavery in the State on July 4, 1827. Free Negroes had the rights of citizens, including the right to vote.

Barred from the professions and most of the trades, Negroes found that whites accepted them more readily as owners of taverns and inns. Samuel Fraunces, a master steward, operated a famous tavern (still standing at Broad and Pearl Streets) where on December 4, 1783, Washington delivered the "Farewell Address" to his army. "Black Sam," as Fraunces was called, owned the "Mason's Arms" on Broadway from 1759 to 1762; and he later purchased the Delancy Mansion—on the site of New York's first hotel—where he conducted an inn known as the "Queen Charlotte."

Fraternal lodges, churches and mutual aid societies began early to play a prominent part in the social and educational life of New York's Negroes. Most of the freedmen belonged to the New York African Society for Mutual Relief, founded in 1808. Negroes made an appeal to the American Odd Fellows for a charter, which was refused. After a special dispensation granted by the English branch, the Philomathean Lodge of the Grand United Order of Odd Fellows was formed in 1843. A fusion of social welfare work with the operation of the Underground Railroad came about through the establishment of the Moral Reform Societies.

One sign of cultural advance manifested itself in 1821 with the establishment of the first Negro theater, at the corner of Mercer and Bleecker Streets. The company gave performances of *Othello* and other Shakespearean dramas. The *National Advocate* of September 21, 1821, reported that James Hewlett was acting his most famous role, that of Richard III. The authorities finally enjoined the company from playing Shakespeare, doubtless because of growing antagonism toward the Negro.

After the abolition of slavery in New York State in 1827, the struggle of the Negroes to improve their status and to help their enslaved brothers in the South changed gradually from intermittent outbursts to a planned movement. The struggle for human rights, equality and liberty which was agitating the minds of men in the post-Revolutionary period had its effect upon the Negro. The latter, having made some cultural progress, began to see his problems in realistic terms and organized accordingly.

A number of New York Negroes were ardent and prominent workers in the abolitionist cause. In 1827, nearly four years before the appearance of William Lloyd Garrison's *Liberator,* a group gathered in the home of M. Boston Crummell and launched the first Negro newspaper in America, *Freedom's Journal,* under the editorship of John Russwurm and the Rev. Samuel E. Cornish. This journal not only helped to shape the ideas of Negroes on the burning question of slavery, but also appealed to many anti-slavery whites and influenced the policies of the abolition societies that were organized soon after.

In 1830, Peter Williams published an eloquent protest against racial discrimination in New York City. Theodore S. Wright, a graduate of Princeton, also wrote on the subject with vigor and logic. David Ruggles published *The Genius of Freedom,* a quarterly magazine called *The Mirror of Liberty,* and several sardonic anti-slavery pamphlets under such titles as "The Extinguisher Extinguished" and "An Antidote for a Poisonous Combination Recently Prepared by a 'Citizen of New York' *Alias* Dr. Reese." Ruggles was one of the first promoters of the Underground Railroad in New York, officially termed the Vigilance Committee, and he was later connected with the New York Reform Society. By means of the "Underground," he is said to have aided 600 fugitive slaves to freedom. One of these, destined to become much more famous than his benefactor, was Frederick Douglass, who in 1838 was sheltered in Ruggles' home at the corner of Church and Lispenard Streets.

Other Negro leaders in the struggle for human rights were Henry Highland Garnett, preacher, orator and pamphleteer, who issued the first call for a general strike among the slaves; Samuel Ringgold Ward, son of fugitive parents, one of the most effective lecturers for the Anti-Slavery Society; J. W. C. Pennington, who in 1841 wrote *A Text Book of the Origin and History of the Colored People,* a pioneer contribution on this subject; James McCune Smith and Charles Bennett Ray, who published the weekly *Colored American;* and Alexander Crummell, son of M. Boston Crummell, who became a prominent scholar and agitator against slavery. Well known in anti-slavery circles were two Negro women—Harriet Tubman, who brought slaves out of the border states and worked as well in western New York, and Sojourner Truth, who took part not only in the anti-slavery struggle but in the woman's suffrage movement.

White abolitionists worked side by side with their Negro comrades in Underground Railroad service and in propaganda activities. Important among these were James Birney, who freed his slaves in Kentucky and became secretary of the American Anti-Slavery Society in New York; Horace Greeley, editor of the New York *Tribune;* Richard Hildreth, historian and author of the first anti-slavery novel; Charles A. Dana, editor of the New York *Sun;* Sydney Howard Gay, who conducted the *Anti-Slavery Standard* and was an effective "underground" agent; William and John Jay, two jurists who by their anti-slavery services nobly upheld an eminent name; Theodore Weld, one of the most devoted workers in the Anti-Slavery Society; Angelina Grimke of South Carolina, a forceful speaker at the women's anti-slavery auxiliaries in New York City; and the Tappan brothers, Arthur and Lewis, prominent merchants and philanthropists.

But the Negroes' economic and educational progress was checked in 1850 by the enactment of the Fugitive Slave Law, and many of the anti-slavery leaders fled to Canada and Europe to escape being subjected again to bondage. Though there existed in New York no definite laws restricting Negroes, the general attitude was so strongly pro-southern that prejudice acted in place of law. Anti-abolitionist feeling grew rapidly, in spite of efforts of the churches and the Anti-Slavery Society.

At a time when slave rescues were common throughout the North, New Yorkers were sending fugitives back to the South. The debts of southern planters to New York merchants, the pro-slavery influence of Governor Horatio Seymour, the increasing antagonism between the slaves and the newly arrived immigrants—these factors served to intensify anti-Negro feeling up to the very brink of the Civil War. As the war progressed, anti-abolitionist feeling heightened in New York, and during the early part of the conflict the army refused to enlist Negro troops. When emancipation was proclaimed as a war measure in 1863, the bitterness grew. In spite of this, however, Lincoln authorized the recruiting of Negroes.

The draft law of 1863 created such resentment that a three-day riot followed the first efforts to enforce it. During the riots hundreds of Negroes were killed or badly beaten. Business stopped, and mobs controlled the city. The Colored Orphan Asylum on Fifth Avenue was burned. Conditions became so appalling that the Merchants' Committee had to grant relief to nearly 11,000 Negroes.

After the war, the nation centered its attention upon the ex-slaves of the South, and the problems of northern freedmen were more or less neglected. Many of the New York leaders went South to work among their freed brothers. Frederick Douglass moved to Washington in 1869. The failure of New York State to ratify the 15th Amendment caused many northern Negroes to realize that emancipation was but a first step toward freedom.

Business establishments conducted by Negroes became fairly common in New York during the last two decades of the 19th century. Hotels, restaurants, "honky-tonks," saloons, professional clubs and small stores were opened. In 1881, the Nail brothers operated a well-known restaurant and billiard parlor at 450 Sixth Avenue. Jockey Isaac Murphy, three times winner of the Kentucky Derby, Pike Barnes, winner of the 1888 Futurity, the pugilist Joe Gans, and many other Negro celebrities of turf and ring were patrons of this resort.

The fields of amusement and personal service offered the Negro his most promising opportunities for advancement. Ford Dabney led the singing Clef Club orchestra at Ziegfeld's Roof Garden; Williams and Walker, Cole and Johnson, and Ada Overton were notable successes in New York and London. *Oriental America,* with an all-Negro cast, opened at Palmer's in 1896, displaying the talents of Sidney Woodward, Inez Clough, William C. Elkins and J. Rosamond Johnson, all of whom were destined for stardom in the years to come. Will Marion Cook's *Clorindy,* with lyrics by Paul Laurence Dunbar, starred Ernest Hogan at the Casino Roof Garden. Although minstrelsy was originated by white actors in the 1830's, it was in this field that the Negro distinguished himself most highly and made an indubitable contribution to the American theater.

One of the worst of Manhattan's several race riots occurred in August 1900, following a quarrel between a Negro and a white man in which the latter was killed. Negroes were seized and beaten throughout the city, with policemen often assisting in the assaults. In the following year, more than a hundred Negroes were lynched throughout the United States. The response of Negro leadership was immediate and impassioned. W. E. B. Du Bois wrote *The Souls of Black Folk,* a sensitive interpretation of the Negroes' plight at the beginning of the 20th century. The book proved a turning point in the history of Negro thought, and had a tremendous influence upon the Negroes of New York. In it, Du Bois took sharp issue with the philosophy of Booker T. Washington, who at that time was the recognized leader of his race.

Growth of Negro leadership during the early years of this century was evidenced by the organization of business men's leagues, in New York and other large cities, by Fred R. Moore, editor of the weekly *Colored American*. But while the Negro middle class was developing measures of organization and self-protection, the larger part of New York's Negro population, numbering some 60,000 in 1901, was excluded from trade unions, and Negro workers had to compete for jobs with newly-arrived immigrants at unequal odds.

For several decades after the Civil War, most of New York's well-to-do Negroes enjoyed a fairly stable community life in Brooklyn. But on Manhattan Island, where the poorer class predominated, the Negro population was scattered and shifting, though with its largest numbers in the blighted areas of the lower West Side. Moving slowly northward as the city expanded in that direction, the chief center of Negro population was by 1900 in the region of West Fifty-Third Street and the neighboring San Juan Hill district. But it was not long before the region became so congested that many Negroes were seeking homes still further north.

At this time, scores of modern apartment houses that had been built in Harlem for white tenants were largely empty, owing to a lack of adequate transportation facilities. Philip A. Payton, a shrewd and enterprising Negro realtor, persuaded the owners of one or two buildings on 134th Street to fill them with Negro tenants. Before long, other buildings were taken over and filled. This invasion, as it was termed by white residents of Harlem, evoked an organized social and economic war. As though they were fighting plague carriers, the Hudson Realty Company, acting for white property owners, purchased all West Side property owned or rented by Negroes and evicted the tenants. Payton, with J. B. Nail, Sr., in retaliation organized the Afro-American Realty Company, which purchased buildings occupied by white tenants and in turn evicted them. Also St. Philip's Episcopal Church, one of the oldest and wealthiest Negro churches in New York, purchased 13 apartment houses on West 135th Street, and rented them to Negroes.

The white tenants gave way, and block after block of apartment houses stood deserted. Reluctantly, the landlords leased them to Negroes. As the years passed, the "black blocks" spread and the present "city within a city" took form. The migration to Harlem was immensely augmented by the large-scale influx of southern Negroes who came North during the World War in search of higher wages. At the end of the war, the Negro population of New York was estimated to be four times greater than when the movement to Harlem began.

But after the larger part of New York's Negro population had settled in Harlem, owners of apartments elsewhere refused to rent them to Negroes; consequently, rents in the highly congested Harlem area are often twice as much as in other comparable sections of the city. This district's density of population and the extremely high rentals have created alarming conditions. In 1935 it was found that as many as 3,871 Negroes lived in a single city block, and that many families were paying half or more of their incomes for shelter. Eighty-four percent of the residential buildings are from 20 to 34 years old. These conditions account in some part for a death-rate that has reached 15.5 per thousand. Early in 1934, exasperated tenants organized the Consolidated Tenants' League to combat high rents and improve living conditions. The Federal-built Harlem River Houses, a Public Works Administration project accommodating 527 families, has shown the way to better things although it has accomplished little in relieving the congestion of Harlem's wide-spread slums.

But not all of Harlem is slum area. Scattered throughout the district are many well-built homes. The section on 138th and 139th Streets between Seventh and Eighth Avenues is known locally as "Strivers' Row," because so many middle-class Negroes desire to live there; and "Sugar Hill," on upper Edgecombe and St. Nicholas Avenues, possesses the newest and tallest apartment buildings in Harlem, as well as many fine private homes.

The Negro's restriction to certain trades and professions has made him particularly vulnerable to suffering during times of depression. As early as 1910, when Negroes comprised less than two percent of the city's population, the majority were employed in domestic service. The labor shortage caused by the World War, however, enabled a few to enter the fields of transportation, mechanics and manufacture. When the depression struck in 1929, many actors, musicians, messengers, porters and domestic servants were thrown out of work. The extent to which Negro income depends upon domestic employment is evidenced by the fact that more than 85 percent of employed Negro women are in domestic and personal service. Though today they account for only a little more than five percent of the city's population, Negroes comprise more than 20 percent of the total number of persons on relief rolls.

Although Harlem is the largest Negro community in the world, most of its restaurants, hotels, saloons and retail shops are owned by Greeks, Germans, Jews, Italians, Irish, and other white groups. In business, more than in any other field, the Harlem Negro has shown a lack of initiative that puts Harlem in sharp contrast with many Negro communities throughout the country. Negro boys and girls are rarely employed as clerks in Harlem stores, but work downtown as maids, porters, elevator and errand boys. Most of Harlem's Negro-owned businesses are in the field of personal service. The community contains more than 2,000 Negro barber shops and "beauty parlors." On the other hand, Harlem has proved a haven for the professional class, which numbers about 5,000. Physicians and dentists are especially numerous.

Catering to the inner man is one of Harlem's chief industries, and eating-places are to be found everywhere throughout the district. These range from tiny Negro-owned restaurants in private homes and basements to large chain-cafeterias controlled by white capital and the cafes and cabarets that play a prominent part in New York's night life. Prominent in this field are Father Divine's 15 restaurants, where a meal featuring chicken or chops is served for 15 cents.

During the Prohibition era, many of the Negro-owned saloons passed into Italian hands, and remained open in spite of the law. Most of Harlem's saloons are still Italian-owned; but some of the better known taprooms and cabarets are conducted by Negroes.

Playing the central role in the life of the Harlem Negro is not the cabaret or cafe, as is commonly supposed, but the church. Thousands of the early southern migrants met for religious services in apartments and homes. Later they purchased the existing churches of white Baptists, Methodists, Episcopalians and Presbyterians in the Harlem region. The actual surrender of a white church to Negroes was done with something approaching ritual: a joint service would be held at which the out-going white congregation would welcome the in-coming black.

It is difficult to say which is the more numerous of Harlem's two largest religious sects, the Baptists or the Divinists. The Baptists have the largest churches, such as the Abyssinia and Mt. Olivet, but it is possible that Father Divine has more followers in his many "Heavens" throughout the city. There are two general types of churches in Harlem: the conventional, which embraces the long-established organizations, including the Methodist, Baptist, Episcopalian, Presbyterian, Congregationalist; and the unconventional, consisting of the tabernacles of "prophets," the "storefront" meeting places, the synagogues of Black Jews, and the houses of various sects and cults. The "Church of the Believers of the Commandments" may be across the street from a Daddy Grace "House of Prayer." The "Metaphysical Church of Divine Investigation" may be a few doors from the Black Jews' "Commandment Keepers." Add to these the Moorish Temples, Sister Josephine Becton's churches, the tabernacles of Prophet Costonie, the "Heavens" of Father Divine, and the sanctuaries of Mother Horne, and some conception of Harlem's many diverse religions and cults may be had.

Because of its highly sensitive social and political temper, Harlem has been termed the "focal point in the struggle for the liberation of the Negro people." It was but natural that the long effort to free the Scottsboro boys should begin in Harlem, and the greatest demonstration in connection with the release of four of them occurred when thousands of Negroes jammed the Pennsylvania Station to welcome them to New York. During Italy's invasion of Ethiopia, anything concerning Italy on the movie screen brought forth immediate hisses and catcalls. In the consciousness of this oppressed community, current events are commonly interpreted as gains or set-backs for the Negro people. This social restlessness results in many public demonstrations. Harlemites in increasing numbers attend street meetings protesting evictions; picket stores to compel the hiring of Negroes, or WPA offices to indicate disapproval of cuts in pay or personnel; parade against the subjection of colonial peoples, or to celebrate some new civic improvement; and march many miles in May Day demonstrations.

Harlem's peculiar susceptibility to social and political propaganda is well illustrated in the case of Marcus Garvey, a West Indian, who for a few years in the early 1920's was known as "provisional President of Africa." He advocated the establishment of a Black Republic in Africa, and preached racial chauvinism. As head of the Universal Negro Improvement Association, Garvey was the first Negro leader in America to capture the imagination of the masses, and no one else has so stirred the race consciousness of the Negroes in New York and elsewhere. The Negro World, once powerful organ of his Universal Negro Improvement Association, attracted such contributors as Edgar Grey, Hubert Harrison and William Ferris to its pages. Garvey's financial manipulations in connection with his steamship company, the Black Star Line, led to his downfall. He was indicted by the Federal Government for using the mails to defraud, served a term in the Atlanta penitentiary, and was later deported.

The most serious rioting that Harlem has known occurred in the spring of 1935, at a time when many of the white-owned business establishments on West 125th Street were being boycotted for their refusal to employ Negroes. A leading figure in the attendant agitation was a person calling himself Sufi Abdul Hamid, who in gaudy Egyptian uniform preached anti-Semitism on the street corners and was regarded by Harlem's Jewish merchants as a "Black Hitler." On March 19 a Negro boy was caught stealing in one of the boycotted stores. Rumors immediately spread throughout Harlem that the boy had been beaten and killed by the white proprietor; large crowds gathered in and near West 125th Street, and in spite of police efforts an orgy of window-smashing and store-looting followed. As emphasized in the report of an investigating committee appointed by Mayor La Guardia, the outbreak had its fundamental causes in the terrible economic and social conditions prevailing in Harlem at the time.

When the Federal Emergency Relief Administration began operations, it found a majority of Harlem's population on the verge of starvation, as a result of the depression and of an intensified discrimination that made it all but impossible for Negroes to find employment. Landlords, knowing that their tenants could not move to other neighborhoods, had raised rents exorbitantly, and wholesale evictions followed. The FERA, with its successors the Civil Works Administration and the Works Progress Administration, brought a new lease on life to Harlem's underprivileged. WPA's monthly checks constitute a considerable part of the community life-blood, and white storekeepers are quick to join with Negro relief workers in protesting against any threats to their jobs. Today one notes a very decided lessening of the dangerous tension that pervaded Harlem in the dark winters of 1934 and 1935.

Although New York had had a few scattered Negro writers before that time, what is sometimes termed the "literary renaissance" of Harlem dates from about 1925. The movement was in large part initiated by the publication of the *Survey Graphic's* special "Harlem Number" and of Alain Locke's interpretative anthology entitled *The New Negro*. A host of young writers made their appearance in the middle and late 1920's, among them Walter White, Eric Walrond, Rudolph Fisher, Jean Toomer, Claude McKay, Countee Cullen, Langston Hughes, Wallace Thurman, Jessie Fauset, Nella Larsen, Zora Neale Hurston, George Schuyler and Arna Bontemps. Confined almost exclusively to Harlem, this literary movement was notable in that for the first time the American Negro depicted his own life with a wide and varied range of talent and feeling. For a few years Negro writers created more than they ever have before or since that period. Joyce's *Ulysses* influenced some of them; and even the gospel of Gertrude

Stein claimed a number of Negro adherents. Some members of the movement were apotheosized in Carl Van Vechten's *Nigger Heaven*, a novel that New York read with avidity. The poetry of McKay, Cullen and Hughes expressed in new rhythms and beauty and vigor the bitterness and despair of Negro life in America. Toomer, in *Cane*, sounded a new and lyric note in American prose; and Walter White, in *The Fire in the Flint* and *Flight*, dealt with the Negro's struggle in both South and North against the barriers of color. Jessie Fauset, Nella Larsen and Claude McKay frequently depicted Harlem life in their novels. James Weldon Johnson, long a Harlem resident, and later a professor at Fisk and New York Universities, elaborated in *Black Manhattan* the description of Harlem that was a prominent feature of his earlier *Autobiography of an Ex-Colored Man*. Rudolph Fisher, Wallace Thurman, George Schuyler and W. E. B. Du Bois wove fantasy and satire into their descriptions of Negro life. With the beginning of the national depression in 1929, the movement largely disintegrated.

Among the Negro artists of Harlem are Augusta Savage, Aaron Douglas, Richmond Barthe, Charles Alston, E. Sims Campbell, Vertis Hayes, Bruce Nugent, Henry W. Barnham, Sara Murrell, Romare Beardon, Robert Savon Pious, and Beauford Delaney. Of these Aaron Douglas, painter and mural artist, Richmond Barthe, sculptor, Augusta Savage, sculptress, and E. Sims Campbell, painter and cartoonist, are the most prominent. Many Negro artists are employed on the Federal Art Project, under whose direction they have executed murals for the new wing of the Harlem Municipal Hospital. Harlem now boasts of 15 art centers, in churches, the Y.M.C.A., the Y.W.C.A., and neighborhood houses, where classes are conducted in painting, ceramics, carving and sculpture. Best known for its exhibitions is the Uptown Art Laboratory. The Federal Art Project in New York has discovered an immense amount of latent artistic talent among the Negro children of Harlem.

Until very recently the doors of the American theater have not been open to the Negro playwright, who has therefore had no opportunity to master the technique of the stage. Only in rare instances have producers presented plays written by Negroes. Willis Richardson's one-act plays were produced in some of the little and commercial theaters; and in 1925, Garland Anderson's *Appearances* ran in the Frolic Theatre. Wallace Thurman collaborated on *Lulu Belle* and *Harlem*, both well known on Broadway. In 1937, Langston Hughes entered the field of the drama with his *Mulatto*. The Krigwa Players were pioneers in the little theater movement.

Today Harlem's thespians are for the most part associated with the New Theater League and the Federal Theatre Project.

Prominent among those plays written by whites in which Negro actors have had an opportunity to depict the lives of their people are Eugene O'Neill's *The Emperor Jones* and *All God's Chillun Got Wings*, produced in 1920 and 1924; Edward Sheldon and Charles MacArthur's *Lulu Belle*, which opened in New York in 1926; Paul Green's Pulitzer Prize play, *In Abraham's Bosom*, produced in 1926 at the Provincetown Playhouse; Marc Connelly's *The Green Pastures*, which started in 1929 on its long career of sensational success; and Paul Peters' and George Sklar's *Stevedore*, first presented in 1930.

New York, like Boston, Philadelphia and Chicago, has its celebrated music schools and opportunities for musical expression, which have always attracted Negro artists. The successes of Hall Johnson, Roland Hayes, Paul Robeson, Jules Bledsoe and Marian Anderson are nationally known. Many of Harlem's Negro musical artists are now associated with the Federal Music Project.

Of all the popular personalities whom Harlem has shared with America, Bill "Bojangles" Robinson has evoked the most lasting and genuine affection. As the world's ace tap dancer, he has appeared on the stage or screen of every city and town in this country, and has earned a reputation as a philanthropist in his private life. In 1934, he was elected "unofficial mayor" of Harlem.

By adoption, Harlem claims the Negro show girl, Josephine Baker, who came out of the slums of St. Louis and earned the title of "Empress Josephine" during her stay in Paris in 1931 with the "Dixie Steppers," a company that had begun by touring the South in a series of one-night stands. She became a European celebrity as star of the Folies Bergère, and married Count Pepito De Albertini.

The late Richard B. Harrison, whose theatrical career knew only one role, made his debut at the age of 66 and achieved the greatest fame of any Negro actor. His life was closely bound up with "De Lawd" of Marc Connelly's play, *The Green Pastures,* and little is recorded of his earlier career. When the play was awarded the Pulitzer Prize in 1930, Lieutenant Governor Herbert Lehman presented "De Lawd" with the Spingarn medal at the Mansfield Theater before an enthusiastic audience. In 1936, the entire nation mourned the death of the man who "brought God to Broadway."

Florence Mills, who ranks as one of America's greatest musical comedy stars, came to New York after a Chicago cabaret career, and was featured by Paul Slavin at the Plantation Cafe. She made her first Broadway appearance in the popular *Shuffle Along,* and achieved her first European triumph in *Dixie to Broadway.* She died in 1927, shortly after a successful European tour in *Blackbirds.*

Paul Robeson, a graduate of Rutgers College who achieved national reputation in his student days as a football star, made his first appearance on the professional stage in Mary Hoyt Wiborg's *Taboo.* Later he replaced Charles Gilpin in *Roseanne,* and in 1924 he became a national figure in the American theater by starring in Eugene O'Neill's *All God's Chillun Got Wings.* After appearing in *Show Boat* in London, he played the title role of O'Neill's *Emperor Jones* in Berlin in 1930. In 1926 he appeared as the star of Jim Tully's *Black Boy.* He has sung and acted throughout Europe, has played prominent roles in many motion pictures, and is the outstanding Negro actor of today.

Though Negroes are considered to be an exceptionally musical people, Harlem's general interest in music is largely limited to those popular jazz orchestras that originated within its boundaries. Some of the greatest of Negro bands—Will Vodery's, Leroy Smith's, Duke Ellington's and Fletcher Henderson's—acquired their initial fame in downtown New York. It was through their often startling innovations in jazz and swing music that Negro orchestra leaders held sway. Whether it was jazz as it was "jazzed" by Cab Calloway in the 1920's, or swing as it was "swung" by Jimmie Lunceford in the 1930's, the white popular jazz and swing orchestras took most of their cues from Harlem orchestras and their Negro leaders. Most of the prominent Negro bands have reached a large public through their phonograph recordings, and Negro band-members are protected by the powerful Local 802 of the American Federation of Musicians, affiliated with the American Federation of Labor—though there are evidences of discrimination against Negroes in the matter of wages.

Harlem's boast that it is an area where new dance steps are created is indisputable. Just who initiated the "truck" is not known. Cora La Redd of the Cotton Club, "Rubber Legs" Williams, Chuck Robinson, and Bilo and Ashes have all put forward their individual claims. It is interesting to note that there are many kinds of "trucking,"—the "picket's truck," the "politician's truck," the "Park Avenue truck," the "Mae West truck," and the "Hitler truck." Among other contemporary Harlem dances is the "shimsham," a time-step featuring the "break" with a momentary pause; and the "razzle-dazzle," which involves a rhythmic clapping of hands and a rolling of hips. The riotous "Lindy Hop" is a flying dance done by couples in which a girl is thrown away in the midst of a lightning two-step, then rudely snatched back to be subjected to a series of twists, jerks, dips and scrambles. All of these and many more can be seen in Harlem's dance halls, at house parties, on beaches, and in the streets in summer to the tune of WPA Music Project bands.

There is but one legitimate theater in Harlem, the Lafayette, upon whose stage the greater part of Harlem's theatrical tradition was made. For years the Lafayette was the home of the Lafayette Stock Company; and together with the Lincoln Theater, home of the Anita Bush Company, it catered to Harlem's smart set. Andrew Bishop, Inez Clough, Rose McClendon, Abbie Mitchell, Anita Bush, Laura Bowman and Leigh Whipper were among the most popular of Harlem's matinee idols.

Gradually the Lafayette's legitimate drama gave way to vaudeville, movies replaced vaudeville, and finally in 1935 the house closed its doors altogether. In 1936, the Federal Theatre, working with a Negro cast, opened the Lafayette again to legitimate drama, producing Frank Wilson's *Walk Together Chillun*, Rudolph Fisher's *The Conjure Man Dies*, and Orson Welles' production of *Macbeth*, which attracted national attention because of its Haitian locale and unusual interpretation by Negro actors. *Macbeth* was followed by Gus Smith's and Peter Morrell's *Turpentine*, Carlton Moss's adaptation of Obey's *Noah*, George Kelly's *The Show Off*, George McEntee's *The Case of Phillip Lawrence*, Dorothy Hailpern's *Horse Play*, four of Eugene O'Neill's one-act plays of the sea, and William Du Bois' *Haiti*.

A number of prominent motion picture actors have come from or been associated with Harlem—notably Bill "Bojangles" Robinson, who has ap-peared with Will Rogers, Shirley Temple, and other screen favorites. Be-ginning in 1910, before the industry moved to Hollywood, West Jenkins appeared in many pictures over a period of years. The cast for King Vid-or's *Hallelujah* was entirely recruited and organized in Harlem, then trans-ported to Los Angeles. Nina Mae McKinney, star of the picture, was a Harlem chorus girl. The first effort of Negroes to produce their own pic-tures was made by the Micheaux Corporation of Harlem, which has more than 30 pictures to its credit.

Negroes have participated in sports and athletics in New York since 1800. Tom Molyneaux, a Negro ex-slave who became champion boxer in 1809, made the old Catherine Market his headquarters. Almost all the Negro boxing champions and near champions—Joe Jeanette, Sam Lang-ford, Joe Gans, Tiger Flowers, Battling Siki, Jack Johnson, Harry Wills, and Kid Chocolate—lived for most of their fighting careers in New York. Canada Lee, now an actor, and Buddy Saunders were born in New York. Joe Louis, the present heavyweight champion, is an adopted citizen of Harlem.

The most popular of Harlem sports is basketball, and during the long season various expert Negro teams, among them the famous Renaissance quintet, provide entertainment for many thousands. The sporting consciousness of Harlem is evidenced by the huge Negro attendance at baseball games in the Yankee Stadium and at the Polo Grounds. Thousands acclaimed John Woodruff, Jesse Owens, Eulace Peacock and Cornelius Johnson when they broke world records at the new Randall's Island Stadium; and other Negroes have been prominent in New York track meets from the days of Howard Drew down to Ben Johnson. Bicycling and horseback riding are popular among the theatrical and sporting sets, while golf is played to some extent. Cricket is popular among the West Indians, who are so adept that they meet many of the world's leading teams.

For the most part, Harlem gains its knowledge of current events in the outside world from the Negro weeklies of New York and other large cities rather than from the metropolitan dailies. The leading Negro weeklies published in New York are the *New York Age,* a Republican journal which under this and various other names has appeared continuously since 1880; the *Amsterdam News,* a supporter of the New Deal; and the *New York News,* which is widely read among Father Divine's followers.

Harlem's best known and most widely used library is the 135th Street branch of the New York Public Library, which houses the famous Schomburg Collection of material relating to Negro life. This collection is the result of 30 years of research by Arthur Schomburg in the United States, Central and South America, the West Indies, Haiti and Europe. It comprises more than 8,000 volumes and 1,500 manuscripts, numerous engravings and specimens of primitive African art.

The community's facilities for public education are woefully inadequate. Although the population of Harlem has more than tripled since the World War, not one new school building was constructed in this region during the post-war period until 1937. Many of the buildings are antiquated firetraps, without playgrounds or auditoriums. In one school, lunch is served to 1,000 children in a room designed to seat only 175. There are no specialized or nursery schools, and because of discriminatory zoning Negro students are not permitted to attend newer and better-equipped schools in adjacent areas. According to Mayor La Guardia's Commission on Conditions in Harlem, one of the contributing factors in connection with the rioting of March 1935 was the deplorable conditions prevailing in the public schools.

Harlem's importance in New York politics has grown along with its increase in population. In 1897, Tammany Hall gained dominance over the Negro vote through "Chief" Lee, a noted Negro leader, and until recently it has retained control by dispensing political patronage. Of the nine Negroes elected as New York aldermen, seven have been Democrats and two Republicans. But because of the depression, increasing economic and racial discrimination, displacement in jobs, and the rise of workers' organizations, thousands of Negro voters have deserted the two older parties to join or support the Labor, Socialist, or Communist groups.

In 1920, Harlem elected its first Negro alderman, George Harris, an Independent Republican. To maintain its prestige among the Negroes, Tammany in the following election ran a Negro candidate for alderman, and regularly since then Harlem has been represented in the Board of Aldermen. When the Tenth Municipal District was created in 1930, two Negro attorneys, James S. Watson and Charles E. Toney, were elected judges. The recent appointments of Myles A. Paige as city magistrate, of Hubert Delany as commissioner of taxes and assessments, and of Eunice Hunton Carter and Ellis Rivers to District Attorney Dewey's staff have placed Negroes in new and important fields of public service.

Legally, there is no racial discrimination in New York. Negroes were not excluded from or segregated in vaudeville and legitimate theaters until the early 1920's. Some New York theaters practice discrimination by refusing to sell tickets to Negroes or by maintaining that all seats are sold; others admit Negroes only to certain sections of the house. Except for some of the "little cinemas," there has never been discrimination on the part of motion picture houses.

Twenty years ago only Negroes of unusual distinction would dare to ask for accommodations in downtown hotels. Gradually, however, the larger hotels have become much more liberal in this respect. But discrimination in restaurants is still common. Of late, law suits have compelled many restaurants to alter their policy, and today a Negro can eat in many downtown restaurants without being asked to sit behind a screen or without finding that a cup of salt has been stirred into his soup. In some sections of Harlem itself there are bars and cafes that discriminate against Negroes;

and the windows of many rooming-houses carry the familiar southern sign: "For White Only."

Present-day Negro organizations, both national and local, represent many varying schools of thought. Some advocate amalgamation, passive resistance, colonization, salvation through "art and joy"; others favor collective political and economic action on the part of white and black. The National Association for the Advancement of Colored People was organized in May 1909, and in the following year Dr. W. E. B. Du Bois became its director of publicity and research and editor of its national organ, *The Crisis*. In his words, the aim of the Association was to create "an organization so effective and so powerful that when discrimination and injustice touched one Negro, it would touch 12,000,000 . . . an organization that would work ceaselessly to make Americans know that the so-called 'Negro problem' is simply one phase of the vaster problem of democracy in America, and that those who wish freedom and justice for their country must wish it for every black citizen." The Association's militant legal struggle against segregation and for civil rights and its long fight against lynching are now known throughout the country. In 1931, James Weldon Johnson resigned as executive secretary of the Association and was succeeded by Walter White.

To assist the thousands of southern migrants coming into the city, and to make investigations into social conditions among Negroes, the National Urban League was organized in 1911. Under its auspices many of the Negro professional social workers in New York have received their training; and through its Industrial Department it has aided thousands of unskilled Negroes to equip themselves with trades. More than any other social agency, the League has fought for a better community life among Negroes, better housing conditions, and against crime, disease and unemployment. Its official organ, *Opportunity Magazine*, edited by Elmer A. Carter, interprets the changing social and economic scene for the American Negro. The New York Urban League was organized in 1918 as a separate and distinct branch of the national League. Besides maintaining a playground and a summer camp for Negro children, it has helped to form and guide several WPA projects. The League has emphasized its fundamental concern in securing better working conditions for Negroes, exposing unfair labor practices, fostering unionism and aiding in the education of workers in the lower and unskilled ranks.

The youngest and largest of the mass organizations devoted to the social, economic and political equality of the Negro is the National Negro Congress, a federation of Negro organizations which attempts to unify the activities of all groups, particularly trade unions. The Congress is wide in scope and purpose, and active in the prosecution of its aims. It has held two national meetings, one in Chicago in 1935, the other in Philadelphia in 1937.

Since the founding of the New York African Society for Mutual Relief more than a hundred years ago, Negro fraternal societies have increased so rapidly that they now comprise the greater number of organizations among the Negroes of Harlem. They are motivated by the need for mutual aid and companionship. There are Negro Elk, Odd Fellow, Mason, Pythian, Woodmen and Philomathean lodges, whose large membership makes possible the maintenance of mountain homes, bands, athletic leagues and summer camps, along with various other activities.

The Young Men's and Women's Christian Associations in Harlem differ little from the white Associations throughout the country. They are cultural centers, meeting places, educational institutions, as well as centers for sports and recreation. The buildings of both organizations were built recently and are imposing structures, designed to serve the manifold interests of thousands of youths and adults. The forums and debates held here often emphasize the economic plight of the Negro.

Perhaps the strongest of Negro organizations in Harlem are the trade unions. The Brotherhood of Sleeping Car Porters, with a national membership of more than 6,000, maintains elaborate headquarters under the leadership of its president, A. Philip Randolph. In 1929 the Brotherhood affiliated with the American Federation of Labor, and in 1936 it was accorded an international charter. Since the depression and the inception of the Committee for Industrial Organization, there is hardly a trade or profession in Harlem that is not organized. Barbers, clerks, laundry workers, newspapermen, bartenders, teachers and domestic workers have all formed unions for mutual protection. Most of these unions are affiliated with the Negro Labor Committee, a representative central body that gives common guidance to Harlem's trade union activities. The problems of the unemployed are dealt with chiefly through the Workers' Alliance, which maintains several branches in this area.

Harlem is the home of one of the outstanding units of the New York National Guard, the 369th Infantry, organized in 1913 as the 15th Regiment of State militia. These Negro troops were under fire for 191 days on the western front during the World War, and were the first Americans to reach the Rhine. On December 13, 1918, they received from the

French Government a collective citation for conspicuous valor, and the *Croix de Guerre* was pinned to the regimental colors.

The question of what will ultimately happen to the Negro in New York is bound up with the question of what will happen to the Negro in America. It has been said that the Negro embodies the "romance of American life"; if that is true, the romance is one whose glamor is overlaid with shadows of tragic premonition.

The Local Vernacular

PRODUCT of scores of nationalities, thousands of occupations and millions of people in necessary and constant contact, of whom some never leave the city while others come and go in a day, the New York language reflects every facet of a multifarious environment: the clatter of riveting-guns, the sighs of the weary, the shrill warnings of policemen's whistles, the sunny chatter of perambulating nursemaids, the jittery laconisms of waiters, countermen, cabbies, musicians, busboys on the run, doctors, lawyers, nurses, thieves and radio entertainers. To suggest the quality of this ever-bubbling linguistic amalgam and to give some indication of its hows and whys is the intention of this brief survey. A few of the more representative words and phrases have been selected as examples in each category.

At the outset the reader should be assured that the New York language is no strange cacophony of foreign tongues intelligible to trained linguists only. Full of Americanisms now standardized by wide currency (*nertz*, *baloney*, *in your hat*, *wise guy*, etc.), and containing expressions which originated in other sections of the country (*yippee*, *yowzuh*, *you bet*, *whoopee*, etc.), the town's talk reflects the alertness of its writers, entertainers and everyday folk in picking up colorful new expressions irrespective of origin. Foreign influences emanating from the last half century's great immigration streams seem definitely on the wane, judging by the 1930 census, which places nearly two-thirds of the total white population in the native-born column. Furthermore, according to the best authorities, the presumable importance of the foreign influence on language in New York has been neither well established nor accurately measured.

Professors William Cabell Greet of Columbia University, Margaret Schlauch of New York University and Robert Sonkin and David Driscoll of Brooklyn College all agree as to the difficulty of placing definite carryover tendencies in the speech of recorded subjects, though Driscoll points out the emphasized articulation of the so-called "dental consonants"—

"d," "ts," "z," "sh," "ch" and "n"—as indicating foreign influence. But since phonetics as the study of speech sounds bears a somewhat ambiguous relation to semantics as the study of word-meanings we may mini mize this evidence, especially if we grant that language as communication-activity reflects, in its way, the total environment of which it is a part. Most of the existing foreign language influences, among which Yiddish probably ranks first in the number of carryovers, have been more or less thoroughly assimilated. Witness *kosher* (literally, sanctioned by Jewish law, but extended to mean genuine, *straight goods, the real McCoy;* a *right gee* or *guy*); *kibitzer* (an unwelcome adviser, one who intrudes); *shikse* (a Gentile girl); *schnorrer* (a beggar, also a haggler over small things, a picayune *chiseler*); *schlemiel* (a gentle fool); *schmegeggie* (a stupid person); *nebach* (term of condescending affection for a weakling); *shiker* (a drunkard); *mazuma* (money, the *dough,* the *chips*); *meshuggah* (crazy); *pfui* (an exclamation of disgust or contempt); *schlepper* (a *poor slob,* also a customer who doesn't buy); *kishkes* (literally intestines, tripe, but expanded to the Hemingway sense of *guts,* basic courage) and *mazzaltov* (congratulations, best wishes).

The League of Nations vocabulary of food—*shaslik* (segments of lamb broiled on a skewer, Russian style, sometimes with vegetables); *blintzes* (fried rolls containing cheese or meat, etc.'); *bouillabaisse* (the fish chowder of Marseilles); *ravioli* (small flat dumplings filled with chopped meat or sausage); *smörgasbord* (Swedish *hors d'oeuvres*)—has long been a part of the city's cosmopolitan language. Idiomatic expressions of foreign derivation, such as the droll *He should have stood in bed* (it would have been better for him if he had never got into this situation) and the hortatory *Poosh 'em opp!* (a call to action in the sense of *Get going! Get rolling! Let's see you go in there now!*), are definitely limited in usage.

If we align the 1933 U. S. Census Bureau estimate of population (7,-154,300) with figures for the combined average circulation of the city's English-language newspapers for the six-months' period ending September 30, 1935 (weekday, 4,663,283; Sunday, 5,862,823), we shall get some indication of the heat turned on under the melting pot of speech. Trains, buses, automobiles and planes have telescoped the wide-open spaces, so that people from all regions of the country now come to New York and leave their impress. It is estimated that no fewer than 50 million persons visit New York yearly. No longer a shining city of the East much discussed but seldom experienced by the average American, New York may impress him as provincial, despite its size and "style"; but he is likely to find it "different" rather than foreign.

The New York language, then, is no babel of patchwork patois; neither can it be considered a well-established body of jargon, slang and varied colloquialisms fitting into a loose but rather recognizable syntax, like the special dialects of the American South and West. The character of language in any given region is related to the education, hereditary background, occupations and economic status of the people of that region; generally speaking, in the South and West language has become standardized to some extent because the factors mentioned have been relatively pegged by the given elements of development. For example, Burke and Jefferson Counties in Georgia, adjacent to each other as are Manhattan and the Bronx, have a population which speaks a language distinct in color and idiom but which has varied little in decades; whereas in New York, an environment subject to innumerable factors in a flux of constant change, it is entirely possible to ask "Where are you going?" one instant and "Whe' yuh goin'?" the next, without the slightest trace of self-consciousness in either case, depending upon the auditor and the urgency of the moment.

"The Big City rhythm" has been dealt with in the movies, radio, books and magazines, but the fact remains that everything which has been told is no more than a pale suggestion of the dominant moods of the town, the qualities that place it by itself in the world: the whirling, driving tempo of existence, the efforts to relax within the battle to exist, the complicated individual adjustments to myriad personal relationships and to the whole process of the living city. But make no mistake, the average New Yorker loves the town. Though he may never have been to the Aquarium or climbed the insides of the Statue of Liberty, it's his town for better or worse. Never does he consider the permanent possibility of renouncing the subway or wearing a gas mask against the traffic-generated monoxide fumes. Hand him a deed to a hundred acres in the country and more than likely he will return it with: "What? No Hubbell-Mungo Sunday duels? No ice hockey? No Monday Winchell column on Sunday night?"

Swift tempo, high pressure, more retail sales each year, more per capita sales, nearly eighty-one millions spent for amusement in 1935, more than 656,000 registered passenger automobiles, close to half a billion dollars a year in wages (excluding salaried employees), hotels taking in nearly sixty-five millions yearly, value of produced goods close to three billion yearly—is it any wonder that the language of the city should project tension and release epigrammatic terseness when the economic machinery operates, and slacken to a grateful legato when night comes and one prepares for another day?

Unless it's out! Out to theater, recital, movie or nickelodeon, mingling with the gay Broadway or Second Avenue or Grand Concourse or Fourteenth Street or Coney Island crowds. Then, if the mood is strong and the purse not too light, on to the *downbeat* (the accented basic rhythm of hot music) at the Onyx, the intimate Caliente, the Roseland and Savoy ballrooms, the sepia Uptown House, Childs—and never mind tomorrow, here it is!

Yet to presume on the part of first-time visitors a total ignorance of the metropolitan argot would be incorrect. The movies (*Three Men on a Horse, Lady for a Day, Little Miss Marker,* etc.) ; radio (Harry Hershfield, *Gang Busters,* Walter Winchell, *Manhattan Moods,* etc.) ; the "funnies" (*Moon Mullins, Popeye the Sailor, Barney Google, Grossly X-aggerated,* etc.) ; the syndicated columns (Winchell's *On Broadway,* Sobol's *The Voice of Broadway,* Beebe's *This New York, Lyons Den,* etc.) ; the magazines (*The New Yorker, Variety, Time,* etc.) ; and books (*Guys and Dolls, Bodies Are Dust, Brain Guy, Thunder Over the Bronx, The Thin Man, Butterfield 8, I Can Get It for You Wholesale,* etc.) have certainly introduced the "New York style" into the contemporary national culture. Within these media the Dorgans, Conways, Lardners, Winchells, Bacrs, O'Haras, Kobers, Durantes and Runyons have given the nation *scram, lay an egg, palooka, belly-laugh, Reno-vate, yes we have no bananas, twenty-three skiddoo, Alcoholiday, Park Rowgue, wisecrack, applesauce, you said it, hard-boiled, pushover, click, laugh that off, yes-man, middle-aisling it, socko, step on the gas, kiss the canvas, throw in the sponge* and many others. Our slang-makers may be separated into two classes: those who listen and repeat, and those who simply sit down, concentrate and create. Among the latter are Dorgan ("Tad" of fond memory), Jack Conway and the practically inimitable Winchell, well on his way to becoming the nation's official chronicler of Things About Somebodies That Everybody Never Even Dreamed Of. Among the efficient leg-and-ear men, class John O'Hara, Damon Runyon, Leonard Lyons and the late Ring Lardner.

Inoculated with these influences, the out-of-towner may be able to translate the following: "Pipe the pushover, he thinks he's a click with his doll because she told him she'd lohengrin and bear it, but all she wants is a stand-in to pinch hit for the last heart, who lost all his what-it-takes in an under-the-bridge-at-midnite payoff." But to conclude that New Yorkers converse in this cryptic manner would be contrary to fact. The truth is that the average talk of the town is more of an attitude than a vocabulary. The same person who puts your breakfast on the table and remarks, "I hope everything is to your taste, sir," may, after receiving a lavish tip, say to the headwaiter, "Keep a gander on the visiting fireman with the ice on his cuffs, he's out to make a flash," or perhaps simply, "The guy in the corner just held up a bank."

Similarly, a girl or *bimbo* may be perfect or *the business,* may maneuver or *play for a break,* be cheated or *gypped,* unbalanced or *screwy,* have a nose or *schnozzle,* become angry or *griped,* be informed or *know her onions,* leave quietly or *take a run-out powder,* gamble everything or *shoot the works,* and be a nuisance or a *stiff pain.*

Also one may buy on credit or be *cuffed,* ask permission to leave or *see a man about a dog,* engineer a difficult coup or *pull a fast one;* and, with no malice whatsoever, one may be told that he *takes it in the arm* (ex-aggerates), is *cockeyed* (fantastically in error), and that he'd better not get his *bowels in an uproar* (excited). Heard each day are countless similar expressions, some going strong after years of usage (*you said a mouthful*), others quickly discarded (*ish kabibble, so's your old man*). H. L. Mencken believes that span of usage depends somewhat upon the logical content. This is borne out by observing the relationship between logical content and flexibility of use. *Go peddle your papers* is colorful, clear and refers to a precarious, generally humble function of city life; and since its basic sense is universally understood, it lends itself to many nuances of meaning, depending on the individual who uses it, and to whom. It may mean *go away; be a good fellow and leave; go away before you get hurt; mind your own business, you lug* (or *sweetheart*); or *leave us alone, can't you see we're busy?* And in the case of the universal *oh yeah?* we have an expression wherein the logical content is no less power-ful for being somewhat subtle. It reflects an attitude toward the city's life-processes—the good-humored cynical reproach, the brief signal of frank disbelief, the useful beats of *stalling* in the rhythm of a situation, the projection of the speaker's hope, disgust, anger, love, philosophy, politics or unqualified withdrawal. In his routine chatter, the New Yorker cannot get along without his *oh yeah?* It is his most valuable buffer, knout, pacifier and bubble-pipe, a necessary protective lubricant in the daily wear and tear.

Of late a humorously conceived system of language corruption called *double talk* or *talking on the double* has made itself felt. Its function is to seduce or *rib* the unknowing listener into believing that he is either deaf, ignorant or ready for a lifetime run in the part of Napoleon. *Double talk* is created by mixing plausible-sounding gibberish into ordinary conversation, the speaker keeping a straight face or *dead pan* and enunciating casually or *off the cuff*. If he is a true practitioner of this insane craft he will always speak with a slight mumble; and it is no wonder that this folk-variation of Gertrude Stein should manifest itself in theatrical and pugilistic circles, where the ability to master an intelligible yet *sotto voce* mumble is considered a prerequisite of the trade. Among the leading exponents of this mad jargon, which Clem White, ice-hockey promoter, characterizes as "the quickest way to poison your mind," are Lou Raymond, Whitey Bimstein, Phatzo Zuckerman, Hymie Caplin, the Ritz Brothers and Mushky Jackson.

Observe in this sample of Mr. Hymie Caplin's double talk the creation of gibberish having a distinctly "sensible" sound, and the ingenuity with which it is woven into the entire melody line: "Well, take now you're in a restaurant. So you say to the waiter, 'Gimme the chicken and vegetables but portostat with the chicken with the fustatis on it.' So he says 'What?' and you say 'You know, the portostat, and moonsign the savina on the top, with the vegetables.' " Note also the bizarre sympathy of Mr. Whitey Bimstein in conversation with a defeated pugilist: "Sure ya got pressed in the third, kid. You done all right, but your trouble is ya fonnastat when you go forward with your left hand. That's a pretty bad fault. All ya have to learn is ya come forward when ya fest 'em up on the referee with the old sedda m'credda."

Delectable though it may be, double talk is surpassed as the crowning contribution to the fantasy of the New York language by the verbal nuggets of Jimmy Durante of the East Side, Coney Island, Broadway, Hollywood, London "and all pernts to a disasterous season." His prodigious vitality, boisterous pseudo-arrogance and unabated cosmic self-affirmation are startlingly projected in the documentation of his categorical imperatives and in the frothy rhythms of his strange, valid furies. His *It's mutiny!* and *Am I mortified!* are best known to the nation, but no catalogue of Durante-cisms can suggest the hysterical tension he brings to a situation and the overbounding exaggeration he gives to its essential quality. His famous nose—large, acute, and shrewd—is but an extension of his heart. "I get you!" he will shout. "A story on Jimmy the Man! A story on Jimmy the Human Bein'! The idea is terrific! It's marvelous! It's dynamite!" Or on the melancholy of fame: "Many's the time I'd like to go into the Automat for a cuppa coffee. But I can't do it. They would reckonize me. I'd be mobbed. I can't disguise my probiscuity! Jimmy the Man! Jimmy the Human Bein'!"

Once, as Michael Mok relates in the New York *Post*, Jimmy noticed an extremely thin and anemic little man wearing a tiny feather in his hatband. At his side walked a very tall and very stout woman. Jimmy's reaction was instantaneous, explosive and complete: "Lookit! Lookit! A mountain climber! Intrepid! Intrepid!"

Only a New York could have produced a Durante, for in New York of all places one can appreciate the comic aspects of widely disparate individuals forced to try to understand each other. This is a result of the social cosmopolitanism of the town, made necessary by its complex socio-economic relationships. Jimmy the Well-Dressed Man is its comic symbol, its Fantasia No. 1, and those pricked by his linguistic darts laugh the loudest.

These words-patterns are an accurate reflection of the exciting and heterogeneous life of New York. The complexity of the economic process produces super-specialization in occupations, many of which create their own jargons. In them are to be found the "typical" elements which energize the language as a whole. Scores of these jargons exist. Just as it would be impossible for the tourist to encounter them all in one visit, so is it impossible in the short space of this article to give more than a few brief samples.

In using taxicabs the visitor will do well to keep his ears open, for the talk of the *hackies* brims with imagination based on an extreme sense of reality. Evidence of the heavy pressure of their work, the epigrammatic nature of their patter is traceable to the necessity for quick, succinct language. Pausing at the red light, they will shout to each other. "Hey, *hoople* [a *hackie* working on a 24-hour stretch], howza clock on 'at *stone-crusher?*" (what's the meter-reading on that cab with the knocking motor?). The answer may be: "It's the *ice-breaker* [his first fare that day]; *see you on the show-break*" (time when the theaters discharge their audiences, but also an expression meaning "au revoir").

Should the visitor be fortunate enough to receive special permission, he may attend the morning lineup at Police Headquarters, where persons *picked up* during the previous day are brought for examination before an audience of detectives and plainclothes men. He will hear more strange talk in an hour than he can possibly remember. The *bad actors* may include youngsters up for their first *rap* (sentence) for *crashing a joint* (burglary);

cons (convicts) caught after *lamming a joint* (escaping from the scene of a crime) or *crashing the stir* (escaping from jail); *shady shonnikers* (pawnbrokers), sleek *valentinos* (young men kept by older women), and perhaps a stolid *chopper* (machine-gunner) on his way to the *hot seat* (electric chair) or extradition to a State where convicted killers *do a dance* (are hanged) rather than *burn* (are electrocuted).

In cafeterias, diners, lunchettes and luncheonettes the cries of counter-men repeating orders to the chefs will prove amusing to the out-of-towner. Staples surviving the introduction of microphones include *nervous pudding* for Jello; *burn the British* or *toasted Wally* for a toasted English muffin; *smear one, burn it* for a toasted cheese sandwich; *bottle o' red* for catsup; *one to go* for an order to be taken out; *one cow* for a glass of milk; *stretch it* for a large glass; *burn one with a feather* for a chocolate malted milk with an egg in it; and the strident *eighty-six,* a warning to the cashier that a customer is trying to leave without paying his check.

Radio has introduced many new expressions into the national language. Easily recognizable are *hog the mike, wanna buy a duck?, check and double-check, are ya listenin'?, ether* and *theme song.* Equally colorful is an *inside* (professional) lingo which employs *killie loo bird* for a flighty coloratura, *old sexton* for a bass with a sepulchral voice, *talking in his beard* for a muffled voice, *fax* for facilities, *town crier* for one who sings too loud, *fighting the music* for lack of ease in singing, *down in the mud* for very low reproduction volume, *line hits* for occasional chirps on trans-mission circuits, *fizzy* for an unclear voice, *fuzzy* for an unclear program, and *on the nose* for ending a program on schedule to the second.

The instinctively creative qualities of the Negro are fully brought into play in his use of language, and no trip to New York should omit a visit to the Savoy Ballroom, where all Harlem comes to dance and gossip. Re-flecting an abounding interest in theater, music and dance, the Harlem lingo contains the rich impressionism and conscious emphasis characteristic of people living as special minorities; for vitality, variety and quality of imagery, it rates as one of the most exciting elements of the New York language. Harlem folk talking amongst themselves never feel "all right" —they're *mellow as a chick;* or if the opposite happens to be the case, they're *beat to the bricks,* or *beat to the socks.* One who talks too much is a *gum-beater* or *solid gum-beater,* while an unclassified nuisance is a *bring-down* or a *hanger.* Uninhibited dancers or party men are called *rugcutters,* sometimes with a lowbrow connotation; highbrows are *high-jivers.* The word *jive* has many meanings, among which are to joke with or *kid,* and to court a girl, as *I'm jiving a chick. The jive is on* refers to group excitement, healthy or otherwise. When one owns a car he's *on rubber,* and to pretend is to be *stiffin'. Lace up your boots, baby* is a cryptic admonition to *get wise to yourself.* Anything wonderful is *murder* or a *killer,* and to call out "Stop!" one says *Blackout!* Hundreds of similar expressions make the Harlem lingo a pleasure to listen to, albeit sometimes difficult to understand or *dig.*

Of all New York jargons, the most colorful and original is the popular or jazz musicians' language. The Negro's contribution here has been as significant as his influence in modern folk music. Greatest of all the great trumpeters of the day, Louis (Satchelmouth) Armstrong has created more of this language than any other individual. The imaginative and freely relaxed quality of the best modern dance music is found in this lingo.

Loiter near the bandstands at Roseland and the Savoy, get a table up close in some of the smaller places such as the Onyx, the Uptown House and Hickory House, or simply stand on the sidewalk among the crowd of musicians gathered outside union headquarters on Fiftieth Street just off Sixth Avenue, and you will catch words and expressions no more comprehensible to uninitiated non-musicians or *ickies* than Sanskrit. How are we to know that a *Dracula* is a key-pounding pianist who lifts his hands up to his face, or that the bass fiddle is the *doghouse,* or that *shmaltz* musicians are *four-button suit guys* and *long underwear boys?* Similarly, the initiate must learn that the *gutbucket* or *riding chorus* is the polyphonic climax to the playing of a tune or recording; that to be *in the groove* is to be playing very well; that *riffs* are deftly improvised rhythm phrases; and that a *solid sender* is a musician who is master of his instrument and who can do expressive things with it. Who in the world but a jazz musician would suspect that *B-flat* means dull, *G-flat* brilliant, and *out of this world*—though it has taken on *ickie* connotation—most completely *in the groove?* Jazz musicians relish their lingo and invariably say *cat* for musician, *Hi Gate!* for hello, *stinkeroo* for poor, *shmaltz* for sugary music and *wacky* for anything stupid or foolish. They are thrilled or *sent* in their *jam sessions* (informal and experimental collective improvisations), and have little respect for the *papermen* of the craft, or those who play only written music. *Gettin' off* or *going to town* on the last chorus or *gutbucket* is one of the thrills of the business to good *hot men.*

The word *swing,* now popularly used as a noun to denote music in the most recent phase of the ragtime-jazz tradition, originated and is properly used as a verb to describe a method of playing in exceptionally expressive rhythm patterns, either individually or collectively, and with organized freedom of improvisation. *Swing, gate!* is an exhortation to a *solid sender* to *take a Boston* or let go with all the *riffs, licks* and *kicks* in his repertoire. And as the sun rises over the housetops and the last bottle of milk is set down at the last apartment door, the *cats* deposit their instruments in their cases and depart with: "Take it easy, Pops, see ya on the downbeat."

In conclusion, it can safely be said that the New York language as a whole mirrors accurately the characteristic social relations of this immense and prodigiously busy city. Propriety may be the rule in courts, hospitals, conference rooms, employment bureaus, schools, waiting rooms and in all situations wherein each person according to his station must exercise proper restraint. But when these restrictions are absent, in shops and subways, cabs and cafeterias, children's playgrounds and grownups' night spots, in all the gay sparkle and grinding routine of the New World's Number One Metropolis, you will find a language as stunning and stimulating as the city itself.

Market Place for Words

NEW YORK CITY is frequently referred to as the "literary capital" of the United States. It would be more accurate to say that it is the nation's outstanding literary market place, one of the great publishing centers of the world. American publishers have tended more and more, since the middle of the 19th century, to concentrate on Manhattan Island; although a number of important houses are still to be found in other cities. The same thing is true of magazines, literary syndicates, etc. New York is also the chief production center for the playwright. Literary and dramatic agents naturally have their offices where the largest amount of business is conducted; and aspiring or successful writers, if they do not migrate here, frequently have occasion to visit the city. Not to be overlooked is the influence of New York reviewers and other groups in shaping the critical opinion and reading tastes of the country.

By virtue of the size of the reading public which it commands and the consequent size of the author's potential royalties, New York has come to acquire international importance as a publishing center. Whether or not it may accurately be termed the country's "literary capital" is a more or less academic question. Earlier in the century, when the "midwestern renaissance" was at its height, H. L. Mencken created a tempest in a teapot by conferring the title of "literary capital" upon Chicago, withdrawing it later when the movement headed by Sandburg, Masters and Anderson appeared to have spent itself. Until then, aside from the growing consciousness and fast-spreading reputation of its Greenwich Village in the earlier years of the century, New York does not seem to have given the question a great deal of thought, but busily went on with its publishing, editing, printing, book reviewing, its occasional making and unmaking of reputations; with not a little writing, though by no means all the writing in the country, being done in the shadow of its skyscrapers. In other words, it remained essentially a market rather than a self-conscious "capital"; and much of the same unsentimental, hard-faceted spirit that went into the building of its financial supremacy was manifest in its literary production. Relatively few of America's better-known writers, past or present, have been native New Yorkers; and there is little real basis for the common belief that as soon as a writer has made or is beginning to make a success he moves to Manhattan. As to the influence of New York in determining the literary taste and reading habits of America, something in the way of qualification and distinction is called for. Through such book supplements as those of the *Times* and the *Herald Tribune,* such weeklies as the *New Republic,* the *Nation,* the *Saturday Review of Literature,* and the *New Masses,* and such newspaper columns as those by Harry Hansen, Lewis Gannett and others, New York exerts a ponderable influence upon reviewers and readers in other sections, and so has a large share in molding literary opinion. But no one can accurately gauge the influence of New York critics on the great mass of book buyers. The latter are perhaps more inclined to be governed by local opinion; and reviewers in smaller towns and cities, while sometimes swayed by the metropolitan verdict, are as likely as not to display independent reactions. On the whole, it is probably in the higher realms of literature that New York's critical influence is operative. That influence obviously has nothing to do with the huge sales of such contemporary authors as Lloyd Douglas and Temple Bailey, any more than it had with the sales of Harold Bell Wright and Gene Stratton Porter in former years; and it is decidedly open to question how much of its success such a book as *Main Street* owes to what the metropolitan reviewers may or may not have said about it.

All this is in no wise intended as a refutation of New York's claims to literary eminence. Those claims are very real ones; the city occupies a place all its own, and one that it will probably retain for some time to come. But a "literary capital" it is not, in the sense, for example, that Philadelphia was during the last half of the 18th century, when, with such writers as Tom Paine and Benjamin Franklin in the foreground, literature was closely associated and frequently fused with national politics. Neither does New York hold the cultural—one might say, the spiritual—hegemony that was Boston's from about 1820 to shortly before the Civil War, during the period of the Unitarian revival, the Transcendentalist movement, and the early abolitionist movement. It was in the decade or two immediately preceding the Civil War that New York began coming to the front as the country's most important literary center, gradually taking the position that Philadelphia had more or less unconsciously lost and that Boston was slowly but surely relinquishing. This transitional phase may have been initiated as early as 1845, when Edgar Allan Poe's "The Raven" appeared in the *New York Mirror* and attracted national notice. However, it is not easy to confine such shifts within definite dates, as a very brief sketch of the highlights in New York's earlier literary history may indicate.

That history might properly be said to begin with Washington Irving, the first outstanding man of letters that New York can claim. But a few men before Irving had been prominent in the city, though they lived and wrote elsewhere as well. One of these was Tom Paine, already mentioned in connection with Philadelphia. For three or four years after the Revolution, Paine was frequently in New York; and the last seven years of his life were spent here and on a farm in New Rochelle that had been given him by the government for his services to the Revolutionary cause. Philip Freneau, most important of American poets before Bryant, was born in New York City in 1752, and for nearly a decade after his marriage in 1789 he was chiefly engaged in journalistic work here, editing first the *Daily Advertiser,* then later (following the failure of his *National Gazette* in Philadelphia) the *Time-Piece.* Though Charles Brockden Brown, the first American to make a profession of authorship, belongs to Philadelphia, his more noteworthy novels—including *Wieland* and *Arthur Mervyn*—were written while he was living in New York, from 1798 to 1801.

In connection with the pre-Irving era, note should be made of the existence in New York City, beginning as far back as 1752, of a number of periodicals of a literary or semi-literary nature: the *Independent Reflector,* the *Occasional Reverberator,* the *Instructor,* the *John Englishman,* the *American Magazine,* the *New York Magazine,* the *American Minerva,* the *Literary Magazine,* the *Lady and Gentleman's Pocket Magazine,* the *Monthly Magazine and American Review* and the *Rush Light.* All of these were decidedly provincial in character.

It is more than birth and long residence in New York, more than the brilliant reputation he achieved in this country and abroad, that make Washington Irving the city's outstanding literary figure of the early period. He was the first important American writer to deal with New York as material for literature, the first to animate it with the breath of a larger cultural world. His earliest published writing, the essays in *Salmagundi* (1807–8), was largely concerned with the Manhattan background; and his first book was the humorously satiric *Dietrich Knickerbocker's History of New York* (1809). Returning in 1832 from a sojourn of 17 years in Europe, and establishing his home near Tarrytown on the Hudson, Irving continued to dominate the New York literary scene for more than a quarter-century, until his death in 1859.

Of Irving's minor literary contemporaries in New York, the best known were his intimate friend and *Salmagundi* associate, James Kirke Paulding, a pioneer in the field of realistic American fiction; and the two poets, Fitz-Greene Halleck and Joseph Rodman Drake, who collaborated in a series of satiric verses on contemporary New York celebrities, published over the signature of "Croaker & Co." in the *Evening Post*. Paulding's novels *(Köningsmarke, The Dutchman's Fireside, Westward Ho!* etc.) are little read today; but Halleck's "Marco Bozzaris" and Drake's "The Culprit Fay" still survive in the standard anthologies.

Much of James Fenimore Cooper's early life, from 1811 to 1835, was spent in New York City or its suburbs; and it was here that he wrote the earliest and in some respects the most successful of his novels—*The Spy, The Pioneers, The Pilot, Lionel Lincoln, The Last of the Mohicans.* As founder and leading spirit of the Bread and Cheese Club, and in numerous other activities, Cooper played a prominent part in New York literary affairs of the 1820's and early 1830's. One of his later novels, *Le Mouchoir* (1840), deals with fashionable life in Manhattan.

With his reputation as the author of "Thanatopsis" and other notable poems already made, William Cullen Bryant came to New York from Massachusetts in 1826 as sub-editor of the *Evening Post.* He was advanced to the post of editor-in-chief three years later, and for half a century thereafter he was one of the most influential and elevating forces in New York journalism. Another poet-journalist of this early period, though one who ranked very considerably below Bryant, was Nathaniel Parker Willis, who for a decade or two before the middle of the century was associated with George Pope Morris on the *New York Mirror,* and later contributed to the *Home Journal* a colorful weekly interpretation of the Manhattan scene. It was Willis who accepted Poe's "Raven" for publication in the *Mirror,* and who later gave the poet regular employment as well as the benefits of a generous friendship.

If New York, after adopting William Cullen Bryant, has no writers of eminence to show down to the time of Poe and Whitman and Melville, this does not mean that the city was barren of literary activity. During the first half of the 19th century, more than 50 magazines were published in Manhattan or nearby, among them the *American Review and Literary Journal,* the *American Monthly Magazine and Critical Review,* the *New York Mirror,* the *New York Review and Atheneum Magazine,* the *New*

York Literary Gazette, the *Knickerbocker Magazine,* the *American Monthly Magazine,* the *New York Review,* the *Columbian Lady's and Gentleman's Magazine,* the *Literary News Letter,* the *American Review and Whig Journal* (later the *American Whig Review*), the *Broadway Journal* and the *Literary World.*

Edgar Allan Poe's life in New York divides into two periods. A few months after his marriage to Virginia Clemm in 1836, the poet took his child-wife and her mother to New York, where they boarded on Carmine Street until the summer of 1838. Then, unable to make a living, Poe removed his family to Philadelphia. In the spring of 1844 they were back in New York, boarding in a farmhouse near Eighty-Fourth Street and Broadway, and it was here that "The Raven" (begun in Philadelphia) was put into final form. The publication of this poem early in 1845 brought to Poe his one brief experience of a favoring fortune. Willis found a position for him on the *Mirror,* other editors sought him out, and the fashionable salons paid him homage. For a few months in 1845, he was editor and nominal owner of the *Broadway Journal.* Early in the following year he moved his household to "Turtle Bay" on the East River, then to the cottage at Fordham that is now New York's chief literary shrine. But by this time the clouds were gathering about him once more. The winter of 1846–7 was one of desperate poverty for the poet and his family, and in its midst occurred the death of Virginia. Soon after this event, Poe began the tragic wanderings that ended with his death at Baltimore in the autumn of 1849.

Less brief and fortuitous than in Poe's case was the association with New York of two other literary titans, Walt Whitman and Herman Melville. Both were born in 1819—Whitman at West Hills, Long Island, Melville in New York City. Except for the three years of sea-wanderings that generated the immortal *Moby Dick* and three or four lesser classics, and for the period of 1850–63 when he lived on a farm near Pittsfield, Massachusetts, virtually all of Melville's mature life was spent in New York. For two decades, from 1866 to 1886, he was an out-of-door inspector of customs on the Gansevoort Street pier—the name Gansevoort, ironically enough, being that of his maternal grandmother and a preceding line of affluent ancestors. What Melville in those 20 years might have contributed to American literature, had his genius received anything but the scantiest critical recognition and material reward, is a matter for tragic speculation.

Yet while Melville was renouncing authorship for a life of routine drudgery, Walt Whitman was serenely though stubbornly maintaining his artistic purposes in the face not merely of critical indifference but of violent critical abuse—along with poverty as well; and he continued to pursue them with equal vigor and equanimity almost to the end of a life longer by a year than Melville's. Beginning in boyhood as "printer's devil" on the *Long Island Patriot,* Whitman spent more than 25 years in association with various Brooklyn newspapers, making frequent trips by ferry to Manhattan, where he roamed the streets at night, hobnobbed with convivial cronies at Pfaff's, or haunted the gallery in opera-houses and theaters. These experiences, along with wanderings in eastern Long Island and (for a few months of 1848) through the South to New Orleans, distilled in the alembic of Walt's unique genius, went to the making of *Leaves of Grass,* first issued by a Philadelphia publisher in 1855. Midway in the Civil War, Whitman left Brooklyn for Washington, and the remainder of his life was passed in the capital and in Camden, New Jersey.

With the close of the Civil War, a host of figures begins to crowd the local literary stage; so that such a brief sketch as this must henceforth emphasize groups and main tendencies rather than individual writers. The decade or so immediately following the war constituted that "Gilded Age" of which Mark Twain and Charles Dudley Warner wrote in 1873. Their novel has been described as a collaboration of the frontier and the effete East; for Clemens was at this time fresh from the mining camps, river boats, and printing offices of the pioneer West, while Warner was a perfect representative of the Genteel Tradition. Together the two men viewed their country, in all its sprawling, promising, menacing inchoateness— viewed it, significantly, in relation to the new and disquieting civilization that Wall Street appeared to be imposing upon the nation at large and its public life, a civilization dominated by New York City, capital of the financial North and East. For while the transition from the rule of industry to that of modern finance had not as yet been effected, Wall Street already was rapidly assuming the role that it has played for the past half century and more—the Wall Street that Melville had written about in *Bartleby the Scrivener,* that was to be the despair of Lafcadio Hearn and the inspiration of Theodore Dreiser.

Meanwhile, the Genteel Tradition in American letters, which had stemmed in large part from Washington Irving, was finding its last local representatives in such competent poets, critics, and journalists as Richard Watson Gilder, George William Curtis, Edmund Clarence Stedman, and Richard Henry Stoddard. The work of its earlier representatives was now little more than a lingering scent of lavender, soon to be dissipated in the heady ozone of the new industrial day and the new American life with which Howells and James were to grapple with so poignant a sincerity.

It is in William Dean Howells' *A Hazard of New Fortunes* that Boston may be said to have had its definitive, its more than a little bewildered, look at New York City and the commercial spirit that seemed to pervade the metropolis and to emanate from it, spreading over the rest of the land to the imperilment of higher values. Virtually all the characters in the book either take a definite attitude toward or stand in a definite relation to the world of business. And Howells, the Ohio farm boy become the perfect Bostonian, is at a loss to grasp it all, but remains the Bay State visitor, doing his best to be understanding and polite.

The short of it is that the United States of America, in the eyes of the sensitive observer, was becoming that "banker's world," that "banker's Olympus," which is described in *The Education of Henry Adams* and in Adams' novel, *Democracy*. From now on for several decades, down through the era of the "muckrakers" and after, the financier "Titan" was to be a luring theme, and the rise of many a Silas Lapham was to be traced. It might seem, accordingly, that the preeminence of New York's Wall Street would confer upon the city a moral-literary ascendancy comparable to that of Transcendentalist Boston in its prime. What militated against this was the vastness of the new American nation, and the resulting diffuseness as well as complexity of the American scene—as is apparent in those two outstanding novels of the post-bellum years, *The Gilded Age* and *Democracy*.

The pioneers, from Daniel Boone to the gold-seekers of 1849, had pushed back the physical frontier; it remained for the writer to take possession of the new and uncharted provinces, in the form of literary regionalism or sectionalism. Bret Harte had made a beginning before the Civil War, and he was followed by Mark Twain, Edward Eggleston, George W. Cable, and numerous minor figures; by the southern regionalists, Sidney Lanier, Thomas Nelson Page, Joel Chandler Harris, James Lane Allen, and others; and by the New Englanders, Sarah Orne Jewett, Mary E. Wilkins, and Harriet Beecher Stowe. A California gold camp, a flatboat on the Mississippi, the backwoods of Indiana, Creole New Orleans, the Tennessee Mountains, the Ozarks, sentimental Dixie, a village on the Maine coast—these were subjects, seemingly, far from the madding Stock Exchange, far from the tide of metropolitan streets and the rhythm of metropolitan life (though not so far, after all, as Sarah Orne Jewett and Mary E. Wilkins, among others, were to discover).

The regional theme had its day and passed, tending to merge in the end with the Genteel Tradition. One thing it revealed was the fact that America henceforth was too large and varied a country to be subjected to the cultural sway of, or even to take its prevailing literary tone from, New York, Boston, Philadelphia, or any other single center of population. The later and less conscious regionalists of the 20th century, such as Sherwood Anderson, Willa Cather and Zona Gale, were to go on writing of the Nebraska, Ohio or Wisconsin that they knew. They were also to keep their places of residence in the hinterland; yet, like so many of the earlier sectional writers, they were to come to New York to make their publishing arrangements and to enjoy occasional intervals of recreation. And New York, being not merely the market place but the editorial workshop, somehow feels that they belong to her.

Some of the writers who did try living and working in New York were having none too pleasant a time of it. That exotic citizen of the world—and of no world—Lafcadio Hearn, was one of these. Having failed to find among the natives of Martinique the superior way of life that he craved, Hearn came to Manhattan. He found it a nightmare—"frightful, devilish." It led him to the conclusion that "civilization is a hideous thing," and to the exclamation, "Blessed is savagery!" Nothing short of an earthquake, as he saw it, could produce any improvement. He was, in brief, hopelessly stunned by it all. Nevertheless, Hearn's was too keen a mind not to perceive that there was a story, a very big story, even in Wall Street. But it was a story that he could never write, and he did not see how any writer could manage it. "Fancy," he said, "a good romance about Wall Street, so written that the public could understand it! There is of course a tremendous romance there; but only a financier can really know the machinery, and his knowledge is technical. But what can the mere *littérateur* do, walled up to heaven in a world of mathematical mystery and machinery."

Hearn refers here to a basic problem of the novelist who would deal with the unfamiliar world of big business—the problem of documentation. But it was not an insolvable one, as Dreiser, Norris, and others were to prove. It was, however, a very real problem for the writers of this era who saw the full complexity of the theme, and who were not so sure of their bearings as was Emerson when he wrote: "It is only the young man who supposes there is anything new in Wall Street. The merchant who figures . . . is very old business. You shall find him, his way, that is, of thinking concerning the world and men and property and eating and drinking and marriage and education and religion and government—the whole concatenation of his opinions—in Rabelais and Aristophanes. Panurge was good Wall Street."

What Emerson is saying, of course, is that the mercantile spirit, the commercial attitude of mind and outlook upon the world, is the same down the ages. This does not take into account the economist's distinctions with regard to the forms of capital. The truth is that the industrial capital of Emerson's day was not the same as the merchant and usury capital of a former day; and by now, industrial capital was about to undergo a further transformation into monopoly finance capital. Hearn was no more an economist than Emerson, but at least he realized that things were not quite so simple as the Sage of Concord would make them out to be. There was something there; he took one look and gave it up, leaving the problem to other men, who were to wrestle with it with varying degrees of success.

But there was another side of the picture, another aspect of the civilization that Wall Street, the commercial spirit, big business (call it what you will) had come to typify. That civilization was one of violent extremes and violent contrasts of wealth and poverty, of senseless luxury and unspeakable destitution—contrasts that nowhere took on a more sharp-edged quality than in the nation's metropolis, with slum and aristocratic mansion often within stone's throw of each other. This was apparent even before the Civil War, at the time when George Lippard, pioneer of proletarian literature and a "Marxist before Marx," wrote his *New York: Its Upper Ten and Lower Million*. Now, in the last decades of the century, New York's famous "Four Hundred," under the leadership of Ward McAllister and like arbiters, was disporting in luxurious orgies at Newport and on Fifth Avenue; while on the Lower East Side and the Bowery, and in other tenement sections of the city, there were hunger, want, overcrowding, crime and prostitution, with conditions rendered worse by New York's vast and constantly increasing immigrant population.

It was this other New York that Stephen Crane saw, and that he pictured in his masterpiece, *Maggie,* the story of a slum girl. With his clear and honest vision, his bitter hatred of human stupidity and corruption, Crane succeeded in creating the classic of the Bowery, home of the "creatures that once were men," the *lumpenproletariat.* It is true that he failed of an ultimate, penetrating comprehension of slum and slum-dweller; he was considerably frightened by what he saw. But his unrelenting integrity and straightforwardness of vision carried him far, and paved the way for the social realism that was to spring up in the later 1890's.

As for New York's moneyed aristocracy, it was not until the early years of the present century that it began to inspect itself, in the novels of Edith Wharton. In *The House of Mirth* (1905), and later in *The Custom of the Country* (1913), Mrs. Wharton subjected the social group of which she was a member to a searching criticism within a distinctly class-limited set of values. The aristocrat had failed of being an aristocrat, and the fault lay with money, in the hands of the *nouveaux riches;* which was much the same point of view, with the same element of snobbishness in it, as that of Henry James in his fragmentary *Ivory Tower.* Mrs. Wharton finally, in her popular success, *The Age of Innocence* (1920), was to take refuge in nostalgia for the 1870's, when "society" was truly "good," having not yet been corrupted by the newcomer from "the Street" with his facile millions and his ignorant disregard for the aristocrat's code of conduct.

It is interesting to note that the publication of *The House of Mirth* virtually coincided with that of Upton Sinclair's story of the Chicago stockyards, *The Jungle.* The new social realism that has been spoken of was now finding expression in the writings of such authors as Frank Norris, Sinclair and Robert Herrick; and it appeared that Chicago, with its stockyards and its wheat pit, was to be the principal locale of the impulse. It was certainly a sturdier-seeming if a cruder brand of realism that Chicago offered at this period; and this it is, according to H. L. Mencken, that accounts for the first westward shift of the "literary capital," a transference that was to be repeated in the second decade of the century, when Chicago's "renaissance" began to flower.

Meanwhile, in New York the eight years from 1902 to 1910 might almost be called the "O. Henry Age." Fresh from an Ohio prison where, whether guilty or not, he had served a term for embezzlement, the "king of story tellers" had at once entered upon his task as chronicler of the little lives of New York's little people—in Upton Sinclair's words, "the obscure and exploited masses of New York, the waitresses and hat-pressers, soda-jerkers and bums, the taxi drivers and policemen, O. Henry's 'Four Million.' " Fearful as he was of the dark and pain of life, he was yet no more fearful than were his readers, those same little people for whom he wrote; and they loved him for it. They loved him, too, because he did know their lives, even though the meaning of it all eluded him as it did them. His faith in the "order of things that be" was little less than sublime, his gaze was never too prying, and his humor was a healing balm.

Someone has said that O. Henry made the short story "the most democratic form of literature in America." Critics will point to the mechanical quality of his tales, which is not to be denied; those tales are the culmination of that technique of the "well-made story" which was begun by Poe and carried on by Bret Harte. Yet O. Henry contributed much to modern interest in the short story form; and his works, like those of Jack London and Upton Sinclair, are eagerly devoured all over the world today. Hundreds of thousands of copies have been printed in the Soviet Union; and the native of South American pampas or Siberian steppes may still lose himself in the joys and sorrows of a department store salesgirl in a New York hall bedroom of the 1900's.

If New York in these early years of the century was not displaying the vitality of that "hog butcher to the world," Chicago, it was, by way of compensation, beginning to take on the cosmopolitan cast of culture that it has worn ever since, as entrepreneur between the Old World and the New. This was the era of Sloan, Luks, Bellows, and Henri in the graphic arts—each very American in his way, but each aware of European currents. The "Nude Descending a Staircase" appeared in 1913. And James G. Huneker, most cosmopolitan of American critics, was commuting between New York and Philadelphia. It was in this period that Greenwich Village, the only section approaching a Latin Quarter that America has been able to claim, assumed a place upon the cultural map, as artists and writers alike took possession of the little old houses below Eighth Street. For a decade or two it was to be the romantic thing for the budding young genius to move down to the Village and "starve it out." Many writers who, like Theodore Dreiser and Sinclair Lewis, were to achieve literary and commercial success spent their hopeful earlier days in New York's little Bohemia. Later, from about 1916, the Village became the home of the social radical—of Max Eastman and Floyd Dell, of Art Young and Bob Minor; and as Freud appeared above the horizon, the Villagers went in heavily for psychoanalysis, including the psychoanalysis of literature, and there was a strenuous revolt against "Puritanism." All of which, needless to say, added to the "color" and the increasingly noisy reputation of the American Montparnasse, which came to be associated with free love, free verse, and all the isms, social and esthetic.

New York may be the common gateway for European literature and literary trends; but even here, on at least two occasions, Chicago has stolen a march. The first time was in the 1890's, when, with such a periodical as the *Chap Book* and such a firm as Stone & Kimball publishing the work of such men as Ibsen, Maeterlinck and Beardsley, the city at the foot of Lake Michigan contrived to out-yellow the *Yellow Book*. The second occasion was in the 'teens of the present century, when the British Imagists, Aldington and others, saw fit to ignore New York and send their wares to Harriet Monroe, the elocution teacher who, casually enough, had founded *Poetry: A Magazine of Verse*. It was also in Chicago that Margaret Anderson and Jane Heap, with the ideological backing of Emma Goldman, launched that intelligentsia-shocking organ, the *Little Review*, "making no compromise with the public taste." The *Little Review* did not tarry long in Chicago, however, but after exhausting the list of printers who would extend it credit, moved on to New York City, to be followed by a small group of those who wrote for it. In Manhattan this periodical enjoyed its most hectic days, centering about the banned publication of the first instalments of James Joyce's *Ulysses*.

While the Midwest was engaged in discovering itself in terms of literature, New York writers were about to embark upon another and more ambitious voyage of exploration, their objective being nothing less than the "discovery" of America, of the continent's "soul" and the meaning of its vast sprawling civilization. There was a feeling in the air that the "great American novel," the "great American poem," were yet to be written. Out of this was to grow one of the best, if shortest lived, literary magazines that the country has known, the *Seven Arts*, which numbered among its editors and contributors Waldo Frank, James Oppenheim, Randolph Bourne, Van Wyck Brooks, Louis Untermeyer, Conrad Aiken and others. The *Seven Arts*, unfortunately, was started on the eve of America's entry into the World War, and its career was cut short by governmental suppression; but that career is notable in American literary history.

The fostering impulse behind the *Seven Arts* was one of "back to our native roots"—the same impulse that was to find expression, some years later, in Hart Crane's poem *The Bridge,* and that eventually, in the 1920's, was to degenerate into a sterile cult of the skyscraper, of a skyscraper civilization and its "Lively Arts." Combined with the expression of this impulse was a new note of social liberalism, sounded with particular force in the pages of the *Seven Arts* by Randolph Bourne, one of the most promising critics America has had. His name and that of Van Wyck Brooks stand out conspicuously in the field of native criticism in the first quarter of the present century.

Short lived as it was, the *Seven Arts* had its effect, not only upon individual writers such as Waldo Frank as evidenced in his *City Block* and later works, but upon the war and post-war generation as a whole. Some members of that generation, after having gone through the blood and mire of the trenches, might come back to America, take one look, give it up as a bad job, and return to the terrace of the Café du Dome and the falling franc; but liberalism henceforth was in their blood—a liberalism that was to enable them to withstand the finely carved disillusionment of a *Wasteland,* and that in the end, after 1929, was to bring them into the social mêlée. In passing, it may be remarked that most of these "Exiles" chose New York for home and workshop, after their season of expatriation. It was, in fact, from New York that the expatriate movement started, in 1922, after Harold Stearns and his 29 fellow-Americans had sat down to look at their country, had found it sadly wanting, and had penned their *Civilization in the United States.* All of which may be regarded as the bitter frustrate end of that impulse for which Randolph Bourne and the *Seven Arts* had stood.

While young Europeans of the post-war period were giving vent to their disillusionment in the tragic clownings of Dadaism, America was witnessing the spectacle of "flaming youth." The Prohibition Era was on, and in New York the speakeasy took the place of the café. As one poet of the day has put it:

> The philosophy of our time was written by bootleggers,
> And we went to the speakeasies for knowledge and hope,
> And the taste was bitter in our mouths.

This was the generation whose higher despair found voice in Scott Fitzgerald's *This Side of Paradise.* It was a generation that read the *Smart Set,* and later found hilarious and "sophisticated" consolation in the *American Mercury.* "Debunking" was an essential phase of the period.

All, however, was not levity and smartness in this too tinny interlude. The era had its serious—possibly a trifle over-serious, not to say ponderous —expression in the magazine, the *Dial,* which had come to New York in the year following the Armistice. The *Dial* was not a new periodical, having had an existence of nearly forty years in Chicago. Under the distinguished editorship of Francis F. Browne, it had been a conservative but authoritative medium of American thought. It now underwent a reincarnation, or rather two reincarnations: the first under Robert Morss Lovett, assisted by Randolph Bourne, Harold Stearns, John Dewey, Thorstein Veblen, and others, when it became a militantly liberal organ with a "reconstruction program"; then under Schofield Thayer, when it put on a quiet yellow garb, put aside liberal things and social-minded contributors, and began publishing what was taken by the intelligentsia of the 1920's to be the last word in art and literature, from America and abroad.

The list of *Dial* contributors makes curious reading today, including as it does Anatole France, Oswald Spengler, Benedetto Croce, Paul Valery, T. S. Eliot, Ford Madox Hueffer (now Ford Madox Ford), Van Wyck Brooks, William Butler Yeats, Arthur Symons, Ernest Boyd, Hugo von Hofmannsthal, Thomas Mann, George Saintsbury, Maxim Gorky, George Moore, Conrad Aiken, Paul Rosenfeld, Sherwood Anderson, E. E. Cummings, Amy Lowell, Carl Sandburg, George Santayana, John Dos Passos, Edmund Wilson, Lewis Mumford, Hendrik Van Loon, Kenneth Burke, Hart Crane—even Michael Arlen. The managing editors under Thayer were, in succession, Stewart Mitchell, Gilbert Seldes and Marianne Moore.

The *Dial* was noted for its annual writer's award of $2,000, instituted in 1921, which went in turn to Sherwood Anderson, T. S. Eliot (for *The Wasteland*), Van Wyck Brooks, Marianne Moore, E. E. Cummings, Ezra Pound, William Carlos Williams and Kenneth Burke. The magazine passed out of existence in 1928.

Another of New York's serious periodicals that expired in the 1920's, and one whose passing is still regretted by many, was the *Freeman*, edited by Albert J. Nock. It was especially noteworthy for its news of English and Irish as well as continental literature.

But, on the whole, literary seriousness was at something of a discount; the "light touch school," *à la* Carl Van Vechten and the earlier Aldous Huxley, was more popular. For these were the boom years of Harding "normalcy" and Coolidge prosperity, when, riding high on a bull market, the stock broker and uptown New York began discovering Greenwich Village as a slumming ground. True, a few pioneer left-wing writers were at work—John Dos Passos, Michael Gold, John Howard Lawson, Isidor Schneider, Joseph Freeman, and others; but they were definitely in the minority, and with the exception of Dos Passos they were little heeded. In his *Ten Days That Shook the World*, John Reed had founded a new tradition; but that tradition, with the exception of such a notable early work as Gold's *Jews Without Money*, was yet to burgeon. In *Manhattan Transfer* (1925), Dos Passos conveyed upon a remarkably ambitious canvas the surging and tumultuous rhythm of the metropolis—a rhythm that springs from the interplay of social forces, mass action and events, mass emotions and the like—and succeeded in achieving a certain epic quality.

Following the stock market crash of 1929, the New York literary scene took on a decidedly different aspect, even though the change was not at once highly visible. The economic crisis that oppressed the nation as a whole could not but have its effect upon writers; and it was from New York that the first literary reactions to the depression were to come. After an initial period of bewilderment, there was much talk of "proletarian literature," and a whole new school of young novelists and poets sprang up almost overnight. As it happened, the earliest "proletarian" novels (Albert Halper's *Union Square* is an example) dealt with the New York scene, and the *New Masses* became the center of critical controversy on the subject, with Granville Hicks, Joseph Freeman, Isidor Schneider, and others seeking to provide a critical orientation.

Out of this movement were to come a number of writers who have since established themselves: Robert Cantwell, Albert Halper, Josephine Herbst, Grace Lumpkin, Fielding Burke, William Rollins, Robert Gessner, Edwin Seaver, Clara Weatherwax, Leane Zugsmith, Edward Newhouse, Ben Field, among the story tellers; Kenneth Fearing, Horace Gregory, Harry Kemp, Alfred Hayes, Genevieve Taggard, Langston Hughes, among the poets; Clifford Odets, Albert Bein, Em Jo Basshe, George Sklar, among the dramatists. Not all of these writers are from New York, but a majority of them have lived here. The settings they choose for their work are widely divergent, each writing of the social scene that he knows best; for the proletarian school seems to have ushered in a fresh kind of sectionalism— one that might be described as an industrial regionalism in literature. New York, none the less, remains the ideological seat of the movement, and perhaps since 1929 it is nearer than it ever was before to being the country's "literary capital," since it is here that the major critical battles—and there have been some spectacular ones—are fought out, over literary-social-economic questions. After occupying the center of the literary stage for several years, the proletarian movement seems to have subsided a little, as did the left-wing drama on Broadway; but there are signs that, like the drama, it is due for another period of popularity.

Out of the heightened social thinking and social awareness of the depression era came the first Writers' Congress, held in New York City in June 1935. At this meeting, the League of American Writers was formed, on a broad basis of opposition to fascism and imperialist war. A second

Congress was convened in New York in June 1937. Waldo Frank was the League's first president; he was succeeded in 1937 by Donald Ogden Stewart. A record of the first Congress will be found in the volume entitled *Proletarian Literature in the United States;* the papers read at the second meeting are given in *The Writer in a Changing World.* The Writers' Union, organized in 1934 and disbanded in 1937, was among the leaders in the campaign for a Federal Writers' Project. The Authors' League functions as a trade union and advisory agency for writers.

Of the New York reviewers, Harry Hansen is one of the most popular; his air of "Olympian serenity," as some one has described it, is seldom ruffled. Lewis Gannett of the *Herald Tribune* and Robert Van Gelder and Ralph Thompson of the *Times* are widely read over the breakfast table. Herschel Brickell of the *Post* is an intelligent commentator in his field. John Chamberlain's reviews in the *Times* were formerly a popular feature of that newspaper; but Chamberlain, and formerly Archibald MacLeish, the poet, is now with *Fortune,* one of the leading de luxe magazines. The *Herald Tribune's* literary supplement is piloted by Irita Van Doren, that of the *Times* by J. Donald Adams. The *Saturday Review of Literature,* edited for many years by Henry Seidel Canby and now under the direction of George Stevens, is lively and informative. The *New Republic,* with Malcolm Cowley as literary editor, maintains its reputation for liberalism in the literary as in the social-political field; as does, though less consistently, the *Nation's* book section, now edited by Margaret Marshall. Clifton Fadiman's page in the *New Yorker,* a bit out of place amid the studied lightness of that publication, is thoughtful and discriminating in its comment and reaches an audience that might not otherwise be attained. The left wing is represented by the *New Masses,* which in addition to a regular weekly book department has a monthly literary section; and by Edwin Seaver's column in the *Daily Worker.* Several of the monthly magazines, such as *Harper's, Scribner's,* the *Forum,* etc., contain book review sections.

It is magazines of the type just mentioned that continue to reach the general reading public of the country and to preserve for that public a link with metropolitan life and modes of thinking. In this field, more than one landmark has disappeared. The *Century,* which for some thirty years was edited by Richard Watson Gilder, is no more; it ended under the editorship of Glenn Frank. The *Bookman* is another memory, a fond one for many readers, who recall its intimate glimpses of writing celebrities; no publication today covers precisely the same ground. Attempts by Burton Rascoe and others to revive this magazine in the after-war years proved unsuccessful. There are those, too, of an older generation, who remember the *Nation* under E. L. Godkin, a long vanished *Critic* under Jeanette and Joseph Gilder, and the days when William Dean Howells conducted the "Editor's Study" in *Harper's* and was engaged in discovering Stephen Crane and other promising young men.

From all the writing, editing, and publishing that goes on in New York, it might well be assumed that there is a great deal of "literary life" in the city. Such life is not lacking, but it follows a pattern of its own. With the exception of the Café Royal on the lower East Side, where Jewish writers and theatrical people gather, there is little in New York to recall the café life of the continent. Even the Algonquin, once frequented by Dorothy Parker, Franklin P. Adams, Robert Benchley, Dashiel Hammett, Alexander Woollcott, and many others, is now almost a tradition of the past as a haunt of the literati. The salon, which plays so prominent a part in French literary life, seems to have attained little popularity in New York. One exception is to be noted in Muriel Draper's "at homes," discontinued and resumed at intervals, which are attended by publishers, writers, musicians, and artists. The favored relaxation of the city's literati is the author's tea, given often by a book or magazine publisher or by a bookshop proprietor. As a rule, writers living in New York tend to frequent literary or political rather than social sets.

As for the literary club of the type popular in the 19th century, it is now practically non-existent, in New York as elsewhere. From 1815, when the Literary and Philosophical Society was formed, there were at various times many of these organizations in Manhattan: the famous *Salmagundi* group, the Bread and Cheese Club, the Fortnightly Shakespeare Club, the Quill, the Century, the Authors, the Lotus, the Knickerbocker, the Irving, the Seventy-Six Society, and others. Today, about the only kind of "club" in which the up-and-coming New York writer is interested is the Book of the Month Club or the Literary Guild, which denote sales, royalties, and a nation-wide reputation.

When all is said, New York City is the writer's market rather than a "literary capital." Publishing houses, magazines, literary syndicates and agents—these are the things that, to the average writer, mean a livelihood, economic security, success, possibly lasting fame. The rest is more or less in the nature of window trimming, very attractive after bread and butter are assured, and useful at times in assuring bread and butter. In this respect, literature in New York is true to the temper of modern Manhattan.

The Federal Writers' Project

The economic plight of the writer not endowed with an independent income has even in periods of general prosperity been discouraging. The few writers who starved it out until fame reached their garrets have been memorialized in many romantic biographical sketches; but of the many who were forced by want to abandon their literary aims no record exists.

In New York City, where struggling authors are to be found in greater numbers than anywhere else in the country, the depression of the early 1930's had unusually severe effects, and there was a united demand that the Federal government should include in its work-relief program a plan to employ the writer in work suited to his training and talent.

With the inauguration of the Federal Writers' Project of the Works Progress Administration, late in 1935, the New York City division of the project was organized on the same basis as in each of the States. At its peak, the project employed more than 500 workers; in July 1937 the number had dropped to below 400. Some were employed as administrators, supervisors, photographers, map-makers, typists, filing-clerks, proofreaders, and in other necessary non-literary capacities. The writers included research workers and those who in the past have devoted themselves to newspaper reporting and the writing of magazine articles, radio scripts, poetry, plays, novels and short stories.

The primary task of this project was to prepare an inclusive guide book to New York City, for publication in the *American Guide Series*. But it soon became apparent that only a small part of the valuable material gathered by the project's research workers could possibly be included in the New York Guide. A number of secondary enterprises were then evolved, among them an annual *Almanac for New Yorkers*, of which the volumes for 1937 and 1938 have received wide distribution; a series of racial studies, the first of which, *The Italians of New York*, has already appeared; a number of volumes for children, after the manner of *Who's Who in the Zoo*, published in 1937; a *Bibliography of Bibliographies Relating to Labor*, an *Encyclopedia of New York City*, a *Motion Picture Bibliography*, and others.

Though the technique of planning creative work for so heterogeneous a group and within the necessary limitations of the national program has not yet been fully perfected, it has been clearly demonstrated that a high degree of cooperation may be secured among the writers on a large collective task.

The encouragement that this project has afforded to aspiring writers in their individual strivings may be gauged in part from the fact that several of those on the project have published books written "off-time" while their daily needs were supplied by the project for work done on the Guide and other books, that one of the New York WPA writers has been awarded a Guggenheim fellowship, one has received a prize in a nation-wide *Story Magazine* contest, and still another has been given the Shelley Memorial Award for Poetry.

VIII. ART

In Studio and Gallery

Early American painting developed along two main lines: the tradition of the professional artist, working under the influence of European training and models; and the handicraft tradition, improvising an art in connection with the making and decoration of useful objects. For two centuries these two lines of creative activity continually crossed and recrossed each other under the pressure of American social and cultural conditions. Often they converged in the individual artist—an artisan coming in contact with imported paintings and, through copying or belated schooling, acquiring a professional manner; a studio-trained artist turning his hand to the popular demand for inn-signs, "limnings" or ornamentation. But while American handicraft art lay outside the main currents of traditional art-values, American professional painting remained a provincial version of the European schools. And it was not till past the middle of the 19th century, when the country commenced to grow into its present industrial stature, that an independent American art arose.

In the Dutch settlement of New Amsterdam art was, necessarily, a chance pursuit. The colonist who had acquired an art-training before leaving for the New World was compelled upon his arrival to devote his energies to more practical pursuits. Severed from the art and teachings of Europe, a continued development of technique was impossible. The artist inclined to employ his talents in this raw country could resort only to drawing upon his memory of the masters he had seen back home. Where memory failed, invention supplied what it could. Jacobus Gerritsen Strijcker found relief from his duties as farmer, merchant and magistrate by painting a number of portraits indicating that he must have had occasion to study the approach of the prominent Dutch painters of the 17th century. Evert Duijkinck, glass-maker and limner by trade, appears, however, to have been far removed from any contact with Rembrandt or Hals. On the purely utilitarian side were those engravers of maps and views who came with the explorers and early settlers as gatherers of "news," and who from their sketches supplied the Old World with reports, often fantastic enough, of life among Indians, monsters and an abundant nature.

The colony that fell to the British in 1664 had reached a population of some 10,000. The century that followed was marked by an almost uninterrupted expansion. The increase of commerce and of immigration brought in its train new public buildings, fine residences, schools and newspapers. Paintings and engravings found their place on the walls of homes and public buildings, and artists continued to arrive from abroad. Native painting thus became a colonial transplanting of the English portrait school. At length a few artists found it possible to maintain themselves by obtaining portrait-commissions from the commercial and official aristocracy. The most memorable among these early professionals are Copley, Earl and Feke. Neither Copley nor Earl is associated with New York City, except through an occasional commission. John Singleton Copley, "the best painter produced by colonial America," passed his early life within a small circle in Boston and his later years in the English homeland. Ralph Earl was a native of Connecticut. Robert Feke is sometimes connected with New York, but little is actually known of the background and studies of this artist. An important visitor to the colony was Joseph Blackburn, who arrived from Bermuda in 1754 and remained for nine years. His style is typical of the period. In a three-quarter portrait of a rigidly posed figure the artist displays his virtuosity by the detailed reproduction of the designs and textural sheen of his sitter's carefully draped garments. The drawing and modeling of the face emphasize the hard, linear quality of his English contemporaries. A rectangular upper corner of the canvas opens upon a landscape of clouds and classical architecture receding into the distances. The total effect is one of dignity, and of extreme, if somewhat strained, orderliness—appropriate, apparently, to the patron's own conception of his class distinction. With individual variances and with different degrees of success, this basic pattern of colonial painting was repeated by other New York professionals, Lawrence Kilburn, William Williams and John Durand.

Until the Revolution, studio art in New York consisted of such portraits, painted for the satisfaction of native and newly arrived merchants and officials. Into the modeling of these worthies and their ladies creep traces, often hardly perceptible, of the local rigors of living—of a certain severity and bareness, a certain impulse towards simplicity and directness, a pioneer forthrightness of arrangement, reflecting the artisan regard of a practical people for things that are above all well-made and useful. It is this narrowing and concentration that constitutes the identifying sign of colonial painting within the English school to which it belongs.

But beneath the art addressed to the "high people" of the colony had already sprung up the multiple manifestations of an art, rarely recognized as such, of the common folk: the work of the craftsmen and amateurs of the 18th and 19th centuries who supplied a popular demand for art— house painters, sign painters, portrait limners, carpenters, shipwrights, wood carvers, stone cutters, metal workers. In the busy port town of New York, makers of ships' figureheads, weather vanes, shop and inn signs, decorative grave-stones and carvings, lawn figures and hitching posts found a ready market. For many years sculpture in America con- sisted solely of the work of these artisans. William Rush, the first notable American sculptor, was a carver of figureheads and portrait busts. Itinerant artists, commonly self-taught, supplied more modest homes with portraits and landscapes, many ground out in stereotyped repetition, others, more rare, revealing the operation of an original genius for character, color and design, and achieving with their makeshift knowledge startling harmonies and insights. To the folk tradition of this horde of anonymous artists belonged Pieter Vanderlyn, who as a youth emigrated to New York from Holland. His portraits and sign paintings indicate that he was an impor- tant popular artist, an American "primitive" of high caliber. To this same popular tradition belongs also, though in a different sense, the famous series of lithographic prints—historical scenes and portraits, country and city views, sentimental and sporting subjects, etc.—published in the mid- dle and later 19th century by Currier and Ives of New York, which served as models for many a homespun artist.

Previous to the War of Independence, New York City had already become a center of resistance to the authority of the Crown. Having risen to social ascendency, its merchants, though still considering themselves loyal subjects, were prepared to assert and defend their own interests and their own version of life. The war, which drove out or discredited the adherents of nobility, cemented the prestige of the local financial and trading classes. By 1790, when the Federal capital was removed from New York to Philadelphia, the city had already become, in the scale of the period, a metropolis. Outwardly, this growth was accompanied by cultural advance. New schools and universities were established and news- papers and public institutions multiplied. Essentially, however, commer- cial activity submerged all other pursuits.

Benjamin West, called the "Dean of American Painting," had left the American colonies towards the middle of the 18th century and after three years of study in Italy had settled himself in London as a painter of portraits and historical subjects. He attained great prominence under George III, and in 1792 succeeded Sir Joshua Reynolds as president of the Royal Academy. This honored ex-American set up a school of art in London which came to be known as "The American School." To West and his school early Republican painters, almost without exception, owed some part of their training. The esthetic principle with which West animated his pupils was that the story depicted upon a canvas ought to exert an elevating influence, through its appeal to moral, patriotic or religious emotions. It seemed to the artists of the young Republic that American history demanded to be treated in precisely this manner.

Returning from West's studio imbued with the expectation that extensive commissions would be proffered them by the new government, the pupils of West were doomed to deep disappointment. The officials of the new Republic participated but slightly in the artists' grandiose conceptions of history and allegory. For the art of the capitol they turned to French decorators and architects. American artists soon found themselves compelled to apply their main energies to the painting of portraits and family groups, or to abandon painting altogether for activities more harmonious with the temper of the times. A number of historical paintings were executed, however, for private and public purchasers. John Trumbull's familiar *Battle of Bunker Hill,* painted in West's studio, dates from this period, as well as his *The Surrender of Cornwallis, The Signing of the Declaration of Independence, The Surrender of Burgoyne, The Resignation of Washington.* Trumbull had been in personal contact with the Revolution and its heroes. He had served with the colonial army, had sketched plans of the enemy's military works at Boston, and later had been arrested in London and released through the mediation of West. His full-length portraits of Washington, George Clinton, Hamilton and Jay, executed during the 1790's, became part of the collection of the City Hall of New York. Trumbull was also president of the American Academy of Art founded in New York in 1802.

Gilbert Stuart, whose Athenaeum portrait of Washington remains the accepted likeness, also studied under West, but his work shows little of West's influence. Like most artists of his period he passed some time in New York, but his career can scarcely be identified with the art of this city. The same must be said of that remarkably versatile craftsman, entrepreneur, soldier, lecturer, naturalist, artist, Charles Willson Peale, whose history belongs to that of colonial Philadelphia. His son, Rembrandt Peale, trained by his father and by Benjamin West, served, however, as president of the American Academy and was one of the original members of the National Academy of Design. Other portrait and historical painters of the school of West who worked in New York include Thomas Sully, William Dunlap (author of a *History of the Rise and Progress of the Arts of Design in the United States*), and the inventors, Robert Fulton and S. F. B. Morse. It was characteristic of the age that the two latter should have divided their art with other interests. John Wesley Jarvis, who contributed a number of portraits to the City Hall gallery, was Sully's partner in a portrait-painting enterprise in New York. Among the recorders of historical events was also Robert Walter Weir.

The war of 1812 brought great hardship to the advancing city, but its termination was followed by a new spurt in business, building and population. When in 1825 the great Erie Canal was officially opened, the increase of wealth and immigration and the expansion of the city's area moved forward still more rapidly.

This intensive material aggrandizement, however, brought with it no corresponding improvement in cultural and esthetic taste. The mechanical, the spectacular and the didactic proved more engrossing to the imagination of both upper and lower classes than the serious historical and legendary themes of the West school. Waxworks, stuffed animals, natural curiosities, geographical views and melodramatic tableaux drew crowds and money for their exhibitors. The question of artistic quality received little attention.

The controllers of public life augmented their esthetic anesthesia with moralistic intolerance. When John Vanderlyn attempted to exhibit his *Ariadne* at the American Academy, its withdrawal was demanded by parents who feared the depraving effects upon the students of the presence in the building of an image of a nude reclining in a landscape. Thus Vanderlyn's early attempts to introduce the influence of the French school of David was met not with appreciation and intellectual interest but with a scandal. In sculpture the effects of prudery were even more disastrous; the study of the human figure was fatally impeded in a society where even a cast of the Venus de Milo had to be locked up out of sight.

Legislative intolerance brought to an end an interesting experiment, begun in 1838, in the popular dissemination of art. The Apollo Association, later renamed the Art Union, was formed on the plan of collecting five dollars from each of its members and spending this fund on works of art which, after being exhibited, were distributed by lot. A copy of an engraving, a critical bulletin and free admission to the exhibitions were included in the membership fee. This forerunner of the modern book club proved very successful, soon reaching a subscription of one hundred thousand dollars a year. Many talented artists were thus brought before the public. The enterprise was terminated, however, when it was found to violate the law against lotteries.

In this epoch of the settlement of new territories, the eyes and fancies of the city turned towards the rural life from which it drew its substance. A sentimental naturalism varying from the melodramatic panoramas of Cole, Church and Bierstadt to the literalist pastorals of Inman and Mount succeeded the decline of portrait and historical painting in the English manner. Art of the pre-Civil War decades is identified with the landscapes of these and other nature-painters who collectively came to be known as the Hudson River school.

The "Father of American Landscape," Thomas Cole, was born in England and during his youth spent in Ohio learned the rudiments of painting from a wandering German portraitist. Arriving in New York in 1825, he exhibited his landscapes in the window of an eating-house in Greenwich Village where they attracted the attention and patronage of Trumbull. With the funds earned by the sale of paintings he departed for the Hudson River Valley to work directly from nature. In later years he studied abroad, and, inflating his notions of art with meditations on grand allegorical themes, produced such series as *The Voyage of Life* and *The Course of Empire*. These, with his *Expulsion from Eden*, acquired by the Metropolitan Museum, and his Catskill landscapes, gained him considerable fame.

The Hudson River painters, like those whom their canvases were intended to please, found themselves absorbed almost exclusively by subject matter and story-telling. A panorama limited only by the four boundaries of its frame and leaving its sentiment with the beholder completed the purpose of the artist. Color, form or compositional value can scarcely be said to receive more than elementary consideration; occasionally, certain touches of virtuosity in lighting intervene as a relief. Flat, diffuse and unevocative, thin in pigmentation, over-detailed with static and unresolved superficialities, the landscapes of the Hudson River group lacked as a rule both esthetic harmony and psychological incisiveness. Yet to the Hudson River painters belongs the important distinction of having been the first (with the exception of isolated folk artists) to take American painting out of doors.

Asher Brown Durand, another "father" of this movement, first gained attention through his popular engravings of Trumbull's *Declaration of Independence* and Vanderlyn's *Ariadne*. After a period of portrait painting and of study abroad he returned to America and became prominent as a landscape painter and president of the National Academy. Cole's pupil, Frederick E. Church, preferred the melodramatic in nature to the moral and metaphysical romanticism of his master. Natural marvels—volcanoes, icebergs, tropical daybreaks, giant waterfalls—attracted his fancy, and in search of these vistas he traveled over the world. His work was well calculated to achieve immediate success; he was elected to the Academy in his early youth and subsequently found many purchasers both here and abroad. Other successful academicians were the genre painters Henry Inman and William Sidney Mount, both of whom did much work in New York and are well represented in its museums; also John Frederick Kensett and Eastman Johnson, whose methods, derived from the disciplined and unimaginative Düsseldorf school in Germany, were applied to reproducing the American scene in a manner similar to that of the Hudson River school.

The impulse to record nature in detail also inspired John James Audubon, whose *Birds of America*, originally engraved and published in London, quickly brought him a lasting success. Audubon, whose artistic training developed for the most part outside the schools, ought perhaps to be linked with American folk art, which reached its culmination around the 1850's. His fresh and dynamic renditions of bird-plumage and bird-posture reveal the utilitarian objectives and the freedom from school restraints of the gifted artisan. His art is achieved through the immediate sincerity and faithfulness of his recording. The preservation of the house he built on the Hudson, near what is now 158th Street and Riverside Drive, and the recent popular reprint of his book testify to the continued regard in which his work is held.

In recapitulating the development of American art up to the Civil War, this relationship of Audubon to folk art is extremely suggestive. It exemplifies the constant tendency on the part of the two main currents in American art—local craftsmanship and European borrowing—to flow together at the center: on the one hand, through the transformation of self-trained amateurs and shop-skilled handworkers into disciples of some European school, and on the other, through the application of art to popular demands. But while this flowing together occurs repeatedly in individual artists, the currents themselves remain at their extremes rigidly apart: a cultivated art of the upper class and a makeshift art of the common man.

This separation of cultivated education from popular life affected both our pristine native art and our borrowings from abroad. Since only the rich or the protégés of the rich could acquire a European schooling, the requirements of the wealthy patrons were bound to determine the perspective in which European culture would be approached. Merchants, landlords and public officials decided, in the last instance, what ought to be borrowed from Europe. And with their naturally conservative and esthetically indifferent tastes they inevitably demanded the "best," that is, the most established artistic articles Europe could supply. Hence the more forward-moving of the European schools, the early appreciation of which could rest only upon an impulse towards artistic and theoretical discovery, were for a long time avoided by American students.

With the fixing of the boundaries of American "fine art" in this manner, the social origins of individual artists became a matter of merely personal importance. The artisan-turned-artist who "arrived" as a fashionable portraitist or landscapist came to produce his work in competition with and in the style of the European academician. There remained no center of resistance which would enable him to place the stamp of a different kind of life upon his necessary derivations. His transformation into a European was too complete: the "American" characteristics of pre-Civil War art are, essentially, *negative* characteristics, arising from unconscious limitations rather than from positive esthetic purposes. The American student not only increased his education by his study abroad—he capitulated to it.

The rigid duality of American creative currents left its effects also upon the artist who remained true to the native traditions. Here the remoteness of cultural forms forced expression into crude, primitive moulds, and, by preventing an interchange of ideas and methods, condemned folk art to isolated, atomic "springing-up," with no hope of a unified organic development.

These tendencies are especially obvious in sculpture. We have referred above to the masterful achievements of American makers of figureheads, weather vanes and trade symbols. Of these folk artists William Rush and John Frazee succeeded in leaving an individual impress on their products and in extending their skill into portrait modeling of a high order of characterization. Frazee, proprietor of a marble-cutting shop in New York, studied at the American Academy and applied both artistic training and artisan skill to his carvings of tombstones, busts and decorative mantels. Clark Mills, cabinet-maker and sculptor, fashioned America's first equestrian statue. But while these laborers in the wilderness were forging the beginnings of American sculpture, often without having seen a single example of what the masters of this art had accomplished, their contemporaries who studied abroad promptly succumbed to an abject conservatism and a loss of identity. The Italian school of the expatriate Dane, Bertel Thorwaldsen, became the center to which American students were drawn in the pre-Civil War epoch. Numberless imitations of classical models were produced. A prominent member of this school was Thomas Crawford, who was born in New York but made his permanent home in Rome. He gained success with his mythological groups and figures: *Orpheus Entering Hades in Search of Eurydice, Hebe and Ganymede, Sappho*. The many commissions which he executed for American purchasers were typical of the sculpture of the Italianate school.

If in the two centuries before the Civil War American art remained nothing more than "a local dialect of the great language of European art"—the phrase is Holger Cahill's—and even fell in the middle decades of the 19th century into an insensitivity deeper than ever, the explanation is to be found in the lack of free play between the cultivated tradition upon which it drew and the ever-changing needs of the American people. In 19th century Europe, the old culture, striving to maintain its stability, was from generation to generation taken in hand by and made to serve the interests of new social elements. Within these tensions the successive schools of European art replaced one another. Nowhere so well as in America did European culture retain a relative stability; America was the Academy of Europe. Before an American art could appear it was necessary to begin borrowing in a new and more radical way.

In the decades following the Civil War, America lifted itself out of its agricultural and mercantile past and entered its industrial phase. A vast national expansion followed which sent wealth and organizational power pouring into and through the port city of New York. The embryonic metropolis matured, rapidly taking on the physiognomy which it bears today. Its size and tempo increased at an enormous rate: skyscrapers, traffic, advertising, newspaper extras and ornate residences; standardized housing blocks, tenement slums and street markets composed its visible reality.

Social and cultural life were thrown into new relations by this upheaval beneath it. Europe, brought closer by the improved methods of transportation, by the gigantic flood of immigration, by new political and trade arrangements, saw industrial New York mounting the historical incline that was to achieve the level of its own capitals. The spiritual lag of the province gave way as the city took its place in world-civilization.

New museums and schools of art in New York made study abroad no longer an absolute necessity in education. Private purchases continued to augment the available store of European examples. Newspapers, art magazines and reproductions carried art far down into the mass of the people. Soon the ingression into art of the lower social strata was no longer attended by an abnegation of previous values; instead there commenced the preparation of that succession of violent revolts against the academic which was to shake the art-world in the years to follow, and from which art in New York was to derive so much of its energy.

Under these conditions the two earlier currents in American art came together in a synthesis which for the first time raised American painting to an independent position. Fundamentally, this synthesis represented the spiritual encounter of city and country, of rural and cosmopolitan values, of the farm handicraftsman and the trained urban technician.

Slowly American art intensified its searching, broke more and more decisively with the prettiness and sentimentality of earlier styles, became harsher and more nakedly critical, absorbed and exchanged its European teachings at an accelerated speed. A genuine, serious American art came into being, attended by anguish and rebuffs but persisting defiantly out of a new sense of inner necessity, a new conviction of possessing a role and a function. American art acquired a core of critical resistance which brought selection and purpose to its derivations.

At the moment when this new birth occurred began the exhaustion of the older strains: the rich production of folk art dwindled after 1860 and ceased almost entirely by the end of the century; the talented American apprentice of the European atelier lost his educational monopoly and was relegated to the dim halls of the Academy.

The art of Homer, Eakins and Ryder, the pioneers of the new spirit in American art, breaks decisively both with the sentimental scene and the classical tableau. For the realists, Homer and Eakins, art is an instrument of research into and communication of objective facts; to the mystic and

Waterbound City

OFF MANHATTAN'S SOUTHERN TIP, THE STATUE OF LIBERTY GREETS
INCOMING SHIPS

LOWER MANHATTAN CASTS ITS REFLECTION IN THE EAST RIVER

BEYOND THE TIP OF MANHATTAN, BUTTERMILK CHANNEL APPEARS
BETWEEN THE BROOKLYN SHORE AND GOVERNOR'S ISLAND

BROOKLYN BRIDGE, FIRST TO SPAN THE EAST RIVER, CONNECTS
MANHATTAN AND BROOKLYN

FISHING CRAFT FIND A HARBOR CLOSE TO THEIR DESTINATION, THE
FULTON FISH MARKET, NEAR BROOKLYN BRIDGE

EXCLUSIVE TUDOR CITY, BEEKMAN PLACE, AND SUTTON PLACE BORDER
THE EAST RIVER IN MID-MANHATTAN

AT THE JUNCTION OF HARLEM RIVER AND EAST RIVER, TRIBOROUGH
BRIDGE CONNECTS MANHATTAN, QUEENS, AND THE BRONX

NEWTOWN CREEK, BRANCHING FROM THE EAST RIVER BETWEEN LONG
ISLAND CITY AND GREENPOINT, IS AN IMPORTANT INDUSTRIAL
WATERWAY

WHERE THE HARLEM SHIP CANAL JOINS THE HUDSON RIVER, WITH
NEW JERSEY IN THE BACKGROUND

GEORGE WASHINGTON BRIDGE SPANS THE WIDE HUDSON BETWEEN
UPPER MANHATTAN AND THE PALISADES AT FORT LEE, NEW JERSEY

STEAMER DOCKS AND FERRY SLIPS FRINGE THE WESTERN SHORE OF
LOWER MANHATTAN

BATTERY PARK WITH GOVERNOR'S ISLAND AND BROOKLYN IN
BACKGROUND

ERIE BASIN LOOKING TOWARD THE BAY

ascetic Ryder the transcription of an image brought into being by an inner state demands no less faithfulness and accuracy. All three are far removed from mere "good painting" according to the tenets of some esthetic school.

Winslow Homer began his self-instruction by persistently drawing from life, deriving his teaching, so to speak, from the objects he was attempting to render. In New York he refined this amateur approach by periods of professional instruction and through study of native and imported lithographs and paintings. He opened a shop for wood-engraving, and found employment as a lithographer and as a magazine illustrator, reporting the Civil War from the front for *Harper's Weekly*. The water-colors of his maturity reflect the ability thus gained to seize quickly the immediate appearance of events. If the rough and ready tradition of the shop and the finesse of the studio had alternately characterized the education of Peale and Durand, shop and studio came together stylistically in Homer, in the break with "finish" for the sake of accurate depictions of light and form relations. In his travels, he was the trustworthy reporter of peoples, occupations and natural phenomena, finding little to attract him in the art of Europe—though he studied in Paris for a year—yet expending great devotion on the movements of the sea off the coast of Maine, or on the palms and colored races of the South.

Thomas Eakins was a realist in a deeper sense. His artistic insight cuts beneath the surface like the scalpel of the surgeon in his famous *Clinic* canvases. Thoroughly trained, familiar with the schools and masterpieces of France and Spain, a pupil of Gérôme in the Ecole des Beaux Arts and of Leon Bonnet, he applied his technique not to the reproduction of the artistic manner of some European movement but to the direct analysis of local personalities and activities. The cosmopolitan language of his art probed the prose-world of contemporary life with the simple directness and adherence to fact with which the farmer-painter of early Pennsylvania might have attempted his colloquial reproduction of environing hills and streams. Thus genre painting in his hands, as in Homer's, had nothing in common with the smooth surface attitudes of Inman and the Düsseldorf *decor*. Playing over the details of muscles, nerves, veins and dress, strong contrasts of light and shade point consistently to his major emphasis, the anatomy of human character. To this he willingly subordinated color and composition in his portrait, sport and genre studies.

The new social life of post-Civil War America affirmed itself in the critical and often harsh observations of Eakins. The grace and beauty which Eakins was accused of neglecting in his canvases were lacking too in the young industrial civilization which he accepted as his subject. These were the days of Thomas Nast's effective cartoon attacks on the Tweed Ring, an epoch which this tireless draughtsman characterized politically by introducing the symbols of the Republican Elephant, the Democratic Donkey and the Tammany Tiger. Says Parrington in his *Main Currents of American Thought:* "The idealism of the Forties and the romanticism of the Fifties, the heritage of Jeffersonianism and of the French Enlightenment, were in the Seventies put thoughtlessly away, and with a thorough lack of social conscience, with no concern for civilization, no heed for the democracy it talked so much about, the Gilded Age threw itself heedlessly into the rough and tumble business of money getting and money grubbing." The tough-minded talents of Eakins reflected this spectacle, attempting neither to reject nor to gloss over its meanings.

At the moment, however, when industrial society began to observe itself realistically, a powerful force of negation sprang up within it, equalling in its lyrical intensity the violence of the life which it thrust aside.

Despite all obvious differences, Albert Pinkham Ryder might be called the American Van Gogh. In his work, as in Van Gogh's, imaginative conceptions, founded upon strong religious and ascetic emotions, modify and exaggerate natural appearances; direct and simple statements break through inadequate training and subject drawing and color to new needs of expression. Ryder never underwent the radical modifications which the influence of the Impressionists wrought in the development of Van Gogh. Nor could the skies of New England and smoky New York pour down upon him the sunlit intoxications of Provence. It is night, not sharp daylight, that inspires Ryder. His landscapes and fables are heavy and brooding, like the thick solemn impastos of the Dutch modernist's early isolated gropings towards a significant language. Ryder worked slowly and painfully, endlessly painting and repainting, never completely satisfied that his inner image had been conveyed. His moonlit subjects, drawn from midnight walks at the Battery or from folk tales, Shakespeare, the Bible, or some self-invented legend, became friezes of overpainting or were destroyed in the effort towards perfection. Out of his nights of sharply jutting masses, emerge the incandescent green, silver and blue apparitions of ships, clouds, seasurges, allegorical horsemen, in a sweeping simplicity of shapes which links his work to the best of the romantic modernists. This real opposition to the realities of modern industrial life already foreshadows in Ryder one of the major esthetic attitudes of the art to come in America.

About the dominant figures of these three pioneers whose work constitutes the Declaration of Independence of American painting other changes were affecting New York City's art. In landscape painting the influence of Düsseldorf had yielded to the "new naturalism" of the Barbizon school. Of the purposes of this school Millet, one of its leaders, had written: "I try not to have things look as if chance had brought them together, but as if they had a necessary bond between themselves." As this French influence began to mount, artists turned their backs upon the labored pastorals of Düsseldorf and the picturesqueness of the Hudson River style and strove for the mellow harmonies of Millet and Corot. Sponsored by the landscapists Inness and Martin and by the sensitive and cultivated artists and travelers Hunt and La Farge, French art now became the predominant European source of American instruction. George Inness, the slowness of whose development testified to the difficulties of self-training, progressed from the formless panoramas of his earlier years to the controlled atmospheres of his maturer landscapes. Homer Martin, who began by pursuing the traditions of Cole in his renderings of the untamed scenery of the Adirondacks, was in time so far penetrated by French examples that in his last paintings he proceeded to break up his tones and lay them side by side in heavy strokes in order to achieve the effects of the Impressionists. The cultured eclecticism of Hunt and La Farge ranged as far as the Italian Renaissance; and in the windows and murals which the latter executed for several New York churches he attempted to recapture the transcendental quality of the masters. Alexander Wyant died in New York after painting landscapes which showed an English rather than the general French tendency. Another important landscapist of this period was Ralph Albert Blakelock, in whose original and largely self-tutored talent resemblances are sometimes found to the genius of Ryder.

Succeeding the Barbizon influence, Impressionism became the dominant American derivation from European sources. Weir, Glackens, Twachtman and Hassam are the outstanding American reputations of this phase. Of these, Childe Hassam and William Glackens painted street scenes of New York City. The fate of Impressionism in America, however, wherever its teachings were not leavened with fresh purposes, is perhaps best summed up in the following quotation from a recent bulletin of the Brooklyn Institute of Arts and Sciences: "The strangest thing about impressionism is that when it was invented, it was attacked as a radical movement subversive of established traditions and public morals. Now it is the manner of the academics."

Thus the absorption of European trends continued throughout the last quarter of the 19th century. During this period many of the famous New York collections, including the Frick and the Havemeyer, were established. The Municipal Art Commission was created in 1898. It was an epoch of vigorous learning and assimilation. All foreign trends were attentively and sympathetically scrutinized by American artists, if not by the buyers and the officials of art. The upsurge of original energy which had produced Homer, Eakins and Ryder was not to spread into new local channels until it had enriched itself with a thorough education. By the turn of the century this had been accomplished: the expatriate Whistler had studied Japanese prints and had declared for "musical painting" in the jargon of modernist theory; Mary Cassatt, another expatriate, had been accepted as a ranking artist among the followers of Degas and the Impressionists; the poetry and art criticism of Baudelaire had stimulated a new romanticism; "art for art's sake" had become a slogan; ideas, mystical, socialist and scientific, had infiltrated the minds of American artists both at home and abroad; the effete superficialities of Sargent had dazzled wealthy New Yorkers with the prospect of sitting for a portrait by a fashionable American "master"; Chase and Duveneck had drawn art back to the studio with the emphasis in their teaching on the brush drawing and heavy paint-mass technique of the Munich School.

In sculpture important strides had been taken by the pioneering efforts of Henry Kirke Brown and his pupil, John Quincy Adams Ward. Brown had spent four years of study in Italy, but unlike so many of his compatriots abroad he succeeded in retaining his native character. His *Abraham Lincoln* and equestrian statue of Washington, both at Union Square, show a rugged originality rare in his period. Ward, though American trained, was a finished craftsman whose realism has evoked comparison with Eakins and Homer. His bronze *Washington* at the Subtreasury Building and his *Pilgrim, Shakespeare* and *Henry Ward Beecher* are important city monuments.

At the time when the Paris influence became dominant in painting, it was brought forward also in sculpture in the plastic romanticism of Saint-Gaudens, who studied in New York and worked with La Farge before leaving for Paris. Saint-Gaudens is represented in this city by the *Admiral Farragut* monument in Madison Square and by his *Peter Cooper* and equestrian statue of Sherman. Other practitioners of the new style.

though without the verve and feeling of Saint-Gaudens, were Frederick MacMonnies, modeler of *Nathan Hale* and *Civic Virtue* in City Hall Park, and George Gray Barnard, familiar to New Yorkers through his fountain at Columbia University, his *Pan* in Central Park, and his unique museum "The Cloisters."

By the end of the 19th century American art was prepared to set a fast pace for itself. The decades to follow were to witness a veritable cloud-burst of creation in the plastic and graphic arts. But certain obstacles had first to be met and overcome. The conservatism which had shackled pre-Civil War art still retained powerful strongholds. True, the Academy had changed its style and was to change again in the future. But it had re-mained constant in its procedure of barring the road to the new wher-ever it appeared, as something radical, destructive and artistically mean-ingless. In 1877, New York artists had already felt compelled to set themselves into organized opposition to the esthetics of the Academy. In emulation of their Paris colleagues, who in an analogous situation had defied the Paris art authorities with their Salon des Refusés, they formed the Society of American Artists. The stale eclecticism of the Academy with its lucrative control over commissions had felt in itself an inner resistance to all living currents in American art, both to the direct and forthright discoveries of Ryder and Eakins and to the intellectual and technical innovations of the more significant importations. Ryder, Eakins, Inness, Wyant and Martin, who had been consistently ignored by the offi-cial cliques, were joined by La Farge and Hunt in the exhibitions arranged by the new society.

The Academy, however, proved to be not merely an Organization but a Process. By the time the first decade of the 20th century had been reached, the art rejected by the Academy in the 1870's had won its way to emi-nence, and had begun to yield to still fresher forces, which it had helped to create. The moment had now arrived for the Academy to accept the former outcasts, in order to gain their support in opposing the new threats to its prestige. In 1906 the Society of American Artists amalgamated with its old foe to form the present National Academy of Design.

But a tremendous secret accumulation of artistic energies was to alter radically the character of art production in New York. And against the flood of painting, sculpture, graphic art and photography that swept up out of this first decade of our century the excommunications of the Acad-emy proved of little avail.

The "refusés" of the 1900's consisted of artists who in the 1890's had been coming together in the Philadelphia studio of Robert Henri and quietly preparing a revolt against all that was dead in American art. The majority of the "Henri Group" were newspaper illustrators whose art was produced in direct contact with the life of the times. Technically, they had developed in themselves an alert workmanlike ability to faithfully reproduce the tonalities and atmosphere of streets and public gathering places. Intellectually, they had immersed themselves in social and political currents, familiarizing themselves, more or less deeply, with the ideas of Bellamy, Henry George, Nietzsche, Tolstoy, socialism, individualism and the labor movement. Through Eakins and his disciple, Thomas Anshutz, who taught at the National Academy, members of the group had acquired a taste for an esthetic of uncompromising realism. Henri himself had practiced an independent approach to the masterpieces of Velasquez, Goya, Hals and Rembrandt, as well as to the realists and Impressionists of France. In the words of one observer, the Group "cared more for life than for paint."

In 1908 "The Eight," as they were also called, presented their work before the eyes of New York. Exhibitors included Henri, John Sloan, George Luks, William Glackens, Arthur B. Davies, Everett Shinn, Ernest Lawson and Maurice Prendergast, the latter having discovered for himself the work of Cézanne and the post-Impressionists. The variety of their techniques reflected the backgrounds of American and foreign art from which they had emerged—romanticism, realism, impressionism, commercial illustration. It was against the academic and all that it stood for that they were united. But what was more important was that once again the influences of the past both native and foreign had been absorbed into an idiom of American experience. In this sense their work was a direct continuation of the spirit of Homer, Eakins and Ryder.

The reaction to their show could not have been unexpected: from their critics the "Henri Group" acquired the additional colorful labels of "The Revolutionary Black Gang" and "The Ashcan School." Their paintings and prints of slums, race tracks, park benches, bathing beaches, busy thoroughfares, rooftops, backyards, old paupers and children of the poor seemed no more to belong to art than had the dots and dashes of color of the early Impressionists.

Most of the "Henri Group" had come to New York by 1900. In a spiritual sense, these artists might be said to constitute the first "New York School." For their work was of and concerning the city, both subjectively and with respect to its material. In any event, these streets and inhabitants of New York now became the concern of a whole corps of artists, who bestowed upon their subjects not the remote touch of Hassam's *Madison Square* or *Fifth Avenue* but a close intruding observation into the condition and habits of the people. In addition to the city-scene paintings by "The Eight," poolrooms, restaurants, prizefights, circuses, beauty parlors and human types belonging exclusively to the city made their appearance also in the canvases of Glenn O. Coleman, Jerome Meyers, George (Pop) Hart, Reginald Marsh, George Bellows and Kenneth Hayes Miller.

Out of this realistic movement and animated by its spirit of critical opposition arose also the satirical social and political cartoons of Bob Minor, Art Young and Boardman Robinson, and in succeeding decades the caricatures and social commentaries of Peggy Bacon, Mabel Dwight, and the sharply conceived lithographs and paintings of William Gropper. A determined impulse to speak to the broad masses had brought a new vitality to the graphic arts. Lithography as an art medium had declined towards 1900, leaving etching as the sole important graphic medium. Whistler, Cassatt, Duveneck, Twachtman, Joseph Pennell and Hunt had practiced the printmaker's art. The situation in this field at the opening of the century is summed up as follows by Carl Zigrosser in his *Fine Prints Old and New:* "The favorite etchers of that period made romantic views of foreign architecture, or pretty landscapes, or sentimental portraits of animals or of human 'types.' They spoke in the language—though not always in the spirit—of Whistler, Meryon, Haden, Cameron."

The new realistic and analytical spirit inaugurated by "The Eight" brought a return of lithography and wood-engraving. In the expansion of techniques that followed, with the rise of photography and the motion picture as independent arts, with the development of color-reproduction of painting, the making and circulation of prints became part of a great movement to render art easily accessible to all and to cause it to form a normal element of daily life. Among the etchers and lithographers of the past 25 years are Sloan, Hassam, Bellows, Hart, Coleman, Rockwell Kent, Miller, Weber, Hopper, Davies, Albert Sterner, Ernest Fiene, John Marin, Marsh, Hugo Gellert, Alexander Brook, Louis Lozowick, John Taylor Arms, George Biddle, Kuniyoshi. Other printmakers of New York include George Constant, Adolph Dehn, John Groth, Kerr Eby, Wanda Gag, Isami Doi, Philip Reisman, Raphael Soyer, Howard Cook, Emil Gauro, Doris Rosenthal; and such newspaper and magazine cartoonists as Rollin Kirby, Peter Arno, Otto Soglow, Denys Wortman.

On the heels of the realistic commentators on social life came the experimental "modernists." In the year of the first exhibition of "The Eight" Alfred Stieglitz had opened his "291 Fifth Avenue," which soon became a center of authentic novelty in art. In a long series of exhibitions "291" brought under one roof the works of the European modernists, Rodin, Matisse, Toulouse-Lautrec, Cézanne, Picabia, Henri Rousseau, Picasso, Braque, Severini, and of the Americans, Marin, Hartley, Dove, Steichen, Weber, Walkowitz and O'Keefe. Stieglitz himself was essentially committed to "spirit," a yearning vague enough to allow a broad range of choice—from a photograph of the *Five Points Clothing House: The Cheapest Place in the City* to the passionate markings of the first American abstractionists.

The most memorable event in the American art world, the famous "Armory Show" of 1913, whose aim was to bring together everything that was vital in modern art both here and abroad, arose from the currents that flowed through "The Eight" and "291." The Association of American Painters and Sculptors which prepared the International Exhibition at the armory included seven members of the original "Henri Group." In the American Section, alongside the works of the realists, Henri, Luks and Sloan, and of the Impressionists, Glackens, Weir, Twachtman and Hassam, emerged the *avant-garde* canvases, watercolors and sculpture of Karfiol, Lachaise, Walkowitz, Marin and Prendergast, as well as of the modernist forerunner Albert Ryder. The publicity, consisting mostly of abuse, which this exhibition received enabled the New York public to encounter for the first time, and to ridicule in its turn, the discoveries of post-Impressionism, Fauvism and Futurism.

Thus, arm in arm, modernism and realism in American art came into prominence during the second decade of this century. The modernists found in the museum, in machinery, in dreams and in reveries and in mathematical relations the life which the realist sought in the street and the subway. The European masters of the American modernists had pursued the trail of art through antique, Oriental and primitive styles; they had borrowed from Egypt, Persia, East India, China, Japan, Byzantium, from classical Greece as well as from savage Africa, Polynesia and the Oceanic Islands, from Mexico, Peru and the North American Indians. The Americans, almost without exception, applied these teachings to contemporary experiences. The structural delicacy of the watercolors of Dickinson, Demuth and Marin; the mystical and sensitive landscapes and the allegorical nudes of Davies; the post-Impressionist, Cubist and Fauvist figures of Weber, Walkowitz, Kuhn and Karfiol; the mechanical designs of Stella; the eclectic experimentalism of Morris Kantor and Samuel Halpert—these reflect the reality of our epoch no less than the photographic factory scenes of Charles Sheeler or the night-life of Guy Pène Du Bois. In spite of the differences and the polemics that were to divide realist and modernist schools in later years, the two movements thus showed themselves at their inception to be two branches of a single stalk, the art of the city, both in its local life and in its world-relations.

The analysis, historical and theoretical, to which the modernists subjected all art brought to sculpture a new point of departure. Cubism, Futurism, and Fauvism had found in Negro and primitive figures a simple and striking embodiment of the principles of rhythm, design, architectonic balance and significant relation of plane and mass. A new analytical acid had also been applied to the classics of Greece, Rome and Florence. The modelings of Crawford and the Thorwaldsen school now seemed remote indeed from sculpture's essential aims. The rough-surfaced monuments of Jacob Epstein, an expatriate, evoked startling and often disturbing conceptions of a kind not hitherto associated with the art of sculpture. Gaston Lachaise's *Figure of a Woman* became a familiar example of modernist treatment of mass, balance and subtlety of form-relations. William Zorach's more easily assimilable subjects achieved wide circulation. Others working in the modern manner included Maurice Sterne, Robert Laurent, Alfeo Faggi, Elie Nadelman. Paul Manship made an academic utilization of modern archaeological research and produced a style of decoration which became a fashionable adjunct of architectural design. Jo Davidson executed portraits of the famous. Among the many sculptors of recent years whose work is worthy of attention are Mahonri Young the realist, Isamu Naguchi, Ahron Ben Shmuel, Chaim Gross, Arthur Lee, Heinz Warneke, Boris Lovet-Lorski, Harold Cash, Hunt Diederich, Reuben Nakian, Aaron Goodleman, John Flannagan, Marion Walton, Sonia Brown, Dorothy Greenbaum, Duncan Fergusson. Especially interesting are the accomplishments of the abstractionists Alexander Calder, John Storrs, and the Russian, Alexander Archipenko.

It was under modernist influence that American folk art was rediscovered, its best examples collected and exhibited, and its esthetic value brought into focus with the art of the world. Modernism, with its historical perspective, found more to admire in the rudimentary but sound artisanship of a Pickett or Hicks than in the studiously elaborated graces of the Düsseldorf professionals.

Since the Armory show and the annual exhibitions open to all artists of the Society of Independent Arts, the division between realism and modernism has grown more conscious and more pronounced, though an overlapping has been constantly visible in the majority of American artists. Extremists are rare in American art. Such artists as Georgia O'Keefe, Peter Blume, Francis Criss, Stefan Hirsch, Stuart Davis, Edward Hopper, Niles Spencer, Walter Pach lean towards formalism without fully discarding realistic elements. Marsden Hartley, Louis Eilshemius, Yasuo Kuniyoshi, Alexander Brook, Reginald Marsh, Andrew Dasburg, Ernest Fiene, Leon Kroll are romantics with varying modernist and realist stresses. These main trends are expressed in the two most active of the recently established art centers, the Whitney Museum of American Art and the Museum of Modern Art. As their names suggest, the Whitney emphasis is upon local tendencies and the American scene, while the Modern Museum seeks out all manifestations, wherever they be found, to which the modernist spirit is attracted. In these two major divisions of 20th century art the two main currents in early American art, localism and the foreign influence, reappear in a more mature form.

The conflict between realism and modernism has brought about the organization of an "Abstract Group" and the establishment of collections sponsoring the non-representational in art. This difference of approach was also reflected in the debates concerning the new social art brought forward during the late 1920's and the 1930's. In connection with this social art, the murals of Thomas Benton received a varied response and a new source of inspiration was contributed by Mexico in the murals of Orozco and Rivera. The rejection for political reasons of the decoration executed by the latter for Radio City led to bitter controversy.

Economic problems of artists produced novel events in New York City during the 1930's. Semi-annual outdoor shows established an informal art market in Washington Square. During the economic crisis which began in 1929, depressing art sales and stifling private patronage, artists organized themselves into the Artists Union to demand Federal support for art. The Federal Works Art Project was set up in 1933 and later the Federal Art Project of WPA. The latter has brought vast changes in the art situation in New York. Its mural decorations of public buildings, its allocations of easel and graphic work, its art center and public exhibitions, its Art Teaching Department, the faithful copying of old art objects by its Index of American Design division—all have served to bring indigenous American art before an immense new public. Its encouragement of talent, through providing the means of subsistence and contact with the public, has served to bring forward such excellent younger artists as Ashile Gorki, Philip Evergood, Gregorico Prestopino, Joe Solman, Max Spivak, James Newell, Lucienne Bloch, Alfred Crimi, Louis Guglielmi, William de Kooning, Joseph Pandolfini, Harry Gottlieb, and others, as well as such sculptors and graphic artists as Eugenie Gershoy, Anton Refregier, Hubert Davis, F. G. Becker. At present a number of artists' organizations, together with organizations of writers, musicians and actors, support a Congressional measure calling for the establishment of a permanent Federal Art Project.

Thus the program of "The Eight," aiming to connect the activity of art with the life about it, has continued, in changing forms, as a dominant factor in the art of New York. The Artists Congress, a national organization stressing the political and social values of art, holds frequent exhibitions in New York and sponsors conferences here to discuss the artist's responsibilities in modern society and to protest against reaction and fascism. The city's public museums and private exhibition galleries provide the means for continual intercourse with the outside world of art. New York City is no longer merely the chance birthplace or residential choice of individual artists, schools and collections—it has become a national clearing-house and a world-center of art.

Bricks of the City

WHAT American has not desired to ascend to the top of the Empire State Building, or stand on the footwalk of the Brooklyn Bridge? High on his vantage point on the bridge, the wind blowing a metallic whistle through the wires above, the boats far below his feet, he looks through the mighty network at those towers of Manhattan, still higher than himself, the most awe-inspiring of all architectural views afforded by the modern world. Below the towers, the shore is fringed with docks, the ocean vessels—chiefly freighters on this side—delivering cargoes that explain the strong odor of coffee and spice that blows from the waterfront warehouses. It is not the "immense tremor" of the open ocean that surrounds us here, but the busy motion of the quiet harbor, so shut in as to appear like a lake. Far off on the horizon to the southwest, beyond the Statue of Liberty, is the graceful arc, dimly visible, of the Bayonne Bridge, connecting the largest of New York's islands except Manhattan to the New Jersey mainland; on the opposite side of the Brooklyn Bridge and in close proximity to it are the other famous "East River" bridges: far from beautiful, some of them, but all brutally business-like and immense, their feet not in fresh water but in salt. They dwarf, as if from another world, the bridges of the other river cities such as Florence or Paris or London. Looking at Manhattan itself, one sees the second skyscraper cluster at midtown: the Empire State Building slightly off to the left, the Chrysler Building's fountain-like pinnacle to the right, the broad slab of the R.C.A. Building of Rockefeller Center remotely visible in the distance, while numerous less famous structures serve to fill out the group.

But even as his eye sweeps this view at the magnificent portal of New York, the judicious visitor is aware that not all is splendor. The great downtown skyscrapers do not simply rise from the water's edge. In front of them, especially to the north of the bridge, is a great low nondescript area, block after block of shabby brick dwellings whose sides are covered with fading patent medicine signs, an area like eroded debris at the foot of a cliff—the notorious New York East Side. If one leaves the bridge to walk these streets, one is confronted again and again by the kind of view that shocked the world when a German architect photographed it and put it in a book: the sight of the unmitigated meanness of the tenements smacked against the very walls of the "cathedrals of commerce." This is one example of the many kinds of abrupt contrast that are far more truly characteristic of New York than the selected magnificence that appears in the Sunday papers. More than any other American City, New York pitches high against low, rich against poor, the elegant against the squalid. All occur juxtaposed, with scarcely a buffer and rarely a disguise.

The energy, the brutality, the scale, the contrast, the tension, the rapid change—and the permanent congestion—are what the New Yorker misses when he leaves the city.

The study of the almost volcanic eruption of New York's skyline should not be pursued without a word of caution. Almost anyone can glibly explain the skyline in terms exclusively economic. The narrow island, the great influx of population, the consequent scarcity of land, and as a result the towering buildings—thus runs the argument that is almost universally accepted. Accurate as far as it goes, it has misled countless people into believing that a skyscraper was always the result of a simple calculation in profit and loss. The development of New York is actually far more enigmatic. Without digressing into a sociological or economic essay, we might barely mention a few factors slurred over by this simple account; the fact, for example, that the giant buildings occupy only a very small fraction of the land actually available, and that, right into the depression, there was a tendency to move offices into fewer, taller buildings, occupying less and less of the land that *was* available, meanwhile leaving surrounding areas in financial straits. Again there is the fact that New York pays far less than an "economic" share of many essential services; for example, freight is lightered across the harbor without charge but at great expense, and if these and other items had been charged against the city in advance, the net profitability of New York's congested building habits might have been called into serious doubt, and this without even mentioning the incredible costs of such items as building the subways.

The point is not that economic explanations of the skyline are wrong, but that taken by themselves they are incomplete. The business nature of the town is to be far more completely understood if we know the nature of its history. In this historic past, three successive powerful impulses acted on New York. Like a series of great waves, they drove the vessel always in the same course. Any major force that might have diverted the city from its single-line development seems to have been lacking, or to have just touched and then passed the city by.

New York from the very beginning was devoted single-mindedly to commerce. It was superbly situated for a port. The Hudson had made New York the chief outlet of the West and permitted it to surpass Philadelphia in population even before the completion in 1825 of the Erie Canal. No religious oppression affected the Dutch who founded New Amsterdam, to render them philosophic or to put them under the leadership of learned parsons like those who established the Puritanic culture in New England. The Dutch spent their energy on developing trade.

Next, the port of New York developed into a manufacturing center. This was largely due to a second stroke of luck: vast coal deposits were found highly accessible in nearby Pennsylvania. Labor came in a great wave from Europe. The effect of industry piled on commerce was cumulative, and cumulatively utilitarian.

Immediately after the Revolution and at the beginning of this new industrial expansion there occurred a brief episode that might have broadened the city's permanent nature. New York became the national capital. But before the city's outlook and planning could adapt themselves to the new situation, the seat of the Federal Government was moved elsewhere and the comprehensiveness of viewpoint and breadth of planning that might have ensued yielded once more to the one-sided attitude of the market. The results will be clearly seen expressed in the city's street plan —and its lack of park plans.

Finally, the effect of its combined trade and industrial leadership was to give New York dominance in finance. Hereafter the metropolis wielded a new power which permitted her to be ruthless even in the face of geography, and to call this ruthlessness "strictly economic." The river and the port had produced trade; the coal and the labor combined with the trade had produced industry; the two together had created the dominating power of money, its influence reaching like radio across all physical barriers and helping to rivet together a purely business culture that piled the profits and the buildings higher and higher in the same places. The psychology of the people was profoundly influenced by the history of the place; and that, as we shall see, has had quite as much to do with the architecture of present-day New York as have land values. If, in the course of the headlong development of the city, a New Yorker without hesitation tears down a historic Vanderbilt mansion for the sake of erecting a block of stores, his action in refusing to be diverted is more eloquent of the historical tradition and culture of New York than the mansion itself. Again, New York began to regulate the shape of tall buildings only after they had already transformed many of the streets into permanently sunless canyons, whereas Boston laid down in advance regulations against what were considered excessive building heights; which showed the effect of historical tradition rather than the relative chances of profit and loss in the two cities.

The Seaport Colony

Of the New Amsterdam period, the architectural remains are few. The Dutch fort stood with its center at about the site of the present Custom House, the Governor's House being inside the fortifications. Wall Street derives its name from having run along the north wall or rampart hastily erected against the English. Of the little Dutch town with its two-hundred-odd houses not a trace remains. The houses of Dutch origin still standing within the present boundaries of New York are those that were outlying farm houses, chiefly in the western sections of Long Island and on Staten Island.

Perhaps it is just as well. The town houses as we see them on the old maps were the familiar trim Dutch houses as found in Holland itself, often with the characteristic stepped gables turned toward the street. The outlying houses, on the contrary, gradually evolved a character all their own, existing in New Netherland but nowhere else in the world, a type we call Dutch Colonial. Its two chief earmarks are its diminutive size and the handsome roof that was gradually developed to curve outward, forming an overhang protruding well beyond the wall. The Dutch, says Miss Bailey in her admirable monograph on these houses, had less use for the upper or garret floor than the English; and when they began to use a gambrel roof they sacrificed bedroom space to achieve a handsomer and steeper roof line.

The oldest known example in the city is the Schenck-Crooke House, at East Sixty-Third Street and Mill Avenue, Brooklyn, set in a lane in a little hollow behind Public School 236. The steepness of the plain gable roof is evidence of its great age. The overhang, as often happened, is said to have been added later, and so were the sloping dormers. There remains unchanged the unusual inside framing, built shiplike with curved timbers and an arch-like inverted frame; for the Schencks were shippers as well as millwrights and built a dock in the adjoining Mill Basin. Scholars can find a number of other Dutch houses of historic interest; the casual visitor would probably prefer a visit on Staten Island to New Dorp, where three charming examples exist close together. The oldest is the Britton Cottage in New Dorp Lane, now belonging to the Staten Island Historical Society, simply and neatly built of random fieldstone; the plain gable roof, however, is scarcely typical, having an unusually flat slope and no overhang at all. Another is the so-called Lake-Tysen House, a larger example than most, built probably 1720–40, with the typical Dutch gambrel roof (the graceful overhang is supposed to have been added later) and the typical three chimneys. The plan is characteristic: a wide central hall with two rooms on each side. A charming house is the Lakeman-Cortelyou-Taylor House, though its gambrel is of the New England type—two equal sections instead of a short nearly horizontal one at the top and a long one on the side. Still another excellent composition is the Stillwell-Perine House, 1476 Richmond Road, Dongan Hills, really two houses separately occupied for 100 years, the older part dating from about 1680, the front from about 1713. In Brooklyn, the Lefferts Mansion in Prospect Park furnishes a precedent for "Hollywood Dutch," the deep curve being carried through the whole lower leg of the gambrel instead of being confined to the overhang. The Lott House and the Remsen House show the earlier, diminutive, thick-walled, small-windowed and steep-gabled construction of their older wings in contrast to the full development of the later period, at the end of the 18th century.

"Dutch Colonial" continued to be built long after the English occupation, for the Dutch and English inter-married and lived peaceably side by side. A very handsome late example is the Dyckman House, at Broadway and 204th Street. This was not built until 1783, at the end of the Revolution. Carefully restored, it is now a city museum. It displays the charming use the Dutch made of varied building materials. The front wall is brick; the end walls are uncoursed fieldstones in heavy mortar; and the gables are covered with wide clapboards.

The Dutch imprint on the city remains chiefly in a line of distinguished families and in the realm of tradition, rather than in buildings. Names survive—the Bowery, which was the road leading past the chief farm or *bouwerie* of the Dutch West Indies Company; Coenties Slip, which according to legend is a compound evolved from the names of the Darby and Joan of New Amsterdam, Coenrat and Antye's Slip; Spuyten Duyvil, which memorializes Trumpeter Anthony Corlear's watery bout with the devil; Pearl, Beaver, Vesey, Hague, and John Streets, Maiden Lane (*T'Madde Paatje*) and others. The stoops of the houses, splendidly adapted to the early New Yorker's living habits, had their origin in Dutch lowland building customs; it was not the fault of the Dutch that in the later brownstone houses the stoops were carried over from mere habit and their earlier purpose completely misunderstood. Of this, more will be said in the discussion of the average New Yorker's dwelling quarters.

English Colonial houses go back to a fairly early date. High on a mound overlooking the sea at the southern end of Staten Island in Tottenville stands the Billopp or Conference House, erected by Captain Christopher Billopp in 1677 on an early patent from the Duke of York. Quite as simple as the Dutch houses, its lines are nevertheless English, standing higher and more openly to the air. In this house on September 11, 1776, Benjamin Franklin, John Adams and Edward Rutledge met Lord Howe and rejected his demand for unconditional surrender of New York. Another Colonial house, Fraunces Tavern, dating from 1719 and still in use as a restaurant, at the southeast corner of Pearl and Broad Streets, earned its fame at the end of the Revolutionary War, when Washington was banquetted in the large second-floor room and there took leave of his officers. Of New York's later and larger Colonial mansions, the country houses are the ones that remain: Alexander Hamilton's "Grange," the Van Cortlandt House, and the Jumel Mansion built in 1765—the last-named for its scale and detail and for its exceptionally delicate and effective two-storied portico.

Federal New York

After the Revolution came an episode that might have changed the entire history and appearance of the city. New York, a small city in what was then considered the most beautiful setting on the continent, was chosen the nation's first capital. It was in this connection that L'Enfant remodeled the Federal Hall (on the site of the present Subtreasury Building on Wall Street), where Washington was inaugurated as first President; and that Government House, a stately porticoed mansion long since destroyed, was built on State Street, in the vicinity of the present Custom House, for occupation by the President. When the Government was moved, first to Philadelphia and then to Washington, this building was converted into a customs house.

Of the row of city dwellings originally adjoining Government House, there remains only Number 7 State Street, now used as a rescue mission. Its tall full-height columns, arranged in a picturesque if awkward curve, are supposed to have marked the termination of the row, of which Mc-Comb is reputedly the architect. The exceptionally handsome interior of this house is unfortunately closed to the public. At Number 9, the house once immediately adjoining, Lafayette was given his great New York reception on the occasion of his return to the United States in 1824.

Had the seat of Government remained in New York, the city might in time have acquired some of the breadth and dignity of planning associated with the capitals of great states—such as the L'Enfant Plan attempted to secure for Washington. There might still have occurred disputes about the appropriateness of geometric monumentality in the layout of a city, but it seems impossible that New York would have developed as it did in almost defiant crowding on part of the tip of an island.

In the early years of the 19th century, Joseph Mangin, a French engineer, with John McComb as partner, created one of the finest buildings in the city—the present City Hall. Few buildings in America of any period are as gracious, as beautifully poised, and as felicitous as the City Hall. The two wings are nicely balanced against the central section and the handsome cupola, now fortunately restored after being for a time replaced by an ugly dome. The windows are large and beautifully proportioned. The detail has a Gallic liveliness and deftness; due to Mangin it savors somewhat of Louis XVI instead of the grave King George. The interior should not be missed by the visitor to the city; the rotunda contains a beautiful circular stairway, while the upstairs rooms not only display the felicitous interior style of the building but show a good many of New York's early treasures of art and furniture.

On April 3, 1807, a commission was appointed to lay out a city plan. On March 22, 1811, it submitted its report, with a map by John Randel, Jr. Its recommendation drew the hand of a heavy fate upon New York, for it proposed the gridiron street system. The commission decided that "a city must be composed principally of the habitations of men, and straight-sided and right-angled houses are the most cheap to build and the most convenient to live in."

Elsewhere in the present volume is discussed the effect of this plan on topography and traffic; we confine ourselves here to its effect on architecture. It permanently limited the shape, the outlook and the surroundings of every kind of future building. It meant, to begin with, that for better or worse every house was to be fitted to a lot, regardless of such considerations as sunlight, prevailing winds and view. The plan divided the city into uniform building lots, always 100 feet in depth, easy to transfer and to speculate in. Consideration of the stages whereby this made rational building more and more difficult instead of simple must be left to the section on housing; suffice it to say that only within the past few years has it been possible for a few large-scale enterprises, usually in outlying sections, to cut across the gridiron plan in the interest of restoring on modern terms the rational type of building that prevailed before the mischief of the plan began. A second effect has been that only rarely does a building in New York possess a vista; so that, paradoxically, in just the city of the United States where the greatest amount of "architecture" has been produced, that architecture is most difficult to see. The skyscraper architect must compromise on embellishing the entrance visible from the street and then apply himself to that part of the mass which will be visible from a distance if it towers above its neighbors. A corollary is that in New York the conspicuous buildings are not the high ones but the low ones, especially those low ones favored by a few feet of open space—such as the Public Library and the City Hall.

Besides the examples already mentioned, the Federal era has left a sprinkling of other buildings worth attention, especially because they preserve the architectural record. There are a few late Colonial houses, such as the charming one with its fan doorway at the end of Cherry Street (built about 1790), and a scattered group (to be described more fully in another context) that survives in Greenwich Village. Another monument is the famous St. Paul's Chapel on lower Broadway, by James McBean. It is perhaps one of the best of the American churches modeled on James Gibbs' work, and is very handsome with its grayish stone hall and tall lively spire.

When we come to the Subtreasury Building on Wall Street we are confronted by a totally different trend from the Colonial. Though no longer the capital, New York continued to share in the architectural ideals of the young republic. Just why these turned to classical models, first Roman and then Greek, is a scholars' dispute. Some believe that it was political enthusiasm for the Roman republic and for the 1821 war of independence of the Greeks; others believe that the Greek, at least, was purely a turn of taste. At any rate, whether the American felt like a Greek or had merely decided to dress like one, Latrobe's Bank of the United States in Philadelphia, with its Doric temple porticoes, built in 1799, took the country by storm.

In New York the old Custom House, now called the Subtreasury Building, shows this somewhat heavy classical hand. It is a crude version of the Parthenon, with changes for the sake of windows. It was erected during the period 1834–41. At the same time on the opposite side of Wall Street, the Merchants Exchange was built, fronted by another colonnade, considerably more refined, above which a second was later imposed when a story was added for its present occupant, the National City Bank.

Churches diverged somewhat from the common mode, since Classical Revival churches were soon followed by Gothic Revival ones, and both kinds were built, according to preference, at the same time. The best known Gothic Revival churches are the late ones, built just before or shortly after the Civil War and therefore belonging to a rather later time. They are Grace Church (with an elaborateness that drew the ire of Whitman), Richard Upjohn's Trinity Church, and St. Patrick's Cathedral by James Renwick. However, there remain numerous other and older examples. On the lower East Side, four old churches typify the two parallel architectural trends. The old St. Patrick's, at Prince and Mulberry Streets, is the earliest example of the Gothic Revival; designed by Joseph Mangin (the interior and upper part of the wall were rebuilt after a fire later), it is "terrible but big." Another more pleasing pointed-arch church, built 1817–18, stands a block east of Knickerbocker Village on Market Street, and has been recorded in detail by the Historic American Buildings Survey. Two of the Greek Revival instances are the Church of St. James (probably by Maynard Lefevre), on James Street east of Chatham Square, and the Marinist Temple just off Chatham Square. On West Thirteenth Street between Sixth and Seventh Avenues stands another example, with a Greek Doric portico in granite.

American houses built at this time resembled Greek temples to a degree never approached in Europe. New York shows very few such houses entirely surrounded by columns; but precariously surviving on Lafayette Street is a part of a Colonnade Row, a block-long series of dwellings erected in 1827, with a Greek Corinthian colonnade across the whole length.

Another once extremely handsome row, built in the 1830's and lingering now in disrepair, is found on Richmond Terrace, Staten Island, near Westervelt Avenue, New Brighton; it sadly reminds us that our forefathers knew how to make the waterfront of what is now the dirty Kill van Kull a handsome and stately drive. In the opinion of Professor Talbot

Hamlin, a special authority on the Classic Revival in New York, the finest single example in existence is the old merchant's house on East Fourth Street between the Bowery and Lafayette Street. But the most accessible and best preserved group in the finest setting is the splendid collection of mansions existing both singly and in connected rows on Washington Square. The example on the eastern corner of Fifth Avenue is of noble simplicity. It has no porticoes or pediments, only a modest Ionic canopy over the door, three stories of well proportioned and beautifully spaced fenestration, a simple wooden entablature painted with a Greek fret, and over the plain cornice a simple balustrade: yet one might search far for a calmer or more felicitous statement.

The Young Industrial City

New York of the early 1800's was rapidly finding new ways of earning a very handsome living. When Washington bade farewell to his Revolutionary officers at Fraunces Tavern, the removal of British restrictions on trade made a rapid commercial expansion certain. Not so many decades later, New York became, among other things, the chief builder of the superlative Yankee clipper ships and operator of the Black Ball and other ocean packet lines. From this glorious period date the few remaining sail-lofts and ship chandleries on Front Street, then South Street.

One of the next phases in the development of New York's history was the growth of industry in the wake of commerce. By 1820 New York already had a desperate housing problem, which helps to explain the building boom that carried straight through into the panic of 1837.

The effects of manufacturing and immigration on the architecture of New York ever since the first quarter of the 19th century have been beyond calculation. Therefore, instead of following the usual procedure, and expounding the decadence in residential and public building that followed the classic revival—a dreary subject—it might be wiser to speak of one type of structure, still existing by the hundreds, which though usually awkward and unlovely nevertheless marked the inception of a totally new technique in the old art of building.

We refer to the despised "cast-iron front." Lewis Mumford in *The Brown Decades* ascribes the introduction of cast iron as a material not only for interior columns but for the façade of buildings, to Bogardus in 1848. The exact date or architect is of minor importance, however, for the use of iron had long been increasing—first in ugly sheet-iron cornices as well as handsome wrought-iron fences, then in "tin" roofs supplanting wooden shingles.

With a kind of naive surprise, those of us who have been told a great deal in recent years about a new architecture of metal and glass—as if there had been a hiatus between the Crystal Palace and the recent 1920's —walk along lower Broadway and the streets heading from it to the westward, noting one after another of these "cast-iron fronts," built not long after the Civil War, in which the proportion of glass to frame compares favorably with present-day standards. After viewing these early examples, even our "glass houses"—such as the new one by the Corning Company on upper Fifth Avenue—seem a little less than revolutionary departures.

What put a stop to the "cast-iron front" was the hazard revealed by the Chicago fire—that the iron, unprotected by masonry, would warp in intense heat. Nevertheless, here was the beginning of the great modern surge toward a strictly industrial building technique, since neither the iron nor the glass could be found, like wood or stone, in a natural state, but had to be fabricated.

It is curious to note that among architectural critics only the German, Werner Hegeman, has thus far had a kind word to say for the "cast-iron front." Hegeman declared a preference for the Stewart Building in New York (now the older part of the Wanamaker store) to the vaunted Field Warehouse by H. H. Richardson in Chicago, on the score of "greater simplicity and less pretension." Whatever may be the opinion of other observers on the point of taste, it is clear that in efficiency, lightness, airiness, and simple order the Stewart Building is on the more progressive side. It is this type, rather than the heavy fortress of Richardsonian Romanesque, that lies in the direct line of modern building.

In contrast with their industrial and commercial structures, the houses of the men who brought industrial preeminence to New York were not of the sort to inspire architectural history. The exotic residences of the early get-rich-quick Wallingfords represented every sort of opulent excess: Moorish castles, Gothic fabrics, mock Italian villas, Swiss chalets, whatever fancy might desire. Inside, these monsters were decked out with nooks and alcoves marked by wooden spindle screens, ottomans, whatnots and sentimental statues. One picture of a "millionaire's parlor" shows even the legs of the grand piano tied up in huge bowknots of ribbon a yard wide.

Hotels are among the structures readily accessible to the public which retain some of this exuberance; and a good measure of gilt and voluptuous accessories will be found in such a house, for example, as the Ansonia. An English visitor to a New York hotel during President Grant's administration, when asked by his wife why he did not put out his shoes to be shined, replied that he was afraid he would get them back gilded in the morning. Some of the energy of those times is carried over today in the sumptuous lobbies and auditoriums of the more overpowering movie houses—the Paramount, for example, of which it was said that its owners "spent a million dollars and made every nickel show." Houses of the parvenu, Victorian and romantic types are perhaps more numerous in Brooklyn or on Staten Island than in Manhattan, a good Brooklyn district to study being the one surrounding Prospect Park. The drab brownstone types here were chiefly speculative residences that mushroomed during the 1870's and later. They may be found on almost any downtown cross-street.

The Great Bridges

Brooklyn Bridge was the greatest achievement in New York architecture after the Civil War. At a time when the architects were producing brownstone fronts, Victorian Gothic churches, and strangely stiffened and distorted Renaissance post offices and court houses, the only fresh blood seemed to flow in the veins of an engineer. When the bridge was completed in 1883, the event was celebrated as a national holiday. The President attended the dedication. The city was hilarious. In their desire to venture out on this "eighth wonder of the world," the citizens rushed forth in such crowds that a moment's panic on one of the first days after the opening caused two people to be trampled to death.

The bridge represents an American epic of heroism. Everyone knew that throughout 12 years, while the bridge was being built, the chief engineer had lain partially paralyzed on a bed in Brooklyn Heights. Everyone knew that the lady to take the first drive across the new structure was his faithful and highly capable wife, who had acted as the engineer's intermediary throughout the whole tedious work.

The bridge was not, as a matter of fact, designed by Washington A. Roebling, the man who actually built it, but by his famous father, John A. Roebling—an energetic, careful, hard-driving man, pitiless with himself and with his children, a student of Hegel who had written his own "View of the Universe" but who with the same thoroughness devised a ropewalk on his Pennsylvania farm, inventing designs, methods and organization as he went along. In the Brooklyn Bridge, John Roebling drew up the last and best of his bridge designs; his son was there to carry on when a stupid accident caused the fatal infection of the father's foot with tetanus. Despite increases in cost and numerous delays, the bridge eventually emerged, a triumph of the engineer's art. And even though thoughtful critics had fault to find with the somewhat stiff and bluff use of Gothic forms in the towers, the artists loved it from the very start and continue to celebrate it in prints and paintings today. The soundness and sincerity of Roebling somehow managed to come through.

The Manhattan Bridge, with steel towers instead of stone, is just matter-of-fact; the Williamsburg Bridge, with towers like contorted peach-basket masts from a battleship, is aggressively ugly; the Queensboro canti-lever bridge is merely quaint. Indeed, the Queensboro structure, with its romantic cast-iron pinnacles, stands at the opposite pole from the three sober bridges located around the bend, and crossing the Harlem River. Both the Washington Bridge of 1889 (not the *George* Washington Bridge across the Hudson) and the High Bridge consist of large steel arches in the central span, joined to a range of solid stone arches on land at the abutments. The High Bridge is quite narrow; originally it was of stone all the way, and carried the famous Croton Aqueduct across the Harlem River. The third Harlem River bridge is the steel one now being double-decked for the Henry Hudson Parkway.

New York takes especial pride in two great recent bridges—the George Washington and the Triborough. Both won the medal of the Institute of Steel Construction as supreme architectural achievements in their respective years of completion. The George Washington Bridge with its central sus-pension span of 3,500 feet has been surpassed in length by the Golden Gate Bridge of San Francisco; but the citizen of New York is still will-ing to pit it against the Coast bridge, asking no favors on the point of design. Curiously, its towers were intended by Cass Gilbert, the architect, to be clad in stone, a fact that explains the arches and the big hooks still protruding from the concrete foundations; but the plan was defeated on the score of cost, and the city is happier with the steel of Amman the engineer. Since the completion of the Henry Hudson Parkway, this colos-sal and magnificent bridge has come into its own, for there is scarcely an architectural landscape anywhere else in United States to vie with the river, the Palisades, the escarpments of Riverside Drive, and (tying it all together) the grace and majesty of the George Washington Bridge.

The Triborough has a setting that will vastly improve with the completion of the West Side Highway. It is really a series of bridges, clean-cut and exciting in the operation of its functional units; for it has a suspension span, a lift-bridge span, and a third span that is cantilevered. A small point, but an important one so often and irritatingly overlooked by engineers when they build bridges, is that the railing is safe yet low enough to allow the automobile occupant a view of the horizon.

Skyscraper Background

The skyscrapers are the children of the bridges. Few realize that the greatest school for steel construction was the bridge school, and that to this day the beams and trusses for tall buildings are fabricated in the "bridge shop." From the bridges, then, we might step to their off-spring on the shore.

Among these, Rockefeller Center is the largest and most spectacular group. The Empire State is the tallest single building, though it is equaled in cubic content by the R.C.A. Building at Rockefeller Center. The old Woolworth Building, opened in 1913, perhaps ranks as the most famous; dated or not, its soaring proportions and fine detail stamp it as an architectural masterpiece. The Municipal Building, largest of the city's administrative units, with its tremendous street colonnade, its fussy and disproportionate circular tower, represents one more effort to prove the classical style adaptable to tall steel-cage construction.

Why are skyscrapers built? The reasons generally given have been business reasons, but underlying these are others of a less abstract kind. Cass Gilbert, the architect, liked to tell how Frank Woolworth came to put up the tallest building in the world at a time when the New York skyline was still dominated by the Metropolitan Tower. The Metropolitan Insurance Company had refused Woolworth a loan, and in so doing had roused his ire. He happened to see a postcard from Calcutta with a picture of the Metropolitan Tower—its fame as the tallest building had spread all over the world. Woolworth made a survey to determine the Metropolitan's exact height, and then ordered his architect to exceed it. Many skyscrapers, large or small, owe their origin to similar rivalries; and the march of the bigger-and-better white elephants, goaded along by such fortuitous competition, was not halted until two or three years after 1929.

On Lexington Avenue between Forty-Third and Forty-Fourth Streets, one block beyond the enormous Chrysler Building, it was found profitable to erect a three-story structure that houses a Childs restaurant. This is a direct outcome of the usual "skyscraper economics," which are too complicated to explain in a brief analysis. One fact, however, can easily be understood: the comparatively enormous expense of skyscraper building. A 30-story building costs not merely ten times but often 30 times as much as a three-story building. The foundations alone, going down to bedrock, are extremely costly; the earth and rock removed to prepare for the Empire State Building weighed three-quarters as much as the building itself. Other costs increase in proportion.

The age of the various skyscrapers can be roughly gauged by their height. Just as, generally speaking, the youngest mountains are the highest, so the very tallest of the skyscrapers are the latest.

New York and Chicago

The skyscraper originated not in New York but in Chicago. Apart from its early introduction of the cast-iron front, New York contributed to the skyscraper only one indispensable element—the elevator. The first commercial passenger elevator installation, in 1857, was in a building on the corner of Broadway and Broome Street, though the honor is claimed for Cooper Union and others. The old Fifth Avenue Hotel was famous for its "vertical screw railway," installed by Otis Tufts in 1859 as the first passenger elevator run by steam. The "screw" was a hollow grooved tube surrounding the whole car and revolving around it on the principle of a worm gear. The first office-building elevator installation was in the first Equitable Building on Broadway, designed by George B. Post and completed April 19, 1871. This installation cost $29,657. Its success was infectious.

The first skyscraper, it is now generally conceded after violent controversy, was the Home Insurance Building in Chicago, designed by William LeBaron Jenney and erected 1883-4. The New York architect George B. Post made plans in 1880, accepted 1881, for the Produce Exchange Building in New York, which was finished simultaneously with the Home Insurance Building, but used metal framework only in the inside courts. New York's building code—then as now a source of anger to the progressives—forbade the use of metal framing in outside walls. Not until 1892 was this code amended, permitting New York to limp along after Chicago; and not until 1899, with the erection of the St. Paul Building, could New York claim a structure taller than any in Chicago.

The St. Paul Building, still standing east of St. Paul's Chapel on lower

Broadway, showed the complete ineptitude of the first attempts in New York City to stretch the classical formula over vertical buildings. It looks like a series of one-story structures piled on top of one another, each with its own pilasters and cornice. An even more glaring example of inappropriate design is found in the American Telephone and Telegraph Building at 195 Broadway (not to be confused with the New York Telephone Building on Vesey Street).

When these landmarks were erected, Louis Sullivan of Chicago had already proclaimed the gospel of the skyscraper as a single soaring unit, setting up his own world-famous Wainwright Building in St. Louis as an example. But New York passed Sullivan by. Of his work the city possesses only a minor example, the building at 65-69 Bleecker Street. Saarinen removed the last horizontal emphasis left by Sullivan—the flaring roofline. He allowed the vertical piers to run to the very top of the structure, where he simply cut them off. A good later application of this method is evident in Howells' Pan-hellenic Building at First Avenue and Forty-Ninth Street; while an even more daring example is the *Daily News* building on East Forty-Second Street, by Raymond Hood.

Cubes and Setbacks

The Equitable Building, designed by Frank Graham and erected in 1912, was the last great skyscraper of the pre-setback era. Its "cubage" is colossal in proportion to the ground it occupies; in fact, this structure of 42 stories carries the highest tax assessment of any real estate in New York—$29,000,000, exceeding the assessment on the 85 stories of rentable floor space in the Empire State Building, and that on the 70-story R.C.A. Building. The Equitable roused fears that future skyscrapers might cut off all light and air from the streets, besides reducing the value of neighboring real estate, if remedial measures were not taken.

New York devised the setback principle to provide at least a partial remedy. Under the law embodying this principle, the city is divided into zones, each of which has its own individual requirements, though in all cases the rule is that at a certain height every building must recede from the street, the degree of recession to be calculated in relation to the width of the street upon which the building stands. This law had a vast effect in altering New York architecture from a sheer vertical to a modified pyramidal shape. The setback rules are not entirely rigid, and slight differences in interpretation have led to considerable variety along any given street.

However, the uniform general requirements have brought about some semblance of order in the chaos of styles and mass effects characteristic of our buildings. The most famous of the early setback buildings is the Shelton Hotel, erected in 1924, in which the utmost care was employed in the designing and balancing of masses.

It has not generally been noticed, in the common preoccupation with copying setback effects, that Rockefeller Center embodies a still later principle. The setbacks here are mere vestiges. The larger buildings rise sheer, but with the radical difference that they do so at a distance away from the street line. There is perhaps the first step toward a possible future transformation of the city, in which extremely high buildings might go up without a break, provided they were entirely surrounded by a sufficient amount of open space. This idea, promulgated by the French architect Le Corbusier in the early 1920's, would call for a degree and extent of centralized control over land holdings that not even a Rockefeller could achieve.

Skyscraper Groups

To describe even the most important of New York's skyscrapers individually would require the space of a whole book; and therefore the present remarks will be confined to characterizing a few groups in various sections of the city. Each district seems to have its own special character in this respect: there is a distinct Wall Street skyscraper type and another distinct midtown type.

In the Wall Street region, the most striking impression of all—apart from the stalagmitic tower shapes—is that the whole agglomerate looks not like steel but stone. These are lithic monuments. They aspire toward "monumental mass," with emphasis on the weight. Apart from the competition of styles and detailed treatment, the chief long-range competition seems to have consisted in seeing who could build a structure with the greatest appearance of stability and permanence. The street has gone beyond making its towers heavy and solid: it has decorated them with classic symbols, thus adding the lure of antiquity to the promise of safe investments. Hence the whole northern front of Wall Street from Broadway to Pearl Street is taken up by different varieties of classical treatment. Even the Bank of the Manhattan Company, trying a venture in "modern," has retained an adequate repertory of free classical allusions. Here and there during the last afterglow of the boom, in 1930 or 1931, a few lighter and more business-like structures made their appearance, such as the North American Insurance Building by Shreve, Lamb and Harmon; but the familiar, older type of the street is still predominant.

Among downtown buildings, the most interesting are the Woolworth Building, still holding its own by virtue of its fine soaring quality and its fine subtly colored detail; the fortress-like Telephone Building at Barclay and Vesey Streets, by McKenzie, Voorhees & Gmelin and designed by Ralph Walker; and No. One Wall Street, with its compact shape, and the remarkable effect of the fluted surface of its entire wall (this also by Ralph Walker, the firm having changed to Voorhees, Gmelin & Walker). For vigor one might want to add the tower of the National City Bank and Farmer's Trust Company, if one could be excused from examining the base.

Bordering Madison Square is what might be called the insurance group, more stately than the bunched towers farther downtown because arranged to be seen from across the park. This group includes the Metropolitan Tower, a handsome coronet-shaped new Metropolitan building to its rear on Fourth Avenue, and the New York Life Insurance building in a converted "American Gothic"—one of the last works of Cass Gilbert.

In the midtown section, the buildings of Raymond Hood seem to express the aspirations of the region. On East Forty-Second Street stands his *Daily News* building, mentioned above, with its simple square-cut shape, its few easy setbacks, its flat striped walls like giant curtains, and its bright orange window-shades that give the building a festive appearance at night, like the paper illuminations in a parade. It was erected in 1930. On West Forty-Second Street, Hood made another strikingly modern attempt in the vividly colored, blue-green, terra-cotta faced McGraw-Hill Building, with its tan window shades, the windows in banks of four creating a decidedly horizontal emphasis. These two have the marks that in the 1920's were considered "modern": the bold color, the sharp outline, the uniform treatment of the envelope, the simplicity of massing, the avoidance of all tags of the traditional styles. In cleanliness they vie with two other groups that are perhaps still more successful because of greater openness in setting—the great hospital aggregations at the Presbyterian and the Cornell Medical Centers. Here we can see what the commercial skyscraper might become, when its architecture is not conditioned by the high value of restricted areas of land.

Buildings for Industrial Work

A person accustomed to the factories of the usual industrial town might easily be baffled, in a hasty survey of New York, to know where so many of its people follow industrial pursuits. The answer is "in lofts." Factories of the traditional type exist, to be sure—numbers of them border the route to Queensboro Plaza on Long Island, others are strung out along the Long Island Railroad, and so on. But in midtown Manhattan the ubiquitous garment and fur trades occupy anomalous loft buildings, some six or eight stories high, reaching back the full depth of the block with just room enough for an air shaft. The loft is "architecture" only when it grows to vast proportions, becoming essentially a big ventilated box enclosing a series of huge floors. In such a loft building there are no light courts or other interruptions, because the lighting is artificial.

Some of these structures, such as the Port of New York Authority Building, though not especially distinguished architecturally, are enormous affairs, embracing far more acreage of floor space than any skyscraper. A frequent and traditional method of decorating these huge cubes is a modification from old fortress structures such as the Palazzo Vecchio at Florence, Italy: a collar-band supplied in the form of a cornice or corbel table —as, for example, in the Furniture Exchange on Lexington Avenue at Thirty-Second Street, where the decorative details are actually geometric and modern. At No. 2 Park Avenue stands a variation, remarkable for the spangling of bright colors in its terra-cotta sheathing. For a time this was the city's chief exhibit of modernism.

Sometimes a cross is made between the loft type and the factory type. One of the most interesting structures in the city, from the standpoint of both function and form, is the Starrett-Lehigh Building on 26th Street at Thirteenth Avenue. Here smaller manufacturers may take individual floors or parts of floors. The railroad tracks come into the building at ground level, and a highly ingenious interior system of elevators and loading platforms permits truck or rail shipment of materials and finished goods without the necessity for street transfer at any point in the process. Except for the tower at the entrance, the building has remarkably clean lines. As all the weight is carried by interior columns, there are no bearing members in the outside walls, but only an exciting combination of alternate full-length strips of horizontal glass windows and brick fill. Not even at the angles are the window lines broken.

In another version of the same basic design, the Cashman Laundry in

Where New Yorkers
Eat and Shop

ROCKEFELLER CENTER'S SUNKEN PLAZA—FOR THOSE WHO CAN AFFORD IT

FRESH FRUITS AND VEGETABLES ARE LESS EXPENSIVE IN THE PUSHCART MARKETS

WEST WASHINGTON MARKET SUPPLIES POULTRY FOR THE MILLIONS

SHOPPERS SWIRL ABOUT FIFTH AVENUE AND 42ND STREET

LARGE DEPARTMENT STORES DRAW CROWDS TO HERALD SQUARE

NEW YORK ABOUNDS IN COLORFUL FRUIT AND VEGETABLE STANDS

GARMENT CENTER OF NEW YORK AND AMERICA

UPPER FIFTH AVENUE—LUXURY STREET

AN EAST SIDE HOUSEWIFE CHOOSES HER LINGERIE

SEAFOOD FOR LOW-INCOME
EPICURES

SEAFOOD BY THE TON, FULTON FISH MARKET

PRETZEL VENDOR, UNION SQUARE

A PARISIAN CUSTOM TRANSFERRED TO CHATHAM WALK

MCSORLEY'S, WHERE MEN ARE MEN AND WOMEN ARE NOT ALLOWED

the Bronx, the same architects (R. G. & W. M. Cory) achieve an even more successful effect of lightness, the broad white wings being canti-levered from the entrance tower, which is treated in four vertical pilasters.

Any account, however brief, of New York's industrial structures would be incomplete without mention of the monumental warehouse in South Brooklyn, built of reinforced concrete as an Army Supply Base in 1917 from designs by Cass Gilbert.

Recent Public Buildings

As contrasted with some of the office and industrial structures, the recent public buildings of New York hold no promise of lasting fame. The chief group, around Foley Square, composes into nothing in particular, and competent mediocrity is the usual attribute in the public buildings in other districts as well. There is, nevertheless, one very promising new trend, namely that shown in Federal post office substations—as for example, at Fourth Avenue and Thirteenth Street, or again on Twenty-Third Street east of Lexington Avenue. Compared to recent European buildings for similar purposes, these American examples have a merit that must be called very mild, but compared to the kind of structure that most of the typical substations continue to occupy in America, or more specifically in New York, the advance is almost revolutionary. The new attitude seems to claim, for the institutions of the great American People, at least a fraction of the dignity and grace that are normally expected in the branch offices of a private city bank.

Colleges and Universities

Among the numerous attractive college groups in New York City there are two that have had an influence on college architecture: City College and more especially Columbia University. The uptown City College quadrangle at 135th Street is a competently planned group, draped in late Gothic forms and made pleasing to regionalists by the use of a local material rarely employed in New York buildings—the Manhattan schist. The trim is equally unusual—a terra cotta so white that only the grime of the city has saved it from an appearance of jumping entirely out of the picture!

Columbia University was one of the earliest American institutions of learning to achieve a flavor of urbane maturity, attained through the consistent use (due to the notable architect Charles McKim) of exterior treatment based upon the Italian Renaissance. Columbia's appearance of maturity rested upon the fact that she did not seek to mimic whole Renaissance buildings but employed her chosen "style" rather as a decorative accessory, furnishing colonnades and uniform cornices to buildings that were essentially a series of large cubes arranged around squares. In recent years Columbia has lost conviction, so that her latest buildings are neither studied Renaissance nor clear-cut expressions based upon modern engineering. The older, domed library by McKim at the center of the university group was long a focal point of architectural discussion, alternately admired for its classical composition and criticized for its functional limitations.

More serious than criticisms of this library are the criticisms that could be made of the layout as a whole. The university chose to surrender to apartment-house use its land holdings that extended straight to the escarpments of the Hudson River, and in so doing let business considerations destroy what was perhaps the most spectacular architectural opportunity that had ever been in the possession of any American university, an opportunity never to return.

Churches

The churches of present-day New York are too numerous for comprehensive treatment in limited space. It must suffice to present a note or two on the examples that are outstanding by virtue of beauty, size, or historical associations. As to outstanding architectural beauty, few competent critics will be found to challenge the great claims of the Church of St. Thomas on Fifth Avenue, by Bertram Goodhue. This church is accounted by some authorities as one of the finest architectural achievements of any sort in the United States, by virtue of the remarkable combination of delicacy with great strength, by virtue of beautiful balance, and (in the interior) by virtue of the unprecedented effect of a magnificent reredos. Goodhue, a designer whose personal romanticism gave individual character to all the Gothic studies he made, produced two other outstanding church buildings in New York, St. Vincent Ferrer and the Chapel of the Intercession.

Goodhue's warmth is lacking in the city's largest church, designed by the great master's surviving partner, Ralph Adams Cram. This church, the Cathedral of St. John the Divine, will when completed be one of the three or four largest cathedrals of Christendom. (Statistics purporting to give it exact rank, whether as "first in the world" or something else, are not really decisive and must be interpreted with care.) The fervor that has gone into raising this immense structure has a heavily intellectual cast, delighting those scholars who like to watch the solution of an intricate problem in Gothic, a problem which the architect set himself not as a copyist but *as if* he were a Gothic architect working in medieval times.

A church preeminent for a still different reason is the Riverside Church, in the building of which John D. Rockefeller was heavily interested. Though the Gothic architecture of this high-towered steel-skeleton pile has excited no great critical approbation, there are certainly no Gothic vaults and pointed windows in existence anywhere that house so complex a set of facilities of a social-service nature. The building is an architectural *tour de force* putting the Gothic libraries and gymnasiums of our colleges to shame, by incorporating the essential facilities of them all.

Among Jewish synagogues, the outstanding example is the richly executed Temple Emanu-El on Fifth Avenue, by Butler, Stein and Kohn; the outstanding "modern" church to date is the First Swedish Baptist Church on East Sixty-First Street, by Martin Hedmark. The single district, however, that is most rewarding to the connoisseur of church architecture is Brooklyn Heights. Here, within walking distance of one another, are churches of great interest and widely varying type. At one end is Plymouth Church, made famous by Henry Ward Beecher. Though designed in "congregational" fashion by an amateur committee, with an exterior somewhat barn-like, this building makes a deep impression by its "meeting-house" character: sunlit, chaste, democratic and withal graceful. The region abounds in interesting Gothic Revival churches, such as Grace Church. One other church building on the Heights must be launched at last into architectural history—the modest Church of the Pilgrims. Designed by the well-known architect Richard Upjohn in a manner very unusual to him, and built with extreme simplicity in fieldstone, this church has been obliged to wait for both the classical and the Gothic Revival to lose their force before being recognized as a remarkable precursor of the tendencies we now call "modern." Unfortunately, poverty has already lost for this church its former graceful steeple.

Hotels

New York is a city of big hotels. Nothing is left of the famous hostelries that once marked lower Broadway, and perhaps the only house that recalls the orderly and quiet style in which the best of them were built is the Brevoort, on lower Fifth Avenue. Midway between the Brevoort and the modern hotels in respect to period is the Chelsea Hotel on Twenty-Third Street, with its picturesque tiers of balconies against a Victorian red-brick front. More characteristic of the country-wide type of modern hotel are the Pennsylvania, the Commodore, and the Roosevelt, built around a system of long corridors running through a main building slab and its series of wings projecting at a right angle.

What might be called the typical New York hotel is the hotel in a tower. This tower may take the shape of a broad truncated pyramid with intricate and interesting setbacks, like the New Yorker, or it may rise sheer, like the Savoy-Plaza, the Sherry-Netherland, and the Pierre, a stately group of big hotels at the Central Park Plaza. The older Plaza Hotel in the same setting is a fine example of relative restraint exercised upon the florid baroquish hotel style of the turn of the century.

Twin towers are to be found not only along the western boundary of Central Park but in the most modern and perhaps the most pretentious of all hotels in New York, the Waldorf-Astoria. This edifice, apart from its lavish appointments, has interest as an engineering feat, since it spans the tracks of the New York Central, and makes use of this fact to furnish the Waldorf guests with private railroad sidings. The problem of carrying a frame down through the track tunnel and still insulating the building against vibration was a formidable one. It calls to mind that all the big hotels have to solve still another spanning problem, of which the general public is quite unaware. Over the ceilings of the large lobbies and dining rooms of the first floors lies the enormous weight of floor after floor of small rooms up above, with the result that the trusses over these first-floor ceilings are colossal.

"Genteel Houses" of the Middle Class

Architectural histories have generally dealt with the living quarters of only those New Yorkers who occupied houses very imposing or very old. As a matter of fact, such structures have formed but a small part of the living accommodations of New Yorkers, and the really fascinating story lies elsewhere. It is easily possible to find houses that trace a complete cycle of domestic evolution, beginning more than a century ago and concerning the great middle class.

Though the oldest of these houses are to be found on Cherry Street, where they were built very early in the 19th century, the largest number survive in Greenwich Village. Here is to be found a special type of early New York residence of the highest excellence, one that Fenimore Cooper referred to as "a species of second-rate genteel houses that abound in New York, into which I have looked in passing with utmost pleasure." It is a house two stories high, with an attic under the pitched roof above, which had two—or very rarely three—dormers; the frontage is only exceptionally more than 20 feet, but almost never less. As originally constructed by mechanics working from manuals rather than from architects' plans, this house sat behind a tidy wrought-iron fence, and showed the street a face of bright red brick above a basement of brownstone or occasionally marble. The details are exceedingly simple. The windows are under plain stone lintels; but the doorways, though always chaste, show considerable spirited variety in the handling of classic details. These doorways always have some form of transom light, sometimes a fan-light, in addition to side-lights, giving an effect of bright welcome and insuring a well-lighted hall. The main doorway is always reached by a stoop; and this is important, for it relates to one of the most practical house-plans for a modestly comfortable scheme of life ever adopted throughout large areas of a city.

The stoop was important because it neatly separated the formal entrance from the service or basement entrance, permitting the living quarters in a highly practical way to occupy two floors, while the whole house could be kept only two rooms deep. The apparently simple arrangement of these straightforward houses of the 1820's is remarkable chiefly because, after more than a century, persons of modest means in New York are once more beginning to dream of living in new houses with every window freely open to unobstructed light, instead of facing a narrow alley or a "light shaft." The principle of city dwellings only two rooms deep, which a hundred years ago was taken as a matter of course, has become an "idealistic" demand of modern housing.

The basement of these old houses was a pleasant affair looking out on the small planted court in front and the garden in the rear. These basements are still considered desirable now that most of the houses are used as small apartments. In the original scheme, the front room of this basement was either the dining room or the family living room (in the latter case the dining room was upstairs); while the kitchen was always to the rear, deliveries being made through the side-hall. Guests could come up the stoop and be properly received in the upper hall and in the "drawing room" that opened from it, the latter being usually connected with the rear room by a wide doorway. The upper floors contained front and rear bedrooms, with sometimes a third hall bedroom at the head of the stairs. A simplifying factor was the total absence in the house of bathrooms; the "temples of Cloacina" were balanced at the two rear corners of the lot. Even the stairway in the house we have described was pleasant, for it began well back and had its own window at the landing.

Speaking of these houses, Montgomery Schuyler said: "They were more than decent; they were 'elegant.' The adjective cannot be applied to the contemporary small houses of Philadelphia or Boston. They were decent, in the one case with a Quakerish simplicity, in the other with a Puritanic bleakness; but they were decidedly not elegant." Schuyler considered that a large part of the charm of the New York houses came from the visible roof and the dormers; but both these features tended gradually to be suppressed as the century progressed, until in the 1840's the full-fledged Greek revival demanded that the roof be concealed behind a cornice.

The Brownstone Front

The change to a cornice, and incidentally to greater severity of line, brought gradual deterioration; for the cornice was most frequently of tin, opening the way to the horrors of the brownstone and parvenu periods. Nevertheless, the first corniced houses, scattered examples of which may be seen on some of the streets opening westward from Seventh Avenue below Tenth Street, were chaste and dignified.

More ominous than the tin cornice was the concurrent shrinkage of the house front. It is no accident that the charming small dormered houses are still chiefly found in the irregular streets of Greenwich Village. When the planning commission of 1807–11 made the standard New York lot 100 feet deep, it unwittingly struck a mortal blow at the comfort of the merchant or professional man who had been paying a rental of from $300 to $500 a year for his small house. Land became too expensive, and the only way out was to build houses with a narrower frontage. Contracted in width, the house required greater depth, with the result that the brownstone and other later individual city houses, even of the well-to-do, possessed an interior not only cavernous but wastefully arranged. As Lewis Mumford points out in his book, *The Brown Decades*, not even the stone itself was suitable for the use to which it was put. In the earlier houses it had been employed structurally in basements, and occasionally as bonding stones in the brick walls above; but now it was used as a veneer to conceal the real structural facts behind a smooth and slick façade. The grain of the stone now went the wrong way, and it frequently spalled; so that a coat of stucco was often added by later builders over the stone.

This type of house, as Schuyler points out, still retained one virtue that later individual houses built by private owners were to lose. The brownstone fronts were speculatively built in large groups, and they had a saving monotony. Since there was no excellence to show, this lack of assertiveness was a positive virtue. But the later private builder, when he employed an architect of his own, endeavored to give his dream-castle a degree of distinction that would knock out all the rest of the street. Hence the fist-fights and shoulder-turnings of turrets against loggias, and loggias against cornices.

To dwell on this combat would be tempting, were it not for the fact that our original New York average professional man or merchant had in the meantime fled. He could afford neither an architect nor his own four-story house, whether brownstone or any other. So he took the new elevated railway to the outlying districts of the Bronx, or the ferries to New Jersey; or he helped to fulfill John Roebling's prophecies about the heavy use of the Brooklyn Bridge; or he began living in Manhattan in a new type of dwelling—the flat.

Homes of Today

Since that time the average New Yorker's solutions to his problem have provided little to brag about. For some reason, owning one's own home in the outlying regions no longer permitted the owner to build compactly up to his neighbor, as had been done when the "outlying region" was still Greenwich Village. Every individual home had to be free-standing, with its own driveway, its own row of windows looking into the neighbors' instead of facing on the street and yard; later every home needed its own garage. Only when limited-dividend corporations undertook large-scale operations was it possible to build, on modern terms, something approaching in both layout and amenities the little "genteel houses" of which Cooper spoke. At Sunnyside, Long Island, was set the leading example; the houses were joined end to end, only two rooms deep; the wasteful driveways and individual garages were eliminated, making way for continuous garden space and park; in addition, since this is a noisy automobile age, very different from the age of carriages, a beginning was made toward turning the face of the houses away from the street. The later developments at Hillside and under the PWA will be discussed in the separate article on housing.

Attention has been concentrated here upon the homes of the middle class, because unfortunately a discussion of past and present dwellings for the great mass of the city's workers would deal not with architecture but with its negations. New York had a desperate housing problem as early as 1820; the problem remains a desperate one as this book goes to press; and as such is dealt with in a separate article.

The rich, too, have been obliged to adapt themselves to the high value of land. The fine homes that used to line Fifth Avenue have been fighting a losing battle for survival against the great apartment and office buildings. Only one of the original Vanderbilt houses now remains; the most famous, the best known work of the architect Richard M. Hunt, disappeared long ago. On Madison Avenue at Fiftieth Street, the old Villard Mansion stands in gloomy isolation, the design of its windows still boldly declaring its free derivation by the architects, McKim, Mead & White, from the Renaissance Cancelleria Palace in Rome. The wealthy have found it more convenient, on the whole, to live in great roomy country mansions on Long Island, and to camp, as it were, in New York. Though the city contains large areas of "blighted" districts bringing no return to their owners, the difficulty of assembling a sufficient number of plots to secure spacious layouts for the wealthy is still apparently greater than the difficulty of coping with traffic problems to reach spaciousness at some distance from the center.

Within the city, there exists a situation perhaps unique in the United States—namely, that rich and poor rub elbows, and an address indicates little or nothing concerning social status. As one after another of the older fashionable districts has lost its social standing, its occupants have moved restlessly about to new locations; and of these, some of the most available have been surrounded by slums. The most dramatic of such contrasts is the one chosen by Sidney Kingsley for his play Dead End, supposedly inspired by the famous River House at the foot of East Fifty-Second Street, with private yacht landings for its wealthy tenants, in an environment of old-law tenements. The most imposing group of fashionable apartment houses fronts on Park Avenue, the so-called "gold-diggers lane"—a double line of vast boxes conservatively designed; while a late development is the special type of Bronx apartments lining the Grand Concourse, none being in the fashion of the day unless equipped with "corner windows."

One glance at almost any rental plan for one of the more expensive apartment buildings will show why the real fascination of this type as an architectural problem lies not so much in the façades as in the planning. Within the one external cube there must be all sorts of irregular accommodations. Apartments vary considerably in the number of rooms to be provided on a single floor. But this is only a beginning. Apartments can also embrace two or more floors and use their own interior stairs. Moreover, the chief room can be two stories high. The result is a three-dimensional fitting together of irregular units that puts the average Chinese puzzle in the shade. The irregularity is perforce mirrored in the disposition of the windows.

Many wealthy districts are solidly built with almost no provision for outside light and air, and have been scorned by reformers as "super-slums." Life for the occupants is not too rigorous, however, since they are rarely at home, and since they enjoy the benefits of such improvements as sun-lamps and air-conditioning. The latter puts a strain on the city water supply; indeed the whole business could be managed more simply by less crowded use of what is now idle blighted land. But simple answers have no appeal for the "sophisticated" New Yorker.

Rockefeller Center

Every city has some outstanding monument that characterizes it in the eyes of the world. For New York, perhaps the most appropriate expression is found in Rockefeller Center. Anyone viewing this great complex is aware of a departure in architecture from long accepted tenets not only of construction but of esthetics. In the great knife-like prow and cliff-like side of the R. C. A. Building there is no easy flowing harmony. This mass that dominates the whole development typifies, on the contrary, the suddenness, the brutality, the overpowering scale of New York. The building seems almost to have been forced upward by pressure from both sides. The "Channel" through which it is approached is no wide avenue but an enlarged fissure. In the whole group there is the squareness, the blockiness, of a project that means business. At night, when the Center takes on a certain softness, its taller elements losing themselves in enveloping mist, there is some semblance of an Egyptian calm; in daylight this effect is instantly dispelled. The proportions are not classic. Their play against one another is restless. From certain angles, the jagged rhythm of the buildings appears to endow them with motion. In minor details, such as the grouping of windows, there is a certain harshness; the harmony is only occasionally resolved. The light blue and gray tone of the buildings, derived from the combined effect of limestone and aluminum in the walls and the color of the window shades, is cool and aloof. In the few places where it is permitted, the ornament is fragile and sentimental; and the sculpture in general can scarcely be said to have reached emotional maturity.

Apart from its physical form, the economic organization of Rockefeller Center is expressive of New York. It sucks tenants out of a large area of smaller obsolescent buildings into one close-packed super-center. Moreover, it is an organization of amazing complexity, a city in miniature, where a tenant need not leave the premises in order to see the latest first-run movies, or buy a complete outfit of clothing, or study the newest manifestations of art and science, or engage passage to foreign countries with visas to match.

The complexity of the endeavor is mirrored in the architectural forms. Everywhere one senses that the architects struggled to do their best with problems just a little too big for complete mastery. Hence, pieces of work that are the flattest kind of failure stand next to fragments brilliantly successful. Thus, although the foyer of the Music Hall contains what is probably the largest and emptiest mural in the world, the auditorium with its vast arched and banded ceiling is a conception of great daring carried through to a stunning effect.

In its way, the Center is an effort to reduce New York to order, still keeping it New York. The Center retains the gigantism, the ruthless preying of the large upon the small, the close packing, the impersonality of the whole; and yet attempts to secure sunlight and air (at least for itself), pleasant promenades, gardens (with Hollywood costumes for the attendants), art, a sense of scale and drama, and such other pleasures as the metropolis can afford.

Program Notes

IT IS always a bit hazardous, in any period of transition such as we are passing through today, to attempt to fix the musical character of a city, either from what has gone before or from what may be happening at the moment. New York is a sovereign case. What shall we say about it without seeming to say too much or too little? One thing is reasonably certain. The many and diverse elements in New York's musical caldron have been seething too long not to have fused at last into an amalgam having recognizable qualities and characteristics. The consideration that, in a single afternoon or evening, performances are given over to such diverse forms of expression as opera, swing, symphony and chamber music, oratorio and madrigal singing, vocal and instrumental recitals, need not cloud the issue. Out of all the sound and fury, the clash of credos orthodox and unorthodox, the invasion of schools foreign and domestic, it should yet be possible to distinguish signs of the genuinely indigenous and collective voice of New York.

The beginnings of music in the city can be traced back to the liturgies brought over by the early Dutch settlers, but records on the subject are scant. These practical and hardy pioneers were undoubtedly more tolerant than the Puritans, who believed music was not something to be enjoyed for itself, but was rather an adornment to religious services. What little secular music flourished at the time (confined for the most part to street tunes and romantic ballads) was commonly frowned upon, by and large, as worldly and unworthy, even when it bore the Continental tag. This was not, it is only fair to add, an exclusively Colonial attitude. The same feeling about secular music obtained abroad, where composers of the day were devoting their best talents to the service and glorification of the church, creating a wealth of oratorios, canons, motets and anthems.

Music proper—that is to say, music divorced from its role as handmaiden to the church or as an interlude to dramatic skits, music composed and listened to for its own sake—may be said to date in New York from an event known as Pachelbel's Recital, which occurred on January 21, 1736, at the home of one Robert Todd, vintner. It was a concert for the benefit of Charles Theodore Pachelbel, a German organist, who came to New York from Boston, and who, on this occasion, played the harpsichord part. No other musical event of any importance is recorded until April 30, 1750, when John Gay's ballad divertissement, *The Beggar's Opera,* with music by John Christopher Pepusch, was presented at the Nassau Street Theater, with an orchestra supplied by the British Military Band (the British military, by the way, directed at this time most of the secular musical activities in the city). This event, too, seems to have been a seed cast on stony ground, for not until a score of years afterward do the records begin to indicate musical events of more or less regular frequency, and an audience that could be depended upon to support them.

The earliest figures in the field of local music, pioneers whose work as composers, performers, or conductors is identified with New York, are Francis Hopkinson, James Hewitt, James Lyon, William Tuckey, John Henry Schmidt, Gottlieb Graupner—to mention only the more prominent. All of them leaned heavily on traditional forms and ready-to-hand subject matter, though they made brave if ineffectual attempts at originality. It took courage in those days to deal with one's own background, for anything native in art was considered of dubious worth and rather a presumption. But men like Hopkinson and Hewitt managed to make themselves not merely heard but also respected; and in some measure they helped to break down a little of the prejudice (which still persists in some quarters) against both native and contemporary music.

Hewitt's fame rests largely on his Clementian piano sonata, *The Battle of Trenton* (1792). Grove also credits him with the ballad opera, *Tammany* (1794). The date and title of the "first" American ballad opera are matters of some dispute. John Tasker Howard goes so far as to suggest that ballad operas were probably performed in New York from 1732 on. In any case, it is fairly certain that Hewitt collaborated with William Dunlap on *Pizarro,* which was given a New York hearing in 1800. Four years earlier, Dunlap had worked with Benjamin Carr on *The Archers of Switzerland* (1796) and with Victor Pellisier on the score of *The Vintage* (1799).

To Hopkinson, a Philadelphian by birth, friend of Washington and signer of the Declaration of Independence, belongs the distinction of having written, when he was only twenty-two, the first secular musical composition of native origin to be published in America, a song called

My Days Have Been So Wondrous Free (1759). In addition, Hopkinson composed *O'er the Hills,* for tenor and harpsichord, a very popular piece in its time; and the *Washington March,* which was played whenever the President and his family appeared publicly. Hewitt later converted this march into the *New York Patriotic Song,* which enjoyed a vogue.

Lyon, whose compositions were mostly anthems and hymns, is another contender for the title of "America's first composer." Tuckey is known chiefly for having directed the earliest American performance of Handel's *Messiah* in 1770, two years before it was heard in Germany. Graupner's contributions to the technique of the popular concert were made mostly in Charleston and Boston. He is often referred to as the "father of American orchestral music."

But audiences of the post-Revolutionary era still lacked a proper understanding of musical values. They sought quantitative rather than qualitative programs, and there arose virtuosos fully prepared to meet that demand. A tenor of the day, one Signor de Begnis, announced that he would sing, at a forthcoming concert, "six hundred words and three hundred bars of music in the short space of four minutes."

Music in New York first began to assume a serious character with the forming of musical societies. The initial attempt in this direction goes back to 1773-4, with the founding of the Harmonic Society, which followed the lead set by the Orpheus Club in Philadelphia (1759). Others in New York were the Musical Society (1788), the St. Cecilia Society and the Apollo Society (1791), the Uranian Society (1793) and the Euterpean Society (1799). Apart from the artistic and financial value that these pioneer musical organizations had for their own members, they were important in spreading the gospel of good music by sponsoring concerts and creating audiences. The foremost orchestras of that day generally comprised an ensemble of not more than 25 instruments, but even so they were sufficient to acquaint New Yorkers with the compositions of Bach, Mozart, Haydn, Beethoven—and occasionally also, as a concession, Hewitt and Hopkinson. By 1819 New York boasted a musical audience large enough and dependable enough to support entertainment of a substantial order. Accordingly, preparations were made for the presentation of grand opera. Rossini's *Barber of Seville* was the first given (1821). It was followed in 1823 by Mozart's *Marriage of Figaro,* and two years later by Von Weber's *Der Freischütz.* All these were sung in English. The first grand opera to be presented in the original tongue was probably *The Barber of Seville.* The event occurred at the new Park Theater in 1825, with the celebrated Garcia family (Manuel and his two daughters, Maria Malibran and Mme. Viardot) heading the cast.

The success of these presentations encouraged an influx of Italian with some French and German operas, mainly through the efforts of Lorenzo da Ponte, Mozart's librettist, a celebrated adventurer who was possessed by the dream of a permanent opera in New York—with himself as chief librettist. He pinned his hopes at first on Garcia, who had brought the original Italian opera company to New York in 1825. Later he turned to Montressor's Richmond Hill Theater, where Signorina Pedrotti was the current attraction. She had taken the place of Maria Malibran (heroine of a modern opera by Robert Russell Bennett and Robert A. Simon), who had deserted the American musical stage for Europe. Thirty-five performances were enough to convince all concerned that the experiment was a failure; but Da Ponte, still persisting in his plan, decided that the only solution was a theater especially built for opera. His tenacity resulted in the elegant and lavish Italian Opera House, the first theater to "boast a tier composed exclusively of boxes." Rossini's *La Gazza ladra,* with Signorina Fanti as prima donna, occupied the stage on opening night. This time two seasons went by before Da Ponte realized the futility of his endeavors in the New York operatic field.

Max Maretzek, cited in Arditi's memoirs as the cleverest of all impresarios, began his American career at Palmo's, which opened in 1844 with Bellini's *I Puritani.* In the cast were Borghese, the prima donna, and Antognini, mentioned by a contemporary critic as the greatest tenor ever heard in New York. During Maretzek's regime at Palmo's and later at the Astor Place Opera House, a long list of great singers performed under him: Pedrotti, Fanti, Caredori, Grisi, Mario ("for a generation afterward all tenors were measured by Mario's standard"), Sontag, Jenny Lind, Alboni, and Salvi.

Most of this constellation passed over to the Academy of Music when the latter was founded in 1854, to be joined subsequently by Patti, Vestvali, Badiali, Amodio, Brignoli, Lagrange, Mirate, D'Angri, Piccolomini, Nilsson, Lucca, Albani, Gerster, Maurel and Campanini. Many American singers who began to appear in opera for the first time scored their initial successes at the Academy. Among these were persons whose glamor endured as long as the generations of opera lovers who thrilled to their voices were alive: Clara Louise Kellogg, Annie Louise Cary, Minnie Hauk, Alwina Valleria, Emma Nevada, Lillian Nordica, Adelaide Phil-

lipps and Josephine Yorke, all of whom made later successes in the opera
houses of England, France, Germany and Italy.

The Academy's star began to set when the Metropolitan Opera House
was opened in 1883. The Metropolitan is, of course, the outstanding name
in the long history of New York opera. Krehbiel, the eminent critic, attributes its founding to social rather than artistic impulses; and this is
confirmed by the fact that the Academy had everything requisite for opera
except the genteel sufficiency of boxes necessary to take care of the rapidly
expanding moneyed classes in New York, to whom a box at the opera
was the symbol of social success. Henry Abbey was first in the long roster
of the Metropolitan's great impresarios; he staged Italian opera the first
year to the tune of a $600,000 loss. The next year, Leopold Damrosch
persuaded the directors that the way to success lay in the presentation of
German opera.

Except for a brief interregnum, again under Abbey, this second period
showed the mark of Damrosch's "fatalistic belief in Wagner opera."
Anton Seidl, who had been associated with Wagner as a young man, was
looked upon as the Wagnerian "prophet, priest and paladin." Great stars
in the operatic firmament under the new dispensation were Amalia Ma-
terna (who had participated in the Wagner festivals at Bayreuth since
their inception in 1876), Marianne Brandt, Mlle. Schroeder-Hanfstangl,
Frau Auguste Seidl-Kraus, Anton Schott, Jean de Reszke, Emma Eames,
Katharina Klafsky, Milka Ternia, Ernestine Schumann-Heink, Lilli Leh-
mann, Emil Fischer, Ernest van Dyck, Anton van Rooy and Albert Nie-
mann. Caruso's acquisition in 1903, engineered by Conried the impre-
sario, and the signing of Gustav Mahler, who became conductor of German
opera in 1907, were other milestones in the history of the Metropolitan.

There have been many lesser shrines, notably Pike's Opera House
(1868), which became the Grand Opera House when it was taken over
by Jay Gould and Jim Fisk in 1869. Oscar Hammerstein entered the field
twice, in 1892 and again in 1910, with two separate Manhattan Opera
Houses. In 1913–15 an energetic effort was made to establish a new
rallying-point in the Century Opera House. Italian, German, French, Russian and American opera companies also invaded the scene at various
times; but though a number of them were competent and worthy of surviving, they were all short-lived. There have been recent ventures of opera
at the Hippodrome and elsewhere in the city, sponsored by rival companies,
but the Metropolitan remains, today as formerly, in full possession of the
field.

While opera was thus becoming established, the musical organizations, all active but none too prosperous or effective, were casting about to pool their interests and identities. In 1842, under the inspiration and leadership of Ureli C. Hill, a Connecticut Yankee, a merger was accomplished. The name chosen was the Philharmonic Society of New York. This organization, which merged with the National Symphony in 1921 and combined with the New York Symphony in 1928, functions today as the Philharmonic Symphony Society of New York, the oldest and most justly celebrated of the city's orchestral organizations.

However, the prejudice against native compositions, soloists and themes still persisted. The music-publishing houses found a very limited market for domestic wares, and the orchestras maintained that they could hold their audiences only when they featured the classic European masters. Even the Philharmonic accepted native works only on condition that the Board of Governors approved them, and about one native composition a season was the maximum presented.

This prejudice was not limited to music: it obtained in practically all the arts. Provincialism was a stubborn root and hard to eradicate. Here and there attempts were made at promoting native productions, but with indifferent success. On September 27, 1850, New York heard its first homespun opera, *Rip van Winkle,* composed by George F. Bristow, the Philharmonic's first violinist for 30 years. American Indian, Negro and local compositions were also making some headway. The Civil War, in particular, gave impetus to the Negro spirituals, the war songs of Henry C. Work and George F. Root, and the Stephen Foster songs—*Swanee River, My Old Kentucky Home* and the rest. But all this was a cry in the wilderness.

A great step forward was taken in 1864 when Theodore Thomas, a conspicuous figure in the musical life of his day, inaugurated orchestral concerts at Irving Hall. Conducting in America before Thomas' advent was rather a haphazard affair, although in Europe Berlioz already had perfected a conducting technique. Thomas—with Leopold Damrosch, who was adding to his European achievement by organizing the Symphonic Society—was the first in New York to turn conducting into an art and a profession. These two men and Berlioz are regarded as the chief forerunners of the great symphonic conductors of our own day.

With the founding by Leopold Damrosch in 1874 of the Oratorio Society; with the introduction in 1879 of the first Gilbert and Sullivan light operas; with the grand music festival celebrations in 1881, when Berlioz'

Requiem, excerpts from Wagner's *Die Meistersinger,* and Beethoven's *Ninth Symphony* were given by an orchestra of 250 pieces and a chorus of 200; with the start of the Wagnerian music dramas at the Metropolitan in 1884 (though *Tannhäuser* had a hearing as far back as 1859 at the Stadt Theater); and with the building in 1891 of Carnegie Hall, at first known as Music Hall (the occasion marking Tschaikovsky's first appearance in America)—with these events music in New York may be said to have passed definitely out of the experimental or provincial stage.

The prejudice against living talent was still strong, however. The advent of such conspicuous native composers as Edward MacDowell, Henry K. Hadley, Rubin Goldmark, Daniel Gregory and Charles T. Griffes should supposedly have left no doubt in the minds of our people that the American composer really had something to say and that what he had to say was eminently worth listening to. But prejudice, stronger than conviction, continued to hold its own.

After the Spanish-American War and the turn of the century, New York, because of its financial preeminence, became a kind of world clearing house for music and performing musicians and ensembles. Experiments at the Manhattan Opera House, the Kneisel Quartette, the foreign opera ventures, the Beethoven Society, the Mendelssohn Glee Club, the Flonzaley Quartette, all flourished. The accent, however, was on money rather than on music. This "gold standard" provided a dangerous basis for artistic values. Tempting sums brought the greatest singers, dancers, instrumentalists in a mad scramble to America's shores. New York, the new Eldorado, witnessed as a consequence an unbroken pageantry of front-rank musical talent, such as it had never known before: Kubelik, Ysaye, Thibaud, the De Reszkes, Paderewski, McCormack, Melba, Casals, Kreisler, Caruso; from La Scala came Toscanini and Gatti-Casazza, the one as orchestral conductor, the other as managing director, of the Metropolitan Opera. But concurrent with the coming to New York of all these distinguished foreigners was the gradual elevation to stellar rank of our own divas and virtuosos: Victor Just, Maud Powell, Horace Britt, Albert Spalding, Guy Maier, Lillian Nordica, Leon Barzin, Louise Homer, Marie Rappold, Geraldine Farrar, Clarence Whitehill, Reinald Werrenrath and others.

The World War, which confirmed New York's position as the premier power in the international money marts, also decisively established its preeminence as patron of music. The Jazz Age, following close upon the war, brought into sharp relief all the vernacular influences—Negro spirituals, blues, hot music and work songs; military, circus and Broadway night-club bands; hillbilly and Western ballads—that had been animating and shaping our musical idioms and trends since the Civil War. Jazz was and is—in its later metamorphoses—a definite contribution to American folk music; its value lies not so much in the usually trivial or derivative songs and compositions written for it, as in its assertion of the principle of free improvisation, a principle that has developed instrumentalists of remarkable technical dexterity and considerable creative resource. But in the early 1920's it constituted a challenge to the future of American formal music. Out of jazz and the other folk idioms, a group of young modern composers in the 1920's and later (George Gershwin, Leo Ornstein, Robert Russell Bennett, Randall Thompson, Deems Taylor, Werner Janssen, Samuel Barber, Roy Harris, Roger Sessions, Walter Piston, Aaron Copland) adapted whatever elements they found useful in creating new patterns for a native American music in the classical mediums—symphonies, concertos, operas, tone poems. Today, among others, Alec Templeton, the English composer-pianist, and Robert McBride, a young composer from the West, are experimenting with the jazz idiom as a primary musical structure, sometimes with brilliant effectiveness.

In other directions the war also caused considerable confusion in musical values. But it accomplished one thing at least—it focused attention on talent flowering in America. More than that, it stressed the need of actively encouraging that talent and of securing to it an adequate monetary return. In time, as an answer to the first need, there were established foundations (Juilliard); scholarships (Naumburg, Schubert Memorial, Philharmonic); awards (Guggenheim, Pulitzer, National Broadcasting Company). In answer to the second need, a host of musical organizations sprang into being. Among the most active are the American Guild of Musical Artists, the National Federation of Music Clubs, the National Music League, the League of Composers, the American Society of Composers, Authors and Publishers, the American Music Alliance, the American Guild of Organists, and (most recent of all) the Affiliated Grand Rights Association.

The post-war era brought with it radio, community concerts and the revival of song festivals, music in the films, the popularization of outdoor summer concerts and national "music weeks." These have democratized music by making it available in every village and farmhouse in the country. Radio, with its numerous excellent programs, its scope and variety, its incomparable facilities for reproduction, has earned the lion's share of credit for this result in terms of audience. The democratization of the control of music was not an overnight phenomenon. Throughout the years various orchestral, vocal, and even purely philanthropic organizations sought to bring music and the people closer together, by way of free or low-priced admissions to concerts, free instruction in schools and settlements. The Mendelssohn Glee Club, the music federations, the MacDowell Chorus (which became, in 1912, the Schola Cantorum) helped considerably toward that end. But these were individual, isolated, and for the most part fugitive attempts. What was needed was a concerted and sustained effort, backed by a powerful agency and directed by musicians with a strong social consciousness. All this was inherent in the establishment of the Federal Music Project of the Works Progress Administration. Almost before anyone was aware of what had happened, the direction of the country's musical destinies, controlled heretofore by a relatively small group of directors and patrons, was transferred to the people. The significance of this change, this musical *coup d'état,* may be summed up by saying that, as a result of it, music today is no longer caviar for the privileged few but meat and drink for the millions. And these millions are not merely passive listeners—they are active participants. They go to music with a will and an open mind; they come away from it as from a service in which they have had a part. An art that began as part of a communal service is once more serving the community.

The activities of the Federal Music Project in New York are extensive. From December 1935 to November 1937, the Concert Division and the Music Education Unit of the project gave 6,971 concerts to an aggregate audience of 4,903,458 and made 4,010 radio broadcasts. The performances, most of them free, were held at more than 350 churches, museums, public libraries, parks, etc., in the five boroughs. The project also presented 147 paid concerts to an aggregate audience of 75,417 at the Federal Music Theatre in 1937. The Music Education Unit, composed of two sub-projects, (1) the Teaching of Music and Music Appreciation and (2) the Recital Division, instructed thousands of New Yorkers in 36 music subjects ranging from piano tuning to musical therapy. During 1935–7 there was a total attendance of 4,029,069 at 267,312 classes held in 150 centers. The unit sponsored 2,028 extra-curricular activities (student concerts, operettas, recitals, etc.) that drew an attendance of 228,791. The Recital Division has 11 groups of performers.

As for the American composer, his day seems also to have arrived at last. Through the WPA Composers' Forum-Laboratory, a device perfected by Ashley Pettis, entire evenings are given over to the presentation of a single composer's works. On such occasions, the composer himself is required to be present to answer questions put to him by the audience. If the compositions performed find favor, the bay and laurel are his; otherwise he must be prepared to take the consequences. This immediate judgment is, of course, not final, nor is it meant to be. Besides the Composers' Forum-Laboratory, there is the opportunity offered by WPA orchestras all over the country, which are eagerly receptive to native talent. Their programs have included the work of such Americans as Copland, Hadley, Goldmark, Chadwick, Mabel Daniels, Roy Harris, Daniel Gregory Mason, Edgar Stillman-Kelley, Charles Wakefield Cadman, Quincy Porter, John K. Paine and others.

Folk Tune to Swing

WHEN the old Academy of Music was being razed in 1926 to make way for the Consolidated Gas Company building, there was a feast of reminiscence in the metropolitan press. Tony Pastor's, formerly in the same block, got almost as much space as its more dignified neighbor. The names of great concert stars who had appeared at the Academy shared the fading limelight with Weber and Fields—Helene Mora, the female baritone, who helped to popularize Harry Kennedy's *Say Au Revoir But Not Goodbye* and sang it at the composer's funeral; and the original Pat Rooney, with his soft-shoe interpretation of *Sweet Rosie O'Grady*. This demolition was a love feast at which there were few guests. Most of the excavation watchers were curious but frankly unaware of the significance of this particular part of Fourteenth Street at Irving Place. Those who knew best what the name of Tony Pastor signified had long since moved on to the Tin Pan Alley of the Times Square district.

With the world's biggest song business well in hand—in 1936 Tin Pan Alley wrote the nation's songs to the tune of $5,000,000—the metropolitan music manufacturers nevertheless occupy an anomalous position. By and large, the products of the Alley are not folk music; nor can they, except by the kind of musical chicanery publicized by tune detectives, claim relationship with the classical composers. This does not mean that individual songwriters lack distinction but simply that the products of the Alley, with exceptions to be noted, have followed the trend of popular taste—a taste dictated less by the will of the people than by the social patterns of the time.

Popular art, in the sense in which we use that term here, is created not by the people but for them. The distinction is particularly obvious in the case of popular song, which as a rule is musically less distinguished than the folk or classical music from which it so often derives. This is not because popular art of a high standard is impossible but because, by its very nature, it rests on the structure of the society in which it exists, reflecting in an exaggerated fashion the virtues and weaknesses of that society. In a field that has more than its share of the false and the artificial, popular song manages to convey, to those who take stock of its limitations, a surprisingly accurate picture of the times and the people.

We learn from George Stuyvesant Jackson's *Early Songs of Uncle Sam* that such songs were used in 1815 to popularize the issues which divided the forces of Thomas Jefferson from those of Alexander Hamilton. These verses, for example, celebrate the Jeffersonian point of view:

> Your union's a knot no intrigue can untie,
> A band which the sword of no tyrant can sever;
> Chased by Reason, the shades of Opinion shall fly,
> And the murmurs of faction be silenced forever.
> From the father to son, every blessing you've won
> Unimpair'd to the last generation shall run.

The same device combines with modern advertising in *Those Foolish Things Remind Me of You,* composed by Jack Strachey, Harry Link and Holt Murrell in 1935, to suggest that in that year of grace women smoked cigarettes, used lipstick and traveled by airplane to romantic places, the probable mingling with the improbable in the process of melodic wish-fulfillment in reverse—a new variation on the *torch song* (related to blues but limited in its subject matter to the theme of frustrated love).

Our Tin Pan Alleyites, sponsored for the most part by big business (the majority of popular songs today are published by companies under control of the large Hollywood film studios), tend to avoid the purely political, though a tinsel patriotism is often assumed. Exceptions are rare but notable. The Yacht Club Boys, who made their hit at one of the more exclusive upper East Side night clubs, poke fun at alphabetic government agencies in such a way as to indicate not so much their knowledge of government as their awareness of what will please their special audience. The capable composers who scored *Modern Times* for Charles Chaplin did a very fine job of adapting wordless but significant variations on songs by Joe Hill, balladist of the Wobblies, and *The Prisoner's Song.*

Pianos in the Alley

There is no better vantage point from which to see the panorama of popular music in America than New York's Tin Pan Alley, that shifting section now more or less bounded on the north by Fifty-Second Street, the swing sector of the Rialto; on the east by Fifth Avenue; on the west by Eighth Avenue, which, like Sixth Avenue, flanks Times Square with the backstage poverty of pawnshops, rooming houses and small hotels; and on the south by Thirty-Eighth Street. The flippant name for the Alley is supposed to have had its origin in the offices of a music publisher-composer of the 1890's. This is possible; but in the Bryant's Minstrels program for November 25, 1861, the show is described as a "Grand Tin-Pan-O-Ni-On of Pot Pourri." Aside from being a heavily loaded pun, this suggests that the Alley need not have waited for a piano with mandolin attachment to acquire its name. Today its most famous composers, and some of its most capable, spend more time in Hollywood than in New York. But New York may still lay claim to most of this music publishing business, which has flourished since the earliest days of the Constitution. One of the first smash hits of the Revolutionary period was more in the nature of an already well-seasoned folksong than what is now called a *commercial pop tune*—the intrepid *Yankee Doodle,* which turned Tory derision into democratic pride.

Though native music was published here so long ago (and occasionally even an English importation, such as *The Girl I Left Behind Me,* attained wide popularity), the national song hit was not to become a reality until almost 50 years later. Troupes of minstrels did for 1840 what nation-wide hook-ups do for the present—that is, they made it possible for the song hit of the day, more often than not of New York origin, to be sung, hummed and whistled simultaneously in diverse parts of the country. There is no doubt that in this manner they helped to shape a national pattern of thought, particularly on such compelling subjects as home, motherhood and young love. But to trace the moral atmosphere of the 19th century to the influence of popular music would be inaccurate. The popular music of that era emerges as part of a social pattern. Whatever the crime, the guilt of the Alley has never been more than that of aiding and abetting.

This it has done, with a frankness always surprisingly unabashed. Thus more than one sentimental pop tune had an origin as immediate as the song's content. *In the Baggage Coach Ahead,* written by the Negro composer Gussie L. Davis, is said to refer to an actual (and harrowing) incident; and the charming *Wait Till the Sun Shines, Nellie,* by one of Tin Pan Alley's finest melodists, Harry von Tilzer, was inspired by a newspaper clipping read in the lobby of the Hotel Breslin on a rainy day. With a superior knowledge of its technical apparatus, Tin Pan Alley has remained faithful to this tender tradition. In the year 1937, for example, it promulgated *My Cabin of Dreams, Sailboat in the Moonlight, Where or When?* and *That Old Feeling.*

The popular conception of Tin Pan Alley, a conception aided by Hollywood and its talent for hyperbole, is still that of an uninhibited madhouse, with composers and their lyricists in the role of zanies who nail the reluctant publisher to a chair while he listens to the year's (unpublished) smash hit. A sober tour of the district, however, is enough to convince anyone that the glamor-and-screwball atmosphere has long been concealed behind polite but firm secretaries; executives who, aside from their Broadway tastes in haberdashery, might as well be in the cream separator business; mahogany desks and, more often than not, photo-murals in place of the old-time collection of autographed pictures of stars who plugged the firm's songs. Here and there, of course, an office typical of the Alley in its halcyon youth can still be found. Here the telephone girl reads *Variety* as she hums one of the firm's numbers; zanies scramble hither and thither; and from innumerable cubbyholes fitted out with antiquated uprights come (with or without words) the unpublished and, alas, often never-to-be-published smash hits of the season.

Statistically, the shorter-lived hits of today are written by fewer songwriters as the new century's downbeat sounds its accent. A closer concentration of the music business, the decline of the sheet music and phonograph record industry, and the rise of radio and moving pictures—these factors augured ill for the many. The lucky few among the nation's songwriters were rewarded with air-conditioned bungalows in the glamor City of Celluloid. The less lucky stay-at-homes obligingly ground out *You Ought to Be in Pictures* and continued to take schnapps with their *schmaltz* (cheaply sentimental sweet music) in the depths of the Fifty-Second Street underground.

The Rise of the Minstrels

If there is any single factor that encourages a study of chronology in popular song, it is the distinction that within a hundred years—whatever may be the case with America's classical composers—songwriters, while confined pretty much to the limitations of the popular music field, have nevertheless used their source material with a naturalness not possible a century ago. Gershwin's *Summertime* shows that the composer understood the richness of theme inherent in American Negro music, and one hardly needs to be told that Gershwin felt this music as part of the American scene, or that he looked upon Bessie Smith, the blues singer, as a creative folk artist. This is a sign for the future. In the past the unassimilated elements in American popular music were very evident, as was also the indication of an emergent pattern in which these elements—native folk music, classical and popular music from abroad—were to take their places.

Almost from the beginning, one of the dominant influences in American popular music has been the folk music of the American Negro, which in turn utilized to great advantage the old English folk music, hymns and a diversity of other folk sources, particularly in such places as New Orleans—a port of entry for French, Spanish and Italian emigrants and a center of the slave trade from all parts of Africa. *Old Zip Coon* (now known as *Turkey in the Straw*) was adapted from Negro folk music for the burnt-cork business back in the 1840's; and certainly since that time the most typically American strains of popular music have derived largely from the folk music of the Negro. The first important influence was a melodic one, as revealed in the work of Stephen Collins Foster, who wrote for minstrel shows. The second influence—though chronology here is a matter of conjecture—was that predecessor of jazz, ragtime; and of course the third was jazz itself, which came to its lusty infancy in the city of New Orleans at about the turn of the century

Stephen Foster lived and wrote in New York. He died miserably at Bellevue Hospital in January 1864, after his friend and collaborator, George Cooper, had found him lying naked and wounded in the hall of an old lodging-house at No. 15 Bowery. Foster's work need not be confused with folk music; but the influence of American folk music upon it was more profound than is usual in the case of popular balladists. To fastidiously musical ears there is, even in the best of these songs—*My Old Kentucky Home, Old Black Joe, Old Folks at Home*—the strain of sentimentality that mars so much of our popular music. But there is also something indigenous and genuine about them, notably in the Poesque darkness (Foster could recite Poe's verses "with thrilling effect") of *Nellie Was a Lady* and in the up-and-coming *Susannah*. One can hardly imagine an American background without the songs of Stephen Foster. It was quite natural that the melody of *Camptown Races* should be utilized to help describe the Lincoln-Douglas debates in a quasi-folksong of the time, *Lincoln Hoss and Stephen A.;* just as it was natural that Dan Emmett's *Dixie*, written for a minstrel show in 1850, should have been accepted by the rank and file of the Confederate South. *Carry Me Back to Old Virginny* was perhaps even more indigenous in inspiration. Written by a Virginian, James A. Bland, the offspring of former slaves, it has the slow solemnly rhythmic quality that characterizes so much Negro folk music. Bland also gave to the quartet contingents *In the Evening by the Moonlight*.

Many colored song writers, taking their cue from white writers for the minstrels, composed songs about themselves and their way of life. Irving Jones' *I Live as Good as Any Other Coon* was typical of their output; though here and there, as among the white composers, an outstanding talent such as that of Bland revealed itself.

Later, Ernest Hogan, a Negro comedian who is said to have been almost as good as Bert Williams, wrote a song entitled *All Coons Look Alike to Me* (1896). This song was justifiably resented; yet when two Negroes, Bert Williams and George Walker, came to New York as the century was turning the corner, their act was a great success, though it was in out-and-out coon style. They did the cakewalk, a fad with both black and white; and Williams challenged William K. Vanderbilt, who had taken up the dance, to a cakewalk contest for a side bet of $100. The repertoire of Williams and Walker featured the coon song tradition. Walker died and Bert Williams went on alone to success on the New York stage, starring in the *Ziegfeld Follies* until his death in 1922. Despite the limitations of his subject matter, which was sometimes an unconscious slur upon his own people, Williams was a great entertainer, and his many imitators still pay tribute to his talent.

With the demise of the coon song era and its undesirable (however unconscious) humorous disparagement, there appeared a new type of Negro performer and a more self-respecting style of entertainment. When Billy Johnson of the comedy team of Cole and Johnson died, Bob Cole sent to the south for a new partner, J. Rosamund Johnson, a young Negro musician. The team of Cole and Johnson made a hit in vaudeville and became even more famous as collaborators in song writing. Rosamund's brother, James Weldon Johnson, who later became a leader of his race in America, quit school teaching in the South and joined them. He and Cole wrote lyrics and Rosamund the music. Their songs were varied—sometimes romantic, sometimes quaint and humorous, but never in the old clownish coon style. During their rise the coon song went into the discard; and the *coon-shouter* (loudly exuberant singer of Negro songs) disappeared from the theater.

While W. C. Handy was notating the blues and New Orleans composers were participating in the development of the still nascent jazz strain, Negroes in the North carried on their work in the popular music field. Hallie Anderson, the capable singer and musical director, supplied orchestras for the Lafayette Theatre in Harlem and the Howard in Washington, D. C. For the most part, her efforts were in the channels of conventional popular music, as were those of James Reese Europe, founder of the Clef Club in New York, who studied under Hans Hanke of Leipzig, Germany, became a renowned figure in the field of popular music, and wrote *Castle Walk*. Later he gained greater fame as leader of what was perhaps the outstanding American band in France during the World War. In discussing a concert under the auspices of the Clef Club given at Carnegie Hall in May 1912, Schirmer's *Musical Quarterly* said: "Few of the players in that great band of more than a hundred members had received any musical training whatever. They were, by profession, elevator men, bell-boys, porters, janitors or followers of still humbler tasks, for few trades-unions then admitted colored men, so that the vocations open to the Negro were about as restricted and over-crowded as the Negro streets themselves." In the program for that concert one or two ragtime pieces are listed, a similar number of pieces that suggest the minstrels, and one number that was to become a swing standard, *Panama*.

In summarizing some of the important Negro influences of the 19th and early 20th century on popular music, two interesting developments may be noted. The first, and most important, is that Negro folk music, along with white folk music, proved a constant freshening influence on popular music, even though the latter most often referred back to this source material only in diluted form. (White folk music influenced our popular song by way of individual composers rather than in waves of influence. It was also an indirect influence, in its inter-relatedness with Negro folk music.) The second development is that the direct Negro contribution to the popular music field became to some extent merely a corollary of the white influence. Thus the impact of new materials, felt so definitely in the 19th century (as exemplified, say, in the source-materials of a Stephen Foster or a James Bland) was to subside until the emergence of jazz music, except in the case of individual composers. The popular music field was sufficiently strong, economically if not culturally, to take into its maw a variety of influences, assimilate them and utilize them in songs the patterns of which continued to show a fundamental vitality despite the lukewarm sentimentalism that usually marked their construction.

Tony Pastor and Tin Pan Alley

To bring this story up to the birth of jazz—the second major folk influence after that of the minstrels—it is essential to review the latter part of the 19th century, this time confining ourselves to the immediate environs of the Alley. No mention of that period would be properly documented without the name of Tony Pastor. His first theater was at 585 Broadway; his second at 201 Bowery, that thoroughfare whose venal glories were celebrated in *The Bowery Lass, The Boys in the Bowery Pit, One of the Boys,* and (most famous of all) *The Bowery,* by Charles H. Hoyt, introduced in *A Trip to Chinatown,* which had its debut in Madison Square Theatre on November 9, 1891. Tony Pastor's third theater, the one usually meant when Tony Pastor's is referred to, was on East Fourteenth Street. It opened October 24, 1881, and one of its specialties was the topical song, a sort of *March of Time* to music.

From Tony Pastor's came such variety stars as Pat Rooney (who sang his own *Are You the O'Reilly?*), Nat Goodwin, Gus Williams, Denman Thompson, Neil Burgess, John and Harry Kernell, May and Flora Irwin, Evans and Hoey, Delehanty and Hengler. Appearing at Tony Pastor's in that era of minstrels was to the profession what "playing the Palace" became in the great Keith days before Hollywood took Broadway over the hurdles and national networks brought in the era of "guest stars." Harrigan, of Harrigan and Hart, was also one of the song-writing team of Harrigan and Braham. They composed many comic Irish songs, among them *The Mulligan Guards,* a number satirizing the pseudo-military groups that sprang up after the Civil War. Subsequently, as Kipling relates in *Kim,* this became the rallying song of British Tommies billeted in India. Tony Pastor was himself an entertainer who introduced to the pre-automobile age the lilting strains of *Daisy Bell.* Most of us have forgotten the title but not the words of this song about the-bicycle-built-for-two, a song that the English composer, Harry Dacre, first conceived as he was trying to get a bicycle (built for one) through the American customs.

Tin Pan Alley was by 1880 the leading musical machine-shop in the land, though its prominent composers were not always New Yorkers. From 1880 to 1900 there were, however, several New Yorkers who contributed to the annual crop of popular songs. *In the Good Old Summer Time* was written by Roy Shields and George (Honeyboy) Evans, natives, and the number had its debut in the Herald Square Theatre. *Sweet Genevieve* was the work of Stephen Foster's erstwhile collaborator, George

Cooper. *Walking Down Broadway* (which Spaeth puts in the 1850's) was the work of William Lingard and Charles E. Pratt, and used the expression "O.K." Joseph J. Sullivan, whose father owned a small dairy farm in what is now Long Island City, wrote *Where Did You Get That Hat?* and introduced it at Miner's Eighth Avenue Theatre. *The Band Played On* was also written by a New Yorker, John F. Palmer, and had its debut in the Harlem Opera House.

The 20th century, so far, has made a much more impressive showing in respect to composers of New York origin. Several of the big names in the song-writing field are those of natives of Manhattan or its sister boroughs. But the point is of only relative importance. The Alley belonged to New York, and the tyros from the hinterland could take it or leave it. Usually they took it. Meanwhile, of course, the regional aspects of the country were beginning to be submerged in a national pattern, a process facilitated by the development of transportation. Witness Charles K. Harris's *After the Ball*, written in Chicago and introduced in Milwaukee in a New York show, Hoyt's *A Trip to Chinatown*.

While the Alley ground out its lesser products, the predecessors of commercial pops, it also developed a tradition of songs worthy of comparison with folksong. Paul Dresser and Harry von Tilzer were in their time outstanding exponents of this tradition. Both were from the midwest and brought with them the genuineness that characterized the best American folk music. Among their works, the commercial pops they ground out for the *ickies* (persons lacking in taste) of their day have been forgotten, or are remembered only in a spirit of whimsy; but their contributions to the heritage of popular music remain significant. Paul Dresser was immensely popular in the 1880's and 1890's. A New Yorker from the midwest, he is mainly remembered for *On the Banks of the Wabash* (words by brother Theodore Dreiser); but the number of his that is most played today, a favorite of the jazz improvisers, is *My Gal Sal*.

Dresser died in 1906. By that time the second great composer of popular music in the period was enjoying a fame that was to be his for years to come. Harry von Tilzer was not a New Yorker, but he spent the greater part of his life in Tin Pan Alley—it was he, in fact, who is said to have given the Alley its name. Von Tilzer, like Dresser, produced the kind of popular music that seemed to be in demand. His songs, sentiment and all, emerged from the social environment of which they were a part. Thus we have a number in the coon song tradition, *What You Goin' to Do When the Rent Comes Round?;* a toast to his own background, *Down Where the Wurzburger Flows;* a rousing predecessor of the motherhood cycle, *I Want a Girl Just Like the Girl Who Married Dear Old Dad;* a few lines, much parodied, anent the popularity of excursion steamers, *On the Old Fall River Line;* a triumph in teardrops, *A Bird in a Gilded Cage;* and an easy-to-sing perennial, *Wait Till the Sun Shines, Nellie.*

In the early years of the 20th century, an up-and-coming New Yorker with an eye to the main chance wrote *Will You Love Me in December As You Did in May?* This young man, James J. Walker, subsequently found other niches for his talent, not the least of which was the Tammany mayoralty of New York City. Tiger or Indian, Tammany itself had made one of several comebacks. Gus Edwards and Vincent Bryan were all set to give the National Democratic Club smoker the season's *bringdown* (deflationary influence or person) in the way of a ditty entitled *In My Merry Old Oldsmobile;* but the Tiger's whiskers were out, and the boys gave them *Tammany* instead. That was in 1905. In those days Tammany Hall was next door to Tony Pastor's, and *Casey Jones* was just a scab who hadn't joined the Brotherhood of Locomotive Engineers. Those who tripped the light fantastic did it in the genteel measures of the period, by gaslight.

William Jennings Bryan took his cue from Tin Pan Alley and told the world to take back its gold and change to silver. In 1907, a line of chorus girls in daring knee-length bathing suits tripped out across the stage of the Jardin de Paris, on the roof of the New York Theatre in Longacre Square, singing: "And they'll say on the beach, there's a peach, there's a peach of a Gibson bathing girl." This first *Ziegfeld Follies* established the Ziegfeld spectacle as an annual event. It had "The Taxi Girls" with "To Hire" signs on their red tin flags. It also featured May MacKenzie, a principal figure in the Harry K. Thaw case, and the comedienne, Nora Bayes, who sang *When Mother Was a Girl.* This period might also be called *The Merry Widow* or *Floradora* era. The former (first produced in New York in 1904, at a Third Avenue beer hall known as the Orpheum) gave birth to reams of romantic melodies and led directly to the musical "production" films of Hollywood; the latter went lightly operatic and heavily platitudinous with *Tell Me, Pretty Maiden.*

Some years before the World War, a singing waiter at the Chatham, a drinking place on Doyers Street near the Bowery, wrote *Alexander's Ragtime Band.* This composition showed the influence of the improvised ragtime that was to lead into jazz. Aside from being of sufficient musical importance to give its composer a place in the annals of hot music, the words of *Alexander's Ragtime Band* were prophetic—especially the lines about the bugle call, played as it was never played before, that would make you want to go to war. The war clouds were over Europe, and before *jass* had quite become *jazz* the Alley, like other moulders of popular opinion, had fallen into a kind of anticipatory war propaganda, in the midst of which *I Didn't Raise My Boy to Be a Soldier* was a still small voice, rather badly pitched.

The period between 1900 and the World War witnessed a great general enthusiasm for dancing, in which ballroom dancing, a particularly urban phenomenon, replaced group and folk dancing. The ragtime dances, for the most part, were hybrids, representing the current interest in ragtime music and in Continental light music. The latter was epitomized so ably by the *Merry Widow Waltz* that there appeared *I Want to Be a Merry Widow, Since Mariutch Learned the Merry Widow Waltz,* and finally (from the pen of a gentleman who sensed the shift in public taste) *I'm Looking for the Man Who Wrote the Merry Widow.*

Another phenomenon that persisted into the 20th century was the dialect song. At about the time Robert Cameron Rogers' poem, *The Rosary,* was being set to music by Ethelbert Nevin and designated "semi-classical," Harry von Tilzer ground out a commercial pop called *Mariutch Make-u da Hootch-a-Ma-Cootch.* This and many other numbers celebrated the Italian immigrant; and the Italian dialect comedian became a familiar type along with the Irish, Negro, German and Jewish.

The smash hit of the 1920's, *Yes, We Have No Bananas,* has Papa Handel to thank for its resounding invocation. It was a pure nonsense song and a relief to the public from the usual run of sentimental trash foisted upon them by a music-publishing tradition that had, and still has, some pretty low ideas about the mass mind. But the fruit business takes us ahead of our story. By 1914, Irving Berlin was well on the way to his transposing piano and the exploitation of his talent for the production of melodic pops. Other composers already in the limelight were Lew Brown, Jerome Kern and Gene Buck.

The foundations for modern ballroom dancing had already been laid before the war. The old-fashioned waltz gave way to more intimate steps: the hesitation, the turkey trot, the bunny hug, the grizzly bear, the tango and later the fox trot. A popular turkey trot was *Tres Moutarde,* imported from France, the title of which indicated that ragtime music was considered *hot,* in somewhat the same sense that jazz is today. Sigmund Romberg, who subsequently gave his all to the sweet school and to operetta, wrote a few turkey trot pieces—*Some Smoke* and *Leg of Mutton*. Mayor John Purroy Mitchel invented a step called the "twinkle" and Bernard Baruch, better known as a banker, also won cups in dancing contests. Mrs. Stuyvesant Fish, however, disapproved of such abandon and per-suaded Vernon and Irene Castle to invent the "Innovation," a touchless tango, which was introduced at one of her parties but did not become popular.

Dance fads brought prosperity to such dine-and-dance places as Busta-noby's and Louis Martin's Café de l'Opera. It also popularized the tea dance, which had seemed so extraordinary when it was inaugurated at the Café des Beaux Arts. But jazz, full-blown, had hardly reached Chicago when the country embarked on its first World War. Dance orchestras were, in fact, orchestras, not bands. The bass was still self-respectingly bowed, and music made up in manners what it lacked in melody.

The New York regiments had gone to the Civil War singing *Shoo Fly, Don't Bother Me*. The song favorite of the Spanish-American War was taken from the minstrels, *There'll Be a Hot Time in the Old Town To-night*, the music of which was written in 1886 by Theodore Metz, band-leader for the McIntyre and Heath Minstrels. Words by Joe Hayden were added in 1896. As for the World War, Sousa's *Stars and Stripes Forever*, played amid scenes of marching men in uniform and flying regimental colors, probably made more business for the recruiting sergeants than any-thing especially written for the purpose. And while the folks at home were being stimulated with *Prepare, U.S.A.* and *Just a Baby's Prayer at Twilight*, the doughboys themselves were entertained with similar num-bers, including the revived *Silver Threads Among the Gold*. Parodies on this and other wartime songs were discussed by Philip Sterling in the April 1935 issue of *New Theatre* magazine. One of the *Silver Threads* variations begins in this macabre fashion:

> Put your wooden arms around me,
> Hold me in your cork embrace.

We can find sufficient evidence, too, that the Negro regiments had songs in their kit other than *They'll Be Mighty Proud in Dixie of Their Old Black Joe*. There was a characteristic stanza that went:

> Joined the army for to get some clothes,
> Lordy, turn your face on me.
> What we're fightin' about nobody knows,
> Lordy, turn your face on me.

Among the major numbers that helped to build up and sustain the war psychology were George M. Cohan's *Over There;* Johnson and Wenrich's *Where Do We Go from Here?;* the enormously successful *Keep the Home Fires Burning; Goodbye Broadway, Hello France;* the sentimental *Rose of No Man's Land;* and that most popular of the stuttering songs, *K-K-K-Katy.* But before passing judgment on composers who helped put the war across, it might be well to recall our original premise: that popular music—and this applies particularly to its shortcomings—emerges as part of a social pattern.

At the top of the sheet-music business in the early 1920's, after the World War, a smash hit might last more than a year and reach a sale of 5,000,000 copies. By 1931 the life-span was reduced to three months and the probable sheet sale to a mere 300,000 copies. Several factors brought about this change. While the phonograph did much to reduce sheet-music sales, the radio was the main factor in cutting down the life expectancy of a song hit. That anguished request, *"Please* turn off the radio," is occasioned as often by the monotony of hearing the same tune time after time as by the undistinguished quality of so much of the popular music on the air.

When the radio came in, it edged out the phonograph and all but sounded the knell of sheet music. As usually happens in such crises, the composers and lyricists were left holding the bag. But recently, through the organization of the American Society of Composers, Authors and Publishers, the claims of the rank and file song-writers have been getting more attention. It is significant that the 20th century witnessed not only a rehabilitation of the popular music field but of its composers and interpreters as well. At the same time that ASCAP began to come to life to express in some measure the needs of composers, Local 802 of the American Federation of Musicians cleaned house and elected a rank and file progressive slate of officers. The new administration of Local 802 has done much to protect and improve the status of musicians in general.

Blues into Jazz

In bringing the story of popular music up to the 1920's, the introduction of jazz into this music is of sufficient importance to warrant separate treatment. Among the elements that went to make up ragtime were those that were later to engender the jazz strain itself—the potpourri of the American songbag and particularly the folk music of the Negro people.

In ragtime a sense of its quasi-folk origins was preserved in low places. The pianist of the honky-tonk and working-class dance halls improvised ragtime and played the blues as well. It was this improvised ragtime that showed the closest relation to the jazz that succeeded it.

Late in the 19th century this style produced its greatest composer, the Negro Scott Joplin. He wrote *Maple Leaf Rag,* still a favorite with hot musicians, and he also tried his hand with ragtime material in classical forms. Among other numbers that have come down into jazz is *Ida, Sweet As Apple Cider,* written by Eddie Leonard, the minstrel star, in 1903. Long before 1900, honky-tonk pianists were encouraged with the admonition "Jass it up!" and someone who shouted this at the Original Dixieland Band in Chicago is indirectly responsible for the use of the word as applied to New Orleans hot music. The most reputable evidence places it as slang, neither Northern nor Southern, traceable to Elizabethan usage. In ragtime, two features of jazz were already in evidence: rhythmic variety and emphasis, and melodic improvisation.

In the realm of popular music, ragtime was not jazz, yet what distinguished them was less a treatment of different materials than a greater refinement of melody and rhythm. In dance rhythm this was particularly obvious—the jerky gyrations of ragtime gave way to the rhythmically more graceful variations of the foxtrot. Perhaps the toddle, which celebrated in dance form the early days of the new music, best exemplified this. Rather silly as viewed from the sidelines, this dance step of Chicago emphasized all four beats of the measure and the vibrato as well. Subsequently the development of improvised jazz to its highest point was to find its accompaniment in an urban folk dance, the Lindy Hop. The name identifies it as to period. As to style, it varied from city to city, sometimes descending to vulgar and senselessly rhythmic elaborations, but never losing sight of its fundamental steps. In New Orleans it utilized the shag as well. In the Carolinas it achieved in city-country dances what the Manhattan supper clubs achieved years later in their publicity columns—the Big Apple. In Harlem's Savoy Ballroom during the year of the Lindy Hop many of the greatest jazz improvisers were playing—Louis Armstrong, Earl Hines, Coleman Hawkins, Joe Smith. These are names of perhaps little significance to the public today, but to musicians and composers who know their indigenous music they are names that immediately suggest the tremendous creative force that went into the development of jazz.

Distinctions of rhythmic and melodic refinement aside, more important differences between ragtime and jazz become perceptible only as one looks into the history of jazz music. First of all, this music was discovered in the South, where it had become an urbanized folk music. Negro and white, the bands of improvising musicians in New Orleans played "ear music"; and while they picked up odd jobs here and there, they were considered "fakers" (faking was, in fact, an early word for jamming, very free and spirited group improvisation by a small or jam band) as far as local musical circles were concerned. New Orleans papers became alarmed when New York announced jazz as of New Orleans origin, and they relinquished all claim to this new product of an urban life. It was solely this improvised music of New Orleans origin, however, that had first claim to the word. That it was radically different from popular music of the day should be obvious from the above. It was to become patently so in 1917, when Victor issued two records—one by Joseph C. Smith's orchestra, the other Livery Stable Blues, a recording by the Original Dixieland Jazz Band then playing at Reisenweber's in New York City. It is of some significance that when jazz bands play this latter piece today they usually conform to a modification of the original orchestral pattern.

This music was born of various elements—of Negro worksongs, spirituals, and blues; of ragtime, Creole songs and mountain "ballets"; and, curiously, of military and brass band music. Early in the 20th century, funeral music—already an established tradition in New Orleans—featured what came to be known as the nucleus of a jazz band (minus piano, which couldn't march): cornet, clarinet, trombone, drums. The usual procedure at funerals was to play a slow blues (vernacular lament, usually but not always statement, repetition, response; usually but not always, pentatonic scale) on the trip to the graveyard. For the return, something lively and gay would be featured, such as that favorite of New Orleans clarinets, High Society Rag—still to be a featured item in 1937 with Sharkey Bonano and his New Orleans Sharks, Manhattan's most popular Dixieland-style band. High Society seems to have been inspired by the flute passage in a John Philip Sousa march.

The irrepressible gaiety of this number makes people question its use at funerals. A similar question was asked in the winter of 1936–7, when Tamiris and her group, aided by an orchestra and a Negro chorus, all of the WPA Dance Theater, interpreted On to de Buryin' from Negro Songs of Protest, a collection by Lawrence Gellert. Krehbiel, an authority on folk music, remarked that most Negro spirituals and worksongs were in major keys, the blues finding expression in the minor scale. He discovered also that Negroes were encouraged to sing happy songs, since the melancholy sort might remind them of their miserable lives; their folk singers also believed in a hereafter that would reward them with all that had previously been denied them. As for the forceful rhythms, some plantation owners paid bonuses to singers who could increase the output of work through the use of fast tempo.

One of the most interesting aspects of early jazz is that for the most part it is a folk music without words. *Tiger Rag, High Society* and other important numbers had no words until their acceptance in the popular music field demanded that lyrics be added to them. The blues did have words, and many of them had words of social significance; but when it came to recording the blues, the many significant lyrics, for fairly obvious reasons, were neglected and emphasis was placed on the sexually conditioned blues. It is important to understand these blues, if only so that one may clearly evaluate the cheap and tawdry imitations of them which emerged from Tin Pan Alley.

The folk music of the American Negro has never been without social connotations. Spirituals were the language of the Underground Railway in the 19th century, just as they are the language of unity today in those parts of the South where the right of collective bargaining is denied sharecroppers and they must organize secretly, and just as in Harlem they have gone into the making of "Rent Blues" or theme songs of a housing problem. Industrialism and the gradual urbanization of the South brought the folksong to the city; but there was little place for it there in a milieu already dominated by popular music, and it retreated to the honky-tonk. A honky-tonk car was sometimes hooked on to the train that carried itinerant workers from job to job; and Meade (Lux) Lewis, one of the greatest of blues pianists, celebrates this in a wordless but beautifully composed piece of music called *Honky Tonk Train Blues*.

A majority of the early jazz songs that have become known in orchestral repertoires as swing standards evolved as the result of collective improvisation. The Dixieland Band is responsible for several, as is King Oliver's Creole Band. The New Orleans Rhythm Kings, a band of New Orleans and Chicago musicians, contributed *Farewell Blues, Bugle Call Rag, Tin Roof Blues,* and other numbers. Hoagy Carmichael, for many years associated with New York's Tin Pan Alley, composed *Washboard Blues* while still at the University of Indiana leading a jazz band there and working with other bands such as the Wolverines, the midwest organization that featured Bix Beiderbecke. All in all, the South and the midwest gave the Alley a score or more of talented composers who brought into popular music the refreshing strain of jazz as it emerged from folk music itself. George Gershwin, Jerome Kern, Irving Berlin, and other New York composers participated in this development. In many cases, however, the Alley composer, smothered by his environment, was forced to bend his talent to the will of the publishing houses; this was particularly true in the early days when jazz was looked upon as more or less of a novelty.

In the early 1920's the situation had changed very little from what it was in 1916, when the Dixieland band came to New York. The site of Reisenweber's in 1937, however, revealed a former movie palace, its box office boarded up, the fake Roman pillars fronting the second floor already showing an appearance of age. Behind these pillars late in 1916 the Original Dixieland Jazz Band gave New York City its first taste of jazz. For a number or two the diners sat at their tables, listened, and stared. The boys were playing their own New Orleans music—*Tiger Rag, Ostrich Walk, Bluin' the Blues*—and the New Yorkers didn't know what to do about it. Finally the manager explained that it was dance music and the couples came out on the floor, one after another, and stayed there until the band was exhausted.

The orchestras that still put manners before melody were startled to see the commercial record companies playing up "the jass" for all the novelty there was in it—and there was certainly an excess of naïveté and novelty in early jazz. Some of the "name-band" boys caught on, though often they headed directly for the *cornfield* (from *corn, corny, cornfed,* indicating faked, inept or hackneyed attempts at hot music; generic metropolitan synonyms for the rustic and countrified). Earl Fuller's orchestra was at Rector's; and with Ted Lewis playing clarinet, Fuller, coming under the Dixieland influence but not quite up to it, could lay claim to the dubious honor of being the first important *corn band.*

Meanwhile, in the country at large and particularly in the midwest, hot musicians, Negro and white, played in honky-tonks, ginmills, working-class dance halls. In these places the improvisational spirit of early jazz was preserved, and its instrumental contributions were developed. The musicians played what they felt, as LaRocca of the Dixieland band expressed it, "from the heart." Their music also caught on with the college crowd; the young men and women of the early 1920's have been its most fervent supporters. Bix Beiderbecke and the Wolverines, encouraged by Hoagy Carmichael, played many college engagements. There and then began the practice of *cats* (fans) "freezing" before the band to catch the hot choruses which, with the Wolverines, were strictly variations-on-theme. Although they played the college circuit, the Wolverines had a minimum of pops and no waltzes in their repertoire.

Frank Signorelli, a Dixieland pianist of the 1920's, joined the Memphis Five and the first Cotton Pickers. The second Cotton Pickers, a recording set-up, enlisted pianist Rube Bloom, author of *Swamp Fire* and a talented composer in the hot music field. Both bands included a trombone player, Miff Mole, who made great contributions in solo work and in stylistic influence on the bands in which he played. Red Nichols' Red Heads were perhaps the first New York band to show the Chicago influence in effects that displayed a mingling of the quite distinct Negro and white traditions. Already, in the small Gennett recording studio at Richmond, Indiana, Negroes and whites were playing together as they did in the ginmills on Chicago's South Side. In New York during the 1920's, white improvisers *sat in* with the Negro bands in Harlem; and by 1936 both Negroes and whites were sitting in with the jam bands in the drink-but-better-not-try-to-dance places along the section of West Fifty-Second Street called Swing Lane. For a few eventful nights the Negro trumpeter from Luis Russell's band, Henry (Red) Allen, Jr., of New Orleans, sat in with Chicagoans Joe Marsala (clarinet) and Eddie Condon (guitar) at Hickory House.

The Nichols bands, which are everywhere in the history of jazz, contributed a note of suavity to the hot strain. To some extent they helped carry along the improvisational and rhythmic tradition that was to emerge, again in Chicago, in a period jazz (*ca.* 1927–32) called *Chicago style.* (This is not to be confused with *classic swing,* sometimes called *Chicago swing,* which developed much earlier.) In line with New York's reputation for heading the parade, the two bands that developed hot arrangements, paving the way for the influence of hot music on popular music as such, were those led by Duke Ellington and Fletcher Henderson. The list of their personnel reads like an honor roll of musicians who have contributed to hot improvisation and instrumental style.

The younger generation growing up with the new music gave it a substantial following. Their dance-steps—cake, collegiate, and the Charleston —that led into the Lindy Hop developed parallel to the development of jazz itself. When Red Nichols and his Five Pennies were at Roseland playing the precise stacatto jazz audible now only on the records made under the name of the Red Heads, there were always several couples dancing *cake* style, a style significant both for its complications and for its casual restraint. Broadly speaking, this was the Flapper Age, in retrospect an age of wise-cracking innocence. For New York's growing crowd of *jitter-bugs* (synonymous with *cats*) there were increasing numbers of hot spots—the Colonnades, Connic's Inn, the Savoy, the original Cotton Club—where the flavor of jazz, elsewhere obscured by the prevalence of popular music, was showing that, like old wine, it could and did improve with age.

From a musician's point of view, New York was never the hot-music center that Chicago so decidedly was in the 1920's. For this reason it points up what happened to hot music and its exponents in that decade. Popular music was called jazz, and musicians began to call the music that was improvised, or of that spirit, *hot* jazz, sometimes referring to it, even in those days, as *swing*. (Today *swing* has no more specific significance to the public than did jazz in, say, 1926; though it has been assimilated more generally through *hot* orchestrations and the popularity of a few of its "names.") The California Ramblers (many of them bona fide New Yorkers, as were the Memphis Five) adapted hot materials to an early variety of "commercial swing." To a Detroit orchestra led by Gene Goldkette goes much of the credit for introducing into name-bands small nuclei of hot musicians. In this band was Joe Venuti, hot fiddle; Eddie Lang, greatest guitar soloist in hot jazz; Don Murray, of the silver clarinet; Frankie Trumbauer, C-melody sax; Bix Beiderbecke, a jazz composer whose improvisations on cornet are fully as important as his compositions; and Steve Brown (from the New Orleans Rhythm Kings) who slapped the bass fiddle and called it the *doghouse*. Red McKenzie, who organized the Mound City Blue Blowers with Eddie Condon, the fine rhythm guitar, induced the Goldkette hot nucleus to make records. Their first recording as a hot unit was *Singin' the Blues,* a Dixieland piece. Paul Whiteman took over this hot nucleus almost intact; and it became customary for name-bands to include a few improvisers who could *swing out for the cats*. Thus, the inculcation of popular music with the hot music germ took place largely in New York City. Hot bands, as such, found it difficult to earn a decent living, and the improvisers were gradually absorbed in name-bands, playing hot style for records only.

This is an important point to bear in mind, for a technical reason. The hot bands on platforms, and subsequently in recording studios, used about the same number of rhythm and melodic instruments. Of the melodic instruments, one of each was standard—clarinet, sax, trumpet, trombone—a disposition that allowed for more counterpoint, in keeping with the folk music from which hot music derived. The emphasis on rhythm was obvious, particularly in such record bands as the Chicagoans, in the formation of which Red McKenzie and Eddie Condon were again prominent. It was only in the *commercial hot bands* (bands that play hot arrangements, as against hot improvisations) that the stiltedness of harmonic arrangement was avoided. Consequently these bands—Fletcher Henderson's, Duke Ellington's and the rest—had a great influence on popular orchestration.

Throughout the development of present-day jazz, the most important single influence has been that of the Negro. When, in more recent years, the Benny Goodman band was packing them in at New York's Paramount Theater and Pennsylvania Hotel, the arrangements were often the work of Negroes: Fletcher Henderson, Jimmy Mundy, Mary Lou Williams. As a unit of the large band, the Goodman Trio—Goodman (clarinet), Wilson (piano), Krupa (traps)—was perhaps the first Negro and white combination to fill important ballroom, theater and hotel engagements from coast to coast. The same personnel, with vibraphonist Lionel Hampton, also played as the Goodman Quartet. Both groups were everywhere acclaimed. Just as the music had from the first vaulted color barriers, so the men who played it—with a few unhappy exceptions—refused to be limited by invidious standards. And the public itself, steeped in prejudice, was beginning to come round to the idea that pigmentation might have less to do with personality and talent than innumerable other factors.

The Negro, with his wealth of folk-music background, was also to create two of the important band styles of 1937: one represented by Andy Kirk's orchestra, with Mary Lou Williams as pianist and arranger, the other by Count Basie's orchestra, with Basie himself, composer of *Roseland Shuffle,* as pianist. Both bands came out of Kansas City. The discovery of the latter, like the first public notice accorded to Goodman, Bob Hackett and others, was largely due to John Hammond, who has devoted so much of his time to the cause of hot music in general and the rank-and-file musician in particular.

Negro composers have also produced some of the best hot jazz compositions. Duke Ellington, of course, stands first, with half a hundred numbers running from the Debussyan *Misty Mornin'* through *Black and Tan Fantasy* and *In a Sentimental Mood* to *Caravan.* The list also includes King Oliver *(West End Blues, Sugar Foot Stomp);* Jelly-Roll Morton *(Wolverine Blues, Kansas City Stomps);* Fats Waller *(Honeysuckle Rose, Wringin' an' Twistin');* Eubie Blake *(Ain't Misbehavin', Love Me or Leave Me),* who collaborated with Milton Reddie on one of the most charming numbers of 1937, *I Praise Sue,* for the WPA production *Swing It;* Fletcher Henderson; and Don Redman.

Of the many concerts that have set out to "explain" hot music to the public, only two or three have been primarily concerned with it. The celebrated Paul Whiteman concert at Aeolian Hall in 1924 presented only one favorite of the swingsters, a pop tune called *Whispering*. At that time George Gershwin was still much more influenced by popular music than by hot jazz. It was only in his later work that he began to utilize hot instrumentation, though such European composers as Ravel, Stravinsky and Les Six had perceived immediately that the great contribution of hot music, apart from its melodic improvisations, lay in the imaginative freshness of its instrumentation. In 1928, Whiteman participated in another "jazz" concert, this time including several authentic hot numbers and performers; but unfortunately both Grofé the arranger, and Whiteman himself leaned heavily on the much diluted classical forms that had seeped down into what was euphemistically called the semi-classical field.

In 1936, a concert of hot music at the Imperial Theater in New York lost money, though the SRO sign was out. At that time a song called *The Death of Swing* had already been published. Something more than a year later, the Columbia Broadcasting System sponsored a concert in one of its Times Square radio theaters to celebrate the first anniversary of the Saturday Night Swing Club. Standees packed every corner of the house.

Between them, these concerts signalized two important developments in latter-day swing. The first was a return to the small three-to-seven-piece band (Raymond Scott's Quintet, Bob Crosby's Bobcats, Benny Goodman's Quartet and Tommy Dorsey's Clambake Seven) usually as a big-band unit. The popularity of the Goodman four and of Raymond Scott's admirably stylized but rather mechanical compositions *(Dynamo, Twilight in Turkey)* set off this revival. In these new small units the rhythm instruments were often predominant, as against the accented horns and reeds of the Dixieland and modern jam bands.

The second development is suggested by the fact that the Imperial Theater get-together was sponsored by the Onyx Club, a late hangout for hot orchestra men, who often "sat in" with the band. It was soon discovered by the *cats* and the curious. A faintly lighted blue-and-orange music box and bar with the photographs of hot immortals dim on its walls, the Onyx Club sponsored Leo and his Spirits of Rhythm, a jam band that included such performers as Buster Bailey (clarinet) and Frankie Newton (trumpet); Martha Raye, in 1937 the gate-mouth singing star of Hollywood; Stuff Smith's fervid jam band; and Eddie Riley, whose demonstration of the internal economy of a battered old horn made *The Music Goes 'Round and 'Round* a national furore in 1935. The Onyx Club's 1937 find was Maxine Sullivan, a handsome Negro vocalist from Pittsburgh, who reinterpreted such old favorites as *Loch Lomond* and *Annie Laurie* in relaxed and subtle swing style.

Along with hot instrumental technique, a hot vocal technique had developed. It was Louis Armstrong who pioneered this technique, as it was Louis who replaced a cornet with a trumpet and gave jazz its hot style on the latter instrument. Armstrong could take an authentic hot tune and give it out "from the heart"; or he could take a pop tune and reinterpret it, often *ribbing* (satirizing) it. He contributed largely to that wealth of humor which developed as one of the features of hot jazz. Ribbing was to culminate in *jive* treatment—at its worst so abandoned that it had lost touch with itself and was a sign only of creative sterility. Hot men jive a great deal—the environment encourages it; but they also reserve their talent for genuinely hot interpretation and melodic improvisations, as anyone may learn by listening to Joe Marsala, Taft Jordan, Bobby Hackett, Eddie Condon, Pee-Wee Russell, Bud Freeman, George Brunies, Harry James, Jesse Stacy, Tommy Dorsey and others in the New York night spots. Among the better hot vocalists should be listed Louis Armstrong, Henry Allen, Jr., Jack Teagarden, Red McKenzie, Mildred Bailey, Ella Fitzgerald, Adelaide Hall and Billie Holiday. Bessie Smith, regarded by most hot singers as the standout in their field, was fatally injured in an automobile accident in September 1937.

This hot talent—at least a hundred gifted improvisers could be listed —has begun to affect the popular music field (witness the success of such bands as Tommy Dorsey's, Count Basie's, Bob Crosby's, Benny Goodman's, Bunny Berrigan's, all of which may be called commercial swing bands); but composers *per se* are still proscribed by the moguls of music, who argue that the public isn't ready for originality. Raymond Scott, Reginald Foresyte and other composers whose work is related to hot music find this work more acceptable when it is tagged with "funny" titles. Aside from a few hot composers such as Duke Ellington, the upsurge of creative talent to be expected in an era of hot music is apparent for the most part in the originality of arrangements rather than of compositions.

The Alley Today

Meanwhile, the commercial pops followed the times without probing too deeply. Prohibition gave us *Come Down and Pick Out Your Hus-*

band; the year 1929 inspired *I'm in the Market for You.* There was a sentimentally effective vulgarization of the jobless in *Brother, Can You Spare a Dime?* from J. P. McEvoy's revue *Americana,* which opened in 1932 with a sardonic line of ticker tape moving across a translux screen: "My country—may she always be right; but right or wrong, Mickey Mouse." It was that sort of year. The musical field had been doubly hit: by the depression, and by musical mass production in the radio and the talking picture. Sound pictures had come in with Jolson's *The Jazz Singer* in 1927. As usual, the evil of plagiarism continued. The publishers of *Avalon* were required to pay $25,000 because the tune derived a little too obviously from Puccini's *E Lucevan le Stella.* The Alley public was less shocked by this $25,000 duplicity than by the fact that a composer of Italian opera was still alive.

There were innumerable other pops related to the depression of 1930–5; but the Alley songs, held down as they were by publishing restrictions, had little direct significance. The beginning of a recognition that social conditions entailed social responsibility popularized the heroic mood of Disney's *Who's Afraid of the Big Bad Wolf?,* which had been preceded by Harold Arlen's implicitly topical *Stormy Weather* with its melody suggestive of Joe Oliver's *West End Blues.*

With the depression came a greater interest in labor organization; and the folk tune of *John Brown's Body,* which had been adapted to Civil War use in *The Battle Hymn of the Republic,* was adapted to labor use in Ralph Chaplin's *Solidarity Forever.* Perhaps none of the later songs had quite the folk quality of the Negro soldiers' war blues, *Black Man Fights Wid De Shovel,* or of Joe Hill's *Casey Jones* (which implies that there is labor justice only in hell). An exception was *Death House Blues (Scottsboro Blues),* refrain by Peter Martin and music by Earl Robinson, with its moaning

> Nine nappy heads wid big shiny eye,
> All boun' in jail an' boun' to die,

lifted up by the chant of the chorus:

> White workin' man goin' to set dem free,
> Black workin' man goin' go set dem free.

There were other effective compositions, such as the anonymous *Hold the Fort,* which began as a song set to a gospel hymn by English transport workers; *Abe Lincoln,* derived from Lincoln's second inaugural address, rearranged by Alfred Hayes and put to music by Earl Robinson, in 1937 the song of the American Abraham Lincoln Battalion in Spain. *The Cradle Will Rock,* by Marc Blitzstein, and *Pins and Needles,* by Harold J. Rome, brought to the stage an original musical treatment of material relating to the everyday life and problems of the people.

Isolated and fragmentary, the social forces that inspired this new material began to penetrate the Alley. Popular composers were becoming increasingly aware of the public demand for less *schmaltz* and more significant compositions. The late 1920's and early 1930's produced an encouraging number of songs whose lyrics were not thick with romance and whose melodies had something of the elasticity of good musical thinking. In the smart revue and musical field, Cole Porter *(Gay Divorcee, Fifty Million Frenchmen)* and the English Noel Coward *(Bitter Sweet, This Year of Grace)* brought quick wit and an engaging dilettante freshness to the job in hand. Among the better revue composers and lyricists were Jerome Kern *(Show Boat, Roberta);* Vincent Youmans *(Rainbow, Hit the Deck);* Richard Rodgers and Lorenz Hart *(A Connecticut Yankee, Babes in Arms);* Howard Dietz and Arthur Schwartz *(The Band Wagon);* Irving Berlin *(Music Box Revues, Face the Music);* Harold Arlen and Ted Koehler *(Cotton Club Revue);* and Dorothy Fields and Jimmy McHugh *(Blackbirds of 1928).*

But the foremost composer of this period was George Gershwin, who died in 1937. His work ran all the way from the earlier George White's *Scandals* through *Girl Crazy* to the political satire *Of Thee I Sing* and the Negro folk-opera *Porgy and Bess.* Gershwin earned the unspoken tribute of the hot musicians, who have a highly selective ear for the popular tunes that lend themselves to improvisation. His *I Got Rhythm* was the number played most frequently at a jam session held in 1937 at New York City. In one set Artie Shaw (clarinet), Chick Webb (traps) and Duke Ellington (piano) improvised for more than ten minutes on this composition by one of New York's finest native musicians.

No doubt there would be more composers of Gershwin's caliber if the younger men were encouraged to recognize the tradition and to utilize the discoveries of hot music. This applies, of course, as much to the so-called serious composers as to those in the popular field. In the future it may quite possibly come to be regarded as sheer musical ignorance that an American composer should be unfamiliar with the hot choruses or variations-on-theme created by such improvisers as Bix Beiderbecke, Sidney

Bechet, Frank Teschmaker and the early Louis Armstrong. The composers of the future will not look down on this music of their progenitors. They will understand it as a product of its environment, and its composers as workers in a songshop that did not always favor the best talent or the finest exercise of talent. This understanding, with a more courageous approach to the environment itself, may lead to a music as true to the life of its times as is the best folk music.

Entrances and Exits

THE CURTAIN rose on the New York stage more than two hundred years ago—on December 6, 1732. A circle of candles stuck on nails projecting from a barrel hoop illuminated the Honorable Rip van Dam's very honestly labeled "New Theater," and a stove in the foyer provided little more than a fire hazard. George Farquhar's *The Recruiting Officer*, revived many times since, was the offering. The bench-lined room, otherwise bare, displayed a large notice exhorting the audience not to spit.

David Douglass, another pioneer of the theater, who offered the first play based upon an American theme and whose presentations were often attended by George Washington, thirty years later found himself constrained to offer "a Pistole reward to whoever can discover the person who was so very rude as to throw Eggs from the Gallery last Monday."

One of Douglass' theaters, the Park, on Park Row near Ann Street, was the city's first playhouse of real architectural pretensions. Here the "star" system, the practice of subordinating vehicle and cast to the celebrated actor, was definitely established. This house, built in 1798, was destroyed by fire in 1820, and the new theater that went up on the same site ruled the American stage for half a century thereafter. Here Edmund Kean acted in Shakespearean drama; the first American production of Italian opera, with Italian singers, was presented here; James Hackett, W. C. Macready, Charles Kemble, Tyrone Power, Junius Brutus Booth and Charlotte Cushman (the greatest tragedienne of her day) were among the celebrities to appear upon its stage.

In 1796, William Dunlap acquired an interest in the old American Company, and began a notable career as playwright-manager. After a term with this company in the John Street Theater, he took over the New Park Theater as director and manager. He introduced many of the plays of Kotzebue, and through his promotion of horror subjects did much to bring about the vogue of the mystery play. Although he was America's first professional dramatist, he is chiefly remembered today as the author of the first documented *History of the American Theater* (1832) and a *History of the Rise and Progress of the Arts of Design in the United States* (1834).

The Bowery era of the New York theater, extending from about 1800 to around the middle of the century, would seem in the light of historic fact to have held even more glory, gaudiness and turbulence than legend attributes to it. Built in 1826, the Bowery Theater that year presented Edwin Forrest in *Othello*. It burned down no fewer than three times within the next ten years, and again in 1845. Incidentally, in the history of the early theater the phrase "destroyed by fire" recurs with sinister monotony. It is usually followed, however, by the statement that "a new structure was promptly erected upon the ashes of the old."

Although the early New York stage was dominated by the European, and no responsible group could be found to challenge this supremacy, there were certain critics who dared to hope that the American theater would develop its own native actors and plays. Washington Irving thus disposed of such persons: "Let me ask them one question. Have they ever been to Europe? Have they seen a Garrick, a Kemble, or a Siddons? If they have not, I can assure you (upon the word of two or three of my friends, the actors) they have no right to the title of critics." Nevertheless, during the Bowery Theater fire of 1845 the audience prevented firemen from reaching the burning structure because uniforms recently issued to the police too closely resembled those worn by English bobbies to suit freeborn American taste. In 1849 the great English actor W. C. Macready was driven from the stage of the Astor Place Opera House by a mob that gathered in response to the anti-English demagoguery of Edwin Forrest. When Macready tried again, a few nights later, more than ten thousand exasperated critics assembled in Astor Place and stoned the theater. Macready fled to the then distant village of New Rochelle, and later to Boston and England.

Evaluating the drama of the Bowery era, and of the decades immediately following it, is a matter that demands caution in the use of generalizations. If some of the offerings seem at this date incredibly puerile, surely no one could complain of the frequent presentations of Shakespeare, of Congreve and Steele, of *The Beggar's Opera*. And if there is a belief today that much of the old-time acting was overdone, full of sound and fury, it must be noted that theatrical conventions change. Authorities have pointed out that the lighting of the early stage was so uncertain and dim that the actor, fearful of not being seen, at least wanted to make sure of being heard.

With the middle of the 19th century, the pace of affairs in the theater perceptibly quickened. Dion Boucicault arrived from London in 1853, to become later on, with his novel production devices, "the upholsterer of the American stage." Boucicault, a man of prodigious energy, staged and adapted many plays that did much to set the fashion of the period. Aside from his many activities as writer, actor, director and producer, he exerted sufficient pressure on Congress to secure the first passably sound copyright laws protecting the previously victimized dramatist. Although dominated for the most part by European models and tastes in the theater, with Joseph Jefferson he adapted and produced *Rip Van Winkle*, which helped to focus attention on American folklore as fertile material for the playwright.

Such offerings as *Fashion, Under the Gas Light, The Black Crook, After Dark* and *The Drunkard* were the popular highlights of a period that extolled violent melodrama, permeated with moral fingerpointing. It is instructive to note that these plays, taken so seriously in their day, served as satires on the same period when revived in the early 1920's and played as faithfully as possible to the original versions. But their melodramatic structure may be partly justified from the fact that life itself in relation to these subjects was then something of a melodramatic experience. Straitlaced Victorian morality, however, was slow to disappear from the theater. It is difficult today to take seriously an innocence that could be shocked by Maude Adams in a role calling for *feigned* tipsiness. Not until the post-war period was Victorianism laughed from the boards. It had, nevertheless, its triumphs, notably in the operettas of Gilbert and Sullivan and of Victor Herbert.

The period from the middle of the 19th century to well into the 20th was the halcyon age for actors, when individual stars and such all-star stock companies as Augustin Daly's dominated the stage. Edwin Forrest, Edwin Booth, Mrs. Gilbert, Ada Rehan, James Lewis, John Drew, Maude Adams, the Barrymores, Mrs. Fiske and many other Americans, along with a host of noted artists from abroad—Sarah Bernhardt, Eleanora Duse, Salvini, Henry Irving, Ellen Terry, Forbes-Robertson, the two Coquelins, Réjane, Mounet-Sully, and others—attracted large audiences that cared less for the content of the plays produced than for the brilliance of the acting. The star system is still prominent on the New York stage, though very few present-day actors and actresses wield the compelling influence that was exercised by the great figures of the theater's halcyon period.

As early as 1847, Walt Whitman had been calling for a distinctly American drama. "If some bold man," he wrote, "would take the theater in hand in this country, and resolutely set his face against the starring system . . . some *American* it must be, and not moulded in the opinions and long established ways of the English stage . . . [if such a man would] revolutionize the drama, and discard much that is not fitted to present tastes and to modern ideas—engage and encourage American talent, look above merely the gratification of the vulgar and of those who love glittering scenery—give us American plays, too, matter fitted to American opinions and institutions—our belief is he would do the Republic service, and himself too, in the long run."

Even the European-minded Augustin Daly in the late 1860's and 1870's had challenged certain restrictions under which the native playwright labored. Why, he asked, must American dramatists select a foreign background for a play about a "wild, whooping American girl" when "a respectable New York, Boston or Philadelphia family would be equally distressed and amazed by such a girl"? This may seem an extremely left-handed plea for an American drama, but Daly's conception of the latter's future was a large one. He predicted that "our national drama will be established without restriction as to subject or plot. The coming dramatist will be indifferent on that score. Neither Shakespeare nor any of his contemporaries . . . made the national drama of their native lands by the delineation of national character only. We must not exact of the American dramatist more than has been demanded of its dramatists by any other country." Daly pictured "the silent brooding observant boy in the gallery" who was to write the play of the future—a perennial picture and prophecy, it must be noted.

The production of Ibsen's best work and the early plays of Bernard Shaw, who was successful as a playwright in New York before he was in London, and of the problem plays of Arthur Wing Pinero and Henry Arthur Jones, was destined to exert the most considerable influence, however, on the theater to follow, particularly upon the playwrights. Previously in the theater, controversial social subjects had been either ignored altogether or glossed over with romanticism. After Ibsen and Shaw (with the latter's provocative prefaces), the serious-minded playwright could feel that almost any subject was material for dramatic treatment. Even such a Messianic play as Jerome K. Jerome's *The Passing of the Third Floor Back* may be considered one of the first steps toward a more robust and serious theater.

The immediate American predecessors of today's celebrities, the men who made possible the achievements of our contemporary drama, were David Belasco and Charles Frohman among the producers, and Clyde Fitch, Augustus Thomas, Eugene Walter, Edward Sheldon and William Vaughn Moody among the playwrights. Belasco's chief contribution consisted of innovations in the mounting of plays. He was the first to introduce from Europe such important devices, now an integral part of stagecraft, as reflectors, borders and spotlights. He had also, at times, a fondness for literal realism in his settings. But Frohman, a less legendary figure than Belasco, probably made the more substantial contribution by encouraging many young writers and by his skillful production of classic and modern plays. Under these two men, the stage presentation tended to become more the group-effort that it is today, rather than a blind gamble in which the efforts of designer, producer, director and actor were pieced together at random.

Augustus Thomas, who died in 1934, was "the playwright to whom America turned with confidence for the drama that clothes significant ideas with power and restraint and the comedy that delights through kindly and adroit revelation of human frailty." This appraisal by Arthur Hobson Quinn is doubtless accurate. Even today Thomas is regarded as the most completely American playwright of the pre-war years. His plays dealt with themes of sectional, historical and social interest. They were plays about cowboys, Mexicans and army officers, plays that popularized certain homely American situations.

The career of Clyde Fitch as a playwright began in 1890 with his romantic *Beau Brummel*, and for twenty years thereafter he was one of America's leading dramatists. For the most part he pictured the life of New York's upper classes; and although his plays were rarely profound or original, he was an unusually accurate observer of externals, of the curious and amusing, and his work discloses a groping for fresh values.

Eugene Walter first attracted attention in 1907 with *Undertow*, a drama of journalism, politics and railroads. *The Easiest Way*, produced two years later, brought him his greatest fame. Contemporary critics hailed it as "realistic" and "epoch-making," though critical opinion today commonly regards it as no more than skillful melodrama.

Edward Sheldon rendered some aspects of American life never before portrayed on the stage. His first success, *Salvation Nell,* gave a realistic picture of slum existence; and his next play, *The Nigger,* dealt with a racial theme in the tragedy of a southern governor who discovers that he has Negro blood.

William Vaughn Moody, as far as his prose plays are concerned, is chiefly remembered for *The Great Divide,* which ushered in the "drama of revolt" and which many critics consider of permanent value. *The Faith Healer,* produced four years later, was a failure on the stage, though it still finds readers to whom anything written by Moody has importance.

In 1909, a group headed by Winthrop Ames built the New Theater at Sixtieth Street and Central Park West. Structurally, the New Theater was considered a progressive step in theater architecture. But it seated 2,500 people, its acoustics were bad, and Ames soon found it unsuited to his purposes. In accord with his altered conception of the drama as requiring an intimate relationship between audience and the stage, in 1913 he built his Little Theater, seating only 299, on Forty-Fourth Street. Ames brought to the New York theater an elegance and a refinement that were soon to be adopted by a number of other producers. He represented a reaction against the growing power of the chain-producers, exemplified so strongly for the next two decades by the Shuberts, and set an example for the many "independents" who despite economic handicaps have long maintained a measure of idealism and held to a relatively high standard in their productions. Arthur Hopkins, Jed Harris, Guthrie McClintic and others owe much to Ames.

As far as the commercial theater is concerned, one of the peculiar features of its post-war history is its continued concentration in what is generally known as the theater district. Forced by high rentals, huge production costs and the fickle taste of the public to be highly competitive in every branch of his trade, the New York producer regards as more than dangerous any attempt to show his wares very far east or west of Broadway below Forty-Second Street and above Fifty-Second. An occasional attempt has been made to break away from this area; but the spell of the "Great White Way" continues to hold, and both audience and producer are soon found back in the district.

The Broadway theaters have to some extent been in forced competition with the Hollywood producers from the early days of the silent screen; but since the advent of "talkies" and color films this situation has grown acute. Producers are often subsidized by Hollywood and plays are written and produced with the picture rights in mind, the New York production being regarded as a sort of preview test before an audience and a means of securing preliminary publicity for the picture version. The playwright who is eager to reach a large audience is forced to yield to this procedure, since even the most successful play on Broadway is seen by only a small portion of the American public and Hollywood controls the only medium that reaches the masses.

That the legitimate theater has been able to survive at all under these conditions, or to save itself from deteriorating beyond any semblance of dramatic respectability, has been due largely to the work of a number of special groups—principally the Provincetown Players, the Neighborhood Playhouse, the New Playwrights, the Theater of Action, the Theater Union, the Theater Guild, the Group Theater and the Mercury Theater. In their various theories and methods, these groups have done more to invigorate the theater, both legitimate and otherwise, than any other force. They gathered audiences for new playwrights and artists that Broadway producers were often quick to take advantage of, and their ideas are reflected in Hollywood pictures; for Hollywood, with all its technical efficiency and splendor, still relies largely on the legitimate theater for ideas.

The earliest and perhaps the most important of these groups was the Provincetown Players. In 1915, a few summer residents at Provincetown, Massachusetts, organized for the purpose of presenting original plays written by members of the group. In 1916, they made their first New York appearance in MacDougal Street, in what soon became known as the Provincetown Playhouse. Although the leadership and personnel of the organization underwent many changes during its career, it clung consistently to one important principle—that the playwright's work should not be a mere vehicle for the actor, the designer and the director, but rather that the work of these theater craftsmen should serve the dramatist. Leadership and inspiration for the early Provincetown group came largely from George Cram Cook, although John Reed was very active and had much to do with its success. Later a triumvirate composed of Eugene O'Neill, Kenneth MacGowan and Robert Edmond Jones assumed control; while in its final period on MacDougal Street it was under the direction of Henry Alsberg, M. Eleanor Fitzgerald and James Light.

The Provincetown Players presented play after play by Eugene O'Neill before he was taken up by commercial managers and became a popular playwright; and it gave a first hearing on the stage to many other writers. Sherwood Anderson, Djuna Barnes, Louise Bryant, E. E. Cummings, Floyd Dell, Theodore Dreiser, Max Eastman, Edna Ferber, Virgil Geddes,

Susan Glaspell, Paul Green, Michael Gold, Alfred Kreymborg, Edna St. Vincent Millay, David Pinski, John Reed, Michael Swift, Edmund Wilson, and Stark Young are some of the authors who at one time or another figured in its program. Such sensitive directors as Jasper Deeter and James Light were developed here, while more than a score of actors and actresses famous today had their start at the Provincetown. A notable accomplishment of this group was its work in bringing the Negro actor to the legitimate stage. Paul Robeson, Charles Gilpin, Frank Wilson, Jules Bledsoe, and Rose McClendon were made known to the public largely by way of MacDougal Street. No more brilliant array of literary and theatrical talent has enriched the American stage than that assembled by the Provincetown Players.

The Neighborhood Playhouse, organized in 1915, was the pioneer of the Little Theater movement in and around New York City. Originally this group had been an expression of East Side settlement activity, intended to provide slum-dwellers with good drama and to give people in the neighborhood who had talent a chance to act in it. Later, under the management of Irene and Alice Lewisohn, the small house on Grand Street became a significant drama center that attracted discriminating theatergoers from all parts of the city and assumed a degree of national importance. The project was abandoned in 1927, by which time it had made nearly a hundred productions, many of them New York premières. It first produced *The Dybbuk,* and a number of dramatic curiosities such as James Joyce's *Exiles.* Its *Grand Street Follies* became such a success in 1922 that the versions of this and later seasons were reproduced in an uptown playhouse.

An outgrowth of the Washington Square Players, founded in 1915 and organized in 1919 on a season subscription basis, the Theater Guild under Philip Moeller, Theresa Helburn, Helen Westley, Lawrence Langner, Lee Simonson and others did much in its early period to encourage higher standards of playwriting and production and the treatment of controversial themes. Its first production, *Bonds of Interest,* failed in a financial sense; but its second offering, *John Ferguson,* was a great success. By its fourth season, the Guild had 12,000 subscribers, and was planning for its own million-dollar theater on Fifty-Second Street. The latter opened in 1925 with an elaborate presentation of Shaw's *Caesar and Cleopatra.*

Operating at times as many as three theaters at once, the Guild has been in the nearly twenty years of its existence the most prolific and consistent producing stage organization in New York—perhaps in the world. Its repertory has ranged through a wide variety of classics, modern plays and revivals. It has produced most of the later plays of Eugene O'Neill and a considerable number of European adaptations. Its productions of Elmer Rice's *The Adding Machine* in 1923 and John Howard Lawson's *Processional* in 1925 were important events, while *From Morn to Midnight, Liliom* and *R.U.R.* had a stimulating effect upon the American theater.

Although a few foreign language groups and occasionally an independent producer brought the social dramas of Ibsen, Galsworthy, Gorki, Hauptmann and others to New York, and pageants had been staged to further the interests of labor, notably at the old Madison Square Garden under the direction of John Reed, it was not until 1926 that New York had its first organization to concentrate on labor drama for a labor audience. This was the Workers' Drama League, which is mentioned farther on in this article. In 1927, a few writers, most of them previously associated with this league, organized the New Playwrights. The enterprise was not self-sustaining (the late Otto Kahn financed it), but it paved the way for numerous successors. Its productions of plays by Paul Sifton, Upton Sinclair, Michael Gold, John Howard Lawson, Em Jo Basshe, and John Dos Passos provoked controversy and helped to clarify issues to be debated later on a wider front.

In 1926, Eva LeGallienne founded her Civic Repertory Theater on Fourteenth Street. Devoted principally to modern classic dramas, Miss LeGallienne's company had a considerable following. But although the admission rates were low in comparison with other New York houses, it was not a self-sustaining venture; and when its subsidy gave out in 1932 the enterprise was discontinued.

Other important influences on the New York theater of the 1920's were the visits of the Irish Players from the Abbey Theater, Dublin, and of the Moscow Art Theater company. The Irish Players came first before the World War, bringing plays by Synge and others that set a new standard for serious playwrights. Later, their presentation of plays by Sean O'Casey and other Irish dramatists, left an indelible impression. In 1923, Morris Gest brought to New York the Moscow Art Theater, with its great actors taught by Stanislavsky and its repertory of plays by Chekhov, Andreyev, Tolstoi, and other Russian writers. The Stanislavsky method of acting has been adopted, in its most complete form, by the present Group Theater. The Habima Players, a Hebrew group from Russia, played for a time in New York in the late 1920's to a considerable following.

It was not until the economic misery of the depression began to penetrate more and more deeply that increasing numbers of people, rejecting the commercial theater that breathed no hint of this, turned to the social drama and gave it a variety of forms. The sponsors of this development believe that drama should reflect the lives and problems of the masses. Workers, labor organizers, the people of average or sub-average economic means, are the heroes and heroines of their new plays. The theater, they say, must be no longer preoccupied with drawing-room and boudoir crises, but with current issues in political and economic affairs.

In 1929, the Workers' Laboratory Theater found an audience for a new type of stage production that needed no more than a hall or a street corner for its production. Using a technique that could easily adapt the vital news of the day to stage production, this group, later known as the Theater of Action, adopted methods later expanded and employed with considerable success by The Living Newspaper unit of the Federal Theater Project. *Unemployed, Scottsboro* and *Newsboy* were typical titles and themes among its productions.

Peace on Earth, an anti-war play, inaugurated the activities of the Theater Union in 1933. It was received by the labor press and audience with enthusiasm but by the Broadway critics with anguish. This play was followed by *Stevedore,* an analysis of race prejudice and oppression that brought down both the left and the right sides of the house. Plays by Paul Peters, George Sklar, Friedrich Wolf, Albert Maltz, Albert Bein and John Howard Lawson figured in the Theater Union program. When the group suspended its collective activities in 1937, it announced that the purpose for which it had been formed was being adequately served by other organizations and individuals.

Although critics were reluctant to see the value of the social-minded theater, the militant and vital theater folk were not without their propagandists. In April 1931, the Workers' Laboratory Theater issued two hundred mimeographed copies of its bulletin, *Workers' Theater.* In September 1933, this bulletin was renamed *New Theater Magazine,* and under the audacious editorship of Herbert Kline it soon became the most important publication of its kind in America. It fought for truth in the theater, and introduced in its pages such sensational hits as *Waiting for Lefty, Bury the Dead* and *Hymn to the Rising Sun.*

Broadway, however, was slow to accept the strongly motivated social-minded play. *Grand Hotel,* employing all the old tricks of melodrama, was among the hits in a season when the theater was beginning to be darkened by a crisis the existence of which it did not openly admit. Paul and Claire Sifton's *1931*, a tragic transcript of unemployment, produced by the Group Theater, drew so little of the Broadway trade that it closed within a week and a half.

It was the Group Theater, originally a subsidiary of the Theater Guild, that reacted most sensitively to the drama with a strictly social or labor theme and (despite the failure of *1931*) proved the box-office value of such drama. Its announced policy was to present plays based upon contemporary social issues. It has shown some confusion in following this aim; and had it not been for the short but vivid career of the Theater Union, it might not have reached its present importance. The organization produced Sidney Kingsley's Pulitzer Prize play *Men in White*, Paul Green's *House of Connelly* and *Johnnie Johnson*, and several plays by Clifford Odets.

It would be wrong to assume, however, that until the voice of labor was heard within the independent theater movement there had been no plays or playwrights with keen social awareness. Prior to the World War, such plays as Augustus Thomas' *The Copperhead*, Eugene Walter's *The Easiest Way*, Edward Sheldon's *The Nigger* and William Vaughn Moody's *The Great Divide* were concerned with themes certainly no further removed from the reality of their times than, for instance, such major works of Eugene O'Neill as *All God's Chillun Got Wings*, *The Emperor Jones*, and *Mourning Becomes Electra*. A comparison of the works of these dramatists brings to light more similarities than differences. All were more concerned with the stage possibilities of their material than with the underlying import of their themes. All wrote more or less around and on the surface of important questions; none was a dramatic genius whose ideas and methods have had much to do with revolutionizing either ways of thinking or the stage, and all wrote in a similar romantic and melodramatic vein.

Furthermore, these men were not the first dramatists to deal with controversial social themes. Before and after the Civil War, many plays on vital and even revolutionary issues of the day were produced on the New York stage. On December 16, 1859, just fourteen days after the execution of John Brown at Harper's Ferry, a dramatization of the event was produced at the Bowery Theater, under the title of *The Insurrection, or Kansas and Harper's Ferry*. As a forerunner of The Living Newspaper type of theater, so popular at the moment, this is not without significance. Technical innovations have been added aplenty since then, but the idea of dramatizing current issues close on their happening is not new.

Uncle Tom's Cabin was also an early social play, and the *New York Herald* in 1852 advised "all concerned to drop the play at once and forever. The thing is in bad taste—is not according to good faith to the constitution . . . and is calculated, if persisted in, to become a firebrand of the most dangerous character to the peace of the whole country."

Nor would it be correct to assume that outside the independent theater movement the New York stage was altogether lacking in vitality. Maxwell Anderson dramatized current issues in *What Price Glory* (written in collaboration with Laurence Stallings), *Gods of the Lightning* (an exposition of the Sacco-Vanzetti trial and its implications, written in collaboration with Harold Hickerson), and a few of his other plays. Elmer Rice has been consistently sensitive to major conflicts and modern problems. Plays like Martin Flavin's *The Criminal Code,* John Wexley's *The Last Mile* and *They Shall Not Die,* Sidney Howard's *Yellow Jack,* and Sidney Kingsley's *Dead End* show to what extent the theater in general has become socially conscious. Ever since the production of *Beyond the Horizon* in 1920 and *The Hairy Ape* in 1922, the many plays of Eugene O'Neill have had their considerable influence on both the so-called sophisticated and the socially responsible playwrights, and have attracted international attention, climaxed in 1936 by the award to their author of the Nobel Prize for literature.

The commercial theater, while for the most part lagging considerably behind the experiments of others, has nevertheless created several types of theatrical entertainment very much worthwhile in their own right. Of these, perhaps the outstanding example is the light, satiric, fantastic revue, found at its best in the various Kaufman-Connelly-Ryskind-Gershwin-Hart combinations. *Beggar on Horseback* in 1924, by George S. Kaufman and Marc Connelly, was one of the earliest of these theatrical cocktails to win wide popularity. They appeared regularly thereafter, welcomed by a diversion-seeking public that had wearied of Ziegfeld's and Earl Carroll's and George White's "glorified girl" in a Taj Mahal setting—itself an innovation in its day. The song and dance type of musical play is still popular. Plays or musical comedies of political satire continue a tradition that began in the days of Weber and Fields and of Harrigan and Hart, and still employ many of the methods characteristic of those comedians.

A second type of strictly American theater is exemplified in *Spread Eagle* and *What Price Glory.* The latter play, by Laurence Stallings and Maxwell Anderson, was the first popular drama in our time to "debunk" war sentiment, and is still a reference point in the drama. It marked with considerable emphasis the theater's liberation from some of the more persistent Victorian taboos. After *What Price Glory* there were plenty of plays whose language and conventions still reeked of refinement, but the unwritten and immutable law that they had to do this was now repealed. *Broadway* by Philip Dunning and George Abbott, and *Chicago* by Maurine Watkins, both produced in the 1926–27 season, continued this vein of hard-boiled, high-speed realism. They were followed by George Manker Watters' and Arthur Hopkins' *Burlesque,* and then by Ben Hecht's and Charles MacArthur's smash-hit *The Front Page,* which like their predecessors effectively caught the gaudy colors and staccato rhythms of the times. This is true also of the plays written and produced in collaboration by George Abbott and George Kaufman. These easily recognizable types— swift paced, dexterous and sparkling—were the commercial theater's unique contribution to Hollywood and to world drama.

Craig's Wife, by George Kelly, the 1926 Pulitzer Prize winner, and Sidney Howard's *The Silver Cord* of the following year, both of them Guild productions, opened a new vein in the perennial domestic-problem play. Many of the plays of Eugene O'Neill were concerned with domestic tragedies and various underlying falsities in our social life. This vein was continued with distinction more recently by Lillian Hellman in her sensational *The Children's Hour.* Philip Barry's plays show excellence of dialogue, not always used to important advantage. As for the contribution —perhaps it should be called the touch—of Noel Coward in recent years, among such diverse proclivities as his it is difficult to say where the facile leaves off and real talent begins. George Jean Nathan labels him a "stagewright"—an unusual but by no means rare phenomenon in the theater— and diagnoses his plays as containing situations but not characters. *Private Lives* and the widely known *Design for Living,* among the many Coward plays, are modernizations of the Victorian drawing-room drama. They belong, in a sense, to impolite comedy, just as the many plays of Rachel Crothers belong strictly to polite comedy.

New York has had a foreign language stage for a considerable period. A pioneer in this field was the German Theater, on Irving Place, which had considerable influence and a devoted following in the 1890's. Here the plays of Lessing, Sudermann, Hauptmann and others were given in the original, with prominent German actors and actresses in the leading parts. Another notable influence on American stage setting and acting, though for a much briefer period, was Copeau's Théâtre du Vieux Columbier. Maurice Schwartz's Yiddish Art Theater was long an important dramatic center in New York's East Side, with which Stella and Luther Adler, Paul Muni and other prominent actors and actresses have been associated. This organization now makes its productions in the uptown theater district. The Artef, a Jewish group organized on a cooperative basis in 1935 by Jacob Mastel, has won a distinctive place among the city's art theaters; and many of its productions, directed by Benno Schneider, have been notable. Since the early 1920's the musical comedy star Molly Picon has been one of the most popular individual figures in the Jewish theater of New York.

No development of recent years in the theatrical world has more significant implications than the Federal Theater, a part of the national relief program inaugurated in 1935 under the Works Progress Administration. Productions of new plays and revivals of old ones, minstrels, marionette and children's theaters, circuses, light opera, vaudeville, a training school and studio theater for drama teachers installed in the old Provincetown Playhouse, even a showboat anchored off a Hoboken pier opposite Manhattan's Twenty-Third Street—all of these sprang into being in the most sudden rejuvenation the New York theater has ever known.

Employing at its peak more than 5,000 persons, mostly actors, theater technicians, writers, etc., the Federal Theater in New York in 1936-37 had more than fifteen distinct units operating more than a dozen theaters. Its principal units near the theater district, the Experimental Theater, the Popular Price Theater, The Living Newspaper, and "891," as well as the Negro Theater in Harlem, were tremendously successful. These units, under the supervision of Hallie Flanagan, Philip Barber, Virgil Geddes, Edward Goodman, Walter Hart, John Houseman and Morris Watson, produced play after play that ran to packed houses for weeks in the very midst of the depression. Plays on contemporary themes such as *Chalk Dust, Battle Hymn, Class of '29, Native Ground, Professor Mamlock* and *Hymn to the Rising Sun,* and revivals of classics such as *Dr. Faustus* and *Macbeth* were among its more notable offerings.

Perhaps the most successful of the WPA producing units, however, was The Living Newspaper. Using a technique combining journalism and the theater by means of actors, a voice amplifier, charts and signs, "stills" and moving pictures, it presented several significant productions. *Triple-A Plowed Under* dramatized effectively the plight of the farmer; *Power* tackled the subject of public versus private ownership of the utilities as exemplified by hydro-electricity and the TVA; while *One Third of a Nation* successfully dramatized the housing problem.

The Federal Theater is the first subsidized theater on a large scale ever attempted in America. Offering almost every form of stage entertainment and playing to millions of people, it has clarified a number of issues. It has proved, first, that there is a large public anxious to see living actors on the stage in plays dealing with living issues, providing the prices are low; second, that to exist on an impressive scale the theater needs Federal subsidy, unburdened by censorship; and third, that at no time in the past has the theater absorbed more than a very small part of the talent at its disposal.

With Broadway producers and the Federal Theater presenting socially minded plays, the 1937–38 season offered only one militantly left production by an independent theatrical organization—*The Cradle Will Rock*, originally rehearsed as a Federal Theater production but presented by the Mercury Theater, whose most important members were drawn from the Federal Theater group. *Pins and Needles*, an outstanding musical revue of the season, was sponsored by the International Ladies Garment Workers Union. The production of this revue by a recognized trade union has important implications. It has been evident for some time to those of experience in theatrical production that the "left theater," like any other today, cannot exist long as an independent organization. It also must be subsidized. Should the day come when a large and progressive labor organization can sponsor a theater for and about the people, then and only then will we have a people's theater.

In 1937, along with its presentation of *The Cradle Will Rock*, the Mercury Theater staged a production of *Julius Caesar* in modern clothes and with a contemporary emphasis on the theme of dictatorship. On a virtually bare stage, lighting effects swiftly and vividly painted the background. The play had all the force of a present-day "thriller," and became an instant hit. The same group has since presented Thomas Dekker's *The Shoemakers' Holiday* in a similar manner and with similar success.

Behind the scenes as it were, the men and women who make up the great rank and file of the theater have long been struggling to improve conditions of existence that were frequently deplorable. Among the earliest of their organizations was the White Rats Actors' Union, formed in 1900 "for the purpose of founding a brotherhood among all vaudevillians, perhaps with a view of eventually embracing all those who act or perform on the mimic stage." In 1916, when vaudeville was about at its zenith, the union had 25,000 members in good standing. Today the leading organization devoted to the cause of the actor in the legitimate theater is Actors' Equity Association, which is affiliated with unions embracing screen actors and radio performers. Equity's great triumph came in 1919 when, after the managers' association refused to deal with it, a strike was called that lasted for 30 days, spread to eight cities, closed 37 plays and prevented the opening of 16. The result was a decisive victory for the actors. Since then even the playwrights have organized (as a branch of the Authors League), and today nearly every type of theater worker belongs to a union.

The financial depression that began in 1929 brought the New York theater to its greatest crisis. It had already been heavily undermined by Hollywood, which had lured away many of its most talented actors, writers and directors. "Broadway" as traditionally known was in truth no longer on Broadway, for the motion picture firms had been steadily purchasing the existent theaters and erecting huge houses on "the Great White Way," until the legitimate stage found itself pushed around the corner east and west on the side streets. Even there, and overbuilt with theaters as the city was (more were erected between 1900 and 1929 than in the entire preceding century), huge rentals prevailed. What Lee Simonson has called "smash-hit economics" dictated, and still dictates, the dizzy rules of the theater game. Rents, salaries, production costs are all based upon the premise that the producer either has a tremendous success that will bring him millions or he has nothing at all, and as a result, credit expansion has reached giddier proportions in the theater business than it has in other spheres. The once prosperous "road business" has declined to insignificant proportions. Except in the case of a few unusually successful Broadway hits and some of the more important Theater Guild productions, companies are seldom sent out from New York. But by developing production groups in many other cities, the Federal Theater is going a long way toward the establishment of locally supported theaters for the presentation not merely of New York successes but of indigenous regional plays as well. From these large cities as production centers, the Federal Theater plans to send out its plays to communities in the neighborhood of each city; and thus to some extent the "road" will be revived.

Vacillating between the extremes of industry and art, the commercial theater represents a complicated problem, and its progress is necessarily slow. During the 1937–38 season, the idea of plays without scenery as adapted by the Mercury Theater was taken up by other producers. The scenic designers' union, seeing a threat to its craft, threatened to impose a $1,000 fine on all productions not using scenery. Strindberg was kicking useless canvas walls and shrubbery off the stage back in the 1890's, and the resources of light as expounded by Adolph Appia years ago have long been available. Broadway, however, discovers all this as a great innovation in the year 1937.

The New York theater is the sum of many influences that are often contradictory in motives and ideals. It will adopt a method or style used fifty years ago as readily as it will the newest innovation, providing either brings money to the box office. While probably the most active theater in the world, it is still on the whole an old-fashioned affair that lags in the rear of progressive theory and experiment. Its buildings are obsolete— uncomfortable to sit in and out of keeping with new esthetic standards; even the newer ones have had to imitate the horrible examples of theater architecture of the past because they must squeeze in between two other buildings in order to find a place in the district.

Realistic settings were a fetish with Belasco. It is recorded that on one occasion, to provide an accurate background for a scene in a theatrical rooming house, he bought the furnishings and decorations of a room in such a house and removed them, wallpaper and all, to the stage. A revolt against such hard-and-fast literalism set in; but the stage, particularly since the World War, is still too much preoccupied with the man who designs the sets and mounts the play.

The theater, commercial or otherwise, is of course an ephemeral affair if it does not produce a dramatic literature. The New York theater has occasionally done something toward this end, although writers and authors as distinguished from "stage carpenters" still have only a small part in it. The gulf between literature in print and on the stage has been lessened only slightly. The printed play is seldom reviewed in literary journals, and our established authors seldom think in terms of dramatic writing.

The New York theater belongs—when it does not belong to the real estate agent—to the showman, the entrepreneur, the director, the personality actor and actress, the promoter, the press agent, the dramatic critic and the high-priced box-office clientele. It rarely admits the independent thinker. In a negative way it may arouse and provoke through satire; it may even finance plays of popular protest; but aside from novel interpretations of Shakespeare and other classics, it cannot support dramatic literature. Nevertheless, it would be far less than it is without its Brady, Gordon, Harris, Hopkins, Miller, Pemberton, among the producers; its Barrymores, Lunts, Katharine Cornell, Helen Hayes, on the stage; and the many competent directors and craftsmen who have made it, in its way, famous.

Vaudeville, once immensely popular, has all but perished before the onslaught of radio and the sound films. In its pure form it was still to be seen in 1938—as an adjunct to a screen program—in only three New York theaters, one of them on Broadway. And remnants of it still survive as part of the stage presentations in such movie houses as the Roxy and Radio City Music Hall. But vaudeville's less·respectable sister, burlesque, is well patronized in New York. Although the word "burlesque" is officially taboo in advertising, the houses presenting this form of entertainment flourish in considerable number, both in and outside the regular theater district.

As far as the drama is concerned, theatergoing in New York City may be an uncertain adventure—we no longer have a "comedy theater," for example, where one can be somewhat sure beforehand what to expect; but a little investigation proves one thing to be true, that in the course of a few seasons, providing one has the price of admission, almost all types of theater may be found, in productions that are unmatched anywhere else.

Pleasures in Palaces

THE AMERICAN cinema has impressed its influence on a thousand communities from Bucharest to Surabaya, New York among them; but the influence of New York on the cinema constitutes a unique cultural relationship. Indirectly but unmistakably, the metropolis puts its stamp on American motion-picture art.

The keen-eared movie-goer may have observed that Popeye, gnarled knight of the clenched fist and the corncob pipe, speaks Tenth Avenue's indigenous tongue. Betty Boop, epitome of short-skirted innocence in the 1920's, scolds her little dog and sings her copyrighted ditties in exaggerated New Yorkese. It is not unlikely that her creation was suggested by the personality and appearance of a musical comedy and screen actress, Helen Kane, whose short-lived star rose in the Bronx.

New York's vital contribution to screen acting art lies not alone in the number and quality of actors it claims as natives. It has produced individuals whose screen personalities and acting style symbolize America and its people.

Just as William S. Hart was a national idol during the period of pre-war growth and the World War itself, so it is entirely logical that James Cagney should have become the embodiment of the Great American Male during the Babylonian years of the Coolidge era. Hart's vast popularity was based on the vitality with which the pioneer tradition persisted in the life of the American people. This tradition gave way in part, however, before the increasingly urban substance and coloration that American culture began to assume in the post-war period.

In the unsophisticated years when Bill Hart and his pony were idols of the screen, the ideal man was straightforward, fearless and pure. But in the sybaritic 1920's, this paragon of American manhood, imbued with the ideology of speedy success, turned tough, unscrupulous and glib. Because his acting embodies all these qualities and modifies them with a subtle warmth of attractive personality, Cagney and his tommy-gun became the

284

apotheosis (almost the caricature) of this spirit, replacing Hart and his six-shooter as symbols of America. Such observations are necessarily over-simplified, perhaps too exclusive; but they help to illuminate certain major changes of emphasis in the national psyche.

Again, as a cinematic reflection of its own admittedly insular life, New York has contributed such a typical personality as Lionel Stander. No one who has ever elbowed his way through the lower East Side will fail to recognize the raucous voice, the good-humored sneer, the compressed lips, the critical lift of the eyebrows, the noisy obtuse cynicism—even the callous deadliness he displayed in *A Star Is Born*—that mark Stander as New York's own.

Equally indigenous to New York's celebrated sidewalks is that night-club fish-out-of-water in the motion pictures, Jimmy Durante. He represents New York of the 1920's not merely as a living caricature of New York's Al Smith. His characterization of the unlettered but shrewd polit-ical adviser in *The Phantom President* was a pat, if accidental, commentary on New York politics; and his self-libelous label, "Schnozzola," could have blossomed only in New York's polyglot give-and-take. Moreover, his vio-lent self-assurance smacks of a cross between the slightly bewildered but intensely adaptable immigrant and the youth whose haywire eagerness to make good often develops into a burst of confusion-for-its-own-sake. At his liveliest, Durante combines the best features of a good terrier and a typhoon.

Conversely, another character actor, Allen Jenkins, symbolizes still an-other variety of New Yorker: the hardboiled and amiable *cluck,* an un-derprivileged, frustrated individual who mistakes his own boisterousness for good-fellowship, his obtuseness for deep thinking and his vulgarity for wit.

Nor is New York extravagant in claiming at least two of the Marx Brothers. Harpo, by virtue of his pantomime and his music, is universal; but Groucho, with his be-moustached aplomb, his cocked eye and his omi-nous walk, is a travesty on every phase of metropolitan ambition and pre-tense. Chico represents the glib ingenuousness masking a predatory shrewd-ness that is essential for survival in most of New York's foreign quarters. The character he has created of the foot-loose and tongue-loose vagabond may be obsolete in its externals, but it has strong roots in the life of New York's ghettos.

Edgar Dale, in *The Content of Motion Pictures,* a study published by the Payne Fund, reports that out of 115 pictures on which his researches were based, 37 had their settings in New York, while 13 others were set in other large cities. Undoubtedly the New York skyline and Times Square have become two of the most common bits of scenery on the world's screens. It is not the whim of urbanized and sophisticated writers that makes the metropolis so common a locale for screen dramas. It's simply that the most crowded cage in the zoo attracts the greatest number of specta-tors. If the essence of all drama lies in a conflict of forces, then New York must necessarily continue to be one of the screen's principal sources of material.

Broadway's close-packed ranks of picture palaces reveal at a glance, for better or worse, the city's chief agency of entertainment and culture. The self-same glance also points out the New Yorker's easiest avenue of escape from the strident realities and the gruelling tempo of metropolitan en-deavor. Perhaps New Yorkers have greater need for short and frequent re-laxation. Often the dwellers in other American cities may escape to a small garden plot, to the open road, to playing fields, even to mere restful idle-ness among quiet houses and streets whose tree-lined aspect offers relief from the grimness of factories and the austerity of office buildings. The New Yorker lacks such workaday variety. The end of his day's work, or his day's search for work, brings no relief. On the contrary, it intensifies his feeling of oppressive concern.

The sense of physical confinement that lurks in a remote corner of his consciousness during the day becomes overwhelming as he goes down into the crowded subway. Even his cramped living quarters offer no room for the unbending of his weary spirit. The apartment houses in which he lives are as closely packed as the office buildings where he works. The tenements look as grim as the factories. His mild but recurrent claustrophobia is fully roused by the time he has finished his evening meal; and the habit of a narrow but intense physical activity urges him like a drug. Where to go? There is a motion picture house in every second block. The answer is, in-evitably, the movies.

Yet among New Yorkers there has grown up a very strong demand for the creation of a motion picture art that has greater consonance with reality. Those few motion pictures that reach beyond the fixed Hollywood pattern to deal seriously with social realities are always certain of an audience in the metropolis. Pictures like *Fury*, *The Black Legion*, and *They Won't Forget* are seldom failures in New York.

The movie-goer who is not isolated from his neighbors by the darkness of a theater and the physical hypnotism of the screen may discover that most audiences seldom betray a great variety or intensity of reactions. New York audiences, however, are critical. The vast number of movie houses permits them to express their criticism of any single picture in the manner most profoundly understood by producers—non-attendance.

The comparatively discriminating tastes of New York fans have led to a marginal revolt against Hollywood on the adjacent fronts of exhibition and production. At about the time the Paramount Building first reared its precariously balanced globe against the midtown sky, the little cinema movement was sprouting roots among a new type of movie-goer. German importations such as *The Cabinet of Dr. Caligari, Variety, The Last Laugh,* and Russian epics on the order of *The End of St. Petersburg, Potemkin* and *Ten Days That Shook the World,* had suddenly revealed to aloof esthetes that the motion picture could be more than a form of slow and painless intellectual suicide. Their appetites whetted by foreign achievements, these esthetes rediscovered Charlie Chaplin, canonized Krazy Kat and well-nigh deified Mickey Mouse. New York entrepreneurs, adept in exploiting even the most obscure and exotic desires of the paying customers, began to import foreign pictures and to revive meritorious domestic productions. The logical next step was the establishment of houses that specialized in the showing of esoteric films. In the first years of sound, when the picture shortage was acute, the exhibition of foreign pictures attracted another new audience from the foreign-born communities.

In the field of production, the revolt against Hollywood followed similar lines. Those who had come to regard the cinema with intense seriousness sought to drive home their strictures by example. Isolated experimenters tried to develop a new camera technique that would liberate the film from the Hollywood idiom. Others made films that were clearly under the influence of the English documentalists, who apply their creative imagery to such ordinary undramatic topics as the fishing industry, the radio and the postal service. Ralph Steiner made films without actors—the hypnotically rhythmic *Surf and Seaweed* and *H_2O.* Robert Florey made *The Death of a Hollywood Extra* and *The Loves of Mr. Zero;* James S. Watson and Melville Weber produced *Lot in Sodom;* and news of even more daring ventures began to filter across the ocean from France and Spain and Germany. Recently, the traditions of this energetic if somewhat directionless movement have been absorbed and revised in a trend toward the production of documentary films under Government auspices, resulting thus far in two distinguished efforts, *The Plow That Broke the Plains* and *The River,* both made by Pare Lorentz.

No matter where these new films were made, they had their greatest repercussions in New York. They spurred the intellectuals to louder cries against Hollywood and stronger efforts to make their own films. Unofficially, Hollywood producers welcomed although they did not support this movement, because it diverted pressure formerly exerted on them for the production of unprofitable films. Labor groups turned to movie-making in a valiant effort to counteract what they considered anti-labor propaganda incorporated in many Hollywood films. They even avowed the intention of taking Hollywood's audiences away from Hollywood. The Workers Film and Photo League, probably the most energetic and clear-headed of these insurgent groups, produced a series of newsreels, the documentary film of a hunger march on Washington, and the semi-documentary *Taxi.* Nykino Films made *Pie in the Sky,* an experimental satire of high cinematic quality and engaging ribaldry. Significant in this connection was the cooperation of actors from the Broadway legitimate stage. The rapid development of amateur film equipment, which made it easier and cheaper to get high-caliber results, gave further stimulus to the movement away from Hollywood.

New York's importance as a center of advanced ideas, coupled with its dominant position as an exhibition center, has made it the logical mecca of the serious film student. What cinematic work cannot be seen in New York? There are new releases, old pictures, foreign pictures. Academic research in the film art is further facilitated by the existence of the Theatre Collection of the New York Public Library and the Film Library of the Museum of Modern Art. The latter, a privately endowed project, has attained international importance, in the few years since its foundation, as an institution that serves with equal facility the demands of the industry and the investigations of the film esthetician.

The art of the cinema has grown apace since the first public exhibition of the Edison-Armat Vitascope in 1896, drawing without discrimination from all the intellectual treasures of the ages on which it could lay a profitable if heavy hand. But New York, fountainhead of the nation's contemporary culture, fostered the motion picture palace that has made a place for itself in every metropolitan community.

Its origins were probably innocent of any motive save profit. In 1912, when Adolph Zukor imported the four-reel picture *Queen Elizabeth,* movie houses were for the most part unpretentious. His importation demonstrated the success of pictures longer than the customary two reels. As a more or less direct result, George Kleine, one of the leaders of the Motion Picture

Patents Company, brought over the eight-reel spectacle, *Quo Vadis*. Because the film's length put it beyond the scope of the nickelodeon, Kleine resorted to the large legitimate theaters and succeeded, intentionally or accidentally, in giving an impressive setting to his spectacular film. It opened at the Astor Theatre on April 21, 1913, and ran for 22 weeks at a one-dollar top.

When Mitchell Mark opened his Strand Theatre in 1914 and the Triangle Film Corporation followed suit with the Knickerbocker Theatre, there was more than immediate profit at stake. These houses represented a conscious effort on the part of the motion picture industry to cloak an accomplished fact in respectability. The motion picture had become a purveyor of culture and amusement to the intellectually hungry immigrants of the lower East Side during the first teeming decade of the century.

The nickelodeons, when silent movies had barely developed the elementary device of written subtitles, were offering primitive two-reel versions of *Romeo and Juliet* to the accompaniment of passionate but unpolished rendition of Shakespeare's lines by an off-screen reader. From the wells of contemporary reminiscence there often bubble up stories by born-and-bred New Yorkers who tell how "we used to take our lunch to the nickelodeon and stay all day."

Long before Mitchell Mark achieved the splendor of the Strand, earnest discussion raged in trade papers and general publications about the nickelodeon as a substitute for the saloon; about the nickelodeon as the poor man's theater; and about the motion picture as an agency of great potential if not actual social value.

But Mark's pretentious theater was more than the first modern "cathedral of the motion picture." It was the star to which were later hitched such stratospheric wagons as those of the late Roxy (Samuel L. Rothapfel), and Hugo Riesenfeld. The quoted phrase is Roxy's—in concept, if not literally. Until Mark's and Roxy's arrival in the field of exhibition, the respectability of the motion picture had been in doubt. Mark's money and Roxy's resourcefulness allayed that doubt forever. Music, originally a superficial refinement, became essential to cinema expression. The physical setting of film exhibition became important. Mark's coup in the establishment of the Strand on Broadway set the inexorable laws of competition in motion.

The old Rialto and the Rivoli rose on Broadway in quick succession. In 1919 the Capitol opened as the largest theater in the world and the era of the super-movie house became an accepted fact. The Paramount, the

Roxy and Radio City Music Hall followed at comparatively short inter-vals. Perhaps the evidence of a distinct pattern in the motion picture cathe-dral's development is due to the fact that all of those named, save the Paramount, felt the guiding hand of the same man—Roxy.

Unfortunately the magnitude of these theaters outstripped the caliber of the films they sheltered. Perhaps also because vaudeville still made strong competitive claims as a form of popular entertainment, the cathedrals con-tinued to present stage shows; and the term "presentation house" became common in the industry's parlance during the Harding-Coolidge-Hoover era.

These presentations grew increasingly lavish and spectacular, but their quality remained negligible. They were, for the most part, competently pro-duced, but they lacked the intimacy and informality of vaudeville; and they failed to make good their claim as spectacle, partly because the images on the movie screen dwarfed the live actors and dancers on the stage.

The super-theater was, on its economic side, a reflection of the struggle for monopoly control of the motion picture industry. In the years following the war, the major film companies were preoccupied with consolidating their positions as producers and distributors. The competition for markets, always keen, assumed a new and two-fold aspect in the 1920's. Each major producer turned his energies to the acquisition of a nation-wide theater chain large enough to insure the minimum of showings consistent with a profitable return on every picture he produced. At the same time, the super-theater in New York became a potent force in attracting bookings from independent theater owners. The phrases "three smash weeks at the Roxy" and "a box-office record-breaker at the Paramount" are still frequent in ad-vertising intended for exhibitors. The glamor of a gala first night made good publicity for general consumption. In cities like Chicago, Cleveland, Detroit, Philadelphia, the huge presentation houses yielded a profit; in New York, the super-theater was often a financial liability maintained only to heighten the prestige of a producing company and its interlocking thea-ter chain.

If the super-movie house began life as an awesome and forbidding ca-thedral, it now exists as a castle in whose sheltering shadow the humble serf and artisan may work and play. "Early-bird matinees" and "midnight shows" have made it a haven for the footsore and discouraged job-hunter, the venturesome housewife, the impromptu family party and the city-bound victim of summer's heat or winter's cold. The interior of the modern super-cinema is far more than an auditorium and a screen. The galaxy of paintings on the walls, the elaborate lounges where one may sit for hours in upholstered comfort, are standard equipment. The immaculate and imposing appointments of the washrooms are almost a consolation for the occasional disappointments of the screen. No cathedral is without an infirmary for emergencies; one even boasts a maternity ward. Of all the super-houses, the Radio City Music Hall has been least compromised by the tastes and practices of misguided architects and decorators. Its architecture is recognizably modern, and its decorations bear the effective stamp of muralists and sculptors whose esthetic sins, if any, are easier to forgive than those of their predecessors.

The sound film and the era of economic depression have wrought changes in the cathedrals. The stage show persists in the larger ones, but it has lost the hectic overtones attendant on its determination to be regarded as super-spectacle. The stabilization of the industry and the improved quality of films have contributed a quieter atmosphere and tone.

The heyday of the presentation palace for silent pictures was concurrent with the rise of the little cinema movement. Discriminating intellectuals and faddists alike shrank from the ballyhoo, the impersonal and often ill-considered splendor, of the big houses, as well as from the mediocrity of the films. The little cinema houses, as they sprang up in response to the demand for unusual films, sought to create an atmosphere of intimacy and informality. The architecture and decoration were frankly modern, in contrast to the corrupted classicism of the big houses. Unable to offer mother-of-pearl washroom fittings, the little cinemas held out ping-pong tables, demi-tasses and cigarettes in the lounge. One such house with a Park Avenue clientele installed a checkroom for pets. The intimacy and informality in these theaters are more than artificial atmosphere; they help to induce moods of lively and intelligent reaction to the program.

The newsreel theaters, particularly the Trans Lux houses, have contributed notably to the architecture and decoration of small theaters. They have also given a new and healthy direction to movie-going habits. The wide variety encompassed by their programs in the course of 60 minutes—news, comedy, travel and educational films—is making for a greater catholicity in audience tastes. Again, the newsreel theater offers the usually articulate New Yorker a public forum for the expression of his political and social faith, whatever it may be, in a period when aloofness from politics has become a rarity. During the Roosevelt-Landon campaign in 1936 the newsreel houses resounded perpetually with cheers and hisses, applause and boos, as the opposing candidates appeared on the screen. Any student of politics and government might have gauged New York's reaction to President Roosevelt's proposal for enlarging the Supreme Court by the applause and dissent of newsreel audiences, as protagonists or opponents of the plan spoke from the screen.

Booing has become a prevalent form of expression for movie audiences, carried over perhaps from the tradition of the baseball park; and politically minded film-goers seem to consider two current European dictators especially as fair game. Following the outbreak of the Spanish civil war in 1936, many a theater resounded with cries of "No Pasaran," slogan of the Spanish Loyalists and their sympathizers. Such expressions have been emphatic and widely distributed.

In one instance, probably unique in movie history, audience disapproval was aimed, not at the content of the newsreel, but at the producer. Hearst-Metrotone News was compelled to withdraw its name from the screen because of wide public displeasure at the policies espoused by publisher William Randolph Hearst. An account of the matter in the issue of *Time* magazine for November 23, 1936, contains the following: "Unfortunately, while Metrotone was scrupulously avoiding every trace of partisanship, its famed producer's newssheets were doing nothing of the sort. By last summer cinemaddicts who objected to Hearst's newspaper policies had taken to booing Hearst Metrotone News whenever it appeared on the screen, picketing theaters that showed it. First move of theater managers was to cut the titles with the Hearst name on them and insert substitute titles and sub-titles. Last week, after his return from Europe, William Randolph Hearst made the change official."

The wedding-cake architecture of many American office buildings, the elaborate appointments of business offices, the glimmer of a young girl's platinum blonde hair, the familiar utterance of words derived from unfamiliar lexicons—these are the externals of the influence the cinema wields on New York and Kamm's Corners alike.

The more basic forms and content of this influence, however, have been subjects of perennial discussion by sociologists, clergymen, clubwomen and art critics. None has hesitated to cast a stone in the direction of the screen (though perhaps only the little cinema has been immediately constructive). The sociologists and clergymen have approached unanimity in their charge that the cinema is dangerous as a social force; they sometimes fail to take note of the social forces that shape the cinema and are reflected in it.

Art critics have protested (though not so loudly in recent years) that the cinema is *per se* not an art at all, because it employs industrial methods, machinery and organization; they ignore the fact that artists in all ages have sought to make their art greater by applying to it all the resources of science. No one reproached Leonardo da Vinci for his work as a scientist—or for discovering, incidentally, the principle of modern photography. And no one effectively discounted the French impressionist painters for their preoccupation with Cherreul's spectrum analysis and the physics of light.

For the rest, the social ends and esthetic resolutions that this most social of the arts may attain in the future are limited only to the progressively higher levels of social organization and cultural development achieved by American civilization itself.

World of Wireless

IN THE world's intricate spiderweb of radio communication, New York forms a central node. The city's radiotelegraphic facilities, day and night, keep up a running conversation of war, business and politics with the rest of the world in the dot-and-dash language of telegraphy. The city is also the central link of two international chains in the transmission by radio of the human voice. International short wave programs, originating abroad, are retransmitted from New York to other radio stations in the country via the broadcasting chains and telephone wire systems, and the city is the radiotelephone "bottle-neck" where international messages are handled. Yet these are by now commonplace aspects of the routine workings of civilization's underlying machinery of communication.

It is in broadcasting, where radio most vividly touches the lives of the people—where it enters their homes with words and music to become part of the daily routine of living—that New York plays one of its most significant and popularly appreciated roles.

Much of radio's latter-day development may be credited to America, and in that development New York has played an important part. Knowledge of the fundamental phenomena upon which radio is based dates back nearly 26 centuries, when the Greek experimenter, Thales of Miletus, caught a glimpse of electrical attraction induced by friction. More than 22 centuries passed before this phenomenon was described by the English scientist, William Gilbert, in his work *De Magnete,* where the word "electric" appears for the first time. Gilbert heads the long list of distinguished experimenters who formulated the basic laws of electricity, a list that includes Volta, Coulomb, Gauss, Ampere, Ohm, Cavendish, Faraday and a host of others. But the birth of radio proper did not take place until the 1870's, when the great Scottish mathematician, James Clerk Maxwell, developed the wave theory of electromagnetism. He calculated that electromagnetic waves travelled at the speed of light, and showed that the length of these waves depended on the electrical "length" of the circuit producing them, just as the pitch of a harp's note depends on the length of the string that produces it. Thus radio was born—on paper. In 1888, a German professor, Heinrich Rudolph Hertz, succeeded in producing the radio waves Maxwell had predicted by discharging sparks of "static" electricity across the gap between a pair of small metal balls, and was able to send his "Hertzian" radio waves over a distance of several hundred feet. In the 1890's, Guglielmo Marconi took Hertz's apparatus, connected one of the metal balls to the earth, the other to an "antenna" strung in the air, and shot his sparks across the gap between them. By 1903 he was sending and receiving radiotelegraph messages across the Atlantic Ocean.

Shortly thereafter the American physicist, Professor R. A. Fessenden, pointed out that radio could be used to carry the human voice as well. In 1905, J. A. Fleming, an English inventor, produced his two-element "valve" or vacuum tube; and in September 1906, Professor Fessenden was able as a result to install an experimental radiotelephone transmitter at Brant Rock, Massachusetts. Here he arranged transmissions of voice and music that were picked up by startled ship operators at sea in what was undoubtedly the first successful radio broadcast in the world. In the same year, Dr. Lee De Forest of New York added another element to the Fleming "valve," and thereby evolved the three-element radio tube, called by him the "audion." This third element was the "grid"—a kind of electrical trigger which made it possible for a tiny electric current to reproduce an exact duplicate of itself on an enormously amplified scale. This invention above all others was responsible for the development of radio as it is known today.

In the winter of 1909, Dr. De Forest used his audions to arrange a radiotelephone broadcast of Caruso singing *Pagliacci* at the Metropolitan Opera House, and picked it up at his home for the benefit of a circle of invited guests. Radio broadcasting as a commercial possibility was then just around the corner. But De Forest's radio tube was technically an improvement on the Fleming "valve"; the Marconi Company held the Fleming patents and by court decision was able to enjoin De Forest from manufacturing his tube, but could not itself make the three-element audion so far superior to the Fleming tube. Other patent holders entered their claims as well; and there matters stood deadlocked in one of the most costly, infinitely complicated and confused series of patent litigations on record—until October 1919, when the various conflicting interests pooled their patents and formed the Radio Corporation of America.

In 1919, the ban on amateur radio which had been imposed during the World War was lifted, and amateurs returning from military service opened their radiotelegraph and radiotelephone stations again. Among them was Dr. Frank Conrad, an engineer of the Westinghouse Electric and Manufacturing Company, who rigged up an experimental radiotelephone amateur station at his home in East Pittsburgh, and conducted regular musical broadcasts for the benefit of an audience of 15 or 20 fellow amateurs. By the summer of 1920 his audience had grown to several hundred, and Pittsburgh department stores were advertising "approved radio receiving sets for listening to Dr. Frank Conrad's concerts." Now fully aware of the implications of this experiment, the Westinghouse Company installed a new radiotelephone transmitter in one of its buildings under Dr. Conrad's supervision, just in time to broadcast the Presidential election returns of 1920 to an audience estimated at 1,000. The broadcast was an immediate success.

The new station—the first regular broadcasting station in America— received the call letters KDKA. Other stations followed rapidly and the sale of radio receivers and parts began to boom. By 1922 there were several stations in New York, among them station WEAF, established by the American Telephone and Telegraph Company as the first station offering its facilities for rental on a time basis to commercial sponsors. By 1923 the licensed radio stations in the country numbered 573.

In 1922 a New York station sent its program by wire to a Chicago station to be broadcast there simultaneously, in the first successful "chain" broadcast. WEAF, the pioneer toll station, then became the central point where programs were originated and sent by wire to other stations of the country in a broadcasting chain of ever-growing size. The cost of these programs was distributed proportionately between the commercial sponsors and the chain stations using the programs. In 1926 the National Broadcasting Company was organized by Radio Corporation of America, the General Electric Company, and the Westinghouse Electric and Manufacturing Company to take over stations WEAF and WJZ in New York for service as the cores of two national broadcasting chains—the so-called "red" and "blue" networks. The Columbia Broadcasting System and other chains were quick to follow the precedent set for nationwide program release.

Until recently, New York's dominant position in the nation's broadcasting scheme remained unchallenged in every phase, but New York, once supreme as the point of origin of chain programs, has since given way to Hollywood. A current report shows that of 44 top-bracket commercial radio programs, Hollywood was originating 36, Chicago six, and New York only three. Yet New York is still the financial and administrative headquarters of more than half the country's stations; the point where radio-control circuits are planned and managed; the focal point where radio advertising—the life-blood of American broadcasting—is bought and sold; and the center of radio's comparatively new subsidiary industry, the making of "electrical transcriptions"—the phonograph records that are used by all the smaller stations.

New York City is now the home of the four largest national broadcasting networks, of two regional networks, and of a tributary station of a seventh chain. Of the "big four," the National Broadcasting Company owns and operates two—the "red" (WEAF) and "blue" (WJZ) networks. Though their studios are in Rockefeller Center's "Radio City," their transmitting equipment—the real "station"—is housed outside the city boundaries: that of WEAF at Bellmore, Long Island, and that of WJZ at Boundbrook, New Jersey. The Columbia Broadcasting System, for which station WABC is the local outlet, maintains four "studio theaters" in the city; all of them connected by wire circuits to the station's transmitter at Mountain View, New Jersey. Station WOR, the metropolitan outlet of the Mutual Broadcasting System, is a New Jersey station owned by the Bamberger department store in Newark. A number of its studios are in New York; others, along with its transmitter, are in Newark.

The smaller regional networks are the Intercity, with station WMCA, and the Empire State, with the Hearst-owned station WINS, as New York City outlets. Station WHN, noted as the original home of the "Major Bowes Amateur Hour," is an affiliate of the country's most powerful station, WLW in Cincinnati, Ohio. How powerful this station is can be grasped from the fact that its maximum power reaches 500,000 watts as compared to 50,000 each for such well-known stations as WEAF, WABC, and WOR.

Of the dozen or so other stations in the city—all of them small, unaffiliated with networks, and intended for local service only—the reputations of three in particular, because of the unusual type of service they render, have spread beyond the metropolitan boundaries. These are WQXR, WNYC, and WEVD.

WQXR is the first of the country's so-called "high-fidelity" stations. Its channel in the radio spectrum occupies 20 kilocycles instead of the usual ten—an advantage which makes possible the faithful transmission of music, so that this station is noted for the quality of the classical music it specializes in broadcasting.

WNYC, "New York's Own Station," is owned and operated by the city, and for that reason belongs to the limited category of broadcast stations that are non-commercial and accept no advertising. It has been of civic value in publicizing announcements, programs and advice from the police, fire, health, sanitation and educational departments of the city. Although it lacks funds to attract high-priced performers, it is one of New York's most popular stations because of the high quality of its musical programs, its lectures in a variety of fields by college instructors, and its experiments in radio school-room educational programs. Its transmitter, with a power of 1,000 watts, is in the Greenpoint section of Brooklyn.

Station WEVD, founded in 1927 as a memorial to the Socialist leader, Eugene V. Debs, occupies a position unique among the city's stations. It is identified with the slogan "Voice of Labor," and serves as a channel for full discussion of labor problems. It accepts no compensation for time on the air taken by political discussion; it invites leaders in all phases of labor, politics, education and economics to use its facilities; and it claims to broadcast a wider educational program than any other comparable station. Station WEVD has produced one of its most popular programs in its "University of the Air," under the direction of Hendrik Willem van Loon, noted historian, author and artist. A distinguished volunteer faculty conducts four nightly periods a week. The success of the "University" has been such that transcriptions of its courses in philosophy, psychology, art, history, labor, economics, literature and drama have had a country-wide distribution to other radio stations on a non-profit basis. Oswald Garrison Villard, Heywood Broun and Norman Thomas, along with other nationally known persons, are associated in the administration of WEVD.

Station WBNX, sometimes called "The Voice of the Bronx," is typical of the several smaller stations of the city that make a special appeal to the polyglot section of New York's population by means of foreign language broadcasts. These statio..s find audiences large enough in almost any nationality group to make their entertainment commercially worth while. WBNX has gone further into a systematic nationality approach than any other New York broadcaster. Nearly one-fourth of its programs combine both racial and language appeals, and include Italian, Irish,

Jewish, Negro, Polish, Spanish, Hungarian, Ukrainian and Greek periods. Through the local outlets of the big chains New Yorkers hear the same radio programs that reach the smallest hamlet of the country. But in the quality of these programs, even more than in their variety, New York has made its most important contribution to broadcasting. It has raised the level of the musical taste of the nation, for here originated, and originate, the great opera and symphony broadcasts. To the excellence of the music selected, New York adds what no other city in the country —or even the world—can add: the excellence of presentation. Great operas are presented in their entirety by the Metropolitan Opera Company; great symphonies are played by the world's finest orchestras, led by the world's greatest conductors. The audience of these broadcasts has grown to an incalculable size. Likewise in drama, the plays of Shakespeare and Ibsen, as well as of numerous later dramatists, have been presented by many of America's best known actors and actresses. In political education, Town Hall forums, held in New York weekly during the winter months, have revived a democratic institution that in similar form exists now in other communities. The New York forum, however, has the advantage that its platform attracts the outstanding political and social leaders of America.

A phase of broadcasting most important to the buyer of radio advertising is the time-of-day placement of programs, and of the day of the week as well. The value of the period from Monday to Friday is fairly uniform, as a whole, the important distinction lying in the hours of each day. Saturday and Sunday have special values, and are considered good for some programs and less good for others. The summer months give an expectancy of fewer listeners than the winter months; but the greatest difference appears in the values before and after 6:30 P.M. Advertisers usually deem the early evening hours the most valuable, and pay double for the privilege of using them. To the advertiser, the cost of sponsored programs, from morning to night, may run as low as $50 an hour on a small station to $15,000 an hour on a nation-wide broadcast over a major network.

Radio stations, advertisers, and advertising agencies find it imperative to ascertain the comparative popularity of various types of radio programs. Acting for an association of advertisers, a New York statistical firm through branches in 33 cities annually makes 400,000 telephone calls to determine what radio-set owners are listening to. The highest rating during the latter part of 1937 was accorded to "Charlie McCarthy," the ventriloquist's dummy, whose Aristophanic remarks and opinions have earned deferential comment even in the dignified editorial pages of the New York *Times*.

A universal program feature worthy of special comment is the "news flash." It was made possible by the establishment in 1934 of two specialized radio news services, the Press Radio Bureau and the Transradio News Service. Press Radio presents Associated Press news through the networks of both the National Broadcasting Company and the Columbia Broadcasting System in two five-minute broadcasts each day, as well as supplementary flashes on occasions of special importance. The Mutual Broadcasting System, represented by station WOR in New York, is provided with United Press news flashes by Transradio. Press Radio has 12,000 miles of leased teletype wires in the United States, and serves some 300 radio stations and 40 newspapers. It does not operate a radio station itself, but daily transmits through the short wave radio transmitter of Press Wireless, Inc., at Little Neck, Long Island, to isolated points in this country and abroad where the teletype service is not available. Press Radio evolved from the discontinuance of a similar service by the National Broadcasting Company, under pressure applied by the powerful American Newspaper Publishers' Association. The employees who had been conducting the news services of NBC promoted Press Radio, which was an instant success and compelled other news services and newspaper rivals of radio stations to flash news by radio, in modification of the newspaper publishers' original ban.

A promising new trend in program content has been brought about by the work of two Works Progress Administration units: WPA Radio, organized in April 1937, and the Federal Theater Radio Division, organized in March of that year. The Federal Theater Radio Division gave Shakespeare and Eugene O'Neill to its listeners a year before their plays were featured by the major networks. Its program series included an educational innovation, a dramatization of James Truslow Adams' *Epic of America,* sponsored by the American Legion Auxiliary. Through the New York City Board of Education and station WNYC, this feature was rebroadcast to 49 high schools in New York City, reaching a million and a half students (1937-38).

Witnessing a broadcast is one of the keenest delights of the radio fan, and this fact has been utilized by New York stations to bring the public to the threshold of the microphone. Those who will take the trouble to arrange for passes from one to three weeks in advance have the choice of more than a score of broadcasts weekly. Most stations welcome visitors to the limit of their capacity, but the very small stations do not encourage them. The Columbia Broadcasting System maintains four "studio theaters" in New York, in addition to 15 other studios on company premises or leased property; the Mutual Broadcasting System, one. Activities of the National Broadcasting Company are confined to Radio City in Rockefeller Center. There, under one roof, is housed one of the most elaborate radio organizations in the world. Of its more than 40 studios, one is a guest theater.

No discussion of New York's radio facilities would be complete without mention of broadcasting's quiet step-sisters—the governmental and emergency services. In the Greater New York area, four direction-finder stations and ten radio beacons, all using telegraphic code, are scattered along the coast to guide ships in and out of New York harbor. Five code stations broadcast weather warnings to ships at sea. Now that the range of radio receivers has been extended to include the short-wave bands, the average listener can hear the clipped, monotonous voice of New York's police radio stations. Three such transmitters flash orders to the roving radio-equipped police cars—WPEE, WPEF and WPEG. Station WPY keeps in contact with the police boats in the harbor. The fire department maintains a similar station, of 500 watts power, to keep in touch with the harbor fireboats. And New York's radio amateurs maintain more than 2,000 private radio transmitting stations that chatter endlessly with amateurs in the rest of the country and in almost every foreign nation of the globe.

Television, though still within the realm of experiment, antedates successful voice-broadcasting radio. As far back as 1842, more than 60 years before the Fessenden broadcast, a Scotsman, Alexander Bain, devised the first known apparatus for the electrical transmission of visual images at a distance. A more efficient device serving the same purpose was produced independently in 1847 by an Englishman, F. C. Bakewell. In the latter's machine, the picture to be sent was drawn on electrically conductive paper with an insulating ink; the paper was placed on a rotating drum, and a metal stylus in contact with this drum was connected by wire to the receiver, where the pressure of an inked brush poised against another rotating drum was controlled by an electromagnet. As the stylus moved over the picture at the transmitting end, the inked brush traced an identical path on a blank piece of paper in the receiver. When the stylus touched a dark area, the brush pressed down hard; when the stylus touched a white area, the brush lifted itself off the paper—and in fifteen minutes or so the original picture in the transmitter was reproduced in facsimile by the receiver. The most modern television equipment is precisely analogous in its method of operation. For the stylus it substitutes a swiftly moving finger of light, for the inked brush a cathode-ray pencil in the receiver that "paints" an immediately visible image on a fluorescent screen; in place of the inter-connecting wire it uses an ultra-short-wave radio circuit —and in order to produce the illusion of moving pictures, it works several hundred thousand times as fast, sending and receiving some 30 or 40 pictures a second instead of one every fifteen minutes.

In 1884, the so-called scanning disc used in television transmission today was invented by Paul Nipkow, a young German; not for so inconsequential a use as television, but in connection with his amazing "electrical telescope," a device intended ultimately to be used in astronomical observation for the purpose of magnifying distant stars and planets electrically instead of optically—and a possibility still far beyond the reach of present day television. In 1890 an American, N. S. Amstutz, successfully transmitted a photographic half-tone over a twenty-five-mile wire line. At about the same time the photoelectric cell was invented; and in 1895 another American experimenter, C. Francis Jenkins, who has worked on television ever since, conceived on paper the idea of substituting "wireless" for wire line circuits and sending motion pictures by radio. By that time television had gone so far that it had to stand still and wait for radio to catch up with it.

It was not until 1923, when Jenkins successfully transmitted a portrait of President Harding from Washington to Philadelphia, that television as such took its next important step forward. Meanwhile engineers had been working behind closed doors. In 1927 the Bell Telephone Laboratories sent television pictures from New York to Washington; in 1928 the first television drama was broadcast by the General Electric Company from Schenectady; in the same year a special television broadcast from England was received by R. M. Hart at Station W2CVJ in Hartsdale, New York; and in 1929 Dr. Vladimir Zworykin announced his new "kinescope," or cathode-ray television tube. In 1931 Jenkins opened the first television station in New York, station W2XCR, broadcasting television programs on regular schedule. It was quickly followed by several others: stations W2XBS, W2XBO, W2XAB, W2XF and W2XR; and New York became the center of a television boom that lasted until 1933. Thousands of television outfits were constructed by amateurs, manufactured receivers were offered for sale in the department stores, and television "fan" magazines appeared on the news stands. But the boom was premature and proved to be something of a fiasco. The stamp-size pictures were very poor in quality, New York's regularly broadcasting television stations disappeared, and television retired again behind closed doors. There it now remains, issuing reports from time to time of brighter and larger images, of television in natural colors, of stereoscopic television in three dimensions—but still awaiting the day when it can emerge as a commercially practicable reality.

As the connecting link between radio and the talking movies, television opens up a host of possibilities, with innumerable psychological, social and political as well as technical implications. With its coming, there is the certainty that radio's influence will be woven even more deeply into the pattern of American life.

Newspaperman's Mecca

On November 8, 1725, William Bradford put forth the initial issue of his *New-York Gazette,* the first newspaper to be established in the colony. In the more than two centuries since that event, journalism in New York City has had a notable and colorful history. To recount that history even in broad outline is a task that cannot be attempted in such a book as this. What follows here is no more than a brief record of the city's present-day facilities for the gathering and presentation of news, with some notes on the evolution and character of those facilities.

Eight major dailies harvest the current crop of news events for metropolitan readers. The *Times,* generally considered the best all-around newspaper of the lot, has been characterized as "the newspaperman's newspaper." This is a distinction previously held by the *Sun,* in the heyday of Richard Harding Davis, Frank Ward O'Malley, Will Irwin and the rest; and by the old *World,* when it boasted a staff of such brilliant special writers as Walter Lippmann, Laurence Stallings, Alexander Woollcott, Franklin P. Adams, and Heywood Broun, and a crew of star reporters under Frank Cobb, Herbert Bayard Swope, James W. Barrett and other city editors.

The encyclopedic *Times* acquired its formidable reputation under the late Adolph S. Ochs, a Chattanooga publisher who took it over in 1896 and who was responsible for the policy that established it in the front rank of newspapers. From that time on—and especially since the World War, when public interest in European affairs reached a new high—the *Times* has steadily increased its foreign news-gathering facilities. Now it excels all other American papers in the amount and quality of its foreign news coverage. It has also been in the forefront in the general tendency toward specialized reporting. At home and abroad it employs a distinguished staff of reporters, some of whom have achieved spectacular feats.

In the days of its founder, Henry J. Raymond, the *Times* displayed a notable zeal for political reform. Its most glorious successes in the role of crusader were scored in 1857, when a Washington correspondent's exposure of the Land Grab Deal resulted in the expulsion of four members from the House of Representatives, and in 1871, when it helped to bring the Tweed Ring to book. Under the guidance of Adolph S. Ochs and Arthur Hays Sulzberger, Ochs' son-in-law and successor, it has striven to make its appeal, *qua* newspaper, nationwide. That it has succeeded in becoming America's foremost newspaper not even its severest critics will deny.

The *Times'* most formidable New York rival in the dissemination of news is the *Herald Tribune,* which leads it in popularity in the wealthier sections of the city and suburbs. The *Herald Tribune* is notable especially for the crisp contemporaneity of its local coverage, in which respect it is considered in some quarters the superior of the *Times;* while its editorial page is much livelier than that of its foremost rival. It resulted from the merger in 1924 of two of New York's oldest newspapers. In 1872, Whitelaw Reid, members of whose family are the *Herald Tribune's* present proprietors, bought the *Tribune* equity from its owner-editor, Horace Greeley, one of the first in the long line of great American editors. Greeley cherished high political ambitions, so high that certain contemporaries charged that he was suffering from messianic delusions (an affliction attributed to editors and publishers to this day). A master in the art of political diatribe, he enjoyed, through the paper he had founded in 1841, a power and prestige that lasted until his death in 1872.

The Reid family acquired the *Herald* in 1924 from Frank Munsey, who four years earlier had bought it from the estate of James Gordon Bennett, the son of that paper's eminent founder. The elder Bennett was one of the earliest pioneers in the field of sensational journalism, author of the remark that a newspaper's function was not to instruct but to startle. Modern reporting owes much to both Bennetts for their conception of what constitutes news. Stories other papers would not touch—scandals, chancy bits of gossip, neighborhood trivia—were all printed in the *Herald,* side by side with news of national interest. This paper, founded in 1835, was the first to report events in the realms of Wall Street, society, sports and the weather.

But the last straw for the contemporary London *Daily News* was the *Herald's* inauguration of the interview. The *News* commented severely on that "portion of the daily newspapers in New York" which was "bringing the profession into contempt so far as they can by a kind of toadyism or flunkeyism which they call 'interviewing'." Bennett would stop at nothing to get the news—even if he had to make it himself, which he did often enough—or to scoop a rival for circulation purposes. It is said that he spent a half million dollars reporting the Civil War and considered it well worth the price. The younger Bennett, carrying on the family tradition from 1866, sent Stanley out to Africa to find Livingstone, exclusively for the *Herald*.

By the 1890's the Bennetts had come to be regarded as conservative influences in comparison with the current crop of sensationalists who were frantically stirring up the journalistic waters around New York in quest of higher circulation. Chief among these was Joseph Pulitzer, who had acquired the *World* in 1883 in an effort to duplicate his St. Louis successes in New York. Pulitzer outdid Bennett in sensational circulation schemes intended to attract the barely literate masses of New York. Appropriately enough, the term "yellow journalism" originated in the office of the *World*, when a Pulitzer cartoonist in an idle moment created the famous "Yellow Kid" cartoon character.

When Pulitzer died in 1911, he left to his three sons an immensely successful paper, the name of which was everywhere synonymous with militant and courageous liberalism. Twenty years later, on February 27, 1931, New York was reading the story of "The End of the *World*." The journal's death was mourned by the entire newspaper profession, especially those members who still regard the old *World* as their real Alma Mater.

The Scripps-Howard interests acquired the assets of the *World* after its demise, and Roy Howard combined it with the *Telegram* to form the present *World-Telegram*. Though this paper boasts of progressive tendencies, it is indefinite in character and not too firm in its convictions. Stanley Walker in *City Editor* characterizes the *World-Telegram* as "alive in its news, but skimpy and shot through with dubious semi-crusades." Its chief distinction is its battery of distinguished columnists, including Mrs. Franklin D. Roosevelt, Heywood Broun, Westbrook Pegler, Hugh Johnson and others.

William Randolph Hearst has been the *enfant terrible* of local journalism ever since he burst upon the New York scene in 1895, flushed by his California triumphs, and began to publish the *Morning Journal* (afterwards the *American*). Although he made some popular innovations that have been adopted by many other newspapers, he has contributed nothing lasting to New York journalism. Even the *American*, his personal mouthpiece and considered the darling of all his papers, was never a profitable business and not solid enough to last. It was finally merged (1937) with his tabloid *Mirror* and the *Evening Journal.* The former—except for Walter Winchell, the tattletale of the big city, who invented a private vernacular for the double purpose of enlivening gossip and avoiding libel, and Mark Hellinger, the mass-production O. Henry of Broadway—is a cross between the superior *Daily News* and the *Graphic* of horrible, if sometimes amusing, memory. The present *Journal-American* suffers from a plethora of features, and its news pages have gained little or nothing in caliber as a result of the merger.

Another entrepreneur who failed to contribute anything solid to the city's journalism was Frank Munsey, who invaded New York in 1891. He was responsible for the death, by merger or otherwise, of so many papers that a wit was finally impelled to remark that "good newspapers when they die go to Munsey." Yet the *Sun* was one sheet that managed to survive the fatal Munsey touch, perhaps because it had preserved some of the strength once imparted to it by its great editor, Charles A. Dana, and the long line of newspapermen who worked in the shadow of his formidable reputation—Samuel Hopkins Adams, Will Irwin, Edward ("Chimmie Fadden") Townsend, David Graham Phillips, Ray Stannard Baker and (greatest legend of them all) Richard Harding Davis.

After Munsey's death in 1925 the *Sun* was acquired by a group of his former employees. It caters to the ultra-conservative elements of the city, and its inside pages reveal a fondness for the antiquarian and other features which are of less than cosmopolitan interest. Though its news stories are usually well written, there is little about it to suggest that it was once the "newspaperman's newspaper."

New York of the early post-war period broke out with a rash of tabloids. There appeared, within a few years of each other, the *Daily News,* Bernarr Macfadden's now defunct *Graphic,* and Mr. Hearst's *Mirror,* already mentioned in this article. The *Daily News,* first in the field and the most successful of the lot, was started in 1919 by Captain Patterson of the Chicago *Tribune,* and in less than ten years its circulation had soared well over the million mark. George Seldes attributes the amazing popularity of the tabloid at this time to the current disillusionment with the more sober press in the post-war years. But a more convincing explanation of that popularity must take into account a physical form far more convenient for subway and streetcar reading than that of the "full size" papers, an abundance of more or less sensational news pictures, and a condensed style of news treatment that requires little time or effort for its mental digestion.

In 1933, J. David Stern, who had been operating several Pennsylvania and New Jersey newspapers, took over what was left of the *Evening Post* and restored its original name, the *Post*. New York's oldest surviving journal, it had been founded in 1801 by Alexander Hamilton and edited at one time by William Cullen Bryant. Under E. L. Godkin, a firebrand of New York journalism, and later under Oswald Garrison Villard, it had acquired a reputation for liberalism. This liberal inclination survived in part even after it was taken over by Cyrus H. K. Curtis of Philadelphia. Its news section and editorial page salaamed to Wall Street (a ritual gesture of the 1920's) and New York was mildly titillated each autumn by *Post* editorials thundering against Harvard and Princeton teams for playing football with their social inferiors. But it supported many worthy causes, including municipal reform, and it played a strong hand against John H. McCooey, late Tammany leader of Brooklyn, and throughout the Seabury investigations.

When Stern took it over in 1933, he immediately converted the *Post* into a forthright New Deal supporter. The paper stresses news of intrinsic social importance. Its editorial page, manned by a group of younger men, is a trifle shrill at times but easily the liveliest and most outspoken in the city. Altogether the *Post* has made more impressive gains than any other newspaper in New York in the last few years, though there is still a touch of the small town about its make-up and circulation methods.

Every borough has its own newspapers but the Brooklyn *Daily Eagle*, once edited by Walt Whitman, and the Bronx *Home News* are the only ones that can be considered of metropolitan stature. Among dailies of closely specialized or "trade" character, the *Wall Street Journal* and *Women's Wear* are conspicuous.

The *Daily Worker*, official organ of the Communist Party of the United States, occupies an important place among New York's labor newspapers. Many well-informed persons outside the labor movement now find it necessary or desirable to supplement their reading of the regulation newspapers with a perusal of the *Daily Worker* in order to obtain a balanced and comprehensive view of current affairs. The *Jewish Daily Forward* is also notable for its labor news coverage, and it has played a prominent part in furthering trade union organization among New York's workers— the needle trades workers in particular.

In the foreign-language field, no fewer than 35 dailies, with a combined weekday circulation of approximately 800,000, are published in New York City. Chiefly prominent among these, with respect to the number of readers that they reach, are the *Forward, Jewish Morning Journal, Der*

Tag, and *Freiheit,* in the Jewish (Yiddish) field; *Il Progresso Italo-Americano, Corriere d'America* and *La Stampa Libera,* Italian; *New York Staats-Zeitung und Herold,* German; *Amerikai Magyar Nepszava,* Hungarian; *Nasz Przeglad,* Polish; *Novoye Russkoye Slovo* and *Russky Golos,* Russian; and *New Yorsky Dennik,* Slovak. Others of the city's foreign-language newspapers are mentioned in the various sections of the article on Nationalities, contained in the present volume.

New York's very large Negro population has no local daily of its own, but it supports three weekly papers—the *New York Age,* the *Amsterdam News,* and the *New York News.*

That special phenomenon of the American newspaper world, the Sunday edition, attains in New York a bulk and comprehensiveness not to be matched elsewhere. Of the foremost metropolitan papers that inundate the Sabbath with countless reams of news-print, the *Times* and the *Herald Tribune* offer by far the most palatable and nourishing fare. Each has its separate magazine and book-review supplements, its rotogravure picture sections, and its many pages of feature matter written by competent specialists in every main field of current interest—along with a vast array of advertising that makes these other things possible.

Though they contain special features of various sorts, the Sunday editions of the *Journal-American* and the tabloid *News* and *Mirror* for the most part merely increase the volume and speed the tempo of these papers' regular week-day editions. Each is blanketed in several layers of colored "funnies," and the *Journal-American* carries as a supplement Mr. Hearst's widely syndicated *American Weekly.*

Outside the borough of Manhattan, the only metropolitan newspaper that publishes a Sunday edition is the Brooklyn *Eagle,* which follows the general pattern of its more affluent contemporaries on the other side of the East River, while maintaining an individual emphasis on matters of especial interest to residents of Brooklyn, Queens and the rest of Long Island.

New York's lone Sunday afternoon newspaper, the *Enquirer,* employs most of the devices known to sensational journalism in an effort to gain patronage from those who throng the city's restaurants and theaters on Sunday night.

Twenty-one New York newspapers in the foreign-language field appear on Sunday, several of them with magazine supplements, rotogravure sections and other special features. The *Daily Worker* also has its Sunday edition, with a magazine section.

The circulation of New York's principal Sunday newspapers is by no means confined to the metropolis, but reaches out to nearly every town and hamlet in the country. The *News,* with a total of more than three million readers, heads the list in this respect. Through book stores and other special distribution channels, the book supplements of the *Times* and the *Herald Tribune* attain a large national circulation.

The most remarkable journalistic development of the New Deal period was the first stirring of labor consciousness among newspapermen—a phenomenon that finally flowered into the present American Newspaper Guild, with Heywood Broun as its national president. The Guild was given considerable impetus by the NRA, and after a while picked up power enough to go ahead on its own. Its declared purpose is that of all labor unions—collective bargaining to obtain better conditions and wages, with the addition that it seeks to raise the standards of the profession. It has met with the bitter opposition of many publishers, who were quick to raise the cry of "freedom of the press"; but it has already won several notable victories. A few old city-room die-hards mutter darkly about the impending doom of a noble calling; but the majority of news gatherers, especially in New York, have rallied to the movement with great enthusiasm. The Guild's more sanguine supporters even look forward to the time when, by the strength of their organization, they will be able to demand a more complete freedom in factual reporting. Carl Randau, president of the New York Guild, has revealed that "a few alert publishers are already recognizing that only through constant honesty in the news can they retain the confidence of the public—a confidence that has been largely sacrificed through the flagrant special pleading many editors have injected into the news columns."

All the major press associations make New York their headquarters. The first to begin operations here was the Associated Press, which began as a purely local affair in 1848 and gradually developed into the vast and powerful world organization that it is today. It was followed by the original United Press in 1882; this service was soon forced to discontinue, but it was later revived by the Scripps-Howard interests. Hearst's International and Universal News Services, which followed soon after and have since been merged, serve the Hearst papers as well as others. The New York City News Association, a cooperative enterprise to which most of the major papers belong, covers the routine stories in Manhattan and the Bronx, including news from most of the far-flung municipal buildings. The Standard News Association provides a similar service for a territory that takes in the remainder of the metropolitan area.

The trend toward "chain" journalism has been increasingly apparent in New York, as elsewhere throughout the country, in recent years. Today, four of the city's eight major dailies are in the hands of men who own newspapers in several other cities. In the resulting standardization and loss of individuality, journalism is slowly losing its glamor and interest. A symptom of the public craving for more individual fare is seen in the current vogue of the columnists, both serious and light, who sometimes give the only personal touch to a paper, by providing the interpretation and comment that were once functions of the editorial page.

Many of Manhattan's most celebrated newspaper workers have deserted journalism for more lucrative fields. Radio has claimed a number of those with good voices, others have succumbed to the lure of Hollywood's lush pastures, while still others have retired to do the "free lance" writing that all newspapermen dream of doing some day and so few accomplish. But notwithstanding these defections, Manhattan remains the newspaperman's mecca. From the journalistic backwaters of the republic a steady flow of seasoned veterans and aspiring neophytes pours Manhattan-wards, their ears humming with the roar of its giant presses. They flock to New York for the greater rewards held out to those who "make the grade," and for the chance it gives the working reporter to see for himself at close hand the vast and lavish spectacle of the great metropolis.

Athletics by Proxy

THE NEW YORKER—the average insensitive resident—is conditioned, even oblivious, to crowds. He is a member of many publics; his life is spent among great crowds of his fellows, herded together in search of happiness or trains. He belongs at one time to the subway public, at another to the theater audience or the fight mob. But he always belongs to a crowd, and except at rare moments (in telephone booths or shower baths) he is only one of the faces one sees without recognition in such crowds.

That is why, to look at New Yorkers, one goes to the Garden, or the Yankee Stadium or even the subway. In those places the New Yorker is immersed in his native mass; he is excited or delighted, irritated or tired, but safe and with his guard down. Look as long as you please.

This crowd-man, if he has come from the outlands, tends to balk at his fate when he first becomes aware of it. But that soon stops. On some unmarked day he doesn't care any more, one way or another. He's a New Yorker then. He knows the high-sign.

But, the laws of motion being what they are, one doesn't get much recreation in crowds. Most citizens, condemned to lives in which the elbows of other people are jammed into their patient ribs, don't get much play. And, because of that, New Yorkers make the world's greatest audiences. They will wait in line longer, they will pay more, they will gamble more on a bad fight than will the citizenry of Elyria, O., on a good one.

Supposing these assertions to have been admitted into evidence, it follows that any discussion of the place of sport in the city's life must deal primarily with those games in which a few men participate, to be watched by thousands of others. But first a word about the men—and the women —who watch.

There was a time when a fight fan was not to be seen at a tennis match, and the baseball mob spent dull winters because they didn't like basketball. Crowds were typical then; now they tend to coalesce, to represent as audiences not a single New York type but New York in the mass. You may see top hats at the fights and low brows at the Metropolitan Open. A number of forces worked for a number of years to bring this about. There were, for instance, the great 1920's, the Big Money, and such great national movements as Tex Rickard, Jack Dempsey, Babe Ruth, Bill Tilden, Bobby Jones.

Each of these men, by the power of his personality or—in the case of Rickard—the depth of his guile, caught the fancy of population brackets which had never thought before of the specific sport in which the individual hero was engaged. Each man arrived at the right time, a point not to be lost sight of in considering their titles to greatness.

Dempsey and Ruth, of course, simply took advantage of an increasing national interest in old and established sports. Tilden and Jones foisted their games onto the public consciousness by dint of sheer technical virtuosity. But Tex Rickard created a cult and a mystery—ballyhoo.

Rickard, too, came along at the right time. But, more than the others, he helped to fashion the time. Dempsey swung a hook or Ruth a bat out of a deep physical necessity. Rickard created the million-dollar gate only after due process of intellection.

He appeared on the New York scene in 1915, and took the Garden for his own. The old Garden, to be sure, had been in Madison Square long before Rickard had been anywhere. It had been Madison Square Garden since 1879, following an early career as a railroad station and successive incarnations as Gilmore's Garden and Barnum's Hippodrome. Giants had rebuilt it in 1890, the elder Morgan and P. T. Barnum using their money, Stanford White his ill-starred genius. White had lived atop the building in one of the first penthouses, in sight of the ornate if nude *Diana*.

But it didn't suit Rickard for long, memories or no memories. In March 1916 he staged the Willard-Moran fight in the old building, but by 1920 he had envisioned the Big Money. The million-dollar gate arrived with the Dempsey-Carpentier fight in July 1921, and in 1923 Dempsey pulled another million through the turnstiles to see him in there with Firpo for about four minutes.

In spite of the sociologists of the sports pages, Tex wasn't thinking about a monument to play when he got the ear of John Ringling and started his "Association of 100 Millionaires." Tex was thinking that now the fight racket was respectable; that he, Tex Rickard, wanted dough and needed more room.

The new Garden was capitalized for $5,650,000 and completed in 1925 at Eighth Avenue and Fiftieth Street. It's still there.

Nowadays, if New York has a heart, it might be the Garden. Almost everyone goes there, for one purpose or another. There are dog shows, and Sonja Henie and mass meetings; one may pay 25 cents to sit through a mass meeting or $300 for a box at the horse show. *Les Canadiens* may do battle with the Americans on the night after Henry Armstrong has knocked over another featherweight.

The Garden is probably America's greatest spot for ethnic research; it has a lot of influence on cultural values, and no top-flight anthropologist would be lost in one of its crowds; it contributes to the social well-being of the community, and it earns a pretty profit. It's quite a place.

The Garden (always excepting the ball parks in summer, which become gridirons in fall) is in almost absolute control of professional and semi-professional sport in New York. Boxing, hockey, and (in recent years) basketball have become its special charges.

In the city of New York 15 corporations are licensed to operate 20 clubs or arenas in which pugs may throw punches at one another for a fee. But under the iron hand of Mike Jacobs, who learned at the feet of Rickard, only the Garden has access to the top-notchers. Every high ranking heavyweight is contracted either to the Garden or to Jacobs personally.

Jacobs came into control during 1937, after a long and bitter duel with Jimmy Johnston, the colorful "Boy Bandit." Since the death of Rickard the associates of the Madison Square Garden Corporation had cast about here and there for a successor. They didn't find one. Johnston did well for a time, but he never came within shouting distance of Rickard's $3,000,000 dividends in four years.

Jacobs, who had been the power behind the throne of the Twentieth Century Sporting Club, came into the Garden on a pay-as-you-go arrangement during 1937. Jacobs' sagacity in judging the crowd's temper is shown by his gamble with Sonja Henie in January 1938, in which the Scandinavian ice star carted off about $300,000, and the Garden directorate smiled from the windows of various exclusive clubs.

The Garden is indisputably a great cultural center and a good solid investment. At least a carrying income is assured each year from rentals— the circus, rodeos, horse and dog shows, mass meetings and conventions. And the increasing mass attention to spectator sports, nurtured in some cases by the Garden management, makes the gamble with the gate more and more of a sure thing.

The directors seem at present inclined to play safe, taking an assured income rather than the bigger risks for greater gains of the days of Rickard. But that assured income is greater today than in Tex's time. The Garden controls the New York Rangers and has a receipt-sharing agreement with the Americans, while even the amateurs use the place for hockey and pull big gates.

So it may be that the high-flying days are over. Maybe the Garden *has* become just an investment, with no stake in the great outdoor fights or any other of the bigger promotions. But for a long while to come one may see claret on its ring floor or hockey players (they paid the directors $640,-000 in 1935) bashing one another with their sticks. The color and noise are not gone. It's just that business is indisputably business.

Spectator Sports

The great divide in sports used to admit of clarification. There were professionals and amateurs. It was all as simple as that. Today only one generality, and that very rough, is admissible. There are people who play and people who watch.

Consider the players. Collegiate basketball, in New York, has become a highly profitable sport. The game has moved from the smaller gyms into the Garden, and a promising double-header between two New York teams and two visiting quints will fill that great cultural center on any night you care to name. And filling the Garden for basketball means seating more than 16,000 addicts.

Now then. Are the players amateurs? They get no money for their services; their schools insist that no advantage, monetary or scholastic, accrues to them as a result of their efforts. They must be satisfied, it seems, with the things of the spirit. Yet they are engaged in a strictly commercial enterprise, from which one commercial institution (the Garden) and various educational institutions profit. The methods employed in attracting big gates are those of the prize-ring or hockey promoters. A column of newspaper publicity is so much cash in the bank to the participating firms—or institutions, if you like.

This subtle distinction, which makes amateurs of persons engaged in professional activity, extends to every sport that draws an audience. An amateur sport used to be one which great numbers of people played, for pleasure only, and without reference to the number of onlookers. But for the purposes of the present term paper it becomes simpler to forego the amateur-pro hairline. There remain, then, sports which great masses of the people play, and sports which great masses of the people watch.

Batter Up!

Among watched games, of course, baseball comes first. And in baseball New York comes first.

The three major league teams draw each season almost three million customers. The Yankees top the list. Their stadium accommodates more than 83,000 for baseball, and in addition they've been the best team in the game for the past two years.

The Yankees are a well-mannered group of business men, highest paid on a team average the game has known. They seldom have fights on the field; they are courteous, if cool, with the umps. They can hit harder as a group than the opposition, and their pitching and fielding are as good as the best. They have a great farm system, and can outbid any club in sight for new talent. Some New York sports writers, after the 1937 nickel series (that's carfare, not gate receipts), seriously suggested that the Yanks were too good for the present major leagues, and that their proficiency, if carried out on so high a plane much longer, would lessen interest in the game. That hasn't happened yet, evidently. People still go to ball games.

The Giants are gentlemen off and on. One of the greatest defensive combinations ever, they defend themselves at one and the same time from hot grounders, internecine strife and public vilification. Giant players never look on the flowing bowl, and are respected by one and all. Even the Yankees respect them.

Another aspect of the purely professional game is presented by the teams which make up the National Negro Baseball League, in which New York is represented by the Black Yankees, who play at Dyckman Oval. Though Negroes have been playing professionally since the 1880's, and have developed more than one authentic star of the diamond, none has yet appeared in major league baseball.

New York has a fair representation of amateur and semi-pro teams, but the paucity of diamonds throughout the greater city restricts their growth. Land values, in most cases, make city purchase of ground prohibitive, and the parks have almost reached the point at which one more diamond wouldn't be fair to people who don't play baseball.

Thus variations of the game have taken hold in New York. In point of numbers participating, "stickball" is easily the city's greatest summer game. For this variant, the required equipment is a rubber ball, a broomstick, and a street with or without traffic.

Primarily a kid's game, it often enough pulls papa off the front stoop of an evening to do or die against the kids from the next street.

Softball, because most playgrounds offer space for it, and any vacant lot (there *are* vacant lots) is large enough for a diamond of sorts, is played by thousands. Organized teams and leagues account for 25,000 adult players alone, while the playground pits many more thousands of kids against one another in dubious battle. Dubious, since neighborhood teams often lay bets against one another, and when the dough's on the line . . . Even rumors of thrown games occasionally float ominously about the lower East Side.

The Manly Art

In point of annual attendance boxing would seem to rank an easy second to baseball in the collective New York mind. In the professional ranks, of course, the Garden dictates. There were times when Mike Jacobs was the Garden's only serious rival, with his lease on the Hippodrome and his position as head of the Twentieth Century Sporting Club. But, during 1937, Mike consolidated himself. He runs the Garden, and he runs the Hippodrome. The really top-line bouts go into the Eighth Avenue tabernacle. The Hipp may be regarded as a testing field for talent.

Among the larger of the second-flight clubs are the Windsor Palace (the fans still call it St. Nick's), the Broadway Arena and Dyckman Oval. They all do well enough, and the very small temples throughout the five boroughs seem still able to pay the rent.

The amateur game flourishes, with the *Daily News* Golden Gloves tournament leading the way, and other organizations sponsoring occasional simon-pure bouts. The boys are sometimes, alas, not amateurs. But they fight, and how they fight!

For figures on the real love-of-the-game variety of boxing one would have to post checkers outside the various institutional gyms and count the busted noses as they pass out the doors.

Wrestling, too, was once regarded as a manly sport. But that was before Bill Muldoon (now among the shades) took over the cult and the mystery. Nowadays, though lots of people attend matches, the State Athletic Commission will have little or nothing to do with the business. These affairs are held weekly at the Hippodrome and fairly regularly at most of the town's small clubs, and must be billed as "exhibitions." The artists, of late, have taken to beards in alarming numbers.

Hell on Ice

Ice hockey, after all these years, has hooked on in New York. The Rangers and Americans fill the Garden regularly, and pay handsome dividends.

The rise of the game really dates from 1925–26, when the Americans and Rangers joined the newly organized professional loop. The amateurs had been at it regularly since the 1880's, but their audiences were then, as they are now, restricted to a few fans and the student bodies of participating schools.

Then the pros arrived, swinging. They have made it the fastest and roughest game now played anywhere; they have created probably the most fanatic sports audiences to be found. They have littered the Garden's fancy icing with opposing players, and they have made money in scads.

Very nearly 500,000 fans see the Rangers and Americans each winter at the Garden.

Hockey is probably directly responsible, incidentally, for the astonishing vogue of winter sports which has swept the city and the country. New Yorkers, a few of whom skated, seem never to have thought of what might be done on skis, snowshoes or bobsleds. But, with the rise of hockey, they began to see the ingenious uses to which a pair of skates might be put. The 1936 Olympics, with their stress on winter sports, finished it off. Nowadays an astonishing number of our citizens, who naturally can't ski or toboggan in a borough like Manhattan, hopefully watch the winter skies and keep posted on the snow trains.

The professionals have entered here, too. The 1937 Winter Carnival at the Garden was a smashing success, what with a real ski-run and all. But Sonja Henie, who does "Tales of the Vienna Woods" and such things, came along in January of 1938 to make that money look like peanuts.

Dying for Dear Old . . .

Even men now living can remember when football had to do only with colleges. Now, in New York at least, the pros threaten to give the collegians a run for it.

College football, of course, still dominates the situation. On any Saturday through the season there's at least one important game in town, since Fordham and N.Y.U. like to be at home when Columbia's away, and since the feeling is mutual.

New York is a big-time football town these days. True, during the 1937 season New York University was something less than a ball of fire, and Columbia never reached the boiling point. But Fordham? Indeed, yes. The only game the Rams didn't win was a tie, and it took Pitt to do that to them. New Yorkers are hard put to it to understand those Rose Bowl people.

The Army-Navy game or the Army-Notre Dame classic can always fill the Yankee stadium.

Manhattan and City College have been coming fast of recent years, but they're still far from the class of the others. The five local teams draw something like a million persons at the gate each season, and the Army-Navy or Army-Notre Dame session pulls about 90,000 more.

It's the pros, though, who provide the really astonishing feature of football in New York. They've only been at it for about ten years in these parts, but they've arrived. The Giants, of the National Professional League, last fall played to almost 250,000 spectators in seven home games. The old charge that the pros were inclined to take things easily is heard no more; possibly the greatest game played in New York during the 1937 season was the Giants' 10-0 win over the Green Bay Packers—great because with a skill never seen on a college field was combined a viciousness in tackling and line play that even the collegians at their maddest couldn't surpass.

Naturally this new dispensation needed a patron saint to guide it on its successful way. His name is Tim Mara. He books the horses here and there about the land; he is a shrewd father to his players, and nourishes carefully the growing "Die for dear old Mara" spirit among the fans. The Giants organization is often referred to as Mara University, which tells the story.

Disorder on the Court

Collegiate basketball has come in for some previous attention, but it's worth another word. For the game about here has risen to an eminence that it boasts in few other sections. On the basis of year-in and year-out intersectional play only the Pacific Coast teams can claim an advantage over the big town schools, though few of the far westerners have appeared here.

In spite of the changes in rules there is little uniformity of basketball method throughout the country. Western teams shoot fast and often, and

when two such teams meet the resulting score may be anything at all.
Defense is the word in the Midwest. But in New York it's all floor play—
passing to the point, sometimes, where the spectators stagger slightly on
the way out. New York teams, City College, notably, tend to overdo the
passing game, sacrificing points to technical brilliance.

In basketball the minor schools hereabouts play on an equal footing
with the bigger ones; as often as not City College (one of the outstanding basketball schools of the nation) is better on the court than such giants
as N.Y.U. or Columbia. St. John's of Brooklyn, Manhattan and Long
Island University draw crowds as great as those which watch Fordham or
Columbia.

While the five other teams meet one another every season, Columbia, a
member of the Eastern League, is inclined to be a bit coy with the local
talent. The Lions met only N.Y.U. during the 1937–38 season.

The pro game in New York is at the moment in a bit of a muddle.
Despite its great influence on the collegiate brand of play, it has undoubtedly suffered at the hands of the schoolboys. Good gates are still the rule
at the Hippodrome, but the accruing prestige isn't what it was.

There are too many teams, for one thing. There are the Celtics (now
owned by Kate Smith), the Visitations, the Jewels, and a host of other
less conspicuous pro clubs. It is not uncommon for a player during a single
week to appear with two or more teams, and the loosely-organized pro
loop tends to take on the aspect of a wrestling troupe, with the difference
that the pro basketballers play to win.

Probably the oldest and the best team now playing professional basketball is the great Renaissance Five of Harlem. This Negro club, members
of no league, can beat almost any pro team in the business, and their audiences are constant and large. Of late they have taken to protracted tours,
but they make an occasional stand against local teams, to the acute discom-
fort of the latter.

The game is popular in every one of the city's thousands of gyms, and
several amateur leagues for men and women flourish.

Some Others

Track and field events, long handicapped by lack of facilities in and
about New York, have come to the front recently as spectator sports, with
the indoor version bulking ever more large in the public eye. The Knights

of Columbus games and the Millrose meet, with its famed Wanamaker mile, attract outstanding men in every event. Of the track events, sprints and the mile are favored by the fans, with such figures as Cunningham, Venzke, San Romani and Lash making the mile run a highlight of any meet. Field events suffer somewhat indoors, though the high jump and the pole vault, granted that topnotchers are participating, will evoke a cheer or two.

Completion, during 1936, of the Randall's Island Stadium has given the city a fine outdoor field. Its cinder track is said to be the best in the country, though no spikes have yet cut it in record time.

The city's outstanding outdoor meet has come to be the annual Labor Games at the Island stadium. It attracts stars and crowds, and presages labor as a growing force in sports. Track and field sports among the youngsters are principally under the supervision of the Public School Athletic League and the Parks Department.

Golf, too, has a bright future in the city. There are ten civic links within the town's area, but they were something to be ashamed of until a while back. But WPA, in collaboration with Commissioner of Parks Robert Moses, has taken the tin cans out of the fairways and sodded the greens, among other things.

Golf in New York is still far from a mass game, and not many of the citizens ever see an event like the Metropolitan Open. But the sport is coming along, and will come faster when equipment prices fall within the range of the average purse.

Not a great deal of competitive swimming is done around New York. Such amateur competition as occurs is confined to indoor pools in various clubs and institutions. But from the public standpoint swimming is the greatest mass sport of all.

Here again WPA takes a bow, for since the beginning of the work relief agency 11 great public swimming pools have been opened in the five boroughs, and two beaches have been made habitable for humans. Orchard Beach, opposite City Island in the Bronx's share of the East River, is alleged by experts to be one of the world's outstanding examples of reclamation.

Then, of course, there remain such beaches as Coney Island, Brighton, Rockaway and (farther out) Jones Beach, as well as several others along the Long Island and Jersey shores, with their immense summer crowds.

Then there's tennis. The game grows and grows, but if one comes down to it it's not a mass game in New York, even today. Some few hundred thousands hold a racquet at one time or another, but the number of real devotees looms very small, to use a paradox, on the New York scene. There's a distinct lack of public courts, and a noticeable lack of money to pay rental fees or club dues.

Forest Hills may be regarded as a New York enterprise, but the galleries at the annual National Amateur tourneys or the not-annual-enough Davis Cup finals represent a very, very small segment of the populace.

Pro tennis, meanwhile, isn't as important as the newspapers once claimed it to be. A Vines-Perry match once filled the Garden, but filling the Garden once in a year is no criterion. The case could be clinched by pointing out that New York has never produced a great hand with the racquet, but why labor the point?

The six-day bike races have two functions: they keep people away from home nights, and they bring the Garden about $170,000 a year. But they occur only once or twice during each year, which may be just as well, all things considered.

Polo is played indoors and outdoors by men who can afford polo ponies. They're strictly amateurs, because they have money enough or resources enough. Pros are pros because they need the money. Polo is played and watched by people who don't need the money.

Auto races haven't attained much foothold around and about New York, in spite of the reopening of Roosevelt Raceway at Westbury, L. I. The Vanderbilt Cup races were held at this road track in 1937, but one race, even a big one, is still one race.

There remain other games which New Yorkers watch while other New Yorkers play. Soccer, for instance, boasts 700 teams in various city leagues, but attendance is pretty well restricted to the foreign born. Rugby is played occasionally, but there are no figures on where, when or why. People fence, shoot arrows at targets, play lacrosse and field hockey, bowls and billiards. But they do these things because they like to do them, and you could count the gate on the fingers of one billiard cue.

The usual gym games—handball, volley ball, and the rest—haven't the appeal in New York that they have in other cities, because we have here too many people and too few gyms. The court games, such as court tennis, squash racquets and squash tennis, are prohibited to most, since relatively few people belong to private clubs. There is, incidentally, only one public court tennis layout in the entire city.

National Games

The Italians are steeped in a very old culture, and any one of them could beat you at bocci. The Irish sing well, have elected a lot of aldermen, and play hurley better than the Sassenach. West Indians are polite, wear white flannels, and will take you on at cricket and trounce you in a genteel manner.

These are the three great national games still flourishing hereabouts. You may see bocci on any vacant lot where Italians gather, and if you want to cheer at the sight of one wooden ball colliding with another wooden ball that's up to you. The Irish lay the caman fiercely about every Sunday at Innisfail and Van Cortlandt Parks. The West Indians stand around Van Cortlandt Park weekly with those funny bats and that mysterious manner affected by cricketers.

Sailboats sail, yachts yacht, and shooters shoot here and there. People play lawn bowls, roque and croquet. But not many people could name one star in these sports.

Supervised Sports

One doesn't have to tell the young how to play. They seem to figure it out for themselves. But in such a city as this other considerations enter uninvited. How are the kids to be kept out of the way of trucks, trolleys, and gangs? How are they to learn other games as well as, unattended, they would learn dice, blackjack and pitch-penny?

The Public School Athletic League tries to answer the question during those days and hours when the kids are within the League's range of fire. The Police Athletic League (on the badge it says PAL) supplements the effort of the schools.

PAL—a branch of the Juvenile Aid Department—had a membership of 74,260 boys and girls at the close of 1937, each a dues-paying member at ten cents per year. Adults may become associate members at a cost of one dollar, and it's worth it.

The organization boasts a double-barreled value. It teaches a boy or girl how to play team games—off the streets—and it unlearns a lot of what the streets teach him about cops. The kid who is taught to box by a cop is never likely to become a cop-fighter, the Juvenile Aid Department reasons. The cops seem to agree.

New York, more than any other city in America, is dotted with institutions devoted to the welfare of the young. The welfare of the young is partly bound up with games, so the kids do fairly well. They could do a lot better, but housing has nothing to do with an essay on sports.

On a Moral Note

The horse is admittedly a noble beast which runs at four tracks in or adjacent to New York City. The primary idea in a horse race is to see which horse is best in a given group. In an effort to determine this superiority men have lost their shirts, homes and happiness, and have made merry and money.

The four metropolitan tracks are Belmont, Jamaica, Acqueduct and Empire City, and during 1937 they played to more than 1,300,000 fans. So racing is a mass sport; but that isn't the half of it.

Of each hundred persons who follow the races one may say conservatively that 30 will see a race at one time or another during their lives. The others are occupied only with the possible riches to be gained by monetary insistence on the quality of some particular horse. According to the estimate of a large booking syndicate, about 950,000 New Yorkers lay a bet with the corner bookie at one time or another. (The track-goers usually bet with the books there.)

The bookies are much less numerous than the bettors, and the bookies take rather than lay bets. In the long run, against any run of luck by any number of bettors, a bookie will win. He will win because he risks only his theory that horse players really don't know horses, or anything.

Here are some figures:

About 10,000 horses are raced in the United States each year. Of these about 500 are fairly consistent winners. About 1,500 are in-and-outers ("give him a heavy track and he'll deliver"), and the remainder are plugs, a charitable enough term. The bettor doesn't know which of his picks belong to the 8,000 and which to the 500. The bettor, therefore, loses.

Horse-racing, a great sport in itself, has tended to bring about the extension of small-time gambling into every other game. This gambling has always been a business with a small portion of the population. Today it has become a pastime among a great number of people. One bets on the horses, the fights, football, baseball—and the game ceases to be a game.

But in the end it's hard to blame the bettor. He likes to play; there isn't quite enough room or time, so he plays at a distance. That's the tragedy of that typical crowd.

Water Gate

EMBRYONIC New York evolved from the germ of ocean commerce, and the infant settlement was nurtured on salt water. Salt water provided its nourishment during more than three hundred years of prodigious growth. Salt water conveys sustenance to the modern city's gargantuan anatomy. Without its great harbor, in short, the New York of today would have been impossible. By the same token, commerce and shipping have molded the city's destiny.

One hundred years ago, your average New Yorker was acutely port-conscious. Even more than Broadway, South Street was the Main Street of the little metropolis; and virtually every stream of metropolitan life—financial, commercial, industrial and social—flowed into the "street o' ships." Here was the profitable outlet for accumulated capital; this was the happy hunting ground for enterprising traders, where golden opportunity beckoned—and rewarded—the ten-dollar-a-month clerk no less than the established merchant. Here ships were bought and sold, within earshot of the famed East River yards that laid them down. Here too were the gala launchings and Liverpool packet sailings, always attended by vast throngs and not a little conviviality. The New Yorker of 1837 could boast something besides a trace of salt in his veins; there was inevitably a wisp of seaweed in his hair. "The beach" evoked aspirations and images not even vaguely resembling those that contemporary New Yorkers associate with Coney Island. There was an immediate tie-up between what happened on South Street and a man's bank balance or his butcher bill.

One hundred years ago, the Port of New York was the City of New York. There were distinctions, of course, but historically they are unimportant. New York in 1837 was America's premier seaport, but hardly more than that. It was primarily a mercantile city. And precisely at that time ships and shipping were laying the foundations of an edifice that would engulf South Street and require water frontage extensive beyond the wildest dreams of early 19th century merchants. The City of New

York today is more than the port; and the port includes more than the waterfront of the city.

In less than 100 years New York was transformed from a seaport town, maintained by a few docks, warehouses and shipyards, into a great world metropolis, supported by tens of thousands of factories and countless other wealth-producing enterprises. And while that aggregate of water-front activity which may loosely be called maritime industry is not the city's only industry—as, practically speaking, it was a hundred years ago —it is still the city's basic industry.

The waterfront is the heart of a gigantic metropolitan organism. Before we dissect this mighty heart and investigate some of its mysteries, we might consider our initial postulate that New York City without its harbor would have been impossible. On the surface, this is almost axiomatic. But, as we shall see in our observations on the Port of New York's life-and-death struggle with competing ports, this obvious proposition requires frequent argument and proof.

Nature was unusually beneficent with New York Harbor. This body of water is one of the largest natural harbors in the world. Seven major bays (Jamaica, Upper and Lower, Raritan, Gravesend, Newark and Flushing), some of them bigger than well-known harbors abroad, plus the mouths of four large rivers (Raritan, Passaic, Hudson and Hacken-sack), plus four estuaries (Arthur Kill, Kill van Kull, East River and Harlem River), go into its composition. Its 67 well-defined anchorage grounds have an area of 92,500 acres. Heavy ocean fog is infrequent in the harbor. In addition to being virtually landlocked, it is never ice-bound; its mean tide range is only four and a half feet; and it is equipped with exceptionally deep channels, both natural and dredged. New York's main channels have a depth of 40 feet, practically a minimum requirement for such modern liners as the *Normandie* and *Queen Mary*. What nature marred or forgot man has remedied or supplied; since 1853 the Federal Government has expended more than $10,000,000 on harbor improvements here.

Besides these outstanding physiographical features, New York Harbor is blessed with an extraordinary geographical location. It is directly accessible to the Atlantic Ocean, only two hours' steaming time, or about 17 miles, separating the Manhattan waterfront from the open sea. The good fortune of New York in this respect is doubly apparent when we note that Philadelphia and Baltimore, two of the port's chief rivals, are situated 102 miles and 179 miles respectively from the sea. New York is likewise remarkably favored with a short all-water route to Boston, via the sheltered East River, Long Island Sound and the Cape Cod Canal; and from 1835 until 1933 there was an inland all-water barge route from New York to Philadelphia via the Delaware-Raritan Canal.

This combination of factors would have been sufficient, in itself, to insure the port's popularity with shipping interests. But the harbor has another geographical virtue as well, equalling and at one time surpassing all others in economic significance. It is connected, by inland water routes, with the Great Lakes, Lake Champlain and the St. Lawrence River. The general and historical importance of this circumstance is clearly demonstrated by a simple statement of fact and a few well-worn statistics. New York is the only port on the Atlantic coast of the United States connected by waterways with the interior. In the decade 1811–20, before the Erie Canal (which completed the inland route to the interior) was opened, New York exports were valued at $88,000,000, as compared with $65,000,000 for South Carolina, which was second, and $50,000,000 each for Louisiana and Georgia. Between 1840 and 1851, as canal traffic steadily mounted, New York exports increased to $302,000,000; while the exports of South Carolina, its nearest rival on the Atlantic coast, amounted during the same period to $86,000,000, and those of Massachusetts to $76,000,000.

Given a harbor naturally magnificent, plus a great estuary located at "the seaboard portal of the best highway approach to the West," plus the Erie Canal linking that harbor with a fabulously wealthy interior, and the sum spelled immense advantage to trade. It is self-evident that trade attracts vessels and vessels attract trade. This is not necessarily an endless process; and it is, of course, subject to a multiplicity of other factors. But with the opening of the Erie Canal, New York decisively captured supremacy from her rival ports. She retains that supremacy today, on a scale beyond comparison in the western hemisphere.

Radius of the Port

Before surveying that colossus, the New York waterfront, it may be advisable to glance briefly at the map in order to understand exactly what constitutes the Port of New York. Your average New Yorker thinks of the shores of Manhattan and Brooklyn, and lets it go at that. But not so the scientific student of port affairs.

Considered as an economic unit, the Port of New York embraces the entire area within a 25-mile radius of the Statue of Liberty. It extends westward beyond the Passaic River and southward beyond Perth Amboy in New Jersey, farther than Jamaica Bay on the east, northward to Tarrytown on the Hudson River, and as far as Port Chester on Long Island Sound. This territory of more than 1,500 square miles, with a population of between 11 and 12 million persons, contains some 40,000 industrial establishments, which produce annually goods valued at about $8,000,000,000. Altogether, the port district ranks as the country's greatest commercial, financial and residential community.

Rail and Road

Serving this community overland are upwards of 300 motor truck lines and 10 great trunk line railroads, competing thunderously for the millions of tons of freight dumped and loaded on port district shores annually. The importance of these railroad systems in the port economy cannot be overemphasized. Shipping in the port constitutes the right arm of the giant organism, and railroad transport is the left. Deprived of one or the other, the organism would be disastrously crippled.

As another glance at our map will show, the difficulties of railroad freight distribution in the port district are enormous. The Cyclopean body of the metropolis was conceived on Manhattan Island. As it grew and became cramped in these narrow confines it spread, perversely, not to the mainland but to Brooklyn and Long Island. This anatomy was reasonably in harmony with the times in which it was molded. But under the conditions and demands of a voracious and prolific hinterland, whose very life-blood flowed through railway arteries, it was bound to be an exasperatingly inefficient structure. Long before railroads appeared on the scene, shipping had taken root on the east bank of the Hudson, next to the center of population. In order to reach this rich source of revenue and compete successfully with canal and river carriers, the railroads had no alternative but to occupy the west bank of the Hudson and go nautical. Rails cannot be laid on a river, but they can be bolted to a scow. And freight can be transferred to lighters. Thus the Port of New York's free lighterage and carfloat system, which makes every dock in the port available to every railroad in the port, came into being. We shall have occasion to consider this system later.

The first railroad to connect the port with the interior, the New York Central, alone succeeded in establishing passenger and freight terminal facilities on Manhattan Island. Most of the great railroads that followed had to accept the Jersey shore as the end of their lines and, as indicated above, very grave maritime responsibilities for the delivery of freight. The consequent investment in terminals, classification yards, pier stations, towing vessels, float bridges, carfloats, lighters, barges, ferries and other marine equipment runs into hundreds of millions of dollars.

The complexities and ramifications of railroad transportation in the port district require far more extended discussion than is possible here. Elsewhere in our survey of harbor activity we shall find it necessary to outline certain phases of railroad marine operations. It is sufficient now to note that in the development of Port of New York's waterfront, railroads have played a part that equals and may even exceed that of the strictly seagoing enterprises.

The Waterfront

We have already alluded to the magnitude of the New York waterfront. In order to enjoy a close-up view of its vast contours, we should need a launch capable of turning up some 16 miles per hour, with provisions and gasoline for a 48-hour run. This would be the equivalent of a voyage from Sandy Hook to Savannah, Georgia—a rather exhausting journey, even if it were done in easy stages. A much more convenient, if not quite so comprehensive, concept of the waterfront can be gained from a few statistics.

Of the 771 miles of direct shoreline fringing Port of New York bays and waterways, 578.4 miles are waterfront boundaries of the five boroughs of New York City. Measured around the 1,800 piers, wharves and bulkheads in the port, developed waterfrontage covers 350 miles. The city's share of this stretch of developed frontage is about 285 miles, including a greater frontage on deep water, probably, than any other port in the world—certainly greater than that of any other port in the United States. Along the waterfront of the city proper are more than 700 piers and wharves, from 50 to 1,700 feet in length, some of them antiquated, but many ultra-modern and equipped to accommodate the world's largest steamships. Of these piers about 270 are owned by the city, 410 are privately owned, 27 belong to the Federal Government and nine to the State. The New York City holdings are concentrated along the Manhattan waterfront for the most part, although certain sections of the Brooklyn and Staten Island waterfronts also belong to the city. A few of the city-owned piers are reserved for departmental and public use; most of them are leased for five-year periods to railroad and steamship companies. Rentals on piers such as those comprising the new Transatlantic Terminal from West Forty-Eighth to Fifty-Fourth Streets run as high as $200,000 annually. Smaller piers, of the type used by the railroads, rent for about $40,000 a year.

State ownership of waterfront property in the city is limited to the barge canal terminals in each of the boroughs, except Staten Island. Federal Government waterfront property includes the Navy Yard and the Army Base in Brooklyn, and the Staten Island lighthouse basin. Several islands in the harbor and the shoreline of a number of army reservations are also owned by the Federal Government.

The extent and distribution of New York City's shoreline holdings are best indicated by the following figures: Along the Hudson (North) River waterfront of Manhattan the city owns 12 miles of a total of 13.33 miles; along the East River waterfront of Manhattan and the Bronx, 7.9 miles of a total of 13.3 miles; and on the East River waterfront of Brooklyn and Queens, 2.4 miles of a total of 27.7 miles.

Private ownership of waterfront property is nearly at a minimum along the North River-Manhattan waterfront, totaling only 1.2 miles; on the East River waterfront of Queens and Brooklyn it totals more than 23 miles.

Hub of the Port

The North River waterfront of Manhattan is the most valuable and intensively developed section of the port. It unquestionably ranks, in this respect, with any similar area in the great ports of the world. Here are located the terminals of most of the express lines in the European passenger service; the terminals of the lines engaged in South American, West Indian and coastwise service; and the pier stations of eight major trunk line railroads. There are no large industrial establishments along the North River waterfront, almost the entire section being devoted to passenger and freight facilities.

This area contains more than 110 piers, 24 ferry slips, and 8 float bridges, where freight cars are transferred from shore tracks to carfloats and vice versa. Between 25 and 30 of the total number of piers are used in foreign or intercoastal trade, a few more than 40 in domestic trade, and about 40 serve the railroads. Since most of the latter are south of Fifty-Ninth Street, these figures reveal one of the troublesome problems created

Education and Science

EDUCATION WITHOUT TUITION: NEW YORK LIBRARY

ALMA MATER, COLUMBIA UNIVERSITY

LIBRARY AND CHAPEL, COLUMBIA UNIVERSITY

CAMPUS OF CITY COLLEGE, WHERE STUDENTS TAKE LIFE AND POLITICS
SERIOUSLY

EDUCATION BY OBSERVATION: BROOKLYN BOTANIC GARDENS AND
(below) THE ZOO IN CENTRAL PARK

BUILDINGS OF THE COLUMBIA PRESBYTERIAN MEDICAL CENTER, IN
UPPER MANHATTAN OVERLOOKING THE HUDSON

EAST SIDE PUBLIC SCHOOL

Above: ENTRANCE HALL, BROOKLYN MUSEUM. *Below:* A ROOM IN THE
AMERICAN WING, METROPOLITAN MUSEUM

THE UNIVERSE BROUGHT TO EARTH: HAYDEN PLANETARIUM

THE NEW SCHOOL FOR SOCIAL RESEARCH: TWENTIETH CENTURY ADULT
EDUCATION

by railroad marine operations. Forty percent of the most valuable steamship frontage along the West Side of Manhattan—perhaps the most valuable in the whole port district—is devoted to railroad freight operations having no direct relation to shipping. This state of affairs was made inevitable, of course, by the fierce competition among common carriers for the large volume of domestic freight consigned to Manhattan Island.

A primary task of the Port of New York Authority was to bring about a consolidation of the many duplications of service that sprang from this carrier competition, so that deepwater frontage might be released for ocean terminals. In spite of considerable effort by the Port Authority to accomplish this end, progress has been hampered by various factors, not the least of which is the sharp rivalry among carriers. Eventual solution of this problem may well rest with the fate of legislation proposing national consolidation of the rail systems.

Ever since the opening of the present century, steamship operators and the city government have been confronted with the problem of supplying adequate berthage, in close proximity to railroad passenger terminals and hotels, for ships that are constantly increasing in number and size. The general progress in this direction is demonstrated by the fact that approximately half of the steamship piers in the port can accommodate oceangoing ships. This means that more than 100 miles of side wharfage are available for deepwater berthage. A few years ago it was estimated that new dock construction in the Port of New York in a single year equalled the entire deepwater dockage of Portland, Maine. Since 1920, between 75,000 and 80,000 feet of wharfage have been constructed for ocean steamship use. At the present time the city is proceeding with a comprehensive plan for the development of its North River property. Several modern pier projects are in progress or nearing completion.

Along the East River waterfront of Manhattan and the Bronx there are 108 piers, 16 ferry slips and eight carfloat bridges, as well as nearly 100 bulkheads and shore wharves. The piers along the Manhattan waterfront of the East River comprise approximately 90 of the total, but only about seven of these are used in foreign trade. A few of the piers are employed in the coastwise freight trade, and about 20 are used by the railroads.

We have already had occasion to mention the role of South Street in the city's development. The East River waterfront of Manhattan was, of course, the nucleus of the port. For the student of American merchant marine history, this stretch of beach swarms with the phantoms of famous clippers and the ghosts of the men who built them. But the forests of towering masts and jaunty bowsprits that shaded South Street in the clipper ship era have disappeared forever. Only a handful of ocean-going vessels continue to dock in this area, barely keeping alive South Street's 19th century packet tradition. Although it has a deep channel, the East River is narrow and handicapped by treacherous tidal currents—conditions poorly suited to the docking problems of a modern super-ship. Various industrial and other establishments, ranging from gas and slaughter houses to hospitals and luxurious apartment hotels, have covered the retreat of shipping from this area.

A large percentage of the 196.8 miles of Queens Borough shoreline is undeveloped. But the banks of Newtown Creek, which separate Brooklyn from Long Island City, are crowded with a conglomeration of industrial plants, and harbor activity in this region is particularly marked.

The most intensively developed portion of Brooklyn's 201.5 miles of waterfront extends from the mouth of Newtown Creek south to Bay Ridge. This area is occupied almost entirely by facilities for ocean-going cargo carriers, intraport lighterage and railroad carfloatage. Passenger and freight terminals of steamship lines to all parts of the world, hundreds of large industrial plants, dozens of warehouses, as well as the most extensive dry-docking and ship repair facilities in the port, are in this section.

Most important among the developments along this stretch of the Brooklyn shore are: (1) Brooklyn Eastern District Terminal, one of the principal warehousing and freight transfer enterprises in the port. Various commercial and industrial concerns make use of its facilities, foremost among which are carfloat connections with all the major trunk line railroads. (2) Jay Street Terminal, nine piers comprising 91,000 feet of side wharfage, one float bridge and more than 1,000,000 square feet of warehouse space. (3) New York Dock Company Terminal, extending for a distance of 2.5 miles along Buttermilk Channel and consisting of the Fulton, Baltic and Atlantic Terminals. In addition to its 27 piers and two float bridges, the New York Dock Company development includes 89 warehouses and 91 factories, 35 miles of track and a fleet of 50 motor trucks. Nearly 25 percent of the entire ocean freight tonnage of the port moves through the company's property. (4) Erie Basin, one of the oldest terminals in the port, which comprises ten piers—three of them more than 1,000 feet in length—several warehouses, a sugar refinery, and ship repair establishments ranking with the greatest in the country. We shall come back to these later. (5) The New York State Grain Elevator, operated by the State of New York in conjunction with the Barge Canal

Terminal adjoining it. This elevator has a storage capacity of 2,000,000 bushels. (6) Bush Terminal, one of the major docking, storage and industrial developments in the world. Behind its eight piers, offering side wharfage for 35 average-size steamers, are approximately 140 warehouses and industrial loft buildings, served by a marginal railway affording 35 miles of trackage and carfloat connections with all trunk line railroads. It has been estimated that 20 percent of the entire export and import traffic moving through the port is handled at this terminal.

Like the Borough of the Bronx, Staten Island's role in the port economy is rather modest. Except for the Kill van Kull waterfront and certain sections between Brighton and Rosebank, its 57.1 miles of direct shoreline are largely undeveloped. The unfortunate chance whereby the large-scale waterfront enterprise of the port has, comparatively speaking, avoided the Borough of Richmond, is one of destiny and geography. Whereas the Dutch preferred Manhattan in the 17th century, the railroad and steamship lines in the 20th prefer the shortest path between two points. Staten Island, in short, is somewhat out of the way; traffic lanes point in other directions. The late Mayor Hylan attempted to challenge this scheme of things, but his accomplishments were regarded by New Yorkers at large as a monument to his lack of business acumen. The 13 piers constructed by his administration along the Stapleton waterfront at a cost of $30,000,-000 were promptly dubbed "Hylan's Folly," for the ocean-going vessels they were built to accommodate did not materialize.

However, if "Hylan's Folly" failed to reshape Staten Island's destiny, his project is scheduled finally to obtain at least a measure of its original objective. The Federal Government approved four of these piers as a terminal for the Foreign Trade Zone opened in 1937 in the Port of New York. The announcement of this decision was made by the Secretary of Commerce on January 29, 1936. Under the terms of the act authorizing this zone, the first in the United States, goods may be brought into the restricted area from any foreign country, without passing through the cumbersome red tape of customs inspection; they may be processed or stored within the zone, and then passed through American customs or transshipped to a foreign country. Responsible authorities maintain that the zone will eventually prove of incalculable value to the Port of New York.

Flanking the Foreign Trade Zone are the only two private terminals on Staten Island—the American Dock Terminal, consisting of four piers and 31 factory and storage structures, which have the advantage of being served directly by standard-gauge railway trackage, connecting by way of the B. & O. Staten Island system with the major trunk lines; and the Pouch Terminal, which has three piers and 25 factory and warehouse units, also served directly by the B. & O.

Although the New Jersey waterfront is an inseparable part of the whole port organism, extended treatment of its ramifications belongs in a survey of common carriers in the port. This is not to say that New Jersey's part in ocean-going trade is negligible. Indeed, a number of outstanding steamship lines operating out of the port maintain terminals in Jersey City, Hoboken, Weehawken or Newark.

Considered from the point of view of foreign commerce, however, the Brooklyn and Manhattan waterfronts are by far the most strategic. The great majority of the passenger lines employ terminals on Manhattan Island; most of the freight lines operate from Brooklyn.

Close to 200 vessels of one kind or another tie up at the piers and wharves of the port every day. An analysis of the distribution of inbound ships on a typical day, made by the Port of New York Authority, shows that more than one-third, or 36 percent, docked in Brooklyn and nearly one-quarter were berthed in Manhattan, while 16 percent docked along the principal sections of the Jersey waterfront—Hoboken, Jersey City, Bayonne, and so forth.

Approximately 90 steamship lines are engaged in foreign trade out of the Port of New York. Operating for the most part on regular schedules and with frequent sailings, they supply the shipper and importer with direct service to and from the major ports of Europe, South America, the West Indies, Africa, India, Australia and New Zealand. Many of the world's outposts are also reached by steamers operating regularly out of New York. In addition to fast freight service, many of these lines offer passenger service and vacation cruise itineraries duplicated at no other American port. Some 25 lines operate vessels accommodating passengers to the more important ports of Europe and the Near East. Nine lines are engaged in regular passenger service to Africa, the Far East and around the world; and about 18 lines maintain passenger vessels on regular schedules and cruises to ports in the West Indies, South America and Canada.

Since 90 percent of the sailings on these itineraries are *direct* (no intermediate calls at other domestic ports), New York appeals particularly to exporters of high-grade manufactured goods and importers of quality merchandise, as well as to overseas travelers. In consequence, this port has become the gateway for approximately 50 percent by value of the foreign trade of the United States and 85 percent of the country's foreign passenger traffic.

In addition to the steamship companies operating vessels in foreign trade, there are seven lines in the intercoastal or Pacific Coast service. Passenger accommodations are available on four of these intercoastal lines, with facilities ranging from the "luxury" type on Dollar liners to the informal one-class type on Luckenbach freighters. At least seven steamship companies operate vessels to ports on the Atlantic seaboard and the Gulf; and a few lines dispatch freight vessels to Sound and inland points.

Waterborne Commerce

The amount and value of the commodities dumped on New York piers every year by vessels engaged in foreign and domestic trade are enormous; and the commodities they take away are only a little less considerable. Let the figures for the calendar year 1936 tell the story.

During the course of that year, 13,479,929 tons of commodities of almost every conceivable kind, valued at $2,913,001,116, were landed in the Port of New York out of the holds of ships from foreign ports. With deduction for gold and silver shipments valued at $1,149,225,000 that were included among the 48,784 tons of "precious metal" imports, the value of merchandise and raw materials brought into the port during 1936 amounted to $1,763,776,116. Compared with the Philadelphia port district imports of 4,765,115 tons valued at $169,207,820, Baltimore's imports of 4,519,970 tons worth $70,777,740; and the imports of the entire San Francisco Bay area imports of 959,688 tons worth $98,006,187, during the same calendar year, the colossal character of the port's import business becomes readily apparent.

In the sphere of export trade the port's national supremacy is likewise unchallenged. While the San Francisco Bay area was exporting 2,462,131 tons valued at $102,937,822, Baltimore 765,600 tons worth $14,907,322, and the Philadelphia port district 1,159,903 tons valued at $62,454,393, the Port of New York loaded 5,926,044 tons of cargo worth $1,130,891,-305 (exclusive of gold and silver) on foreign-bound ships. The high quality of merchandise exported from the Port of New York is revealed by the fact that while tonnage volume was considerably less than one-half the volume of imports, the total value of exports was nearly two-thirds the total value of imports.

In round numbers, the entire foreign trade of the port during 1936 amounted to 19,400,000 tons, with a total valuation of $2,894,000,000. During the same period, the total waterborne foreign commerce of the entire United States, again in round numbers and excluding gold and silver, amounted to 90,000,000 tons valued at $5,307,000,000. Thus in the calendar year 1936, the Port of New York handled approximately 54 percent by value and 21 percent by volume of the nation's grand total of foreign maritime commerce.

In the field of domestic waterborne commerce, traffic in the port attained even more enormous proportions. No less than 91,291,715 tons of everything from adrenalin to zwieback, having a total valuation of $4,969,671,721, moved through the port during 1936. In comparison, the entire waterborne commerce, *both foreign and domestic,* of the Philadelphia port district amounted to 34,171,000 tons, valued at $1,081,800,-000; the entire waterborne commerce of the San Francisco Bay area was 25,685,000 tons, valued at $1,062,177,000; and Baltimore's entire waterborne commerce was 21,886,000 tons valued at $695,838,000—a combined total of 81,742,000 tons of waterborne freight worth $2,839,815,-000. These three ports certainly cannot be called sluggards, but their total waterborne commerce was exceeded by the Port of New York's domestic waterborne traffic alone.

There are four general types of domestic waterborne commerce: (1) coastwise, (2) internal, (3) intraport, (4) local. *Coastwise* traffic, of course, is self-explanatory, but brief definitions of the other types may be necessary. *Internal* traffic refers to traffic between a port and an inland point via a tributary waterway, such as the Hudson River. *Intraport* traffic is that between the several arms or channels of a port—i.e., traffic involving the use of more than one channel or waterway. Traffic between Brooklyn and the North River waterfront, or between Hoboken and the East River waterfront, for example, is intraport traffic; the use of more than one channel is involved in these movements. *Local* traffic refers to freight movements involving the use of no more than one harbor channel or waterway. Thus, traffic across the North River between Manhattan and Weehawken, or across the East River between Manhattan and Brooklyn, is local.

Of chief importance in 1936, with respect to both value and volume, was the port's coastwise traffic. Receipts attained the tremendous total of 28,554,604 tons, valued at $1,186,430,648. Shipments came to 7,608,499 tons, valued at $1,000,109,270. Coastwise tonnage was 32.6 percent of the entire waterborne tonnage of the port—nearly double the foreign traffic tonnage, which amounted to 17.5 percent of the total.

Next in value and tonnage were intraport shipments and receipts, totaling 34,810,231 tons valued at $1,751,214,961. This traffic constituted about 31.4 percent of the port's total waterborne volume of freight.

Local traffic followed, with 14,129,888 tons, or about 13 percent of the total waterborne tonnage, valued at $862,846,490.

The final category, internal traffic, accounted for only 5.6 percent of the total waterborne tonnage, or 6,188,493 tons, valued at $169,070,352. Since the origin or destination of most of this freight was the New York State Barge Canal System, it may be permissible to discuss briefly, at this point, the relation of the canal system to port economy. As previously noted, Erie Canal commerce played a decisive part in the early development of New York as a city and port. The importance of the canal diminished rapidly, however, after the appearance of the New York Central Railroad on the scene. By 1873 the New York Central was carrying as much tonnage as the canal; by 1884 it was carrying twice as much; and in 1915 it transported 64,000,000 tons of freight, as compared with about 2,000,000 tons handled by the canal system.

Traffic on the barge canals has been increasing steadily since 1919, when it amounted to only 1,238,844 tons. The present volume represents a rise of approximately 500 percent over the bottom of 1919. Despite rate cutting tactics—favorite and efficient bludgeon used by the rail systems to squelch competing canal operators—the canal system is regaining a constantly increasing quantity of bulk freight from the common carriers.

If present plans of the State of New Jersey to widen, deepen and reopen the Delaware and Raritan Canal under Federal auspices should materialize, a general resurgence of internal water-transportation in the New York area may very conceivably develop. Certain shippers would unquestionably regard with favor an inland water route linking the Great Lakes with Baltimore and points in the South. Such a route would benefit the New York State Barge Canal System, but the port's coastwise traffic would be affected, since the projected canal would shorten by 264 miles the present voyage from New York to Baltimore.

Returning to the subject of Port of New York's waterborne commerce, and recapitulating: During the calendar year 1936, 110,697,688 tons of cargo valued at $7,864,339,142 moved over the waters of New York Harbor. During the same period, all waterborne cargoes moving through

Houston, Texas, Baltimore, the San Francisco Bay area and the Philadelphia port district totaled 105,543,787 tons and were valued at $3,459,-235,455. In other words, although the Port of New York moved only 5,153,901 more tons of cargo, the total tonnage handled had nearly twice the value of the combined cargoes moved by the other four ports.

A glance at a small cross-section of the mountainous cargoes passing through the port is not without interest.

Unusually large exports in 1936 included the following: 872,000 tons of general merchandise, 467,000 tons of motor vehicles and parts, 641,000 tons of wheat, 258,000 tons of flour and meal, 197,000 tons of hay and feed, 169,000 tons of kerosene and gasoline, 546,000 tons of lubricating oil and grease, 277,000 tons of iron and steel manufactures, 107,000 tons of coal-tar products, 135,000 tons of copper manufactures and 450,000 tons of scrap iron. The smallest export item was one ton of mats and matting.

Conspicuous in the vast bulk of imports poured into New York docks during 1936 were the following: more than 4,500,000 tons of petroleum products, 735,000 tons of coffee, tea, cocoa and cocoa beans, 535,000 tons of fruits and nuts, 905,000 tons of raw sugar, 346,000 tons of flaxseed, 309,000 tons of paper manufactures, 263,000 tons of inedible vegetable oils, 101,000 tons of bags and bagging, 217,000 tons of wood pulp, 366,000 tons of gypsum, 358,000 tons of iron ore, 414,000 tons of crude rubber. Cargoes of almost every commodity and raw material under the sun followed the above in varying volumes. The smallest import was airplanes and parts, 6 tons; the next smallest was office appliances, 14 tons.

"Duty-Free" Imports

The only commodities brought into the port from foreign lands during 1936 of which there is no record were smuggled goods. The total value and volume of this traffic were probably unimpressive.

Time was when smuggling was a highly respectable practice in New York and its environs, some of the city's most reputable citizenry not only encouraging this practice but even participating in it on occasion. There is no question that many early New York fortunes were erected on such a basis. How vigorously smuggling once flourished in this area is indicated by the state of affairs that prevailed at Oyster Bay early in the 18th century. The Customs Officer, who received 30 pounds as salary and one-third of all seizures, begged to be relieved of his duties; for although most of the inhabitants were relatives of his, he had been threatened with bodily violence.

Nowadays the United States Treasury Department, through the Commissioner of Customs and a special staff of agents, keeps a vigilant eye on duty-evasion rackets in the port, which fall into four general categories. Least spectacular are the *drawback fraud* and *undervaluation*. The former is a method employed by dishonest commercial firms to collect illegally the refund of import duty allowed by law on certain raw materials that have been processed or made into manufactured articles. "Undervaluation" is chiefly practiced by returning globe-trotters, but even large-scale importers have been known to indulge in it.

The most spectacular duty-evasion rackets are classified as *miscellaneous* and *narcotics*. Under *miscellaneous* fall such practices as the smuggling of watch-movements, diamonds, etc. Recent tariff revisions have deprived the watch-movement racket of its lucrative character, but illicit traffic in high-quality optical equipment, such as binoculars and cameras, has been increasing. Although diamond smuggling remains a constant challenge, "Miscellaneous Division" agents in the port dealt the trade a severe blow in 1937 when they seized more than $200,000 worth of gems in a single haul.

The narcotic traffic is most vexing of all. Usually operated by syndicates or big-time mobsters, this traffic is not necessarily checked for long by apprehension of the carriers. In spite of the strictest vigilance, a certain flow of drugs into the port is inevitable. Seizures and arrests are frequent, however; during the fiscal year that ended June 1937, drugs—mostly opium—valued at approximately $2,350,000 were seized in the port district.

Handling the Cargoes

The main bulk of New York's waterborne freight moves, of course, through the normal channels of trade; and when this deluge of freight descends on the waterfront, processes far more involved and impressive than duty evasion are brought into motion. To the uninitiated, the result is chaos and bedlam. The discharge, loading and transfer of waterborne freight are accompanied, indeed, by great confusion and travail. But the latter are surface phenomena. Beneath tumult and turmoil the waterfront functions with the smoothness and precision of a new Diesel engine.

Consider the following: During 1935, 21,589 cargo carriers of all types and sizes passed through Ambrose Channel. (Figures showing similar traffic bound in and out via East River are not available.) In their cabins were 1,106,260 passengers; in their holds was an overwhelming proportion of the port's 55,569,076 tons of foreign and coastwise freight. The great majority of these carriers arrived and sailed on schedule time.

This remarkable accomplishment was made possible by the highly co-ordinated activities of three armies of labor: one inland, one alongshore and one afloat. Equipped with tens of thousands of trucks, the inland army storms the waterfront from near and far, bombarding it with freight and being bombarded in return. Making use of a harbor fleet second to none, the army afloat storms the waterfront from every point of the compass, likewise bombarding it with freight and being bombarded in return. Finally, equipped with more freight-handling machinery than is available in any other port in the world, the alongshore army stands on the docks between, giving and taking in both directions, and maintaining in addition a private feud with the ships. On the shoulders of this "middle" army of longshoremen, numbering from 30,000 to 40,000, rests the heavy and dangerous responsibility of moving freight into and out of the cargo carriers.

The port's supply of machinery for this work consists chiefly of esca-lators, trailers, skids, and lift-trucks. The lift-trucks, of which there are well in excess of 1,000 in the port, are usually electrically operated, rubber-tired and self-loading. They can be turned in their own length, and are fitted with special equipment such as small crane hoists, cradles, tiering apparatus, chisel prongs and newsprint scoops. With the last-named appliance, newsprint rolls weighing 1,700 pounds can be automatically tiered three high. These trucks are also used to shuttle trailer and skid loads of freight about the docks and warehouses. The number of trailers and skids in the port has been estimated at 150,000.

Cargo is transferred from the lower holds of ships to pier or lighter by the ship's tackle and winches. Some 50 piers are equipped with special cargo masts. For use in handling extra-heavy cargo, 150 floating hoists are on call in the harbor, together with 70 floating derricks, some of them built to handle weights up to 300 tons.

In spite of this mechanization, or perhaps because of it, longshoremen in the port nurse many grievances. "Speed-up" causes the loudest and most frequent complaint. Others include (1) the "shape-up" system of hiring, which is said to breed favoritism and the "kick-back" or buying of jobs; (2) excessive "sling-loads," dangerously heavy load hoists out of the hold; and (3) the 44-hour week. The loudest demand is for "West Coast conditions," which include: (1) union hiring halls and the rotation system of hiring; (2) 2,100-pound maximum sling load; and (3) the 30-hour week.

Completely organized in the International Longshoremen's Association, Port of New York longshoremen are under conservative American Federation of Labor leadership. While rank and file sentiment (1937) looked toward the swelling Committee for Industrial Organization tide, ILA officialdom dropped its anchor and prepared for storm.

As figures already cited will indicate, 48,940,000 tons, or about 44 percent of New York's waterborne commerce, is strictly inner harbor traffic, classified as intraport and local freight movements. The operation of this traffic requires, as has been pointed out, a harbor fleet second to none.

This fleet numbers no fewer than 6,000 barges, scows, lighters, carfloats and tugs, and the "army afloat" that mans it approximates 15,000 men. Functioning on the port's water highways as efficiently as switching engines on a railroad belt line, this harbor fleet is indispensable for the distribution of general freight, food products and building materials throughout the port district.

These operations are conducted by scores of private firms and eight of the great trunk-line railroads—the Central Railroad of New Jersey, the Baltimore & Ohio, the Lehigh Valley, the Pennsylvania, the Erie, the Delaware, Lackawanna & Western, the New York Central and the New York, New Haven & Hartford. In addition to *lighterage* (towed barges that have been loaded from freight cars or terminals), the railroad lines employ *carfloatage* (towed barges carrying freight cars on rails) as a means of harbor freight transfer. Carfloats may transfer freight cars via float bridges to the tracks of terminals, such as Bush and New York Dock; or they may tie up alongside a pier or ship. Much to the annoyance of competing ports, both services are performed by the railroads without extra cost to the consignor or consignee, since they are merely the equivalent of terminal extensions of the carriers' rails.

Lighterage service in the harbor may originate at any of the following general points: (1) rail terminals; (2) local points; (3) vessels from foreign ports; (4) vessels from coastwise ports; (5) vessels from internal ports. Since traffic may move from each of these general points of departure to each of the other four and to destinations identical with the point of departure itself (with two exceptions: "local" and "vessels from internal ports," which naturally dispatch lighterage only to each of the other four), there is a total of 23 possible forms of lighterage freight-transfer in the port. All of which helps to explain the endless and discordant whistling and lowing of New York harbor craft. The infinite possible combinations of lighterage routes intersect at an infinite possible number of points, and the result is a kind of efficient bedlam in mid-channel.

Railroad marine equipment in New York Harbor represents an investment of $35,000,000 in 150 towboats, 323 carfloats, 1,094 lighters and barges and 44 ferryboats. This fleet is manned by 3,400 men. Carfloats from 257 to 360 feet long, some of them carrying 23 cars, float a monthly average of 75,000 freight cars loaded with about 940,000 tons of miscellaneous freight. In this connection, it should be noted that carfloat freight tonnage is not included in the "local" and "intraport" statistics previously cited in this article.

The magnitude of private and industrial lighterage operations in the harbor is indicated by the fact that more than 500 tugs are owned by towboat and lighterage companies; about 50 by oil, coal and terminal companies; and 20 more by steamship companies. Although tugboats are generally associated with the drama of ocean liner sailings and arrivals, this is but a minor phase of their role in port economy. In addition to the lighterage and carfloat towing duties already mentioned, their work includes removal of waste material, wrecking and salvage operations, transfer of ships from pier to pier or from pier to drydock, towing of cargoes to coastwise and internal ports, and so forth. Docking the *Normandie* is merely a detail in the average work week of a towboat.

Shipbuilding

Between the close of the War of 1812 and the outbreak of the Civil War, shipbuilding in the port of New York rivaled and possibly outranked even the shipping industry. More correctly, perhaps, these were facets of the same gem: an increase in the luster of one added to the brilliance of the other. In those days, American cargoes were carried in American ships. The East River yards were known the world over for the quality and numbers of packet and clipper ships sliding down their ways. There was a world demand for East River products, and tens of thousands of skilled artisans labored in the vicinity of South Street to supply it.

The Civil War drove American shipping from the seas and New York's shipyards into oblivion. Except for a brief upsurge during and shortly after the World War, American shipping in general and New York construction in particular have drifted in the doldrums.

Facilities for ship construction in the port, however, are still plentiful. Disregarding those of the United States Navy Yard, the city proper contains 26 shipbuilding plants. Four of the largest in the United States are in Brooklyn; and several other large yards operate on the Kill van Kull waterfront in Staten Island. But except for some city ferryboat and naval destroyer work during 1935-7, new construction in the port area has been limited in recent years to scows, barges and a few towboats.

Although 15,000 workers are engaged in this industry in the port area, the majority of them are employed on ship repairs. The fact that most of the yards in the port are accessible for ship repair work has naturally increased the popularity of the port among ship operators. Special equipment and skilled mechanics are always available in the event of damaged hulls or machinery. Drydocking facilities include 50 floating docks, six of which can handle ships of 10,000 to 27,000 tons. In addition there are two commercial graving docks, one of which can care for ships up to 713 feet in length. In case of an emergency in which no commercial drydock is available, the four graving docks at the Navy Yard may be used. All but a dozen of the largest ships afloat can be serviced at port drydocks.

In ship repair facilities, as in all other facilities related to the flow of water-borne commerce, the Port of New York is first in the United States.

The Port of New York Authority

New York's ascent to supremacy in the world of shipping and commerce was conditioned by the major factors of a superior physiographic situation plus the methods of hand-to-mouth commercial development. Long-range planning has been notably absent throughout the whole course of its development. The port just grew; and men hurried along in the wake of its growth, striving breathlessly to adjust old conditions to new situations. Inefficiency and waste in port economy were consequently inevitable.

Makeshift compromises with the demands of progress were permissible in the era of transition from Hudson River sloops to Hudson River steamboats. In the era of transition from side-wheelers to the steel leviathan, makeshift compromises were injurious to the best interests of the port. And since the contradictions thus engendered were aggravated in direct ratio to the growth of the whole organism, these compromises were bound to become downright dangers. The usurpation of valuable steamship frontage by competing common carriers is a case in point. The senseless duplication of harbor freight services, inevitably reflected in higher freight rates for the inland shipper, is another. These problems were in turn complicated by a more serious circumstance.

Although natural geography, as we have seen, especially favored the port, political geography has not been so kind. The Port of New York is an economic unit, but the harbor and district are divided by state lines. There were—and are—not only state rivalries to complicate matters; municipal jealousies flourished—and still flourish—as well. New Jersey fought for the Foreign Trade Zone; Port Newark demands a rate-differential on railroad freight. And looming in the background are the ambitious designs of other Atlantic and Gulf ports on New York's foreign commerce.

The compulsive need for a joint agency to correct the anarchies of port economy was finally recognized, and in 1921 the States of New York and New Jersey created a medium charged to protect their general mutual interests and to plan for the port's future.

A thorough discussion of this medium, the Port of New York Authority, is hardly possible within the limitations of this article. We have already had occasion to note its efforts to obtain the release of Manhattan railroad piers for steamship use. Several steps in this direction have been made, the most recent being the coordination of less-than-carload freight deliveries, initiated by the railroads in 1935 after 14 years of Port Authority agitation. In addition, the Authority has built in Manhattan a $16,000,000 union inland freight terminal which is served by the trucks of all the trunk line railroads.

Balked, on the whole, in its efforts to remedy the hardened harbor arteries, the Port Authority tackled the problem of efficient freight distribution through the port district from another angle. Since the motor truck was becoming an increasingly important factor in the delivery and pick-up of freight at the port piers, interstate highways by bridge and tunnel were the logical solution. Port Authority accomplishments in this field—the Holland and Lincoln Tunnels, the George Washington Bridge, the Outerbridge Crossing, the Goethals and Bayonne Bridges connecting Staten Island with New Jersey—are too well known to require comment here.

The organization's activities behind the scenes are less well known but no less vital. Port Authority lawyers are in the midst of a grim and bitter warfare that rages in the chambers of the Interstate Commerce Commission and elsewhere between the port and combinations of its eastern seaboard and Gulf rivals. Arguing that New York's great volume of foreign trade is due to certain unfair preferences and practices, these rivals are more or less continually initiating or preparing wholesale assaults on the railroad rate structures. Differentials of two and three cents per 100 pounds are already in the trophy rooms of Philadelphia and Baltimore respectively. New Orleans has differentials, and wants them improved. Galveston occupies a similar position. Even tiny Port Albany is frowning at New York. The warfare is deadly serious, of course; much of the port's bulk traffic has already been diverted to rival ports. New York's high-class freight traffic, however, is the coveted plum.

But the Port of New York, as we have demonstrated, is a Brobdingnagian structure, equipped with almost limitless facilities and resources. Whatever the outcome of the differential wars, it will long continue to be the outstanding port of call in the western world.

City in Motion

IN WHAT is perhaps its most striking general aspect, the island of Manhattan may well be likened to a gigantic ant-hill, teeming with an incessant and almost furious intensity of motion. Along the shadowed canyons of its streets, through vast stretches of tile-lined or whitewashed tunnels piercing its foundational rock, and over many miles of sky-effacing trestlework roars a ceaseless traffic of human freight exceeding in volume and density that of any like area in the world today.

Besides this centralized activity within the confines of Manhattan, there is a large and constant movement of traffic to and from the other boroughs of Greater New York. A river runs between Manhattan and the Bronx; another river cuts it off from Brooklyn and Queens; and the Upper Bay spreads out between Manhattan and Richmond. These barriers to land travel from borough to borough have resulted in an almost unbelievable concentration via ferries, bridges and tunnels, nearly all of which lead to Manhattan. There the greatest traffic flow of its kind in the world occurs twice each business day, this borough being the bottle-neck into which millions of passengers are poured between eight and nine in the morning, and from which these same millions are siphoned out again between five and six in the evening.

The public carriers involved in New York City's huge intracity passenger movement are: (1) Subway and elevated lines, the rapid transit system; (2) street surface railways; (3) motor buses; (4) taxicabs. For the year ending June 30, 1937, the combined traffic of all these carriers consisted of more than three billion passengers, or (reckoned on the basis of 340 "full traffic" days) a daily average of more than nine million. Of this total, approximately 60 percent was handled by the subway and elevated lines, 18 percent by street surface railways, 19 percent by motor buses, and three percent by taxicabs.

But for a complete picture of the "city in motion," one must take into account also the vast commuting army that like an ebbing and receding

346

tide daily flows into and out of New York; the horde of transient visitors, arriving and departing by railroad, bus, airplane and steamer; the hundreds of thousands of private motor cars and commercial trucks that throng the city thoroughfares. Some of the commuters and perhaps all of the transient visitors, while they are within the city, figure in the intracity passenger totals above cited. But in their coming and going, at any rate, these groups as a whole comprise a separate and very considerable element of traffic movement.

Highlights of Transit History

Traffic has been a matter of public concern in New York since the days of the Dutch, as is indicated by an ordinance of June 27, 1652, prohibiting "fast driving" and forbidding cartmen to stand or sit in their vehicles "except on the Broadway." Seventy-nine years later, the revised laws and ordinances of the English included regulations concerning "carts and cartmen" on the public highways; and in 1786, the first hackney coach, forerunner of today's taxicab, was introduced by James Hearn, whose stand was outside the historic coffee house at Old Slip.

Stages running at short intervals along regular routes included lines from Wall Street and the lower city to the Dry Dock, Greenwich Street, and Fourteenth Street; and from the Bowery and Bayard Street to Yorkville, Bloomingdale, Harlem and Manhattanville. There were more than 120 vehicles on all lines to and from Wall Street, some drawn by two and others by four horses. The fare below Fourteenth Street was generally 12½ cents; to Yorkville, 18¾ cents; and to Harlem and Manhattanville, 25 cents. On all days except Sunday, when the horses were permitted to rest, the average number of passengers carried was about 25,000. The rush period came between noon and three P.M., when merchants and others were returning to their homes for dinner. The hackney coaches in 1837 totaled more than 200; and fares, fixed by law, were 37½ cents for less than one mile and 50 cents for from one to two miles.

In Manhattan, horsecars were operated at this time by the New York & Harlem Railroad Company, which dispatched cars every 20 minutes from the Bowery, opposite Prince Street, to Harlem—a distance of seven miles. At first, mules were used as motive power, especially in Brooklyn, but they were abandoned later in favor of the more popular and less opinionated horse. Street cars were introduced in Brooklyn on July 3, 1854, by the Brooklyn City Railroad, after New York had been using them for more than 20 years. These Brooklyn cars hauled a comparatively enormous traffic in the 1850's, the total in 1858 being 7,500,000 passengers, drawn from a population of only 225,000. After 1864, when the first open cars were introduced in Brooklyn, the popularity of horsecars and the consequent passenger totals steadily increased.

Meanwhile, in 1846, the Harlem Railroad was operating steam trains as well as individual horsecars, the latter running chiefly to Thirty-Second Street. Above that thoroughfare, steam power was permitted. Schedules show that cars were dispatched from City Hall to Twenty-Seventh Street at six-minute intervals throughout the day and every 20 minutes throughout the night, at a fare of 6¼ cents; to Harlem, every hour during the day, at a fare of 12½ cents; and to White Plains, four times daily at a fare of 50 cents. Below Twenty-Eighth Street, transportation facilities in 1846 consisted chiefly of 12 lines of omnibuses, operating 258 vehicles.

By 1860, six street railroad lines were running horsecars and steam trains on a city-wide five-cent fare; and 16 omnibus companies controlled 544 licensed stages over fixed routes to all parts of the city below Fiftieth Street, as well as to neighboring villages, at a six-cent fare.

The need for better transit facilities was reflected seven years later in the beginnings of elevated rapid transit. In 1867, an experimental half-mile of elevated track for a projected cable-operated road from the Battery to Yonkers was built, but it proved a failure. In 1875, the mayor was empowered to appoint a board of commissioners to study the problem of rapid transit. This board chose elevated railways as the best rapid transit medium, and selected Second, Third, Sixth and Ninth Avenues as routes for such railways.

On June 5, 1878, the Sixth Avenue elevated line was opened from Rector Street to Central Park; and in August 1878, the Third Avenue line was opened to Sixty-Seventh Street. Steam locomotives had been definitely selected as the motive power, much to the annoyance of the citizenry, who complained about soot, cinders and live coals dropping in the streets. In 1902, the elevated system did away with locomotives and live coal showers by electrifying all the lines.

In 1880, the lines on both sides of the city reached Harlem, about one year after all elevated properties in New York had been leased by the Manhattan Railway Company; and on January 1, 1903, the Interborough Rapid Transit Company, which was to operate the subways then being built, leased the Manhattan Company's elevated railroads for a term of 999 years.

Meanwhile, plans for subways were being proposed. In 1868, the New York Central Underground Railway Company was incorporated to build a line from City Hall to the Harlem River. It built nothing. In the same year, the Beach Pneumatic Transit Company was formed to carry parcels underground by means of compressed-air tubes, the terms of the incorporation being broadened the following year to include transportation of passengers. On February 26, 1870, the Beach Company completed and opened to the public an eight-foot brick tunnel under lower Broadway, between Murray and Warren Streets, as a one-block sample of the subway it proposed to construct under Broadway and Madison Avenue.

The experimental run with a car propelled by compressed air was successful, but engineers at that time regarded a railroad beneath the streets as unsound, and laymen lampooned the project in a popular song of the day. Beach and his subway were soon forgotten. Years later, when the first of the present systems was proposed, no less a figure than Russell Sage, millionaire Wall Street operator, declared: "New York people will never go into a hole to ride. . . . Preposterous!"

Cable traction for surface routes was introduced in 1885 on the 125th Street and Amsterdam Avenue lines, and this form of motive power was widely adopted within the next few years. The year 1885 also witnessed construction of the Broadway street-car line, after severe opposition had previously defeated the scheme. Work progressed rapidly, so that cars were being operated over the entire line from Bowling Green to Union Square by June 21, 1885; and omnibuses, which had been running on Broadway for many years, were now withdrawn—a situation that was to be reversed 51 years later.

In 1891, a State legislative act created the Board of Rapid Transit Railroad Commissioners. Three years later, this act was amended to provide for municipal ownership and construction of a rapid transit line, if the people approved such a move—as they did by a large majority. Soon thereafter, the commissioners laid out routes, despite opposition that included a test case to determine the constitutionality of the Rapid Transit Act. In its decision of July 28, 1896, the Appellate Division of the State Supreme Court declared the act constitutional.

Four years later, after continued legal and other opposition, the first subway contract was awarded to John B. McDonald. This contract was for the IRT route from City Hall northward through Manhattan and into the Bronx. It was dated February 21, 1900, about five months after the first electrification of street railways had been effected on the Third Avenue line, between Sixty-Fifth Street and the Harlem Bridge, as a forerunner of city-wide electrification. Even increased speed, however, did not solve the problem of congestion, which was indicated by New York's amazing passenger traffic as far back as 1903, when the number of street car and elevated passengers exceeded the total for all trunk line railroads in North and South America.

On March 24, 1900, ground was broken for the first subway at City Hall Park. On July 21, 1902, bids for the Brooklyn extension were opened and the contract awarded to the Belmont-McDonald syndicate, which was already building the original subway. In 1904, this original subway was opened from Brooklyn Bridge to 145th Street and Broadway on October 27, to 157th Street on October 12, and to West Farms on November 26. In 1905, it was extended farther northward to 180th Street in the Bronx via the Harlem River tunnel, and southward from Brooklyn Bridge to Bowling Green. In 1906, it moved northward in Manhattan as far as 221st Street. Two years later, the southward extension was completed to Borough Hall, Brooklyn, in January, and to Atlantic Avenue in May; while northward progress was made from 221st Street to 242d Street and Broadway, in the Bronx, present terminus of the IRT's West Side line.

Although these subway developments added materially to the city's rapid transit facilities, they were still not sufficient to keep pace with a constantly increasing population. The so-called "dual contracts" for further subway construction, signed on March 19, 1913, provided for a total trackage of 620 miles, as against 296 miles then in existence. The new or added facilities were to be built by the original subway company (the Interborough) and the Brooklyn Rapid Transit Company, this latter being the operator of the elevated railroads in Brooklyn and Queens. By 1916, subway congestion was such that 1,200,000 passengers were sometimes being transported daily by lines with a rated capacity of only 400,000 passengers a day. This congestion was noticeably reduced by southward extension of the IRT lines to Utica, Flatbush and Nostrand Avenues, Brooklyn, in 1920; by another extension to New Lots Avenue in 1924; and by completion of the Brooklyn-Manhattan Transit Corporation's new lines.

Greatest of all aids to improvement of the situation was the municipally constructed, owned and operated Independent system, the trunk line of which was opened on September 10, 1932, from 207th Street to Fulton Street in Manhattan. On February 1, 1933, the Independent's trunk line had been extended southward to Jay Street, Brooklyn, via the Cranberry Street tunnel; on October 7, 1933, it was carried to its terminus at Church

Avenue, Brooklyn; and on April 9, 1936, Independent trains began to operate publicly through the Rutgers Street tunnel from Manhattan to South Brooklyn.

In 1938, the Independent system was actively concerned with a large development designed to provide additional underground rapid transit, especially in Brooklyn. In Manhattan, construction of the Sixth Avenue line, planned to run from Eighth Street to Fifty-Third Street, was well under way, adding one more link to the world's largest municipally owned, constructed and operated rapid transit railroad.

Financial and Political Imbroglios

Underground rapid transit was not easily won in New York. The so-called traction lobby, representing the street car and elevated railroad interests, fought the idea vigorously, as it had fought other advances for more than half a century. Since 1832, when the introduction of horse-drawn street cars on metallic rails had demonstrated the possibility of profits in large-scale passenger traffic for a small per capita fee, the moneyed class had looked upon transportation as a matter to be handled between itself and the politicians. The latter, suddenly finding themselves in a position to grant or withhold a privilege for which certain interests were willing to pay a high price, developed what might charitably be termed the bargaining instinct. This was not surprising, for the idea that charters might be worth anything to the city itself did not develop for many years. On the contrary, transit operators were looked upon as benefactors, since they furnished cheap transportation in a period when that commodity was scarce.

The idea that private interests should pay to the city part of the profits they reaped as the result of charters took hold eventually, although even then the traction lobby defeated the purposes of bills introduced to that end by inserting the word "net" before "proceeds" and letting bookkeepers do the rest. This era of private ownership was at its height between 1865, when the first rapid transit bill was passed by the legislature, and 1880, when the elevated railroads were completed. The next 15 years—1880–95—have been termed "the era of public ownership" by James Blaine Walker, an authority on the subject. "During that time," Mr. Walker points out, "the perpetual and gratuitous franchise was abolished and the right of the public to build, pay for, own and if necessary operate street railroads was successfully asserted."

The change in sentiment toward municipal ownership did not dismay the traction lobby, which continued its obstructionist tactics. As far back as 1873, it had defeated a bill introduced in the legislature to authorize the city to build and operate a rapid transit railroad; and in 1888 it killed off Mayor Abram S. Hewitt's idea for a rapid transit set-up substantially the same as that later incorporated in the act passed by the legislature on May 22, 1894, after the voters had emphatically approved municipal ownership. In the 68 years from 1832 until 1900, when the people finally got their way, the graft in New York City rapid transit paralleled the legislative corruption of steam railroad financing in the State.

In 1894, the Board of Rapid Transit Railroad Commissioners was given State legislative authority to utilize the city's credit and to proceed on the basis of municipal ownership of the proposed subway. This aroused the street car and elevated railroad interests, whose lobby had already engineered legislation so drastic that only those able to command tremendous financial resources could hope to submit a bid on subways. Such action eliminated virtually all interests except those in control of—or in sympathy with those who controlled—the existing street railway and elevated properties.

The rapid transit commissioners were unquestionably honest men, but they were also conservatives who thought in terms of private enterprise and were not sympathetic toward the new-fangled notion of "municipal ownership." For six years after the rapid transit act had been amended in 1894, the commissioners were parties in fact, even against their wishes, to the time-killing tactics employed by street car and elevated railroad interests. Neither of these factions wanted an increase in transportation facilities. "The more congestion the bigger the dividends" was then a demonstrated fact, and the private capital that controlled the situation did not relish the idea of seeing its highly profitable congestion reduced by new facilities. Every possible obstruction was thrown in the way of the new legal machinery designed to put an end to, or at least to lessen, the congestion.

The traction interests were successful. Indeed, they were too successful, for they finally overreached themselves and produced that rare phenomenon—a thoroughly aroused public opinion. This was the result of three moves. First, the Metropolitan street railway interests asked bluntly for a perpetual franchise. Second, Mayor Van Wyck, who had been doing everything he could to help the street railway and elevated people, introduced an innocent-looking resolution before the rapid transit board, asking for power to contract for construction and operation of the proposed subway by private capital instead of on a municipal ownership basis, as then provided by law. Third, a bill was introduced in the State legislature to take municipal ownership out of the transit act and to give the rapid transit commissioners power to grant to the Metropolitan interests, without competition, a perpetual franchise for a subway, with the privilege of charging a ten-cent fare on express trains. Oddly enough, this bill was not noticed even by civic organizations until well on toward the end of the legislative session. When it was brought to light, however, the voters who had previously approved municipal ownership at the polls staged mass meetings such as New York had seldom seen before, and convinced the rapid transit commissioners that New Yorkers didn't intend to be put off any longer.

This result, however, by no means ended the efforts of powerful groups and individuals to manipulate New York's transportation necessities for their own private gain. The development of underground rapid transit during the early years of the present century was attended by much shady dealing on the part of financiers, contractors, and politicians; as was also, though on a smaller scale, the development of motor bus transportation in the 1920's.

Efforts Toward Unification

After the original subway was completed and opened, the Interborough Rapid Transit Company—which had withdrawn from a series of conferences with the Public Service Commission and the special Transit Committee appointed by the Board of Estimate and Apportionment to cooperate with the PSC—reentered the picture on February 12, 1912, with a new plan for city-wide rapid transit development. This reentry of the IRT displeased the Brooklyn Rapid Transit Company, which had no subways at that time but was making application to the State and city conferees for construction and operation of the proposed new lines. The issue was further sharpened by the fact that the Board of Estimate had formally notified the Public Service Commission that it would approve construction contracts on the proposed subways for operation by the Brooklyn company; and the BRT had signified its intention to operate the lines now being reconsidered for the IRT.

Thereupon a handsome battle-royal was staged between the two companies. For more than a year they fought to gain public support of their respective proposals. Finally, on March 19, 1913, the so-called dual contracts were executed, certain lines being apportioned to the Interborough, others to the Brooklyn company. Under these contracts the city was to get, among other things: (a) rentals from the companies; (b) taxes, etc.; (c) 12 percent of revenue for maintenance exclusive of depreciation; and (d) compensation for depreciation at the rate of five percent from the IRT and three percent from the BRT. Five cents was stipulated as the fare to be charged by both companies.

Almost from the day they were executed, the dual contracts, under which subway facilities were considerably expanded, have been a subject of bitter debate. This has resulted in the drafting of four major "unification plans" since 1931, all designed to "recapture" the subways for the city and to retain the five-cent fare. These plans differed so sharply in detail that agreement between the three parties concerned was virtually impossible.

"Unification" is a convenient term intended to describe the idea of putting all subways and elevateds, with their related properties, under one operating system. In 1937 there were two operating companies, the IRT and the Brooklyn-Manhattan Transit Corporation. Transfers between the trains or stations of one carrier and those of the other, or even between subway and elevated properties controlled by the same parent company, could not be effected without payment of an additional fare. Under unification, all lines would constitute one system and, as some proposals suggest, transfers to all lines would be possible at stated points on a single fare. Millions of words of testimony by experts have been recorded on this subject; but even the experts disagree among themselves, thus making it extremely difficult for the layman to understand the situation.

The first step, of course, is that the city must make arrangements to pay for the private holdings at once instead of at the stipulated expiration date of contracts under which these holdings are being operated by private interests. Today, the price to be paid depends upon the willingness of the private interests to terminate the operating contracts before the legal dates set therefor, at a price and under conditions that must be approved not only by the companies and the city but by the Transit Commission as well. So far, it has been impossible to secure agreement among these three parties.

As previously stated, four major unification plans have been proposed. In June 1931, Samuel Untermyer, special counsel to the Transit Commission, proposed a gross purchase price to the private interests of $489,804,-

000. In December 1931, the Transit Commission submitted its own tentative plan, the gross price being set at $474,500,000. On November 1, 1935, Samuel Seabury, special counsel to the Board of Estimate, and A. A. Berle, Jr., Chamberlain of the City of New York, submitted to the Board of Estimate the so-called Seabury-Berle report, proposing a gross price of $430,751,000, together with a "Memorandum of Understanding" between themselves as representatives of the Board of Estimate and "committees for the various classes of securities of Interborough Rapid Transit Company and Manhattan Railway Company." This understanding did not bind the city and the private security holders, but merely cited terms and conditions upon which final negotiations might be approached or based. On May 1, 1937, John J. Curtin, special counsel to the Transit Commission, reported to the commission on the Seabury-Berle Definitive Plan and the memorandum, and submitted his own alternative recommendations, fixing the gross price at $343,469,000.

As of June 30, 1937, the total stake of the city in privately operated subways owned by the city, as against the total stake of the private companies, was as follows:

	City	Private Interests
IRT	$180,890,000	$188,953,000
BMT	208,313,000	69,535,000
	389,203,000	258,488,000

In addition to the total of $389,203,000 shown above, the city also had $729,193,000 tied up in its own municipally-operated subway—the Independent System. Thus New York City's grand total stake in all subways was $1,118,396,000.

Analysis of rapid transit traffic in New York for the 12-year period of 1925–36 (selected because its sharp variations in economic conditions provide a fair average) shows that the total of 1,898,104,385 passengers for 1936 was nearly six percent more than the yearly average for the period, with the Independent's gain of about 65 percent over its 1932–36 average accounting for the general increase. In other words, rapid transit continued to be the chief agent of passenger movement within New York in 1936, carrying more persons in that year than surface railways, buses and taxicabs combined, and showing a three-to-one lead over its nearest competitor.

Street Cars

This competitor, the street car, dominated all transportation facilities within the city's present corporate limits from shortly after 1832, when the crude forerunner of today's streamlined car was first run on flat metallic rails, to about 1915. In 1860, the passenger total of street surface railways was more than 50,000,000; in 1900, it exceeded 600,000,000; and as late as 1915, subways and elevateds combined were carrying fewer passengers than the street cars. Seven years later, though rapid transit now held first place, the street surface railway total exceeded one billion. The effect of motor bus transportation was not seriously felt by the street cars until 1930; but thenceforward the descent was rapid, the number of passengers carried in 1937 being fewer by nearly half a billion than in 1930.

Chiefly responsible for this tremendous loss was a carrier that had been little more than a minor item in the 1925 totals. Insignificant then, the motor bus steadily increased in importance until in 1936 it was literally pushing the once-mighty surface railways off the streets that they had dominated for so many years.

Street cars are apparently doomed in New York. In one borough, Richmond, they were completely superseded by buses in 1934. In Manhattan, street railway passenger totals dropped from more than 345,000,000 in 1925 to less than 85,000,000 in 1936. In Brooklyn, where street cars have played an enormous role, the 1936 total was about 135,000,000 less than in 1925, while Queens slumped more than 50 percent from its 1925 total. Only in the Bronx did 1936 fail to show a decided loss as compared with the figures for 1925.

Further indication of the swift decline of the once-mighty street car is to be found in statistics of the number of passenger cars owned or leased by all common carriers within the city. In 1900, street surface railways operated 81 of every 100 such cars; in 1930, 38 of every 100; in 1937, 17 of every 100. The decline is still further evidenced in the loss of trackage. In 1919, when the "emergency" buses first began to operate on a five-cent fare, street car tracks extended over the city's five boroughs to a total of 1,344.37 miles. By 1937, this total had been reduced to 811.07—a loss of nearly 40 percent within seven years.

Motor Buses

More than a century ago, horse-drawn stages and omnibuses were transporting passengers over fixed routes, precisely as motor buses do today.

But they rapidly disappeared after the introduction in 1832 of horse-drawn street cars running on metallic rails; and from about 1860 to 1915 the street car was the undisputed leader in interborough traffic totals.

About midway in this period, however, a company was organized to transport passengers once more by bus. This was the Fifth Avenue Transportation Company, Ltd., incorporated October 29, 1885, and still in business as the Fifth Avenue Coach Company. The Fifth Avenue buses did not threaten the street car's supremacy, since they carried and still carry a special class of traffic, necessarily limited because of the ten-cent fare. Nevertheless, this pioneer in the revival of bus transportation did a large business, and as late as 1925 it carried 67,700,517 of the 68,713,208 passengers credited to all buses in that year. The effect of the "emergency" bus lines inaugurated in 1919 did not begin to be decidedly evident in bus traffic totals until 1926. This was 19 years after the Fifth Avenue Coach Company had introduced the first gasoline-motor buses in New York.

The gradual city-wide replacement of street cars by buses operating on a five-cent fare began in 1919, when the New York Railways Company obtained legal permission to abandon four of its crosstown trolley lines in populous lower-Manhattan districts, thus leaving those areas without adequate transportation facilities. The city's Department of Plant and Structures thereupon obtained buses from neighboring cities, which it placed in operation under temporary revocable permits issued to owners and operators. As the result of court actions brought against the city in this connection, many of the bus lines were stopped and the purchase of buses by the city was enjoined. But the authorities went ahead with other "emergency" operations, gradually spreading out to boroughs other than Manhattan.

The tremendous development of motor bus transportation in New York is evidenced by the total of 587,595,507 passengers carried during the year ending June 30, 1937. This total represents a gain of more than 28 percent over the figures for the previous year, when 45 major companies were operating 2,763 vehicles over about 170 routes totaling more than 785 miles in length.

Buses have brightened the streets up a bit. They differ in color and in interior appointments. Some, for example, are upholstered in a smooth leather-like material, while others have brightly colored fabric coverings. Many are automatically ventilated, and all are infinitely less noisy than the street car. This latter advantage has contributed to a rise in real estate values, as has also the removal of street car tracks, largely by WPA workers, an improvement that gives an appearance of greater width to the street and provides a smooth-surfaced roadway from curb to curb.

Hacks and Hackmen

The advantages of bus operation, including the highly important five-cent fare, have cut heavily into the passenger totals of taxicabs, New York's fourth largest carrier. The hackmen once enjoyed a heavy business transporting people to and from the comparatively isolated sections not served by crosstown trolley lines. Now bus routes are so frequent that their passengers have access to many districts hitherto served only by cabs. Cabs are not passing from the picture; although the 1936 total of about 73,000,000 passengers was far below the yearly average of about 135,-000,000 for the period from January 1, 1926, to March 31, 1937. During this period, the number of cabs decreased from an average of 26,504 for the whole period to 13,555 on March 9, 1937, or about 48 percent; the number of drivers dropped from an average of 67,660 for the whole period to 40,871 on March 31, 1937, or about 39 percent.

Back of today's huge taxicab fleets stands the memory of October 1, 1907, when motor cab service was inaugurated in New York by 35 bright-red four-cylinder Darracqs, which appeared before leading hotels and set out to compete with the old hansom cabs. From that day on, taxicabs have been a perpetual source of discussion, first as to their desirability in the horse-and-buggy era, later as to the number necessary for the city's needs. The latter question has often been before the Board of Aldermen, whose last attempt at control, before the Board went out of existence on January 1, 1938, was the ordinance signed March 9, 1937, by Mayor La Guardia. This gave the Police Department discretionary power to fix the number of cabs as of that date, the total then being 13,555.

The outcome of this and other measures has had, and will very likely continue to have, very little effect on the men who drive the cabs. They are a colorful lot. Drawn from many nationalities and including all types, they know New York from end to end. They work hard, play hard, and talk among themselves in one of the most interesting of New York's many jargons. They are *hackies* and their job is *hacking.* Sometimes they ride *stick up,* which means carrying passengers without running the meter; at other times they *ride the ghost,* which refers to running an empty cab with the flag down in order to bring the metered mileage to the minimum required by the company. *Canaries* are company inspectors, *beefsteaks* are policemen, and *neutrals* are crazy people. These are only a few of the many odd terms one hears in the early morning hours at some *beanery* where drivers have gathered to eat and to talk things over.

In 1934, the large-fleet drivers struck. Since then, efforts have been made to stabilize the business, especially that of the independently-operated cabs, which are outnumbered two to one by the fleet cabs. Rates are usually "20 and 5"—20 cents for the first quarter-mile and five cents for each additional quarter. Some independents charge 20-and-10, or 25-and-5, these rates being for converted private cars of the de luxe type.

Hacking is one job at which women have proved almost a total failure. On March 31, 1937, there were only about 18 licensed women taxicab drivers in the city, not one of whom appeared actually to be driving a cab.

Ferries

All the major carriers within the city utilize one or more of three means of transport—ferries, bridges and tunnels—between boroughs separated by water.

Ferries are the oldest of the three, the first ferry having been operated in 1641 by Cornelius Dirckman, a farmer who plied a rowboat between New Amsterdam and the straggling settlements on Long Island. This type of service was followed by the pirogue, a two-masted flat-bottom sailboat supplemented by oars. It was with a pirogue plying between Staten Island and Manhattan that the first $1,000 of one of the country's great fortunes was earned by Cornelius Vanderbilt in the 17th century.

Steam supplanted oars and sails on May 10, 1814, when the *Nassau* made the first steam ferry run between Brooklyn and New York at an average speed of five miles an hour. It was owned and operated by the Fulton Ferry Company, headed by Robert Fulton and William Cutting, who had a 25-year lease on service between Beekman Street slip and the old ferry slip in Brooklyn. This side-wheel type of ferryboat gave place to the modern screw-propeller vessel after 1885, when the *Bergen* was launched by the Hoboken Company from the Delamater Iron Works at Newburgh, New York. Latest of all developments is the electric ferry, introduced in 1926, and capable of a speed of from 15 to 18 miles an hour.

That the ferries still being used for interborough traffic have an important part in that movement is shown by the figures for 1926–36, during which period the ferries carried a yearly average of 32,384,566 passengers and 3,318,936 vehicles. In 1936, passengers totaled 29,237,507 and vehicles 2,621,652—a decrease of about nine percent for passengers and 21 percent for vehicles from the yearly averages for the period.

Municipal ferries and those owned by railroads having their terminals on the New Jersey side of the Hudson do the largest share of this business. The city operates boats over six routes, with a uniform five-cent fare for passengers and a sliding scale of rates for vehicles. Service on these lines has been greatly improved since the city took them over from private owners and operators. In addition to its six public routes, the city runs several departmental ferry lines serving city institutions on islands in the East River.

Bridges

As four of its five boroughs—Manhattan, Queens, Brooklyn and Richmond—are either islands or parts of islands (only the Bronx is on the mainland), New York has always had to consider the problem of water in its larger transportation plans. Before Brooklyn Bridge, first of the great East River crossings, was completed in 1883, a score of ferry lines crisscrossed the rivers and bay. Now almost all of these are gone, replaced by 62 bridges and 16 tunnels—railroad, rapid transit and vehicular—which bear the tremendous daily flow of traffic within and to and from the city. Manhattan Island itself, surrounded by the Hudson, Harlem and East Rivers, resembles a many-legged insect, with all the tunnels and 15 of the bridges radiating from it into Long Island on the east, the Bronx on the north and New Jersey on the west.

Except for the Outerbridge Crossing and the Goethals and Bayonne Bridges, which span the waters between Staten Island (Richmond) and New Jersey, and the famous Hell Gate railroad bridge connecting the Astoria section of Queens with the Bronx, all of the city's notable bridges have a base in Manhattan. Over the East River are the Brooklyn, Manhattan, Williamsburg, Queensboro and Triborough Bridges; and above the Hudson is the George Washington Bridge. Nine smaller structures over the Harlem River join Manhattan and the Bronx. Within the boroughs outside Manhattan—and connecting some of them—are 43 other bridges, from 65 to 1,900 feet in length, which span such inlets as Gowanus Canal, English Kills, Beach Channel, Shell Bank Basin, Bronx River and Newtown Creek.

Best known of all these structures is Brooklyn Bridge, which for many years after its opening on March 24, 1883, was considered one of the engineering wonders of the world. Costing more than $25,000,000 and with a span of 1,595 feet, it was designed mainly for pedestrians between Brooklyn and Manhattan, but is now used almost entirely by surface cars, subway trains and automobiles. Brooklyn is further linked to Manhattan by the Williamsburg and Manhattan Bridges, opened in 1903 and 1909 respectively. Together with Brooklyn Bridge, they bear the bulk of the Long Island-Manhattan traffic over the East River. Only occasional pedestrians use most of the large bridges, but the Williamsburg is a favorite promenade of tenement dwellers from both sides of the river.

Queensboro Bridge casts its shadow on fashionable Beekman and Sutton Places, Manhattan, as well as on the city hospitals and the home for the insane on Welfare Island in the center of the river. This structure, of the cantilever type, with a span of 1,182 feet and two upper levels—one for elevated trains, the other for vehicular traffic—was completed in 1909; and until the Triborough Bridge was opened in 1936, its narrow roadways were packed day and night with motor traffic between midtown and uptown New York and Long Island points. Now the Triborough, which cost $60,300,000—more than half of it from PWA funds—connects upper Manhattan, the Bronx and Queens with a gigantic Y-shaped crossing, linking the highways of Westchester and Long Island and relieving the traffic burden on the streets and bridges of lower Manhattan. This newest of the city's bridges is a model express sky-highway system with 19 miles of roadway, including the approaches. In 1937, it was used by 11,171,956 vehicles, which paid tolls amounting to $2,845,109.

For a while after its completion in 1931 the George Washington Bridge, whose main span is 3,500 feet long, was the longest suspension bridge in the world, but it is now surpassed in length by the San Francisco-Oakland Bridge over San Francisco Bay. Built at a cost of $60,000,000 over a period of 4½ years, the George Washington rears two majestic towers on each bank of the Hudson River—at Fort Lee, New Jersey, and 180th Street, Manhattan—and provides Manhattan with its only direct overwater link with the west. The slender span between the towers is 250 feet above the water and has two roadways and a footwalk, which afford an incomparable view of the Jersey Palisades, on one side, and of upper New York on the other.

High Bridge, connecting Manhattan and the Bronx, is the oldest of the city's bridges and most notable of the Harlem River crossings. It was built in 1839–48, long before modern bridge-building principles were known.

In addition to its other facilities, this massive masonry structure carries an aqueduct of the city water supply.

Three bridges link Staten Island with New Jersey and provide additional outlets between New York and points west and south. The Goethals Bridge and the Outerbridge Crossing, both opened in 1928, are sister spans of the truss type, overhanging each end of Arthur Kill ("kill" is the Dutch equivalent for "stream") on the west side of the island. On the north side, Bayonne Bridge, with a span of 1,675 feet, crosses Kill van Kull into Bayonne and leads directly to the Jersey entrance of the Holland Tunnel in Jersey City. The three bridges cost a total of approximately $30,000,000.

Particularly impressive is the East River span, more than 1,000 feet long, of the Hell Gate Bridge, above mentioned. The bridge in its entirety carries the four tracks of the New York Connecting Railroad, linking the Pennsylvania and the New Haven railway systems; and it is used for through freight and passenger trains between the areas covered by those systems.

Some idea of the traffic flow across New York's interborough bridges may be gained from the fact that during the period 1926–36 an average of 15,104,815 subway and trolley cars, 289,741,745 vehicles, and 1,100,-318,425 persons (passengers and pedestrians) crossed these structures yearly.

Tunnels

Far below Manhattan's bridges and the waters they cross, nearly a score of tunnels burrow into that island from adjacent land areas. Beneath the East River are eight arteries of the city's subway systems and one of the Pennsylvania Railroad. Three more subway tubes underlie the Harlem River. Under the Hudson are the Pennsylvania Railroad tunnel, the uptown and downtown Hudson Tubes used exclusively by the Hudson and Manhattan Railroad (a Newark-New York system), the Holland Tunnel and the new Lincoln Tunnel. Underlying Newtown Creek on Long Island is a tunnel that connects Brooklyn and Queens over the Independent subway system.

The oldest of the under-river crossings is the Harlem River Tunnel of the IRT's Lenox Avenue line, connecting Lenox Avenue between 142d and 143d Streets in Manhattan with 149th Street in the Bronx. It was opened on July 10, 1905. The latest tunnel within the city, the Independent subway's East River crossing from Fulton Street in Manhattan to Cranberry Street in Brooklyn, was completed on December 12, 1933.

The average length of the East River transit tunnels is about 2,500 feet, while those beneath the Hudson are as long as 6,000 feet. They cost from three to seven million dollars each. Although most of the under-water crossings are at about the same general level, at some points they are sunk so deeply, because of obstructing bedrock or intervening land subways, that elevators or escalators are needed at their terminals to carry passengers to the surface.

The Holland Tunnel, a double-tubed vehicular passage between Canal Street in Manhattan and Provost Street in Jersey City, is one of the world's greatest engineering feats. Built by the States of New York and New Jersey, it required more than seven years to build and cost $50,000,000. It was opened on November 13, 1927. Its two tubes lie 72 feet below the surface of the Hudson River; the northern one, for west-bound traffic, is 8,557 feet long, and the southern, for east-bound traffic, is 8,371 feet. Each tube has a 20-foot roadway. The interiors are white-tiled, brilliantly lighted, and ventilated by 84 huge fans. Policemen, stationed at intervals on a catwalk along the walls, supervise the movement of traffic.

Two important vehicular tunnels are in course of construction as this book goes to press—the Lincoln, under the Hudson River from West Thirty-Ninth Street in Manhattan to Weehawken in New Jersey; and the Queens Midtown, under the East River from East Thirty-Eighth Street in Manhattan to Long Island City in Queens. One of the Lincoln Tunnel's two tubes was opened late in 1937; the other is expected to be ready for traffic in 1940. The Queens Midtown Tunnel will be completed in time to serve as the pivotal link in a direct motor route from Manhattan to the grounds of the great World's Fair in 1939.

Commuters and Transient Visitors

What may for want of a better term be called the "in and out" traffic movement of New York, as differentiated from traffic confined within the city limits, comprises an annual total of considerably more than 300,000,000 passengers, although its exact volume is for various reasons rather difficult to estimate. By far the largest number of these passengers are either commuters or transient visitors; but they include also a relatively small number of resident New Yorkers who travel either habitually or occasionally beyond the city boundaries.

Those who work in New York and live outside the city constitute the largest army of commuters in the world. On every business day throughout the year, this army converges upon and moves into the city from the west, the east and the north—to retreat later in the day over the same routes into a far-flung suburban area.

Of the commuting traffic that originates on the New Jersey side of the Hudson River, the largest part is handled by the Hudson & Manhattan Railroad, an inter-city system between New York and Newark via Jersey City and Hoboken, with its own under-river tunnels (known as the Hudson Tubes), its own terminal and subway in Manhattan. In addition, New Jersey commuters utilize six major railroads—the Pennsylvania, the Erie, the Lackawanna, the Lehigh, the Central of New Jersey, and the West Shore. Of these roads, the Pennsylvania and the Lehigh run their trains directly by tunnel to the Pennsylvania Station in Manhattan. The four others terminate on the Jersey shore of the Hudson, and their passengers are transferred to Manhattan either by ferries owned and operated by the railroads or through the Hudson Tubes—as a service included in the original fare.

Commuters from the east stream in from Long Island, where the Long Island Railroad dominates the whole area beyond the limits of Brooklyn and Queens. In 1936, this railroad carried a total of close to fifty million passengers. No such traffic volume was ever dreamed of when the Brooklyn & Jamaica Railroad Company completed connections between Brooklyn and Jamaica on April 18, 1836. Even in 1861, when the road opened its first South Shore division to Islip, or in 1883, when the Montauk division was opened, the 1936 totals would have been considered fantastic. As a matter of fact, the company's original plan was not so much to handle Long Island traffic as to provide a short cut to Boston by ferry across Long Island Sound at Greenport, that being the primary purpose of the Brooklyn-Jamaica-Hicksville line, opened July 25, 1844. But the New Haven's all-land route to New England proved much more attractive, and the Long Island Railroad turned instead to the business of transporting Long Island-New York passengers almost exclusively. The railroad uses the Pennsylvania's tunnel under the East River, and lands its passengers at the Pennsylvania Station in Manhattan.

Commuters from the north and northeast are for the most part residents of Westchester County or of the neighboring Connecticut area to the east. They travel to and from the city on two principal railroads, the New York Central and the New Haven, both of which utilize the Grand Central Terminal in the midtown section of Manhattan. Certain of the New Haven's trains, however, run directly to another Manhattan terminal, the Pennsylvania Station. The volume of this commuting traffic from the north and northeast is considerably smaller than that of either the New Jersey or the Long Island traffic.

In addition to the army of commuters that daily throngs the city, New York is host each year to a tremendous number of transient visitors from every part of the United States—and indeed, from every part of the world. They are constantly coming and going, by railroad, bus, private motor car, airplane, and steamer.

An average of between 60 and 70 million passengers, other than commuters, enter or leave New York annually by means of the trunk-line railways and their subsidiary facilities, making this city one of the busiest centers of railway passenger travel in the world. The more important of these railways are mentioned above, in connection with commuting traffic, but there are some others that serve the city. Four of them—the Pennsylvania, New York Central, New Haven, and Lehigh—land their passengers in Manhattan, at either the Pennsylvania Station or the Grand Central Terminal. The others have their metropolitan terminals on the adjacent shore of New Jersey, chiefly in Jersey City.

The extent of New York's in-and-out motor traffic cannot be estimated, because one of the five boroughs is part of the mainland and two others occupy only a relatively small section of Long Island—so that vehicles may enter or leave these three boroughs by many thoroughfares. But some notion of the volume of motor traffic into and out of the island of Manhattan may be formed from the fact that (taking into account only two of several main connecting links) nearly twelve million motor passengers were carried through the Holland Tunnel and more than seven million over the George Washington Bridge, in 1936.

A large proportion of these passengers, whether commuters or transient visitors, consisted of bus patrons. New York is the most important motor bus center in the United States, being served by lines to every part of the country and to hundreds of suburban points. In midtown Manhattan are half a dozen principal bus terminals, with ticket offices, waiting rooms, information booths, etc.; and subsidiary stations are scattered all through the main business sections of the five boroughs.

Although by no means inconsiderable in itself, the total number of New York's transient visitors who arrive and depart by steamship constitutes less than one percent of the in-and-out traffic as a whole. The facilities and other factors involved in this particular phase of the city's passenger movement are described elsewhere in the present volume (see article dealing with Maritime Affairs).

Airports

Air travel to and from New York is chiefly served by the Newark Metropolitan Airport, at Newark, New Jersey. This is the metropolitan port of entry and departure for four major airlines—the American, Eastern, Transcontinental & Western, and United. New York business accounts for about 90 percent of this airport's traffic. Passengers are transported between Manhattan and the airfield by special limousine buses. During the first nine months of 1937, 227,252 passengers arrived at or departed from the Newark Airport—an increase of 42,486 over the corresponding period in 1936.

Most important of the ports within the city is Floyd Bennett Field, municipal airport of the City of New York, at Barren Island, Brooklyn. When dedicated in 1931 this was considered one of the best fields in the East, but so far it has had small success in competing with Newark for a major share of the metropolitan air traffic. At present (1938) the city is spending several million dollars upon improvements and additions here, in an effort to bring more business to airports within the city limits.

Even more extensive is the projected development of North Beach Municipal Airport in Queens, which was purchased from the Curtiss-Wright interests for $1,300,000 in 1937. In collaboration with the Federal WPA, the city will spend approximately $12,000,000 in a large-scale improvement program to be completed before the opening in 1939 of the World's Fair, the site of which is only a short distance from the airport.

The city is also pushing a proposal designed to utilize part of Governors Island as an air field. This move has the support of many civic leaders and is being urged vigorously before Congress, which must grant permission to use this Federal property for the purpose.

Commercial airports of minor importance in the metropolitan area include Holmes Airport, in Queens; Flushing Airport, near Flushing, L. I.; Brentwood Airport, Brentwood, L. I.; American Airport, Farmingdale, L. I.; and Patchogue Airport, on Great South Bay, near Patchogue, L. I. Seaplane anchorages for aerial commuters include the Wall Street Skyport, foot of Wall Street, East River; the Thirty-First Street anchorage on the East River; and the 125th Street facilities on the Hudson River. Anchorages are also provided at North Beach Airport, in Queens, and at Edo Seaplane Anchorage, College Point.

Mitchell Field, near Hempstead, L. I., is the principal United States 'Army airfield in this area; and Miller Field, at Dongan Hills, Staten Island, is a subpost of Fort Wadsworth used by a squadron of the New York National Guard Aviation Corps.

Forward Look

Two proposals of major importance in the extension of New York's existing transportation facilities were advanced in 1937. On February 8, Mayor La Guardia requested the New York City Tunnel Authority to study plans for a vehicular tunnel that would link Staten Island with the adjacent New Jersey mainland. The second proposal, submitted March 1 by the Port of New York Authority to Governor Hoffman of New Jersey and the legislature of that State, contemplated linking the communities of northern New Jersey with midtown Manhattan by means of a new rapid transit system costing $187,500,000. The outstanding feature of this enormous development would be the creation of a new rapid transit center at Fifty-First Street, Manhattan, in the vicinity of Rockefeller Center, with an extension of the Hudson Tubes and other existing facilities to this center.

By such constant planning for the future, New York has in recent years kept abreast of its traffic needs and moved steadily forward in the developments necessitated by a population pressure that has no equal anywhere in the world. To a city thus able to cope with its own perennially evolving situation, population density and other primary factors hold no terrors.

World Market Place

UNDERLYING the diverse factors that brought about New York's ascent to supremacy among cities, trade—the buying and selling of goods—was, and still is, that function with respect to which all other of the city's localized economic processes occupy an ancillary position. New Yorkers were traders before they were colonists, they were tradesmen before they were industrial entrepreneurs, and they were merchants before they were bankers. Whether it consisted of bartering with the Indians, dealing with richly laden pirates, marketing the prizes of privateers, selling the Government condemned ships and rifles, or simply carrying on a legitimate exchange with the general public, trade was the driving force that overcame all barriers and reduced all obstacles to New York's future greatness.

To sell something for more than it cost, to buy something at less than it could be sold for—this was the key that unlocked the door to riches, this was the formula that engendered New York's great fortunes. Shipping, transportation, banking, even industrial production, were but necessary appendages of trade, grafted to the primary economic organism as the urge and possibilities for greater profits increased.

This was not peculiar to New York alone. It was characteristic of the entire historical epoch and civilization that sprang from the wreckage of feudal society. But New York, more than any other of the world's metropolitan monuments to the glittering achievements of trade, symbolizes the fabulous chemistry of the buying and selling formula. In most modern cities one or another particular auxiliary of trade has acquired greatness in its own right, usurping or overshadowing its progenitor. In the case of New York, however, *all* the auxiliaries of trade—shipping, transportation, industrial production, and banking—have acquired greatness in their own right, but with the exception of banking alone they remain in subordinate positions. Because of Wall Street's national and international ramifications, New York as a financial center outranks New York as a commodities market. From an appendage of New York trade, Wall Street has developed into an appendage of world trade. In this respect Wall Street may be said to have independence, greatness in its own right. Within the bounds of metropolitan economy, however, trade retains its basic and historic function. New York is more a city of merchants than of bankers, of shopkeepers than of stockbrokers, of clerks than of industrial workers. It may not be World Market Place No. 1, but it is indisputably and demonstrably United States Market Place No. 1.

In round numbers, the entire United States in 1935 recorded wholesale transactions approximating $42,803,000,000. In the same year New York did a wholesale business valued at $9,618,000,000, or more than 22 percent of the national total. Among all American cities, Chicago made the closest approach to New York's accomplishments in the wholesale field, but its transactions were but slightly in excess of one-third of the New York total. Only three other American cities, Boston, Philadelphia and San Francisco, did a wholesale business amounting to more than a billion dollars in 1935, and New York's wholesale business far exceeded the combined total of all three *plus that of Chicago.*

In the field of retail trade, New York likewise occupies a predominant position among American cities. In 1935 its total retail sales amounted to $2,847,000,000, which was about eight percent of the national total. No other American city could show anything like this figure, the closest being Chicago with less than half the New York total. As a matter of fact, New York City transacted more retail business in 1935 than did any state in the Union except the state in which it is situated; and this business was conducted in more stores (numbering 115,500) than were in operation in any state except New York and Pennsylvania. Employed in the retail and wholesale establishments of the city in 1935 were 522,908 persons, or 37,764 more than were employed in the city's industrial plants. Supervising this great army of wage-workers were 114,882 proprietors and firm members. Employees in the city's retail and wholesale establishments received an average of about $1,500 each for their labor in 1935, as against an average of about $1,200 paid to the city's factory workers.

The foregoing data establish the general quantitative picture of marketing in the metropolis. In a qualitative examination it should be noted, first of all, that retail establishments in New York City can be classified in three main categories characteristic of retail marketing in any community. Briefly, these categories are as follows: (1) stores engaged in the selling of "convenience goods," such as groceries, meats, drugs, baked goods, tobacco, etc.; (2) stores selling the so-called "shopping lines," consisting of wearing apparel, house furnishings, dry goods, etc.; (3) stores that sell "luxury goods," such as expensive jewelry, furs, antiques, etc.

In New York, as in every other community, an overwhelming majority of retail establishments belong in the first category. Engaged in the marketing of commodities that have a generally low sales price, such retail establishments find it profitable to cluster close to the heart of comparatively small residential districts. In 1935 almost one-half of all the retail stores in the city, 52,161 to be exact, were engaged in the marketing of food stuffs. That these stores were, for the most part, small-scale neighborhood enterprises is shown by the fact that they were operated by a total of only 60,300 employees. Stores of this type are scattered, in proportion to population concentration, over all five boroughs of the city. In themselves they are no more distinctive of New York than of any other city.

New York's world-wide reputation as a shopping center derives primarily from retail outlets that belong in the last two categories above mentioned—the great department stores, the countless "specialty" shops, the "exclusive" gown, millinery, art and antique stores. These establishments, particularly the department and specialty types, constitute the shopping mecca of the entire metropolitan district. They cater to the varied tastes and needs not only of New York's millions, but of additional millions in New Jersey, Long Island, Connecticut and upstate New York. Unlike the "convenience goods" shops, the location of such establishments is determined more by their accessibility than by their proximity to the buying public. During the past 30 years, consequently, New York's retail shopping district has shown a marked tendency to crystallize in the area of Manhattan bounded by Thirty-First Street on the south and Fifty-Ninth Street on the north, between Third and Eighth Avenues on the east and west—the area that is most accessible to all parts of the metropolitan district. This area receives a majority of the quarter-million or more who daily visit the city, for most of these visitors arrive at the Pennsylvania and Grand Central Terminals. Since all the city's rapid transit systems converge on the center, the area is also directly accessible to the hordes of bargain hunters among the native population, whether they come from the outermost reaches of the Bronx or from the depths of Kings or Queens.

The central retail shopping district, conforming to this first principle of profitable retail operation, is distinguished first of all by intensive concentration of retail outlets. Here are a majority of the most modern and best equipped metropolitan agencies that retail service and amusement as well as merchandise. Definite location patterns are discernible in the district, but little homogeneity. Certain shops that handle similar goods or serve similar social strata tend to develop a location center peculiar to their special function. Along and in the vicinity of Thirty-Fourth Street, for instance, are many of the mammoth department stores, which sell the most goods to the most people. Along Fifth and Madison Avenues, between Thirty-Fourth and Fifty-Ninth Streets, are most of the "quality shops," where the cost of an article is reputedly a secondary consideration with the patrons. Then there is "automobile row" on Broadway between Fifty-Fifth and Sixty-Fifth Streets, the art galleries and antique shops in the region around Fifth Avenue and Fifty-Seventh Street, and a number of other distinct centers in each of which are shops specializing in a particular type of merchandise. This clustering trend is a response, for the most part, to consumer desire to "shop around," to deliberate and compare before making a purchase. To some extent, too, clustering develops in the vicinity of establishments that do extensive advertising, the reason being obvious.

Before the development of modern methods of transit and transport, proximity to the buying public was the decisive factor in determining the location of New York's central retail shopping district. The history of this central district, accordingly, has been virtually identical with the history of Manhattan's residential development. Originally, of course, the district was in the lower end of the island. By 1850 it had pushed northward to Canal Street, only a short distance south of the newly developing residential area. Thirty years later the shopping center had effected another northward migration, this time to Fourteenth Street and again in the wake of the residential movement. By 1900 a further move had been made, along with the northward-bound populace, to Twenty-Third Street. The movement toward Thirty-Fourth Street and beyond began early in the present century. Very gradually, and virtually in inverse ratio to the tempo of transit development, proximity to the buying public ceased to be a location determinant.

There is every reason to believe that New York's central shopping district will remain permanently rooted in the area that it currently occupies. City planners have called attention to the fact that only the financial district has the economic power to displace the retail merchants, should it ever feel the urge to move north. Business and banking firms have shown a tendency to move their administrative offices northward in recent years, but the only apparent effects on the central shopping district have been new skyscrapers, greatly increased street and sidewalk congestion, and a still further influx of retail establishments stocked with wares to catch the fancy of the new armies of office employees.

Retail merchants in the city as a whole manage to retain their traditional enterprise, even in the face of adversity. There were nearly 12,000 more stores in New York in 1935 than in 1929, although the total 1935 dollar volume of business was only about one-half the 1929 total. Whether in a boom or a depression year, however, the lion's share of the city's retail business is transacted in Manhattan. Thus, in 1935 the total dollar volume of sales in Manhattan exceeded by $77,666,000 the corresponding total in the other four boroughs combined.

Wholesale marketing is concentrated in Manhattan even more intensively than retailing, 91 percent of the city's vast volume of wholesale business in 1935 having been transacted on the island. Although virtually all this business was carried on below Fifty-Ninth Street, Manhattan contains no central wholesale area comparable to the central retail shopping district. With few exceptions, each of the 20 or more well-defined wholesale market sections in the city is composed of all the agencies dealing in certain products, clustered together in a specific neighborhood. The wholesale market for butter, cheese and eggs, for example, is concentrated on Greenwich Street, on the west side of downtown Manhattan; most of the wholesale leather establishments are in the old "Swamp" district, below the Brooklyn Bridge; the wholesale shoe distributors are on Reade and Duane Streets in downtown Manhattan; the wholesale fish market centers around the intersection of South and Fulton Streets. Similarly concentrated in particular neighborhoods are the fruit and produce markets, the coffee and tea markets, the women's garments market, the men's garments, the headwear, jewelry, silk goods, woolen goods and cotton goods markets. The wholesale hardware, drug and paper markets, on the other hand, are composed of scattered agencies, although the latter remain in the central area. Only the groceries and fresh meat markets are made up of widely scattered agencies.

This tendency of some wholesale agencies to cluster and of others to scatter is created by factors peculiar to the selling process in each case. Where price fluctuations are frequent, where buyers come to the market, or where the determination of quality is important, the market is composed invariably of clustered agencies, since the proximity of every dealer to all the others in each case is essential to the efficient transaction of business. Where, on the other hand, price and quality are standardized, the market tends to disperse over a wide area.

The forces determining the locations of the various clustered markets are less easy to define. Generally speaking, the markets in which fashion is a factor, such as fur, women's garments, millinery and silk, have gravitated uptown toward the central retail shopping district; markets where trucking economy is a paramount consideration, such as the fruit and produce market or the butter, eggs and cheese market, tend to concentrate near the railroad pier stations on the lower west side. In at least one case, that of the leather market, the location seems to have been established by tradition, the "Swamp" having been associated with New York leather operations since earliest times.

Unlike the retail merchant, whose existence depends upon his ability to attract the public eye, the wholesaler as a rule operates behind the scenes, generally in an out-of-the-way neighborhood and usually in obsolete premises. Of his role in the city's economic life, the public at large knows little and cares less. Nevertheless, that role is of primary importance. The wholesaler is the stoker who feeds the city's mighty productive machine; he is the distributor of its million-fold products. He is host to much of the avalanche of rail and water-borne cargoes that descend daily on the city. Such functions will be necessary to the end of time.

In addition to being America's greatest commercial center, New York is also this country's major industrial city. More workers are paid more wages for producing more goods in more manufacturing establishments here than in any other American city—or, indeed, than in any one of 43 states. In 1935 (the latest year for which figures are available) 485,144 workers were employed in 26,061 factories scattered throughout the five boroughs of the city. For converting $1,756,000,000 worth of raw materials (including fuel and power) into $3,666,000,000 worth of products, these workers were paid $582,000,000 in wages. Only the states of New York, Pennsylvania, Michigan, Illinois and Ohio paid more wages to more factory workers, and produced manufactures of greater total value. New York City contained twice as many manufacturing establishments as any state in the Union other than New York and Pennsylvania, the latter having only 20 more than one-half the New York City total. With reference to the United States as a whole, New York City factories employed six percent of all the workers, who were paid nearly eight percent of all the wages for manufacturing eight percent by value of all the products of the country.

While 77 percent of all the manufacturing establishments in New York

State during 1935 were situated in New York City, these gave employment to only 54 percent of the total number of workers in the state and manufactured only 60 percent by value of all the products. This indicates that New York City industrial establishments were, as compared with those of the rest of the state, generally small-scale enterprises. The output per factory, from the point of view of value, was considerably smaller in New York City than in the rest of the state. On the other hand, the city's highly skilled wage-earners were producing, man-for-man, more valuable commodities, and were being paid higher wages. The raw materials passing through the hands of the average New York City worker annually were increased in value by $3,900, while raw materials passing through the hands of the average worker up-state were increased in value by only $2,600.

The preponderance in New York City of highly skilled workers engaged in the manufacture of high-quality articles is one of the primary reasons for its dominant position among American industrial cities. Some of the other factors that helped to mold the industrial pattern were the ready accessibility of capital, raw materials and specialized machinery. Of great importance also were the geographical peculiarities of the city region, creating grave transportation problems, and the concentration of population on Manhattan Island, leading to excessive land values, high rents and acute traffic congestion. In addition to these basic factors, which conditioned the establishment and growth of industry in general, were numerous minor factors peculiar to specific industries. In certain trades, as for example, the making of women's cloaks and dresses, it was essential that the plants be located in close proximity to the favorite haunts of the buyers, in this case the mid-town hotels near the Pennsylvania and Grand Central Terminals.

Industrial establishments engaged in the fabrication of products that require large reduction in bulk or weight of raw material avoided Manhattan because of space and transport problems. The water barriers separating Queens, Brooklyn and Richmond from the New Jersey railheads discouraged such establishments from taking advantage of the large tracts of undeveloped acreage in these boroughs. Conversely, industries manufacturing products that involved little or no reduction in the bulk or weight of raw materials took early root in Manhattan and (in cases where immediate juxtaposition to the market was not a primary condition of survival) in the adjoining boroughs. Where quick accessibility to the great

East Side labor market was a major consideration, as in industries subject to seasonal fluctuations in demand, Manhattan factory sites were vitally necessary. In the same fashion, Manhattan became, and continues to be, a favorite locale for industries that find it possible to function in run-down and obsolete buildings.

Despite transport, traffic, warehousing and realty difficulties probably unparalleled in any other important manufacturing area, Manhattan Island is today, as it has been from the beginning, the hub of industrial activity in the metropolitan region. Since 1910, when nearly 49 percent of the city's population was concentrated in Manhattan, there has been a steady exodus to Brooklyn, the Bronx and Queens, until today only 22 percent of the population remains in Manhattan. But there has been no proportionate dispersal of manufacturing establishments. Some industries, such as tobacco products, have fallen from a position of importance to one of relatively minor consequence. Certain branches of the garment industry, such as underwear, shirtwaists, kimonos, children's wear and house dresses, in which both the operation and the product are more subject to standardization than cloaks and dresses and men's wear, have shown a tendency to favor the outlying boroughs. Similarly, the heavier branches of the metal products industry and most of the chemical establishments have drifted to the environs. In the main, however, Manhattan is still the favorite site for New York's industrial activities.

Turning again to the 1935 statistics, we find that of the city's 26,094 industrial establishments 18,694, or about 72 percent, were situated in Manhattan. Employed in these latter were 288,000, or about 59 percent, of the city's industrial wage-earners—an average of about 15 workers to each factory. The value of the commodities manufactured in these Manhattan establishments amounted to $2,432,000,000, which was 66 percent of the total value of all the products manufactured in the city. Of the total value of commodities manufactured in Manhattan, more than $1,-322,000,000 was added in the course of manufacture, representing nearly 70 percent of "added value" for the entire city. Thus, while output per factory on Manhattan Island was less than in the other four boroughs, the Manhattan factory workers as a whole were performing more skilled operations and turning out more valuable merchandise than workers in the other boroughs of New York City.

A few city-wide statistics for 1935 concerning those industries in which Manhattan holds undisputed leadership will convey, to some extent, an idea of the scale of operations. Engaged in the manufacture of fur goods were more than 2,000 shops employing about 9,500 wage-earners. The value of their product exceeded $124,000,000, which was 86 percent of the value of all fur goods manufactured in the United States. There were 10,272 apparel and accessories plants (nearly triple the number of plants in the city's next most important industry), which employed an average of 187,334 workers and manufactured goods valued at $1,383,000,000, more than $675,000,000 of this sum being added in the process of manufacture.

Next in importance with respect to the number of plants involved and value produced was the printing and publishing industry, with 3,159 establishments, employing 49,783 wage-earners and turning out products valued at $490,357,000. Book, music and job printing was the largest division, with 1,886 establishments in which were employed 20,631 workers. The total output of this division exceeded $155,519,000 in value, which was about 22 percent of the national total in the same division. The newspaper and periodical publishing division of the industry followed next in number of plants and wage-earners, but the value of its products exceeded the value of the first division's products by nearly $100,000,000, and amounted to 21 percent of the national total.

Of greater importance than the city's printing industry, from the point of view of value produced, and nearly equaling it in total number of plants in operation, was the foods and beverages industry, with 3,072 establishments, employing 49,906 wage-earners and producing commodities valued at nearly $545,000,000. More than 2,100 of these plants, employing 24,100 workers, were engaged in the manufacture of bread; the total value of bread products exceeded $157,000,000, nearly one-half of this amount being added in the process of manufacture. In the next largest division were 132 confectionery establishments, manufacturing goods valued at more than $28,500,000 and employing 6,329 wage-earners. Among the various other establishments in this division were 99 ice cream plants, 28 malt liquor plants and three sugar refining establishments.

Establishments engaged in the manufacture of metal and machine-shop products, ranging from boilers to structural and ornamental ironwork, numbered 1,689. There were 1,031 textile plants, 898 wood products plants, 653 chemical plants, 414 establishments making stone, clay and glass products, 378 paper and paper products plants, and 129 establishments manufacturing tobacco products. The manufacture of jewelry, precious articles of metal, and similar products occupied an average of 3,388

New Yorkers Relax

Above: THE POLO GROUNDS, HOME OF THE NEW YORK GIANTS

Below: ALL SET FOR A TRIP DOWN THE BAY, OR UP THE HUDSON

THE EARLY BIRD CATCHES THE BEST SEAT IN RADIO CITY'S MOVIE PALACE

SHAN KAR PRESENTS THE DANCES OF INDIA IN THE RAINBOW ROOM
ATOP THE R.C.A. BUILDING

Above: ROCKEFELLER CENTER'S SUNKEN PLAZA TURNED SKATING RINK FOR THE WINTER

Below: BROADWAY PLAYGROUND

ANY SUMMER DAY IN PROSPECT PARK, BROOKLYN

HEAT WAVE ANTIDOTE FOR EAST SIDERS AT HAMILTON FISH MUNICIPAL
POOL

HOT WEEK-ENDS FIND MILLIONS OF NEW YORKERS ON MUNICIPAL
BEACHES. THIS IS JACOB RIIS PARK

A WPA CARAVAN THEATRE ON STATEN
ISLAND

Above: "JAM SESSION" IN A 52ND STREET BARROOM
Below: A NEW STEP IS BORN AT A POPULAR NIGHT CLUB

workers in 466 plants. Their output was valued at $32,679,000, nearly $12,000,000 of which was added in the course of manufacture.

In the miscellaneous category were 3,805 establishments, 212 of them making signs and advertising novelties, 152 making toys, 106 making trunks, suitcases and bags, 80 making windowshades and fixtures, and various others manufacturing everything from feathers and plumes (95 percent of the national total) to buttons (27 percent of the national total).

While Manhattan Island contains a disproportionate number of these manufacturing establishments, industries that require spacious plant facilities or that are unaffected by the whims of fashion have shown in general a preference for the Bronx, Brooklyn and Queens. Industrial establishments in the Bronx are of about the same average size as those in Manhattan, but in the other two boroughs they are generally larger. The average number of workers per factory in 1935 was 27 in Brooklyn and 32 in Queens, whereas the average in Manhattan was only 15. But Brooklyn, with 24 percent of the total city area and 37 percent of the total population, contained only 17 percent of the city's manufacturing plants; and Queens, with 35 percent of the total area and 17 percent of the total population, contained only five percent of the city's manufacturing plants.

Industrial planners have long been conscious of the maladjustment of uses to areas which these figures reveal. Yet the heavy tribute in overhead, street congestion, trucking costs, transport demands and human misery exacted by the over-concentration of industry on Manhattan Island has not resulted in any appreciable shift of manufacturing to the outer boroughs. Even in the period immediately following 1933, when the financial crisis reduced the number of industrial plants in operation in New York City to 19,233, fewer by far than at any time since 1899, location trends remained in the traditional groove. Between 1933 and 1936 the number of reopened and newly established plants in Manhattan increased by 37 percent, while the increase in Brooklyn and Queens amounted to only 28 percent and 27 percent respectively.

Even more distressing than the failure of industry to effect a more logical site distribution in New York City is the closing of many of its plants since 1929. By the end of 1935, when the incidence of industrial production was approaching its post-depression peak, 3,300 fewer plants were in operation in New York City than when the financial crisis began. Idle, along with these plants, were more than 76,000 wage-earners who had been working six years before. The drop in wages from the 1929 total exceeded $328,000,000. Products manufactured in 1935 were worth $3,-

666,000,000—a drop of $2,242,000,000 from the 1929 total of $5,908,-000,000. The economic losses resulting from this reduction in industrial activity were catastrophic; the consequent suffering and misery have probably surpassed anything ever before experienced in a modern industrial community.

Mechanics' Bell

In THE Webb Institute of Naval Architecture in the Bronx there has rested silently for several decades a great 900-pound throat of bronze. This is Mechanics' Bell, which shipwrights hung a hundred years ago at Stanton and Goerck Streets, in lower Manhattan. From its point of vantage near the shipyards on the East River, this bell signalled the end of each ten-hour day, in defiance of the custom of the 1830's which demanded that artisans work "from dark to dark." The shipwrights who rested its shoulder on odd pieces of scaffolding and tied a length of tarry rope to its tongue were unaware that its pealing symbolized not only their struggle for a ten-hour working day but something much more significant—a new division of society and the emergence of a new class of which these artisans as yet but dimly felt themselves a part. Mechanics' Bell rang in the rise of the merchant-capitalist and the first of a cycle of financial crises which were to become so terrible a part of the new economy; the separation of trade societies, where masters and men were on an equal footing, into trade unions of workers on the one hand and associations of employers on the other; the beginning of a remarkable series of intellectual movements clustering around workers' educational, political and economic aims.

The storing of Mechanics' Bell in the Bronx, several miles from the mouth of the East River, in 1897, was coincident with the close of a great era. The technique of collective bargaining had been adopted and perfected. Trade unions, at first regarded as conspiracies, had become legally recognized bodies. The vote had been gained for wage earners, imprisonment for debt abolished, education made universal and free. Thomas Skidmore, George Henry Evans, Robert Dale Owen, Frances Wright, Albert Brisbane, Horace Greeley, William Weitling, Joseph Weydemeyer, J. P. McDonnell, John Swinton, Henry George, Father McGlynn, Daniel DeLeon, had spoken to two generations of workers in New York City. The Workingmen's Party, the Equal Rights Party, the Phalanxists, the Single Taxers, the Workingmen's Alliance had embodied the political aspirations of various groups. The Knights of Labor had yielded to the American Federation of Labor. For the first time in American history, national trade unions had succeeded in weathering a major business crisis, and felt confident that they could survive future crises. The population of New York City was about three million, a rush of foreign-born was storming Ellis Island, and Wall Street was the symbol of a concentration of wealth that in the next 30 years was to have as profound an effect on the lives of the majority as had the rise of the merchant-capitalist.

By 1930 the working population of New York had grown to a figure greater than the city's entire population in 1897. More than three million persons worked for wage, salary, fee or commission. The majority of wage earners were engaged in manufacturing. More than a million persons were employed in the manufacture of iron and steel, leather and shoes, paper and printing, textiles, clothing and in other manufactures. Clothing was the largest single manufacturing industry, with 141,202 persons engaged therein. Building trades mechanics accounted for nearly a quarter million workers, including 53,569 carpenters, 54,122 painters and glaziers, and 62,528 laborers. There were 297,809 transportation and communication employees. Among the largest groups of workers were domestic and personal service employees, numbering 448,838, of whom 135,939 were house servants other than cooks.

When New York became the nation's business and financial center, every important national firm felt a need, real or fancied, of maintaining an office in the city. This contributed to the growth of a comparatively large white collar class. In 1930 there were more than a half million office or clerical workers not in stores, and a quarter million professional and white collar workers other than clerks and sales persons, including 49,381 teachers. Retail store and commission salesmen totalled 195,358.

New York also became a major intellectual center, not only for literature, science and art, but for labor. New developments such as the American Labor Party, originating in New York City, had profound influence on the direction of workers' political movements throughout the country. Also of importance to workers elsewhere was the fact that in the nation's business, financial and cultural center and in its greatest industrial city at least one-third of all those who worked for a living belonged to labor unions. By 1938, union organization was the rule in New York City in all manufacturing industries, in transportation, and in the building trades and miscellaneous industries. Unions were established in a less degree among municipal employees, professionals and utility workers. Largely unorganized, though there was some unionization among them, were domestics and other servants, clerical and office workers and store salesmen. Company-dominated organizations or company unions in 1938 were established chiefly among clerical workers in some of the larger offices.

An organized class of highly specialized workers did not exist in colonial New York. Labor was not hired, but bound, and consisted of indentured servants and apprentices, or of convicts and slaves. Among the indentured servants were not only skilled workers such as dyers, weavers, carpenters and barbers, but doctors and surgeons, dancing masters and teachers of fencing, writing, drawing and arithmetic. Many of these indentured servants became freemen, joining the large body of free residents —merchants, retailers, mechanics and free servants—in the New Amsterdam of the 1650's. Unless he managed to acquire land, however, the freeman had no voice in the management of the colony.

When in 1628 a body of emigrants erected on Manhattan 30 rude loghouses thatched with reeds, a counting house, a sawmill and a flour mill were all that their simple community economy required. In the century and a half following, the number of skilled workers gradually increased. Many mechanics fought as soldiers of the Revolution. But the winning of political freedom for the colonies did not yet mean political freedom for the mechanic. Under the constitution of New York of 1777 he could vote only if he held land in freehold.

Negroes acquired rights gradually and incompletely. Under the Dutch, enfranchised Negroes were allowed to acquire and hold land. After the English acquired possession of the Colony, however, this practice was expressly prohibited. As early as 1684, the colonial General Assembly passed a law that "no servant or slave shall either give, sell or truck any commodity whatever during their term of service." This law was reenacted in 1726, and again in 1778. By 1790 there were 5,915 Negroes in New York City. With the emancipation of Negro slaves by the acts of 1799, 1817 and 1827, Negroes began to engage in the trades and professions, and records indicate the existence in 1835 of Negro carpenters and joiners, shoemakers, tailors, dress and cloakmakers, clockmakers and teachers.

Many a master workman successfully operated his own business, and after the Revolutionary War masters and journeymen banded together in common organizations for the purpose of furthering their trade. The General Society of Mechanics and Tradesmen was founded in New York in 1785 to resist the competition of foreign goods, and held meetings and parades to influence public opinion. In 1821 this society founded a school and a library to further the education of apprentices. But the position of the master workman slowly grew less secure, and from George Washington's to Andrew Jackson's day he struggled desperately to retain control of his trade. By the 1830's the merchant-capitalist was definitely in command. As early as 1817, New York printers expelled an employer member from their society and declared, with italic emphasis: "This society is a society of *journeymen* printers; and as the interests of the journeymen are *separate* and in some respects *opposite* to those of the employers, we deem it improper that they should have any voice or influence in our deliberations."

Union organization, however, was still regarded as a conspiracy against the public order, and in 1818 the New York Typographical Society was refused articles of incorporation because these did not provide that the society would not "at any time pass any law or regulation respecting the price or wages of labour or workmen." Eight years before, the cordwainers of New York had been forced to defend themselves in court on the charge of conspiracy. At the trial their counsel put the case for the "closed shop" as follows: "If an individual will seek to better himself at the expense of his fellows, when they are suffering privation to obtain terms, it is not hard that they leave him to his employers; and the most inoffensive manner in which they can show their displeasure is by shaking the dust off their feet, and leaving the shop where he is engaged." The term "union" was used for the first time in New York in its modern labor sense in 1825, with the forming of the Nailers' and the Weavers' Unions.

In 1830 Manhattan was about the size of Syracuse a hundred years later, with a population of 202,589. Many poor workingmen owing sums from $2 to $100 were annually sent to debtors' prison, where they were given a single quart of soup every 24 hours, but neither bed nor fuel. There were no tax-supported schools, and the Public School Society of New York City estimated that some 24,000 children between the ages of five and 15 years were deprived of schooling. Even in the so-called public schools a fee was charged until 1832.

Male citizens had held the vote since 1821, but not until 1829 did mechanics organize a political party of their own—the Workingmen's Party of New York City. After a whirlwind campaign of two weeks in 1830, the party elected an assemblyman and a State senator. A New York assemblyman of the old school described this political organization of workmen as "more dangerous than any . . . in the days of the French

Revolution." The press called members of the Workingmen's Party "levelers" and "workies," and described their movement as the "dirty-shirt party" of a "ring-streaked and speckled rabble," whose leaders were "lost to society, to earth and to heaven, godless and hopeless, clothed and fed by stealing and blasphemy." The *Commercial Advertiser* and the *Journal of Commerce* attacked the system of universal suffrage that could bring into being a party "which is emerging from the slime of this community, and which is more beastly and terrible than the Egyptian Typhoon." Yet the platform of the Workingmen's Party called merely for the establishing of free public schools, the reform of banking, the curbing of monopoly, the abolition of imprisonment for debt, improvement in election methods, reform of the militia system, payment of adequate fees to jurors and witnesses, civil service reform, religious freedom and the abolition of capital punishment.

Prominent in the political and reform movements of the 1830's was Thomas Skidmore, a machinist strongly influenced by the ideas of Thomas Paine. Skidmore published in 1829 *The Rights of Man to Property* in which he maintained that the unequal division of property caused the ills of society. George Henry Evans, brother of the famous Shaker, became editor of the New York *Working Man's Advocate* in 1829, and devoted his life to land reform. Robert Dale Owen, son of the famous philanthropist, became editor of the *Free Enquirer* in New York, where he was associated with Frances Wright, rationalist, social reformer, and champion of women's rights. Other workers' papers established in these years were the *Daily Sentinel* and the *Evening Enquirer*.

New York workers supported the free land movement for which Skidmore and Evans carried on unremitting propaganda for a generation after 1828. It was the alliance of Eastern wage earners interested in stimulating emigration to the West (thus improving the market for their own labor) with frontiersmen in national politics that made possible the election of Andrew Jackson and later the election of Abraham Lincoln.

As the century advanced, however, and the infant commercial system grew stronger, political action yielded to the more immediate task of union organization. In 1833 there were at least 15 organized trades in New York. These included several trades mainly employing women, such as bookbinding, in which the binders formed in 1835 the Female Union Association and struck for higher wages, and the garment industry, in which seamstresses organized a union in 1836. From February to December of 1836 no fewer than 13 strikes of skilled workers were recorded—in addition, no doubt, to many others unrecorded. A central union body organized in 1833, published a paper, *The National Trades' Union,* from 1834 to 1836. Most of these early unions feared that participation in politics would bring division into their primarily economic organizations, and they adhered to immediate demands for higher wages and shorter hours. The first national convention of trades unions was held in 1836, and the first national body set up; it prematurely and unsuccessfully attempted to represent all working men. In its place, national organizations of various crafts were formed.

With the panic of 1837, the labor movement was crushed out of existence. Unions, city trades unions and councils, national federations, and the labor press disappeared. Wages were reduced and thousands lost their jobs, 6,000 building workers being discharged in New York City alone in 1837. A "dense multitude of many thousands" gathered in the park in front of City Hall in February 1837 to demonstrate for "bread, meat, rent and fuel." This demonstration and others were sponsored by the newly organized Equal Rights Party, formed by workingmen who had seen their trade unions dissolve in the panic and who sought some alternate means of gaining security. The party defeated Tammany in the city elections in 1837. Tammany, now early in its career putting into effect its principle of "if ye can't lick 'em jine 'em," in the next elections placed on its ticket five members of the Equal Rights Party, on condition that the latter withdraw its other candidates—and thus embarked on a policy, the main source of its strength for almost a hundred years, of organizing the labor vote.

The panic of 1837 deepened into a long depression, the "hard times" of the 1840's. The merchant-capitalists, who had been busy fighting the trade unions, now turned to fighting the business crisis—a large part of their strategy consisting in attempting to undermine one another. Although the weaker ones vanished, the remaining merchant-capitalists became stronger than ever.

The "occult power" of machinery, as the land reformer Thomas A. Devyr phrased it, was now rapidly overtaking handicraft, and in the consequent shifts and readjustments the new class rung so bravely into being by Mechanics' Bell suffered incredible hardship. The first great wave of unskilled laborers from Europe arrived to swell the labor market. "Hard times" brought to the working men a feeling of frustration. Their unions had all but vanished, the Workingmen's Party was a thing of the past, the Equal Rights Party had been absorbed by Tammany. The right to vote, held for about 20 years, had served only to strengthen merchant-capitalist policies. Small wonder that a band of beckoning spirits, the intellectuals, found in the 1840's many followers among workers. Robert Dale Owen, in New York after the failure of New Harmony, Josiah Warren, the founder of "time stores" and of the American school of intellectual anarchists, Albert Brisbane, and the rest, although preaching diverse methods of solving the problems of society, had a common aim: the introduction of "harmony" into the productive world, the collaboration of the consumer with the producer and of the entrepreneur with the laborer. They opposed both political action and trade union organization. Brisbane, returning to America in 1834 a convert to Fourier, announced that society must be organized into "groups," "series," and "sacred legions" based not on modes of production but on men's passions and desires.

As editor of the New York *Tribune* from 1841 to 1872, Horace Greeley had an enormous influence on the temper of the age. His philosophy, never clearly defined, contained elements of land reform, currency reform, Fourierism and abolitionism. William Weitling, a German immigrant, who in 1850 founded in New York the *Republik der Arbeiter,* saw more clearly than Brisbane or Greeley that producing and distributing cooperatives remained at the mercy of the bankers who supplied the capital. He therefore proposed the organization, not of more cooperative ventures, but of "banks of exchange," or cooperative banks, which in his view would effectively displace the merchant-capitalist.

The cooperative propaganda of the 1840's found a fertile field in New York, and a number of societies were set up, both of the producers' and of the consumers' type. Most of them failed. The reason assigned by the workers themselves, as reported in Greeley's *Tribune,* was the rapid turnover of the membership. Too many leaders were drawn away to the West or tried to start little businesses of their own. This factor of mobility also accounts largely for the apparent desultoriness and lack of stamina in the trade unions of these years.

With the rush of immigrants to New York and the rise in business activity in the early 1850's, there began the separation of skilled from unskilled labor, and the rise of craft unions solidly organized on the basis of regular dues, fixed meetings and contracts with employers. As the earlier artisans had expelled employers from their ranks, the skilled workers now excluded from their unions all "friends of labor" not working at the trade. Parallel to the growth of craft unions was the new tendency among workers speaking a foreign language to make up a single local or union. Prices began to rise rapidly, and the skilled workers, whose wages lagged considerably behind the rising cost of living, made great gains in organization. In 1853 and 1854, Greeley's *Tribune* sometimes recorded in a single issue as many as 25 or 30 strikes, while Greeley himself in an adjoining editorial would thunder against the trade unions, which he alternately opposed and cajoled during the rest of his career. Weitling, too, was strongly opposed to trade unionism, maintaining that it was a device of capital to hold the workers in check.

The hard times of the 1840's were scarcely over when a new depression in 1854–5 deepened into the panic of 1857. Mobs of desperate men and women roamed the streets of New York shouting "Bread or death!" and threatened to attack the Subtreasury Building. Had it not been for the safety-valve of the westward migration and the increasing tension over the slavery question, the revolutionary events in Europe might have had a parallel in American industrial cities such as New York.

Many workers in New York had ardently supported the abolition movement, but the attempt made during the Civil War to apply the Conscription Act in New York resulted in mob fighting and the erection of barricades in the streets. The provision of this act permitting a man of draft age to purchase immunity from military service for the sum of $300 was strongly resented. The average worker, to whom the sum represented a large share of his annual income, and who was aware that some of those who thus purchased their freedom were making huge war profits, felt that the entire burden of the war was on his shoulders. Riots began on Monday, July 13, 1863, and continued until Friday. What began as a demonstration against the unfairness of the Conscription Act ended in bitter street warfare, the destruction of property, the sacking of buildings. New York employers had on numerous occasions made use of Negro workers as strike-breakers, and the mob, many of whom saw the slavery issue as the single cause of the war, dragged Negroes from their homes, beat and in some instances killed them, and attempted to sack the office of Greeley's abolitionist *Tribune*. Not until the city had been occupied by 10,000 troops was order restored. Nearly a thousand rioters and three policemen lost their lives during the week.

Organized labor, however, did not participate in these riots. Neither did the German workers, influenced by revolutionary doctrines of Europe which maintained that the Civil War represented a struggle between the merchant-capitalists of the North and the landlords of the South, and hence was generally in the direction of progress. Whole locals of unions in New York, in fact, enlisted on the side of the North.

The period immediately following the Civil War saw the rise of two characteristically American movements. Greenbackism began as currency reform and developed into an attempt at complete industrial organization by displacing bankers and middlemen from their positions in the economy of production. The eight-hour day movement began as an attempt by workmen to shorten their hours of work, but soon accumulated a body of theory aimed at solving the problems of capital and labor by a general rise in purchasing power. Other important developments of this period were the invention of the trade union label, the first national trade agreement, the first eight-hour legislation, the formation of a national employers' association and of a national labor party, the first laws directed against "conspiracy" and "intimidation" by trade unions, and the beginning of jurisdictional disputes between unions.

The National Labor Union, founded in 1866 at Baltimore, held its third annual meeting in New York in 1868; and at that meeting it appointed delegates to the International Workmen's Association, established by Karl Marx and British trade unionists in 1864. The National Labor Union affiliated with the International in 1870, and the American section devoted most of its practical efforts toward international regulation of immigration and the attempt to avert what seemed an inevitable war between England and the United States. A National Labor Congress, representing 600,000 organized American workers and counting among its leaders Ezra A. Heywood, Susan B. Anthony, Elizabeth Cady Stanton and A. C. Cameron met in New York on September 21, 1868.

The Communist Club of New York, organized in 1857, affiliated with the International in 1867; as did the more powerful General German Workingmen's Union, the latter becoming Section 1 of New York of the International. Originally, the German Workingmen's Union, while recognizing that "in Europe only a general revolution can form the means of uplifting the working people," hoped for the abolition of the capitalist method of production in the adopted country by "the education of the masses" and "the use of the ballot." In 1866 the Union received an invitation from the county committee of the Republican Party to send delegates to the county nominating convention. Most sections of the International in New York City were made up of foreign workers, but Sections 9 and 12 were composed largely of native Americans and were headed by two sisters, Victoria Woodhull and Tennessee Claflin. Section 12 was a great trial to the central committee of the International in London, which finally expelled it for addressing, without authority, an appeal "to the citizens of the Union" which called for the right of women to vote and hold office, the formation of a universal language, and freedom of sexual relations. For a while, after the Congress of The Hague in 1872 and the expulsion of Bakunin, the general council of the International, fearing the influence of the Bakuninists, had its headquarters in New York. The International in America was dissolved in 1876.

The panic of 1873 forced about 3,000,000 workers into unemployment throughout the country. In New York State approximately 182,000 skilled union workers were idle, and trade union membership in New York City fell from about 44,000 to about 5,000. A great demonstration and parade of the unemployed was called for January 13, 1874, with permission of the city authorities; but at the last moment, when it was too late for the leaders to inform the paraders, the officials withdrew their consent. At the appointed hour a great crowd of men, women and children poured into Tompkins Square. Suddenly, in the midst of speeches, a force of police charged upon the gathering, and many persons were clubbed or otherwise injured.

Wage cuts, unemployment, and a general lowering of living standards for American workmen brought about the "Great Riots" of 1877, when all over the country workers violently demanded food and jobs. "Contrary to the popular notion," remarks Lillian Symes in *Rebel America,* "that violence in the American labor movement stems from European anarchism, it was this spontaneous uprising on the part of the native American workers in the sultry dog days of July 1877 that first directed attention of European revolutionary anarchists—men like Michael Bakunin and Johann Most—to our revolutionary possibilities. The events that make 1877 the bloodiest year in the history of the American labor movement occurred without benefit of alien theories."

In order to break a strike of the highly organized cigar makers in 1873, the employers transferred cigar making from large shops to tenements. Within a year more than half of the cigars manufactured in New York were being made with tenement labor, under appallingly unsanitary conditions. An appeal to the Board of Health proving unsuccessful, the union began to organize the tenement workers. A strike of 7,000 cigar makers in 1877 included many tenement workers, but it was lost. Although the union was successful in 1883 in securing the passage of a law prohibiting the manufacture of cigars in tenement houses, the highest court of the State declared the law unconstitutional because "it is plain that this is not a health law, and that it has no relation whatever to the public health."

After the disastrous strike of 1877, Adolph Strasser, the union president, began to reorganize the union along the lines of what later became known as "pure and simple" trade unionism. The Cigar Makers International Union became a model organization of highly skilled craftsmen, with many of the characteristics that Samuel Gompers was later to introduce into the American Federation of Labor (established in 1881 as the Federation of Organized Trades and Labor Unions of the United States and Canada).

Although marked by a growing emphasis on "pure and simple" trade unionism, the last two decades of the century were by no means barren of political activities on the part of labor. The "Big Six" typographical union, while engaged in a dispute with the New York *Tribune,* boycotted not only the newspaper and its advertisers but a presidential candidate, James G. Blaine, when the Republican National Committee in 1884 refused to repudiate the *Tribune* as its party organ. In the same year Henry George, author of *Progress and Poverty,* ran for mayor of New York on a labor ticket, opposing Abram S. Hewitt, the Tammany candidate, and Theodore Roosevelt, the Republican nominee. Hewitt accused George of attempting "to organize one class of our citizens against all other classes," to which George retorted that all classes, save the minority that did not work for a living, were with him. Hewitt won the election with 90,000 votes, George polled 68,000 votes and Roosevelt 60,000. Contemporary observers believed, however, that George was fraudulently "counted out" of thousands of votes. As a result of this campaign, the United Party was formed. Its platform, however, neglected labor issues in favor of the single tax; and the party soon disintegrated. During the presidential campaign of 1896 many prominent trade unionists in New York threw their support to William Jennings Bryan.

The closing years of the 19th century witnessed the beginnings of a tremendous consolidation of enterprise in all the basic industries, as far reaching in its effects as had been the rise of the merchant-capitalist class in the 1830's. Coincident with the national growth of monopoly came enormous technological progress, most apparent in transportation and building. Trains were first operated by electricity in New York in 1901; and the first subway unit, from City Hall to 145th Street and Broadway, was completed in 1904. While very few private homes were being built in Manhattan at the end of the century, apartment houses were going up everywhere; and a modern office structure, the Flatiron Building, was completed in 1902.

Union organization kept pace with transportation and building. As early as 1861 there had been a union of street car employees on the Third

Avenue line. Other lines were successfully organized in 1886. By 1903, 1,300 elevated employees had joined a union that in 1904 waged an unsuccessful strike against the Interborough. The United Board of Building Trades was formed in New York in 1902.

The coming of the skyscraper to New York after 1890 brought a new set of problems to the building workers, since the rapid change of technique and the substitution of metal for wood meant the shifting of craft lines, the breaking down of old skills, and the growth of new specialized occupations. Jurisdictional disputes have kept closely related unions at loggerheads with one another for at least a generation. The introduction of new processes has at times been delayed though never prevented by union action.

The relatively strong bargaining position of the building unions has enabled them to secure high hourly wage rates. They have shown a tendency to make exclusive contracts with certain employers' groups, and have at times closed their books to new members and even to union members from other cities. The great power that came to be concentrated in the hands of their business agents, coupled with the presence in the industry of unscrupulous business men, led to some of the most notorious grafting and racketeering in the history of labor. Sam Parks was convicted of extortion in 1902, and Robert P. Brindell was convicted of the same offense in 1921; each was president of the Building Trades Council at the time of his conviction. Many other union leaders in the building trades have been sent to prison for grafting from employers or stealing union funds. The Building Trades Employers' Association was set up among the contractors to check Sam Parks; it has bargained with the unions and protected its members from grafting.

The unethical union practices prevalent in the post-war building boom were coupled with a failure to consolidate the position of the unions in the economic field and to extend their field of operations. The fringes of the industry, in outlying parts of the city and in the suburbs, were never thoroughly organized. Representatives of the International Brotherhood of Electrical Workers even signed an agreement with the Consolidated Edison Company that the union would not try to organize the men in the company's plants, though claiming jurisdiction over them. In the slump after 1929 many more men slipped away from the control of the unions; and the "kick-back," by which part of the worker's wage was paid over to the boss after payday, became common.

Complete unionization, even on the larger jobs, has never existed in the industry since 1904, when the Structural Ironworkers' Union was defeated in a tussle with the employers organized in the Iron League. The faulty tactics of the union leaders cost them the support of the unions in the other trades, and the trade remained technically "open shop" for a generation, though paying union wages and working union hours.

Always there has been at work in each union an element that was revolted by the undemocratic methods and grafting tactics of certain hardboiled leaders. This element became thoroughly aroused when the depression weakened the grip of the old-timers, and the painters took the lead in making a thorough-going change in leadership.

When, at the turn of the century, New York became the garment-making center of the country, the International Ladies Garment Workers Union was formed (1900). With a strike of 20,000 shirtwaist makers in 1909 and a walkout of 60,000 cloakmakers in 1910, this union firmly established itself in the garment shops on an industrial basis. In the men's clothing industry, as the result of a schism in the United Garment Workers Union during the strike of 1914, the Amalgamated Clothing Workers of America was organized. This union ultimately emerged as one of the most progressive and powerful of the garment unions, and by 1937 it had 50,000 members in New York City and 200,000 throughout the country. It created a statistical and research department, and in 1923 established the Amalgamated Bank. Through this bank, owned and operated by the union, labor has often financed its employers—an arrangement unique in large-scale industry. The solidly organized garment unions, through their Joint Boards, exert a stabilizing influence upon an industry that is made up of small units and that is as erratic as the fluctuations of style itself.

The growth of industrial unionism in the garment trade was paralleled by the growth of the Fur Workers Union, at first limited to highly skilled workers but after 1905 broadened to include the semi-skilled. New York was also the chief stronghold of the Steel and Metal Workers International Union.

During the World War, labor gains were notably evident in New York in the shipbuilding industry, the iron and steel fabricating plants, and the clothing industry, with allied industries similarly affected. The building-trades unions also grew in membership. On August 7, 1919, the Actors' Equity Association fired the opening gun in its fight for recognition by the Producing Managers' Association. Twenty-five theaters were kept in darkness during a strike that lasted 31 days and included a spectacular parade down Broadway of more than 2,000 Equity members. The producers granted the actors' demand for a closed shop.

The strike of the New York Newspaper Web Pressmen's Union crippled the newspaper plants of the city in September 1923, and regular editions of the metropolitan newspapers were suspended for a period of 18 days. The *Socialist Call,* which had made an immediate settlement with the union, alone appeared in its usual form. On September 19, the publishers issued the *Combined New York Morning Newspaper,* carrying in miniature the mastheads of nearly all the city's prominent newspapers. International President George L. Berry signed an agreement on September 21 with the publishers providing for a closed shop, shorter hours and a weekly wage increase. Simultaneously, the New York local, which had waged the strike without authority of the international union, was divided, and its members ordered to apply directly to the International for new membership cards.

A tugboatmen's strike in January 1920, resulting from wage cuts and other grievances, led to the issuance of a strike call by the International Longshoremens Association. Twenty thousand members of the Marine Workers Affiliation in New York responded to this call, and the strike was later extended to all southern ports. Vast quantities of foodstuffs and coal were tied up in all terminals. Groups of railroad shopmen quit without warning, and all freight and passenger traffic between Chicago and the East was stopped. The strike became a public issue, and the workers demanded that Samuel Gompers, president of the American Federation of Labor, should call a nationwide walkout. Attorney-General Palmer denounced the strike as the work of the IWW, and threatened to invoke the Lever and Sherman laws. Raids and arrests followed and the Railroad Labor Board declared that it would refuse hearings to all railroad employees who had broken work agreements. Strikebreakers were imported, while college professors and students manned commutation trains as volunteers. Teamsters joined the strike on April 15 by refusing to handle non-union shipments. A so-called Citizens' Transportation Committee began to deliver freight, and broke the strike.

The "New Era" of prosperity between 1923 and 1930 was characterized by a growth of welfare schemes, company unions and various plans for employer-employee collaboration. The American Federation of Labor adopted a conciliatory policy, showing a willingness to cooperate with industrial management so that prosperity might continue undisturbed. There was a constant drop in membership in all but the entrenched craft unions.

For the most part, however, New York unions came through this period better than unions in other parts of the country, losing ground mainly by attrition and apathy.

During the 1920's, New York City became the battlefield for two opposing currents of union philosophy. Left-wing blocs, waging war against organizational inactivity and for industrial unionism, were especially active in the garment unions. Their activities centered chiefly around the Trade Union Educational League, formed in 1920 and headed by William Z. Foster, former American Federation of Labor organizer and leader in the steel strike of 1919, subsequently chairman of the Communist Party of the United States. The League announced its plan "to develop the trade unions from their present antiquated and stagnant condition into powerful, modern labor organs, capable of waging successful war against Capital." This left-wing movement won the allegiance of several locals of the Fur Workers Union, and created opposition blocs in the garment unions and a number of the building-trades unions. In 1929 the International Ladies Garment Workers Union expelled 77 regularly elected left-wing delegates of the New York Joint Board who represented the 30,000 members of Locals 2, 9 and 22. At about the same time, the International Fur Workers Union expelled several left-wing locals, with a membership of 15,000. New independent industrial unions were organized and affiliated with the Trade Union Unity League, itself affiliated with the Communist Red International of Labor Unions. The unions of the Trade Union Unity League led a series of aggressive strikes in New York, notably among shoe and leather workers and cafeteria employees and in out-of-the-way sections of the garment trades.

Although the activities of the Trade Union Unity League caused American Federation of Labor unions and leaders in New York City to define their own policies more sharply, the severe economic crisis of 1929 found organized labor still poorly prepared to meet it effectively. Labor, in New York, again began to express itself politically, as it had in 1830, 1837, 1850 and periodically since. Conscious of its plight and of the dangers inherent in vast unemployment, it helped—although not in any organized way—to elect a national Democratic administration in 1932. It also undertook a series of organizational drives, the success of which was aided by Section 7a of the National Recovery Act, effective June 16, 1933, which acknowledged the right of workers "to organize and bargain collectively through representatives of their own choosing . . . free from interference, restraint or coercion of employers of labor or their agents."

A number of new unions were chartered, among them the American Newspaper Guild, which had its largest local in New York City. The Trade Union Unity League officially dissolved in 1935, its members returning to American Federation of Labor locals. The Fur Workers Industrial Union, one of the strongest units of the Needle Trades Workers Industrial Union, was formally admitted as an entity into the American Federation of Labor, becoming the International Fur Workers Union. The International Ladies Garment Workers Union launched an intensive organizational drive. A stoppage of cloakmakers in 1934 brought 12,000 new members into the fold; and the dressmaking division was reorganized and strengthened by 90,000 members. Passing the 100,000 mark in New York, the union spread its recruiting campaign to outlying towns, where it organized an additional 120,000 workers.

An event of unusual importance to organized labor was the passage of the National Labor Relations Act, popularly known as the Wagner Labor Act because of its sponsorship by Senator Wagner of New York. This measure, as signed by the President on July 2, 1935, provided for "the exercise by workers of full freedom of association, self organization and designation of representatives of their own choosing for the purpose of negotiating the terms and conditions of their employment." Resort to the New York regional office of the National Labor Relations Board became frequent. In the nine months between October 1, 1936, and June 30, 1937, the New York regional office cleared a total of 386 cases, in 213 of which agreements were reached by employers and employees through mediation by the board.

While labor was recovering from its moribund state and taking the offensive, public attention was directed to the extensive racketeering and corruption that had sprung up in a number of unions during the prosperous years of 1923–30. In some organizations in New York City—the Painters' Union, for example—the issue was fought out internally and the corrupt cliques ousted. Later, with the appointment by Governor Lehman of Thomas E. Dewey as Special Prosecutor, indictments were brought in 1936 and 1937 against gangsters and racketeers who preyed upon bona fide unions—in some instances actually becoming officials of legitimate unions, in others forming "associations" disguised as labor unions which attempted to "shake down" employers. Among those convicted and sentenced were three officials of the Hotel and Restaurant Workers Union, who were proved to have engaged in extortion; a notorious gangster, Arthur Flegenheimer ("Dutch Schultz"); "Tootsie" Herbert, described as a leading figure in the underworld, who had become business agent of Local 167 of the Chicken Drivers Union; and officers of the Official Orthodox Poultry Slaughterers of America (orthodox Jewish chicken killers or *schoctim*), who, according to the prosecution, had conspired with members of the New York Live Poultry Chamber of Commerce to monopolize the live poultry business of New York City.

A new element, destined to increase union enrollment at a tremendous rate and to help swell the total number of New York unionists to more than 1,000,000 in 1938, was formed in 1935 as a coordinating body engaged in union activities outside the jurisdiction of the American Federation of Labor. The Committee for Industrial Organization, as it was named, grew out of certain American Federation of Labor unions committed to the structural principle of industrial or "vertical" unionism as against the craft or "horizontal" policy predominant in the AFL. The CIO movement, though deriving its greatest momentum from the enrollment of workers in mass production industries in other parts of the country, proved to be a driving force for unionization in New York City, enrolling organized garment workers, clothing workers, hat, cap and millinery workers, seamen, transport workers, shoe workers, office and professional workers, as well as many others hitherto unorganized.

Many new unions were created as a result of the entrance of CIO into the organizing field. It took the stand that it would not invade AFL territory except where the existing unions included only a small percentage of the workers in the industry and were too weak to undertake organization activities. The AFL charged that CIO was setting up dual unions, and countered by extending the jurisdiction of its existing unions to cover sections of industries not previously enrolled. Despite bitter disagreement between the CIO and the AFL, however, large sections of rank and file workers in both organizations, as well as numerous officials, hope for ultimate unity.

The resurgence in 1936 of broad political action by labor, independent of the old-line parties, was not a new phenomenon in the history of labor in New York. Workers had organized their own political parties for independent action, as has been seen, in 1830 and at intervals since, especially when panics and depressions smashed local trade unions and wrecked national federations. When, on the other hand, labor parties gained the objectives of universal suffrage, free public schools, and the abolition of oppressive legislation, or when workingmen's political groups were absorbed or defeated by other political groups, New York labor abruptly forsook politics, especially in a period of industrial expansion, and turned toward simple trade unionism.

What was striking about the organization, on July 16, 1936, of the American Labor Party was that for the first time in more than a hundred years New York workers turned to independent political action during a period of growth in union organization. Workers now entered politics, not because their trade unions had been smashed by an industrial crisis, but in order to broaden politically the democratic gains being made at the same time in the economic field.

On August 18, 1936, the American Labor Party announced the names of the first labor party presidential electors in United States history. With President Roosevelt and Governor Lehman as its candidates, in the November election it polled 274,924 votes in New York City. Encouraged by this success, its leaders began organization of an electoral apparatus, and proceeded to form Labor Party clubs in the State's more important assembly districts. The party name was kept prominently before the public by vigorous support of the national Child Labor Amendment and the Judicial Reform proposal. On August 4, 1937, the party nominated Mayor Fiorello H. La Guardia for reelection as mayor, and in September it adopted a municipal platform demanding public ownership of those services in which "private enterprise and capital have failed to meet public necessities." Specific planks in the platform called for extensive public housing, municipal ownership of utilities and the traction system, distribution of low-cost milk, extension of free hospital facilities and maintenance of relief at adequate living standards. In the sphere of social justice, the platform called for government aid in the fight against child exploitation, substandard wages, excessive hours, and sweatshop working conditions. Demands for maintenance of the public educational system at a high level and adequate minority representation in city government were also included.

In the subsequent city election of November 1937, the American Labor Party polled nearly 43 percent of the votes for the winning ticket. Five of its candidates were elected to the City Council, along with one Fusion-Labor candidate. Meanwhile, units of the American Labor Party were being formed in many industrial sections of the United States.

In 1938, a century after Mechanics' Bell had pealed its demand for the ten-hour day and the recognition of the needs of the workers in New York, there was again occasion for a mechanics' bell to call attention to new labor problems and the urgent need for new solutions, with unity the most pressing need of all.

The Urban Pattern

As EARLY as 1914, Graham Wallas could write that "the science of city planning is rapidly developing into the master science of the material conditions of modern life." Even into the late 1930's, this remained an effective characterization of the tremendous range and complexity of the "civic art." It also implied basic conceptual limits. In the positive sense, planning had expanded from the nucleus of skills recommended by Vitruvius until it included such highly assorted factors as power, heat, light, commerce, engineering, transport, finance, architecture, industry, education, meteorology, water supply, wharfage, sanitation, physiography, traffic control and landscape architecture in their modern meanings.

On the negative side, the phrase "material conditions" indicates in general how far the science is still bound by historical and technical usage. Especially as regards statutory planning, it has largely failed to establish that degree of removal from politics as a means, that ability to regard politics as a necessary element in the problem rather than an unyielding frame, which has been considered essential in the other sciences. As against such practice, compare Frank Lloyd Wright's free projection of Broadacre City —somewhat Utopian, perhaps, in its detachment from existing dilemmas in the recasting of great cities, but superbly calculated in relation to materials, social use and the prevention of just such future dilemmas.

Again, civic art has made little use of those biological techniques—the genetics of Morgan, Haldane, Jennings and Hogben, for example—which, as Lewis Mumford shows, had begun to reach a flowering in the first third of the 20th century. It has also largely failed to integrate findings in the collateral social sciences: the mass psychology of Allport; Galpin's pioneer study, *The Social Anatomy of a Rural Community,* which analyzed methods of determining actual as against administrative limits of the community. Perhaps the chief criticism of community planning so far has been that it did not find room for these and other contributory techniques in the broad terms of ecology, which considers "the interactions among plants, animals and environment that result in organic communities." Robert Murray Haig mentioned in 1927 that ecological studies were not then sufficiently advanced to be available for immediate use; ten years later, Marie Swabey could write that on the whole the social sciences were still "at the descriptive and classificatory level." But since the planning science is in part an attempt to anticipate future social situations, even the broader and more basic framework of ecology could not help but be invaluable as a more elastic scheme of orientation.

The characteristic terms of the planning science—*land economics, efficient pattern of population, primary and ancillary economic functions, factor of safety, ratio of friction*—indicate that it attempts no primary cultural analysis beyond the exposition of current or anticipated plant and process. Its basic orientation is in effect an extension of civil engineering. Perhaps in part as a reaction from the somewhat wide-eyed school of the City Beautiful popular in America early in the 20th century, or more importantly, out of prejudice for and training in the tradition of the geometric approach and the mechanistic sciences, its sponsors—with certain notable exceptions—have been content to work within the broadened criteria of Victorian utilitarianism.

It is obvious that this must have been influenced to some extent by the necessity for "practical" presentation. The real reasons lay deeper; they were all involved in the fact that modern community planning, from Haussmann to Walter Curt Behrendt, has been in the main a technique of reclamation. "In the larger community," said the architect Clarence Stein in 1938, "we have city patching, not city planning." It could not—except in the new Soviet industrial cities, or in the towns set up by the Resettlement Administration and the Tennessee Valley Authority—begin with a fresh site, as Alexander of Macedon had done, or as Peter the Great did with St. Petersburg: a site so ill-chosen that floods, commemorated in Pushkin's *The Bronze Horseman,* repeatedly overran the city from the Neva and Lake Ladoga.

Paris is perhaps the typical example of a long tradition of city planning as reclamation. Seven times in its history it has broken out of a girdle of fortifications, each time adding one more ring of growth. Under Louis XIV, great monumental buildings went up and the old Portes Saint-Denis and Saint-Martin became triumphal arches. Napoleon Bonaparte developed 60 new streets, among them the Rue de la Paix. Under Napoleon III, Georges Haussmann and his executive engineer, Deschamps, spent $20,-000,000 a year—an enormous sum in those times—toward opening up traffic with great avenues broad enough to serve as military roads. These, of course, were instances of planning by fiat.

In the present century, heights of buildings have been regulated by zoning in the central quarters of the city; but the major problem of Paris, like that of most metropolises, has been the problem of the suburbs. It is, in other words, an end-product of unregulated industrial expansion in the paleotechnic age: the benighting of whole regions with industrial waste products and the housing of workers in semi-rural slums. Jules Romains has made this world and its causes explicit in *Flood Warning;* and in *The Meek,* he recreates a horrifying fragment of squatters' life in "the zone," a former military area outside the fortifications. After the World War, these squatters multiplied until they numbered some 100,000 in 1929. A law regulating the development of such marginal areas was passed in 1924 and a correlating and planning board, Direction de l'Extension de Paris, set up. Since that time the fortifications—400,000 cubic meters of stone work—have been demolished, most of the 59 gates widened and underpassed with tunnels for circumferential traffic.

The area of the old walls and "the zone," long obsolete and now replaced by the new strategy of the Maginot Line, is being occupied by planned developments: University City to the south, the great Boulevards Souchet and Jourdan, workers' colonies and other dwellings (more than 50,000 new apartments were built during the period 1933–7), all interwoven with a green belt of playgrounds, gardens and parks. In 1932 regulations were set up establishing a General Plan of Greater Paris—the area within a radius of 22 miles about Paris proper—intended to provide systematic development zones for housing, business, industry and recreation. These regulations granted certain legal powers necessary to survey and create a coordinated city plan.

This characteristic history of remedial planning has been duplicated all over the modern world. Sir Patrick Geddes suggested a pattern in the biolysis of great cities: *metropolis* becomes *megalopolis,* which puffs itself up like a balloon; next *parasitopolis,* in which every man necessarily turns thief or chiseler; and the end-phase, *pathopolis,* "the city that ceases effectively to function." Nearly every modern world city has gone through one or more of these phases, complicated by the primary and drastic stresses of the first industrial age; all over the world, authorities and advisory boards have been set up to recast cities and whole regions.

In Italy, for example, "the first modern town planning legislation," the Expropriation Law, was passed in 1865; but it turned out to be so complicated that not very much could be done. Under Premier Mussolini, national planning became a major ambition, and the rebuilding of Rome, especially in the central parts, was begun on a scale equalled nowhere else in the world. But this was to a considerable degree a work of archaeological restoration, compromised by an oversimplified system of radial military avenues of the type generally considered unsuitable for modern traffic.

A town planning law similar to the Italian act was passed in Sweden in 1874 and amended in 1907, 1917 and 1919. In Stockholm, a building board—two architects, a physician, a lawyer, a contractor—determine architectural taste and land use. Aside from the older government group, the Stockholm Town Planning Board is developing a civic center in the middle of the city. As Marquis W. Childs has shown, one remarkable feature of Stockholm planning was the early capture of suburban areas and harbor islands for low-cost housing financed in part by municipal loans. Except in scale, Stockholm's problem of accommodation to a complicated system of waterways resembles that of the New York area. It is being solved with a regard to order and the amenities equalled nowhere else, perhaps, but in the more ingenuous disposition of Rio de Janeiro about its harbor.

The Russian single-function industrial cities are related more closely to the ancient Kahun or the modern Dearborn than to multi-functional world cities. In 1932 and later, as Thomas Adams writes, "the Communist Academy of Russia, which deals with the problem of Socialist distribution of the population, has evolved a concrete program of town planning which takes into account all technical and social factors characteristic in the present period of building." A ten-year plan for the development of Moscow, submitted by the Union of Soviet Architects and made effective July 10, 1935, specifies that (1) the area of the city shall be increased from 19,-768 acres to 148,260 acres by 1945; (2) Greater Moscow is to be surrounded by a forest belt some six miles deep (probably for military purposes); (3) there will be three new boulevards of extraordinary width—Ilyich Avenue, for example, is to be 328 feet wide; (4) the new city will converge upon the Palace of the Soviets, 1,360 feet high, one-third of a mile long and 820 feet deep; (5) population growth will be limited to 5,000,000 by means of control of factories, evictions for slum clearance, and a passport system.

At the end of 1937, Albion Ross reported in the New York *Times* that plans were being laid to convert Berlin into a monumental capital city organized about two huge squares and a mall. This Roman pattern was intended to refurbish the old city of "disjointed and formerly independent towns," in which there were few impressive structures other than the Imperial Palace and the Reichstag Building. The latter was to be pulled down to make way for a massive Fuehrer Haus. Near its old site, two of "the broadest avenues in the world" would intersect each other. Behind the Potsdamer Platz, the section in the middle of the city long occupied by railroad tracks was to be built up as a new district.

In England, aside from the establishment of such limited garden cities as Letchworth and Welwyn, London has made notable advances. The capture of the Thames Embankment, beloved of Whistler and Carlyle, in 1862–70, and the commercial developments involved in the Kingsway reconstruction project prepared the way for a combination of local authorities in the Greater London Joint Committee, which deals with coordinated problems involving the greater city and considerable areas in the Counties of Hertfordshire, Essex, Kent, Surrey, Middlesex and Buckinghamshire.

Against this drastically simplified perspective of world planning, which necessarily leaves out of account such projects as the great Ruhr Regional Planning Federation, the situation of any large American city region, New York in particular, shows certain obvious differences. Even among American cities, many of which went up like tent colonies, New York had an excessively rapid growth which did not taper off to any great extent even in the years after the World War. While the French were instituting their national compulsory planning law in 1919–24, the plummets of the land speculator and the hammers of the cheap contractor swung over all the outlying boroughs of the city. Gazing at those interminable rows of houses, often unsound in construction and exorbitantly priced, the observer may reckon for himself the overhead of unplanned and insufficiently regulated development.

Aside from private losses, "it can be shown," as Charles D. Norton wrote, "that without a plan hundreds of millions of dollars have been wasted in and near New York during the past century in desultory or ill-considered public improvements." The cost goes deeper than that. It is reflected, not only in the measurable relation between unhealthy living conditions and disease, crime and misery, but in the whole tone of a society. A policeman standing forever on point duty in the man-made night of lower Broadway may feel that "timeless melancholy, dry, reckless, defeated and perverse," which Malcolm Cowley mentioned as the underlying mood of New York in the 1920's; or a truck-driver, his willing gusto turned sour by an eternity of exasperation in jammed parking, red lights, sidewalk loading, and traffic like cattle in a chute, may wear a chip on his shoulder for all men, as Stephen Crane's Jimmie Johnson did.

More often than not, the functional ills of Manhattan and to an extent those of the other boroughs have been blamed on a single scapegoat: the Randall (Randel or Randell) Manhattan Plan of 1811, which still governed the main pattern of the borough in 1938. This was the gridiron street plan drawn up by the engineer John Randall, Jr., under the direction of a three-man commission appointed by the legislature on April 3, 1807, at the request of the Common Council of New York. The commission was authorized to plot the undeveloped area of Manhattan "in such a manner as to unite regularity and order with the public convenience and benefit, and in particular to promote the health of the city." Under the more precise terms of the act, these large words meant that the commissioners—Gouverneur Morris, Simeon DeWitt and John Rutherford—were limited to the laying out of a system of streets and parks. They had no authority to regulate building on private land, though the necessity of correlating street plan with land use and other elements had been understood as early as the Babylon described by Herodotus. The Manhattan commission plotted a street and park system from the existing limits of the old town at about the present East Houston Street north to 155th Street. The plan was submitted on March 22, 1811, and the legislature approved it in the same year.

Europeans of the day regarded the checkerboard design as a prime stroke of Yankee skill in mechanics, and it was later adopted in the plans for many American cities. When its defects began to appear, especially in Manhattan, the Randall Plan lost face rapidly. Often its mathematical pattern was unfavorably contrasted with the outline for the city of Washington drawn up in 1791 by Major Pierre Charles L'Enfant in collaboration with Washington and Jefferson. This contrast is in part a misconception born of short memory and in part a failure to perceive the relatively light and simple functional demands made upon Washington as against other large cities in the industrial age. The gridiron system, of course, was not original with Manhattan's commissioners. Surveyors in the Roman Empire laid out farms in squares; the 13th century plan of Peking was rectangular to a fault. Traditionally, surveyors tended to carry over rural practice in the city. Thus Philadelphia's virgin start under William Penn was affected by the rectangles of farms and the American householder's determination to build whatever he pleased on his own land.

Thomas Adams has suggested that even L'Enfant's Washington plan

"was a combination of radial and rectangular streets, and its chief defect was that the diagonal lines were superimposed on the right-angled pattern instead of the reverse." Its orientation about the "Federal House," or Capitol, which occupied the central position of the forum in Roman towns; the placement of the Capitol in relation to the "Grand Avenue," the latter-day Mall, which strikingly resembles the configuration of Paris between the Place de la Concorde and the Louvre, even to the right-angled situation of the "President's House" corresponding to the Palais Royal; the "President's park," with its suggestion of the royal parks later converted to public use in many European cities; the satellite squares which answered to the minor squares of Paris; the disposal, more architecturally symmetrical than functional, of the great avenues—all these betrayed the 18th century's charming love for classic geometry, quite aside from the Francophilia of a young French officer in exile and two Virginia gentlemen in a young
. country which had a good deal more than classic charm to be grateful for.

The plan was well suited to display those great masses of showy architecture subsequently laid down on it, many of which, as Lewis Mumford remarks, have developed out of "a common failure of the American imagination—a failure to realize that a mode of building that was in international vogue in 1789 is neither appropriately international nor properly expressive of our much broader and richer national tradition in 1937." But to argue that L'Enfant's design for a single-function city indicated a greater prescience than the Manhattan commissioners showed, or that it would have withstood the torque of rapid industrial and commercial expansion which was mainly responsible for the distortions of the 20th-century multi-functional community, is to defend a case that has never come to trial.

The defects of the Randall Manhattan Plan were for the most part of a different order. No doubt there are things to be said for it. Even in 1938, its simple east-and-west division of numbered streets to either side of Fifth Avenue, traversed by other parallel avenues and bounded by three rivers, remained the simplest and quickest system of orientation available in any world city. The original plan and the slightly later one signed by William Bridges, City Surveyor, apparently did not call for those broader streets at intervals—Fourteenth, Twenty-Third, Forty-Second and so on up to Dyckman (200th) Street—which served as cross avenues and helped to fix the shopping cores of neighborhoods and the placement of subway express stops. In any case, these were a practical extension of the plan. Besides a large public market, the commissioners laid out "ten public places, seven squares and three triangles," including a 230-acre parade ground in the center of the island between the present Madison Square and Thirty-Fourth Street; but these were mostly gobbled up when the reservation of Central Park was approved. Only Manhattan Square, present site of the American Museum of Natural History, and the parade ground nibbled down to Madison Square, survived the rape of commercial development. Too, the commission, limited by instructions and their own good sense, were prevented from attempting what would have been the crowning monstrosity of classical grouping about a plaza on so narrow a strip of land as Manhattan. Quite properly, they saw that the functional nexus of the island would continue to be its waterfront.

The chief criticism usually leveled against the Randall Plan is that it failed to anticipate the much greater volume of north-and-south as against river-to-river traffic. In his excellent monograph on New York's planning history, Henry James, consultant to the Regional Plan Committee, discusses the relevant points in detail. The report accompanying the Plan of 1811 suggested that "it may be a subject of merriment that the commissioners have provided space for a greater population than is collected at any spot on this side of China." (In New York, then and later, there was always the tongue of the satirist to consider. But the commissioners reckoned without their host; the population actually developed about twice as fast as those honorable gentlemen, who were resigned to being called grandiose, had anticipated.)

James shows that Gouverneur Morris in particular, a member of the Manhattan commission and promoter of the Erie Canal, had what seemed to be a very plausible notion of New York's future. He wrote in 1814 that the Erie Canal would "make the shores of the Hudson in sixty years almost a continued village." Seen thus, the contemporary perspective falls together in all its parts. New York traffic would feed up and down the Hudson exactly as the Mississippi steamboats did in relation to New Orleans half a century later. No matter how far to the north the city spread, it would spread along the banks of the Hudson, and water transport would be its dominant means of communication. Easy access between the many expected barge terminals on the North River side and the concentration of ocean vessels along the East River waterfront was therefore the first consideration. It was a sensible view; but in the onrush of the paleotechnic era, in the waves of immigration, and more especially because the advent of the railroad caused a basic division in transport methods and brought its own problems of transshipment by land, most of the hypothesis which had dictated the 1811 plan went by the board. A century later, the automobile broke loose on the narrow deck of Manhattan like the carronade in Victor Hugo's novel.

The commissioners set aside a total area for streets approximately equal to one-third of the whole land surface plotted, exclusive of open spaces; but as James suggests, their too literal gridiron did not make sufficient allowance at intersections or provide the necessary long diagonals. There were broader and graver faults of conception. Mumford mentions that an accurate topographic survey had been made for the commission. Its contour lines appear on the plan; but it was disregarded as completely as if the city were to be laid out with a spirit level. Regard for grades is, of course, as essential in the plotting of a city as in drainage systems, highway or railroad construction. In this case, blocks were laid out even on the escarpments of the island, many of which—Riverside Drive and Morningside Park among them—were subsequently recaptured for public use by the brilliant Frederick Law Olmsted. The old drainage streams, crossed by makeshift culverts, backed up into insanitary areas of swampland. The natural water entrances along the lower island were disregarded or filled in and most of the available waterside preempted for commerce.

These were symptoms: of the plan's inflexibility, of its lack of concern —in part prescribed—with the incidence of any street pattern to topography, land use, character of transport, types of architecture. In a very definite sense, the plan was a portent of advancing Victorianism, with its often exclusive criterion of immediate and immediately "practical" use. More significantly, perhaps, it symbolized a cultural attitude which in other manifestations was to kill off the passenger pigeon and the bison, destroy shelter belts in the plains states, and make the outskirts of most industrial cities and towns so many paleotechnic hells. Framed in the spirit that called for "the conquest of nature" instead of an accommodation between nature and man, it preferred to iron out the hills of Manhattan by force rather than attempt to blend them into the contexture of a more habitable city.

The rectangular plan, in the main unhampered by building regulations, naturally encouraged fliers in land values and helped to develop "the world's greatest real estate enterprise"—an ambiguous honor. This forced speculative development in terms of a rigid plan was the mode of Manhattan's growth through most of the 19th century. It is important to note how the city's most characteristic method of expansion—the gradual emergence of distinguishable but interlinked neighborhoods, in a process which resembles Boveri's classic sketch of the development of a sea urchin—was obscured and distorted by these speculative methods, especially in the later promotion of Brooklyn, Queens and the Bronx.

Meantime there were hitches and starts in city planning. A commission appointed in 1860 to map the island north of 155th Street handed over its powers to the new Commissioners of Central Park before very much had been done. This time topography was carefully considered; and the effects of such concern are particularly evident in the Fort Tryon-Inwood section. The Central Park Commission was given jurisdiction over the Bronx area west of the Bronx River, with fairly broad powers. In 1871 this commission was superseded by the Department of Public Parks, which was also charged with planning for railroads, pier and bulkhead lines. During this period the elder Olmsted worked with Andrew H. Green and J. J. R. Croes on the notable job of laying out upper Manhattan and the Bronx.

Olmsted was everywhere. He drew up a masterly report showing the relationship between high land prices, the standard 100-foot lot depth, and the long, unventilated, sunless houses of the day. He fought as hard for green earth and light in Manhattan as the Michigan or Wisconsin settlers were doing to cut their lands from the wilderness. He sponsored the design for Riverside Park, which was acquired after 1872, and collaborated with Calvert Vaux on Prospect Park in Brooklyn (1864–9) and the superb arrangement of Manhattan's Central Park, opened in 1857. This period between the Randall Plan and the greater city also saw the beginnings of Van Cortlandt, Pelham Bay, Forest and Bronx Parks, the Croton and Brooklyn Water Systems, and the 1867 Tenement House Law—this latter a poor patch on a useless garment.

After the consolidation of Greater New York under the 1898 charter, the Board of Estimate and Apportionment was empowered to pass on street and park plans for each borough, which were to be submitted by the respective borough presidents. Nelson P. Lewis, Chief Engineer of the Board of Estimate during the period 1902–20, did much to establish a provisional order in the hodge-podge of the city. In particular he understood very thoroughly the sea-urchin process of New York's expansion. As secretary to the New York City Improvement Commission—the so-called McClellan Commission of 1903—he pushed hard for anticipatory planning of marginal and other undeveloped areas. This was a shrewd point, as has been noted in the case of Paris and Stockholm. Instead, the McClellan Commission recommended projects which "were confined in great measure to the built-up portions of the city and the cost of acquiring the land needed for them was so great that few of them were ever undertaken."

This commission had been instructed to draw up "a comprehensive plan." The phrase itself indicates a beginning realization that processes interrelated in fact could not usefully be studied piecemeal. The short-lived Committee on the City Plan, 1914, was notable in that (1) it extended the idea of comprehensiveness to include a radius at least as broad as that which might "be reached within one hour by the most rapid means of communication at present developed for the transportation of passengers," and (2) its advisory committee was headed by Charles D. Norton and Frederic B. Pratt. Norton later served as chairman and Pratt as a member of the Regional Plan Committee.

The creation of the Port of New York Authority in 1921, which evolved out of concurrent measures by the New York and New Jersey legislatures in 1917, the report of a commission in 1920, and empowering legislation by the two states approved by the Federal Government, turned out to be the first large-scale attempt at unit planning for communications in the New York port area. Set up as a permanent body freed to a workable extent from the hindrances incident to conflicting political subdivisions, the Port Authority was itself a miracle forced by economic pressure and the designs of far-sighted men. It was commissioned to draw up, recommend and execute broad projects for the interstate port area; more than that, it could finance such projects by borrowing against "the security of the works undertaken and their earning power."

Thus the Port Authority, given a more or less free hand in the kitchen, was made responsible for the proof of the pudding. How well and to what extent—in its visual aspects, at least—that proof has been supplied even the most indifferent visitor may see for himself. Like surgeons' clips, a row of bridges and tunnels joins the New York and New Jersey waterfronts. The George Washington Bridge lifts across the Hudson from 178th Street, Manhattan, to Fort Lee on the Palisades. The Lincoln Tunnel from Weehawken bores into Manhattan at midtown. (When the south tube, ending in a plaza between West Thirty-Eighth and Thirty-Ninth Streets, Manhattan, was officially opened on December 12, 1937, it had already been sanctified by the legend that its glass roof was intended to give travelers a good view of the fishes in the North River.)

The Holland Tunnel—named for its chief engineer, the late Clifford M. Holland, and opened in November, 1927—carries vehicular traffic between Canal Street in lower Manhattan and Twelfth and Fourteenth Streets in

Jersey City. Of the three Staten Island links, the Bayonne Bridge, a sprung bow, arches over the Kill van Kull from Port Richmond to Bayonne; the aqueduct piers of the Goethals Bridge join Howland Hook with the Bayway approach to Elizabeth; and the Outerbridge Crossing wades into the Arthur Kill on legs as slender as a heron's, connecting the Amboy Road north of Tottenville with Perth Amboy. The great Commerce Hall, which takes up the block bounded by Fifteenth and Sixteenth Streets, Eighth and Ninth Avenues, Manhattan, is also administered by the Port Authority. It has become a major factor in the classification of less-than-carload freight for distribution through the port area.

These bridges, tunnels, terminals, with the articulated phases of the commission's proposals for the future, are intended to tie into the larger processes of the New York region. The revenues derived from them have long since proved their usefulness. In the main, the works already in operation stand as evidence of a high skill and probity in design functioning through an extraordinary range of construction, from the bold gangway of the George Washington Bridge to the detail of the beacon pylons at the Weehawken plaza of the Lincoln Tunnel. These latter, designed by Aymar Embury II, show what may be one solution for the problem of a style in modern functional decoration. Here, as in his Marine Parkway span and the bascule bridge over Flushing Creek, Embury makes use of associated engineering forms for decoration intended to suggest the function of the object. Thus the upward lines of the slender gray-green steel light pylons in Weehawken, with their four wing flanges, are broken at intervals by enclosed sheaves of stainless metal discs that resemble the insulators on high-tension towers. A narrow spiral stairway—this might as well have been a vertical ladder—corkscrews up through the center of each pylon to the floodlights clumped like hollyhock blooms at the tip of the stalk.

But the key factor in the Port Authority's effectiveness is precisely that, almost alone among the dozens of public and private groups which have set out at one time or another to put things straight on the map of New York, it was given executive powers and a relative autonomy of action. Contrast this with Mayor James J. Walker's City Committee on Plan and Survey, to which more than 500 members—a metropolitan Who's Who—were appointed in 1926 and later. This group had no funds and no executive authority. Only the energy of the sub-committees in rustling up contributions for surveys and other work made possible the advisory report issued in 1928.

Two points mentioned in this report linked up with major events in the city's planning history. The first recommended that some such regional group as the Committee on the Regional Plan of New York and Its Environs should cooperate with a planning board to be established by the city. The other suggested that the zoning law should be further extended and revised. This referred, of course, to the famous New York City Building Zone Resolution adopted on July 25, 1916. Founded on a broad report by the Heights of Buildings Commission and prepared by a Commission on Building Districts and Regulations appointed by the Board of Estimate, this resolution broke the city up into use zones classified as business, residential and unrestricted areas.

The limitation of building heights was one of its main objectives. Skyscrapers, coming up rank as unthinned plants, had choked off each other's light and air. The most spectacular effect of the zoning resolution was evident almost at once in the new setback architecture: parallelepipeds, the base of each smaller than the one below it, rising in steps like the temple ziggurats of Babylon. Tall buildings were permitted in the so-called *two and one-half times* and *two times* districts. The Grand Central area, for example, was set aside as a two times district. Above the street wall, it was required that each building should set back one foot for each four feet of added height. Towers occupying not more than 25 percent of the plot were unlimited in elevation.

These regulations turned out to be highly beneficial in their degree, but the question as to what should be done about the skyscraper—that bold signature of New York—had become a little academic in 1938, at least so far as present building was concerned. Trading in architectural futures shifted to communications projects, to group housing, even to the so-called *taxpayers*—small structures, for the most part pleasantly designed, of a type that sprouted in the vicinity of upper Park and Madison Avenues, and for which the Greek fret became unaccountably a favorite mode of decoration. In any case, the original zoning regulations were, within their limits, so shrewdly drawn up, so legally sound, and in general so successfully revised and administered that they not only improved the pattern of New York but served as a model for large and small communities all over the United States.

To the extent that the new zoning rush did not merely set up makeshifts to replace the ampler necessity for regional and city plans (zoning in some expensive suburbs even degenerated into a complicated system of residential snobbery) it was a clear advance. Even so, and more especially in New York City, the lack of any total perspective, of a general organizing scheme to which separate agencies might have recourse with a view to straightening out overlaps and harmonizing disparate elements, had from the first led to miscarriages in intent and performance. From the hamstrung Randall Plan commission of 1811 to the largely decorative City Committee on Plan and Survey in 1926, the gains had been piecemeal, the losses wholesale.

But there were large-spirited men who understood what this disease of fractionalism had cost in blood and crime and misery, in high taxes and rents and economic waste, in opportunities missed and the defeat of heartbreaking effort, in the whole tone and texture of city society. For the most part, these were men grimly experienced in what may be called the biostatics and biodynamics of the modern community. First among them was the late Charles Dyer Norton—a name to rank with Unwin, Geddes and Henry Wright among the most distinguished in the planning science—who had worked with Daniel H. Burnham and served as chairman of the 1907 Committee on Plan of Chicago. Struck by the potential magnificence of a coordinated New York, he looked about him and found, as he said, "a hundred citizens—teachers, architects, artists, engineers, bankers, merchants, social workers, lawyers, editors—men and women whose names would be recognized from Maine to California as being specially expert in the subject of city planning. No American city is so rich in competent personnel. None has so superb a situation or presents so great an opportunity for a noble city plan."

So the Committee on Plan of New York and Its Environs—"Plan" later became "Regional Plan" in the official title—was brought together in 1921 as a private five-man body, with Charles D. Norton as chairman. Preliminary surveys directed by Nelson P. Lewis and others staked the tremendous claim. At the first public meeting, which took place on May 10, 1922, Norton announced the project. His eloquent and comprehensive vision, broad enough to conceive the full magnitude of a task which would have disconcerted Swedenborg or Leonardo, was yet solid and prescient; it came out of his experienced regard for the mass and multitude of phenomena whose complex equilibrium, or lack of it, determines the functioning of a modern, first-rank city.

As this outline has suggested, the New York Regional Plan Committee appeared as part of a world renascence in city planning, forced to some extent by the cumulative demonstration of what Norton called "the high cost of not planning." It inherited a considerable tradition. It could profit by the errors and advances in the recent Garden City and City Beautiful movements—especially Burnham's 1907 Plan of Chicago, in itself generous and monumentally striking, but predicated too exclusively on an architectural scheme of order. More significant, perhaps, were the techniques newly available, techniques in statistical method (pioneered by the Belgian astronomer, Quetelet, early in the 19th century) in the correlation of data, in traffic control, zoning, highway construction and a dozen other fields.

Norton and his co-workers honored the challenge. With one stroke they cut away most of the fractionalism which had hampered previous planning efforts, and sheared through the maze of economic, political and topographic divisions to expose the broad intercommunity of the New York region. This master stroke was the proposal that the committee should survey the whole area within, very roughly, a 50-mile radius of City Hall, Manhattan, an area which would include, as Norton first envisaged it, "the Atlantic Highlands and Princeton; the lovely Jersey hills back of Morristown and Tuxedo; the incomparable Hudson as far as Newburgh; the Westchester lakes and ridges, to Bridgeport and beyond, and all of Long Island."

Consider the magnitude of this choice and the complexities it implied. It was delimited in general by the known practicable commuting range, extended to include recreation areas available to the metropolitan centers, boundaries of cities and towns at the periphery, and extensions of watersheds and waterways. Thus, by the very terms of its definition, the regional approach was made in engineering rather than in social science terms. The ecologist R. D. McKenzie, who regards the regional community as "the basic economic and social unit of American civilization," has analyzed the typical "spatial pattern" of such a region.

It is organized about an axis. Its major elements are centers, routes and rims. "It is composed of a constellation of centers, the interrelationship of which may be described as that of dominance and subordination." The main center provides "institutions and services which cater to the region as a whole and which integrate it with other regions. The subcenters"— and this, functionally, is what distinguishes big-city neighborhoods and regional villages alike from the American small town of the 1880's— "are seldom complete in their institutional or service structure; they depend upon the main center for the more specialized and integrating functions."

McKenzie's definition suggests very closely the basic interrelationships of the New York region. As defined by the committee, this region was a little larger than the total area mapped in 24 contiguous United States

Geological Survey quadrangles. At its points of greatest extension, it ran from Wappinger Town in Dutchess County, New York, south to Wall Township, New Jersey; and from Washington Township in Morris County, New Jersey, east to Montauk Point, Long Island, and Bridgeport, Connecticut—some 40 miles into New Jersey, 60 miles into New York State and Connecticut, and out to the tip of Long Island. On the circular map, the region looks like a tremendous clam pie with a broad untrimmed flange along its northern and eastern rim. Nosing into the center, the great sea bass of Long Island—itself a considerable unit in the region— appears to have nibbled away the whole southeastern quadrant between Sandy Hook and Bridgeport. A wide meandering crack from Newburgh to Manhattan is the Hudson River.

Burnham's Chicago Plan covered 200 square miles in what was essentially a single political division. The New York Regional Plan Committee marked out an area of 5,528 square miles in three states, administered by 436 local governmental authorities in 1925. This was a territory five times as large as Rhode Island, 250 times the size of Manhattan Island. Its population and business center was the section of Manhattan south of Fifty-Ninth Street, its focus of activity the whole Port of New York. Thus, geographically, it was composed of two sub-regions divided east and west by the Hudson River and drawn together by the unit character of the port. The eastern sector comprised 2,232 square miles in New York State and 413 square miles in Connecticut; the western sector was made up of 2,328 square miles in New Jersey and 655 square miles, including Staten Island's 57 square miles, in New York State. The whole region had a population of 8,979,055 in 1920 and the committee's *factor of safety* (allowance for future expansion) was calculated on a population of 20,000,000 in 1965.

When Norton died in 1923, Frederic A. Delano—as early as 1911, he and Norton had shared their hopes for a comprehensive New York plan —became chairman of the committee. To the original group—Norton, Delano, Alfred T. White (who died in 1921), Robert W. de Forest, John M. Glenn and Dwight W. Morrow, late United States Ambassador to Mexico—were subsequently added the names of Frank L. Polk, Henry James, Frederic B. Pratt, John H. Finley of the New York *Times,* Lawson Purdy and George McAneny, the latter long prominent in city planning affairs. Thomas Adams, Associate Professor of City Planning at Harvard University, a professional of wide experience in England, Wales, Canada and the United States, was appointed General Director of Plans and Surveys. Among the specialists who worked with the committee at one time or another or served on subcommittees were Raymond Unwin, Jacques Lambert, Frederick Law Olmsted the younger, Cass Gilbert, Harvey Wiley Corbett, William J. Wilgus, Daniel L. Turner, Frederick P. Keppel and Robert M. Haig.

When the Regional Survey, intended to organize a body of basic materials for the Plan itself, was first set up, "the quantity and variety of the detail that seemed to call for consideration were almost terrifying"—perhaps not too grim a word to describe the task of formulating a preliminary harmony out of the chaos of the world's largest city. Terrifying or not, the work went forward, methodically and boldly, in the years between 1922 and 1930. By 1927 the first of the Regional Survey reports had been published. Thereafter, until 1931, these appeared at intervals until the ten volumes (including two bound supplements to Volume I) were complete. The two books of the Plan itself—*The Graphic Regional Plan* in 1929, and *The Building of the City* in 1931—rounded out the original project at a total cost of $1,300,000. Robert L. Duffus published his admirable digest of Survey and Plan, *Mastering a Metropolis,* in 1930. When the committee's work was finished, a permanent Regional Plan Association was organized to further the realization of its proposals and to cooperate with other planning agencies. By the end of 1937, this association had assembled an additional volume of bulletins covering planned development in the region since 1931.

Taken together, these 14 volumes made up the first wide-focus view of a modern metropolitan region in terms of the "economic complements" of site, land use and circulation. Necessarily, in a city that marches back and forth upon itself as swiftly as New York does, a proportion of the data in the Survey Series was obsolescent almost before the books were launched. But these appeared to have permanent value, not only in that they collated an immense statistical and conceptual background for the Regional Plan, but because they checked off that background within a fairly broad period, so that it might stand as a bench mark for the measurement of future trends and developments.

This outline cannot hope to do more than suggest the content of the Survey and the bone structure of the Plan itself. In the main, the Survey tended to corroborate the specialists'—and to some extent the popular—criticisms of New York in the 1920's. Thus, in the three volumes devoted to an economic estimate, Robert Murray Haig and Roswell C. McCrea of Columbia University set up certain working hypotheses. The plan for any city region must be at once a harmonious design and "a productive piece of economic machinery"—a "production good" rather than a "consumption good." This, the analysts inferred as of 1927, must be its justification as an economic unit, its usefulness to the larger territory and the nation of which the city region is a part.

The planner must attempt to reduce the *friction of space* (the economic waste involved in excessive or ill-considered movement) by an *efficient pattern of population* (a population conveniently disposed in relation to its activities). In order to find out approximately "where things 'belong,' " he must have regard to the planning principles that govern selection of definite areas for special activities. But first he must consider which industries, and more especially which functions of industry (shipment, assembly, management, storage), are most likely to be successful in exerting pressure for advantageous urban sites.

With these principles in mind, the economic survey found that managing, administering, buying, selling, financing, risk-bearing, investigating and advising were among the city's preferential activities. Certain types of manufacturing were already being pushed out toward the periphery; this was part of a decentralizing movement not yet broad enough to be called a trend. In the middle of the city, only the printing trade had gained steadily in the period 1900–22. The financial cluster at the foot of Manhattan could outbid any other group in competition for sites and would probably remain where it was.

Next in bidding power came the great consolidation of retail business encamped between Thirty-Fourth and Fifty-Ninth Streets, Manhattan, on its historic march uptown; but there were no considerable factors to suggest that this bloc would be likely to give up its strategic grouping in the neighborhood of Grand Central Terminal and Pennsylvania Station. Haig, McCrea and others examined a score or more typical industries, large and small, using maps, text, scatter diagrams and statistics to indicate the relative position of each in the economic pattern of the New York region.

Much the same procedure was followed in the report covering growth and distribution of population and land values. The traffic study, edited by Harold M. Lewis and Ernest P. Goodrich, showed that the ratio of population to motor vehicles in New York and its environs curved downward from about 35 in 1916 to 7.6 in 1926; that in congested districts—certain sections of Fifth Avenue, for example—the average traffic speed at peak loads sometimes fell to between 2.5 and 3.0 miles per hour; that building heights and densities show a measurable correlation to street widths and capacities; and that physical planning is more effective than regulation in separating through and local traffic.

As might have been expected, the volume on transit and transportation dredged up some very similar specimens. For one thing, it pointed out that rapid transit facilities usually predetermine the location of new centers of population rather than the reverse. (This was an old song-and-dance to the land speculator, who had often been willing to pay well for information on subway or elevated extensions before these were publicly announced.) In 1924—and it was heavier later—subway traffic from residential districts during the morning rush hour jumped to between 380 and 584 percent of the average hourly movement. The survey calculated that as much as one-third of the total estimated railroad freight tonnage for both 1935 and 1965 (the factor of safety limit) could make use of a cross-harbor railroad link.

The survey of public recreation concerned itself particularly with the ratios of free open space to population and with discussion of the large areas available for development in the outlying sections of the region, particularly on Long Island and in northern New Jersey and New York State. The discussion of *Buildings: Their Uses and the Spaces About Them,* an admirably thorough set of monographs by Thomas Adams, Edward M. Bassett and others, emphasized the complexity of factors—land prices, traffic, open spaces, rapid transit, control of amenities, building densities, housing, interplay between urban and suburban land use, zoning, coordinated regulation—which must be pulled into some sort of intricate balance if the physical plant of the region was to achieve even "minimum standards for health, safety and general welfare." The final volume of the Regional Survey, *Physical Conditions and Public Services,* assembled and correlated the soundest available data on the geography and climate of the region, on water supply, sewage and refuse disposal, oil pollution, power, heat and light, food supply, building materials, hospitals and prisons.

Anyone who takes the trouble to look up a copy of Charles Scott Landers' 1929 sub-surface map of Manhattan, on which subway lines in use or projected are shown against the original hills, swamps, watercourses and made land, will get a striking sense of what happened to the island's earth between the Randall Plan of 1811 and the year in which the first volume of the Regional Plan was published. The two dates set a term, an elastic century in the main borough's turbulent career. They pointed up the extraordinary density, expansion, multiplication and diversity of factors which had vitally confused the process-pattern of the city. As a consequence, the need for and achievement of the Regional Plan stood out boldly.

Armed with the lessons of the Survey, the Graphic Regional Plan divided its proposals, for convenient presentation, into two main categories: ways of communication and land uses. The first embraced a trunk line railroad system, suburban rapid transit lines, improvement in the utilization of waterways, a coordinated regional highway pattern and a chain of air terminals. Under the heading of land uses, the Plan made a primary distinction between close development areas, including industrial, business and residential sections, and open development areas, broken down into parks, water supply reservations, bridle paths and hiking trails, airports, open military reservations, and tracts available for private estates, woodlands, pasturage and farming. A third class—extremely important in a region that includes some 1,800 miles of waterfront—was set aside for water areas and the treatment of their shores, subsumed under three heads: areas of water considered as open spaces, beaches, and projects for the employment of submerged land in central areas.

The railroad, rapid transit and highway systems proposed for the region were all modifications of a single basic diagram: the metropolitan loop or open grid pattern. This was a broad central rectangle, criss-crossed by four internal routes each way. Its boundary was formed by the beveled corners of the metropolitan loop proper. Radial routes spread out from it, intersected by two main exterior circumferential roads. Applied to a stylized map of New York City and environs, this scheme showed Manhattan and the eastern section of Hudson County, New Jersey, at the main center of the grid. The Newark district and the western areas of Brooklyn and Queens formed two secondary centers within the loop.

This pattern was favored over the hub-and-spokes and "Main Street" systems for obvious reasons. It adapted itself to the crucial main center of the region, split by the Hudson River. It promised to break up incoming traffic on the periphery and shunt a good part of it into circumferential and by-pass routes. It would help to prevent overcrowding along the radii, offer easy communication between outlying towns, and draw industries toward the outskirts by providing better facilities at the circumference.

Adapting themselves to terrain, the location of communities, and facilities already in use, the systems evolved for trunk line, rapid transit and highway communication differed widely in each case from the abstract pattern. It is impractical to attempt to trace the systems in detail. Only the map can convey an adequate sense of these ground plans for movement; but major proposals must be noted.

The framers of the Regional Plan considered the clarification of railroad services as perhaps the most important factor in the life of the region. William J. Wilgus recommended electrification and unification of all trunk lines. An outer belt, thrown about the region at an average distance of 20 miles from City Hall, Manhattan, was planned to connect with all intersecting railroads. A broad inner-belt loop in New Jersey and two in New York—one following for the most part a proposed underground right-of-way inside the shoreline of Manhattan, the other a lariat flung down loosely over Brooklyn and Queens—would be hooked up by six crossings over or under the Hudson and East Rivers. Six union passenger terminals were proposed for the New Jersey inner belt. In Manhattan, besides Grand Central Terminal and Pennsylvania Station, a new major terminal at about 178th Street and Amsterdam Avenue would be supplemented by others in the neighborhood of 149th Street and Mott Avenue, the Bronx, Queens Plaza in Queens, and Prospect Park Plaza in Brooklyn. The Plan also suggested the transfer of commuting traffic from railroads to rapid transit lines at specified inner points in New Jersey, Queens and the Bronx, as a preliminary to rapid transit extension all over the region.

The regional highway system conformed more closely to the pattern grid than trunk lines or rapid transit. The metropolitan loop, largely an express route, was projected so as to cross from Fort Lee on the George Washington Bridge, traverse Manhattan in an open cut to a proposed new bridge over the Harlem, and so through the Bronx and over the East River by way of an Old Ferry Point-Whitestone Bridge (under construction in 1938) to Queens. A wide obtuse angle through Queens and Brooklyn would carry it to the long-discussed Narrows Crossing, a bridge or tunnel from Fort Hamilton to Staten Island, over the Goethals Bridge to Union County, New Jersey, and deep into Essex and Passaic Counties in a broad curve back through Bergen County to Fort Lee.

As in the railroad trunk line (it was intended, in fact, that trunk line, rapid transit and highway programs should use the same differentiated or parallel routes at many points), radials splayed out from the loop to connect with the main long-distance highways. An express highway circuit about the Manhattan waterfront (more than half completed in 1938) was also projected. Three transverse inner routes, running east-and-west across Manhattan, were intended to facilitate intra-regional traffic between New Jersey and Long Island. The southernmost would use the Holland Tunnel, a Canal Street crosstown express highway, and follow Manhattan Bridge to Brooklyn. The midmost highway would reach Manhattan through the Lincoln Tunnel, underpass at midtown, and go under the East River by way of the Queens-Midtown Tunnel. The most northerly inner route was proposed as a vehicular tunnel from Fort Lee and an express highway crosstown at 125th Street to the Triborough Bridge.

The other major feature of the highway program was the metropolitan by-pass, well inside the extreme circumferential route, which would connect with all the chief radii. This would enable long-distance vehicles southbound from New England on US1, for example, to turn west at Bridgeport through upper Westchester County to Peekskill, cross the Hudson on the Bear Mountain Bridge, and come down through New York State and New Jersey in the vicinity of Suffern, Boonton, Morristown, Bedminster and South Somerville to the mainline south. Besides the major highways, and often consolidated with their routes, the Plan advanced a well-articulated net of parkways, boulevards and freeways laid down over the whole region.

Its proposals in regard to land use are necessarily somewhat complex. Stripped of explanations and coordinating data, these advocated a future policy of regional zoning in terms of fixed qualities legally imposed on land—i.e., areas permanently devoted to business, industry, residence or recreation. They maintained the primary distinction between open and closed development. They favored, whenever possible, the tendency toward industrial dispersal into nuclei on the periphery. It was suggested that these nuclei should be wedge-shaped developments along the radial lines, interspersed with residential areas and green spaces, rather than urban belts woven indiscriminately across sectors better suited to other uses.

Specifically, the Graphic Plan recommended these projects, among others, for industrial close development: satellite districts along the proposed railroad outer belt line; a major portion of the Hackensack Meadows; reclamation of Upper Bay areas in the vicinity of Bayonne and Jersey City; the western shore of Newark Bay and related territory; the Raritan River and New Jersey Ship Canal sector; further concentrations at Newtown Creek, Astoria and Long Island City; and the westerly shore of Jamaica Bay. The larger part of the bay land area was to be reserved for recreation facilities.

Quoting the fact that 75 percent of urban land is normally devoted to residential purposes, the Plan recommended large areas for such use on Staten Island, in Queens, Brooklyn and the Bronx; a 15,000-acre tract at the upper end of the Hackensack Meadows; and portions of Middlesex,

Union, Essex, Passaic and Bergen Counties, New Jersey, and Westchester County, New York. These proposals had special reference to extensions of railroad and highway belt lines, and more particularly to the enlargement of rapid transit routes.

In the category of open development, the Plan submitted an extensive park program considered under two heads: large parks in the environs and New York City parks. These were subdivided into so-called compact and ribbon parks. The environs proposals contemplated, among others, reservations along the Highlands of Navesink, in parts of the Watchung Mountains, and a section east of Lake Hopatcong. A large extension of Bear Mountain Park, a four-by-five mile tract north of Peekskill, and the Lake Ronkonkoma and New Mill Pond sections on Long Island were also picked out for treatment. Among 83 large or small park proposals listed for New York City were those covering areas of the East River islands, Flushing Creek Meadows (the 1939 New York World's Fair site, which has been developed with subsequent park use in mind), the Jamaica Bay islands, a waterfront extension at Canarsie, a Marine Park addition in Brooklyn, and other parks at Willow Brook, Great Kills, Prince's Bay and Ward Point on Staten Island—the least developed borough. Studies of water supply and military reservations and a strategically laid out system of 46 airports for land and seaplanes filled out the program.

The second volume of the Regional Plan, led off by a comprehensive and luminous rationale of the planning art in a democratic society, took up the problems of planned land use, zoning, housing, maritime and railroad terminals, and the dovetail interdependence of streets and buildings. It sketched out plans of treatment for a variety of typical or specific sites, areas and neighborhoods in New York City, metropolitan New Jersey and the outskirts. So far as architecture was concerned the slightly advanced conservatives seemed to be in the majority; but the projects themselves were at worst inappropriately fantastic—the suggested Battery Park restoration, for example, with its armillary spheres and enormous obelisk—and at best brilliantly practical realizations of what the city and the region might become.

Among the major proposals were those for a civic center about City Hall Park and a West Side waterfront development in downtown Manhattan (the Miller Express Highway was roundly disowned); a replanned lower East Side; elevated promenades for pedestrians—once envisioned by Leonardo—in the Times Square district; a watergate on the Hudson for Columbia University, which would form a part of the Riverside Drive apron development; and a tremendous project for remaking the Harlem Valley, tied in with a new railroad terminal and civic center for the Bronx at Mott Haven. The pattern of borough civic centers was further elaborated by suggestions for remodeling the Brooklyn Bridge approach neighborhood in Brooklyn and for the establishment of a borough center and airport just east of the junction of Grand Street and Borden Avenue in Queens.

The selective sampling undertaken in this outline hardly suggests the organizing values of the Regional Plan: its generosity of conception in the democratic idiom, its immense and precise scale, its allowances for time and the unpredictable, its coherent interlinkages, its evidence of cooperative harmony in the labor and vision of many workers. It has been criticized —soundly enough in some cases—for an orientation largely outside the social sciences; for an insufficient realization of the neighborhood's predominant role as the chief unit and type phase in the city's growth; and for various minor errors of judgment or attack.

But the beginnings of the Plan's vindication are woven into the story of New York's change of heart in the 1930's. In the past such changes have been periodic and subject to violent relapse. (A British psychiatrist, S. H. Kraines, diagnosed national psychologies for a professional journal in 1937, with an effect of high satire. He gave as his opinion—no doubt with a particular eye to New York—that the United States was suffering from "a typical manic-depressive psychosis.") Certainly there are Grand Canyons and Himalayas in the landscape of the city's spirit. But after each climb or descent the works remain: the bridges raised, the songs sung, the formulae put to use.

In any case, the city had begun to work toward a negotiable future. At the end of 1937 the Regional Plan could report striking progress in its schedule of improvements. During the first four years after publication of the Plan, 15 out of 51 projects recommended as "urgent" were completed or in process and 13 others had been officially approved or studied. Among items on the agenda for the next four years, a bulletin of December 6, 1937, showed that 20 projects were finished or under construction and land had been acquired for five more, out of a total of 47 "urgent" proposals.

The clover leaf of the Triborough Bridge and the south tube of the Lincoln Tunnel already carried their shining ranks of cars. The Queens Midtown Tunnel shields were inching forward under the plans of the New York City Tunnel Authority. The ribbons of the Henry Hudson Parkway led across the new Henry Hudson Bridge, its Number Two deck still under construction. The Old Ferry Point-Whitestone Bridge was advancing over the East River. The Interborough Parkway from Kew Gardens to Brooklyn had been completed and the Marine Parkway Bridge laid across Rockaway Inlet. In New York and its environs some 207 miles—or about two-thirds—of the express highway system advocated by the Plan were open to traffic or about to be opened.

Even in a city in which school children carve soap models of housing units and adults play a game called "Skyscraper," a city in which acute amateur appreciation of architecture and engineering is by way of being a minor amenity, the carrying out of such projects on such a scale would not have been possible without broad popular support of an extraordinary kind. This same support gave Mayor Fiorello H. LaGuardia the chance to put his intelligent and truculent energy at the service of the city. It encouraged the resourceful Robert Moses, his Commissioner of Parks, in the execution of a program which included Jacob Riis Park and Orchard Beach, the recapture of Wards and Randalls Islands for recreation use, and the development of Juniper Valley Park in Queens and Red Hook Park in Brooklyn. Light began to cut into the dense formations of New York and there was sun over new beaches.

Other influential factors were involved. The Port Authority's achievements have been elsewhere noted. The Mayor's Committee on City Planning had done creditable work and the City Planning Commission authorized under the new charter effective January 1, 1938, made an interesting start early in that year with a project for reclamation of areas on the lower East Side. Most important of all, perhaps, the Federal Government's work relief agencies supplied labor and technicians to do the job of public reclamation and construction.

Such effects signalized a profound change in the social tone and habitude of the city: in what it wished to be, in its conception of a desirable life-pattern. This change was remarked by the French novelist, Jules Romains, who came to the United States in the summer of 1936 and later reported his impressions in *Visite aux Américains*—a Voltairean title for a book that offers New York in particular the tribute of a singularly discriminating admiration. Romains' last previous visit had been in 1924. An expert in the human resonance of great cities, he compared his precise recollections of that earlier year—its equivocal ethics, at home in the guarded half-light of the speakeasy, its neurotic drive to make each moment pay in full, its violent emulation of the machine—with the New York to which he returned in 1936.

The effect was decisive. There had been some extraordinary change in the face and character of the city. Its very streets were fresher, the sky had opened, there was a luster on the flanks of great clay shafts, the intimation of an unbelievable tranquillity. True, it was summer; but the deeper signs were plain. They appeared in the faces of the people, in every turn and feature. The old, abrasive will-to-action for its own sake was gone. These men and women were freer, more open, casually good-natured, even happy. They had time for a new and more relaxed gaiety. He felt in them a profound reinvigoration of the democratic spirit.

So it must come back to the people: the lives they wear—and since, as John Dewey wrote, "walking implicates the ground as well as the legs"— the city they make, the city they hope for. The symbolic instant of light coming up in a face as the coin is dropped in the subway slot and the turnstile jerks, a face unknown before, unlikely to be seen again—nurse, pickpocket, showgirl, newsboy, grandmother, artist, wife—defines the innumerable lives. These are the faces of the city's children, patient and furious, mad or indestructibly calm; relentless, vain, wandering, gleeful, obdurate or lost; faithless and lonely, or ennobled by an infinite practical tenderness for mankind. The city is their companion and their mother, their schoolmaster and executioner. They are constructed in its image; and the city itself is an image of the disparate and enduring heart of man.

New Yorkers in Transit

THE VAULTED MAIN ROOM OF GRAND CENTRAL TERMINAL

WALL STREET'S EMPLOYEES EMERGING FROM THE SUBWAYS AS THE
CLOCK ON TRINITY TOWER POINTS TO NINE

Top: "EL" STATION AT HANOVER SQUARE, NEAR THE FINANCIAL
DISTRICT

Bottom: MILLIONS EACH DAY SURGE THROUGH THE NARROW PLATFORMS
OF SUBWAY STATIONS

Top: THE *S.S. Normandie* NOSING HER WAY INTO NEW YORK HARBOR

Bottom: GIANT PIERS THRUST WELCOMING ARMS INTO NORTH RIVER

Above: "CITY LINE TO CANAL STREET WITHOUT A RED LIGHT," ON THE NEW HIGHWAY ALONG THE HUDSON

Below: TRAFFIC AT COLUMBUS CIRCLE, LOWER END OF CENTRAL PARK

PENNSYLVANIA STATION'S GLASS-ROOFED TRAIN SHED

Above: BUSES, TAXIS AND PRIVATE CARS ON FIFTH AVENUE

Below: THE HOMEWARD RUSH ACROSS THE BAY TO STATEN ISLAND

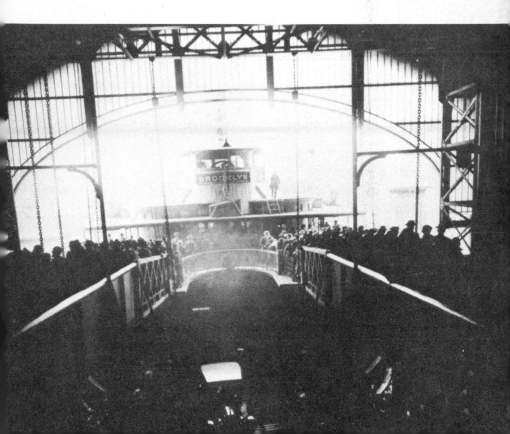

TIMES SQUARE, BUSIEST TRAFFIC INTERSECTION IN NEW YORK

Below: A SUBWAY ROAD COMES UP FOR AIR IN BROOKLYN. (MANHATTAN IN BACKGROUND)

One-Third of a City

THE HOUSING problem in New York, becoming each year more pressing as the city has developed, was already an inherited evil more than a century ago. Today it has grown into an overwhelming menace, calling for heroic measures and large-scale planning to remedy the cumulative effects of greedy land speculation, low building standards, and faulty city planning. Housing designed to bring in a profit from the lowest income group is admittedly no longer possible under existing minimum standards without government subsidy. A century of protest has at last resulted in an awakened and intelligent approach to the problem.

Indeed, analysis has gone sufficiently far to show that even many worthy Knickerbocker landlords are themselves inadequately housed, and that elegant Park Avenue—despite brass-braided doormen, glassed-in showers and air-conditioning—is essentially a super-slum, lacking such fundamentals of good housing as pleasant and wholesome surroundings for each dwelling, plenty of fresh air and sunshine for each room, adequate playspace and other amenities of civilized living. New housing for the underprivileged has gone far to incorporate these standards; and though contingent upon subsidies in one form or another, modern housing developments are progressively tending toward higher living standards. Slum clearance, city planning, government subsidies, improved building practices, and ever more stringent housing regulations are all various aspects of the housing problem as it is envisaged today.

Existing Conditions

In the predominantly residential blocks of Greater New York as a whole, housing of the multi-family type constitutes only a little more than a third of the total. But in Manhattan nearly 94 percent of the housing is of this type, in the Bronx nearly 70 percent and in Brooklyn more than half. In the much newer boroughs of Queens and Richmond, single-family housing prevails to the extent of about 79 percent and 94 percent respectively. Two-family homes, while still relatively numerous in Brooklyn especially and to a lesser degree in the Bronx and Queens, are virtually non-existent in Manhattan.

About 17 square miles, or nearly 10 percent of the greater city's predominantly residential blocks, consist of slums or blighted districts; and of these, ten square miles have been condemned as unfit for human habitation. In extent of condemned slum area, Brooklyn holds first place with 5.3 square miles, and Manhattan follows 4.4 square miles. Throughout the entire area, according to the New York City Housing Authority, "more than a half-million slum-dwelling families are condemned to lives of squalor and degradation." Rents in New York City are higher, both absolutely and in proportion to income, than anywhere else in the world; and these families pay from $10 to $30 a month for their slum apartments.

In few foreign cities outside of Italy and France and Germany, and in no other American city save Boston, are housing conditions comparable to those in New York. Certainly not since the days of Imperial Rome have so many people been so packed and piled together. Most densely populated, of course, are the slum areas of the lower East Side and Harlem in Manhattan; Brownsville, Williamsburg and the Red Hook and Navy Yard sections in Brooklyn. The average population to the acre for the city's residential area as a whole is 266; but in the slums numerous acres contain as many as 600 people each. A single block in Harlem, probably the most densely crowded in the city, has a population of 3,781. Negroes in the city are segregated and exploited, the higher rent they are forced to pay amounting in many cases to 40 or 50 percent of the family income. The congestion in Harlem has made common what are known as "hot beds"—i.e., beds rented in three eight-hour shifts.

As related by the editors of *Fortune,* an architect of model towns in England told a New York conference that he had seen the slums of Europe and South America but had nowhere found conditions that were not preferable to those in New York City. The latter's tenement history, he declared, is "one of the most shameful of human records. Nowhere have the estates of early landowners benefited more richly from an increase in real-estate values for which their founders were very slightly responsible, and nowhere have the heirs ripened their benefice with greater harm." In 1894 the trustees of Trinity Church, richest religious organization in the country and one of the largest of early landowners, refused to heed an ordinance requiring them to supply water to each floor of their tenements in Greenwich Village, in spite of a Board of Health report that the death-rate in 83 of the Trinity tenements was a third higher than the general rate. The trustees have since changed their attitude, but the fact remains that in general even the most elementary advances in the improvement of housing conditions can be effected only through stringent enforcement of the law.

At least a glimpse of New York's principal tenement area is afforded the visitor who speeds over the long approaches to one of the great East River bridges. He will note the monotonous unbroken rows of five or six story structures, the façades of red-brick or brownstone, the outside fire-escapes, the first-floor shops, the interspersed factories and warehouses, the clotheslines and bulkheads and pigeon coops on the huddled roofs, and the teeming activity of the narrow streets. But, perhaps fortunately for his own peace of mind, he cannot see beyond the walls and beneath the roofs into the fetid and roach-infested interiors where slum-dwellers spend by far the greater part of their lives.

A common type of slum apartment consists of four rooms occupied by six or seven persons. It contains no toilet or bathtub. It has beds, a sink (but no hot water tap), a washtub, a dresser, a stove, a table and a few chairs. A public toilet (used by a score or so) is in the hall, either on the same floor or on the floor below or above. If there are windows the outlook is upon a grimy blank wall, an elevated structure, or the windows of a similar apartment.

Where massive Knickerbocker Village now squats Gulliver-like on the lower East Side there stood until as late as 1933 the dark and infamous "Lung Block." Of one of its buildings, known as the "Ink Pot," Ernest Poole wrote: "Rooms here have held death ready and waiting for years. Upon the third floor, looking down into the court, is a room with two little closets behind it. In one of these a blind Scotchman slept and took the Plague in '94. His wife and his fifteen-year-old son both drank, and the home grew as squalid as the tenement itself. He died in the hospital. Only a few months later the Plague fastened again. Slowly his little daughter grew used to the fever, the coughing, the long sleepless nights . . . At last she, too, died. The mother and son then moved away. But in this room the germs lived on . . . they can live two years in darkness. Then one year later, in October, a Jew rented this same room. He was taken ill and died in the summer. The room was rented again in the Autumn by a German and his wife. She had the Plague already, and died. Then an Irish family came in. The father was a hard, steady worker . . . But six months later he took the Plague. He died in 1901. This is only the record of one room in seven years."

The "Lung Block," happily, has been demolished; unhappily, however, nearly all of the vacated tenants were crowded into similar tenements nearby—and at higher rentals. Only three families of the Lung Block were able to pay the Knickerbocker Village average rental of $12.50 a room a month.

New York City has the reputation of ruthlessly tearing down older buildings to make way for new ones. And so it does—but not often its tenements. More than three-fourths of Manhattan's residential blocks are occupied by tenements at least 37 years old in 1938. Fifty percent of the tenements condemned in 1885 as unfit for human habitation are still standing; and human beings are still stifled in 200,000 dark interior rooms of those tenements—rooms with no windows opening to the outer air. The building of tenements of this evil kind was effectively prohibited in 1901; they are therefore known as "old-law tenements," while those constructed since 1901 are referred to as "new-law tenements."

Compared with most of the old-law buildings, new-law tenements are relatively fire-safe. Their ground coverage cannot exceed 90 percent of corner lots and 70 percent of interior lots; their height cannot exceed, by more than one-half, the width of the widest street upon which the building stands. The size of the rear lot must be in definite proportion to the building's height; and there must be interior courts of specified minimum dimensions. Every room of the building opens upon a yard, court, or street, and has a floor area of not less than 70 square feet. Each apartment must have running water and a toilet. While these and numerous other provisions made the Tenement House Act of 1901 "the chief working model for most of the tenement-house legislation of America since that date," they still left much to be desired. Then, too, owing to the increased cost of construction and maintenance under this act, the rental for apartments in new-law tenements is seldom less than $30 a month, thus excluding most families in the lower income groups.

A considerable proportion of the city's ill-housed population lives in old single and double family residences that have ben converted (16,000 of them illegally) for multi-family use, residences that were not fitted for such conversion. Housing conditions for single persons are even more inadequate than for families. One or more persons are lodged with each of 180,000 families; and the resultant problems, both for the lodgers and for the families, can be readily apprehended. Rooming houses are usually converted homes in down-at-the-heel districts; they are characterized by antiquated front parlors and narrow bedrooms separated by flimsy partitions. Though the city now provides beds for an average of 7,000 homeless each night, the "two-bit flophouses" in the Bowery and elsewhere are little better than those described by Jacob Riis at the turn of the century.

At the beginning of 1937 there were 135,949 multiple dwellings in the city, and of this total (which includes dwellings converted for multifamily use, hotels, high-class apartments, rooming and lodging houses) 52,343 were new-law tenements, while 64,888 were old-law tenements. According to the rate at which old-law rookeries were demolished between 1909 and 1925, it would take 138 years to get rid of the still existing structures; while at the current rate, several lifetimes would be required. In view of the fact that few old-law tenements are at present providing any return beyond tax and interest charges, it is unreasonable to expect that a non-altruistic landlord will voluntarily demolish his decayed tenement and erect in its place a modern and wholesome one when the old structure is bringing in all the rental that its tenants are able to pay. Most tenements are torn down only when a bridge or a tunnel is constructed, or (as in the case of Tudor City) when a block or two of slum area can be utilized for high-class apartment buildings.

Origins of the Problem

Some of the peculiarities of bad housing in New York have been determined by the narrowness of Manhattan Island, the tidal waves of immigration that swept into the harbor, and the unexampled exploitation of the land. As the city grew, the rich abandoned their homes and built new ones further north on the island—the only direction for expansion—and their cast-off dwellings were then inadequately converted for the use of the less fortunate. With the exception of Brooklyn, it was not until the era of rapid transit and river bridges and tunnels that the other boroughs shared in absorbing the new immigrants. The first thousands of foreign-born put up with the bad housing that was available or soon profitably made available—some of them because their homes in the old country had been little or no better; others, who had known better homes, because here in the land of opportunity such quarters would be only "temporary." As a result, the demand for better housing was broken down, and a basic standard set up for new construction. The fabulous price of land in New York City did not directly produce its rookeries. This price came about because of the low housing standards tolerated. It was the possibility of congestion, inherent in the gridiron plan, lax building codes, development costs and eventually in taxes, that increased the price of land. In the section between Fourteenth and James Streets east of the Bowery to the river, 531,-000 people were living in 1910, but only 220,000 in 1937. The land of the lower East Side was valued at $187,000,000 in 1912, but only $169,-000,000 in 1929 and $148,000,000 in 1933. Overcrowding is the cause as well as the effect of high land values; and so it is not to be wondered at that the 6,000 owners, 20 or 30 to a block, have not formed a "Society for Decrowding the East Side." The erection of Knickerbocker Village, which houses 5,200 persons on five acres, helped to bolster the declining price of the surrounding land.

But the bad housing in this city, as in cities elsewhere in the Western World, is due primarily to the Industrial Revolution and the consequent growth of the urban centers. Since 1800 the population of Greater London has increased from one to eight millions. In the Paris of 1836 there was an average of 11,000 persons to the square kilometer; in the Paris of 1886, the corresponding figure was 29,000. Comparison of various German and American cities of equal population in 1880 shows that the German cities have grown twice as fast. The story of bad housing is basically much the same in all large cities. The first period was marked by haphazard congestion, with ramshackle structures blanketing all available space in the central sections. In the second period appeared the built-in slum, with standardized tenements constructed expressly for slum dwellers. Unregulated speculative expansion characterized the third period, and slum dwellings were put up in the peripheral districts.

As the population of the cities increased, land values soared. But the wings of wages were tipped with lead; and the average family was allowed a smaller and smaller portion of land. Construction costs began to rise as the result of restrictive legislation concerning the height and density of buildings, and increased immensely because of modern improvements in building materials, in plumbing, and in the utilities. And though these improvements can be sacrificed with less danger in sparsely populated areas, in the crowded cities they are imperative for safety and health. Building evolved into an almost purely speculative business. As a result, the probability of blight entailed high-pressure promotion and sales. The cost of money—the most important single factor in the determination of rentals —increased faster than the general interest rate. In short, all these increased costs raised rents; but as wages did not rise in anything like the same degree, the majority of people went on decade after decade living in evil and obsolescent dwellings.

The Historic Background

When New Amsterdam was only about 30 years old and comprised only 120 houses and 1,000 people, social control of housing had already become necessary. Landowners were obliged under penalty of forfeiture to build upon their land within nine months of residence—"a significant recognition," James Ford comments in *Slums and Housing*, a thorough history of housing in this city, "of the primacy of the community's interest in land." In 1656 a resolution was issued requiring in no uncertain terms that builders consult with the city surveyor, because "a great deal of bad building has been done not only to the disadvantage of the public but also to the disreputation of the City."

Under English rule, "ruinous and decayed houses" were subject to condemnation and qualified expropriation. The Common Council in 1684 prohibited the storage of combustible material within dwelling places, and required that hooks, ladders and buckets be kept in convenient places. The laws governing housing and the general welfare of the community during this early period were notably progressive, and the precedent thus set has been a leavening influence on all subsequent legislation.

Following British withdrawal in 1783, building activity increased greatly and New York became America's largest city in 1800. The growth of the population to more than 60,000 was accompanied by epidemics known to originate in districts where unventilated rooms and damp cellars were the rule. Three Commissioners of Health were appointed, and their chief concern was with sanitary housing conditions. Building on small yardless lots was prohibited, and a law provided for the purchase of such lots and the demolition of the buildings, the land to be re-sold in such manner and for such purposes as would "best conduce to the health and welfare of the city."

There is uncertainty as to when the first tenement designed for multi-family use was built in New York. One writer mentions a "single-decker" for four families built on Water Street in 1833, but the *Plumber and Sanitary Engineer* of December 1879 states that a seven-story tenement at 65 Mott Street had been occupied since 1825. In any case, the New York *Mirror* was complaining as early as the 1830's of the "towering" dwellings.

When Wall Street was the fashionable residential center of the colonial city, the first slums were roofed-over holes in the ground or shanties near the foul Fresh Water. The first up-to-date slum area and the most notorious for half a century was Five Points, where five streets intersected near Foley Square. Conditions in Five Points were as bad as the city has ever known. There were houses in which a thousand persons of all ages and nationalities and of both sexes slept upon one floor. Here was the Den of Thieves and Murderer's Alley and the Old Brewery. The latter in its most sanguine period is reputed to have witnessed a murder a night. Dickens went slumming in Five Points in 1842, recording his shock in the *American Notes*. Long after this area was partly cleared and made regenerate, with missionaries garrisoning the Old Brewery itself, writers were pointing their pens at it with horror. The real thing, however, was no longer there, but in Mulberry Bend, the Bowery, Hell's Kitchen, Frog Hollow, the lower East Side and elsewhere.

A fire in September 1835 destroyed 46 buildings; and in December of the same year, the Great Fire razed 530 more. The combined damage was $16,000,000, but this loss was not followed by any noticeable improvement in fireproofing. The year of the Great Fire was, however, marked by an important event in the fight for better housing. Gerret Forbes, city inspector of health, reported on the high death rate. The city population was then but little more than 250,000. "Some cause should be assigned for the increase of deaths beyond the increase of population, and none appears so prominent as that of the intemperance and the crowded and filthy state in which a great portion of our population live, apparently without being sensible of their situation; and we have serious cause to regret that there are in our city so many mercenary landlords who only contrive in what manner they can to stow the greatest number of human beings in the smallest space."

Another report, made in 1842 by Dr. John Griscom, was the first comprehensive document on the city's housing. When the authorities ignored his report, Dr. Griscom publicized it in the form of an address which was later published. He advocated the prohibition of cellars and basements as living quarters; proposed that regulation should be supplemented by philanthropic building; and assailed the farming out of tenements. Particularly with reference to the foreign-born, Dr. Griscom said: "We are parties to their degradation, inasmuch as we permit the inhabitation of places from which it is not possible improvement in conditions or habits can come. We suffer the sub-landlord to store them, like cattle, in pens, and to compel them to swallow poison with every breath."

The protests of these two men, strengthened by two severe epidemics of cholera which originated in the slums but also visited other parts of the city, were not entirely without fruit. A long era of reform began at the middle of the century. Stimulated by the Association for Improvement of the Poor, which erected the Workingmen's Home in 1855, a number of "model tenements" were built. In each decade tenement legislation was passed, and commissions were appointed from time to time to study the problem.

Regulation and Reform

In 1856 a bill was before the State legislature embodying the recommendations of the first housing investigation commission. The commissioners' findings had been duly shocking, revealing that rooms 12 feet square were occupied by "5 families, comprising 20 persons, of both sexes, and all ages, with only 2 beds, without partition or screen, or chair or table." The cause was ascribed to "municipal neglect" and "exploitation." The bill failed of passage "through press of business," and it was 44 years before the establishment of a Tenement House Department with the powers recommended by this commission.

The first tenement house law was passed in 1867. Most of it was repealed in 1872, and what was left of it was nullified. Though defective in some important respects—as, for example, in permitting complete coverage of building lots—this law required a transom window for every interior room, a proper fire-escape, bannisters, a water closet for every two persons, and the vacating of unrepaired buildings. Its repeal and sabotage resulted in the construction of 90,000 shameless tenements—and all the disease and crime and tragedy that have come out of them.

In 1879, the evils of the "railroad" type of tenement having long been recognized, a competition was conducted for a better plan. The prize-winning design initiated the "dumbbell" type, and thousands of such tenements were put up during the next two decades. An intensive development of the upper East and West Sides began in the 1880's, displacing the Shantyvilles that had always fringed the city. Stereotyped brick "dumbbells" marked the East Side, between Ninety-Eighth and 125th Streets; and on the West Side vulgarly embellished Victorian mansions vied with the similar mansions being put up on Fifth Avenue. Accompanying the extension of rapid transit (the first elevated train clattered above the streets in 1872), the other boroughs were speedily developed. In 1905, 54 percent of the city's population lived within four miles of City Hall; by 1930 the figure had been reduced to but 22 percent.

Agitation for reform reached its height in the late 1890's, partly due to the books of Jacob Riis and others. In *How the Other Half Lives*, Riis describes the *fin de siécle* slums. Names, at least, were picturesque. Among the streets were Blindman's Alley, Penitentiary Row, Battle Row, Poverty Gap, Bottle Alley. Among the tenements were the Ship, Bandit's Roost, House of Blazes, the Dirty Spoon. In the last named, fire broke out six times in one year; the fires, however, were smothered by the dirty walls. There were four grades of licensed lodging houses, with accommodations at 25 cents, 15 cents, 10 cents and 7 cents, respectively. Signs on some tenements proclaimed: "Five Cents a Spot" or "Standing Room Only." Space in hallways rented at three cents.

A third State commission investigated the tenement situation in 1900, and its recommendations resulted in the law of 1901. This law had two distinct purposes—to set up standards for future construction, and to create minimum standards for existing tenements. In attaining the first purpose the law was successful. During the 1920's the conversion into rooming houses of completely unregulated buildings became so important a menace that the legislature revised the law in 1929, 1930 and 1931, bringing under it hotels, lodging and rooming houses, clubs and dormitories. These revisions also legalized the illegally converted dwellings provided that they conformed to certain minimum requirements, but enforcement in this connection was postponed by a moratorium until 1934. Additional moratoriums further weakened the law. The revised act of 1929 is known as the Multiple Dwelling Law, and replaces for New York City the Tenement House Law of 1901.

In spite of sabotage and nullification and moratoriums, many of the worst evils in the tenement situation have been eliminated or alleviated. Due to the comparatively vigorous efforts of the Tenement House Department under Mayor La Guardia's administration—and to the fires of 1934—the number of occupied old-law tenements has been reduced by at least 6,000, and more improvements have been made in those still occupied than during the previous 33 years. Nevertheless, according to a report of the Tenement House Department, "the number of old-law tenements which fully comply with the law is virtually negligible." Experience with moratoriums shows that very few landlords do anything to improve their buildings during the period of grace allowed.

Providing minimum safeguards for the lives and health of the ill-housed one-third of New York's population—the more than 2,000,000 persons who live in old-law tenements and converted dwellings—remains an urgent and tremendous task. But enforcement of the law is also a boomerang: decayed buildings that should be demolished are given a new lease on life. "Even when old-law tenements are brought into minimum compliance with the law," states the 1937 report of the Department, "they are distinctly below any acceptable standard."

The City and Suburban Homes Company, the leading promoter of limited-dividend developments, was organized in 1896, and since that year the buildings under its management have yielded an average annual dividend of 4.65 percent. Its buildings on Marie Curie and York Avenues were the most important model apartments in Manhattan prior to construction of the Amalgamated Dwellings on the lower East Side. Another notable enterprise is the Paul Laurence Dunbar Apartments in Harlem, for Negroes. This co-operative project, completed in 1928, was financed by John D. Rockefeller, Jr. Monthly payments were fixed at an average of $14.50 a room, including upkeep and payments on principal. In 1936, Mr. Rockefeller foreclosed, re-imbursing the former tenant-owners for their capital payments.

The New York State Housing Law, enacted in 1926, created a State Housing Board to co-operate with municipal authorities in constructing and managing limited-dividend and co-operative housing. Fourteen projects, representing an investment of approximately $30,000,000, have been completed under the supervision of the State Board of Housing. One of these is Knickerbocker Village, on the lower East Side. Of the ten others in New York City, the most interesting are the Amalgamated Dwellings in Manhattan and the Amalgamated Housing Corporation in the Bronx. Both are run as co-operatives, and are partly sponsored by the Amalgamated Clothing Workers. Ventures such as these—both started just before the financial crash of 1929—are not likely to be repeated. Few workers can afford to rent a modern apartment, let alone buy one.

Positive Measures

The current intensive concern with housing and slum clearance coincides with hard times. The lowered standards of millions, the evictions, foreclosures, doubling-up, etc., have not been accepted passively. Then, too, building is the country's second major industry, and builders and material manufacturers, as well as disinterested individuals and groups searching for recovery, want a vast housing program. Residential construction dropped from a total $3,500,000,000 in 1928 to $300,000,000 in 1933—a decline of over 90 percent. Building continues to lag far behind other major industries.

In New York City, important housing pressure groups are the Housing Study Guild (led until recently by the late Henry Wright), the Citizens Housing Council, the Housing Division of the Welfare Council, the Regional Plan Association. And, in addition to the trades unions themselves, active tenant unions are now grouped in the City Wide Tenants Council. Rent-strikes, picketing of banks, mass resistance to evictions and foreclosures have done much to publicize the housing problem, secure enforcement of existing laws and enactment of new ones, and in general counteract the powerful pressure of the realty interests.

The Conference on Home Building and Home Ownership set up by President Hoover issued a report (1932) indicating that nearly three-quarters of the country's population was inadequately housed, but the report offered no immediate solution. Late in President Hoover's term, the Reconstruction Finance Corporation aided in the financing of Knickerbocker Village by lending $8,000,000 to the enterprise. At the outset of the New Deal, housing was cast for the major role in the Federal public works program. Many agencies were set up, and housing has been front-page news ever since. But in the four and a half years previous to January 1938, less than $134,000,000 was put into low-cost housing, and only 29,928 dwelling units were constructed—21,800 units in apartment houses in the larger cities, built by the Public Works Administration, and 8,128 farmstead and suburban units built by the Resettlement Administration.

In 1934, ninety-nine years after Gerret Forbes' report, the State legislature passed its first law aimed at slum clearance and government-subsidized low-cost housing. The enactment of the Municipal Housing Authorities Law of 1934 proves by itself the inadequacy of limited-dividend and co-operative housing. Doubt as to the legality of this law helped to hamper the start of any housing for more than a year. Finally the New York Court of Appeals upheld the validity of the statute. "The menace of the slums in New York City," the Court said, "has been long recognized as so serious as to warrant public action . . . The slums still stand. The menace still exists . . . Slum areas are the breeding places of disease . . . Juvenile delinquency, crime and immorality are there born, find protection and flourish . . . Enormous economic loss results . . . The cure is to be wrought, not through the regulated ownership of the individual but through the ownership and operation by or under direct control of the public itself."

At a recent hearing conducted by the New York City Housing Authority concerning the threatening housing shortage, every witness—tenant and bank president alike—testified that government subsidy in one form or another is the only solution of the housing problem. The lowest possible monthly room rental that private enterprise is able to offer is $11. Limited-dividend developments such as Knickerbocker Village, the Hillside project in the Bronx, and other similar projects, average $11.30. And these projects (nearly all tax-exempt) received government loans at 4 percent interest and are limited to dividends of 6 percent. But the unescapable fact is that $6 a room is the highest monthly rent that the one-third of the population now living in the city's unregenerate fire-traps can pay. Only if wages were doubled (and prices kept from rising) would the differential between the cost of building a dwelling unit and what the worker can pay for it be wiped out.

Forward Steps

During the Coolidge period, New York, like the rest of America, was a paradise for land-speculators and real-estate promoters, and the city then experienced its most intense and chaotic building activity. This was a period of unusually rapid development in the suburbs and outlying sections—many of the houses being flimsy frame structures which, though sold to the upper income groups, were soon smitten by blight. Every dwelling begun in the city from early in 1921 until well into 1924 was tax-exempt in part or in whole until 1931. This meant a direct cost to (or subsidy by) the taxpayers of about $200,000,000. The indirect subsidy—the eventual cost of foreclosures, tax arrears, premature utility developments and the other wastes of rapid depreciation—will be much greater. During approximately this same period, Germany, Holland, England and other countries of not-so-prosperous Europe, with a combined population only slightly exceeding that of the United States, built four and a half million government-aided dwellings. These dwellings rehoused about 20 million people, nearly all of them in the lower-half income group. None of these countries cleared its cities of slums or fully solved its housing problem; but the new dwellings did establish concretely the minimum standards of good housing.

Steps forward have been taken in this country. The Public Works Administration of the Federal Government was given $123,000,000 in 1933 for low-rent housing; and on the strength of a promise of $25,000,000 New York City set up a Housing Authority early in 1934, with Langdon W. Post, head of the Tenement House Department, as chairman. The Authority was charged with three duties: (1) investigating housing and living conditions throughout the city, (2) clearing congested areas, and (3) constructing and operating low-rent housing. In fulfilling its first task, the Authority directed 6,000 Civil Works Administration workers in taking an inventory of real property—the biggest task of the kind since William the Conqueror compiled the Domesday Book. The data collected in this eight-months survey served as the basis for a long-term housing program recommended by the Authority. This program involves the expenditure of $150-,000,000 each year for ten years, and the re-housing of 1,320,000 New Yorkers. Such a construction job, if ever carried through, would represent about one-tenth of the capacity of the city's building industry during the 1920's.

In discharging its second duty, during the past four years the Authority has used work-relief labor in demolishing old structures having a total frontage of about eight miles. Never able to get its hands on the $25,000,-000 promised from PWA funds, it has done little in the construction of low-rent housing. By shoe-string promotion, and with the aid of State and Federal work-relief labor, the Authority does have one development to its credit. First Houses, replacing slum property on Avenue A and Third Street mostly owned by Vincent Astor, was ready for occupancy by its 122 families on July 1, 1936. Its coverage is 41.6 percent on the street level, and 36.5 percent for the higher stories. The average monthly rental a room is $6.05. It would take more than 4,000 such developments to care for the 500,000 families living in the slums.

The Authority also had a hand in two demonstration projects built by the PWA—the Harlem River Houses, near the Macomb Bridge in Upper Harlem, and the Ten Eyck Houses in Williamsburg, Brooklyn, both occupied in the fall of 1937. The Ten Eyck Houses, costing approximately $13,500,000, constitute the largest of 51 PWA projects built or being built throughout the country. It has a 12-block site, and consists of 20 four-story apartment buildings and a junior high school, with a park and playground. The Harlem River Houses, built on land bought from John D. Rockefeller, cost $4,500,000; on October 7, the last of the 574 Negro families moved into their new quarters. Average monthly rent a room is $7.10, not including a charge for heat and hot water of about $1.50 a room a month.

Applications for apartments in these developments swamped the Authority; and a strict system of selection was used in admitting the few lucky tenants. While termed "low-rent housing," such dwellings can be afforded only by the middle-income groups. Plans for true low-rent housing—rooms for families with incomes under $900 a year—have yet to be put on paper.

On September 1, 1937, President Roosevelt approved the United States Housing Act, creating a permanent Federal Housing Authority with the power to make loans and annual contributions or capital grants to local housing authorities for financing low-rent projects. The Authority may issue $500,000,000 worth of bonds, guaranteed by the United States, the proceeds to be used for loans during a three-year period. In addition, $26,-000,000 may be appropriated for operating expenses and annual grants. While a stride forward in the history of American housing, this act is in effect a compromise measure. The Wagner-Steagall bill on which it was based had provided for about twice the amount of housing over a four-year period. Rehabilitation of New York's lower East Side alone would require at least a half billion dollars; and it would take more than 20 billions to rehabilitate the slums of the nation. As no State may receive more than 10 percent of the half-billion allocated under the act, the new low-rent housing that can be constructed in New York City from these funds in the next three years is negligible— at the most, $30,000,000 worth, or some 5,000 units. More than two centuries would be required to rehabilitate the city's slums at this rate.

But in 1938, five American Labor Party members took seats in the new City Council and five others in the State Assembly. The Party members in the Assembly sponsored the Minkoff bill, now enacted into law, which in broad effect prohibits the owner of an old-law tenement or converted dwelling from raising rents in his building unless the latter complies with the provisions of the Multiple Dwelling Law. The American Labor Party (in which Mayor La Guardia is enrolled) is also pledged to a program of low-cost housing for the city. And as the post-war record of European housing shows, no group has a livelier or more sustained interest in abolishing the slums than the group that is forced to live in them.

Body Politic

JACOB LEISLER, a merchant-captain stationed at the fort of New York, made in 1689 the first attempt to establish a representative government for the city of New York as part of his plan for governing what was then the Province of New York. The provincial government was in no sense a democratic one. All officials were appointed by the royal governors, whose authoritarian rule was resented by the colonists—with the exception, of course, of the landed proprietors, who were its immediate beneficiaries. For his purpose Leisler took advantage of the prevailing confusion that resulted from the deposition of the Catholic King James and the ascendancy of the Protestants William and Mary of the House of Orange. Governor Dongan, who was a Catholic and therefore in disfavor, fled; whereupon Leisler, proclaiming allegiance to the new British rulers, seized the fort at New York and called for the formation of a representative government for the province. He convoked a convention attended by delegates from a number of villages, who spoke for the merchants, supported by mechanics and artisans—as opposed to the former ruling class, the great landowners, many of whom had never seen their American holdings. A committee of safety composed of ten men was appointed, and with Leisler governed the Province. They established a municipal government for the City of New York; and Peter Delanoy, elected mayor by popular vote of the freeholders, served from October 14, 1689, to March 20, 1691. In the latter year, Leisler's government was deposed and he was hanged as a traitor.

Under the succeeding regime, the Province was granted the right to convoke an assembly, but the status of the city was restored to that existing before the Leisler uprising. The Crown made a concession to popular government in 1731, when the charter granted by Governor John Montgomerie included a provision for the annual election of aldermen and their assistants by vote of the freeholders. These aldermen, with a mayor

438

and a controller appointed by the governor, formed the first common council, with legislative powers.

The Revolution made no change in the immediate form of municipal government or in its relation to the State government. The mayor was still an appointed officer of the State, and suffrage was still limited to freeholders. Political interests were divided sharply between the haves and the have-nots. The Federalists represented the city gentry and the merchant class; the Society of St. Tammany represented the poor and underprivileged. The latter organization was a survival of a group of patriotic societies effective before and during the war in their espousal of the Revolutionary cause. Its name was chosen in mockery. The loyalists, or Tories, had organized in such groups as the St. George Society and the Order of St. Andrew and St. George, pledging fealty to King George III. Derisively, the plebeians chose a legendary Indian chieftain as their patron saint. The society was more or less identical with the group known as the "Liberty boys," politically active in the suppression of Tories immediately after the war, even to the extent of confiscating their property.

At the close of the 18th century, the political star of the Society of St. Tammany dimmed. The Federalists, led by Alexander Hamilton, had wrested control of city offices from the "Liberty boys." The method used was simple. Hamilton's party sponsored the cause of the former loyalists, succeeded in having all restrictions against them removed, and thereby gained their votes. Resentment was widespread, as the patriots, many of whom were still deprived of the vote, saw the pre-Revolutionary status being re-established. As a result, the property qualification for male suffrage became a deeper cause for dissatisfaction. Revitalized as a semi-fraternal organization, the Society of St. Tammany or the Columbian Order (Sons of Tammany) led the movement for popular suffrage. Under Aaron Burr's tutelage, the society became a municipal political organization with control of political offices as its goal. Countering the influence of the one bank in the city under Federalist control, Burr used the Bank of the Manhattan Company, which he had established, as a means of "arranging" property qualifications in accordance with the suffrage requirements.

This means of righting a wrong might well be questioned, but the justice of the cause was such that it won to its support an ever-growing section of the population. Nor was an abstract principle of suffrage the only issue: it was to the interest of the municipality to broaden the base of support for what seemed the larger issue, local versus State control. Dissatisfaction with State dominance grew with the years, stimulated not only by the example of New England towns and cities, but also by that of nearby Long Island communities, where a high degree of democratic local government was accepted. Growth of the city accentuated the contradiction between local needs and State inability or unwillingness to cope with the problems involved. Tammany, which had never renounced its support of universal manhood suffrage although men of property were assuming leadership in the organization, also led the movement against State control. As a result of Tammany's espousal of both popular movements, the State legislature in 1821 voted for a Constitutional Convention and acceded to the municipality's demands in one respect: a suffrage amendment to the Constitution was passed. The effort to gain a greater degree of local control, in a resolution providing for popular election of the mayor and common council, was defeated by one vote. However, the council was authorized to appoint the mayor, and from 1821 to 1834 six mayors were thus appointed.

Eight years after the great Tammany victory, its power was threatened by the Workingmen's Party, composed of artisans and mechanics organized in labor societies. This party, maintaining that Tammany no longer represented the interests of the people, advanced a program of social legislation. In the election of 1829 the new party polled 6,000 votes to Tammany's 11,000, electing one of its candidates, Ebenezer Ford, to the State Assembly. The result was a hurried entrance by Tammany into the field of social legislation with the introduction of a Mechanics' Lien Law, calculated to abolish many abuses suffered by workmen at the hands of unscrupulous employers. Restored thereby to public favor, Tammany next rode the crest of popular sentiment for a fuller measure of local control, doubtless not unmindful of the great political and patronage power that such a victory might mean. It led the fight for popular election of the mayor, and in 1834 the city had its first such election since 1690.

In the next decade the population almost doubled, and its needs brought into sharper relief the failure of State control in the administration of municipal government. Provision for such indispensable services as water, light and sanitation was inadequate; but the inefficiency of the police force, then known as the Watch Department, was scandalous. The fight against State domination broke out sharply when the mayor and common council, sensitive to public anger, created a municipal police force under their own authority, instead of accepting one set up by the State legislature in 1844. The local force proved a failure, however, and in 1845 the State-authorized department was organized.

Early in the 1840's, a system of public schools was established under a Board of Education. Other municipal services were taking form—a process accelerated when the charter of 1849 was granted, giving more powers to the municipality. Executive power was vested in the mayor and the heads of departments. The mayor was still nominally the head of the police department, but a chief of police was given direct responsibility for the department. The charter further provided for a Department of Finance headed by a Comptroller, a Department of Streets, a Collector of Assessments, a Superintendent of Wharves, a Department of Repairs and Supplies, a City Inspector (or Public Health Department), an Alms House Department and a Law Department. The Department of Streets was charged with the lighting of the city and with "cleaning the public streets, and collecting the revenue arising from the sale of manure." Provision was made for the creation of a Croton Aqueduct Board, responsible for "the supply and distribution of water to the City of New York."

The New York City charter of 1849 gave belated recognition to the fact that what in early days was a protective agency had long since become a great administrative enterprise. The government, of necessity, was forced to provide the framework whereby half a million people could live together. That framework—streets, schools, hospitals, transportation facilities, sewers—had to be built, and no great foresight was needed to see the literally golden opportunity inherent in its construction. In consequence, the 1850's were marked by the pressure of utility entrepreneurs upon local government for valuable concessions. Franchises, charters and incorporation papers were obtained through bribery of members of the Common Council. Valuable leases, many granted in perpetuity, were often given without the slightest compensation to the city.

Such corrupt practices went hand in hand with the building of a political machine based upon the patronage involved in an extended public service program. The conflict between the State and Tammany was renewed, but with different connotations. The agitation for local control originally had a popular base, but was now chiefly a partisan fight for spoils. In two battles in the 1850's, the State forces won. A Metropolitan Police District was established in 1857 under State control, and in the same year a Board of Supervisors was created as a county body vested with supervisory functions in Manhattan. By the latter move, the State government adherents controlled a body counterposed to the Common Council.

But these added measures of State regulation did little or nothing to prevent local political corruption of unprecedented proportions. Within a few years after the Civil War, the so-called "Tweed Ring" in New York City plundered the municipality of a sum conservatively estimated at about $75,000,000. Depredations could be made on so large a scale because of the new charter that Tweed fostered and forced through the legislature in 1870. By this charter, State commissions were abolished, and the power of the Board of Aldermen was effectually curtailed. The mayor was given absolute power of appointment; but, what is still more to the point, practically full municipal control was placed in the hands of a Board of Special Audit, composed of A. Oakey Hall, Mayor; William M. Tweed, Commissioner of Public Works; Richard B. Connolly, Comptroller; and Peter B. Sweeny, President of the Board of Parks. No money could be drawn from the city treasury without the permission of this body.

Although millions were appropriated for municipal services, what the people received for their money was little more than a brazen mockery. Sanitary conditions in the city were unbelievably vile. Cholera epidemics swept through the tenements, endangering the entire population. So corrupt had the political machine become, so injurious to the functioning of municipal government and to business, that a great reform movement gathered force. Paradoxically, it had an anti-democratic impetus. Its leaders, some of the most public-spirited men of the time, among them Peter Cooper, opposed the broadening of the base of municipal government by popular election of department heads. Instead, they wanted continuation of State commission rule, in order to keep control of municipal affairs out of Tweed's hands.

Two years after passage of the notorious charter of 1870, the suffering populace rallied under the anti-Tweed banner, and a reform ticket was swept into office, with William Havemeyer at its head. A new charter, intended to correct some of the shortcomings of the previous instrument, was adopted in 1873. The unlimited appointive power of the mayor was checked. Heads of departments were replaced by boards, the reformists believing that board administration would act as an automatic check on individual corruption.

But hopes for permanent reform survived the efficient Havemeyer administration for only a brief period. Thereafter attempts to make the municipal government one of service instead of exploitation were as futile as the legendary efforts of King Canute; for the great immigration wave from Europe broke upon New York. The immigrants represented various things to various groups. To the idealists, the Statue of Liberty was an appropriate welcome; to the industrialists, the newcomers meant a cheaper labor supply; but to the politicians, the arrivals at Ellis Island were merely potential voters. Friendless, bewildered, anxious to become a part of the country of their dreams, the immigrants went through the naturalization mill, grateful to the petty politicians who showed them the way. Their vote was Tammany's, and upon it was built a patronage machine that controlled the city. The singleness of purpose with which the political machines of New York and other cities went after the spoils of office, to the neglect of municipal problems and services, caused James Bryce to say in 1888 that "the government of cities is the one conspicuous failure of the United States."

Then suddenly the voice of righteousness reverberated throughout Sodom and Gomorrah, and was heard. In 1892 the Rev. Dr. Charles H. Parkhurst rallied the middle class, represented by the residual church Puritanism that still wielded some influence, in a campaign against corrupt city officials whose power depended upon vast numbers of immigrants. Like his fellow ministers, he saw the essential degradation of man in commercialized vice; but gifted as he was with some degree of realistic outlook, he knew this evil thrived through collusion with a municipal officialdom that profited from the graft connected with prostitution. Police connivance and protection in return for bribes permitted the existing state of affairs. Dr. Parkhurst's raids on the brothels and his weekly sermons were sensational. His language was fitted to his subject. "The polluted harpies, under the pretense of governing a city, are feeding day and night on its quivering vitals. They are a lying, perjured, rum-soaked and libidinous lot."

Finally, in April 1894, as a result of the Parkhurst agitation, the State Senate appointed an investigating committee with Clarence Lexow as its chairman. The committee's exposure of wholesale police extortion and of corruption in other departments led in 1895 to a thorough overhauling of the municipal government. The commission or board system of administration was abolished, and responsibility for each department was vested in a single executive head. Theodore Roosevelt, then a member of the Board of Police Commissioners, instituted drastic reforms in the police department. A Department of Investigation and Accounts was organized, headed by a commissioner whose duty was to run down graft, favoritism, and bribery in the municipal government. In 1884, the first civil service law for city employes was enacted.

The Parkhurst vice crusade and the ferretings of the Lexow Committee aroused the people, but a deep community interest in the underlying cause of the maladjustment had been evident for some time before. Recognizing that the basic difficulty was, and had been, a proper relation and balance between city and State governments, the State Senate appointed a committee to investigate the subject of municipal government in the State and to make such recommendations as seemed pertinent. The report of the Fassett Committee (as it was popularly known), submitted in 1891, declared that the business of the city was subordinated to the exigencies of State and national politics, and that under the existing circumstances stable city government was impossible. Municipal officials were unable to initiate changes and reforms because of the inevitability of State interference. Any State law affecting municipalities as such was applicable to all cities of the same class within the State; and as few measures could conceivably be welcome to all, political jockeying often blocked necessary adjustments in the governmental machinery of cities.

As a result of the Fassett Committee's report, the State constitution was amended in 1894 to allow some measure of local autonomy to the cities. Municipal authorities were given power of veto over a special enabling act of the legislature affecting them, a veto that could be overridden only if the legislature repassed the act in the same session within 30 days of its passage. The amendment was only a minor victory, but it foreshadowed the charter granted in 1897, which provided the basis for consolidation of the five boroughs and (with revisions adopted in 1901) formulated the general pattern of municipal government followed by Greater New York for forty years—until superseded by the charter that came into effect on January 1, 1938.

So dense was the population of the metropolitan area, and so rapidly had it spread beyond the confines of Manhattan Island, that years before the five boroughs were consolidated in 1898 their political separation had become an expensive anachronism. The city of Brooklyn, which in a half century of rapid growth absorbed a number of adjacent towns and villages, had its own mayor, and in almost every other way duplicated the governmental organization of New York. Queens, Richmond, and what is now the Bronx, the scene of vast real estate developments, were hampered by antiquated or inadequate governmental forms. The separation was expensive because of the duplication of administrative functions; but more important, it prevented the extension and coordination of municipal services to meet the needs of the growing communities.

In the years after consolidation the new metropolis adjusted itself to its governmental framework, free from the restrictions imposed by small governmental units. Municipal services were extended and improved. The boroughs were linked more closely by subways whose trains roared under boundary lines and rivers. New bridges were erected. A water system that is an engineering marvel came into being. Port facilities were enlarged and modernized.

Yet the problem emphasized by the Fassett Committee still remained unsolved. State legislative action in almost all important municipal matters continued, and such action was often not disinterested but tempered by political expediency. Municipal initiative was not free to operate, and city government was largely reduced to routine administrative functions. To the public-spirited New Yorker, the problem of securing good government became irrevocably linked with freedom from State dominance. In the election of November 1923, the so-called "home rule amendment" to the State constitution was adopted by popular vote; and in the following year the necessary enabling act specifying the details of home rule powers and methods of exercising them was passed by the legislature and approved by the governor. Under the amendment, every city in the State was granted "power to adopt and amend local laws not inconsistent with the constitution and laws of the State," and in addition certain specific privileges were granted to New York City alone.

Within less than a decade after adoption of the "home rule amendment," scandal broke anew around the city administration. A series of revelations shocked the nation and impelled the State legislature, on March 23, 1931, to authorize an investigation of the governmental affairs of New York City. This investigation lasted 11 months, coming to a dramatic climax with the resignation of Mayor James J. Walker, during formal proceedings for his removal.

How far-reaching were the consequences of that investigation is a matter for historians to evaluate. Suffice it to say here that the older order was replaced in 1934 by one in which the reform aspects were less spectacular than the adjustment to a changed conception of the municipality's responsibility for the economic welfare of its citizens. The mayoralty election of 1933 took place at a time when the lowest point of a nation-wide depression had been reached. Nearly 700,000 persons in New York were dependent on relief. The state of municipal finances was unsatisfactory, and bankers were clamoring for budget stability. A division in Tammany's ranks gave a new Fusion reform party its opportunity, and its standard bearer, Fiorello La Guardia, was elected mayor. Four years later he was reelected by the support of such divergent groups as the Republican and

Fusion Parties, whose official candidate he was, the anti-Tammany Democrats, the American Federation of Labor, the Committee for Industrial Organization, and lastly, but not least important, the newly organized American Labor Party. He was also the latter's official candidate, and his own vote was cast as a member of that party. The Communists and Socialists, while not officially endorsing the La Guardia ticket, put forward no candidates of their own for the office of mayor.

Thus it was evident that a great political realignment had taken place, one in which many ideas of government were synthesized. There was acceptance of the municipal government as a functioning agent for social welfare and unemployment relief. There was evident approval of the large-scale public works program, especially an increase of recreational facilities, undertaken by the municipality. There was recognition of the city's responsibility in labor disputes, through appointment by the Mayor of special fact-finding committees and his active intervention in some disputes. And, in no less degree, there was general satisfaction with the previous four-years' administration of the city.

A new charter for the city was approved at a referendum held November 3, 1936, after several legal attempts had been made to prevent the vote. This document was drafted by a Charter Revision Commission appointed by Mayor La Guardia, the purpose being to bring the municipal government machinery more closely in line with the modern demands placed upon it. The commission was concerned with the elimination of duplicating functions in municipal, county and borough governments, with securing a larger degree of centralization in the governmental structure, and with setting up a more representative form of legislative body. The last named objective was achieved when, in the first election under the new charter, in November 1937, members of a City Council to replace the old Board of Aldermen were elected in accordance with the principle of proportional representation and preferential voting, whereby political parties are given representation in proportion to their voting strength, in contradistinction to the old system of majority rule. How the principle works out with respect to representation of all sections of the population is indicated by the party affiliations of the first City Council: Democrats, 14, one of whom was not an organizational candidate; Labor, five; Republicans, three; Fusion, three; and Independent, one.

The counting of the vote in the first election took weeks; the organization of the Council, in view of its divergent party representation, took months. Yet by the spring of 1938 the Council was in full action and, as

Heywood Broun remarked, was "putting on a better show than the Planetarium."

The Municipal Government

Only a very brief outline can be given here of the more important elements and workings of New York City's huge governmental apparatus, with particular reference to the new agencies and arrangements instituted under the charter that became effective in January 1938. These latter are of especial interest as indicating the adjustments made by one of the world's greatest cities to the swiftly changing social and economic exigencies of our time.

Although a large majority of the agencies and officers of government function for the city as a whole, the geographic-political divisions of boroughs and counties still retain a place in the governmental structure, with full or limited jurisdiction in certain matters within their respective boundaries. As a result, three more or less distinct forms of local government are operative in New York City: (1) that for the city as a whole—an entirely centralized form; (2) that for the individual boroughs, partly centralized through representation on the Board of Estimate; and (3) that for the individual counties, which is wholly decentralized.

The Mayor is chief executive and magistrate of the city. The City Council (replacing the old Board of Aldermen) is the legislative body. The Board of Estimate, notwithstanding its misleading title, is the general administrative body. The Comptroller is the chief financial officer. Ranging down from these peaks in the governmental structure is an imposing array of departments, bureaus, boards, commissions and other agencies, along with the borough presidents and a number of other special officers.

The Mayor, elected from the city at large for a four-year term at an annual salary of $25,000, is directly assisted by a Deputy Mayor and a Budget Director, appointed by himself. As chairman of the Board of Estimate, he exercises an important influence in that body in addition to casting three of its 16 votes. Local laws enacted by the City Council are subject to his approval or veto, and his veto can only be overridden by a two-thirds vote of the Council. He appoints the heads of departments, as well as the members of various commissions and boards, in the city government, and can remove them at will; he also appoints the city magistrates and the justices of the Court of Special Sessions. He serves as ex-officio member on the boards of trustees of a dozen or more of the city's libraries, museums and other public institutions. Next to that of the President of the United States, his job is perhaps the most difficult and wearing of any in the country.

Members of the City Council, the legislative branch in local government, are elected on the basis of proportional representation within each of the five boroughs, with one councilman for every 75,000 voters in a borough and an additional councilman if the remaining borough vote reaches 50,000. The Council elected in November 1937 on this basis consists of 26 members. The President of the Council is elected by city-wide majority vote at the same time as the Mayor, and for a corresponding term of four years, at a salary of $15,000; he presides at Council meetings and participates in discussion, but has no vote except in case of a tie. The councilmen are elected for a two-year term, at a yearly salary of $5,000. No one already serving the city in any official capacity is eligible for election as councilman. Within certain somewhat technical restrictions, the City Council has the sole power of initiating and passing local laws.

In direct contrast with the Council, the Board of Estimate is of wholly ex-officio composition, its eight members being the Mayor, the Comptroller, the President of the Council, and the five Borough Presidents. The three officials first named above have three votes each in the board's deliberations, the borough presidents of Manhattan and Brooklyn have two votes each, while the borough presidents of the Bronx, Queens and Richmond have a single vote each. The Mayor serves as chairman of the board, whose functions in general are similar to those of the board of directors of a business corporation. It fixes salaries and approves franchises, authorizes sales or leases of city property and exercises final control over matters of financial policy. In these and other affairs it has at its disposal the services of a large technical staff organized in five bureaus, as well as the assistance of any department or agency of the municipal government.

Although, as has been said, the Comptroller is the chief financial officer of the city, his duties under the new charter are largely of an auditing and investigating character. But the charter makes him sole trustee of the sinking funds and of all other trust funds held by the city; and he continues to exercise the important functions of borrowing money and of settling all monetary claims in favor of or against the city, in addition to advisory and other powers. He is elected from the city at large for a four-year term at a salary of $20,000 a year.

The collection and disbursement of city funds, formerly handled by the Comptroller, are assigned by the new charter to a Department of Finance headed by a City Treasurer and two Deputy Treasurers. Within the department are (1) a bureau of city collections in charge of a city collector, with a deputy collector for each of the five boroughs; and (2) a bureau of receipts and disbursements for the reception and safe-keeping of all money paid into the city treasury and for the payment of all money on warrants drawn by the Comptroller and countersigned by the City Treasurer.

Fundamentally important in the city's governmental mechanism is the annual budgeting of finances. In briefest possible statement. prospective expenditures and receipts for an ensuing fiscal year are formulated in two separate budgets—one having to do with current expenses, the other with capital projects (permanent public improvements, acquisition of real property, etc.). Responsibility for preparing the expense budget is vested in the Mayor and his Budget Director; the task of making up the capital budget is assigned to the City Planning Commission—a creation of the new charter. After preliminary investigation and reports involving every municipal agency, tentative budgets are drawn up and presented to the Board of Estimate. When approved by vote of that body, they are certified by the Mayor and submitted to the City Council. Then, after approval by the Council, they are certified by the Mayor, Comptroller, and City Clerk. From beginning to end the parturition of a city expense budget is slow and painful. It is attended by acrimonious official debate, cries of anguish from the taxpayers, inside political jockeying, incessant paring and patching—with usually in the end a compromise result not wholly satisfactory to anyone. But the democratic process has been fulfilled, and the democratic purpose roughly achieved.

A significant feature of the new charter is its recognition of the fact that "the growth and development of a modern city depend upon the wisdom and foresight with which capital improvements are undertaken and the extent to which the integrity of zoning regulations and of the city map is maintained." To eliminate the log-rolling and pork-barrel evils of the past in this connection, the charter provides for a City Planning Commission, comprising the chief engineer of the Board of Estimate and six members appointed by the Mayor for overlapping terms of eight years. The function of this commission in preparing the city's capital budget has been mentioned above. It is also charged with making and maintaining a "master plan" of the city, embodying the most desirable arrangement of all public and private improvements; it is guardian of the official city map; and it has the power to recommend changes in existing zoning regulations. In these, as well as other similar duties and prerogatives, the commission is assisted by an Advisory Planning Board of three members in each of the five boroughs.

Of somewhat closely related significance is the creation of a new Department of Public Works and a new Department of Housing and Buildings. The former supersedes the old Department of Plant and Structures; its duties are to "plan, construct, and repair all public works except those otherwise provided for in the charter or by statute." In the Department of Housing and Buildings, which replaces the old Tenement House Department, are centralized "all functions of government relating to the regulation and control of the planning, construction, inspection and occupancy of private buildings." Each department is headed by a commissioner and two deputy commissioners, and each is empowered to set up special bureaus within the departments.

Except for an occasional shift of duty or authority, many of the departments and agencies of municipal government in New York continue to function as before adoption of the new charter. For the casual reader, the names of these agencies sufficiently indicate in most cases the general field or purpose of each. The problems of local government in New York differ, in the main, only with respect to scale from the corresponding problems of other great American municipalities. Certain unique or unusual features of the city's governmental apparatus and procedure, particularly the progressive features initiated under the new charter, are noted above; but the rest is, for the most part, distinctive only because of relative size and complexity.

The magnitude, if not the complexity, of New York's present-day governmental machinery is perhaps best indicated by the totals of its financial balance-sheet for the calendar year of 1937. In that year the city received in cash from all sources a grand total of $1,402,361,066.03, including borrowings of $614,700,000. In the same year it paid out in cash a grand total of $1,416,487,321.66, exclusive of transfers between funds. The city's proposed expense budget for the fiscal year of 1938 totals $683,261,-660.88. Of that amount considerably more than half is allocated for "personal service"—i.e., for paying the salaries or wages of 155,486 employees.

Borough Government

In addition to their representation in the centralized municipal government, New York's five boroughs enjoy a modest share of local self-government with respect to strictly local improvements paid for by assessment on the property of residents within a single district.

At the same time and for the same term as the Mayor of the city, each borough elects a Borough President, who receives a salary of $15,000 a year. While his chief activities and influence are as a member of the Board of Estimate in the centralized municipal government, he is in some degree a local mayor, responsible for local improvements and with power to appoint a commissioner of borough works, a secretary, clerks, etc.

The five boroughs are divided into 24 "local improvement districts," in each of which there is a Local Improvement Board, presided over by the president of the borough of which the district is a part. With the creation of a City Planning Commission under the new charter, the power of these boards and of the Borough Presidents with respect to local improvements have been greatly restricted.

County Government

Counties as political subdivisions were established in what is now the State of New York in 1684, twenty years after the British capture of New Amsterdam from the Dutch. The present City of New York covers an area that embraces five such political subdivisions—New York County, Bronx County, Kings County, Queens County and Richmond County. These five counties are respectively coextensive with the boroughs of Manhattan, the Bronx, Kings, Queens and Richmond. As counties, the areas are political subdivisions of the State; as boroughs, they are political subdivisions of the city.

The attempt to maintain a county system of government within so large a metropolitan area has proved increasingly impracticable since the Greater New York consolidation of 1898, and many of the functions ordinarily performed by county officials or boards have been taken over by the city. Those that still remain are almost wholly of a legal and protective nature. Each of the five counties elects a District Attorney, a Sheriff, and a County Clerk. A Register (of deeds, mortgages, etc.) is elected in each county except Richmond. A Public Administrator (for intestate property, etc.)

and a Commissioner of Jurors is appointed for each county. A Commissioner of Records is appointed for New York, Bronx and Kings Counties; and New York County has a special Commissioner of Records for its Surrogates' Courts.

With the coming into full effect of an amendment to the State constitution, adopted in 1935, all county offices other than those of the district attorneys, county clerks, and judges of county courts will be done away with and their functions assigned to offices or officers within the centralized city government.

Good Samaritan

OFTEN the visitor who comes to town for two or three days goes home with a sincere but slightly complacent opinion about New York's coldness and inhumanity. To him it is a city of machines in more than the physical sense; he may feel that the people themselves are motivated by the machine spirit. His day-by-day perceptions add up to the impression of a terrible and casual disregard for human life. Too often he is bewildered and appalled by the contrast with his own home town. This latter may be a metropolis of a million or two; but the pace is slower there, the people more relaxed and affable. A more ready sympathy is in the air; disease and want seem to be more obviously the concern of the whole community. But if the humanitarian impulses of a great city can be gauged by the relative number of its social agencies—its home and work relief bureaus, its hospitals and clinics for the poor, its settlement houses, its parks and play spaces, its homes for the aged and orphaned—then New York compares favorably with the most progressive and socially sensitive of American communities. Broadly speaking, for nearly every form of hard luck that flesh is heir to there exists in the city today an institution or an agency prepared and willing to offer alleviating aid. In its broad organization for relief and remedial work, New York stands high among American cities. In the field of prevention it is, like most communities, only beginning to master its job. In eradicating preventable disease, in building the maximum of physical and mental health in the young, in guiding the youthful delinquent away from a career of professional crime, in caring for chronic illness, in eliminating slums and making a minimum standard of decent housing a universal requirement, in absorbing the social shocks and personal tragedies consequent upon unemployment, the city is still in a pioneering stage. It has made a beginning, and in some of these fields has established effective techniques, but many years must pass before results can be obtained comparable to the effort expended.

The present system of social services in New York is the outgrowth of decades of effort, of trial and error, gradually evolving in the direction of orderly planning and execution. The obstacles were uncommonly formidable. The city grew at a prodigious rate, fed by successive waves of immigrants from countries ever more distant, geographically and culturally. It had a disturbing tendency to crowd upward instead of spreading outward. Though it has repeatedly shown a fine frontier impulse to extend a helping hand in great emergencies, it had little of that tradition of continuing public responsibility for distress upon which the social services of the great western European cities were built. It had an almost endemic habit of political corruption, relieved but not checked by occasional reform administrations. And it had, and still has, its peculiar problems in the thousands of sailors daily in port seeking or switching jobs, in the great national market on the Bowery for casual and migrant labor, and in the streams of Negroes from the South and Puerto Rico, unequipped by physique or training for successful life in a congested industrial city.

The earlier history of New York's social services, going back to Revolutionary days, is one of organizing to meet isolated problems as they appeared, or rather as they made an impression on the pity of philanthropists or charitable groups. Hospitals and orphan asylums were an early and obvious need. The New York Hospital was incorporated in 1771; Bellevue City Hospital in 1811; the Orphan Asylum Society in the City of New York in 1806. The needs of the seamen in the western hemisphere's greatest port were likewise evident. Sailors' Snug Harbor for aged sailors was founded in 1806, and has become legendary for the fantastic appreciation in the value of the real estate bequeathed to it in those early days. Characteristic of the period was the Association for the Relief of Respectable, Aged, Indigent Females, organized in 1815. But until well toward the end of the 19th century such efforts to meet the city's welfare needs were impulsive and sporadic, and left vast areas of essential service neglected. In some respects and at certain periods, the city was a leader among American communities. The public health work of Herman Biggs, just after the Civil War, was unequalled in its day. But in many other respects, in the second half of the century, New York's welfare work had merely the same standards, or lack of them, that characterized all large American cities.

Those were the days when the destitute were obliged to stand for hours in bread lines, though Thanksgiving or Christmas might bring a basket of groceries from the neighbors or the district political boss for a treat; when the natural meal for a lonely poor man was the free lunch in the corner saloon; when it was seriously debated whether feeding a destitute man and his family did not deprive him of "self respect" and "initiative"; when homeless children were herded into an impersonal institution (when they were not loaded onto railroad trains for the West, where farmers picked them up as "help"); when abandoned babies were put in congregate institutions where the brand of "illegitimate" was affixed perhaps for life; when the unmarried mother was treated as an outcast and often drifted all too naturally into prostitution as her most natural means of support; when youthful delinquents, even mere children, were regarded as "depraved" and "dissolute" and were hidden away with experienced criminals in institutions where society could forget them; when anyone who contracted "consumption" was given up for lost; when persons found with communicable diseases were rushed off to the pest house, while syphilis, being unmentioned, went unchecked; when babies went blind for lack of a few drops of silver nitrate in their eyes at birth and others died off by the hundreds each year of "summer complaint" for lack of elementary diet knowledge in the home.

At some time before the end of the century (the grouping of many dissimilar agencies into the Charity Organization Society in 1882 marks a convenient dating point) the necessity began to be felt among social workers to know the facts about the unmet needs, to study methods and procedures systematically, to set standards for the measurement of success or failure, to bring some degree of order and method into financial administration, to eliminate duplication of effort. It is hard today to realize that this impulse met with considerable public hostility. "Scientific charity" was commonly regarded by our pious grandparents as a contradiction in terms, almost a sin; the greatest of the abiding virtues seemed somehow soiled and its divine source withered by any admixture of calculation.

The process of transforming the neighborly impulse of charity, which was sufficient to pioneer life, into an instrument that would be effective under metropolitan conditions was slower and more complex in New York than in most other communities, because of the city's sheer size and the heterogeneousness of its racial composition. Nevertheless, by 1910 the social services here had acquired some degree of organization and certain standards to measure professional skill, expressed and stimulated by the New York School of Social Work, incorporated in 1898—the first professional graduate school of social work in the country.

Once the concept of city-wide effort and standards of effectiveness had been achieved, the city's voluntary social services expanded notably. In

1910 these services, exclusive of hospitals, spent some $15,000,000; by 1936 they were spending about $50,000,000, and employing thousands of full-time workers. If all forms of welfare, public and private, except hospitals, are included, the figures for 1936 reach the huge total of $442,-000,000. But more than $379,000,000 of this represented "outdoor" (non-institutional) relief from public funds, inclusive of the cost of administration, supplies and materials; and of this sum two-thirds was spent for the Federal works program. How enormously the depression figured in New York's welfare problem is indicated by the fact that at the peak, in March 1936, 1,550,000 persons, or nearly 20 percent of New York's total estimated population, were receiving some form of public assistance. Reports as of February 1938 showed some diminution, with a total of 1,255,800. At this time, 557,000 individuals were on home relief, and 568,000 were deriving their chief support from 142,000 work-relief employes of the Federal WPA. There were, in addition, the following special classes of relief recipients whose plight was not entirely, or even chiefly, due to general economic conditions: 48,500 recipients of old age assistance, 1,300 blind, 13,000 homeless, 23,500 children in institutions and foster homes, 37,000 children maintained in homes of parents or relatives by payments from the city, and 7,000 youths in CCC camps—a total of 130,300.

Since the beginning of the depression, direct cash relief to the unemployed has come to be recognized as a primary responsibility of municipal and state governments, substantially aided by the Federal treasury. But in earlier years, the private agencies bore the chief burden of unemployment. In 1910, public funds provided only 19 percent of all relief in New York. For years private charity continued to carry the greater part of the load. But by 1930 it had become evident that voluntary agencies could no longer assume such a responsibility, and by 1933 they were carrying only 12 percent of it. By 1936, out of the grand total of $310,000,000 given directly to clients as outdoor relief, largely necessitated by unemployment, and exclusive of administrative and operating costs, the private agencies' contribution had dropped to less than two percent.

Omitting unemployment relief from further consideration, then, how does New York care for its inhabitants when misfortune overtakes them? Most impressive, by its sheer size, is the hospital system. Each year, about two-thirds of a million New Yorkers, or roughly one in ten, are sick enough to need hospital treatment, and at least as many more require clinical care or dispensary service.

The total property investment in New York's institutions for the care of the sick amounts to some $430,000,000. Its 133 hospitals, public and private, contain nearly 38,000 beds and care for a daily average of more than 30,000 patients. Fifty-four of these hospitals specialize in the treatment of cancer, chronic diseases, eye-ear-nose-throat troubles, neurological disorders, orthopedic ills, tuberculosis, and communicable diseases, and in maternity care. The two gigantic medical centers, New York-Cornell and Columbia-Presbyterian, combine treatment and research in nearly all fields of medicine, and make their findings available to the entire medical world.

Somewhat more than a third of the total hospital work is done by the 23 city-owned hospitals, with 14,000 beds and an annual operating budget of close to $23,000,000. In these, in 1936, 267,000 patients were hospitalized, the great majority of them without payment. The present construction budget of the city-owned hospitals calls for an outlay of $60,000,000 for work to be completed by 1945.

The total operating budget of the 110 voluntary hospitals is about $35,000,000, of which in 1936 some $25,000,000 came from service charges ($4,319,369 of it paid by the city for the care of needy patients), and $10,000,000 from donations and income from capital funds. In 1937, 465,000 persons received bed care in these hospitals, and about 1,135,000 more were cared for as out-patients.

The city's clinics, most of them departments of the hospitals, are numerous and specialized. The *Directory of Social Agencies* lists 1,533, under the following general headings: arthritis, asthma, cancer, cardiac, dental, diabetes, ear, nose and throat, endocrine, eye, gastro-enterological, genito-urinary, gynecological, hay fever, health examinations, medical, neurological, orthopedic, osteopathic, pediatric, physical therapy, prenatal and postnatal, skin, surgical, syphilis and gonorrhea, tuberculosis, and vaginitis. Treatment at most of them is free to those unable to pay, and the fees charged to others are in most cases nominal.

New York was the first city in America to establish a convalescent home. Today there are 46 convalescent institutions, with a total of 3,777 beds, some providing medical care and some merely needed rest, but all giving free service when the patient cannot pay. The city pays half a million dollars yearly for care of poor convalescent patients in 23 of these institutions.

Yet there is still another large category of sick persons who often do not go near a hospital or clinic for years, who are only partially incapacitated or not visibly incapacitated at all. These are the chronically ill.

Chronic illness, which frequently is long neglected because it does not present symptoms demanding immediate care, saps the vitality and earning power of a huge proportion of our population, and it is growing so rapidly as to suggest that America may become a nation of invalids. But if New York has not yet adequately met this problem, it has at least been among the first to recognize that chronic disease is not necessarily incurable or incapacitating disease, and to shape a program on that premise. Montefiore Hospital, established in 1884, was the first in America dedicated to the care of chronic diseases. And as these lines are being written there is rising on Welfare Island what will be the first municipally owned and operated hospital of that type in the world. It is intended that this shall be a center of research in the field of chronic disease, which has been one of the neglected stepchildren of medicine, and that its findings shall be made available to other cities. From this experimental research and practice, New York may in two or three decades produce results of inestimable value to all America.

New York has also been a pioneer in the systematic effort to eradicate disease by educational methods. Its campaign against tuberculosis, conducted at the beginning largely by a voluntary association, has been the chief factor in lowering the city's tuberculosis death rate from 280 per 100,000 in 1900 to 59 per 100,000 in 1934, and the work is continuing without relaxation. Diphtheria deaths among children under 15 years of age were reduced from a percentage of 137.5 per 100,000 in 1907 to 3.4 percent in 1937, through a system of immunization inoculations widely advertised and free to those unable to pay. City medical authorities believe that diphtheria can be made as nearly extinct as yellow fever and smallpox. But to achieve this end, 300,000 inoculations of children must be made yearly—a requirement which, at this writing, is being fulfilled only to the extent of about 75 or 80 percent.

Under the national leadership of Dr. Thomas E. Parran, Surgeon General of the United States Public Health Service, New York has intensified its efforts to control and eventually eradicate venereal disease. To this campaign the city is at this writing spending at the rate of nearly $300,000 a year from its budget, plus a like amount contributed by the WPA and the National Social Security Board. From all sources, exclusive of fees paid for private treatment, New York will spend close to $2,500,000 on its antivenereal campaign in 1938. The city Bureau of Social Hygiene issues hundreds of thousands of pamphlets yearly describing for the layman, in simple language, what these diseases are and how they may be cured. Its laboratories issue without charge to all registered physicians the medicines needed for the treatment of syphilis and gonorrhea (as well as those for diphtheria, pneumonia and other diseases). And it is enlisting the cooperation of thousands of private physicians and social workers throughout the city to help educate the public so that these once unmentionable diseases may become as rare in New York as they are, for example, in Sweden, where the number of new cases of syphilis reported has been reduced from 5,976 in 1919 to only 399 in 1935.

Imperceptibly, in the past two or three decades, the city's public and private health agencies have become more and more active as centers of preventive medical work. The Health Department's nine health centers disseminate literature, organize lectures, administer the work of local public clinics, look after the health of public school pupils and arrange health conferences with their parents. They give annually 2,000 lectures on health for the general public, and hold 4,000 classes in health education for parents. In conjunction with the central Health Department office and the city laboratories, they maintain supervision over the 180,000 cases of communicable diseases annually reported and investigated; control the 17,000 cases of ascertained tuberculosis; diagnose 72,000 suspected cases of tuberculosis and 102,000 of suspected diphtheria; perform more than 400,000 Wassermann tests for the detection of syphilis. They dispatch their public health nurses on half a million home visits annually, though this represents but 16 percent of these nurses' work. They supervise the work of 70 infant and preventive health stations, which give a wide variety of service and advice to those who cannot afford a family doctor.

The work of New York's visiting nurses, including the 800 working with the Department of Health and those of the three voluntary visiting nurse services, is educational as well as remedial. In the health clinics, besides assisting the physician, they interpret the doctor's orders to the patients and their families. They teach young expectant mothers how to take care of themselves and how to prepare for the coming baby. They instruct parents in the preparation of food, initiate them into the importance of correct weight, sun, air, cod liver oil and orange juice, into the value of immunization against diphtheria and smallpox. In the fields of tuberculosis and syphilis, they emphasize the importance of early discovery. In their home visits they consider the family's social, economic and mental hygiene problems in relation to health.

New York's hospitals and clinics are laying ever-increasing stress upon the value of medical social work in both the prevention and the cure of disease. In order that the physician may treat not only the disease but also the patient, he needs the assistance of the medical social worker. It is her task to discover the environmental or emotional factors that affect disease in the individual, and to guide him in controlling those factors so as to favor a speedy recovery—at the same time, of course, teaching him how to stay well.

More and more, New York's social and health agencies are recognizing that abnormal emotional conditions may not only complicate and even cause disease, but that they frequently constitute disease in themselves. Many cases, once they are properly diagnosed by the psychiatrist, can be alleviated by comparatively simple common-sense methods—a change of attitude on the part of bullying members of the family, a created job or responsibility for a man whose neurosis is aggravated by unemployment. Often, of course, the mere opportunity to talk candidly with an understanding person goes far toward relieving the condition. A large proportion of future cases of mental illness can presumably be averted by timely treatment of the child, whose behavior peculiarities of today may become the anti-social or criminal tendencies of tomorrow. In New York's 55 mental clinics (those for children are euphemistically called "child guidance clinics") psychiatric advice is given free or at nominal charge to the thousands who visit them either voluntarily or, as is more frequent, on the advice of the family worker or medical social worker, though consistently thorough treatment is an ideal of the future. Five excellent hospitals also give specialized care to the more difficult cases.

The baby who makes his debut in New York City ought to be impressed by the elaborateness of the structure set up to welcome him. Indeed, long before he is born, this system has begun to function through the prenatal clinics and classes and the nurses' visits, already mentioned. Seventy thousand babies are born annually in New York's hospitals, and in every case where the mother comes for early pregnancy examination the Wassermann test is given, and where indicated, the anti-syphilis treatment which will in most cases guarantee the baby against inheriting the disease. And care of mother and child is continued in a large number of cases through the first year of the child's life.

The foundling baby becomes the ward of the Department of Child Welfare, and is taken to one of the three foundling hospitals until he is old enough to be assigned to one of the 72 child-caring homes in the city. Later, perhaps, he is boarded out in a private family. So far as his background can be determined, he is brought up in the religion of his parents.

There are 22 temporary shelters for children and 17 agencies which board out children in family homes, for which definite standards are set. Occasionally legal adoption is secured. Contrary to the usual belief, there are a great many more homes asking for children to adopt than there are children who can be placed.

For the child whose mother has to work, New York has 104 day nurseries, some of them denominational, scattered, unfortunately, all too planlessly throughout the city. Here 7,000 children receive a hot lunch at a nominal charge, and in many instances are given pre-school nursery training.

When the child reaches school age the city attempts to keep an eye on his health, though its resources are at present most inadequate. However, the clinical facilities are fairly abundant. In 1936, 300,000 visits were paid by children to the city's dental clinics and 50,000 visits to the eye clinics. The school and health departments are cooperating with voluntary agencies in an attempt to work out a system of regular health examinations for all school children. Considering how many ailments and pathological conditions can be cured or prevented if the individual is examined in time, this program should have a notable effect in lowering the city's future disease and death rate.

Incidentally, New York is exceptionally thorough in examining its milk supply. All the cans containing the three million quarts of milk shipped to the city daily are examined as they are delivered to the dealer for bottling, and 500 samples from the cows that supply the metropolis are subjected to bacteriological examination every week.

The charge used to be made against New York's public schools, and with considerable justification, that they put all children through the same impersonal mill, without regard to individual aptitudes or disabilities. This charge, as far as it relates to the handicapped child, is no longer true. The Board of Education spends $4,000,000 a year on the latter. Twenty-seven thousand children receive special instruction for the correction of speech difficulties—instruction that is wholly or largely successful in 90 percent of the cases. There are 101 special classes for pupils with defective eyesight—conducted, of course, in conjunction with the neighborhood clinic. There are nine special classes for the wholly blind in elementary and high schools. More than 10,000 mentally retarded pupils are taught in 536 special ungraded classes, the work of which is divided approximately evenly between academic study, physical training and handicrafts.

For the child of normal health the great need is recreation. In this city, recreational opportunities, though numerous, are geographically badly distributed. Public and voluntary agencies are seeking to meet the need. Some 140 non-profit vacation services offer a summer holiday for a week or more to about 81,000 children free or at nominal charge. Playstreets, playgrounds and parks (New York's park area was more than doubled between 1933 and 1938) are the city's answer to the need for outdoor recreation when weather permits. Tennis, baseball, golf, swimming, street games are provided in fairly ample and increasing measure, though in congested neighborhoods the parks are usually too far away and the playgrounds are too few. For winter months and for non-athletic types of play, the private agencies—the Y's, settlements, boys' clubs, scout groups —and the school community centers provide a varied program, with informal classes, hobby groups, esthetic and cultural activities. To get the greatest service from existing facilities, it is necessary to secure the use, with adequate supervision, of all school buildings after school hours. The settlements, of which there are about 40 in the city, with an average of some 1,000 participating members each, offer a wide variety of activities in arts, handicrafts, hobbies and just plain fun. Similar work is carried on by many other social and recreational agencies.

Yet such group activities as these are still but a drop in the bucket. The card catalogue of the WPA's youth department shows no fewer than 4,000 spontaneously organized boys' clubs which rent cellars, back rooms or loft space where they may hold their "business meetings," play cards, or "throw a dance." Some of these are on friendly terms with club leaders from social agencies and federate themselves into inter-club associations for athletic contests and other activities; many are going their chosen and often questionable way with no sort of leadership. Yet according to a summary completed by the Welfare Council in 1935, 65 percent of the males in New York between the ages of 16 and 25, and 75 percent of the females in this instinctively gregarious period of life, belong to no club or organization of any kind.

Every year in New York some 5,000 boys and girls under 16 years of age are brought into court charged with the commission of some crime or misdemeanor which would land them in jail or penitentiary if they were of legal age. But with very few exceptions, these children are not put through the impersonal mill of court procedure. The Children's Court, which deals with these cases (there is a branch in each borough) has wide powers of discretion, and the young delinquent is usually placed in the custody of a relative or friend, or of some social agency, to work out his salvation under friendly guidance. Here the social agency, whether directly or indirectly concerned, has an opportunity to investigate the youngster's problem and give him the help he may need. This help may mean the straightening out of some family relationship or care by a medical or psychiatric clinic, or merely the stimulating influence of a boys' club in a neighboring settlement. In any case, the youthful offender is likely to get humane and sympathetic treatment.

But once he has celebrated his sixteenth birthday his situation before the law is tragically altered. Though he will not be responsible for his acts under the civil law for five years more, before the criminal law he is already an adult and must, in principle, pay in full the penalty for his acts. The five-year span between the ages of 16 and 21 is today a no-man's-land of judicial and social practice in New York. For several years the Crime Prevention Bureau of the Police Department took all youthful offenders between the ages of 16 and 21 out of the dreaded police "line-up" and tried to deal with them if possible, as individuals needing understanding and guidance. At present, boys between the ages of 16 and 19 may be referred to the Adolescents' Court, and girls between 16 and 21 to the Wayward Minors' Court. Here the judge endeavors to give special attention to the circumstances, and often places them on probation under the care of a relative or a social agency instead of sending them to a reformatory or prison. But no student of delinquency in New York is satisfied that an effective method of dealing with the youthful criminal has yet been devised. Evidence accumulates that the average reformatory provides a high school course in the technique of crime, as the penitentiary offers a post-graduate course. It is evident that the courts, the police and the social agencies must between them discover how to deal with the youthful wrongdoer so as to give him the best possible chance, while still protecting society. They are far from having reached any agreement, but at least they have passed beyond the slogan stage—the stage in which phrases like "pampering the criminal" and "environmental causes of crime" do duty as arguments—and they are honestly working together to find a solution.

The adolescent, whether or not he has been fortunate enough to escape the attention of the law, will soon need a job. The public schools, as well as many voluntary social agencies, are expanding their work in guiding the boy and girl toward jobs to suit their aptitudes, and several public industrial high schools train them for types of work in which large numbers of New Yorkers are employed—the needle trades, for example. The city spends more than $2,280,000 a year for classes in evening trade schools and other evening classes. In addition to the public schools, a number of voluntary agencies offer a variety of general and special vocational training courses for from 20,000 to 30,000 handicapped persons in arts, handicrafts and other fields.

In actually finding employment for the boy or girl, the outstanding agency is the State Employment Service, which since January 1, 1938, has reorganized its operations under the provisions of the Unemployment Insurance Law and will in all probability make an increasing number of free placements in the future. An outstanding feature of its work has been the development of its junior employment offices. As in the vocational guidance field, a number of non-profit employment services, dealing with selected applicant groups, are also concerned with placement and find jobs for 50,000 young persons annually. Through a "clearance bulletin" initiated in 1929 under the auspices of the Welfare Council, these agencies and the State Employment Service cooperate in pooling job orders, making available to the applicants of all agencies the openings for jobs which any agency has and cannot fill from among its own applicants. In this field, however, the basic need is not for more guidance and employment agencies, but for more jobs. And while unemployment persists, the social agencies must continue to absorb as best they can the resultant shock and distress.

But most of the problems that confront the social worker are not single and simple—not solely the need for a job or for treatment of a certain acute disease or for a place where the youngster may play baseball. Usually the case that has become desperate enough to demand the attention of an agency is complex, calling for not one but perhaps half a dozen diverse kinds of aid. Here the family social worker, a too often misunderstood ministrant, is called upon to exercise an uncommon degree of understanding, skill, tact, resourcefulness and specific knowledge. A single example from the records of one of New York's largest family welfare agencies will suggest what this work is.

The Jones family is poor, badly fed, half sick, fearful of the future. The father earns about $11 a week as a taxi driver. The three-year old daughter is seriously undernourished. A baby is on the way. The father, approaching the end of his devices, has appealed to the welfare agency for help. A case worker then endeavors to disentangle cause and effect. On her recommendation, the agency supplies the money needed to make up a decent minimum family budget; a nutritionist shows the mother how to make the small food allowance buy really nourishing food; a nurse from the agency arranges for prenatal care at a nearby clinic, secures hospital treatment, provides a layette. After the baby is born it is sent with its mother to the agency's convalescent home in the country for six weeks. Meanwhile, the father, his courage restored and improved in health, has increased his earnings to $17 a week, and expects soon to return to a better-paid former employment.

Multiply this story 18,610 times, with innumerable variations of circumstance and some conception of the work done by this one agency in a single year (1936) will become apparent. That work involved 107,112 interviews and 102,999 medical and dental treatments. The particular agency referred to is one of the few that have a number of diverse types of aid at their command. Smaller agencies usually have to call upon others doing other types of work in order to supply all forms of aid needed in individual cases. Hence the necessity of constant contact and cooperation between them. In all, the family welfare agencies aided nearly 130,000 persons in 1937.

One tragic circumstance that may befall even a self-sustaining family is the temporary incapacitation, from illness or any other cause, of the mother. How will the children manage while the father is at work? Several agencies in New York have in recent years been supplying housekeeper service, or "substitute mothers," to such families. These mothers in Israel, who are usually called in on recommendation of a hospital social service department or of one of the family service agencies, not only see that the children are fed and washed, but leave a good deal of dietary and sanitary commonsense behind them in the home, and not infrequently actually prevent the disintegration of the family.

New York, like other cities, confines its welfare services, in principle, to persons who have legal residence, or "settlement," within the city or the state. But strangers arriving within its gates often have need of help. There are a number of agencies which among their other activities assist such persons, and one agency devotes itself exclusively to such work. This latter organization, whose representatives are found at all railroad and trans-Atlantic steamship terminals, works in conjunction with many of the city's other social agencies and with its 1,200 cooperating agencies in America and foreign countries. In 1936 it gave aid to nearly 50,000 travelers in some sort of trouble, 11,000 of whom presented major problems requiring intensive case work and care. More than 2,000 children under

16 traveling alone were given protection; nearly 1,000 children, girls and women were housed at its Guest House; 228 prospective brides were met and their marriages assisted—or, if marriage proved inadvisable, they were helped to return home or make other plans; and 289 runaways were found and cared for.

The transient, including even the panhandler and the hobo, can get lodging and food for the night in one of the city's two lodging houses for men or in its shelter for women, or in the lodgings provided by several voluntary agencies. In one year of the depression, an average of 12,-000 men and 300 women were thus sheltered in the city's houses or in its Camp La Guardia, regardless of legal residence, or in private rooming houses at city expense. In all, from 16,000 to 18,000 were housed nightly by public and private agencies. When the transient's true residence is established he is of course sent back home—at the expense, if necessary, of the city's Department of Public Welfare.

The figures last cited are exclusive of seamen, several thousand of whom are in port on any given day. Nineteen agencies (including two in Hoboken) care for them, providing club rooms, books, religious services, recreation, shelter, food, employment services, and, when necessary, cash relief. Early in 1938, an average of 1,500 seamen were maintained nightly by the Department of Public Welfare, and several hundred more in contract shelters at city expense. In the homes provided by the Sailors' Snug Harbor, from 700 to 800 aged seamen comfortably pass the last years of their lives.

The unattached and homeless who are properly the city's charge may be lodged and fed in the municipal shelters, in commercial lodging houses, or in contract shelters at the expense of the Department of Welfare. Aged persons without homes are lodged in the City Home for Dependents on Welfare Island which has 2,000 beds, or in the City Farm Colony on Staten Island (with 1,300 beds) where they may do such light work as they are capable of. In the latter part of 1937 approximately 48,000 aged persons were being given old age assistance in their own homes by the Department of Welfare, and some 7,600 were living in the 76 private homes for the aged. The Tompkins Square Apartments building, privately maintained, is something of a model of its kind. In one and two room apartments, single or married elderly persons may live comfortably, doing light housekeeping if they choose or eating their meals in the community cafeteria, their health supervised by a resident professional nurse.

The Department of Public Welfare cares for 1,300 of the city's blind, and private agencies serve 7,000 others, providing instruction in Braille reading, a circulating Braille library, outdoor occupations and vacations, industrial training, and employment that brings a monetary profit.

The poor man who gets into a row with his landlord, his neighbor, or the police can obtain free legal aid from a number of agencies in New York. The one that specializes in this work and does the major portion of it reports that it handled in 1937, 26,439 civil cases and 2,417 criminal cases. Many of its clients come to it on recommendation from other social agencies. In civil cases its activities are confined to New York City, though it acts in cooperation with legal aid societies in other cities. Its criminal work is confined to the representation of those accused of felony in the Court of General Sessions and the Manhattan Felony Court. The larger part of its business consists of the collection of wages and other money claims, assistance in matrimonial difficulties, workmen's compensation and personal injury claims, landlord and tenant disputes, and small matters in connection with estates.

The social agencies, public and voluntary, that perform all these local services, and many others of which space forbids mention, number no fewer than 1,167 according to the 1937 edition of the New York *Directory of Social Agencies*. More than 450 work in the field of family service and relief, including 95 organizations caring for the aged. There are 38 that provide care for the unattached and homeless, 75 that render various services to immigrants, foreign-born and travelers, 88 that provide protective and correctional service, 19 that serve seamen, and 91 that maintain non-commercial residences for men and boys or women and girls. Close to 340 agencies render health services, in addition to the 133 hospitals and the 1,533 clinics already mentioned. There are 90 maternity services and 18 nursing services. Fifty-five clinics and 43 city hospitals and institutions attend to persons who are mentally sick. For children there are no fewer than 366 agencies, among them 83 for dependent children, and 134 non-profit vacation services. In the fields of recreation, education, employment and neighborhood activities, there are approximately 250 organizations.

Such a census is impressive, and our casual visitor, mentioned in the first paragraph, might well conclude that the system of social agencies is organized to meet every human need. But even assuming that all the parts are operating adequately in their several fields, which is far from true, the system still suffers from one vital defect—it is inadequately planned. It grew, as the instruments of democratic society are likely to grow, spontaneously and therefore piecemeal, the left hand not knowing what the right hand was doing. The result has been that there is both too much and too little. Several agencies may be doing the same kind of work in some areas, while other areas are neglected, and major needs of the future loom without any appropriate instrumentality to meet them. There has been in the past a lack of central facilities through which the dozens or hundreds of agencies concerned with a given problem could pool knowledge and create and implement programs.

Crowded Manhattan appealed to the imaginations of philanthropists, hence three-quarters of New York's settlements are situated in that borough, which houses less than a fifth of the city's population. Schools were formerly thought of as merely educational institutions, hence for years their playgrounds and assembly rooms were padlocked after school hours in congested areas which, as social workers knew too well, were crying for recreational opportunities. Even those social agencies that are most susceptible of exact measurement—the hospitals—have more beds than are needed for many acute diseases, while the chronically sick and those suffering from tuberculosis and venereal disease cannot be adequately cared for. The social and medical techniques for handling these diseases and perhaps eventually eradicating them have been splendidly developed— and find progress blocked because there have been no central instrumentalities to plan and provide in advance for the increased hospital and clinical equipment called for by those techniques.

In the past three or four decades definite progress has been made in remedying this defect, particularly in closer cooperation and interrelation of city and voluntary agencies. To bring together diverse agencies operating in a given geographical area of the city, so that they might work smoothly together, regional councils were some years ago organized in 15 districts of the city. In greater or lesser degree, these have served their purpose of making the various services available to the individual or family needing them with a minimum waste of time, energy and money.

In 1925 a majority of the city's agencies, public and voluntary, created the Welfare Council as a central machinery for exchanging information and effecting, on the foundation of exact knowledge, workable techniques and programs of action. The Council now includes some 812 member agencies, of which approximately 150 are bureaus or subdivisions of municipal departments.

One of the primary functions of the Council is the exchange of information. Its Social Service Exchange records in a vast card catalogue all

Art in New York

THE ROMAN COURT, METROPOLITAN MUSEUM OF ART

Above: THE CLOISTERS, AT FORT TRYON PARK, A BRANCH OF THE METROPOLITAN MUSEUM OF ART

Below: FIFTH AVENUE FACADE OF THE METROPOLITAN MUSEUM

Above: MACHINE ART EXHIBIT; *below:* MODERN MURALS EXHIBIT; BOTH AT THE MUSEUM OF MODERN ART

EXHIBITION GALLERY AND SCULPTURE COURT OF THE WHITNEY
MUSEUM OF AMERICAN ART

ENTRANCE HALL OF THE MUSEUM OF THE CITY OF NEW YORK, AND, *above.* DIORAMAS IN WAX OF HISTORIC SCENES

HOME OF THE HISPANIC SOCIETY OF AMERICA, AND *(below)* COURT OF
THE MUSEUM WITHIN THE BUILDING

THE BROOKLYN MUSEUM

THE NATIONAL ACADEMY OF DESIGN, WHICH ALSO
HOUSES THE ART STUDENTS' LEAGUE

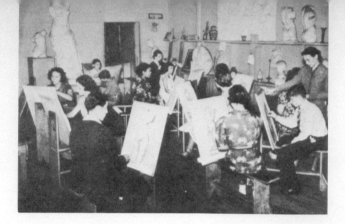

A FEDERAL ART PROJECT CLASS IN THE LEONARDO DA VINCI SCHOOL

NEW YORK'S FIRST OUTDOOR SCULPTURE EXHIBIT (APRIL, 1938)

cases brought to the attention of any of its member agencies, and tells them which other agencies if any, have had the same case before, thus permitting the elimination of a deal of duplicating effort. The Exchange has handled as many as 10,000 inquiries in a single day.

The Council's Bureau of Information Services answers the multifarious questions that member agencies put to it—where John Smith may obtain treatment for his particular ailment, where a certain specialized type of information may be obtained concerning the blind—the hundreds of concrete problems that turn up in the course of the day's work. It also tells the inquiring layman where to obtain the answer to the question that has been puzzling him.

To explore neglected needs and foresee approaching ones, to eliminate duplication and keep procedures fresh and effective, the member agencies of the Council doing similar work are grouped in sections for periodic consultation. These sections, drawing upon their intimate knowledge of daily case work, have set standards and created programs in public health, family and child welfare, group work and recreation, which were later taken over and applied by special agencies or city departments. City and state welfare agencies, foundations and philanthropic groups are more and more looking to such voluntary efforts to explore the field before appropriating money to new fields of work or to an expansion of the old.

To provide hard factual knowledge on which workable programs can be built, the Research Bureau of the Council makes studies of special areas of social work. Some of these have become standard reference works in their several fields. For example, its current records of agencies' expenditures in many fields have provided the indispensable basis for this rational financing.

The Council also constitutes a kind of central forum where the city social agencies can frame recommendations for legislation and constitutional provisions affecting public welfare. The New York City charter which went into effect January 1, 1938, and the later Administrative Code were influenced in no small degree, in their social service and health provisions, by the recommendations assembled through the Council's good offices; and the New York State constitutional convention of 1938 will have for its guidance, in framing the social provisions of the new basic law, the considered judgment of the city's social agencies, framed after long consultation under the Council's auspices.

A further step in the consolidation of a city-wide welfare program was taken with the launching in 1938 of the Greater New York Fund, Inc., to solicit supplementary funds for the city's voluntary agencies from corporations, business firms and their employee groups, leaving agencies free to solicit from individuals as before. The distribution of the sums so collected obviously called for a central admission and distribution committee, under Council auspices, possessed of full information concerning both the work of each participating agency and the needs still unmet. Out of the social service "map" thus called into being, and with the support of specific reports made from time to time by the Council's research bureau and others, a further step, it is hoped, will be taken toward the preparation of a practical city-wide plan for the consolidation and extension of New York's social services to implement its present knowledge and to meet its impending needs.

Among the outstanding items of unfinished business which such a program must take into account are the prevention of crime, the provision of good low-cost housing, the prevention and eradication of certain types of disease, and the care of chronic illness. The soundest basis for the hope that these problems may eventually be solved lies in the fact that today all faiths and all neighborhoods, all types of agency, public and voluntary, are learning to work together toward the fulfillment of a common plan.

Learning for Life

THE FIRST schoolmaster to make an appearance in what is now the City of New York was one Adam Roelantsen (or Roelandsen), a native of Holland who disembarked at the tiny settlement of New Amsterdam in 1633. Evidently the province at that time offered small opportunity for one intent upon teaching the young idea to shoot, as tradition has it that this pioneer disciple of the birch and book was obliged to take in washing, by way of eking out a modest income derived from the Dutch West India Company. But something of Roelantsen's failure as a pedagogue may have been due to a cantankerous disposition, as evidenced by the frequent appearance of his name in provincial court records of the time. Forsaking education after a few years, he achieved minor distinction as Provost and member of the Burgher Corps of New Amsterdam.

The rudimentary instruction dispensed for a fee in private homes or hired rooms by Roelantsen and his successors during the Dutch period was chiefly of a religious nature. So, too, was most of that provided during the ensuing English period. A public school, "free for 20 pupils," seems to have been opened about 1732; but for more than 150 years in province and colony, the clergyman rather than the schoolmaster predominated in the classroom, and free public education in the modern sense was all but unknown. The schools were adjuncts of the churches, conducted by religious sects for the children of their own members. A powerful organization calling itself The Society for the Propagation of the Gospel in Foreign Parts, sponsored by the Church of England, maintained virtually all English schools in the colony from about 1700 to 1776. During that period, the only event of major significance in New York's educational annals was the incorporation, under a royal charter granted in 1754, of King's College, reorganized after the Revolution as Columbia College.

The opening in 1787 of a free school for colored children, under the auspices of the Manumission Society of New York (founded 1785), has been characterized as marking the "first faint impulse towards free public education" in the city. A stronger impulse, and one of much wider scope, came with the organization in 1805 of the Free School Society, under the presidency of DeWitt Clinton, then mayor of New York. The Society's avowed purpose was to provide educational facilities for poor children to whom the existing church schools were not available. The gradual enlargement of that purpose to embrace public education for all, regardless of economic status, led to a change of name in 1826 from Free School Society to Public School Society—a change that marks the real beginning of New York's public educational system.

Supported at the start mainly by voluntary contributions, the Society later received regular grants of money from the city treasury. Its first school was erected in 1809, on a site near the northeastern corner of the present City Hall Park. With its change of name and its enlargement of scope to that of a semi-public agency, it came into sharp conflict with several of the city's foremost church organizations, chiefly on the question of whether a part of its funds should be used for the support of schools controlled by religious groups. This conflict led to the establishment in 1842 of a public Board of Education, which worked in cooperation with the Society until the two bodies were merged by legislative act in 1853.

During the 48 years of its existence, the Society supervised the instruction of some 600,000 children and trained nearly 1,200 teachers. In addition to several elementary schools, it brought into being a free academy—embryo of the present City College. By its merger with the Board of Education, the board acquired property then valued at about half a million dollars.

The subsequent history of public education in New York City is mainly a record of gradual expansion and of frequent organizational changes, to meet ever-growing needs. That history has its shabby as well as its creditable aspects, and the record is by no means one of uninterrupted and unimpeded progression in the direction of high educational ideals. As in other large cities, the public school system of New York City has suffered heavily in the past from stupidity and self-seeking, from lack of understanding and vision, on the part of many of its so-called public servants. In this, as in other fields of community effort, real progress has been painfully slow and difficult.

Educational policies and procedures in New York are at present undergoing the severest test in their history. They are in a state of upheaval and rebuilding, with all the temporary confusion that drastic change and opposition to change of necessity bring about. A campaign for sweeping improvements is only in its initial stages. That campaign is directed against stultifying curricula, inertia, overcrowding, lack of funds, inadequate building and mass methods of teaching. Old-time fixed ideas and old-time powers-that-be oppose the forward movement. But with the present political regime a new era has begun to dawn, and the long struggle shows signs of becoming a gradual victory.

Progressive Education

Early in the present century, the intricate and powerful organization that controlled public education in New York was assailed by a handful of college professors with new-fangled notions about what they called "progressive education." They not only proposed changes in methods of instruction but made forceful suggestions as to how the city's vast school system ought to be conducted. Many a skirmish centered around the demand for a new vocational training for modern life and industry, to replace the dull and outmoded educational methods so long in force. The child's interest in school became a matter of greatest importance—unlike the old philosophy of education according to which, as Mr. Dooley expressed it, "it doesn't matter what you teach a boy so long as he doesn't like it."

Under the old system, which still persists to some extent, dingy and archaic school buildings, most of them destitute of playgrounds and without sufficient sunlight and air, received great crowds of children in double or triple sessions, few of the pupils attending full time for lack of space and adequate teaching staff. Mass education was doled out without regard to the needs of the individual child. A harassed teacher, herself not infrequently ill-prepared for her job, was confronted by a conglomerate of human beings comprising numerous nationalities, of diverse ages and sizes and of widely varying home background and familiarity with the English language.

Packed into crowded classrooms, they received an identical limited education by means of the assigned lesson, the memorized question and answer, the infrequent written test. They left school to face the world equipped with a few facts soon to be forgotten, having little or no preparation for suitable individual occupation, and with only a vague individual appreciation of social and economic factors soon to loom up with terrific significance in their lives. In other words, individual equipment for success, usefulness and happiness in a complex modern world was too frequently absent altogether. The student was hurled forth into the maelstrom of modern life in a great city, to sink or swim as best he could with his latent individual faculties undeveloped.

Such was the old type of school, the old way of learning. What of the new way and its champions? Although there is demand for better teaching, better buildings and more modern equipment, the essential difference between old and new lies in the spirit within rather than in material appurtenances and outward aspects. Emphasis in the new point of view has shifted from school and subject-matter to the pupil himself, to activity and interest rather than passivity and coercion. The new picture shows an alert and expert teacher guiding students eager to learn by doing interesting things, instead of forcing them into unwilling subjection to book memorization. "A fuller, richer school life while learning," "health, fresh air, sunlight, space," "learning by experiences," "developing the whole child," "the aims of education must include personal health, personal happiness and success,"—these statements of objectives are coupled with a demand that active administrative positions in the public school system shall be held by trained educators.

An exact definition of progressive education is not easy to formulate. Whatever the child is interested in or can do, whatever man aspires to, is encompassed within its scope. It has neither confines nor limitations but only horizons, which when approached spread ever outward to wider learning. The essence of the creative school is ever-continued growth. Each generation develops, discards, builds anew for its own day. The teachers must be mature and creative personalities, possessing a flexible and active awareness. They must be able to create an atmosphere of joyful exploration in varying occupations and studies, for the highest type of modern school must never become fixed or static.

The leading pioneer in this movement was Dr. John Dewey, dean of American philosophers, who formulated a new theory of education as far back as 1895 and ever since that time has remained the most influential exponent of progressive education. Dr. Dewey attracted a large following among educators. Especially prominent among those who defended progressive education in New York were William Heard Kilpatrick, for nearly three decades with Teachers' College; Frank Pierrepont Graves, State Commissioner of Education; and Stephen F. Bayne, Associate Superintendent of Schools of New York City. For years these educational leaders brought to the attention of officials and public the great advantages of progressive education for both society and the individual.

Organization and Control

The public school system of Greater New York comprises 54 school districts, covering an unevenly inhabited area of more than 300 square miles. The population of this area is considerably in excess of 7,000,000. On January 1, 1938, the number of school organizations in the city system was 839, and the number of pupils on register in these schools was 1,196,766—more than equaling the total combined population in 1930 of New Hampshire, Delaware and the District of Columbia. The number of employes required for the Department of Education in 1938 was 46,541; and the sum of $97,797,956.93 was provided by the city for the department's expenses, in addition to $54,707,507.44 estimated as receivable from the State.

Responsibility for the general educational policies and management of New York's public school system is vested in a Board of Education, consisting of seven members appointed by the mayor for seven-year terms and serving without salary. Two of the members must be residents of Manhattan, two of Brooklyn and one from each of the three remaining boroughs. A President and Vice-President of the Board are chosen from the members. Although a lay body, the Board "seeks to inspire the professional staff to greater achievement, and often takes the initiative in advocating betterments for the school system." It is assisted by an Advisory Board of Industrial Education, consisting at present of five non-salaried members appointed for two-year terms.

A local school board in each of the city's 54 school districts supplements the work of the Board of Education. Each local board is made up of five members, appointed by the president of the borough in which the school district lies and serving five-year terms without salary.

The chief executive officer of the school system is the Superintendent of Schools, who with eight Associate Superintendents is elected by the Board of Education for six-year terms. The salary of the Superintendent is $25,000 a year, and each of his associates receives $12,500. Collectively they comprise the Board of Superintendents. The Board of Education also appoints, upon recommendation of the Board of Superintendents, 33 Assistant Superintendents, with permanent tenure after a three-years' probationary period, at an annual salary of $10,000.

The Superintendent of Schools serves in *ex officio* capacity on a Board of Examiners, the seven other members of which are appointed by the

Board of Education. They receive annual salaries of $11,000, and have permanent tenure after a probationary period of 90 days.

The administrative division of the city's Department of Education comprises no fewer than 17 separate offices, bureaus and boards, which handle matters relating either to the department as a whole or to various specialized fields within the department's jurisdiction. One of these units, the Bureau of Libraries, exercises general control over the three great public libraries of the city—the New York Public Library, with its 46 branches, 11 sub-branches, a Municipal Reference Library, a Music Library and the Bronx Reference Center; the Queens Borough Public Library, with its 11 main branches, 16 minor branches, 12 sub-branches, 6 community stations and 15 school libraries; and the Brooklyn Public Library, with its 35 branches.

Under the general corporate title of The College of the City of New York, a Board of Higher Education controls the educational policies and general management of the city's four public colleges—the City College, Brooklyn College, Hunter College and Queens College. This board consists of 21 non-salaried members appointed by the mayor for nine-year terms, with the President of the Board of Education as an *ex officio* member.

A very considerable part (more than one-third in 1938) of the cost of operating New York City's public education system is borne by the State, which exercises important powers over that system through the medium of its Education Department. At the head of the latter is a body known as the Board of Regents of the University of the State of New York; and the chief administrative officer of the department is the Commissioner of Education.

Educational Problems

Persons of foreign-born white stock, with their children, number in New York more than 5,000,000, or roughly five-sevenths of the city's total population. The foreign-born alone constitute nearly a third of the population. These facts add greatly to the difficulties of developing an educational program and of gaining public support for such a program. In this connection, the Educational and Recreational Department of the Works Progress Administration in this city has estimated that more than 250,000 persons of native or foreign birth in New York City cannot read, write or speak English, and that another quarter million cannot read or write any language.

Another extremely difficult problem for the schools has its source in the rapidly accelerated emigration of Negroes from the Southern States, Puerto Rico and the West Indies. In 1900 there were 60,000 Negroes in New York City; in 1930, the number had increased to 328,000; and there has been a steady stream into the city ever since.

The flow of population from one borough to another creates another difficulty with which school boards have had to cope. With the opening of each new rapid transit line, there is a considerable shift of population. During the decade of 1900–10, Manhattan's population increased by more than half a million, and gains were large in other boroughs, but during the past decade the density of population in many sections of Manhattan has decreased greatly. "The effect of this flow of population upon the organization and administration of the school program is strikingly illustrated in data from two supervisory districts. One district superintendent reported that during a period of six years, eight school buildings had been closed in his district and that a number of others were shifted from elementary school use to other school purposes. During that time his district had lost more than 13,000 elementary school children. At the other extreme, another district superintendent advised that during a period of six years the elementary school registration of his district had increased from 21,832 to 38,472. Eleven new elementary schools were organized. One of these schools with a registration of fewer than 700 had drawn pupils from 119 different schools. In this and similar areas school building construction could not keep pace with the increase of school registration." (*Report of a Study of New York City Schools*, State Education Department, 1933–4.)

Small wonder, then, that the theories worked out for the public school system are far in advance of its realities, especially since the New York educational budget is so overwhelmed by special emergencies that it can allow only for a minimum of experimentation. Moreover, in times of depression the budget is pared to the bone, so that over-crowded classes, inadequate equipment, old-fashioned buildings and under-privileged children are still to be found in many sections.

Teachers face serious classroom problems. Many have studied the most advanced methods, are imbued with the idea of "individuation," of working out each child's problems sympathetically, apart from the mass; but so long as more than 40 children of widely varying capacities are crowded together on part time in one medium-sized classroom, the teacher is forced back to regimentation methods. Under such conditions the pupils sit, much as they did 50 years ago, with hands folded on the desks in front of them, knowing that certain dry facts will have to be memorized before they will be allowed to enter a higher class.

Considering these problems, together with the political interference that has greatly hampered the school system in New York, one may well wonder that things are as good as they are. But it is precisely because the problems are so formidable that progressive educators demand for the city better teaching, better supervision and administration, the finest available educational talent and the cooperation of the entire city.

Elementar⁊ and Secondary Education

In March 1938 close to 1,200,000 pupils were registered in New York's public school system—1,098,922 in day schools, 95,653 in evening schools. Of the day enrollment, 668,715 pupils were in elementary schools (including nearly 120,000 in kindergarten classes), 130,494 were in junior high schools, 254,624 were in senior high schools, and 45,089 were in vocational high schools. The evening enrollment comprised 27,393 pupils in elementary schools (common branches, commercial subjects, trade subjects), 56,347 in high schools (academic, commercial, and trade subjects) and 11,913 in trade schools. A total of 728 buildings housed the activities of these groups—by far the largest number, 609, being in the elementary field. The others were distributed as follows: senior high schools, 74; junior high schools, 23; vocational high schools, 22.

A notable increase in secondary school attendance during recent years has greatly overtaxed the existing facilities in this field. In both senior and junior high schools the lack of housing has resulted in the use of a large number of annexes, some of which are far from satisfactory, and many pupils attend only part time because of inadequate space and teaching staff. Thus, at the end of March 1938, approximately 77,500 pupils in senior and junior high schools, or about 20 percent of the total number registered in such schools, were on short-time schedules, receiving limited and inadequate high school education. In the field of elementary instruction, the situation is much less serious, the short-time attendance in this classification being only about 28,000, or a little more than four percent of the total elementary registration.

Some relief in the general situation created by a shortage of facilities came with the opening in 1936 and 1937 of several new and beautiful school buildings, with such features as auditoriums, cafeterias, gymnasiums, laboratories, libraries and model apartments for home-making and home economics courses. A huge construction program, involving no fewer than 52 new buildings or additions to buildings, was under way in the spring of 1938. Rooms with removable and adjustable furniture, to permit of progressive experimental class procedures, are contained in the newer buildings.

Extra-curricular activities for pupil development—in music, art, dancing, athletics, language, manual and motor activities, science, business, social studies and other fields—continue to develop, although all too slowly. The State Education Department under Commissioner Graves is conducting valuable research on the city schools, with recommendations for future policies and improvements; and the city Board of Education has enlarged its facilities for the appraisal of new teaching methods. Among other projects, special regard is being given to the problems of retarded children, 11,000 of whom were being helped in March 1938. Many schools have open-air classes for anemic and pre-tubercular children; sight conservation classes and classes for deaf or otherwise physically handicapped children have been introduced. In September 1937, new health regulations and physical education programs were adopted by the State Board of Regents, after a five-year study by leading educators. These regulations are designed to prevent physical, mental and social handicaps in young persons, and are especially aimed at the physical care and development of the individual child.

Noteworthy is a recent tendency to organize segregated classes and schools for children either with special interests, with physical or mental handicaps, or with special artistic talents. The Building Trades School, the High School of Music and Art, and the Speyer School for gifted and sub-normal children exemplify this tendency. In March 1938 nearly 1,600 sick or homebound children were being taught at home by public school teachers. The first of two schools for superior students was opened in Brooklyn in February 1938. Nor is family life overlooked. The school system is employing a number of psychiatric social workers as permanent members of the teaching staff to give special attention to the maladjusted and anti-social child.

Private Schools

New York's private schools, numbering more than 300 in the five boroughs, with numerous others in the city's immediate environs, are of varied types, from nursery schools to college preparatory institutions. Possessed of greater resources in money and equipment, and with a considerably smaller student-teacher ratio, these institutions have so far had much more favorable opportunity than the public schools for making innovations in educational procedure.

To the private as to the public school, the way to "learning for life" is pointed out by the modern progressive experimental schools, many of which began years ago as nursery schools and later expanded to include all grades and in some cases high school and college courses. Their program and policy are in general subject to constant experiment and change, based on continuous research, their aim being to modify and expand the educational program in the light of the stresses and pressures of modern life. Most if not all of them are co-educational, non-profitmaking, and non-discriminating with respect to race and color. In some, an effort is made to approximate in enrollment a kind of cross-section of society, with high tuition fees for some students and for others a sliding scale of scholarships that at its lowest range involves no fees at all.

Private progressive schools in New York and vicinity include the Little Red Schoolhouse, the City and Country School, the Hessian Hills School, the Manumit School, the Cooperative School for Student Teachers, the Harriet Johnson School and others. The Lincoln School and the Horace Mann School are experimental laboratories for Columbia University ideas. Among other progressive institutions are the Walden School, the Dalton School, the Friends Seminary and the Ethical Culture Schools. The famous Ethical Culture movement was founded upon a belief in the "worth, the potency and the promises of every child's individual nature." Its first school was started by Felix Adler as a free kindergarten in 1878, in a dance hall on the present site of the Hotel Astor. Today the main school is in upper Manhattan near Central Park West, and the movement has another center in the Fieldston Day and Country School at Fieldston Road and Spuyten Duyvil Parkway.

The day may come when the public school budget of New York will permit the inclusion in every school of the excellent innovations made by these more favored institutions, together with their type of highly trained personnel.

Denominational Schools

Although several of the principal religious denominations conduct educational activities of one sort or another in New York City, the only church organization that plays an extensive part in elementary and secondary education outside the city's public school system is the Roman Catholic Church. With respect to the Catholic schools, as to private schools in general, detailed and up-to-date statistics are difficult to obtain. But on the basis of such information as has appeared from time to time in recent years, it is possible to give some tentative indication of the present-day figures in broadest summary.

Probably about three-fourths of New York City's private elementary and secondary schools are supported and conducted by the Roman Catholic Church. Most of the elementary schools are parochial institutions, operated in connection with parishes; they are approximately 300 in number, with a total student enrollment of somewhere around 175,000. The secondary institutions (high schools and academies), which are conducted under diocesan or private auspices, number approximately 100 and have an enrollment of about 25,000 students; they include various types of schools—senior high, college preparatory, commercial and trade schools.

The instruction given in both elementary and secondary institutions is free (except in a few private academies) and along the general lines of that offered in the city's public school system, plus certain religious courses. Class-room work is in charge of women and men belonging to the teaching orders of the Church, together with some lay teachers—the former predominating in a ratio of four or five to one.

Some of the New York churches supported by large nationality groups in the city's foreign white stock population conduct Sunday classes in which younger children are taught the history, language, folk-songs, etc., of the countries in which these groups originated, or are given instruction in the religions peculiar to some of the groups.

Special educational activities of various sorts, both religious and non-religious, are conducted by the Jews of New York—as described in the Jewish section of the article entitled "New World Symphony" in the present volume.

Adult Education

For years adult education was directed chiefly toward reducing illiteracy in the city's vast immigrant population. Today it is a part of the regular cultural and vocational program of many organizations. Men and women are taught not only at evening public schools and university extension classes, but also in various lecture halls, forums, museums, libraries, trade unions, political and social organizations. One agency alone, the Adult Education Project of the Works Progress Administration, reported an attendance in February 1938 of more than 130,000 men and women in a total of some 8,800 classes, with the largest enrollment (more than 27,500) in vocational classes.

Various bureaus offer free information for adults on educational and recreational opportunities in New York. One of these, the New York Adult Education Council, aids about 1,000 persons each month, and keeps a record of some 2,000 organizations offering adult education in numerous subjects. It estimates that from 400,000 to 500,000 adults are annually taking advantage of such educational facilities in the city. It is interesting to note that the first school for adults in New York, the Institute for Adult Education, organized by Professor S. Alexander Spear at DeWitt Clinton High School in February 1932, owes its origin to the Parent-Teachers Association.

Students in this field are representative of nearly all racial groups, and range in age from 17 to 80; some are illiterate, some highly educated; many are depression victims seeking economic rehabilitation in new trades, others wish to supplement an academic education. The courses offered, with respect to broad character and purpose, are thus classified in Lyman Bryson's *Adult Education* (1936): Remedial education, bringing the individual's standard up to minimum requirements; Americanization of the foreign born, reading and writing for illiterates, training in health, elementary child care and homemaking; occupational, or improving oneself to obtain a better job, rehabilitating the technologically unemployed, and vocational guidance; relational, including parent education and studies (psychology) to better understand one's own limitations and abilities, and to develop the ability to get along with others; liberal studies, such as art, music, philosophy and science, mainly for self-culture; political studies, to educate the individual for intelligent political action.

The city's evening high, trade and elementary schools provide facilities for adult education, and a variety of courses is offered by New York University with its Washington Square Center of Adult Education, by Hunter College in 30 centers scattered throughout the city, and by City College. Not only are regular academic and vocational subjects available, but the problem of leisure time and how best to spend it is dealt with, and there are courses in handicraft, languages, instructive reading, music and the arts.

Notable for its interest in adult education is the New School for Social Research, an institution interested in making the individual aware of the world in which he lives and his own part in its destiny. It swings widely away from the old theory that, in shaping social and political life, enthusiasm and action are more important than study and thought. The New School advocates that not only the scholar but also the intelligent layman must aid in shaping modern civilization. It stresses intensive cultivation of the arts and sciences, particularly the social sciences.

Facilities for workers' education are abundant in New York City, where hundreds of thousands of wage earners are organized in trade unions, political parties and fraternal and cultural organizations. Socialist, Communist and trade union schools conduct classes in labor history, principles of trade unionism and economics, as well as in the arts and sciences. Especially prominent in this field are the Rand School, a conservatively socialistic institution; the Workers School, which emphasizes the principles and implications of Communism; and the Educational Department of the International Ladies Garment Workers Union, a pioneer in trade union education. The Department of Social Philosophy of Cooper Union carries on an extensive work in adult education by means of lectures and open forum discussions. This department was known until a few years ago as the People's Institute.

WPA in Education

Since late in 1935, the Federal Works Progress Administration has initiated and directed a wide variety of educational projects, as a part of its emergency relief program in New York City. During a single typical month (February 1938), well over 100,000 persons were enrolled in the city's regular WPA classes; nearly 350,000 attended the various forums, institutes and health instruction centers conducted under WPA auspices; nearly 25,000 received elementary instruction in reading and writing English; and within the city public school system, thousands of children participated in many demonstration projects conducted by the WPA.

One project provides a clinical program for problem cases, including medical, psychological, psychiatric and social investigation of various individual cases, together with experimental teaching and group therapy. Other projects are concerned with remedial work in arithmetic and reading, special methods of individuation, health work and examinations, group and individual audiometer tests, the teaching of homebound children, swimming instruction to crippled children, and vocational guidance.

Three timely WPA aids to progressive education are the production and distribution of moving pictures, slides, models, graphs and charts and other objective cultural, scientific and industrial teaching material; the Field Activity Program under which groups of children are conducted to museums, the planetarium, parks, and places of historical interest, to awaken and develop individual appreciation; and the New Reading Materials Project, which creates illustrated matter designed to enlarge the oral and written vocabularies of children.

Hundreds of needy children between the ages of two and four from impoverished families have attended WPA nursery schools, where they were provided with nourishing food, supervised rest periods, recreational and educational play guidance and medical attention. Supervised play and other group activities for city children through the vacation months have also been a part of the WPA program.

To carry on all these and other similar projects, the Educational and Recreational Department of the WPA has given employment to a staff of as many as 8,500 persons in New York, of whom about 70 percent are actively engaged in teaching. In addition to the work of this department, the Art, Music, and Theater Projects of the WPA conduct numerous local activities of an educational nature, some of which are described in other sections of this volume.

Higher Education

Four public colleges, providing free tuition to residents of New York City, are among the more important institutions of higher education in the metropolitan area. The City College, with an average yearly enrollment of some 30,000 students, is the largest municipal college in the country. Its College of Liberal Arts and Sciences, School of Technology and School of Education occupy a large group of buildings on Lower Washington Heights; its School of Business and Civic Administration is at Lexington Avenue and Twenty-Third Street. Brooklyn College, with more than 10,000 students, is a co-educational institution offering instruction in the liberal arts and sciences. Hunter College, housed in several buildings about the city, is one of the largest colleges for women in the country; originally a training school for teachers, it has in recent years shifted emphasis in its curriculum to a general four-year course in the liberal arts. Queens College, in Flushing, was opened September 1937, with a notable faculty drawn from all sections of the country. In addition to the usual college courses, its program stresses the acquisition of primary skills, the acquiring of "tools for study," health and recreational activities, personal and community hygiene, and vocational guidance.

New York University long ago outgrew its original home in Washington Square, and now cares for a large part of its 38,000 students in buildings in lower Manhattan, on University Heights, in the Bronx and at Hempstead, Long Island. It is a typically metropolitan institution of the progressive type, with liberal arts college, professional and graduate schools in subjects varying from medicine and law to business administration, retailing and aeronautics, and a department devoted to adult education. Its activities include summer physical education courses at Lake Sebago and in Palisades Interstate Park, and extension classes in upper New York State, New Jersey, Pennsylvania, Connecticut and Delaware.

Columbia University, the oldest and best-known institution of higher learning in New York State, with its large liberal arts college and numerous graduate schools of advanced study, occupies the area from 112th to 126th Streets between Amsterdam Avenue and Riverside Drive. Its campus is thronged yearly by an average of 20,000 full-term students and 12,000 summer attendants. It offers courses for men and women of all ages in scores of subjects, from advanced calculus to plain cooking, from French literature to tropical medicine. Studying may be done either at the university or by means of extension courses conducted by mail.

The major divisions of the university, aside from the undergraduate liberal arts college, include the School of Law, College of Physicians and Surgeons, Teachers College, School of Engineering, New College, School of Agriculture, School of Journalism, School of Business, Institute for Cancer Research, School of Dental and Oral Surgery, School of Library Service, and graduate facilities in political science, philosophy and pure science.

Affiliated with the university are Barnard College, the College of Pharmacy, Bard College and the New York Post-Graduate Medical School; and it cooperates with the University of San Juan, Puerto Rico, in its School of Tropical Medicine.

The influence of Teachers College, this country's outstanding school of education, in developing and disseminating creative educational ideas and the effect of its long fight against obsolete educational methods are felt throughout the world. Every year, students by the thousands absorb its progressive philosophy and practice.

Close to this fount of growing social knowledge stands Barnard College for women, famed for its progressive work in education for living. Keeping its student enrollment strictly around the 1,000 mark, Barnard uses the whole of New York as its working laboratory.

New College, a recent addition to Columbia, aims to turn out teachers with a full background of knowledge and experience. Its curriculum emphasizes training to meet human problems rather than the acquisition of facts *per se*. Every student is expected to have some experience in industry or on the farm, and wide travel during college years is a requirement.

Fordham University, largest Catholic institution of higher learning in the United States, has more than 7,000 students in its various divisions, which include a School of Law, a Graduate School, a School of Business, a Teachers' College and a School of Social Service.

Another Catholic institution of higher education is Manhattan College, founded in 1849 as the Academy of the Holy Infancy. Its present group of buildings overlooks Van Cortlandt Park in the Bronx. In addition to the usual college curriculum, it offers courses in engineering and business.

Cooper Union, chartered in 1859 "for the advancement of science and art," has given free instruction in general science, engineering and the fine arts to more than 200,000 persons. A large majority of its students are registered in night courses.

Scores of other institutions provide instruction to many thousands of students in various specialized fields (medicine and surgery, law, theology, music, art, technology, etc.), and play their part in making New York City the largest center of educational activities in the country.

Perisphere and Trylon

RETURNING from the tardy Paris Exposition of Arts and Crafts in the summer of 1937, Grover Whalen, president of the New York World's Fair Corporation, was optimistic on the subject of peace. Should his prediction of world peace turn out to be correct—or even, perhaps, if it doesn't—it is reasonably certain that on April 30, 1939, commemorating Washington's inauguration in New York City exactly 150 years earlier, the biggest and costliest of all expositions will open at Flushing Meadow Park, Queens. For the first time in its history, Greater New York will be host to the world; and as a press release of the corporation suggests, this announcement in itself is "enough to set the world agog—for the world well knows New York's reputation for carrying through to spectacular success."

Hourly transportation capacity to the fair will be 160,000, and close to 1,000,000 visitors are expected to storm the entrances on the opening day. The average daily attendance will be 250,000; or 50,000,000 for the season. (Chicago's fair in 1933 attracted 22,500,000; 16,500,000 in 1934.) Between $125,000,000 and $150,000,000 will have been spent on reclamation and construction; and the horde of visitors, at the fair and in Greater New York, will spend $1,000,000,000. These are, of course, estimates before the fact; but even the man from Missouri will not be surprised if the fair lasts two seasons and attracts 100,000,000 people who spend $2,000,000,000. Missouri was not only the first State to pass a legislative measure for participation in the fair; it was also the first State to sign a formal contract for exhibit space and will expend $250,000 in developing the space.

Flushing Meadow Park embraces 1,216½ acres (about two square miles) and extends from the North Shore-Flushing Bay area of Queens southward 3½ miles along the Flushing River Valley, with a width of a mile and a quarter in the north central section, the main exhibit area. Superimposed on a map of midtown Manhattan, the fair plan would reach from the Central Park menagerie deep down into Greenwich Village; and the transverse Central Mall, lying approximately over Forty-Second Street, would extend from Times Square to Tudor City.

In addition to the zone for governments, the main exhibit area will be arranged in six sectors: Transportation, Communications, Production and Distribution, Food, Health, and Community Interests. Most of these nuclear groupings will have their own restaurants, theaters, concert halls and dance floors, supplementing the attractions in the amusement area to the south. Just as each sector will have its focal point—an exhibit in a fair-built pavilion revealing the nature of the entire sector—so the fair itself will have a thematic center. An elaborate prismatic color scheme has been devised for the fan-shaped portion of the exhibit area. From the theme center, which will be white, three ribs—the Golden, Red and Blue Avenues (the Avenue of Patriots, the Central Mall, and the Avenue of Pioneers)— will radiate, cutting the fan into wedge-shaped sections. On the avenue around the edge of the fan—the Way of the Rainbow—buildings and lights will attain the deepest tones, their hues blending into one another as they do in the spectrum. The official fair colors are white, orange and blue.

"Building the world of tomorrow" is the bold theme of the fair. The theme center, situated in the northwestern part of the grounds, will consist of the perisphere, a 200-foot steel-framed globe (comparable in size to an 18-story building occupying a city block); and the trylon, a slender, tapering three-sided pillar rising to 700 feet. These stark structures, designed by Harrison and Fouilhoux, will cost $1,700,000. They will be simple, striking, beautiful. Officially, the trylon symbolizes the finite, the perisphere the infinite.

Two escalators, the longest in America, will be capable of carrying 16,000 persons an hour from the trylon to the perisphere entrance, which is to be 65 feet from the ground. The perisphere, weighing 5,760,000 pounds exclusive of exhibit materials, will rest on eight columns arranged in a circle 81 feet in diameter. The columns, 12 feet high and four feet thick, jacketed with glass, will be concealed by fountains, so that the building will create the effect of a mammoth bubble kept afloat by jetting water. A circular pool, 325 feet in diameter, will be set eight feet below the bottom of the perisphere. Inside the latter will be two revolving platforms or "magic carpets," on which visitors will ride while "seeing the sights and hearing the sounds of the World Tomorrow," an exhibit to be designed by Henry Dreyfuss. A bridge will join the perisphere to the trylon; and the helicline, a ramp 900 feet long, will slope gradually from the trylon to the ground in a great three-quarter turn. The helicline and bridge will afford a view of the whole fair. The trylon will not be illuminated, but batteries of projectors will make a revolving, vari-colored screen of the huge white globe, creating mobile marbled patterns heretofore limited to the Wilfred clavilux or color organ.

The theme center, set in a plaza at the intersection of the north-south promenade and the $60,000,000 Central Mall, will face eastward across an expanse of mirroring pools and lagoons, waterfalls and fountains, pylons and "aqualons," to the commanding Federal area at the far end of the Mall, where nine closely related structures in semi-classic style will border on a large Court of Peace and a large oval Lagoon of the Nations. The Government has appropriated $3,000,000 for this area and appointed Howard L. Cheney as architect. The dominating Federal building will symbolize the three branches of our government, with a central or executive section flanked by a Tower of Judiciary and a Tower of Legislature; additional symbolism is contained in the 13 pillars of the central section. Sculptures, murals and exhibits will illustrate the Government's role in the promotion and protection of individual and collective security. Revolving murals, 23 feet high, will be a notable feature of each of 12 exhibits. The murals and sculptures will be executed by winners of a national contest.

Two of the eight lesser structures will flank the Federal building, four will adjoin the Court of Peace, and two will be situated on the eastern shore of the lagoon. These buildings will form the Hall of Nations, in which all foreign governments participating in the fair will be given exhibit space. In addition many foreign countries will erect pavilions of their own in an allotted space north and south of the Hall of Nations. France and Belgium, however, have choice sites on the western side of the lagoon. The next choicest positions would seem to be those of Great Britain and the Soviet Union. The cost of the exhibits and buildings of foreign countries is expected to total more than $25,000,000.

Between the lagoon and the theme center, the mall will be dominated by a figure of George Washington, one of the largest statues ever fashioned. Its height and bulk are intended to symbolize both the grandeur of Washington's character and the growth of the Washington tradition through the years. The model for this figure portrays Washington in civilian clothes, dressed for the inauguration. In his left hand he holds a cocked hat; his right hand rests gently on the hilt of his sword; a long cape falls to his feet. The model creates an effect of great resolution, dignity and kindliness. This figure is the work of James Earle Fraser.

East of the 65-foot statue of Washington, in a square paved in red, white and blue, there will be a sculptural group by Leo Friedlander: four tall figures representing freedom of the press, religion, assembly and speech. The calm postures of the four figures are intended to express the sense of security and peace fostered by the American Constitution.

A group of statues by Paul Manship, including the largest sundial ever devised, will be placed in front of the colossal Washington. Branches of the Tree of Life will support the sundial; under its branches, the Three Fates carry on their immemorial business. The Future, holding her distaff, passes the thread of life to the Present; she in turn moves it along to the Past, where it is snipped off. A fountain group with 11 jets, suggesting the passage of time, will flow away from the sundial—which symbolizes time in the abstract—toward a second Manship group in a blue-and-white lagoon. This represents the moods of time. Four statues 15 feet in height will be surrounded by misty fountains resembling clouds. The first figure, Morning, is an awakening woman. Day is embodied as a charioteer charging across the clouds, the sun in his hands. Evening is a woman, semi-recumbent, loosely wrapped in the veil of darkness, and Night a prostrate female figure surrounded by stars, her head cradled in the moon beneath two outstretched male figures representing the reaches of space.

Thus the father of his country, with 150 years of democratic government behind him, will turn his confident gaze on the world of tomorrow, represented by the unorthodox trylon and perisphere. Moreover, he will be gazing straight at the Statue of Liberty in New York Harbor. The moral intended is that the four constitutional guarantees of liberty, keys to our country's past progress, are the keys also to American progress in the future.

Dozens of historical murals and reliefs will supplement and harmonize with the main sculptural groups. For example, on the facades of the buildings bordering "Washington Square," colonial scenes will be depicted. Several free-standing relief groups will face the theme center at the western end of the mall. Three sculptures by George H. Snowden will show primitive man learning to employ his mind, learning to control nature, and learning to conquer evil. A group by Edmund Amateis will exemplify stories from American folk-lore, with Paul Bunyan, Strap Buckner and Johnny Appleseed among the characters.

The colorful Central Mall, bordered by some 25 of the fair's most imposing buildings and studded with numerous trees and shrubs, will undoubtedly be the most elaborate esplanade in the history of expositions. The mall was planned under the direction of the fair's Board of Design, composed of Stephen F. Voorhees (chairman), Walter Dorwin Teague, Richmond H. Shreve, Robert D. Kohn, Jay Downer, William A. Delano and Gilmore D. Clarke. The architects are William and Geoffrey Platt.

At the opposite end of the mall-axis from the government sector, and balancing it in magnitude, will be the Transportation sector, with the Transportation building—between the two Corona gates—in line with the Federal building on the Flushing side of the exhibit area. But between the Transportation sector and the theme center lies the New York City structure, a $1,200,000 permanent house of glass. In the Transportation sector will be major buildings devoted to automotive, rail, air and marine transportation, as well as the buildings of the Firestone and Goodyear rubber companies. The General Motors Corporation and the Ford Motor Company buildings will face each other across the mall-axis. The former has contracted for the largest plot taken by any single exhibitor, paying $56,009.15 for 298,719 square feet. The feature exhibit of the Ford building will be a "Road of Tomorrow," an elevated highway half a mile long, rising upon a series of spiral ramps and finally circling the top of the main part of the building.

Twenty-six eastern railroads have contributed to a $3,000,000 fund for a building and exhibits. These railroads will have a larger total of space than any other group of exhibitors at the fair, and theirs will be the largest building. Spur tracks will be extended directly to this building, and there will be 3,600 feet of outside track for rolling-stock exhibits. The main entrance to the elongated S-shaped edifice will carry out the design of a roundhouse. A featured exhibit will be a working model railroad, complete in every detail.

Water will be an integral part of the design for the Hall of Marine Transportation in the southern part of the sector. Twin prows, 30 feet higher than the nose of the *Normandie,* will rise from a moat and tower 40 feet above the roof of the building. A semi-circular wing of the structure will partially enclose a basin in which full-size yachts, cruisers, speedboats and other small craft will be displayed. The entrance ramp to the building will simulate a gang plank; ship railings will border the water; and extending along one wall and out over the basin will be two decks, one above the other.

The Aviation building and the focal exhibit in the Transportation building are bound to attract huge crowds. In the former the activities of a great airport will be presented, and visitors will be privileged to enter the exhibit planes and handle the gadgets. The building will be one of the oddest in the entire fair, embodying architect William Lescaze's idea of "flight in space." A Y-shaped entrance leads to, but does not make contact with, a huge semi-circular rear wall that suggests a wind machine or the back of a bandstand. Entering the building, the visitor will hear the droning of many motors and his eyes will be drawn to the cup-like wall at the far end where a transport plane, propellers whirling and lights flashing, will be "flying" against a background of midday clouds, a sunset, or a moon-lit night. The focal exhibit for the Transportation sector, designed by Raymond Loewy, will include streamlined futuristic models of ships, trains, airplanes, etc. An animated presentation of transportation from the dawn of history to 1939, shown on a map-screen to the accompaniment of sound effects, will be climaxed by a sensational portrayal of a rocket ship taking off from a rocket port for an interplanetary trip.

Richard Kent, writing in *Pencil Points,* an architectural publication, indicates that the approximate symmetry of the fair's main exhibit area was largely an improvisation; it could be planned only after the Board of Design had determined the best foundation site for the theme center and—the problem of transportation being a vital one—the most accessible entrances to the grounds. Lewis Mumford suggests that the ideal plan for an exposition must give the visitor an immediate understanding of the exposition as a whole. As logical designs that successfully oriented the visitor, he cites the Paris Exposition of 1867, whose concentric groups enabled the visitor to walk around the perimeter or to cut in toward the center at convenient points, and the Chicago World's Columbian Exposition of 1893, in which the buildings were grouped about the main watercourse. In the 1939 New York fair, the height and distinction of the theme buildings, together with the zone grouping of related exhibits, will enable the visitor to check his general whereabouts rather readily. The plan is in part logical and formal; but it escapes the rigidly geometric, leaving room for that element of the informal, the unexpected, the casual which is associated with good landscape gardening.

The fair's second main avenue or axis leads southward from the theme center through the Plaza of Light, which is bordered by the General Electric, Consolidated Edison, Edison Electric Institute, and United States Steel buildings; then over the Empire State Bridge across the Horace Harding Boulevard to the New York State building and marine amphitheater. These latter structures will cost the state $1,700,000. The amphitheater, seating 10,000, will remain after the fair is over; on its large island stage, concerts, operas, pageants and aquatic displays will be presented. A Hollywood building, a children's miniature world's fair, and a Music building, together with the State building and amphitheater, will make up the "modern" zone, a transition section between the "ultra-modern" architecture of the exhibit area and the period, national, and exotic designs of the various villages to the south. In the music auditorium, seating 2,500, a festival of music, unprecedented in scope, will be presented by famous artists from all over the world. The Children's World will occupy a five-acre plot, with indoor and outdoor playing facilities, exhibits of children's furniture, clothing and playthings, two theaters (one for living actors and another for puppets), book, doll and toy houses, and other features.

The directors of New York's fair have decided to ban the use of the word "midway," though as yet no substitute term has been coined. Midway or no midway, the fair will have an amusement district on the eastern side of Meadow Lake capable of entertaining 250,000 people at one time. The main thoroughfare in this 280-acre area will be a two-mile loop; and no doubt the 500 concessions will be responsible for a sizable portion of the fair's estimated gate receipts of $25,000,000, at 50 cents a visitor.

Nightly spectacles of color, music, fireworks, flame and water will be presented in Meadow Lake and in the Lagoon of Nations. Installation of the equipment is to cost $700,000. The display to be presented over Meadow Lake is characterized as "the nearest approach to chaos that man can contrive for purposes of sheer entertainment," while the Central Mall spectacle is described as "a Niagara plus a Vesuvius."

The plan of the loop calls for 13 or more villages, and each concession must conform in design and atmosphere to its particular village. "Little Old New York" is one village contemplated. If this village includes a theater, it will be the old Park Theatre; if a café, the concessionaire will be required to reproduce Steve Brodie's saloon. Every employee will be expected to dress appropriately, and no detail of architecture will be permitted which doesn't carry out the approved theme. Other villages planned include Little Harlem, with its Cotton Club and Savoy Ballroom; a winter village featuring a musical comedy on ice; and a Montmartre incorporating a Moulin Rouge or Bal Tabarin and perhaps a theater showing Grand Guignol productions. There will be all sorts of rides and spectacles in the amusement area, and an effort is being made to provide a large number of novel devices. Details of inventions, obviously, will not be disclosed until patents have been granted and the opening date of the fair is near at hand. The two major attractions—"Little Old New York," and a huge night club seating 4,000 to 5,000 people—will be placed at the lower end of the loop to serve as magnets. The plan for the loop was developed by Albert Johnson, who designed the sets for such elaborate theatrical productions as *Jumbo* and *The Great Waltz*.

The western side of Meadow Lake will be reserved for an army encampment and for quiet forms of entertainment, with many rest oases, flower gardens and picnic grounds. Another lake to the south, Willow Lake, will feature tree plantations and parking space. To keep these artificial lakes fresh and prevent erosion of their shores, a tide gate and dam costing $586,365 will be constructed on the Flushing River.

The northeastern corner of the main exhibit area will be occupied by the Town of Tomorrow, pleasantly spaced over ten acres and comprising some 35 houses and apartment groups, a nursery, playground and shops. This model community is intended to show the average man how he may live under "the more nearly perfect flowering of democracy" in the American small town of the future. Adjoining the Town of Tomorrow will be an Arts building, exhibiting hundreds of works by living American artists.

In the southeastern corner of the main exhibit area, at the opposite end of the Rainbow Way from the Town of Tomorrow, will be the Court of States, an 11-acre plot for the exhibits of the various states and territories. Freshly approaching the problem of grouping state exhibits, the buildings will be designed in three architectural styles—Georgian, French, Spanish —representing the three cultures that have influenced, respectively, the Atlantic seaboard states, the Mississippi Valley states, and the southwestern states. Allocation in this area will not be compulsory, however, and some states will erect individual buildings elsewhere on the fair grounds.

The $740,000 Administration building, standing just outside what will be the northwest entrance to the fair, was completed August 13, 1937, two days ahead of schedule. Designed by several architects in collaboration—Harvey Stevenson, Eastman Studds, John A. Thomson, Gerald A. Holmes, Edgar I. Williams, and Kimball & Husted—the two-storied structure resembles a high school building of advanced design. Its special character, however, is indicated by the octagonal entrance and pre-fair exhibit hall, which juts out from and towers above the main mass. The façade above the entrance doors is decorated with a high-relief panel carved by Albert

Steward, which displays a semi-draped woman rising above the skyscrapers of Manhattan and lifting as she rises a veil which screens the world of tomorrow. The figure is executed in pure white plaster; the veil and the skyscrapers are dull gold. The other walls of the façade are relieved by vertical fluting surmounted by rows of five stars, the latter "forecasting a five-star fair." In a handle-like wing to the right are housed the executive offices; the main H-shaped wing to the left contains the other offices and workrooms. The domed ceiling of the octagonal hall is supported by eight columns painted an ultramarine blue; the ceiling itself is ringed with several shades of blue, and the walls are light gray. There are no windows; illumination is provided by overhead disc lights. A bridge leads from the lobby on the second floor to the fair grounds proper.

The completion of the Administration building left some 300 more buildings to be constructed. During the three-day preview held at the fair site one year before the scheduled opening, the thousands of visitors saw 17 buildings in steel and framing or already enclosed, and many more in the preliminary stages of construction. Among the 17 were the Textile, Shelter, Communications, Business Administration, Food, Medicine and Public Health, Mines and Metallurgy, and New York City buildings. Two of them were painted to afford the guests a foretaste of the "color cocktail" that will characterize the completed exposition. The walls of the Business Administration building are in white and two shades of "warm" yellow, with accents of vermilion and grey-blue; its interior court is deep red, violet, white, gold and black. The façade of the Hall of Communications is in white and two shades of "cool" yellow, with accents of vermilion and blue-green. The twin pylons guarding the entrance are in red-orange, blue and white. The fair's color scheme, unique in extent and boldness, has been developed by Julian E. Garnsey. A total of 499 carefully graduated colors is available to the fair architects. White, however, will be used freely "to wash the fair-goer's eyes out and let him start over again."

The Board of Design, in order to enlist new architectural talent for the fair structures, held an open competition in 1936. More than 360 designs for a free-style exposition building were anonymously submitted. Of the numerous prize winners, a majority have been employed by the fair. First prize winner was George Lyman Paine, Jr., and the second prize went to Peter Copeland. The former has designed the Production and Distribution building and the latter the Electrical Production building. The joint designers of the theme center, Wallace K. Harrison and J. André Fouilhoux, were prize winners in the contest. Two others, Leonard Dean and Francis Keally, have designed the Hall of Communications. Plans for all buildings to be erected at the fair must be approved by the Board of Design, but in practice this approval indicates only a corrective supervision of architects appointed by private exhibitors and foreign governments.

Some of the more striking buildings the designs of which had been revealed at the time of the preview, and not mentioned above, include an "inside-out" building, and a building "roofless and wall-less." The former structure, designed by Walter Dorwin Teague to house the exhibits of the United States Steel Corporation, will consist of a hemispheric shell of polished stainless steel supported and segmented by external girders joining at the top. Norman Bel Geddes is the designer of the "roofless and wall-less" building, which will be used by Wilson & Co., the Chicago packing house. This unique structure will consist of a series of huge showcases tied together architecturally by a winding ramp and a 96-foot glass pylon—the only lighting fixture—in the center of the plot. The $750,000 Gas Exhibits building will feature a Court of Flame in which four 90-foot pylons, suggestive of the grid points above the burner of a gas range, will surround a burning 50-foot jet of gas. The motif of the Cosmetics building is a lady's powder box; that of the Radio Corporation of America, the radio tube; while the Continental Baking Company building has been inspired by the doughnut. Less novel architecturally will be the non-sectarian Temple of Religion; set in a cloistered garden, it will rise in the form of a tower, 150 feet high.

Not many designs of foreign government pavilions had been disclosed at the time of the preview, but the announced plans for the Belgian, Italian and Egyptian examples indicate the variety to be expected. The Belgian building will be thoroughly modern, with plate glass forming fully half of the exterior. Italy's pavilion is described as "modern-classical"; rising high above the frontal colonnades and the oblong block of the building itself, a tower surmounted by a statue will be the source for a cascade of water. Egypt's pavilion is in the conventional style commonly associated with that country, with a temple-like façade ornately decorated.

Expositions dramatize architecture to the public. A world's fair, of course, is intended to make money for the sponsoring community and to advertise industry; but a fair also gives architects and designers a chance, in erecting temporary structures out of impermanent materials, to crystallize the art of their time and perhaps precipitate the art of the future. Many expositions have caused major or minor waves of architectural development in the style of the exposition. The Paris fair of 1889, featuring the skyscraper skeleton—the Eiffel Tower—began the *Art Nouveau* movement. The famed Crystal Palace, a huge glass-and-iron edifice designed for the London Exposition of 1851, illustrated the principle of "take down" construction. Erected in Hyde Park, and later removed piecemeal to Sydenham Hill, it was destroyed by fire in 1936. This was perhaps the first definitive monument of modern architecture. The exhibits of the Paris Exposition of 1925 exercised an influence on almost every form of artistic effort. Nothing was exhibited which the authorities considered an imitation or an expression of any ancient style. The two American expositions that perhaps affected architecture most were the Chicago fair in 1893 and the San Diego Exposition in 1915. The magnificent classic architecture of the Chicago display was a revelation to the American people; from that year until about 1915, a majority of the civic buildings erected in Middle and Western America were of classic or pseudo-classic type. At the San Diego fair, Bertram G. Goodhue modernized the ornate architecture of Spain and embodied color in his buildings by the use of tiles. This style spread rapidly through California, Florida and other states. "The ultramodern functional architecture at Chicago's Century of Progress Exposition created a popular furor and good gate receipts and it has exerted an influence, not only on American architecture during the past five years, but on the architecture of the present fair as well."

New York's fair, as indicated by the designs and the already visible structures, will be bold and striking, with much of the architecture—perhaps not inappropriately for an exposition—striving for sensational effects. At the other extreme, scalloped walls, fluted pilasters and old-fashioned columns are not entirely banned. In general, the buildings will be relatively low, discreet and orderly.

To the west of the fair site is Corona; to the east, Flushing; Kew Gardens and Forest Hills lie to the south. The reclamation of the site, originally an old city dump, was completed in 190 working days at a cost of $2,200,000—one of the largest and speediest jobs of the kind ever accomplished. About 6,700,000 cubic yards of ashes, rubbish, etc., were moved and graded. From 12 towers 80 feet high, floodlights were focussed on the area nightly and these consumed $80,000 worth of electric current. Junk trucks, as many as 40 in one day, haunted the cuts; and many thousands of tons of metal in the form of range boilers, bathtubs and bedsteads were salvaged. Hundreds of children organized themselves into salvage gangs: one band taking copper only, another brass, a third lead. One boy found a crusty, battered wallet containing $1,000 in bills—the old-fashioned large kind. A tin can also contained money, estimates of the amount varying from $20 to $700. Many fires, decades old, were uncovered. One singularly wrathful blaze was due to pent-up gases formed by decomposition.

It is planned to convert about 800 cubic yards of excavated meadow mat into a rich topsoil by a process that will effect a saving of $500,000. The salty, fibrous, highly acid mat will be plowed, harrowed, turned time and again, windrowed with lime for five or six weeks, composted with horse manure for another spell, and inoculated with phosphates and nitrogen until it has an organic content as high as 40 percent. Six percent is the State's standard for acceptable topsoil.

This rich soil is necessary, for the fair's $1,500,000 landscaping program calls for 250 acres of grass sod, 250,000 shrubs, 250,000 pansies and 500,000 tulips. Shade must be provided for some of the fair's 50,000 benches. Ten thousand trees, costing $218,000, will be transplanted, brought from points as far away as the State of Washington. Some of these will be 65 years old, 55 feet high, 25 tons in weight. Scouts are searching the country for specimens that meet the stringent specifications.

Storm and sanitary sewers costing $6,000,000 are under construction. These will provide drainage for the fair and 3,000 acres surrounding it. The city dump on Riker's Island will be spruced up, the mounds leveled off and screened with shrubs and trees. The Tallman's Island Disposal Plant, a $4,000,000 project, will rid Flushing Bay of its pollution. More millions will be spent on other collateral improvements such as bridges and highways.

Six main highways lead from Manhattan to the fair site, which is nine miles from Times Square. Northern Boulevard, Queens Boulevard, Horace Harding Boulevard and Roosevelt Avenue may be followed from Queensborough Bridge; Astoria Boulevard and Grand Central Parkway Extension from the Triborough Bridge. Visitors from New England and eastern Canada will be able to follow the Boston Post Road direct to the fair; the city promises completion of an $18,000,000 suspension bridge over the East River between Old Ferry Point, the Bronx, and Whitestone, Queens, to be known as the Whitestone Bridge. The Lincoln Tunnel, between West Thirty-Ninth Street, Manhattan, and Weehawken, New Jersey, one tube of which was opened December 1937, will be fully completed for the fair's opening—possibly also the $58,000,000 Queens Midtown Tunnel under the East River from East Thirty-Eighth Street, Manhattan, to Long Island

City. A third vehicular tunnel, crossing midtown Manhattan and connecting with both the Lincoln and the Queens tunnel approaches, is projected. Once the system of underground passages is completed, motorists can descend in New Jersey and come up on Long Island just short of the fair grounds. Ferry service from the west shore of the Hudson is also probable. A $700,000 boat basin in Flushing Bay will be constructed, and the Federal Government has appropriated $505,000 for dredging Flushing Bay Channel and the basin.

A branch of the Long Island Railroad runs along the northern side of the fair grounds; additional trackage and a large overhead terminal are planned. The IRT-BMT subway lines are a quarter of a mile north of the railroad; the Willets Point Station of these lines will be enlarged and linked by viaduct to the second fair entrance. Running time from central Manhattan will be 14 minutes by rail, 18 by subway, and 25 by motor. A temporary spur of the city subway will be constructed at a cost of $1,700,-000, with a terminal on the shore of Meadow Lake. The IRT and BMT subways will have an hourly capacity of 40,000, the Independent subway 40,000, Long Island Railroad 18,000, street cars 15,000, buses-taxis 28,-000, and automobiles 17,000. The capacity of excursion boats and airplanes has not yet been estimated. The fair is ringed by five airports. The North Beach Municipal Airport for land and sea planes, a mile from the fair, is being improved at a cost of $12,000,000. The fair will have 17 miles of roadways, and parking space for 35,000 cars. Overpass, passerelles, and center lanes fenced and landscaped will keep pedestrians clear of through motor traffic.

Thirty-four million dollars spent by New York City, New York State and the Federal Government provide the firmest official backing ever guaranteed to a world's fair. The Fair Corporation has issued $27,829,500 in four percent debentures to finance development until the beginning of the fair's earning period. About $50,000,000 will be received from exhibitors and concessionaires. The corporation is a non-profit organization, and New York City is assured the first $2,000,000 in profits toward development of the fair grounds as a permanent park. City and State will divide any further profits, the money to be earmarked for charitable and educational purposes.

It is pretty certain that nearly all States and territories and most of the foreign governments will participate in the fair. Oregon, after appropriating money for an exhibit, withdrew in a quarrel about its site. Germany withdrew because of "financial difficulties." Austria simply disappeared.

Manchukuo was not invited, and Spain and China were unable to accept invitations because of the "uncertain conditions" prevailing in their countries. The International Bureau of Expositions has recognized New York's fair as the official 1939 exposition.

A network of committees and advisory committees marshals more than 13,000 prominent Americans behind the fair. Grover Whalen was elected president of the corporation on May 5, 1936, about a year after the fair was conceived. A year before the fair's opening, more than 1,000 persons were on the full-time staff. It is estimated that 50,000 persons will be directly employed in building and operating the fair, and an additional 150,000 indirectly.

World fairs do indeed get bigger, but commentators are not wholly in agreement with popular opinion (as expressed in attendance figures) that they also get better. The Victorian mama of them all, London's Crystal Palace Exposition of 1851, has even been called the best of the lot. Certainly it was a success from every point of view: artistic, scientific, financial. Citizens of the world came to marvel—some 6,000,000 of them; and the show made a profit of about a million dollars. But this exposition presented for the first time the great promise of the machine and machine-products, not only in its exhibits but in its exposition building—the glorified greenhouse designed by gardener Joseph Paxton.

Most of the recent fairs have not pleased the critics. According to Lewis Mumford, writing in the New Yorker, the trouble with world fairs is that their promoters "lack any rational notion of a fair except the now completely tedious and unconvincing belief in the triumph of modern industry. The less said about that today, the better. The peace confidently promised in 1851 is now sour with war, and the plenty that industry seemed about to achieve now intermittently carries with it a threat of starvation. Lacking any effective dramatization or rational purpose, most modern fairs are threatened at an early stage with bankruptcy."

The New York fair, secure in its broad official backing, is very well off financially; it may also break the pattern which has often hitherto evolved into a demonstration that the march of progress is a dance. Whether it does or not, one thing is certain: the City of New York itself will be the smash hit of its own exposition. No vista at the fair will equal the fantastic splendor of the view from a returning Staten Island ferry, and none of its spectacles is likely to match Times Square. The Empire State Building will be something to write home about as the big brother of the trylon.

Index

ABOUT THE AUTHORS

The Federal Writers' Project was established in 1935 as part of Federal #1, a project to provide work relief for artists and professionals under the Work Progress Administration. In the next four years the project produced works on local history, folkways, and culture in addition to the magisterial American Guide Series. The New York City division of the Writers' Project included many writers who were later to become famous, including John Cheever and Richard Wright.

Alfred Kazin is the author of *On Native Grounds, A Walker in the City, New York Jew, Starting Out in the Thirties,* and *An American Procession,* among many other books.